W9-ASJ-306

15 ST. MARY STREET
TORONTO, ONTARIO, CANADA
M4Y 2R5

WITHDRAWN

ISAIAH 1–12

Other Continental Commentaries from Fortress Press

HANS WILDBERGER

ISAIAH 1–12

A Commentary

Translated by

Thomas H. Trapp

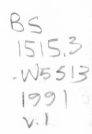

BS
1515.3
.W5513
1991
v.1

Regis College Library
15 ST. MARY STREET
TORONTO, ONTARIO, CANADA
M4Y 2R5

98151

FORTRESS PRESS
MINNEAPOLIS

ISAIAH 1–12
A Commentary

English translation copyright © 1991 Augsburg Fortress.

Translated from *Jesaja, Kapitel 1–12,* second edition, published by Neukirchener Verlag, Neukirchen-Vluyn, in 1980 in the Biblischer Kommentar series.

Copyright © Neukirchener Verlag des Erziehungsvereins GmbH, Neukirchen-Vluyn, 1980. English translation copyright © 1991 Augsburg Fortress, Minneapolis.

All rights reserved. Except for brief quotations in critical articles or reviews, no part of this book may be reproduced in any manner without prior written permission from the publisher. Write to: Permissions, Augsburg Fortress, 426 S. Fifth St., Box 1209, Minneapolis, MN 55440.

Library of Congress Cataloging-in-Publication Data

Wildberger, Hans, 1910–1986
  [Jesaja. English]
  Isaiah : a commentary / Hans Wildberger.
    p. cm. – (Continental commentaries)
  Translation of: Jesaja.
  Contents: [1] Isaiah 1–12.
  ISBN 0-8006-9508-9 (v. 1 : alk. paper)
  1. Bible. O.T. Isaiah–Commentaries. I. Title. II. Title:
Isaiah 1–12. III. Series.
BS1515.3.W53613 1990
224′.1077–dc20

91-8874
CIP

The paper used in this publication meets the minimum requirements of American National Standard for Information Science—Permanence of Paper for Printed Library Materials, ANSI A329.48–1984.

∞™

Manufactured in the U.S.A.

AF 1–9508

95   94   93   92   91   1   2   3   4   5   6   7   8   9   10

Contents

v

Contents

Preface

This first volume of my Isaiah commentary brings the study to the end of chapter twelve. It is both obvious and generally accepted that one comes to a recognizable break in the book of Isaiah at this point. Since the completion of such a study will continue within the context of many unavoidable demands on one's time and because of the almost threatening flood of literature, it has seemed reasonable to bring the sections that have appeared to this point into one volume, the first major part of the commentary.

Because of this decision, it is obvious that the introduction to the entire commentary cannot be placed at the very beginning of the whole study, but must rather serve as a conclusion. Since the overview of the book and its history (both the history of the prophet and his message as well as that of the many unknown personages who make some contributions by way of additions) cannot be written until a study of the entire text has been carried out, one hopes that the reader will understand. Study of the book of Isaiah will continue, and I myself am amazed again and again how intensive work with a particular unit of material leads to new paths of understanding, even when one ventures to tread on territory that has been traveled many times already. In general, whoever uses this commentary will be able to detect very clearly the main lines of argument that set forth my understanding of the book and the prophet.

Whoever writes a commentary on the book of Isaiah must reflect upon the עֵצוֹת (plans) of God, but must also take to heart, from personal experience, that human plans must always remain in doubt. In spite of that, it is to be hoped that the future sections of this commentary will not appear at the present pace but that they will be able to follow, one after the other, in a more fast-paced rhythm. That would not be possible if the author would have to wait until after the many burning issues concerning the understanding of Isaiah—and beyond that the whole question about prophecy itself—would have been clearly solved. The discussion of these issues will and must continue. The interpretation of the text will show how I have sought to listen to and to take seriously the views of others. That I myself have been able to stimulate discussion at certain points is shown as well, both by favorable reactions and criticisms. On a higher plane, hope remains that the message of the prophet and the words of the many interpreters and interpolators within the book itself will begin to speak once again in a new way to our own age. The central theme of Isaiah's proclamation is as timely today as it was in the time of the prophet:

אִם לֹא תַאֲמִינוּ כִּי לֹא תֵאָמֵנוּ

If you do not believe, then you will not remain.

Hans Wildberger

Translator's Preface

It was just four years ago that my Doktorvater, Hans Walter Wolff, arranged for me to sit in on the meeting of the authors who are writing the various volumes of Biblischer Kommentar for Neukirchener Verlag. Many of these volumes have been translated into English in the Hermeneia series or in the Continental Commentaries series. About that same time, initial contacts had been made with me regarding the translation of Hans Wildberger's three volumes on Isaiah 1–39. It is a joy to bring the first volume to a conclusion. Work continues now on the second volume, Isaiah 13–27. The third volume includes Isaiah 28–39 as well as "introductory" materials to which Professor Wildberger made mention. At that meeting in Neukirchen, Professor Wolff shared with the authors what he had written in honor of Hans Wildberger, who had died in 1986. Professor Wolff has shared with me the deep joy which he feels and which Wildberger would have felt to see his efforts of thirty years of research available to a much wider public.

Certain decisions were necessary in translating this very complicated volume. First, a translation of every foreign word is included in parentheses, unless the meaning of the word is brought out by the discussion. Thus the book will be accessible to a variety of readers. For the words used in Isaiah 1–12, the translated foreign word is keyed to the word used in the translation of the text. For the rest of the biblical material, the Revised Standard Version was used. The only change made to that text was to read "Yahweh" instead of "LORD." Beyond that, standard dictionaries were used. Even the advanced scholar will be able to follow the arguments in the text-critical notes without recourse to lexica.

Literature updates are furnished through 1979 (incorporated from the third volume), but time constraints prohibited adding to the overall bibliography of Isaiah 1–39. Texts in the commentary refer to the Hebrew numbering in the Masoretic text. Standard translations were used for extra-biblical materials. I retained some disputed renderings, such as reference to Palestine, but changed others that relate to gender issues.

The notes on meter reflect the occurrence or nonoccurrence of parallelism. A colon refers to the shortest unit of the text. Parallelism is indicated as bicolon or tricolon. In such cases, one might find a 3 + 3 (three-stress) bicolon. A unit that is poetic but not parallel would be designated as a six-stress colon, and the colon would identify the entire line.

I appreciate technical help from members of the religion division at Concordia College, St. Paul, especially Dan Jastram for help with Greek and Latin; Mark Hillmer of Luther-Northwestern Seminary, St. Paul, for an entire morning with about thirty dictionaries for Syriac, Akkadian, and the like; Ray Olson at Luther-Northwestern Seminary, who tracked down many journal articles so that German translations of English articles could be accurately cited, and my now-sainted father, Harvey Trapp, an analytical chemist by trade, for help with the technical aspects of smelting and refining ore. My wife, Kathy, and children, Matthew, JoAnna, and Daniel, have endured much already and have carried the ball and waited patiently many times. I appreciate the trust that Marshall Johnson of Fortress Press has placed in me and the fine work done by Hank Schlau in editing the manuscript.

Thomas H. Trapp

The Superscription

Literature

Concerning chaps. 1ff.: A. Condamin, "Les chapitres I et II du livre d'Isaïe," *RB* 1 (1904) 7–26. K. Budde, "Zu Jesaja 1–5," *ZAW* 49 (1931) 16–40, 182–211, and *ZAW* 50 (1932) 38–72. R. J. Marshall, "The Structure of Is 1–12," *BR* 7 (1962) 19–32. Idem, "The Unity of Is 1–12," *LQ* 14 (1962) 21–38. N. H. Tur-Sinai, "A Contribution to the Understanding of Isaiah I–XII," ScrHier 8 (1961) 154–188. **[Literature update through 1979:** P. R. Ackroyd, "Isaiah I–XII: Presentation of a Prophet," VTSup 29 (1978) 16–48.]
Concerning chap. 1: J. Ley, "Metrische Analyse von Jesaja Kp. 1," *ZAW* 22 (1902) 229–237. F. Zorell, "Is c. 1," *VD* 6 (1926) 65–70. F. Ruffenach, "Malitia et remissio peccati (Is 1:1–20)," *VD* 7 (1927) 145–149, 165–168. E. Robertson, "Isaiah Chapter I," *ZAW* 52 (1934) 231–236. L. G. Rignell, "Isaiah Chapter I: Some Exegetical Remarks with Special Reference to the Relationship between the Text and the Book of Deuteronomy," *ST* 11 (1957) 140–158. G. Fohrer, "Jesaja 1 als Zusammenfassung der Verkündigung Jesajas," *ZAW* 74 (1962) 251–268. **[Literature update through 1979:** L. Alonso-Schökel, "El ritmo hebreo come factor expresivo," *RB* 25 (1963) 24–29. J. Stampfer, "On Translating Biblical Poetry (Isaiah, Chapters 1 and 2:1–4)," *Jdm* 14 (1965) 501–510. A. Mattioli, "Due schemi letterari negli oracoli d introduzione al libro d Isaia," *RB* 14 (1966) 345–364.]
Concerning the chronology of Isaiah's era: J. Begrich, *Die Chronologie der Könige von Israel und Juda,* BHT 3 (1929). S. Mowinckel, "Die Chronologie der israelitischen und jüdischen Könige," *AcOr* 10 (1932) 161–277. W. F. Albright, "The Chronology of the Divided Monarchy of Israel," *BASOR* 100 (1945) 16–22. Idem, "New Light from Egypt on the Chronology and History of Israel and Judah," *BASOR* 130 (1953) 4–11. E. R. Thiele, *The Mysterious Numbers of the Hebrew Kings* (1951). Idem, "A Comparison of the Chronological Data of Israel and Juda," *VT* 4 (1954) 185–195. A. Jepsen, *Die Quellen des Königsbuches* (1956²). E. Kutsch, *RGG³* III, 942–944. C. Schedl, "Textkritische Bemerkungen zu den Synchronismen der Könige von Israel und Juda," *VT* 12 (1962) 88–119. A. Jepsen/R. Hanhart, *Untersuchungen zur israelitisch-jüdischen Chronologie,* BZAW 88 (1964). V. Pavlovský/E. Vogt, "Die Jahre der Könige von Juda und Israel," *Bib* 45 (1964) 321–347.

Text

1:1 The vision of Isaiah, the son of Amoz, which he saw concerning Judah and Jerusalem in the days of Uzziah,[a] Jotham, Ahaz, and Hezekiah,[b] the kings of Judah.

1a In addition to עֻזִּיָּהוּ (see also 2 Kings 15:32, 34; 2 Chron. 26:1–23 [12 times]; 27:2; Isa. 6:1; 7:1), in other places, the MT uses the shortened form עֻזִּיָּה (2 Kings 15:13, 30; Hos. 1:1; Amos 1:1; Zech. 14:5). Q^a: עוזיה. The shorter form is more recent (M. Noth, *Die israelitischen Personennamen,* BWANT III/10 [1928] 105). Concerning the writing of the name with the *matres lectiones* in the handwritten documents of Qumran, see P. Kahle, *Die Handschriften aus der Höhle* (1951) 40ff.

1b Q^a reads חזקיה (corrected to יחזקיה), instead of יחזקיהו. MT uses four different forms in the OT, יחזקיהו, יחזקיה, חזקיהו, and חזקיה, all of them quite often. Concerning the prefixed י, see Noth, op. cit., 246; and also D. Diringer, *Le iscrizioni antico-ebraiche palestinesi* (1934) 74f.

Form

The superscription has been constructed by making use of an established tradition which was used to introduce literary works. The "normal form" for a title at the beginning of a prophetic work is likely that found in Hos. 1:1: "The word of the Lord that came to Hosea the son of Beeri, in the days of Uzziah. . . ." The superscription used here departs from the normal form insofar as it designates the content of the book of Isaiah as a "vision" of the prophet, as is also the case in Obadiah. All of the elements used in this title can also be commonly found in other superscriptions at the head of this type of literature.

The father's name (with בֶּן־, son of) is mentioned in Jer. 1:1; Ezek. 1:3; Hos. 1:1; Joel 1:1; Jonah 1:1; Zeph. 1:1; Zech. 1:1. The expression אשר חזה (which he saw), which would be expected only after חזון (vision) or a synonym of this word, is also used in 2:1 (used there with הדבר, the word), Amos 1:1 (after דברי־עמוס, words of Amos), Mic. 1:1 (after דבר־ יהוה, word of the Lord), and Hab. 1:1 (after המשא, the oracle). The designation of those being addressed by the prophetic proclamation, not mentioned in the example cited from Hosea, is found in Amos ("concerning Israel," 1:1), Micah ("concerning Samaria and Jerusalem," 1:1), Nahum ("concerning Nineveh," 1:1), Haggai ("to Zerubbabel . . . and to Joshua . . . ," 1:1), and Malachi ("to Israel," 1:1). When the time during which the prophet was active is set into its historical context, we notice that the Judean kings who are mentioned here in Isaiah are those that are also mentioned in Hos. 1:1; however, in Hosea, Jeroboam the king of Israel is added to the list. In contrast to Amos, Micah, Nahum, and Jeremiah, Isaiah's hometown is not mentioned. This is certainly not because it was not known, but rather because it would have been immediately clear to every reader of the book that the author could not have come from anywhere except Jerusalem.

It would appear that only a substantive was needed in such superscriptions to characterize the content of the work which would follow, with the author's name following in a genitive relationship. Thus, the superscription over the little book of Obadiah is reduced to the notation חזון עבדיה (vision of Obadiah). We encounter parallel constructions in the wisdom literature: "words of the wise" in Prov. 22:17 or "the proverbs of Solomon" in Prov. 10:1; cf. Prov. 1:1; 25:1; Eccles. 1:1; cf. also Song of Sol. 1:1; Prov. 30:1; 31:1. In contrast to these very short superscriptions, an Egyptian document about wisdom which comes from Ptah-hotep (about 2450) uses a more expanded form of introduction, remarkably similar to that which is used in Isa. 1:1: "The instruction of the Mayor and Vizier Ptah-hotep, under the majesty of the King of Upper and Lower Egypt: Izezi, living forever and ever" (*ANET*² 412); another example comes from Amen-em-het (about 1960): "The beginning of the instruction which the majesty of the King of Upper and Lower Egypt: Sehetep-ib-Re; the Son of Re: Amen-em-het, the triumphant, made, when he spoke in a message of truth to his son, the All-Lord . . ." (*ANET*² 418). From this, it would seem to follow that such titles were at first commonly used for the writings of the wise and were then adapted in whatever way was appropriate to be placed at the beginning of the writings of the prophets.

Setting

Without a doubt, 1:1 is meant to be taken as a superscription for the entire book with all of its 66 chapters. It is possible that it was originally written with only "Proto-Isaiah" in mind; that is, referring only to the first 39 chapters of the book. Even if it is understood in this way, it would in no way have originated with Isaiah himself. Literary criticism has demonstrated that even the first part of the book of Isaiah, as it now stands, did not originate in its present completed form solely with the prophet himself. Against taking this superscription as originating with Isaiah, one must consider the following: (a) the prophet is referred to at this point in the third person; (b) the superscription presumes that the activity of Isaiah is now complete; and (c) the word order "Judah and Jerusalem" was first used in the postexilic era; the prophet himself regularly chooses the opposite word order (3:1, 8; 5:3; 22:21). Even if "Judah and Jerusalem" had not practically become the official designation in the postexilic era, it was still a stereotypical formula used to designate the little community of the true Israel whose center was to be found in Jerusalem after the exile. (For statistical evidence, see D. Jones, "The Traditio of the Oracles of Isaiah of Jerusalem," *ZAW* 67 [1955] 226–246; see 239f.)

The kings who are mentioned in 1:1 are also mentioned in other places in the book of Isaiah: Uzziah in 6:1 and 7:1 (as Jotham's father), Jotham in 7:1 (as Ahaz's father), Ahaz in 7:1, 3, 10, 12; 14:28, and 38:8, and Hezekiah in the narrative section, 36–39 (passim). According to 6:1, Isaiah was called to be a prophet in the year in which King Uzziah died. There is no reason to question the reliability of this notation. It is just as certain that Isaiah was still active during the reign of Hezekiah, even though this king's name is not mentioned, in so many words, in material which comes from the prophet himself. It is possible that 1:4–9, a section which looks back to the catastrophe which took place when Sennacherib besieged the city, is the last message of Isaiah which we have. In any case, no utterance of the prophet is preserved which would give any evidence for presuming that Isaiah's activity would have extended significantly beyond this time, say, for example, through to the end of Hezekiah's reign or even into the time of Manasseh.

Unfortunately, trying to establish the dates of the reigns of these kings has not yet resulted in any measure of relative certainty. The most difficult date to establish in this chronology is the date of Ahaz's death. According to 2 Kings 18:13, the enthronement of Hezekiah as king took place in the year 715, not earlier. John Bright (*A History of Israel* [1959]

461ff.), relying mainly on the research of Albright, arrives at the following dates: Uzziah 783–742, Jotham (co-regent from about 750 on) 742–735, Ahaz 735–715, and Hezekiah 715–687/86. However, 2 Kings 18:13 conflicts with both 2 Kings 18:1 and the text of Isa. 14:29–32, which is dated according to the year in which Ahaz died and also makes reference to the death of Tiglath-Pileser III (727). This would suggest that the earlier dating of Ahaz's death, which Begrich and others use, would be the more likely. Using the studies of Begrich, Jepsen/Hanhart (op. cit., 42) assign the following dates: Azariah/Uzziah 787–736, Jotham 756–741, Ahaz 741–725, Hezekiah 725–697. According to this dating scheme, all of Jotham's reign and even a part of Ahaz's reign would have come during the time when Azariah was ill (2 Kings 15:5); this would mean that Jotham's reign was never more than a co-regency and, thus, Isaiah's activity would have fallen completely within the period of the reigns of Ahaz and Hezekiah. And yet, there is no shred of evidence for this in the OT texts. This particular problem is avoided when one adopts the solution offered by Pavlovský/Vogt (op. cit.), based upon a suggestion from Schedl. They reduce the length of Ahaz's reign from sixteen years (see 2 Kings 16:2) to six years, accept with the others that Azariah and Jotham had a co-regency, and then presume that Judah functioned with a system of postdating a king's reign and a fall New Year while Israel functioned with a system of antedating and a spring New Year. They come up with the following dates for the kings who lived during the time of Isaiah: Azariah/Uzziah 767–739 (co-regent from 792 on), Jotham 739–734/33 (co-regent from 750/49 on), Ahaz 734/33–728/27, Hezekiah 728/27–699. Of course, this solution does postulate that Ahaz died at age twenty-six, having ascended to the throne at age twenty. This would also require that his son and successor, Hezekiah, could not have been twenty-five (see 2 Kings 18:2) but rather only five years old when he took the throne and that he would have been born a short time after the Syro-Ephraimitic War.

Commentary

[1:1] The vocalization for יְשַׁעְיָהוּ is not absolutely certain. In addition to Ησαιας, Gk has a number of other forms of the name, including Ιεσσ(ε)ια (1 Chron. 23:20; 2 Esdr. 10:31 [Engl: Ezra 10:31]). Vulg follows Gk by using either *Isaias* or *Esaias*. It is also not possible to ascertain the meaning of the name with complete certainty. It seems rather unlikely that the first element of the word ישע (deliver) is to be taken as a *qal* perfect, since the verb is used elsewhere only in the *hiph'il* and *niph'al;* the Masoretic punctuation would not speak in favor of taking it as a *qal* imperfect. Therefore, it has already been suggested that the name is derived from the root שעה, "look" (see Gen. 4:4f.; Exod. 5:9), meaning "Yahweh looks." But it seems more advisable to stay with ישע as the root, since it is used in many places to construct names (הוֹשֵׁעַ, Hoshea; הוֹשַׁעְיָה, Hoshaiah; מֵשַׁע or מֵישַׁע, Mesha; and יִשְׁעִי, Ishi). The rendering in Gk suggests that the pronunciation is יְשַׁעְיָהוּ(ו) "Yahweh is salvation." The short form of the name, יִשְׁעִי (1 Chron. 2:31; 4:20, 42; 5:24), might be an abbreviated form of the name יְשַׁעְיָהוּ: "Yahweh is my help" (cf. also names such as חִלְקִיָּה, Hilkiahu; צִדְקִיָּהוּ, Zidkiahu; and עֻזִּיָּהוּ, Uzziahu), which is also worth noting when one takes into account the rendering of the name

4

as Ιεσσια. But since there are other situations in which the *qal* form of the verbal idea is used when constructing names, instead of using one of the derived verbal patterns (see Noth, op. cit., 176; cf. also Delitzsch, 39), it is quite justifiable to establish the meaning based on the *qal* perfect of ישע. Thus, the name means "Yahweh has granted salvation." Though all date from a later time, the OT knows of others who had this name; see 1 Chron. 25:3, 15; 26:25; and, in the later form ישעיה = Isaiah, 1 Chron. 3:21; Ezra 8:7, 19; Neh. 11:7. The Psalms show a preference for speaking of Yahweh's "help," or better yet, that Yahweh is "help" (18:47; 24:5; 25:5; 27:1, 9, and often elsewhere); in the cult, the "help" of God is sought or else there is a confession that Yahweh has "helped"; e.g., 20:7: "Now I know that the Lord has helped [RSV, will help] his anointed" (הוֹשִׁיעַ). Isaiah himself speaks of Yahweh as the "God of your [Israel's] help" (RSV, salvation) (17:10 parallel to צוּר מָעֻזֵּךְ, strong rock). The name of the prophet is a natural reflection on the cultic piety found in Jerusalem; it is also found on seals (see Diringer, op. cit., 209; and *IEJ* 13 [1963] 324).

אָמוֹץ, Amoz, the name of Isaiah's father, is most likely a shortened form of the name אמציהו, "Yahweh is strong." It is also found on a seal of unknown provenance (cf. Diringer, op. cit., 235). It is most doubtful that the seal actually belonged to the father of the prophet (contra R. T. Anderson, *JBL* 79 [1960] 57f.). According to the Jewish tradition (see Delitzsch, ad loc.), Isaiah's father was said to be the brother of King Amaziah; that is, a brother of the father and predecessor of Uzziah (Megilla 10b and Sota 10b), which would make Isaiah a member of the Davidic family. In principle, this would not be impossible—Isaiah did have significant access to the palace (see 7:3ff.), but there is no possible way to substantiate this very late bit of information.

The name Amoz also points back to the world of cultic poetry, where one would confess that Yahweh "makes one strong" or would ask him to make someone strong (Pss. 80:16, 18; 89:22; cf. 27:14; 31:25). Furthermore, the names of the kings who are mentioned in v. 1 are themselves to be explained by referring to the same cultic setting: Uzziah = "Yahweh is my strength," Jotham = "Yahweh is upright," Ahaz (a hypocoristicon for Jehoahaz, known to Tiglath-Pileser as *Ya-u-ha-si*) = "Yahweh has taken hold" (namely, by the hand; cf. Ps. 73:23), Hezekiah = "Yahweh is my strength."

It is striking to note that the collection of Isaiah's words is designated as a חזון י׳ (vision of Yahweh). Though it has often been suggested, the reason for this is not to be explained on the basis of a later Judean theory about how a prophet received a revelation. Isaiah is aware of this term (29:7; cf. חִזָּיוֹן, vision, in 22:1, 5) and also knows about "seers" (חֹזִים, 30:10). It is very likely that he would have characterized himself as a "seer"; thus, he apparently would have belonged to that group of men, according to 30:10, whom some people hoped could be stopped from being "seers." Amos is also called a חֹזֶה (seer) (7:12; cf. 2 Sam. 24:11; Mic. 3:7; 2 Kings 17:13), and the substantive חזון (vision) is also used in 1 Sam. 3:1 and Hos. 12:11, not to mention later occurrences. There is no doubt that the specific conceptualization of what was meant by the term חזה had already become less clear even in early times, so that it did not automatically have to include seeing a vision, but could have taken on the general meaning of a revelation event, and also could have been used to describe the actual reception of a message (see 2:1: "The word which Isaiah saw"; see also 1 Sam. 3:1; Isa. 29:10; Mic. 3:6).

Consequently, the title חזון (vision) corresponds to Isaiah's understanding of himself, and it is appropriate that the prophet is not called a נביא (prophet) in the superscription and that his activity is not described by using some form of the root נבא (to prophesy) (cf. how different it is in Hab. 1:1; Hag. 1:1 and often elsewhere; Zech. 1:1). Only in the narrative sections is he called a נביא (prophet) (37:2; 38:1; 39:3). When he himself talks about נביאים, "prophets" (3:2; 28:7 [9:14 and 29:10 are textual additions]), he does so in a deprecatory sense. He also could have said, with Amos: "I am no נביא" (7:14). It is contradictory for the later tradition to call him a prophet, since, as his own words reveal, he plainly sought to distance himself from the prophetic movement.

It could be that the singular form חזון (vision) was used because originally the (still shorter) formula was used to introduce only a single vision account. Thus, Budde presumes that the superscription stood originally at the beginning of 6:1 (see ZAW 38 [1919/20] 58). Yet, there is no plural form of חזון (vision) to be found in the OT; the term can by all means be taken as a collective (cf. Hos. 12:11; Nah. 1:1; also 1 Sam. 3:1), or it can be taken as being used in an abstract way to refer to the entire series of revelations. It is most likely that חזון ישעיהו בן־אמוץ (the vision of Isaiah, the son of Amoz) served as the superscription for the collection of materials found in chap. 1 and was then used in an expanded sense by a redactor, who used it as the title for the entire work.

"Judah and Jerusalem" are addressed in the proclamation of the prophet. This designation can be considered only approximately correct when one compares it with what one would conclude from the material in the individual textual units. "Israel" is often addressed. That might have served as a reference to the sacred Yahwistic community (1:3; 5:7; 8:14). But, before the fall of Samaria, Isaiah also addressed the residents of the Northern Kingdom; the Jerusalemite Isaiah is also acutely conscious of the fact that the divided kingdoms were actually parts of a greater entity, the people of God, and that the religious leaders were responsible for more than just whatever governmental regulations they artificially established on their own (see 8:23; 9:8ff.; 17:4ff.; 28:1ff.). In addition, foreign nations are also included in the proclamation of Isaiah: the Assyrians (10:5ff.; 14:24ff.), the Philistines (14:29ff.), Damascus (17:1ff.), Cush (18:1ff.; 20:1ff.), Egypt (20:1ff.; possibly also 19:1ff.), and perhaps the Phoenicians (23:1ff.).

And yet, even though these words are formally directed toward the foreign nations, in actuality it is Jerusalem/Judah which is addressed, whether Isaiah wants to show his own people that there is a limit to the "pride" of Assyria or whether he wants to take away from Israel any illusion that it could expect its salvation to come about as a result of an alliance with foreign powers.

Purpose and Thrust

The superscription over the book of Isaiah sets forth a claim that the content of the book ought to be taken as a revelation from God. The reader becomes aware of that which the one who transmits this revelation "has seen"; therefore, what is to be encountered is a message which is both binding and demanding. To underscore the objectivity of this revelation which is being set forth, virtually nothing is mentioned about the details of the life of the prophet except the prophet's name (along with his father's name, which does no more than to help identify him). The prophet is not important because he is a religious personage within the parameters of his own particular existence, but rather because of his function as one who announces the details of the vision which has come to him. Providing information about the dates betrays, of course, an awareness that the understanding of a prophetic message cannot simply ignore details of the time and place in which this occurs. If the reader wants to press on to understand what is written, he or she would have to make an application which is specifically based on what happened "then and there." That is even more necessary in the case of Isaiah, since he, more than any other prophet, illuminated the history of his own people with his message.

Isaiah 1:2–3

Sons of Yahweh
without Understanding

Literature

J. Ziegler, "Ochs und Esel an der Krippe. Biblisch-patristische Erwägungen zu Is 1,3 und Hab 3,2 LXX," *MTZ* 3 (1952) 385–402. E. Nielsen, "Ass and Ox in the Old Testament," *Studia Orientalia Ioanni Pedersen dicata* (1953) 263–274. G. E. Mendenhall, *Recht und Bund in Israel und dem Alten Vordern Orient, TS* (Zürich) 64 (1960); trans. from "Ancient Oriental and Biblical Law," *BA* 17/2 (1954) 26–46, and "Covenant Forms in Israelite Tradition," *BA* 17/3, 50–76. H. B. Huffmon, "The Covenant Lawsuit in the Prophets," *JBL* 78 (1959) 285–295. J. Harvey, "Le 'Rîb-Pattern', réquisitoire prophétique sur la rupture de l'alliance," *Bib* 43 (1962) 172–196. G. E. Wright, "The Lawsuit of God: A Form-Critical Study of Deuteronomy 32," in FS J. Muilenburg (1962) 26–67.
[Literature update through 1979: D. R. Jones, "Exposition of Isaiah, Chapter One, Verses One to Nine," *SJT* 17 (1964) 463–477. M. Delcor, "Les attaches littéraires, l'origine et la signification de l'expression biblique 'prendre à témoin le ciel et la terre'," *VT* 16 (1966) 8–25. I. von Loewenclau, "Zur Auslegung von Jesaja 1,2–3," *EvT* 26 (1966) 294–308. M. Dahood, "אבוס cfr. 'ibsn (ug.)," *Bib* 53 (1972) 386. H. W. Hoffmann, "Die Intention der Verkündigung Jesajas," BZAW 136 (1974) 82ff. C. Westermann, "The Role of the Lament in the Theology of the Old Testament," *Int* 28 (1974) 20–38. E. Zawiszewski, "Synowie niewzięczni (Iz 1,2–20)," *Studia Warminskie* 12 (1975) 419–421.]

Text

1:2 Hear, you heavens,[a] and listen attentively, you earth,[a]
    for Yahweh speaks:[b]
Sons have I reared[c] and brought up,
    yet they have raised themselves up against me.
  3 The bull knows its master,
    and the ass, its owner's[a] manger;
however, Israel has no insight,
    my people,[b] no understanding.

2a Concerning the omission of the article with a vocative in poetic speech, see Joüon, Gr §137g. Qᵃ reads הארץ (the earth).
2b Concerning the word order יהוה דבר (Yahweh spoke) (the subject precedes the verb, for emphasis), see Joüon, Gr §155m.

2c Gk reads ἐγέννησα (I have begotten) for גדלתי (I have brought up) while, on the other hand, Sym and Theod read ἐξέθρεφα (I have brought up). Vulg: *enutrivi* (I have brought up). Exegetes stay with the MT reading. The reading in Gk is not technically impossible, though this presumes that the text read הוליד (to beget), since the Israelites are portrayed as "sons" and Yahweh as "father." But the OT does not use הוליד (beget) with Yahweh as subject, except in Isa. 66:9, where the verb means "allow one to give birth," and God's "begetting" is mentioned only very seldom (Deut. 32:18; Ps. 2:7). It is also very rare to find theophoric personal names in the OT which employ forms of ילד (bear, *qal*) or הוליד (beget, *hiph'il*), so that it seems best to stay with MT.

3a The "plural of majesty" (בעליו, his lords) serves to identify beings who exist on a higher level; cf. Exod. 21:29; 22:10f.; Job 31:39, and elsewhere; on this, see BrSynt §19c and Joüon, Gr §136d.

3b A great number of MSS and Q^a read ועמי (and my people), as do the copies of Gk, Syr, Vulg; yet the MT is to be preferred, since the subject of both halves of the verse is identical (in contrast to the preceding line).

Form

At one time, chap. 1 must have existed as an independent collection; we encounter a new superscription in 2:1 which does not give any indication that it was aware of the superscription in 1:1. Six originally independent messages of the prophet are arranged here so as to form an impressive unity: 2–3; 4–9; 10–17; 18–20; 21–26 (expanded by 27f.); 29–31.

Many modern scholars (Hertzberg, Kaiser, Eichrodt) actually take vv. 2–9 as a single unit. But just the fact that the verses differ in length would call this into question (concerning this, see Ley, op. cit. [in literature for 1:1]; Robertson, op. cit. [in literature for 1:1]; and K. Budde, *ZAW* 49 [1931] 20ff.). Even more significantly, the genres are different and there are differences in emphasis: "The message of Yahweh, which is introduced by Isaiah in 1:2–3, is a harsh and sharp accusation, whereas Isaiah begins the reproach in 1:4–9 with more of a rebuke; then he goes on to make accusations against his people, rather than just to scold them" (Fohrer, op. cit. [in literature for 1:1] 254f.).

Meter: The section vv. 2–3 consists of four verses, each with six stresses; the first has three lines with two stresses each (2 + 2 + 2). The next three have two lines each, with three stresses each (3 + 3). Just the form of 2a is enough to set it off as an introduction, separate from the speech of Yahweh which follows.

The message begins with an appellation to heaven and earth to hear how shamefully Israel has behaved. Without a doubt, we are dealing with a judgment speech ("rîb-pattern"). The closest parallel is found in the introduction to the Song of Moses in Deut. 32:1: האזינו השמים ואדברה ותשמע הארץ אמרי־פי (Give ear, O heavens, and I will speak; and let the earth hear the words of my mouth). In the very same way as described in Deut. 31:28, Yahweh wants to summon heaven and earth to serve as witnesses (העיד); actually, this is to take place in an assembly in which he will proclaim the words of the law in the hearing of the people; cf. also 30:19 and 4:26. In Mic. 6:2, the mountains are summoned to listen attentively to the lawsuit (ריב) of Yahweh, and the enduring foundations of the earth are called upon to lend an ear (according to a widely accepted textual emendation, reading האזין, give ear). In a somewhat altered form, a summons is also to be found in Mic. 1:2, admonishing "all peoples" to hear, imploring "the earth, and all that is in it" to listen attentively. The same formula is used in Jeremiah (2:4), and in Psalm 50 (v. 4) heaven and earth are summoned to appear in the context of the covenant festival so that they can be present when Yahweh judges. Finally, we can find an altered form of this appellation in Job 20:27. As Mendenhall (op. cit., 37) noted, this summons to heaven and earth can be explained by consulting the usage within ancient Near Eastern state treaties, where the gods served as witnesses, a phenomenon particularly noticeable among the Hittites (see *ANET²* 199–206; and V. Korošec, *Hethitische Staatsverträge* [1931]; however, cf. also the treaties of *sefire* in the Aramaic usage; see M. A. Dupont-Sommer, *Les inscriptions araméennes de Sfiré* [1958] 19, and often elsewhere, or consult such writings as the treaty between Suppiluliumas and Niqmadd of Ugarit; see J. Nougayrol, *Le palais royal d'Ugarit* IV [1956] Text No. 17, 340). The commonly used lists of gods include also the deified powers of nature: mountains, rivers, springs, sea, heaven and earth, wind and clouds. No doubt, this "secular" treaty formula had an influence on the terminology used in the form of the OT version of the Yahweh covenant. Here also, heaven and earth, as well as (in certain circumstances) mountains and the enduring foundations of the earth, are characterized as witnesses to the covenant. The covenant oath is called the "oath of heaven (and) the earth" *(mamītu ša šamê irṣiti)* in the epic of Tukulti-Ninurta (see Harvey, op. cit., 182). This is the reason why in this "judgment speech" Yahweh, one of the partners in the covenant, when accusing the other partner, Israel, of having broken the covenant, summons these powers as the ones who were to keep watch over the covenant; those who had witnessed the ratification of the covenant are also witnesses who attest that the covenant has been violated (cf. Job 20:27), so that they might verify the failure to abide by it, and naturally also, that they would set the sanctions in place which were planned for the eventuality that "disobedience" would occur. Of course, though there is still a formal correspondence, the reality of these powers is completely subsumed under the OT belief in God. Yahweh does not need any witnesses to back up his accusations, and he alone is responsible for allowing the curses of the covenant to come upon Israel; the gods are set aside, and the summoning of heaven and earth remains as nothing more than a rhetorical device. H. Schmidt, who first recognized the genre of judgment speech (*Schriften des AT in Auswahl* II/2, 133 and 143), believed that this genre had its roots in a secular judicial setting. E. Würthwein took the exact opposite approach, trying to show that, at the very least, the cult served as the *original* setting in life for the judgment speech, more specifically, in the covenant renewal ceremony ("Der Ursprung der prophetischen Gerichtsrede," *ZTK* 49 [1952] 1–16). Based on considerations from Psalm 50, it is easy to see that a spokesman for Yahweh would have stood up at the covenant renewal festival and raised a cry of lament, in the name of his God, over against the unfaithful partner to the covenant. This thesis has encountered considerable opposition (F. Hesse, "Wurzelt die prophetische Gerichtsrede im israelitischen Kult?" *ZAW* 65 [1953] 45–53; B. Gemser, "The Rîb- or Controversy-Pattern in Hebrew Mentality," VTSup 3 [1955] 120–137; and H. J.

Boecker, *Redeformen des Rechtslebens im Alten Testament,* WMANT 14
[1964]), while E. von Waldow (*Der traditionsgeschichtliche Hintergrund
der prophetischen Gerichtsreden,* BZAW 85 [1963]) adopts a mediating
position when he writes: "On the basis of formal considerations, the
prophetic judgment speeches are rooted in the secular judicial life of the
Hebrew legal community. However, in terms of content, they point back
to origins within the tradition of the covenant of Yahweh with Israel" (p.
20). In light of Psalm 50 or Deuteronomy 32 (on this, see Wright, op. cit.),
but even more so, on the grounds of the connection with the formal
terminology of the suzerainty treaty, it must be questioned whether form
and content can be so completely separate from one another, which
would indeed suggest that the original form of the prophetic speech of
judgment is to be found within the context of the cult. Even if one can
substantiate the claim that there are influences from secular forms which
use forensic terminology, this still does nothing to contradict an origin in
the cult. The central point of this discussion is that one must conclude
that the forms and thought patterns connected with the Yahweh covenant furnish the backdrop for the prophetic judgment speech and, therefore, that Israel is being measured according to the standards of the
covenant stipulations. This does not mean that Isaiah, just because he
uses the genre of a judgment speech (see also 1:18–20; 3:13–15; in a
qualified sense, 5:1–7), is to be considered a cultic prophet or an official of
the Yahweh amphictyony, a thesis which H. Graf Reventlow has put
forth to explain the background of Amos (*Das Amt des Propheten bei
Amos* [1962]) and Jeremiah (*Liturgie und prophetisches Ich bei Jeremia*
[1963]). When viewed in its entirety, Isaiah's proclamation does not simply and solely reflect the traditions of the amphictyony. And yet, it is
fundamentally significant for understanding Isaiah that one is able to
determine that he is cognizant of the covenant tradition and that he considered Jerusalem also to be under a direct obligation to live according to
that which all Israel had inherited. In actual fact, this connection can be
verified on the basis of the overall content of his proclamation, an analysis of which shows that Isaiah's use of the judgment speech, but also wide-
ranging sections of his complete message, do not simply make use of
forms, but also many aspects of the content of the covenant tradition, at
which points one must pay close attention to the way in which Isaiah
reinterprets ideas which have been transmitted from the past.

Setting

Nothing can be established with any confidence concerning the time
when Isaiah delivered this message. W. Zimmerli (*Das Gesetz und die
Propheten* [1963] 114f.), who especially sees a reliance upon Amos and
Hosea in Isaiah's early preaching, thinks that he can detect a theme in
1:2f. which is reminiscent of Hosea's concept of the sonship of the people
and suggests the possibility that Isaiah's demand for obedience might
have pulled together various concepts which are part of Hosea's message
about the "knowledge of God." If this is the case, the present message
might possibly be presumed to come from the time in which Isaiah's
activity first began. But, as will be demonstrated, the message about
"sonship" and "knowledge" has different, very deep roots in another
traditio-historical setting. The short, apodictic form of this section,

which leaves no room for questions and objections and which does not betray the slightest effort at a careful, reasonable assessment of Israel, uses instead a caustic tone to set forth an accusation by God which leads to complete destruction, forcing one rather to conclude that the prophet spoke this message after a great deal of experience with his people.

Commentary

[1:2a] The appellation to the witnesses speaks of Yahweh, the one who laments, in the third person, in contrast to Deut. 4:26; 30:19; 31:28, and 32:1. A fundamental distinction is made here between the prophet, who is the spokesman for Yahweh, and Yahweh, the one who actually laments; the same is true in 3:13, 14a; Mic. 6:1f.; Ps. 50:6 (cf. also the difference in the tense of כי יהוה דבר, "thus said the Lord" versus אדברה, "I will speak," in Deut. 32:1). Here we are no longer dealing with a naive identification of the speaker with Yahweh himself; by the time the proclamation is made, the moment when the revelation was received is already in past time. This shift is an indication that Isaiah is not speaking as one who is directly involved in circumstances connected with the cult in which Θεὸς ἐπιφανής (God manifest) is directly present and allows his word of judgment to go forth (cf. the epiphany of Yahweh which precedes the judgment speech in Mic. 1:3f. and Ps. 50:3). Since heaven and earth are no longer considered, within the context of the Yahwistic faith, to be deified powers of nature who could keep a watch on the covenant, as was typically believed by those who lived in the immediate vicinity around Israel, the question must be posed concerning the way in which Isaiah understood the motif which finds expression in this tradition. One hint which suggests how it was interpreted is furnished for us by Mic. 1:2; when characterizing those who are summoned to hear the accusation, which will be leveled, Mic. 1:2 uses "you peoples, all of you" instead of "heavens" and also uses "earth, and all that is in it" instead of "earth." In a similar way, Isaiah wants to say: All the living beings in the heavens and on the earth should (and can) testify that Yahweh is very much in the right when he brings his accusation concerning the violation of the covenant.

[1:2b] In the accusation, Yahweh contrasts his own good deeds for Israel with the apostasy of the people. Their unfaithfulness is brought into sharper focus by means of the harsh contrast which is portrayed when the people's deeds are compared with the good things which had been received from God, God's care being described with the imagery of a father's loving care. The same imagery is used in 23:4, which also uses the verbs גדל (become great) and רומם (be exalted) but then expands the idea by using חיל (writhe) and ילד (give birth). As a rule, the OT prefers describing the parental care for children by using the two verbs ילד, meaning either "beget" or "give birth," and גדל, which in this context simply means "bring through" (in light of the high death rate among children); see 49:21; 51:18; Hos. 9:12, and 1 Kings 11:20 (text emended); see also Job 31:18 (cf. on that text L. Köhler, *Alttestamentliche Wortforschung, Rektoratsrede,* Zürich [1930] 13). But it can also be that more is meant than just a concern for body and life. The meaning of the verb גדל

becomes more clear already in Job 7:17 where the parallel phrase שִׁית לֵב אֶל, "have deep concern for," says the same thing in a different way (cf. on this also Job 31:18). The use of this imagery is remarkable in many respects. In the first place, it is relatively rare to find the metaphor of Yahweh as father used in the OT. Second, when the concept of father is used in a general sense in the Semitic languages, the emphasis is placed on the aspects of rule, of ownership, and of general authority (see Eichrodt, *TheolOT* I, OTL, 235), but in this case the context suggests that Israel was being confronted with the caring kindness of its God. Evidence for the idea of goodness also being part of the ancient Near Eastern concept of fatherhood is furnished by a Phoenician city gate inscription from Karatepe, in which Azitawadda declares: "On account of my right-eousness and my wisdom *and the goodness of my heart* (נעם לבי), every king considered me his father" (see *WO* I/4 [1949] 274; and *WO* II/2 [1955] 178; cf. the letter of *Yarîm-Lim* from Aleppo to *Yashûb-Yaḥad* from *Der:* "I have been a father and a brother for you; but you have been wicked towards me and an enemy"; see Harvey, op. cit., 183f.). In the third place, according to the parallels which have been mentioned, one would have anticipated that Isaiah would have used the two verbs ילד (beget) and גדל (bring up), which reiterate the details of parental care with an amazing consistency. The Song of Moses, which has noticeable points of contact with this passage not only because of its use of the appellation to heaven and earth but also when it uses other terminology similar to what is employed in this judgment speech, does not only say that Yahweh, as a father, created (קנה), made (עשה), and made Israel ready (כונן) (Deut. 32:6), but risks saying, without any embarrassment, that God is also to be considered the rock who *begot* them (ילד), the God who had labor pains and *bore them* (18). Of course, ילד (bear) is to be taken figuratively, as is also the case in Ps. 2:7. But, as would normally hold true for the OT in general, Isaiah takes great care to make sure not even to hint at suggesting that Yahweh was actually known as one who functioned on the same level as the procreating deities who were well-known in the regions which surrounded Israel. This could also be the reason why, again in contrast to Deuteronomy 32, he does not specifically use the title "father" when speaking of Yahweh (concerning El as father in the texts from Ras Shamra, cf. M. H. Pope, *El in the Ugaritic Texts,* VTSup 2 [1955] 47ff.; and J. Gray, *The Legacy of Canaan,* VTSup 5 [1957] 116ff.). Fourth and finally, although the people are addressed, Isaiah still speaks, in this case in the same way as in the Song of Moses (5), about "sons," thus seeing (as 30:9) the individuals who were standing before him. At other times during the ancient Israelite era, the entire people was called the "son" of Yahweh (Exod. 4:22; Hos. 11:1 [Gk actually reads here τὰ τέκνα, the sons]; Jer. 31:20 [about Ephraim]). However, in later times, "sons" of Yahweh are referred to by Deuteronomy (14:1) and Jeremiah (3:14, 19, 22; 4:22, among others; see Isa. 43:6f.; 63:16; Mal. 1:6; 3:17; concerning the general topic of sonship in the Old Testament, see G. Quell, *TDNT* V, p. 959ff.; and H. W. Wolff, *Hosea,* BK 14/1, 255ff. [Engl: *Hosea,* 197ff.]). How is it that Isaiah comes to speak about the Israelites as sons? In the ancient Near East in general, the king was widely acknowl-edged as the "son" of the deity, the deity as his father; this concept is not completely foreign to the OT either (on this, see H. Frankfort, *Kingship and the Gods* [1958³] 159ff., and 299ff.; in addition, see S. Morenz, *Ägyptische Religion* [1960] 36ff. In the OT: 2 Sam. 7:14; Pss. 2:7; 89:27; in addition, see Isa. 9:1–6; 11:1–9). But, within the domain of the kingship ideology, the "son" is the earthly representative of the heavenly deity, acting on the deity's behalf, and answerable to the deity. There is no mention of this in the present text. The verbs clearly refer to the domain of child-rearing. Child-rearing is the central theme in the arena of wisdom teaching. In reality, from very ancient times, the idea of a spiritual sonship has its roots in the realm of wisdom (concerning Egypt, see H. Brunner, *Altägyptische Erziehung* [1957] 10f.).

In the twelfth precept of *Ptah-hotep* one reads: "When you have become a mature man, then get for yourself a son (that is, a student who can learn), so that God will be kindly disposed. If he is upright and acclimates himself to your nature and is concerned for your welfare in a proper manner, then provide for him everything which is good; then he is your son, then he will be part of that which your Ka has reproduced; if such is the case, you should not cut off your heart from his. Concerning the 'seed' (that is, the physical son), if he causes dissension, if he errs in his ways and transgresses your instructions and fights against everything which is said to him, and if his mouth is filled with wretched words, then reject him; he is not your son. Demote him to be a servant . . ." (according to Brunner, op. cit., 155f.; cf., in addition, L. Dürr, *Das Erziehungswesen im Alten Testament und im antiken Orient,* MVAAG 36/2 [1932] 15). Just as in Egypt and Babylon, the wisdom teacher in Israel is also considered to be "father" and addresses his student as "son" (Prov. 2:1; 3:1; 4:1, 10, 20; 5:1, 20; 6:1; 7:1).

The lack of insight and understanding (3), which the prophet notes when reprimanding the sons, points in the same direction. We can put this even more succinctly: as father, Yahweh is the teacher who passes on well-intentioned and good advice, conveys wisdom which leads to control over one's life, and heads one away from all danger (on this, cf. Job 7:17 and 31:18).

The sons, however, who have been well-schooled, "raised themselves up in rebellion" against him. The verb פשע (rebel) is originally a political term: "Israel has been in rebellion against the house of David" (1 Kings 12:19). However, this Israel which was in rebellion had established a "covenant" with David (2 Sam. 5:3). פֶּשַׁע (rebellion) is the breaking of the covenant (see 2 Kings 1:1; 3:5, 7; 2 Chron. 10:19) which sets in motion the threatened curses which were detailed in the covenant document; thus, it is the opposite of חֶסֶד, "covenant faithfulness," or elsewhere אֱמֶת (faithfulness). The verb פשע (rebel) is thus completely appropriate when it is used in an accusation within the context of the covenant tradition (note the use of the verb in Jer. 2:8, 29; 3:13, and the use of the substantive in Mic. 1:5; 6:7; that is, it is also used in judgment speeches). When פשע (rebel) is used, individual mistakes are not the issue—the substantive rarely occurs in the older texts in the plural; it is rather used to brand those who have essentially given up on being loyal to their Lord God, the one who had given them ongoing proof of his goodness (on this, see Köhler, *OTTheol*, 169f.; and idem, *ZAW* 46 [1928] 213ff.). What the covenant partner raised as an accusation against Israel was already staring them in the face with utter seriousness when this verb was used.

[1:3] However, by using a comparison, the prophet takes great care to make sure that the significance of this reproach from God could not be missed. Both the ox and ass were well-known in Palestine, with both of them being used for farming small plots of land (see passages like Gen. 34:28; Judg. 6:4, and Isa. 32:20; cf. Nielsen, op. cit.); both were used for plowing (Deut. 22:10; see also 22:4). Verse 3a appears to be used in a proverbial fashion, and it seems that this might have been a pedagogical wisdom saying. As a matter of fact, the wisdom teachers love to use imagery from the ways of the animal world for their budding scholars: the ant (Prov. 6:6; 30:25), badger (30:26), grasshoppers (30:27), lizards (30:28), etc. (see 26:2f.); 1 Kings 5:13 also shows that the ways of animals were a favorite theme in wisdom. There are numerous examples of comparisons from the animal world, e.g.: "Fodder and a stick and burdens for an ass; bread and discipline and work for a servant!" (Sir. 33:25). There are other passages which tell us that the ass must be kept in line (Prov. 26:3), as is also true for the ox (Prov. 7:22; 15:17; cf. also 14:4). Sayings like these are used in wisdom for more than just examples and comparisons. Wisdom has as a basic goal that it might demonstrate the basic order which has been set up for everything in the living and nonliving world, the human realm and the universe. Animals can be used as examples insofar as they embody truths about basic order (Egyptian *Maat*) which help one better to understand oneself (see von Rad, *OTTheol* I, 424f.; Morenz, op. cit., 130ff.). Part of the basic order into which one must fit oneself is the realm of the basic structure of human society, in which one is subordinated under the master, the Lord. But now, Isaiah takes the example which has its roots in wisdom and gives it a new dimension; his basic concern is not with the *Maat* type of order which has been established at creation; rather, his concern is with faithfulness to the covenant which was supposed to show a correspondence with Yahweh's gracious turning to his people.

And yet, "Israel has no insight, my people no understanding." Both of the verbs ידע (know) and התבונן (consider intelligently), as used here, are apparently also rooted in wisdom (ידע is intransitive; Isaiah is not rebuking them because of a lack of the knowledge of God). This means that Isaiah can given an interpretation of the violation of the covenant by using wisdom terminology. For him, it is not contradictory to compare demands to be faithful to the covenant to the demands of wisdom for perceptive, "insightful" behavior, which is wisdom's ideal. For him, it is the same thing to practice faithfulness toward Yahweh and to behave in a "wise" way. "The rebellion grows out of the failure to have insight . . . , which here, as in 30:8–11, is in no way to be taken as the result of Yahweh himself causing a hardening, but rather, it is represented as something contrary to what is natural" (R. Fey, *Amos und Jesaja,* WMANT, 12 [1963] 120).

There are other places in Isaiah where the two roots ידע (know) and בין (perceive) stand next to one another (6:9: בין and ידע; see also 32:4), and he uses ידע in an absolute sense in other places as well (6:9; 32:4; 5:13: מבלי דעת [want of knowledge]; 11:2: רוח דעת [spirit of knowledge]; cf. also Hos. 4:6; there, however, דעת [knowledge] as defined more specifically by דעת אלוהים [knowledge of God] in 4:1, and the term תורת אלוהיך [the law of your God], used parallel to it, is also defined more specifically). This intransitive usage is characteristic of wisdom (in Prov. 1:2: דעת [knowledge] is parallel to both חכמה [wisdom] and מוסר [correction]; it is parallel to בינה [understanding] in 4:1; 14:7 speaks about שפתי דעת [words of knowledge]; in Job 34:2 ידעים [knowledgeable ones] is parallel to חכמים [wise ones]; cf. 13:2; in Ps. 73:22 לא אדע [I did not know] is used with בַּעַר ["like a beast, stupid"], which shows, as does Prov. 12:1; 30:2, that it is commonly used also in wisdom. Cf. also Eccles. 9:11).

Even in this accusation speech, which does not allow any room for discussion, Yahweh still calls Israel עמי, my people (cf. לא עמי, not my people, in Hos. 1:9), highlighting both his sovereign authority and his fatherly affection.

With this, the accusation comes to an end. One would expect at this point either that one would be threatened with a judgment, something like what is found in the "Song of the Vineyard" in 5:1–7, or that an admonition to repent would follow, as in 1:10–17. However, in the same way that it is handled in the judgment speech in 3:13–15, the hearer is confronted with the harshness of the accusation, and it remains for the individual to figure out the consequences. What is in store for a stubborn and rebellious son who refuses to be corrected is stated in the law (Deut. 21:18–21), and every Israelite was aware of the threats connected with breaking the covenant. It must have been apparent, to everyone who heard, that the situation had become deadly serious.

This passage, together with Hab. 3:2 (Gk), was used as the basis for the reference to ox and ass at the Christmas manger. In the gospel of Pseudo-Matthew one can read: "On the third day after the birth of our Lord Jesus Christ holy Mary went out from the cave, and went into a stable and put her child in a manger, and an ox and ass worshiped him. Then was fulfilled that which was said through the prophet Isaiah: 'The ox knows his owner and the ass his master's crib'" (Pseudo-Matthew 14, according to Hennecke-Schneemelcher, *New Testament Apocrypha* I [1963] 410; on this, see Ziegler, op. cit.).

Purpose and Thrust

There is little doubt that this section was purposely put at the beginning of the collection of messages in chap. 1 (just as it is not by chance that this collection introduces the whole book). It sets forth Isaiah's major accusation against Israel; all of the reprimands which will follow can be nothing but a host of concrete examples detailing this fundamental faithlessness over against Yahweh. The appraisal which takes these sins as rebellion and stubbornness against God corresponds to Isaiah's basic premise and will therefore be encountered again and again (1:4; 3:8f.; 30:8f.; 31:6). In certain circumstances, that appraisal will be modified somewhat and those sins will be viewed as pride and arrogance (2:6ff.; 10:5ff.). Insofar as these sins are contrasted with the fatherly way in which Yahweh has helped Israel grow up, its reprehensible character will be made abundantly clear. "These few words open up great vistas in the divine action in history"; "a long road in history has come to a completely negative end" (von Rad, *OTTheol* II, 181, and 151). Of course, when Isaiah ponders the way Yahweh dealt with Israel, he does not refer back to the aspects of salvation history which deal with the tradition of the exodus (see T. C. Vriezen, "Essentials of the Theology of Isaiah," in FS J. Muilenburg

[1962] 128f.), but rather, to a description of Yahweh's intervention on Israel's behalf in holy war (see the discussion of 9:3; 28:21), his providing fruits of the ground (see 1:19, but also the "Song of the Vineyard"), and his gifts of justice, righteousness, and peace (9:1ff.; 11:1ff.). Since Yahweh is not shown as a demanding Lord, but rather as a gracious, guiding and protecting father, one would expect a corresponding reaction on the part of the covenant partner Israel within the framework of trust and thankfulness, rather than just in terms of simple obedience. As Isaiah brings his comments to a close, the exact opposite of פשע (rebel) is used, namely, faith (תאמין), which means more than just "rely upon, be held up by leaning upon," but also carries with it the aspect of "look to him," and "trust." Thus, it is an event which takes place on Israel's journey with its God, an event which is observed by Isaiah, with rejection of faithfulness to the covenant characterized as a lack of knowledge and insight. When the people were unfaithful to their God, they also put themselves outside the bounds of the created order and renounced "what was characteristic of all creaturely existence, that which would draw the creature to one's master and provider" (Eichrodt, op. cit., 26). Whoever renounces faithfulness toward God is finally also a fool before the forum of human wisdom.

Isaiah 1:4–9

Almost Like Sodom

Literature

[Literature update through 1979: S. Speier, "Zu drei Jesajastellen (1,7; 5,24; 10,7)," *TZ* 21 (1965) 310–313. W. T. Claassen, "Linguistic Arguments and the Dating of Isaiah 1:4–9," *JNSL* 3 (1974) 1–18.]

Text

1:4 Alas sinful people,
    offense-laden generation,
  pack of rogues,
    sons, who act destructively.
  They[a] have abandoned Yahweh,
    scorned the Holy One of Israel, [b][turned themselves
      backwards].[b]
 5 Why do you still wish to be struck,
    that you persist in revolt?
  The whole[a] head is sick
    and the whole heart ailing!
 6 From head to foot
    [a]no unhurt place is on him![a]
  Only wounds and bruises
    and marks from a fresh blow,
  not pressed out[b] and not bound up
    and not softened up with oil!
 7 Your land: a wasteland,
    your cities:[a] burned up by fire,[b]
  Your tillable ground: before your eyes
    strangers waste it! [c][and it will become wilderness[d] as at the
      destruction of 'Sodom'.][c]
 8 Yes, Zion's daughter is left
    like a booth made of foliage in a vineyard,
  like a shelter[a] for the night in a cucumber field,
    like an [b]ass's foal 'in a pen'![b]
 9 Had Yahweh of Hosts not
    spared for us a small number[a] of escapees,

it would have gone for us as for Sodom,[b]
we would have been like Gomorrah.[b]

4a עזבו (they have abandoned) is a perfect of continuance, which describes an action from the distant past which continues on into the present; cf. Joüon, Gr §112e.

4b–b נזרו אחור (they turned themselves backwards) is missing in Gk, Lat; Gk[h], Theod, Syr[h], and other texts (see Ziegler, op. cit., in literature for 1:2–3) presuppose the same reading as is found in the MT by reading ἀπηλλοτριώθησαν εἰς τὰ ὀπίσω (they alienated themselves by going toward that which was behind). The difficult state of the text itself might be the reason why it is not in the Gk, Lat. נזר is actually the *niph'al* form, from זור, and means "turn oneself from"; אחור means "backside, behind, to the rear" (cf. a phrase like סבב לאחור, [the sea] turned back, in Ps. 114:3, 5). Budde's suggested emendation (*ZAW* 49 [1931] 21), מֵאַחֲרָיו (from after him), would fit better into the context, but there is no real justification for accepting it. G. R. Driver (*JTS* 38 [1937] 36f.) compares נזר with the Arabic *zarra* "squeeze out, drive back," but this is not a satisfying reading in its context. Vulg (*abalienati sunt retrorsum,* they have become estranged backwards) and Targ (אסתחרו והוו לאחרא, they have turned around and they are backwards) seem to be based on the MT (contra BHK³). N. H. Tur-Sinai's suggestion (op. cit. [in literature for 1:1] 155f.) to read יחד (together) or כאחד (all as one) for אחור and to translate it "They have become estranged altogether" would, in fact, make good sense, but it is too uncertain a reading for one to be inclined to accept it. Staying with the transmitted text is still most advisable. However, these two words do extend the line so that it is longer than what one would expect on the basis of the metrical rhythm and are considered a gloss by most contemporary exegetes.

5a Within the confines of poetry, the article will sometimes be missing, which one would expect before ראש, meaning "the whole head"; cf. Joüon, Gr §139e.

6a–a According to H. D. Hummel (*JBL* 76 [1957] 105), אֵין־בּוֹ מְתֹם (no unhurt place is on him) is a copyist's error for the original אין במו תם (there is no sound place in him), but this change in the reading is not recommended (contra Kaiser), since Ps. 38:4, 8 also reads אין מתם (there is no sound place). It is not recommended that one strike the three words from the text just because the Gk does not offer an equivalent phrase ('Aquila, Gk[h]: ουκ εστιν εν αυτω ολοκληρια, there is no soundness in him), since, even on the basis of meter, these words are needed.

6b זרו is a *qal* passive from זרר (cf. Joüon, Gr §82 l), "to be pressed out" (on the basis of the Arabic *zarra,* "press upon, press"), not simply meaning "pinch one's eyes" as suggested in KBL.

7a A great number of MSS, Targ[L], Syr presuppose reading ועריכם (and your cities), but Isaiah's concise style would hardly justify reading it this way.

7b אש (fire) is dependent upon שרפות (burned up), which is in the construct state, mentioning what caused the burning; see Joüon, Gr §121p.

7c–c MT: "and it'll become a desert as when destroyed by foreigners," coming right after mention is made of זרים (foreigners), is not a possible reading. In addition to that, it is without exception in the OT that "Sodom and Gomorrah" follows the substantive מהפכה (overthrow), which means that a standard fixed formula was in use (see Deut. 29:22; Isa. 13:19; Jer. 49:18; 50:40; Amos 4:11). Ewald had already suggested reading סדם (Sodom) for זרים (foreigners). This emendation makes more sense than that recently suggested by Tur-Sinai (op. cit. [in literature for 1:1] 156), who suggested changing it to read זֵדִים (haughty ones). However, the entire little phrase is more than what fits here, if one considers the meter, and should be taken as a gloss, based on similar wording in 9b.

7d Qᵃ reads ושממו עליה (and its destruction shall be upon it) instead of ושממה (and destruction).

8a Qᵃ: וכמלונה (and as a booth); see also Gk, Syr, Vulg.

8b–b כעיר נצורה, "as a guarded (or protected?) city," does not make good sense, even though some have made valiant attempts to suggest what it might mean and thus preserve the reading as is (see, for example, Delitzsch, ad loc., who thinks of a blockade). Gk: ὡς πόλις πολιορκουμένη (like a besieged city), Targ: כקרתא דצירין עלה (like a city which is besieged); Syr reads *hᵉbîštâ* (besieged) for נצורה (blockaded); thus, the versions all have a "besieged city" in mind, which is what made Dillmann, a long time ago, read נְצוּרָה (besieged), reading a *niph'al* participle from צור instead of נְצוּרָה (guarded). But these emendations are also not satisfactory, since they would all compare the inhabitants of Zion to a city. One must also reject the translation "tower for watching" (Hitzig, Duhm, and others) since "נצורה does not mean watching, עיר does not mean tower, and there are no guard cities (castles!)" (Dillmann). Referring to נְצוּרִים (secret places) in Isa. 65:4 really does not help, since there are problems there with both the word itself and its meaning. Maybe the problem is deeper than the textual reading. F. X. Wutz (*BZ* 21 [1933] 11f.) suggests reading כְּעִיר בְּצִירָה, which he translates "as a tent stake in a pen" (according to the Arabic *'ajr*, "tent stake," and the Arabic *sîra*, "pen, fold," which also seems to be the reading in Mic. 2:12). But this use of עיר is not found anywhere else in Hebrew, and one is hard-pressed to understand why just a "tent stake" would be standing alone in a pen. I would suggest, therefore, assuming Wutz is on the right track, that the text be emended so that it reads בצירה, "pen," and then to read עיר (perhaps vocalized as עַיִר), which would mean "the foal of an ass."

9a מעט (a few) can also serve to point out that a number is very small (e.g., מעט מזְעָר, in a very little while, in 10:25; שְׁאָר מְעַט מִזְעָר, those who survive will be very few, in 16:14; cf. also 26:20 and, in addition, Ps. 105:12; Prov. 5:14; 10:20). It definitely fits in our passage here and ought not be removed simply because Gk, Syr, Vulg do not have an equivalent reading. Of course, כמעט also means "almost," and it is at least worth pondering whether the *athnach* should not be placed under שריד (escapees) and whether כמעט (a small number) should then be brought down and read in the next line. But logic would speak against transferring this word, as has often been done, since, without the goodness of Yahweh (Targ correctly points to what is meant here, reading ברחמוהי, "with his mercy"), Zion would not have been "almost" like Sodom and Gomorrah, but would have been exactly like them.

9b Qᵃ reads סודם (Sodom) and עומרה (Gomorrah), which is to be vocalized with the help of the Greek as Σοδομα and Γομορρα. The second vowel was already being sounded when the first short syllable was pronounced (on this, see W. Baumgartner, *Beiträge zum hebräischen Lexikon*, BZAW 77 [1958] 29).

Form

On thematic grounds, v. 4 seems to fit right in with vv. 2f. Once again, the discussion is about "sons" and פשע (rebel) is further explicated by the use of the roughly synonymous verbs עזב (abandon) and נאץ (scorn). But, in actual fact, the הוי (alas) introduces a new section. Yahweh himself does not speak here, as he did previously; instead, the discussion refers to him now in the third person (for more about the delineation of the units, see the explanation above, 1f.). There is no disagreement about the fact that v. 10 starts a new section.

Meter: The meter is irregular. After removing נזרו אחור (turned themselves backwards), each of the first two lines in v. 4 contains a two-stress bicolon, the third a five-stress colon with an uncommon pattern of two, then three stresses (2 + 3), which serves to identify a breaking point. The actual lament ends at this point. In vv. 5 and 6a, 4 two-stress bicola follow; in v. 6b there is a three-stress bicolon, which once again points to the end of another part of the section: the image of a sick, bruised body. In the third section, vv. 7f. (after the removal of 7bγ), once again there are four more two-stress bicola, following which v. 9 closes the section with an impressive three-stress bicolon and then a final two-stress bicolon which concludes the description of the devastation.

The section is thus very artistically arranged in terms of meter; the variation in the metrical rhythm is not arbitrary but gives a clear indication about the thought-patterns in each part.

When one observes this section according to the genre, this is a reproach, more specifically, as is often the case with Isaiah, a woe-oracle (see C. Westermann, *Grundformen prophetischer Rede* [1960] 136ff. [Engl: *Basic Forms of Prophetic Speech* (1967) 189ff.]; on this, see also E. Gerstenberger, "The Woe-oracles of the Prophets," *JBL* 81 [1962] 249–263). This actually comes to an end with v. 4; one would expect that either a word of admonition or threat would follow. Instead of either of these, the prophet continues with a description of the sad state of affairs in which Jerusalem found itself, first by using imagery, then directly by portraying the precarious situation of the city. There was no longer any need for judgment to be proclaimed; it had already come upon Jerusalem. The prophet wrestles with the reality that what had happened was to be understood as a result of having fallen away from Yahweh. Even if it is not stated explicitly, the reproach shifts and turns into an admonition speech.

Setting

The time when Isaiah spoke this word (the authenticity of which has not been questioned) can be determined with great accuracy. The countryside is devastated, the cities of Judah have been burned down, Jerusalem is the only city left and it stands alone, heavily weighed down by its isolation. That can only refer to the situation after the siege of the city by Sennacherib in the year 701 (cf. 2 Kings 18:13–16 and the description of the campaign of Sennacherib as found on the Taylor-Prism, *AOT*² 352ff., *ANET*² 287f., *TGI* 56–58). Apparently the population of Jerusalem was happy about the fact that they were not forced into an unconditional surrender (concerning the mood in the city after the pull-out of the enemy troops, see 22:1ff.). Thus they had not yet reached the point of fully assessing the magnitude of the catastrophe that had struck the land—to say nothing of readiness to reflect on the catastrophe—and thus had not yet reached the point of deciding to repent. On the other hand, the prophet has not yet lost all hope that a new beginning could still come, even after the shock of the punishment which they had managed to survive. This message could not have been spoken very long after the actual disastrous events of 701. Kaiser, who takes 1:2–9 to be a unity (see ad loc.), thinks that "the festive, ancient cultic practice which called for an appeal to heaven and earth as God's witnesses . . . [would suggest] that the temple in Jerusalem was the place where Isaiah would have delivered this poetic message." The setting in life would have been a lamentation ceremony, at which the prophet, instead of delivering an oracle of salvation, would have called for the people to consider their own guilt. But one does not have the slightest impression that Isaiah is talking to people who are participants in a day of confession. The content of the message would lead one rather to conclude that it was uttered at a Zion festival, at which one would have had in mind a celebration of the invincibility and majesty of the city of God (cf. the Psalms of Zion 46, 48, 76, among others).

Commentary

[1:4] The woe is pronounced against the גוֹי חֹטֵא (sinful people) and the עַם כֶּבֶד עָוֹן (offense-laden generation). As quite often happens, the two common terms for "sin" and "guilt" are used in conjunction with one another. Even though פֶּשַׁע (rebellion) is the term which most adequately describes Isaiah's understanding of sin, and would be expected here, as was already mentioned in the commentary concerning v. 2b (see, concerning these three terms, V. Maag, *Text, Wortschatz und Begriffswelt des Buches Amos* [1951] 187ff.), the prophet is certainly not limited to using this term exclusively. The basic meaning of the root חטא is "go astray" (see Prov. 19:2: אָץ בְּרַגְלַיִם חוֹטֵא, he who makes haste with his feet misses his way; see also Prov. 8:36; Job 5:24, and the Arabic *ḥaṭi'a*, which is used when describing an arrow which misses its mark). In juridical terminology, חטא describes the case of someone failing to live according to standards of justice; in the cultic-religious sense, it is used to designate the violation of a firmly established order which is used to give guidance to someone when coming into contact with the deity.

The parallel term עָוֹן is derived from the root עוה, which has a basic meaning of "grow crooked" (see the Arabic *'awā*, "bend"), and the term thus means "go astray." "עָוֹן on the other hand indicates that the sins of commission or omission are sins of men with a wrong intention, an intention not in accord with God's will. . . . עָוֹן always presupposes consciousness of guilt" (Köhler, *TheolAT,* 159 [Engl: *OTTheol* (1957) 170]). However, even when one takes into account the "synthetic view of life" as taught by the elders, a view which does not attempt to make a fundamental distinction between "sin" and "guilt," so that חטא (sin), to a certain extent, is also involved in the concept of "guilt" (cf. K. H. Fahlgren, *ṣ^edākā, nahestehende und entgegengesetzte Begriffe im AT* [1932] 50ff. and 190ff.; K. Koch, "Gibt es ein Vergeltungsdogma im AT?" *ZTK* 52 [1955] 1–42 [Engl: "Is There a Doctrine of Retribution in the Old Testament?" in *Theodicy in the Old Testament* (1983) 57–87]; H. Gese, *Lehre und Wirklichkeit in der alten Weisheit* [1958] 37ff., and often elsewhere; U. Skladny, *Die ältesten Spruchsammlungen in Israel* [1962] 71ff.), it is still true that עָוֹן is much more developed in the direction of pointing toward guilt, so that it is only when one puts the two words next to each other that the sin-guilt connection can be fully understood. In the passage before us, Isaiah's precise wording brings the reality of this state of affairs admirably into focus; the activity of the people is repeatedly characterized as a failure to do what is right (note the use of the participle חֹטֵא, "acting destructively," instead of using a nominal form חֵטְא, "sin," as in 1:28 and Amos 9:8), which results in the people being laden with guilt. At this point it is intimated, once again according to the understanding of the synthetic view of life with its action-consequences sequence, that when the עָוֹן (offense) takes place, the punishment has already been set in

22

motion; however, it should be noted here that, when it is discussed on the level of prophetic thought, this sequence is in no way so locked in that it could not be broken. For even at the very time that Isaiah is making such an effort to bring to light the connection between the oppressive situation in the present time and the guilt which had caught up with the people, Yahweh is and remains still the unfettered lord of history and can, as v. 9 demonstrates, limit the consequences of the guilt which has been set in motion when the judgment takes place. Concerning the notion that the guilt is a heavy burden which weighs the sinner down, cf. Gen. 4:13.

The second line of v. 4 repeats the same idea twice. As in v. 2, the imagery about the rebellious sons is used (see Deut. 21:18–21), which is reminiscent, once again, of phrases from Deuteronomy 32: "A God of faithfulness and without iniquity, just and right is he. His sons have broken (שִׁחֵת!) 'his faithfulness'(?), a perverse and crooked generation" (vv. 4f.; concerning the plural בָּנִים, sons, see the commentary above on v. 2). Procksch (ad loc.) suggests: "In זרע מרעים reference is made to original sin." But when this terminology is used in parallel with בנים משחיתים (sons who act destructively), this can in no way have the meaning "descendants of rogues" (which would suggest that, because of their parentage, one might say that evil has become part of their nature), but it really means "offspring or generation which is made up of rogues" (*genitivus epexegeticus or explicativus,* a formal genitive added to the construct state as nearer definition; see GKC §128k–q). Yahweh is definitely also to be considered as the "father" of this זרע (pack), just as he is the "father" of the בנים משחיתים (sons who act destructively).

Compare this to the text of *Ptah-hotep,* cited in the discussion on v. 2, in which the disrespectful, physical son is called "seed." זרע מרעים (descendants of evildoers) is also found in Isa. 14:20, where, if one accepts our explanation of the way the genitive is used, one can be spared from making the commonly suggested textual change which reads it as a singular מרע (evildoer). Cf. also the use of בית מרעים (house of evildoers) in 31:2, parallel to פעלי און (those who work iniquity), but see also the parallel use of זרע רשעים (children of the wicked), which really means the same thing when it is used parallel to 'עוּלים' (unrighteous ones) (as emended!) in Ps. 37:28. These parallels demonstrate, at the same time, that זרע (offspring) has a scornful, judgmental tone in these contexts.

In v. 4b, the terms חֹטֵא (sinful) and עון (offense-laden), which are rather generic and nonspecific, are now given a more precise meaning. The use of חֹטֵא would lead one to suppose that some sort of legal regulations or cultic norms had been "trespassed against," but the accusation goes deeper than that: "They have abandoned Yahweh, scorned the Holy One of Israel." Once again, when using עזב (abandon) and נאץ (scorn), Isaiah uses two verbs which are rooted in the covenant tradition; cf. Deut. 31:20: "They will turn to other gods and serve them, and despise me (נאץ) and break my covenant," in which case the "trespassing against" Yahweh by the people would be dealt with by a corresponding rejection of the people by their God (Deut. 32:19; cf. also the parallel use of the terms "scorn" and "break the covenant" in Jer. 14:21). There is no doubt that with the use of נאץ (scorn) an accusation is leveled concerning the breaking of the covenant. In the same exact way, עזב (forsake) is used in

Deut. 31:16 with exactly the same meaning as the expression הפר את־בריתי (break my covenant), which is used parallel to it. In the same way, the people's having abandoned God brings on the threat that Yahweh would abandon the people. In deuteronomistic usage, עזב (abandon) (as also נאץ, scorn) can be used to describe the downfall of those who go to worship the heathen deities, without the covenant being explicitly mentioned (Judg. 2:12f.; 10:6, 10, 13; 1 Sam. 8:8; 12:10; and often elsewhere). Isaiah does not understand the "abandonment of Yahweh" on such an external and formal level. In 5:24, mention is made of spurning the word (אמרה) of the Holy One of Israel (parallel to מאס את תורת יהוה צבאות, despised the instruction of Yahweh of Hosts). According to the context of that passage, which is not completely certain, the downfall is directly connected with the perversion of justice (5:23). But that would also be just another one of the concrete examples of actions which come from having abandoned Yahweh himself, rooted in the overall breaking away from the daily relationship with Yahweh, including the refusal to trust and be obedient. In such an instance, there is nothing mentioned which would specifically suggest a "downfall" in the direction of idol worship. When Num. 14:11 describes scorning (נאץ) as the exact opposite of faith in Yahweh (האמין), it gets to the heart of the matter in the same way as Isaiah does here.

Yahweh, the God of Israel, is also called, in the parallel expression, the Holy One of Israel, phraseology which is almost completely limited in usage to those sections of scripture which are connected with the name Isaiah.

In addition to the passage before us, this designation is used by the prophet himself in 5:19, 24; 30:11, 12, 15; 31:1; contested or post-Isaianic passages are 10:20; 12:6; 17:7; 29:19; 37:23 (= 2 Kings 19:22); Deutero-Isaianic passages are 41:14, 16, 20; 43:3, 14; 45:11; 47:4; 48:17; 49:7; 54:5; 55:5; Trito-Isaianic passages are 60:9, 14; in addition, see Jer. 50:29; 51:5, and Pss. 71:22; 78:41; and 89:19. However, the fact that it appears so seldom in the Psalter shows that this name was used only by a narrow circle of those who were connected with the Jerusalem cult.

According to Procksch (*TDNT* I, 93), Isaiah himself was the one who is responsible for creating this name. Whether that is true remains uncertain. Though Psalm 71 is certainly postexilic (see H. J. Kraus, *Psalms 60–160*), it is completely within the realm of possibility that both Psalms 78 and 89 existed before the time of Isaiah (on Psalm 78, see O. Eissfeldt, *Das Lied Moses Dt 32:1–43 und das Lehrgedicht Asaphs Ps 78,* BVSAW.PH 104:5 [1958] 33f.; on Psalm 89, in addition to Kraus [op. cit.], see G. W. Ahlström, *Psalm 89* [1959]). Of course, knowledge about the holiness of Yahweh is something which was part of the Jerusalem theology from ancient times: the mountain, upon which Yahweh is enthroned, is holy (Pss. 2:6; 3:5, and often elsewhere), and so is his temple (5:8; 11:4, and often elsewhere); the habitation of the most high (46:5; 68:6, and often elsewhere), his throne (47:9), and naturally also his name (33:21, and often elsewhere) are holy; and, finally, theologically the most important, God himself is holy (99:5). Procksch (op. cit., 89) suspects that the root קדש (holy) has its roots in Canaanite culture. In actuality, the term also played a rather important role in the Phoenician-Punic region as well. In Ugarit, in the Keret-epic, which develops and shapes the ideology of kingship, the king is considered to be the son of El, offspring of the friendly and holy one (*qdš*) (II K I–II, 10f.; see W. Schmidt, "Wo hat die Aussage: Jahwe "Der Heilige" ihren Ursprung?" *ZAW* 74 [1962] 62–66; cf. also U. Bunzel, *Der Begriff der Heiligkeit im AT* [1914]; idem, *qdš und seine*

Derivate in der hebräischen und phönizisch-punischen Literatur [1917]; J. Hänel, *Die Religion der Heiligkeit* [1931]).

It is certainly not by chance that it is right in Jerusalem that Isaiah is made aware of the holy-holy-holy, uttered by the seraphim at the time of the call-vision, and that, in addition to the designation קדֹשׁ יִשְׂרָאֵל (Holy One of Israel), he also uses הָאֵל הַקָּדוֹשׁ (the holy God) (5:16). It is most certain that reference was made to God as the Holy One in Jerusalem even before the Israelite era. But because of that long history, there was the danger that the concept of holiness could have continued to be used in a magical-cultic context (see a passage like 1 Sam. 6:20 for the first aspect and Hos. 11:9 for the second). But it is by using the genitive determinative יִשְׂרָאֵל (Israel) that a genuine Israelite understanding was assured. One suspects that the phraseology was constructed by using the analogous pattern אֲבִיר יַעֲקֹב (Mighty One of Jacob) (Gen. 49:24; Isa. 49:26; 60:16; Ps. 132:2, 5) or, as Isaiah himself says, אֲבִיר יִשְׂרָאֵל (Mighty One of Israel) (1:24; 29:23 shows that the name קְדוֹשׁ יַעֲקֹב, Holy One of Jacob, could also be used). Based on Psalm 132, it is quite likely that the name אֲבִיר יַעֲקֹב (Mighty One of Jacob) came to Jerusalem in connection with the ark and its traditions, so that קְדוֹשׁ יִשְׂרָאֵל (Holy One of Israel) provides us with an instructive example to show the way in which Jerusalem traditions and old Israelite traditions were synthesized, as can be seen in the way these traditions developed in the city where the temple was located. It is on the basis of this newly established relationship of old and new elements that one should develop an interpretation about the concept of the holiness of God. The parallel expression אֲבִיר יַעֲקֹב (Mighty One of Jacob) gives one reason to believe that Yahweh is called the "Holy One of Israel" insofar as he turns toward Israel, leads and protects the people (see below for a discussion of אֲבִיר יִשְׂרָאֵל, Mighty One of Israel, at v. 24). This review of the history between God and his people takes place because it is in this history that the face of God is revealed. This particular meaning of the name fits very well into the present context; the Holy One of Israel is the God of the covenant who is viewed as the kind father who has raised his people; it is this background which underscores the reason why abandoning him is not only unprecedented but also impossible to comprehend. In analogous circumstances, the same title is also used in 5:24, and, in roughly the same circumstances, it is also mentioned in 31:1, where one must look directly to the Holy One of Israel in order to be strengthened in one's trust and in order to recognize that one does not need the Egyptian horses and chariots. But it must also be noticed that *qdš* (holy) stands next to *ltpn* (kind, fine) in the Ugaritic text which was mentioned already; its meaning can be further clarified by the Arabic *laṭîf,* which means "kind, friendly." Clearly, the concept of the holiness of Yahweh is closely connected with the very times when he bends down toward his people in a friendly way. Yet, Procksch has correctly pointed out the paradox which is a characteristic of this concept: "In itself supreme grace, the establishment of the קְדוֹשׁ יִשְׂרָאֵל in his people will be judgment" (op. cit., 94). The holiness of the holy God must consume everything which damages it, just like a firebrand destroys everything which comes close. In this way, the "light of Israel will become a fire and its holy one will become a flame" (10:17; see, in addition, 5:16;

30:12ff.). Apparently, Yahweh's holiness cannot be separated from the first commandment; holiness and zeal go hand in hand. And yet, it is not true that zeal and holiness are "in fact only differently shaded expressions of one and the same characteristic of Jahweh" (von Rad, *TheolAT* I, 204 [Engl: *OTTheol* I, 205]). Hos. 11:9 itself disproves this, but secondary passages in Isaiah 1–39 speak even more clearly against this view. In those places, the Holy One of Israel is the comfort for the remnant which has survived (10:20), the God in whom the redeemed rejoice, the one upon whom humans can rely on the day of judgment (17:7), and the one in whom the suffering and poorest among humanity can rejoice (29:19). It is no different in passages in Deutero-Isaiah and Trito-Isaiah which mention the Holy One of Israel, at the very point where redemption and salvation radiate out to shine upon Israel or the nations. Since this name is so firmly anchored in the context of the announcement of salvation, it must mean that there was a primary emphasis on this aspect in the original concept.

The addition at the end of v. 4, נזרו אחור, "they have turned themselves backwards," if we have understood it correctly, must be a later interpretive element which seeks to bring out the fact that Israel had at one time stood in a loyal relationship with its Lord. The main point of the verb זור *niph'al* (cf. the substantive זָר, stronger) is to describe the point at which one becomes estranged, when one cuts oneself loose from one's intimate circle where trust is characteristic: "I have become a stranger (מוּזָר) to my brethren, an alien to my mother's sons" (Ps. 69:9). When it defected, Israel walked away from the confines of what it had called home and where it lived under protecting care.

[1:5, 6] Although the destructive consequences of having broken the covenant were right out in the open, Israel persisted in rebellion. By using סָרָה (revolt), Isaiah reaches for another concept, in addition to עזב (abandon) and נאץ (scorn), one which would paint an even clearer picture of the insubordination of the people. He also uses the word at other times; see 31:6 (the participle סורר, unruly, is used in 1:23 and 30:1). This also belongs to what one would say about the obstinate son (cf. 31:1, 6 with Deut. 21:18, 20; see also Prov. 7:11). Hosea already knew that the term could be used in a metaphoric sense (4:16; 7:14; 9:15). The phrase דִּבֶּר סָרָה עַל (he has taught rebellion against), which is used in Deut. 13:6, practically became a technical term for trying to convince someone to rebel (Jer. 28:16; 29:32; Isa. 59:13; cf. Deut. 19:16).

If one persisted in rebelliousness, there would finally have to be further acts of judgment. In the threats of coming curses, one finds a preference for describing them as "blows" (מַכָּה), which really meant various types of wretched diseases (Deut. 28:59, 61; 29:21; Lev. 26:21). Corresponding to this pattern, with which he was already familiar, Isaiah had to announce new "blows" of this type; he actually does speak about מכה (blow) and הכה (smiting), but the blows are of a special nature; he reminds Jerusalem that the "body" of the people had already been "battered" enough. This body, as he views it, serves as imagery for the land which had been devastated by war. G. Fohrer thinks that Isaiah might have been thinking here of a slave who had been mercilessly beaten by his master (*ZAW* 74 [1962] 257).

F. Buhl (*ZAW* 36 [1916] 117) makes reference to Tabari, *Annalen* III, 164f.: a police prefect ordered that a scribe, an associate of the previous governor, was to be mercilessly beaten and had him brought before him. Since his body was nothing but one single wound from the top of his head to the sole of his foot, he asks him: "Where else would you like to be beaten?" To this the scribe answered: "By Allah, there is on my body no place to strike; but if you have to, then do so to the palms of my hands!"

However, according to the traditio-historical background which has already been outlined, this would not bring to mind someone who suffered maltreatment by being struck repeatedly, but rather someone whose body was covered, over every square inch, with running sores (cf. חלי, sick, but also דוי, ailing, said with heartfelt sympathy). Since both the head and heart have been affected by this illness, the disease is described as terribly threatening (besides, דְּוָי, ailing, is the intensive form of דָּוֶה, faint, weak); since there is no healthy spot left, from head to toe, it is shown to be affecting the people totally (on this last point, see ראש וזנב, head and tail, in 9:13). אין מתם (no unhurt place) is also used when one describes sicknesses (Ps. 38:4, 8, where, in 4, it is parallel to אֵין שָׁלֵם, "no health," after the text is emended, and also characterizes the disease as the consequence of God's wrath). When one tries to describe the specific meaning of the three substantives in v. 6a, פצע (wounds), חבורה (bruises), and מכה (blow), it is hard to delineate fine shades of meaning. Heaping up these various expressions is intended to have the effect of intensifying the seriousness of the sickness. All three words are also used in conjunction with one another in Prov. 20:30, and all three can also be used when one is describing injuries. טרי means both fresh and moist (just like the Arabic *ṭarîj*); one is given the impression that it is a sore which is oozing.

Verse 6b helps us to discover a little bit about how wounds were treated. One is immediately reminded of the tender care offered by the merciful Samaritan (Luke 10:34). Even way back in Sumerian times, the doctor could be known as an *iazu*, "one who applies oil," and, in antiquity, oil is often mentioned as something which is applied in an attempt to alleviate pain (e.g., even as late a text as Šabbat XIX 2). The doctor in Babylon carried a satchel with him when he went to visit the sick, in which bandages were to be found along with other implements. Diseased parts of the body could have oil trickled onto them, could be lightly sprinkled, could be rinsed, could have generous amounts of oil poured over them, could be completely washed (see B. Meissner, *Babylonien und Assyrien* II [1925] 284f. and 311; concerning Egypt, see also H. Grapow, *Kranker, Krankheiten und Arzt* [1956] 94f., 106f., 125f.; concerning the OT, see P. Humbert, "Maladie et médecine dans l'Ancien Testament," *RHPR* 44 [1964] 1–29).

[1:7] The actual description of the distress begins, at first, with the use of the words which are typical of such portrayals. שממה (wasteland) (see also 6:11 and 17:9) comes from a setting within the context of promises of blessings and threats of curses which are found in the covenant tradition (Exod. 23:29 = Lev. 26:33, והיתה ארצכם שממה, "your land shall be a desolation"; שמה, "horror," from the same root, in Deut. 28:37). A threat concerning the destruction of the cities is mentioned in Lev. 26:31, 33. In the book of Joshua, it is common to read reports about Canaanite cities

being completely destroyed by fire: Jericho (Josh. 6:24), Ai (8:28), Hazor
(11:11, 13), etc. (cf. also Isa. 9:4); therefore, this means that שׂרפות אשׁ
(burned up by fire) is a term which is rooted in the descriptions of holy
war. What had once happened to their enemies when Israel was still
under the blessing of Yahweh was now happening to them, as part of the
curse. That is the "strange deed," the "alien work," about which Isa.
28:21 speaks (on this, see H. Wildberger, "Jesajas Verständnis der
Geschichte," VTSup, 9 [1962] 100). Also as a motif found in the threats
of coming curses, one hears that Israel would not, in such a case, be able
to enjoy the produce from its fields (Lev. 26:16; Deut. 28:30ff., 38ff.; cf.
also Isa. 5:10; Amos 5:11; Zeph. 1:13; in the exact opposite sense the
phrase is used in the promises of salvation found in Amos 9:14; Isa.
65:21f., and similar passages). This means: word for word, what has
happened corresponds exactly to what had been included in the threats of
what would come upon Israel in case of unfaithfulness. Naturally,
Isaiah's way of speaking presumes that those who listened to Isaiah
clearly caught his insinuations. At the very least, the main ideas, if not the
actual institution of a covenant festival, must have still been an actual
part of the thought-world of his time.

[1:8–9] Making use of terminology which comes from traditional motifs
does not mean that what the prophet presented was not actually connected with historical events. Sennacherib's own report and the information from the books of the Kings, which has been critically examined,
demonstrate that the picture which Isaiah paints concerning the situation
immediately after 701 is thoroughly realistic. Even the motif that there
were only a very few who escaped, which comes at this point, certainly
corresponds to the actual historical facts, even if its interpretive meaning
is provided by making use of the traditions. The concept of a remnant,
brought up for discussion at this point, had a long history already before
the time of Isaiah (see the discussion at 7:3). When one searches for
sources, this concept also has its roots in the descriptions of holy war; in
Josh. 8:22, the Israelites slew the people in Ai עד בלתי השׁאיר־לו שׂריד ופליט
(until there was left none that survived or escaped) (see, in addition to
this, Josh. 10:28–40; 11:8; Deut. 2:34; 3:3). Making use of such formulations, Amos can declare in 1:8 that the remnant of the Philistines (שׁארית)
will also perish; cf. השׁאיר שׂריד (those left who survived) in Josh. 8:22;
10:28ff.; 11:8; 2 Kings 10:11. This must be mentioned here because the
use of the motif of the remnant would tie in with the adaptation of holy
war terminology to describe God's judgment on Israel; when the people
are put under the ban, then destruction is declared, which will finally
catch up with even the very last survivor. Passages such as Lev. 26:36, 39;
Deut. 28:62ff.; 4:27ff., even if they came later than the time of Isaiah, still
lead one to conclude that there was an animated discussion among certain circles about the possibility that a remnant might be spared at the
time of judgment. Now, Isaiah makes mention of the fact that there will
be "escapees," even if "only a small number" (כמעט; see Deut. 4:27). They
are not saved because they are the remnant who might be described as
"all the knees that have not bowed to Baal, and every mouth that has not
kissed him" (1 Kings 19:18); even though one can only read between the

lines, since it is not clearly stated, one can still see that the people are saved only because of Yahweh's faithfulness toward his people, since he will not completely abandon them. His faithfulness, of course, is not intended to give one any reason for self-confidence; the sword of Damocles which could completely and absolutely destroy the people was still ready to strike them. The deep-seated hope of Isaiah, that the escapees could become a "remnant which would return" (שאר־ישוב, Shear-jashub, 7:3), apparently provides us with the only reason Isaiah would have had to speak this message. It cannot be by chance that God is called "Yahweh Sebaoth" in this context. Isaiah operates within a widely known stream of tradition when he makes use of this particular designation for God. Already Amos, who, of course, normally uses the expanded form יהוה אלהי (ה)צבאות (Yahweh, God of [the] Hosts), made ample use of the term. As has been known for a long time (see E. Kautzsch, *ZAW* 6 [1886] 17–22), this name is closely connected with the ark and appears initially in the books of Samuel in connection with the sanctuary at Shiloh, and there it is specifically associated with the war palladium which was carefully protected at that site (1 Sam. 1:3, 11; 4:4; 15:2; 2 Sam. 5:10; 6:2, 18; 7:8, 26, 27; cf. also 1 Sam. 17:45). 2 Sam. 6:2 virtually provides us with a definition: "The ark of God, which is called by the name of the Lord of hosts who sits enthroned on the cherubim." There can be little doubt that this was a fixed term, used by the cult which was centered around the ark, when the ark was brought to Jerusalem; at that point, it also became one of the chief terms used in the description of the theology of Zion (see Pss. 24:10; 46:8, 12; 48:9), just as it must have been deeply rooted at one time in the theology of Shiloh (see F. Baumgärtel, "Zu den Gottesnamen in den Büchern Jeremia und Ezechiel," FS W. Rudolph [1961] 1–29, esp. 12ff.; in addition, see O. Eissfeldt, "Silo und Jerusalem," VTSup 4 [1957] 138–147; and H. J. Kraus, *Psalmen,* BK 15/1, 201 [Engl: *Psalms 1–59,* 85ff.]). יהוה צבאות (Yahweh of Hosts) is found no fewer than fifty-six times in the first part of the book of Isaiah (only in Jeremiah is the name used more often; see statistical evidence in Baumgärtel, op. cit., 1). Though the designation is used in the other prophets almost only in fixed formulas, most of the time Isaiah uses it in a free and creative way. That means that he is very much aware of the way in which he uses it and that it has special theological importance for him.

Unfortunately, the question about the religio-historical source and, consequently, about the original meaning of Yahweh Sebaoth is and remains shrouded in mystery. There is already controversy even about the question of determining whether יהוה צבאות is a careless abbreviation for the longer form י׳ אלהי צ׳ (Yahweh, God of Hosts) or whether the longer form was used to provide an interpretive element at a time when the phrase י׳ צ׳ (Yahweh of Hosts) no longer made any sense. One ought to opt for the second solution as the correct one, since י׳ א׳ צ׳ (Yahweh, God of Hosts) apparently is an attempt to make the difficult shorter form י׳ צ׳ (Yahweh of Hosts) easier to understand. The longer form is used only eighteen times while the short form is used 267 times, and י׳ א׳ צ׳ cannot be shown, according to the evidence from the OT, to be the more ancient form of the name (see von Rad, *TheolAT* I, 27f. [Engl: *OTTheol* I, 18f.]; for a different viewpoint, see V. Maag, "Jahwäs Heerscharen," *STU* 20 [1950] 27–52). According to Eichrodt (*TheolAT* I, 120f. [Engl: *TheolOT* I, 192f.]), when צבאות is used, "the bodies, multitudes, masses" are meant; that is, "the content of all that exists in heaven and in earth." But that still does not get at the original meaning of the term, nor does it take into account the variety of interpretations which are found in the individual layers of the OT. O. Eissfeldt (*Jahwe Zebaoth,* Misc. Acad. Berolin. [1950] 128–150) takes צבאות (Sebaoth) to be an intensive abstract plural, with the meaning "mightiness." In this case, the word would function as an attributive name for Yahweh, which is, of course, more logical than explaining it as if it were in a genitive relationship with the proper name, which makes little sense. But there are also problems inherent in taking an abstract plural as an epithet for God in ancient times. Finally, V. Maag's suggestion that the צבאות are "mythical Canaanite nature powers who are robbed of their strength" (op. cit., 50) loses its appeal when one observes that the OT does not have a single clear example of such a usage. According to 1 Kings 22:19, the "host of heaven" stands around Yahweh's throne; Josh. 5:14 speaks of the "commander of the army of the Lord," and Ps. 103:21 says that "Yahweh's hosts" (צְבָאָיו) are his "ministers," apparently identical to his "angels, his mighty ones who do his word" (v. 20). Although the feminine plural צבאות is not used in any of these passages, it can still be concluded from these examples that the epithet Sebaoth describes Yahweh as the lord of those spirits who are assembled around his throne and are ready, at any time, to fulfill his will. This designation presumes that God is the king, surrounded by a heavenly court, by no means a concept which is unknown in the ancient Near East. It fits in very nicely with the God of the ark, which is to be understood as the throne of God. There is, however, no doubt that the ancient mythological meaning had been long forgotten and that the name was commonly used at a later time with a new interpretation attached. 1 Sam. 17:45 gives a demythologized version of the name, saying that God is "the God of the armies of Israel," and, in Psalm 24, "Yahweh of hosts" is used parallel to "Yahweh, strong and mighty, Yahweh, mighty in battle" (v. 8). This recasting of the term is certainly not impossible, since Israel, as we have seen in Josh. 5:14, had also thought that God became actively involved, along with his heavenly hosts, in the battles of those who belonged to him. It is for this reason that it is so easy to see why Isaiah would use the term "Yahweh of Hosts" precisely in those places where he makes use of elements of holy war tradition.

Since it is someone from Jerusalem who is speaking, it is clear why mention is not made of the remnant of Israel, but rather of those who are left from the daughter of Zion, that is, the inhabitants of Jerusalem (יושב ירושלם in 5:3; 8:14; see also 10:24, 32). Isaiah uses "Zion" and "Jerusalem" without distinguishing them in any way (concerning usage and distribution of the use of "Zion" in the OT—with the most frequent usage in the Psalms and Lamentations—see G. Fohrer, Article on Σιών: *TDNT* VII, 293f. and 300f.).

If one wonders why Isaiah so surprisingly often uses the name Zion (3:16f.; 8:18; 10:12, 32; 14:32; 28:16; 29:8; 31:4; see also 10:24; 16:1; 18:7), it is most likely because the mention of Zion would immediately remind the hearers of the promises about the city of God which were still in force, whereas the use of the word "Jerusalem" would lead one to think much more in terms of the political and secular aspects of the city. Yahweh himself established Zion. The "daughter of Zion" is the one who is the heiress of the promises of God which were so closely associated with the mountain of God, but she would have to know that these promises could not assure her of any ongoing security if the people distanced themselves from the covenant relationship and faithfulness to it. The promises about Zion, which were also the backdrop for the daring rebellion of Hezekiah against the Assyrians, were called into question because the people had rebelled, just as surely as true faith (see 28:16) would have given them the right to ask that these promises be fulfilled. In the sanctuary, on the top of Zion, it was confessed that Yahweh hid those loyal to him in his "shelter" (סֻכָּה) (Ps. 31:21; cf. סֹךְ, shelter, in Ps. 27:5), and it was sung in the song of Zion: "His abode (סֹךְ) has been established in Salem, his dwelling place in Zion" (Ps. 76:3). But now the daughter of Zion is compared to a סֻכָּה (shelter) in a vineyard, a place of rest for the night in a cucumber field (concerning מְלוּנָה, shelter for the night, cf. the word מָלוֹן, quarters for the night, in 10:29, which means virtually the same thing).

Vineyards and cucumber fields were guarded at the time when their fruits were ripening. Jewish justice knows all about "fruit-shelters" and also "cucumber-shelters." The accommodation could be a separate building, comparable to a regular house, but it could also be a temporary shelter, whether this would have been made of mud or rushes (see Dalman, *AuS* II, 61ff., and illuss. 12–16; see also H. Guthe, *Palästina* [1927] 43, and illus. 23); it would have also been possible, at that time and as is still observed in the Near East today, that foliage could have been used to construct it. A graphic portrayal of a shelter, used as a watch house in a vineyard, comes from North Africa in the Pseudo-Cyprian tractate "De montibus Sina et Sion" (see, on this, A. Stuiber, "Die Wachthütte im Weingarten," JAC 2 [1959] 86–89).

It is most surprising to see the comparison with Sodom and Gomorrah, since these cities were actually not destroyed in a war. Above all else, Isaiah's words betray the fact that he knows nothing of the transmission of traditions from Genesis. But the cities are also mentioned in 1:10 (Sodom also in 3:9). The sinfulness and destruction of Sodom and Gomorrah must have become proverbial (see 13:19; Amos 4:11; Zeph. 2:9; and often elsewhere), even being referred to in the NT, where the present passage is quoted in Rom. 9:29 (see also Rev. 11:8). One can explain why the pre-exilic prophets knew of the destruction of these cities, since they are mentioned in connection with the covenant traditions which they knew very well (see Deut. 29:22, where Admah and Zeboiim are both mentioned in addition to Sodom and Gomorrah). The gloss in 1:7 (emended text) with its use of the formula מהפכת סדם (the destruction of Sodom), the exact phrase used in Deut. 29:22 and Jer. 49:18, shows that this tradition must have been very well known. The phrase appears to be an abbreviation which was repeated in a stylized way: מהפכת אלהים סדם (as when God overthrew Sodom) (Amos 4:11; Isa. 13:19; Jer. 50:40). The use of אלהים (Elohim) would suggest that the story, at one time, did not include specific mention of Yahweh (see H. Gunkel, *Genesis* [1910³] 217; and J. Rieger, *Die Bedeutung der Geschichte für die Verkündigung des Amos und Hosea* [1929] 4ff.).

אלהים (Elohim) would be understood in this original phraseology to mean "gods" (or "one god"?). It would seem that the version of the story of Sodom as it is described outside of Genesis differed significantly from the account which is most well known to us. מהפכה (destruction), which is always used when mention is made of the downfall of the cities, actually presumes that the destruction was the result of an earthquake.

Purpose and Thrust

The analysis of the terminology and motifs in the woe-oracle has resulted in a complicated picture. Elements of holy war have been used and there are echoes from Zion traditions. The creative poetic abilities of Isaiah are evident in the metaphor about the body which is covered from one end to the other with wounds or in the description of the isolated city of Jerusalem. Also, when these images are used, we become aware of the traditional elements which were available to Isaiah, and also of how he used them with a great deal of freedom as he takes them as a starting point and then reshapes them freely so that they become his own unique message. The covenant with God—that is, the proclamation concerning Yahweh as the merciful Lord who inclines himself toward his people and lays claim to Israel, and then, his threats of coming curses against this people—apparently provides the central theological theme, on the basis of which one must understand and interpret Isaiah's proclamation. It is precisely when one observes traditio-historical roots which are imbedded in the message that one can bring into sharper focus the particular points which the prophet creatively formulates: Yahweh, who is the Holy One of Israel, is the God who surrounded Israel with all good things before he demanded any responses in the form of obedience, and he was protecting them faithfully; it would have naturally followed that it is God alone who is responsible for keeping the activities of the people from resulting in a complete destruction, which would have otherwise followed, that the remnant which remained still had a chance to make it, but also, that the sins were not rooted in the trespasses of individual commandments, but rather in the total abandonment of fellowship with God. In a way which seldom appears in Isaiah, one senses in the words which we have here that the prophet was very shaken up when he considered the future destiny of Jerusalem and that he was deeply engaged on a personal level, trying to make sure that the people correctly perceived what was going on (see A. J. Heschel, *The Prophets* [1962] 86). When describing the devastated body of the nation, the gripping lament affects him very deeply: "not pressed out and not bound up and not softened up with oil!" (v. 6b). This is not anger speaking and it is not a preacher of judgment, but rather one who loves; it is the compassion of a man who will not give up all hope for his people.

In Rom. 9:29, Paul quotes Isa. 1:9 as evidence for the fact that God had not rejected Israel. Isaiah does not speak of that here; the question of Israel's continued existence is an open one for him, and this is so because it could still be possible that Yahweh would finally and totally reject his people, even though Isaiah's own premises could not lead him to such a conclusion. The Christian community would do well not to shove off to one side this deep, heartfelt concern for the future of the people of God and ought to stay alert so that it might hear when the admonishing voice of God's judgments sounds forth.

True and False Worship of God

Literature

Concerning the meter: K. Fullerton, "The Rhythmical Analysis of Is 1, 10–20," *JBL* 38 (1919) 53–63. J. Begrich, "Der Satzstil im Fünfer," *ZS* 9 (1933/34) 169–209, esp. 204–209 = *GesStud.* 132–167.

Concerning the problem of prophet and cult (selected items): W. R. Betteridge, "'Obedience and not Sacrifice', an Exposition of Isa 1, 18–20," *The Biblical World* 38 (1911) 41–49. M. Löhr, *Das Räucheropfer im Alten Testament,* Schr. Königsbg. Gel. Ges. geisteswiss. Kl. 4/4 (1927). C. R. North, "Sacrifice in the Old Testament," *ExpTim* 47 (1935/36), 250–254. J. Begrich, "Die priesterliche Tora," BZAW 66 (1936) 63–88. P. Volz, "Die radikale Ablehnung der Kultreligion durch die alttestamentlichen Propheten," *ZST* 14 (1937) 63–85. C. Lattey, "The Prophets and Sacrifice, A Study in Biblical Relativity," *JTS* 42 (1941) 155–165. N. H. Snaith, "The Prophets and Sacrifice and Salvation," *ExpTim* 58 (1946/47) 152f. H. H. Rowley, "The Prophets and Sacrifice," *ExpTim* 58 (1946/47) 305–307. N. W. Porteous, "Prophet and Priest in Israel," *ExpTim* 62 (1950/51) 4–9. H. W. Hertzberg, "Die prophetische Kritik am Kultus," *TLZ* 75 (1950) 219–226. A. C. Welch, *Prophet and Priest in Old Israel* (1953). R. Rendtorff, "Priesterliche Kulttheologie und prophetische Kultpolemik," *TLZ* 81 (1956) 339–342. R. Hentschke, *Die Stellung der vorexilischen Schriftpropheten zum Kultus,* BZAW 75 (1957). R. Dobbie, "Sacrifice and Morality in the Old Testament," *ExpTim* 70 (1958/59) 297–300. H. Graf Reventlow, "Prophetenamt und Mittleramt," *ZTK* 58 (1961) 269–284. E. Würthwein, "Kultpolemik oder Kultbescheid?" FS A. Weiser (1963) 115–131. A. Caquot, "Remarques sur la fête de la 'néoménie' dans l'Ancien Israel," *RHR* 158 (1960) 1–18.

[**Literature update through 1979:** D. R. Jones, "Exposition of Isaiah 1,10–17," *SJT* 18 (1965) 457–471. Th. Lescow, "Die dreistufige Tora. Beobachtungen zu einer Form," *ZAW* 82 (1970) 362–379. H. W. Hoffmann, "Die Intention der Verkündigung Jesajas," BZAW 136 (1974) 92ff. M. Modena Mayer, "Ayl-, el-'l'animale e l'albero forte': un'antica isoglossa mediterranea," *Acme* 27 (1974) 99–301. O. Loretz, "Die twrh-Stellen in Jes 1," *UF* 8 (1976) 450–451.]

Text

1:10 Hear the word of Yahweh,
    you princes from Sodom![a]
Give heed to the instruction of our God,
    you people of Gomorrah![a]

11 What should the multitude of your sacrifices mean to me?
  says Yahweh.
 I am fed up with[a] burnt offerings of rams
  and of the fat of well-fed animals,
 and the blood of young bulls [and of lambs][b] and he-goats—
  I do not care for that!
12 When you come to behold my countenance[a]
 . . . .[b]
 Who demands such a thing from you,[c]
  so that my courts[e] are trampled?[d]
13 Do not any longer bring gifts,[a] which are nothing,
  [b]offerings of incense, which are an abomination to me![b]
 New moon, sabbath, festival days being proclaimed:[c]
  I do not care for sacrilege[d] and days of merrymaking!
14 'Your festivals'[a] and your solemn assemblies
  are absolutely hated by me,
 they have become a burden[b] for me;
  I am worn out, having to endure them.[c]
15 And whenever you spread out your hands,[a]
  I will cover up my eyes in front of you.
 And even if you continue to pray over and over,
  I will not listen to it.
 Your hands are full of blood.[b]
16 Wash yourselves, clean yourselves![a]
 Eliminate the wickedness of your deeds,
  so that they are thus out of my sight!
 Stop it, this acting wickedly,
17 learn to do good!
 Seek out what is just,
  make sure the downtrodden one is treated well![a]
 Stand up for the rights of the orphan,
  make sure the cause of the widow leads to victory!

10a Qᵃ reads סודם (Sodom with a different spelling) and עומרה (Gomorrah with a different spelling); see above, textual note 9b.

11a Concerning the fact that שבעתי (I am fed up with) has the sense of a present tense, see Joüon, Gr §112a.

11b וכבשים (and lambs) is missing in Gk; the commentaries vary in their assessments; Procksch thinks that the word should not be eliminated, since the verse would then be too short. In reality, however, this verse is too long unless this word is eliminated. The word is an addition, added by a reader who was trying to make sure that there was a complete listing.

12a Gk: ὀφθῆναί μοι (to be seen by me) is to be read, as is done with one MS, לִרְאוֹת (to see) (cf. also Syr lᵉmeḥzâ 'appaj, to see my face); the change to the *niph'al* was done on purpose, seeking to avoid any mention of seeing God, since Yahweh is indeed invisible. Whoever saw him had to die; cf. Exod. 23:15; 34:23f.; Deut. 16:16; 31:11; 1 Sam. 1:22; Ps. 42:3.

12b It seems that a half-verse has dropped out of the text.

12c "From your hands" does not fit here; in fact, the preceding זאת (such a thing) anticipates the רמס חצרי (trampling of my courts). Thus, it has been suggested that מֶאֶתְכֶם (from you) ought to be read. But זאת (such a thing) most likely refers back to a half-verse which dropped out, which probably said something like "what do your many offerings accomplish?"

12d It has been suggested that רֹמְסֵי (tramplings of) be read instead of רְמֹס (trampling of). Possible, yes, but this change is not necessary. Qᵃ reads לרמוס (to trample), which should be construed as an attempt to make a smoother reading.

12e Gk reads, for the plural חצרי (my courts): τὴν αὐλήν μου (my court). But 2 Kings 21:5 and 23:12 make mention of both of the courts of the temple, and there are also many occurrences of the phrase "courts of the temple" or "courts of Yahweh"; a distinction was made between an inner (Ezek. 8:16, and often elsewhere) and an outer court (Ezek. 10:5, and often elsewhere). In addition to this, the Gk connects the end of v. 12 with the beginning of v. 13: πατεῖν τὴν αὐλήν μου οὐ προσθήσεθε (do not continue to tread about my court), which has been accepted as the correct reading by some modern commentators (Duhm, Gray, Eichrodt, and others); then the translation of the following phrase הביא מנחת־שוא (to bring gifts, which are nothing) presents problems which can hardly be eliminated with the aid of the Gk, so that one would read מנחה (gift) instead of מנחת (gift of) (ἐὰν φέρητε σεμίδαλιν, μάταιον! = if you bring the finest wheat flour, vainly!). The combination of the words מנחת־שוא (gifts, which are nothing) in the construct state finds a parallel in שֵׁמַע שׁוא (false report) in Exod. 23:1; עֵד שׁוא (false witness) in Deut. 5:20; הַבְלֵי־שׁוא (vain idols) in Jonah 2:9 and Ps. 31:7, among others. The phrase should not be moved from its present place in our passage.

13a Concerning the Gk reading, see the previous note.

13b–b Many follow the Gk (θυμίαμα βδέλυγμά μοί ἐστιν, incense, it is an abomination to me), which takes קטרת (incense offering) as if it were in the absolute state and takes תועבה (abomination) to be a predicate. Others, including the *Zürcher Bibel*, take קטרת תועבה to be in a construct relationship: "It is an abominable offering to me." Procksch, along with Buhl, would simply remove קטרת (incense) altogether, since the word overloads the three-stress + two-stress colon. But does it really have only five stresses? Actually, תועבה היא לי (it is an abomination to me) is to be interpreted as a relative clause, which attached itself to קטרת (incense) (on asyndetic relative clauses, see BrSynt §146ff.; L. Köhler, "Syntactica II," *VT* 3 [1953] 84f.). Syntactically, this functions the same way as does שוא (nothing) in 13aα.

13c J. Morgenstern (*JBL* 43 [1924] 315ff.), along with F. Schwally (*ZAW* 11 [1891] 257), and Marti (ad loc.) consider מקרא קרא (festival days being proclaimed) to be an interpolation. But even the meter suggests that these two words ought not be eliminated. There is no evidence to show that מקרא (convocation) is being used as an abbreviation for מקרא קדש (holy convocation), a usage which is first found in passages which date after the exile.

13d The Gk reads, for און (sacrilege), νηστεία (fast), which seems to presume a text which read צום (fast), a reading which has been adopted by many commentators, Kaiser being one of the more recent. 'Aquila (ανωφελες, useless), Sym and Theod (αδικια, wrongdoing) follow the MT. The way one makes a text-critical decision in such a case is based upon one's overall assessment of Isaiah's mind-set about the cult (concerning this, see below). If און (sacrilege) stays in the text, it is hard to see Isaiah as one who was fundamentally opposed to the cult. But it does not make sense that one should depart from the MT reading just so that support can be found for the modern devaluation of cultic activity. In addition to this, fasting did not yet play an important role in the pre-exilic period, so that it is doubtful that Isaiah would have put fasting on the same level with festivals and offerings, especially since none of the other prophets mentions fasting in their polemics against cultic activity (cf., by contrast, Isa. 58:3ff.).

14a It disturbs the flow of the text to find חֹדֶשׁ (new moon) at the beginning of v. 14 just as it is at the beginning of v. 13b. Therefore, the old, generally accepted suggestion is to be followed here, as Tur-Sinai has recently done (op. cit. [in literature for 1:1] 156; that suggestion is to replace חדשיכם (your new moons) with חגיכם (your festivals). חג (festival) is often found in conjunction with מועד (solemn assembly) (see Hos. 9:5; Ezek. 46:11). In Hos. 2:13 and Ezek. 45:17, we find the same sequence of terms חג (feast), חדש (new moon), שבת (sabbath), and מועד (appointed feast), in passages which bear close resemblance to our text; in Amos 5:21 חג (festival) is parallel to עצרת (solemn assembly). These occurrences establish the fact, with almost absolute certainty, that חג (festival) simply cannot be missing from our text, especially since Isaiah does not, in principle, avoid using the word elsewhere (29:1; 30:29).

14b On the vocalization of לְ׳! (burden), see Joüon, Gr §103c.

14c For the infinitive construct used as an object, see Joüon, Gr §124c (see also חדלי הרע [stop it, this acting wickedly], in v. 16 and למדו היטב [learn to do good], in v. 17).

15a Concerning the vocalization of פָּרִשְׂכֶם (your spreading out), see Joüon, Gr §61d, note 1.

15b Qᵃ adds to this: אצבעותיכם בעאון, "your fingers (are stained) by guilt." The addition stands all alone and is the work of a glossator who looked in vain for a mention of fingers at this point.

16a הִזַּכּוּ (clean yourselves) has usually been taken to be a *hithpaʿel* from זכה (be clean) (see GKC §54d, KBL). A. M. Honeyman (*VT* 1 [1951] 63ff.) suggests, by moving the accent, that the word is a *niphʿal* imperative from זכך (be clean), which does make a definite difference in meaning. זכה (be clean) is a forensic term while זכך (clean), like רחץ (wash), belongs to the terminology of the cult (for a different viewpoint, see Tur-Sinai, op. cit. [in literature for 1:1] 156).

17a אשרו חמוץ (correct oppression) is problematic. Gk (ῥύσασθε ἀδικούμενον, rescue those treated unjustly) takes חמוץ (the oppressed one) as a passive (as also ᾽Aquila, Theod βλαπτομενον, "the one who has been wronged," and Sym πεπλεονεκτη-μενον, "the one who has been defrauded," Targ דאגים [sorrowing], Syr *ṭᵉlîmê* [oppressed], and Vulg *oppressus* [oppressed]). Thus, the suggestion has been made that this be vocalized as חמוץ (the downtrodden one) (for more about the meaning of חמוץ, see P. Wernberg-Møller, *ZAW* 71 [1959] 58). This issue cannot be treated separately from the question about the meaning of the preceding verb אשרו (correct). G. R. Driver (*JTS* 38 [1937] 37) makes reference to the Aramaic אשר *peʿal* "be strong," *paʿel* "strengthen," but this Aramaic root can hardly be presumed to be of any help in determining the sense of the word as used by Isaiah, especially since he uses אשר elsewhere (3:12; 9:15) with the meaning "lead." For the same reason, it is doubtful that אשרו should be taken to mean "encourage someone to show restraint" or, with Rignell (op. cit. [in literature for 1:1] 151), to translate, on the basis of the Syr, "Be good to the downtrodden!" which would be based on connecting אשר (advance) with אַשְׁרֵי, "happy." It is best to stay with the translation "lead for one's benefit" (Hertzberg reads "espouse the cause of," Fohrer reads "lead," Kaiser and Eichrodt read this differently), in which case the clear evidence from the versions leads one to read, instead of חָמוֹץ (oppression), rather חָמוּץ (the downtrodden one).

Form

The introductory formula in v. 10 leaves no doubt that a new message begins here; it is equally clear that a new, separate proclamation begins with v. 18. Dividing the material this way is also supported by the change in the theme. A change in theme is not immediately apparent, simply because Sodom and Gomorrah are mentioned in v. 10, which at first seems to be integrally connected with v. 9. No doubt, the mention of these two cities in v. 10 is the reason the section was placed right after v. 9.

Meter: J. Begrich attempted to read five-stress cola throughout 10–14. This forced him to make a great number of questionable alterations to the text. It is indeed true that five-stress cola predominate, and it may be that difficulties encountered when trying to establish the meter may at times be caused by damage to the textual evidence. But, in principle, a uniform metrical pattern can hardly ever be expected. In vv. 10–12 there are 7 five-stress cola (after וכבשים [and of lambs] is removed and if one presumes that only the first colon of one line of the text is preserved in v. 12a). In v. 13, it seems that there are 2 seven-stress cola, the longer verses demonstrating clearly how difficult it is to endure the bustle of cultic and festival activity. In vv. 14–16a, five-stress cola follow once again. (Is v. 15a a three-stress bicolon? Possibly מכם, "from you," is to be removed.) The conclusion is formed by 3 two-stress bicola in vv. 16b and 17. Their conciseness demonstrates the urgency of the demands very effectively.

As in 1:2f., the present passage begins with the imperatives שמעו (hear) and האזינו (give heed), making it seem very likely that this is also to be taken to be a judgment speech. But a closer examination causes one to ponder whether this designation would be appropriate. "Heaven" and "earth" are not directly summoned here; rather, "the princes of Sodom" and the "people of Gomorrah" are called. But they do not serve as witnesses in legal proceedings; it is not a "call for two witnesses" (rejecting the view of L. Köhler, *Deuterojesaja stilkritisch untersucht* [1923] 112). In spite of that, this could still be a judgment speech, but in this case those being accused would be addressed directly. However, in v. 10, the words of God are described with the terms דבר־יהוה (word of Yahweh) and תורת אלהינו (instruction of our God), and it is certainly true that the second expression is not an apt term for what is found in an accusation speech. In terms of content, there is no accusation about breaking the covenant in this word from Yahweh, and the topics which are characteristically mentioned in judgment speeches are also missing (משפט, judgment; שפט, judge [cf. 5:3; 3:14]; דין, pronounce judgment [3:13; Deut. 32:36]; ריב, set up a lawsuit [3:13; Mic. 6:1]; יכח, bring a lawsuit [1:18; Mic. 6:2]). There is no judgment taking place here, but rather, instruction is being set forth, specifically about what is disgusting to Yahweh, what he can no longer tolerate. On the other hand, the instruction also deals with what he expects from the cultic community.

The technical term "summons to receive instruction" suggested by H. W. Wolff (*Hosea*, BK 14/1, 122f. [Engl: *Hosea*, 97]) is very applicable to the circumstances described here (in contrast to its use in Isa. 1:2). Isaiah uses a similar type of formula in 28:23, even though it is in four parts there, clearly as an introduction to instruction. One ought to understand that this formula originated in the realm of wisdom teaching. Formulas of this type also serve to introduce the instruction of wisdom teachers in other places: Prov. 4:1; 7:24; Job 33:31; 34:2; Ps. 49:2. Amen-em-Opet had long ago challenged his "son": "Give [me] thy ears [cf. the Hebrew האזין, give heed, from אזן, ear], hear what is said." What is to be appropriated from the wise is presented as "teaching of life" or "the testimony for prosperity" (*AOT*[2] 38f.: *ANET*[2] 421). When considering the theme itself, it is also not impossible to find criticism that concerns sacrifice and is in the realm of wisdom, not only beginning with Israel, but already in Egypt: "Enrich thy house of the West; embellish thy place of the necropolis, as an upright man and as one who executes the justice upon which [men's] hearts rely. More acceptable is the character of one upright of heart than the ox of the evildoer" (Instruction for King Meri-Ka-Re, lines 127–129, *AOT*[2] 35, *ANET*[2] 417), a passage which reminds one of Prov. 21:3, 27; Song of Sol. 4:17 (but also of 1 Sam. 15:22 and Hos. 6:6). Thus, there are several different reasons for suggesting that Isaiah's criticism of sacrifice has its roots in wisdom. תועבה (admonition) (v. 13) is also a favorite expression for wisdom teaching, being used precisely in the proverbs which call sacrifice into question (see Prov. 15:8 and 21:27). On the other hand, however, תועבה (abomination) is also typical of the vocabulary found in connection with the cult (e.g., Deut. 17:1: an incomplete offering is "an abomination" to Yahweh; see also Deut. 18:9, 12, and often elsewhere; Lev. 18:22, 26, 27, 29, 30; 20:13; Ezek. 18:12, 13, 24, and often elsewhere). תועבה היא (it is an abomination) (Lev. 18:22), expanded at times into תועבת יהוה אלהיך (it is an abomination to Yahweh your God) (Deut. 7:25; 17:1; 18:12; 22:5; 23:19, and often elsewhere), seems almost to have been used in the cult as a declaratory formula which was used whenever an offering was rejected because it was not cultically perfect (concerning these formulas, see G. von Rad, "Die Anrechnung des Glaubens zur Gerechtigkeit," *TLZ* 76 [1951] 129–132 = *GesStud,* 130–135; in addition, see also W. Zimmerli, *Ezechiel,* BK 13/1, 410 [Engl: *Ezekiel 1,* 383]). Even more obviously, we are brought into the priestly realm when the word of Yahweh is given the designation תּוֹרָה (torah) (see Deut. 17:11; 33:10; Jer. 18:18; Hos. 4:6; Hag. 2:11), even though wisdom can also impart תּוֹרָה (torah) (see Prov. 3:1; 6:20; 31:26, and often elsewhere, and also J. Fichtner, "Die altorientalische Weisheit in ihrer israelitisch-jüdischen Ausprägung," BZAW 62 [1933] 82f.), though this was apparently not a common term within the context of wisdom until later times, when the distinction between wisdom and cult was not so carefully drawn. Finally, the demand to "wash one's self" and to "clean one's self" suggests terminology which is connected with cultic requirements.

There are apparently points of contact here with both the world of wisdom and with the world of the cult. But since the section places particular emphasis on the fact that it is תורה (torah) and the individual terms are deeply rooted in the language of the cult, one must take this present message of the prophet essentially to be a priestly torah. But this form has been substantially modified by the prophet, so that one would not be completely in error to designate this a prophetic torah (see O. Eissfeldt, *The Old Testament, An Introduction* [1965] 309). Isaiah uses this term תּוֹרָה (torah) elsewhere: 2:3 parallel to דבר־יהוה (word of Yahweh), 5:24 parallel to אִמְרָה (word), 8:16 parallel to תְּעוּדָה (exhortation), the same way in v. 20, also in 30:9 (Hos. 8:1 parallel to ברית, covenant; cf. also 8:12 and the verb הוֹרָה, instruct, in Isa. 2:3; [9:14]; 28:9, 26). This relatively frequent usage shows that Isaiah considered his prophetic office to be substantially the same as that of a priestly or wisdom teacher, even though the fact that the term was possibly no longer in use by the other prophets allows one to suppose that they thought it was important that they would not be confused with a priest or wisdom teacher. And yet, by means of the other terms which are used by Isaiah parallel to "torah," it is clear that his claim to be a prophet would sharply distinguish him from those other functionaries.

Setting

Isaiah must have spoken this message at an open assembly at which the leading officials of the city and the general population were present. Since mention is made of the great quantity of offerings, of the trampling of the courts of Yahweh's temple, of the festival assemblies, and of the prayers, it must have been an official cultic celebration. Based on Isaiah's condemnation of the many offerings and prayers, it would seem quite likely that this must have been a day of repentance. Since concepts used here remind one of thoughts which are expressed by both Amos and Hosea, this passage might come from Isaiah's early period of activity. Of course, there are others who presume that the situation portrayed in vv. 4–9 also provides a backdrop for this section, since it was particularly in times of great need that cultic activity reached a fever pitch (see Betteridge, op. cit.).

Commentary

[1:10] Leaders and people are to be instructed at the same time. קָצִין (prince, leader) is related to the Arabic *qāḍin,* "judge," which comes from the root *qaḍā,* a verb which means to "judge," but can also be used in the more general sense of "determine, decide" or "carry out, execute." In Josh. 10:24; Judg. 11:6, 11, and Dan. 11:18, military leaders are meant, but in Isaiah the reference is to the magistrates of the city (see also 3:6f.; 22:3; in Micah, see 3:1, 9, which refers to all the responsible leaders of the people). "Princes of Sodom" and "people of Gomorrah" makes the point that the description of the reprehensible activity of the inhabitants of these cities can also be applied to the citizens of Jerusalem. Since, as we have seen above (1:9), traditions were passed on about these cities at the time of Isaiah which do not match up with what is described in Genesis 18f., it is possible that Isaiah is making more specific allusions to that which we are unable to recognize, possibly that, in those cities, offerings were presented and festivals were celebrated with great zeal, but that they made no time available when it came to taking care of their social responsibilities. But since all the OT references to the two cities make it clear that whenever they were mentioned their destruction was always immediately brought to mind, it is most certainly clear that to mention them would make the listeners conscious of the danger which was looming on the horizon for Jerusalem. The gravity of the judgment of God was made clear by using the example of the final destiny of these two cities (cf., even in the NT, Luke 10:12; 2 Peter 2:6; Jude 7, among others).

The critical position taken over against sacrifice, which has been shown above to have definite points of contact with wisdom, had already been very important for early champions of the faith even during the period of the amphictyony (1 Sam. 15:22; on this, see A. Weiser, "I Samuel 15," *ZAW* 54 [1936] 1–28). According to Ps. 50:8ff., an opinion about sacrificial practices was one of the themes of the judgment proceedings whenever the covenant festival took place. Amos (5:25) and Jeremiah (7:22) are of the opinion that Israel was not offering sacrifices at the time of the exodus. Considered historically, that is a bold statement, but of course, it is also evidence that those who felt themselves responsible for preserving the amphictyonic traditions, even already at the time of Amos, were thoroughly convinced that hundreds of offerings, in and of themselves, would not provide sufficient evidence that there was real faithfulness to the covenant (in Hos. 6:6, the bringing of sacrifices is set up over against חֶסֶד [steadfast love], continuing in the following verse by making a very pointed reference to the violation of the covenant).

Does Isaiah reject sacrifice and cultic piety even in principle, as has been maintained over and over again (most recently, once again, in great detail, by Hentschke, op. cit., 94–103)? This simply cannot be considered valid. In the first place, consider the constant usage of the suffix כֶם-: *your* sacrifice, from *your* hands, *your* festivals, *your* solemn assemblies, the stretching out of *your* hands. What Isaiah says here is completely appropriate for a priest to say when imparting torah instruction. Indeed, according to the ancient perceptions, sacrifice is in no way a gift to the divine being, which had to be accepted by the deity no matter what. If it does not square with established norms, then it is a מנחת־שׁוא (gift which is nothing) or a תועבה (abomination) (Deut. 17:1; cf. also Exod. 8:22; 2 Chron. 28:3). Just as with sacrifice itself, the priest also had to fulfill certain prescribed rites in order for his gift to find favor with God; Aaron and his sons had to be washed (רחץ), so that their service could be discharged legitimately (Lev. 8:6), and the Levites were also to be ritually cleansed (טהר) and their clothing was to be washed (כבס; see Num. 8:6ff.) before they were installed. Cultic actions which did not adhere to the prescribed regulations were without effect. Just as a priest had to decree in a particular case that a sacrifice would not be acceptable, in an analogous fashion, Isaiah declared that "your (pl.)" sacrifices and festivals are an abomination to Yahweh. But with this assessment, sacrifice in and of itself is not being rejected. Second, what apparently displeased Isaiah the most was the certainty which accompanied the cultic piety. If one is of the opinion that sacrifice would take effect *ex opere operato* (by the very act of doing it), then one must also succumb to the illusion: The more you do, the better it works; the "fatter" (see מְרִיאִים) it is, the more acceptable it is to God (concerning the commercial aspects of sacrifice in the Jerusalem temple, see a passage like 2 Kings 16:15ff.). When Isaiah utters a sharp No! here, he unmasks the conception of sacrifice as magic, showing it to be nothing more than a dangerous illusion. But sacrifice and festivals are not in any way rejected out of hand. This interpretation is bolstered by the fact that Isaiah also deals with much praying (v. 15b) in the same way as he assesses the multitude of sacrifices and the great number of festivals. Praying also belongs to the "cult"; yet, it is obviously impossible that Isaiah would, in principle, call praying into question. In the third place, the key to understanding this section is found in the declaration: "I do not care for sacrilege and days of merrymaking." Thus, what Isaiah rejects here is clearly the mind-set and impulses of the people who had gathered together for the festival. "The issue, therefore, in the polemic of the prophets is whether the breaking of the covenant can be healed by sacrifice or whether sacrifice has any meaning only within the context of an intact covenant relationship—not an attempt to replace the cultus by morality" (Eichrodt, *TheolAT* I, 103, note 348 [Engl: *TheolOT* 1, 168, note 1]). Attempts have been made to manipulate the text so as to steer away from such an interpretation, as can be seen in the writings of someone like Marti (ad loc.). For the opposite interpretation, one might consult the treatment in the commentaries of Fischer, Kissane, Hertzberg (see also Hertzberg's article "Die prophetische Kritik am Kult," *TLZ* 75 [1950] 219–226), Steinmann, Herntrich, Ziegler, Fohrer, Kaiser, among others; in addition, see Rignell, op. cit. (in literature for 1:1) 147ff.; H. H. Rowley, *ExpTim* 70 (1958/59) 341f. (contra R. Dobbie, *ebenda,* 297ff.).

[1:11] Verse 11 mentions the two principal types of sacrifices, זבח (sacrifice) and עלה (burnt offering) (as is also found in 2 Sam. 15:22; Hos. 6:6;
and often elsewhere; on the terminology for sacrifice, see Köhler,
TheolAT 172ff. [Engl: *OTTheol* 181ff.]). The זבח is the meal offering,
during the course of which the participants in the cultic act and the deity
together consume the animal which was selected for use. The sacrificial
offering meal has its roots in the culture of the shepherds who traversed
the grazing lands. "By means of their participation in the זבח, the deity
puts himself, at the same time, into the position of protecting the shepherd family, which is making the offering, from whatever possible types
of attacks by animals which might threaten them" (so V. Maag, *VT* 5
[1956] 16). Thus, Israel had brought the זבח (sacrifice) along from its own
nomadic wanderings in past times, even if the way they understood it
changed after the settlement in the land, specifically, that it was somewhat harmonized with their understanding of the whole burnt offering,
which takes an entire animal which is burned upon the altar as a gift for
the deity. A shepherd out on the grazing lands could hardly afford an עלה
(whole burnt offering), but, in the settled territory, someone could be
wealthy enough to be able to offer up to the deity an entire animal. The
original significance of the whole burnt offering is undoubtedly the feed-
ing of the deity in order to supply the deity with strength to stay alive (cf.
a passage like the Gilgamesh Epic 11,160, but also the terminology לֶחֶם
אלהים [bread of God] which is found in Ezekiel, Malachi, and in the
Priestly Writing; in addition, note the rejection of the notion, in Ps.
50:12ff., that Yahweh was in need of sacrifice as food; finally, note the use
of the verb שבע [be fed up with] in the present passage, even though it is
now somewhat modified to mean "be disgusted with"). The עלה (burnt
offering) had already been rooted in an agricultural context and was
appropriated from the Canaanite world by Israel as it infiltrated their
culture. During the course of time, there was undoubtedly a reinterpretation, since it would have certainly appeared inadequate, for those who
confessed that Yahweh was filled with power, to think that the deity had
to be strengthened or had to be provided with some life-giving power.
And, in the same vein, the knowledge that Yahweh had freedom, being
seen as a partner in a covenant relationship patterned after a suzerainty
treaty, no longer allowed for the option that the deity could be influenced
in any way by magical rites. One cannot easily determine which specific
notions were held by Isaiah's contemporaries when they thought of sacrifice, since, no doubt, there was no single, generally accepted viewpoint
concerning sacrifice. The use of זבח (sacrifice) and עלה (burnt offering),
without distinguishing them more specifically, shows that the original
concepts which lie behind each of these terms had by and large lost their
distinctive aspects. Wherever there is a critical assessment of sacrifice,
both of these types of offerings always fall under the same verdict. The
specific intention, which shows why they are brought up for discussion, is
made clear only when one takes note of the occasion at which they are
offered. When psalms of lament, either of the individual or of the community, talk about sacrifice, the offerings apparently are to dispose the
deity so that he looks on favorably (Pss. 4:6; 20:4; 54:8). But one also
sacrifices after having experienced the help of Yahweh (see Pss. 107:22;

116:17; 27:6, זִבְחֵי תְרוּעָה [sacrifices with shouts of joy]; cf. H. J. Kraus, *Psalmen,* BK 15/1 on Ps. 27:6 [Engl: *Psalms 1–59,* 334–335]), which is clearly an offering by means of which thanks is being proclaimed openly, but which may also have the idea, in the background, that God might also be kindly disposed toward fulfilling the individual's wishes in the future.

A hint which helps in understanding sacrifice is furnished in our passage by the general term מִנְחָה (gift), under which are subsumed the various types of sacrifices referred to in v. 13a. The term is also used in a secular sense, specifically in the sense of a gift which is presented when offering allegiance, especially by someone who is less important, one who seeks to use the gift to secure the favor of one who is more important (cf. Gen. 32:14–16; 43:11; Judg. 3:15, and often elsewhere). At the same time, מנחה (gift) was used already at an early time as a term for a sacrifice (Gen. 4:3–5; Judg. 13:19, 23; 1 Sam. 2:17; 26:19; Amos 5:22, 25); however, there it did not have the narrow focus which was specifically used to designate a "cereal offering"; this passage certainly does not use it as it was used in that special way in later times. At the very least, the concept of sacrifice, as it is used by those who heard Isaiah, is defined very generally as a gift to the deity, used to assure oneself that the deity will act favorably. However, the addition of שׁוא (nothing) to מנחה (gift) says that this goal was not going to be attained by offering a sacrifice.

In v. 11, Isaiah apparently makes use of established formulas which were already in common usage when one criticized sacrifice. The close agreement with the formulation of 1 Sam. 15:22, החפץ ליהוה בעלות וזבחים כשמע בקול יהוה הנה שמע מזבח טוב להקשיב מחלב אילים (Has Yahweh as great delight in burnt offerings and sacrifices, as in obeying the voice of Yahweh? Behold, to obey is better than sacrifice, and to hearken than the fat of rams), is astonishing. One may not be all that surprised to find that "burnt offering" and "sacrifice" are next to one another, but finding חלב (fat) of the sacrificial offerings mentioned in both places cannot be just happenstance, as is also the case with the use of the root חפץ (care for, delight in) (see also Hos. 6:6). Otherwise, the rest of the OT uses either רצה (be pleased) or רצון (delight) in such circumstances (Pss. 40:14; 50:18; 51:18 [רצה, be pleased, *and* חפץ, delight in]; Am. 5:22; Hos. 8:13; Mic. 6:7; Jer. 6:20). Thus, Isaiah did not only have general knowledge about the questionable nature of sacrifice; there were already fixed formulations which were being used to describe the problem.

Abel had already made a sacrifice of the "fat" of the sacrificial animal. It is that particular part of the זבח (sacrifice) (or else the זבח שלמים, peace offering) which is burned for Yahweh. In fact, a distinction is even made between the fat which covers the intestines and that fat which surrounds the kidneys and liver (Lev. 3:3ff.; cf. 4:8ff.; 7:3ff., among other passages); Lev. 4:26 speaks very specifically about חֵלֶב זבח (fat of the sacrifice). Whenever "fat" is mentioned, it is also common that reference will be made to the "blood" (see Exod. 23:18, "blood of my sacrifice and fat of my feast"; in addition, among other passages, see Ezek. 44:7, 15). Very specific reference is made in Lev. 3:17 to "a perpetual statute throughout your generations, in all your dwelling places, that you eat neither fat nor blood." (Even though the applicable laws for sacrifice are first made known to us through the priestly writings, they were apparently already in force at the time of Isaiah.) One sacrifices the blood to God because it is the source of life; in fact, it is life itself (Gen. 9:4). If one relinquishes it to the deity, then one is magically protected from the vengeance of the spirit which protects the animals. But naturally, the ancient meaning behind this concept had also shifted in focus over the course of time. Since other peoples in the vicinity of Israel included drinking of blood, not only as part of their cultic activity, but also as a means for summoning forth an ecstatic prophetic message, or even used it for achieving, by a wild orgy, a oneness with the divinity (see Eichrodt, *TheolAT* I, 79 [Engl: *TheolOT* 1, 158]), it is very possible that the prohibition of this type of consumption of blood could also be explained as a resistance to incursions from such cults.

Concerning the types of sacrificial animals, rams, fatlings, young bulls, and he-goats are mentioned. Cattle, sheep, and goats are, in reality, the most important animals to be sacrificed. But finding "fatlings" on this list (see also Amos 5:22) has a good explanation: it must have been particularly objectionable to the prophet that fattening up the sacrificial animals was thought to result in a greater effect upon Yahweh. 1 Sam. 15:22 mentions only "fat of rams," but Isaiah is even more pointed in his remarks (cf. KAT³ 595, note 1).

[1:12] The people come to the temple in droves to "behold the countenance of God." ראה את פני אלהים is a technical term for paying a visit to the sanctuary when, as Exod. 23:15; 34:23f.; Deut. 16:16 show, the great yearly festivals took place (cf. F. Nötscher, *Das Angesicht Gottes schauen* [1924]). The phraseology must have come from circumstances in which one would have gone into the sanctuary so as to actually see the god; in fact, this meant one would see an image of the god; this corresponds to the Akkadian formula *amāru pān ili* (to see the face of god). In the cult of the Yahweh religion, devoid of pictorial representations as it was, the formula is still used, because Israel considered God to be really present in the sanctuary. The punctuation as a *niph'al* in the MT, on the other hand, helps one to see how inhibited they were in a later age when it came to using such pictorial forms of speech. It is certainly not the opinion of Isaiah that one should not ever again "see the countenance of God." Also at this point, as the presumably lost bicolon would have made clearer, it is obvious that the prophet had in mind the multiplicity of the cultic celebrations which went way beyond what was necessary. The "courts" of Yahweh were being "trampled" by the very large number of the visitors.

[1:13a] The phrase לא תוסיפו (do not any longer add to) in v. 13a shows that we are on the right track with what has just been surmised. One notices immediately that קטרת (offerings of incense), still another specific type of sacrifice is mentioned after the more general term מִנְחָה (gifts) (see above). The reason for this is the fact that the incense offering was highlighted as being particularly offensive. The verdict תועבה (abomination), which is expressed as a judgment concerning this type of activity, is often chosen when heathen cultic installations or cultic activities are described in detail (Deut. 7:25f., graven images; Deut. 18:9, divination; see, in addition, Deut. 20:18 and similar passages). This is even harsher than the negative assessments which have been expressed up to this point. As finds in Megiddo, Beth-Shan, Gezer, *tell bēt mirsim,* and other places have shown, incense offerings were presented in offerings far and wide and were beloved in the Canaanite regions (on this, see G. E. Wright, *Biblical Archaeology* [1957] 70ff.). Therefore, it is perfectly understandable that Isaiah's (Yahweh's) judgment is so harsh; it is really a heathen "abomination" which Israel has appropriated for its own use.

With the term קטרת, one is not to think of the smoke from the sacrifices, but rather the "frankincense scents," that is, the perfumes which were burned in the sacrificial fires. The fact that this is a very old form of sacrifice is attested by 1 Sam. 2:28 and Deut. 33:10. Jer. 6:20, in addition to sacrifices and burnt offerings, also mentions "frankincense from Sheba" and "sweet cane from a distant land" (cf. also Isa. 43:23f.). Fragrant sacrifices were very expensive to set up and carry out, but, for that very reason, they were thought to be particularly effective. According to 1 Kings 7:48 (see also 1 Macc. 1:21), there was a golden altar next to the table of showbread even in the temple of Solomon, and that golden altar served as an incense altar. The correctness of this statement has been questioned, but Isa. 6:6 makes it very clear that there was an altar for offering incense in the pre-exilic temple (concerning the incense altar in the "tabernacle," see Exod. 30:1ff.; archaeological representations are in *BRL* 19; *AOB*[2] illuss. 466f.; *ANEP* illuss. 575ff.; in addition, consult Löhr, op. cit.; and F. Nötscher, *Biblische Altertumskunde* [1940] 296ff.; M. Haran, "The Uses of Incense in the Ancient Israelite Ritual," *VT* 10 [1960] 113–129).

[1:13b] In vv. 13b and 14, a list of the festivals is presented. It is too bad that only two of them are mentioned by name, new moon and sabbath. They belong together, since they recur repeatedly during the course of a year. They are also mentioned together in 2 Kings 4:23; Amos 8:5; Hos. 2:13, and Isa. 66:23. However, one cannot conclude from this, since there is no reference to the matter in the OT (as has been suggested, in spite of that, by K. Marti, *Geschichte der israelitischen Religion* [1907[5]] 54), that the sabbath originated as a moon day, namely, the day on which there was a full moon. We have no grounds for supposing that the sabbath, at the time of Isaiah, was not already the seventh day of the week, or for supposing that it had not been completely separated from any connection with the journey of the moon and phases of the moon. And yet, our passage leaves us uninformed about the character of this day of celebration. Since the sabbath is mentioned only after the new moon festival, it can hardly have had the very important position which was later accorded it. However, it is made clear from Amos 8:5 that, already in Isaiah's time, there was rest from work on this day (as was equally true for the day of the new moon) (see also Exod. 34:21; 2 Kings 4:23; 11:5, 7, 9; concerning the sabbath, see R. de Vaux, *Ancient Israel* [1961] 475ff. and 550f.; concerning the new moon festival, see H. J. Kraus, *Worship in Israel* [[2]1962] 76f.). We learn very little about the new moon festival in the OT. According to 1 Sam. 20:6, it was the time when the yearly festival of a particular clan took place. According to Ezek. 46:1–7 and Num. 28:11–15, it has a more specific character than the sabbath (Num. 28:9–10) in that it included a sacrifice. It was naturally celebrated as a day of Yahweh in Israel, but, on the other hand, in the surrounding region it would have been celebrated as the day of the moon god Yarikh. In the Ras Shamra texts, mention is made of the *ym ḥdt,* "the day on which the moon renews itself" (III D I:9; cf., in addition, for Ugarit: J. Gray, *The*

Legacy of Canaan, VTSup 5 [1957] 180ff.; for Palestine: note the name Jericho, which one ought not try to explain without some reference to the moon god). The rites for the day of the new moon were, without a doubt, concerned with promoting fertility; possibly the ἱερὸς γάμος (sacred marriage rite) was acted out on that day (see G. Boström, *Proverbiastudien* [1935] 135f.; and H. W. Wolff, *Hosea,* BK 14/1, Hos. 2:13 [Engl: *Hosea,* 38]); in any case, the ideas behind this were closely connected with Canaanite concepts.

Now the festival days follow, those which were "proclaimed." One can proclaim a fast (1 Kings 21:9, 12; Jer. 36:9; Jonah 3:5; Ezra 8:21; 2 Chron. 20:3), an עֲצָרָה (solemn assembly) (Joel 1:14; 2:15), or a מוֹעֵד (appointed feast) (Lev. 23:2, 4, 37). The verb קָרָא (proclaim) is sometimes used in an absolute sense (Lev. 23:21), meaning "make proclamation about a festival." It is from this particular usage that one can easily understand how מִקְרָא could take on the meaning "festival day" (see, on this point, E. Kutsch, *ZAW* 65 [1953] 247–253). When the cultic laws were promulgated, certain festivals were given special attention by being designated מִקְרָא קֹדֶשׁ, "a holy festival day." In this regard, "holy" means that all work of any kind was to be left undone on such a day. One would suppose that the phrase מִקְרָא (proclaimed festival day) would have been used, in the beginning, only for the festival days which did not repeat regularly through the calendar year, for example, penitential days during a particular emergency in the land. Even the present passage would not have to be interpreted any differently. The parallel term עצרה (days of merrymaking) can also be used for such festivals, which would have been set up just for a particular purpose (see 2 Kings 10:20; Joel 1:13f.).

Since the root meaning of the verb עצר is "hold back," it is possible that עצרה or else עצרת might mean "(the day of) holding back from one's work" (concerning which one ought to compare Lev. 23:36; Deut. 16:8, and Num. 29:35, where work is explicitly forbidden on such festival days). That is corroborated by the fact that נֶעְצַר can mean both *desistere ab opere* (desist from work) and *celebrare* (celebrate) in the same way that the German *feiern* has both meanings (see 1 Sam. 21:8; cf. E. Kutsch, *VT* 2 [1952] 57–69).

It has already been demonstrated that the combination of the terms אָוֶן (sacrilege) and עצרה (days of merrymaking) is critical to the interpretation of this passage. As S. Mowinckel (*The Psalms in Israel's Worship* [1967] 1–41) and J. Pedersen (*Israel, Its Life and Culture* I–II [1926] 431) have already noted, אָוֶן is closely related to אוֹן, "power," or, more specifically, "magic power." Of course, it is obvious that this original meaning of the term has lost this specific accent in meaning when used by Isaiah, but it still has some of its effect even at this point; אָוֶן is that which is evil in the sense of the sinister, that power which is at work with a destructive power, even if it is only thinking that comes out of an evil heart and that leads to hatching a plot to bring about a disaster (Prov. 6:18; cf. Ps. 66:18; Isa. 32:6; Ezek. 11:2; Ps. 55:11). אָוֶן (mischief) is on the tip of the tongue of the liar (Prov. 17:4); the mouth of the godless permits אוֹן (iniquity) to gush forth (Prov. 19:28; Ps. 10:7). The concept does not belong to the terminology commonly used in the covenant tradition, but seems to have entered the vocabulary of Isaiah from the world of wisdom. In any case, it provides a significant additional element for Isaiah's understanding of sin when added to his use of פשע (rebel) but also when compared with עון (offense) and חטא (sin): it is the criminal way of thinking which destroys the human community, which only survives when the trustworthiness among its members can be presumed. A commercialized festival, at which און (the criminal) can peddle his wares, has to be something which Yahweh would find intolerable. לא אוכל (I do not care) is, without a doubt, a pregnant expression for the phrase לשאת לא אוכל (I am not able to bear, tolerate) or something similar; cf. Jer. 44:22 and Hab. 1:13.

[1:14] Verse 14 furnishes two additional designations for festivals, so as to underscore the great number and the variety of activities at the sanctuaries. The חגים (festivals) and the מועדים (solemn assemblies) refer to the great yearly festivals. The root חגג seems to be actually connected with "springing about, dancing" (see Ps. 107:27 and 1 Sam. 30:16), so that the חג is, first of all, the cultic dance. Then, in the wider sense, with one part of it serving to refer to the whole event, it comes to designate the cultic festival in its entirety (cf. the similar development of the Arabic *ḥaǧǧ*, pilgrim). As the term is used in the OT, it serves already in the ancient festival calendars as a designation for the festivals of Unleavened Bread, Weeks, and In-Gathering (see Exod. 23:15–18; 34:22, 25; Deut. 16:10–16). In Judg. 21:19ff., the חג יהוה (feast of Yahweh) is clearly the Fall Festival (see also 1 Kings 12:32; Isa. 30:29). It is very common to see חג (festival) mentioned along with מועד (solemn assembly); in fact, the two terms become synonyms at a later time. In keeping with the basic meaning of the root יעד (appoint), the term actually refers to the "place" (or time) where people come together," then, in an expanded sense, to "the agreed-upon time" or "fixed time," and finally, it becomes a technical designation, "festival time." The festivals are fixed points, recurring year after year, being used to mark the passage of time. The word is actually used already in the ancient festival calendars, but at first only with the meaning "set time" (Exod. 23:15; 34:18; Deut. 16:6). But by the time of Hosea, the word means "festival day" (9:5), even though he also uses it with its more ancient meaning (2:11; 12:10). The specific meaning of "festival" is just coming into use at the time of Isaiah and it is not accidental that this meaning is not yet found in Amos.

Yahweh "hates" these festivals, more specifically, Yahweh's נפש (*nephesh,* self) hates them. Included in the meaning of נפש is not only that which makes the individual truly alive, but also one's desires and drives; the term also involves aspects of the emotions (see Eichrodt, *TheolAT* II/III, 87ff. [Engl: *OTTheol* II, 134ff.]). שנא (hate) is the harshest of the expressions which the prophet uses to describe the reaction of God to the cultic activities in Jerusalem. He only uses the word here and apparently makes use of traditional formulations: "I *hate,* I despise your feasts (חגיכם), and I do not want to smell your solemn assemblies," says Amos (5:21; cf. Hos. 9:15; Jer. 12:8; 44:4, and often elsewhere). But, already in the Baal cycle from Ras Shamra, one can read: *hm . tn . dbḥm . šn'a . b'l . tlt . rkb . 'rpt . dbḥ . btt . wdbḥ . dnt . wdbḥ . tdmm . 'amht:* "Truly, two banquets (sacrifices) *are hated by* Baal, a third one which goes up on the clouds, (namely) a banquet of shame and a banquet of quarreling and a banquet (at which) the maidens (have something) to mutter about" (II AB III 17–21, trans. according to J. Aistleitner, *Die mythologischen und kultischen Texte aus Ras Schamra* [1959]). שׂנא (hate) was also used long before the time of the prophets when one discriminated between the types of sacrifices or cultic activities which either did or did not qualify as acceptable to the deity. The cultic language of Israel makes use of this word over and over in the polemic against the Canaanite forms of deity worship. Yahweh hates the heathen cultic practices (Deut. 12:31), the pillars (16:22) (see also other similar passages). Those who listened to Isaiah, and other prophets like him, must have been shocked to hear him announce that Yahweh "hated" the cultic activities of Israel, which had been considered legitimate, just as much as he hated the illegitimate cults which worshiped the idols. The polemic against the cult is thus drawn into the realm of what was covered by the first commandment—one must consider how "our God" is used in v. 10b in light of this.

What Isaiah first said when he used traditional phraseology, he now reiterates in 14aβb as he puts the same ideas into his own words. He also uses לאה (be worn out) in other passages (7:13; see also 16:12); according to Mic. 6:3 and Job 16:7, this verb was used when arguing in the forum of a public debate (see also Deut. 1:12). One who sets forth a complaint explains that he is "tired out" by the machinations of those whom he accuses, leading one to expect that a sentence of judgment would be requested next. One wonders what the object of נשׂא (endure, carry) is supposed to be: "you" (pl.)? (see Deut. 1:9), but one could hardly have omitted the suffix; "them" (namely, the festivals)?, which is possible and is usually accepted as the referent. But נשׂא (carry) could also be understood as an abbreviation for נשׂא עון (carry iniquity), or something like that, so that the verb could have the meaning "forgive," which at least makes some sense in this context.

[1:15] One has the impression that the instruction, which looks more and more like an accusation in vv. 13f., may now have come to a conclusion. But Isaiah brings his "teaching" still more clearly into focus; even the cultic activity of prayer, which would seem to be beyond reproach, has not escaped being listed along with the cultic practices in Jerusalem which are to be repudiated. It certainly cannot be said here that the custom was rooted in practices of the Canaanites, so that it would have been considered an activity which was foreign to the expression of faith in Yahweh. Piling up the suffixes in v. 15a has a forceful effect which prevents a misunderstanding that the very action of praying ought to be considered wrong; it is the prayer of those people whose hands were tainted with blood which would not find any favorable hearing, not even if the prayer was lengthy or was repeated over and over again in an attempt to make a real impression. Naturally, the type of prayer at issue here is the one offered in the sanctuary, which accompanied the sacrificial action, not a private act of devotion; this does not say, however, that such private prayer would have been outside the scope of what could be viewed as open to dangerous abuse. תפלה (prayer) may be connected with the same idea that is found in the Arabic *falla,* "cut incisions" (see J. Wellhausen, *Reste arabischen Heidentums* [1897²] 126; for another view, see K. Ahrens, "Der Stamm der schwachen Verben in den semitischen Sprachen," *ZDMG,* 64 [1910] 163, who posits a connection with the root נפל [fall]; for a discussion of the derivation and root meaning, see D. R. Ap-Thomas, "Notes on Some Terms Relating to Prayer," *VT* 6 [1956] 225–241, esp. 230ff.). Then its most basic root meaning would be the same as that of הִתְגֹּדֵד (cut one's self) (see 1 Kings 18:28, among other passages). In any case, Isaiah completely removes prayer from any connection with a view of the world which thought it could be affected by magic, thereby insuring that God's freedom was still intact and recognizing that the condition of the one who was praying was of utmost importance when the prayer was being answered.

One prays by extending the hands, more specifically: the palms of the hands are extended upwards, so that the deity would allow them to be filled (cf. Vergil, *Aeneid* 1.93: *duplicis tendens ad sidera palmas* [stretching out both of the palms to the skies], and a long list of similar passages). Concerning Solomon, 1 Kings 8:54 says: "He arose from before the altar of the Lord, where he had knelt with hands outstretched toward heaven." But one can also stand up straight when one prays (1 Kings 8:22; 1 Sam. 1:26; Jer. 18:20) or could throw one's self down flat, so that one's face would be touching the ground (see Jehu, *ANEP* 355, and the illustration in *BHH* I, 521ff.; see also deVaux, op. cit., 457f.).

Just as someone who, under certain circumstances, "hides one's eyes" from a poor person who is asking for some help (see Prov. 28:27), Yahweh does the same thing in the presence of the one who prays, but only "honors him with the lips" (Isa. 29:13). The hands which are stained with the blood of the sacrificial animals remind Isaiah of the bloodguilt (the plural of דם, blood, is used in this abstract sense) with which those who are praying have burdened themselves by carrying out their violent deeds. But, as this continues, it shows that the prophet did not only discover "bloodguilt" where blood actually had been shed, but identified it as every instance where the justice due to fellow citizens was short-changed (but cf. Jer. 7:6, 9). Innocent blood which was spilled out "cries out to the heavens" (Gen. 4:10). If humans do not execute vengeance, then God does (cf. 1 Kings 21; concerning this, see H. Graf Reventlow, "Sein Blut komme über sein Haupt," *VT* 10 [1960] 311–327; and K. Koch, "Der Spruch 'Sein Blut bleibe auf seinem Haupt'," *VT* 12 [1962] 396–416). For bloodguilt, the punishment was the death sentence (Exod. 21:14; Gen. 9:6). The accusation could not be stated any more harshly!

[1:16, 17] But now, what follows is neither the death sentence nor the offer of unconditional grace, but rather a reasoned, detailed indication about what constitutes the true path of life. Both verbs which come at the beginning of the verse (רחצו, wash, and הזכו, clean) are still being used in the vocabulary of the cult (see above); however, in this case, they refer to ethical renewal (see Ps. 51:9).

The request is directed to Marduk: "May the tamarisk purify me, the . . . -plant release me, the marrow of the palm blot out my sins, may the font holding the purifying water of Ea and Asarluhi allow good things to come to me!" (A. Falkenstein/W. von Soden, *Sumerische und akkadische Hymnen und Gebete* [1953] 306; see, in addition, Exod. 29:4; 30:18f., and often elsewhere).

However, with 16aβ, Isaiah quits using cultic terminology. "Eliminate the wickedness of your deeds" reminds one of Jeremiah's temple address (7:3; cf. 18:11; 25:5; 26:13; 35:15). One would speak about רֹעַ מַעַלְלֵיכֶם (wickedness of your deeds) when curses were threatened in the covenant tradition (Deut. 28:20). Hosea had already referred back to those (9:15; see also 4:9; 5:4; 7:2; 12:3), and the term is a favorite one, more than anywhere else, in the book of Jeremiah (4:4; 21:12; 23:2; 26:3; 44:22). Thus, it seems to be a common expression, used in admonitions and in announcements of judgment. מַעֲלָל (deed), in and of itself, can designate either good or evil deeds; in actual fact, Isaiah always uses it (see 3:8, 10) in a negative sense, like Hosea, just as the root in the *hithpa'el* has the meaning "satisfy one's wanton craving, deal with someone in an evil way," and thus the special meaning "mishandle" (in a sexual sense in Judg. 19:25) developed from this. מַעֲלָלִים (deeds) are thus "crimes," by which the worth of the individual person is trampled upon because of someone's wanton craving and arrogance (cf. the Latin *facinus,* deed, action, crime).

After the negatives, "eliminate," "stop," there follows in v. 17 first a corresponding positive admonition: "Learn to do good!" It is characteristic of Isaiah that he admonishes the hearer to "learn"; his pedagogical bent discovers a most appropriate expression with this term. It just happens that the way he states the facts does not result in his calling for "turning back"; the demand for repentance is implicit in the three imperatives, "eliminate," "stop," and "learn." One must also take note, however, of the use of the two intransitive *hiph'il* forms, הרע and היטב, which, when taken in their very specific senses, do not mean "do good" or "do evil" but rather mean "behave in a good way" or "behave in an evil way" (and "act in such a way"); this means that his comments do not primarily deal with individual actions and the fulfilling of laws, but rather deal with a fundamentally new direction for human existence. Isaiah is not only looking for a new "way of thinking"; he is actually longing for a new basis for human interaction, which would be visible in one's day-to-day relationships with others who live in the same geographic region. "At the forefront of, and, in reality, in the place of a multitude of the ancient legal demands, which had become nothing more than a collection of individual cases and how to settle them, now the prophetic interpretation of these laws concentrates on the will of God by citing one basic demand: 'Do good,' which removes it at the very same time from being simply connected with what is part of the justice and legal system" (G. Fohrer, "Tradition und Interpretation im Alten Testament," *ZAW* 73 [1961] 27). Some specific demands, which serve as examples, are mentioned in v. 17aβb. Amos demands מִשְׁפָּט (justice) and צְדָקָה (righteousness) (5:24); Isaiah has the same thing in mind, even if he expresses it in a slightly different way. No doubt, when he looks for decisions in court to correspond to the will of God, which was plainly not hidden from view, he thinks of "seeking justice" in the same basic sense as Amos. However, when he employs the verb "seek," instead of his predecessor's "establish justice in the gate" (Amos 5:15), it reflects a concern for the problems connected with just decisions, much like the prophet's use of למדו (learn) in the preceding line. Even if God's overall will is apparent, what is just in each case is still not always immediately

49

obvious: "Justice" had to be a subject for demanding, dedicated perseverance and ongoing attention (see C. Westermann, "Die Begriffe für Fragen und Suchen im AT," *KD* 6 [1960] 2–30; see esp. 15).

Unfortunately, 17aγ cannot be translated with certainty (see above). It is significant that the downtrodden are mentioned in the same breath with the widows and orphans; see also Ps. 10:18 (employing דַּךְ, oppressed, here, instead of חָמוּץ, downtrodden). In our passage, שׁפט can only mean "assist someone in getting justice," as is often the case elsewhere as well (see 23; Ps. 72:4 parallel to הוֹשִׁיעַ, give deliverance; Ps. 82:3 parallel to הִצְדִּיק, maintain the right); it is this meaning which is to be used to explain the use of רִיב (concern, lawsuit) (see 23 and 51:22). The type of justice which the OT expects from the judge is not a *justitia distributive* (dispassionate justice) but a *justitia adiutrix miseria* (justice which helps those who are suffering); see Exod. 22:20–23; Deut. 24:17; 27:19, and often elsewhere). The demands of the law correspond exactly to predicates which describe God as protector of the insignificant and poor, the widows and orphans (Deut. 10:18; Pss. 68:6; 82:3f.; 146:9).

According to our present knowledge of Israel's surroundings, one can no longer hold on to the view that we are dealing with specific ideas which are unique to Israel's concept of the divine justice. Already in a Sumerian hymn to the goddess Nanshe we read: "Who knows the orphan, who knows the widow, knows the oppression of man over man, is the orphan's mother, Nanshe, who cares for the widow, who seeks out (?) justice (?) for the poorest (?) . . ." (cited according to S. N. Kramer, *History Begins At Sumer* [1959] 106). What praises the goddess here is included, in a different setting, in the *Hymn on the Building of the Temple* (in praise) *of Gudea* (of Lagash): "He observed the justice of Nanshe and Ningirsu: The rich did not do anything to cause suffering for the poor; the powerful did not do anything to cause suffering for the widow; in a house where there was no son to inherit, he allows the daughter (of the house) to participate when the fat of the sheep is burned . . ." (cited according to A. Falkenstein/W. von Soden, *Sumerische und Akkadische Hymnen und Gebete* [1953] 180). Hammurabi testifies to being called to make sure "that the strong are not able to oppress the weak, orphans and widows receive justice . . . to judge according to the justice of the land . . . to provide justice for the oppressed . . ." (Epilog, XXIVr, 59ff.; trans. on the basis of *AOT²* 407). The Ugaritic *Aqhat Legend* praises *Dan'el:* "He takes his place at the gate among the elders by the threshing floor. He adjudicates the rights of the widow, he passes sentence for the orphans" (*ydn dn. 'almnt . ytpt . ytm* IID V 6–8 = I D 22–25). Keret's son accuses his father because the latter was giving in to the most irritating sorts of brutal men: "You allow your hand to stoop to doing all manner of injustice, you do not permit the widows to experience justice, you do not speak justice for the one suffering in time of need" (II K VI 32–34; cf. also 44–50; trans. according to Aistleitner, op. cit.). Parallels are sometimes found which even use the very same words as this formulation (on this, see also F. C. Fensham, "Widow, Orphan, and the Poor in Ancient Near Eastern Legal and Wisdom Literature," *JNES* 21 [1962] 129–139). One would request of the king in Jerusalem that he would use his influence to bring about the very same thing, to provide the legal protection for the insignificant (Ps. 72:2, 4), or praise him, because he had done it (Ps. 72:12–14; cf. also Isa. 11:1f.; 32:1ff.; Jer. 21:11ff.; 22:1ff.; 23:5ff.). But this most important obligation of the king in the ancient Near East (it was also expected of a king by those who lived in Israel) has now been "democratized" in the OT system of covenant justice. The very nature of human activity was to be a reflection of the justice which mirrored the righteousness of Yahweh. Then the prophets continued by putting renewed emphasis on these ancient demands of the covenant (Amos 2:6f.; 4:1; 5:7, 10ff.; 8:4ff.; Isa. 1:23; 10:2; and even later, Zech. 7:9–10; Mal. 3:5; and James 1:27; Rom. 12:1ff.).

Purpose and Thrust

The exegesis of the individual verses has shown that 1:10–17 is to be interpreted as instruction for a specific situation, not as a universally valid teaching about the disgusting nature of the cult. Even if Isaiah's intentions are particularly clear and focused, the other prophets of the pre-exilic period are not to be interpreted in any different way when one seeks to understand their criticism of sacrifice. But Isaiah did not feel compelled, just as the other prophets were not so moved, to offer instructions about what would constitute a pleasing sacrifice for Yahweh, how a festival celebration could be made suitable in his opinion, and what meaning it could have for the leaders and people if they fulfilled their cultic responsibilities within a context of being faithful to God. Even concerning the cultic officials, one certainly senses a critical assessment of any attempt at further development of a cultic piety. The reference to ethical demands as a condition for participation in the cult would not, in itself, be ruled out automatically, but if that is what Isaiah had intended, then the positive value of true cultic piety or the methodical instruction about piety would had to have been mentioned directly afterwards. However, in Isaiah's case, we do not get the slightest hint that he was so inclined. Israel, including the prophets, owes much to the cultic traditions. The "entrance liturgies" (Pss. 15; 24:1–6; Isa. 33:14–16), which as a genre are much older than Isaiah, show that thinking about cultic matters did not have to be far removed from the thinking of the prophets who raised criticisms of it. Even when observing Israel's neighbors, one knows that there were certain expectations which were to be fulfilled by those who visited the temple (cf. H. J. Kraus, *Psalmen,* BK 15/1 concerning Psalm 15 [Engl: *Psalms 1–59,* 225ff.]). Concerning Israel, Deut. 26:12ff. shows that the visitor to the sanctuary knew very well that only the gift of one who was obedient could be followed by God's blessing. The "oath of purification" in Job 31 is a late, but richly developed reshaping of such a confession, which would have been expected from one who was participating in cultic rites. "He who has clean hands and a pure heart . . . will receive the blessing from Yahweh" (Ps. 24:4f.). But even though all of these expressions demonstrate an affinity with such instruction, the prophets do not generally voice such concerns. They saw their task in heading off a fatal danger for the faith of their people: the danger that the people would sink into a purely formalized cultic religion, in which the person thought, because of having completed some magically potent rites, that the deity could be forced to act in a beneficial way and also that an individual could manipulate the deity so as to ward off threatening forces. The prophets were speaking with a sharpness which a "cultic official" would never have used, saying that the salvation offered to Israel could be a reality only if Israel persistently sought to be faithful to the God of the covenant, a faithfulness which provided the very foundation of its existence and was in no way separable from the solidarity with— yes, even goodness toward—the "neighbor" (see Matt. 12:7). All participation in acts of cultic piety, all the way from official worship services to the most private prayer, had to come under continual scrutiny, according to the position held by the prophets, so as to determine whether each was legitimate; in fact, each had to be repeatedly exposed as questions were raised about its continuing validity. Where would one be able to find cultic activity being practiced according to a completely unbroken, faithful relationship with God, in which the hands which are "stretched out" in prayer are "pure"? The radical nature of the criticism of sacrifice, as also the strengthening of the prophet's demands for obedience in general, brings one to issues which do not, in fact, find their full explanation until one goes beyond the scope of the OT.

Good Things or the Sword

Literature

J. Schoneveld, "Jesaia I 18–20," *VT* 13 (1963) 342–344.

[**Literature update through 1979**: R. D. Culver, "Is 1:18—Declaration, Exclamation or Interrogation?" *JETS* 12 (1969) 133–141. M. Dahood, "שני 'scarlet' (ug. tn)," *Bib* 54 (1973) 362. H. W. Hoffmann, "Die Intention der Verkündigung Jesajas," BZAW 136 (1974) 96ff.]

Text

1:18 Come, let us enter into a lawsuit, one against the other,
     says Yahweh.
   If[a] your sins are like crimson,[bc]
     can they (then) pass for white, like snow?[c]
   If[d] they are as deep red as purple,
     can they (then) be like wool?
 19 If you are willing[a] and you are obedient,[a]
     you shall eat the good gifts of the land.
 20 But if you refuse and resist,
     then you shall be devoured by the sword.[a]
   For the mouth of Yahweh has spoken it.

18a Joüon, Gr §171d, wants to take אם (if) in a concessive sense ("même si," even if). That is highly unlikely and, based on the sense of the section, not necessary.
18b Instead of the plural of שנים (crimson), some MSS and Qª read the singular, which is also presupposed by the Gk, Syr, Vulg, already having been proposed as an emendation by Michaelis (see G. R. Driver, *JTS* 2 [1951] 25).
18c–c Concerning the article with שנים (crimson stuff) or rather שני (crimson stuff), שלג (snow), תולע (purple stuff), and צמר (wool) (used to designate types of material), see BrSynt §21cβ.
18d Instead of אם (if), many MSS and the versions read ואם (and if).
19a Concerning parataxis (placing together without coordination) instead of hypotaxis (syntactic subordination) when using שמע (obedient), cf. Joüon, Gr §177h, and L. Köhler, "Ein verkannter hebräischer irrealer Bedingungssatz (Jes 1:19)," *ZS* 4 (1926) 196f.

20a Joüon, Gr §128c, tries to take חרב (sword) as an accusative next to the passive תאכלו (you shall be devoured), but this is not supported by evidence from the text. But the punctuation of תאכלו as active ("you shall experience the sword"; see Duhm and G. R. Driver, BZAW 77 [1958] 42) is also too far-fetched an attempt at making the sense more clear. Possibly מחרב (from the sword) should be read here (haplography of the letter מ), but it is more likely that the reading should be בחרב (by the sword) (see Neh. 2:3, 13, אֻכַּל בָּאֵשׁ, destroyed by fire), which is exactly what the Qᵃ actually offers as a reading.

Form

By means of the introductory formula, יאמר יהוה (says Yahweh) and by means of the closing formula, כי פי יהוה דבר (for the mouth of Yahweh has spoken it), the section is marked off as a separate unit. The theme of the "cult" is no longer the issue and thus, there are many (including Kaiser among recent scholars) who are incorrect when they take 1:10–20 to be one unit. The connection with the previous section is based solely on the grounds of association; the forensic terms שׁפט (stand up for the rights) and ריב (cause, lawsuit) seem to lead without interruption into נוכחה (enter into a lawsuit) and into the judgment speech itself, in vv. 18–20.

Meter: The section is composed entirely of five-stress cola (each 3 + 2); ונוכחה (let us enter into a lawsuit) actually has two stresses in v. 18; טוב הארץ (good gifts of the land) in v. 19 is to be read with one "stress." The closing formula stands by itself. It is the same one as is found in 40:5; 58:14; Mic. 4:4; however, it is hardly to be considered as nothing more than a later addition inserted by a compiler (so Marti, Cheyne). It has the effect of underscoring the authority of the message.

The section is a judgment speech, like the one which was already presented in 1:2–3. נוכחה (let us enter into a lawsuit with one another) is a clear indicator. But "judgment speech" is just a catch-all term. In 1:2–3 it was an accusation speech, which summoned witnesses. J. Begrich (*Studien zu Deuterojesaja* [1938] 20 and 27) designates the present section, along with others, as an "appellation speech of one who is an accuser." But no accusations are mentioned at this point; rather, two alternatives are mentioned, which would have to be further clarified in the course of the legal proceedings. H. J. Boecker (*Redeformen des Rechtslebens im Alten Testament,* WMANT 14 [1964] 68f.) is thus correct when he designates this an "appellation calling for the establishment of legal proceedings." As a matter of fact, in v. 18a there is a summons to appear at a judicial session which is to determine the facts of the case. For this reason, no questions are put to the adversary party, which would have then had the tone of a rebuke (as 3:15; Mic. 6:3); instead, there is the imperative לְכוּ (come), which is not to be treated lightly, as in other places, as if it were a simple interjection tossed in for good measure, but it is intended to cause exactly what it calls for. There is a formal parallel with 41:1–4: "Listen to me in silence, O coastlands; and you peoples, wait for my reprimand (יחלו לתוכחתי, text emended); let them approach, then let them speak; let us together draw near for judgment!" This is followed by a string of questions which are to be debated and further explicated in the hearing, and then a decision is to be handed down.

Setting

It could be that Isaiah spoke this message on the occasion of a covenant
festival (see the discussion of 1:2–3). In favor of this viewpoint, one can
take note of the main topic presented in vv. 19f. (see below), which has its
roots in the covenant festival tradition. But we know far too little about
whether and how such a covenant (renewal) festival could have been
observed at the time of Isaiah for us to be able to pass judgment, with
anything approaching certainty, about whether this is a covenant renewal
festival.

The time when this section originated cannot be established with
certainty either. In any case, the land has not yet been devastated by the
Assyrians (as in vv. 7–9). The message may belong to the time when the
leading circles of power in Judah were possessed by the idea that they
would give notice to Assyria that they were withdrawing their pledge of
loyalty, having formed a relationship with Egypt instead, which would
mean that it might have been formulated about 705.

Commentary

[1:18a] Once again, Yahweh himself speaks. No mention is made of the
adversary with whom he will engage in this discussion. According to the
present context, it would be Jerusalem and its leaders (v. 10). But since v.
18 starts a new section and vv. 19f. makes use of the themes of promise
and curse, terms connected with the covenant tradition, one should probably presume that the covenant people Israel are Yahweh's "opponents at
the legal proceedings." The root יכח (enter into a lawsuit, decide) is used
as the basis for various derived forensic terms. The *hiph'il* means "reprimand," which can take place through education or when someone
receives a public reprimand (Prov. 3:12; 9:8; 28:23, among other passages), but can also be issued in a court of justice. The מוֹכִיחַ (him who
reproves) (Amos 5:10; Isa. 29:21) seems to be that particular person who,
as a member of the group which was responsible for justice, denounced
the scheming of selfish rulers courageously and relentlessly. Such a person
is neither judge nor accuser, but an impartial third person (so that הוֹכִיחַ
בֵּין could take on the meaning "be an arbitrator between" [Gen. 31:37;
Job 9:33]) who can "set things right" (יכח is related to נָכֹחַ, straight, right)
and can admonish others to deal justly (see Lev. 19:17; Ezek. 3:26).
Yahweh is able to appear in this role at the covenant festival, as the מוֹכִיחַ
(one who rebukes) (Ps. 50:8, 21). But in this present passage, the rarely
found *niph'al* is used (see also Job 23:7 and cf. the *hithpa'el* in Mic. 6:2,
which has the same meaning). Actually, in the proceedings which were
supposed to be arranged, Yahweh is not simply the impartial מוֹכִיחַ (one
who reproves) but he functions, at the same time, as the accuser. And yet,
by means of the use of the reflexive, it is presumed that Israel, as the
accused, would also have the opportunity, from its side as well, to stand
up as a מוֹכִיחַ (one who reproves) against Yahweh. Even as the בְּרִית
(covenant) between Yahweh and Israel has a secular counterpart in the
suzerainty treaty from the world of ancient Near Eastern politics (see
Mendenhall, op. cit. [in literature for 1:2–3] 31f., 40f.), one must be very
serious when it comes to considering Israel a full partner, so that the

relationship God–people corresponds to a real situation, in which dialogue was to take place.

[1:18b] Verse 18b presents many obstacles to a correct interpretation, which become apparent when a wide variety of attempts to translate it are compared. Gk reads καὶ ἐὰν ὦσιν αἱ ἁμαρτίαι ὑμῶν ὡς φοινικοῦν, ὡς χιόνα λευκανῶ, ἐὰν δὲ ὦσιν ὡς κόκκινον, ὡς ἔριον λευκανῶ (and if your blood is as crimson, I will make it white, like snow; if it is as scarlet, I will make it white, like wool). This rendering speaks very clearly about God forgiving unconditionally. But there is absolutely no doubt that the MT has preserved the original text. As a rule, it is translated as follows: "If your sins are a deep red, they shall yet become snow white; if they are as scarlet, they shall yet become as wool," or something along that line, which is interpreted, also by modern commentators (Ziegler, Hertzberg, Herntrich, Kaiser, Eichrodt, Schoneveld, op. cit.), in a factual sense, according to the meaning furnished by the Gk: "He (Yahweh) thus breaks through the wall which separates humanity from himself; he declares that the guilt, which is so great that all human efforts at atonement run aground, has been atoned for. . . . In forgiveness, as a free act of grace, the question about Israel's destiny is splendidly answered" (Eichrodt, ad loc.). However, it is Duhm who is more correct yet: "Isaiah never offers the people the forgiveness of sins in such a polite manner." If Eichrodt's interpretation is correct, then v. 18b cannot be part of Isaiah's own message. In fact, it also contradicts the rest of the context. For what purpose would a challenge be issued which called for a confrontation? And above all: What would be the meaning of the alternatives offered in vv. 19 and 20? Duhm himself is inclined to take the sentence in an ironic sense: "Let them be white as snow! Let them be as wool!" in the sense: "Turn yourselves into innocent lambs, that is, if you can!" But since the time of J. D. Michaelis, the second clause has been most generally assumed to be an interrogative clause (as it is also handled in the *Zürcher Bibel*). The absence of the particle which identifies it as a question does not preclude this interpretation (see Joüon, Gr §161a; G. Fohrer, *ZAW* 74 [1962] 262f.). In terms of content, this explanation is about the same as that offered by Duhm, but is preferable to what he suggests.

Concerning חֲטָאִים (sins), refer back to what was said about חֵטְא (sin) in 1:4. שָׁנִי (Ugaritic *tn*, possibly "purple"; Arabic *sana'*, "luster"), crimson red, is a dye-stuff (Arabic *qirmiz*) which is manufactured from the clusters of eggs laid by a scale insect, collected from upon the leaves of the *quercus coccifera* (see Dalman, *AuS* V, 84f.). תּוֹלָע (Akkadian *tultu*, worm), normally translated as "purple," actually refers to the material which has been dyed by using this color; these two words are often used together: תּוֹלַעַת שָׁנִי (purple of crimson) (on this, see R. Gradwohl, "Die Farben im Alten Testament," BZAW 83 [1963] 73f.). Since the sheep, the suppliers of wool in Palestine, had a lightly colored coat, it is possible to use "wool" and "snow" as parallel terms.

Since Yahweh demands an appearance in the court of justice in order to clarify the issues, he has to explain why this is necessary. One could have objected, when responding to the proclamation of the prophet, that just by performing certain cultic rites it was indeed possible to make amends for the guilt incurred by the offenses which had been committed, whether these rites would have been sacrifices or ritual washings (on this, see 16aα). The issue did not revolve around the forgiveness of sins, but whether there was a possibility for expiating them on one's own. It is fully in keeping with the line of thought in vv. 10–17 that Isaiah would also respond here with a sharp No! to the notion that one could place any confidence in the fulfillment of cultic rites; thus, Isaiah reduces any such understanding, that such actions could guarantee salvation, to the status of being nothing more than an illusion. It is not that easy to be rid of the guilt of sin, and a human being ought not attempt to toy so frivolously with the long-suffering nature of God. In this matter, Isaiah does not differ from the judgment of Jeremiah, who uses a similar description: "Though you wash yourself with lye and use much soap, the stain of your guilt is still before me, says the Lord God" (2:22; cf. Job 9:30).

[1:19, 20] Does that mean that there is no means of escape for Israel, and thus, that it would have to perish because of its guilt? No, for even in this case the following is true: The future always remains open. Israel is placed before completely real alternatives: blessing or curse.

It cannot be just by chance that the two verbs אבה (be willing) and שמע (hearken) are next to each other in Lev. 26:21, in the "covenant festival Psalm" 81 (v. 12), and in Josh. 24:10 (see also Ezek. 3:7 and 20:8 [here also parallel to מרה, rebel]; cf. also Isa. 28:12 and 30:9). When these vocables are used in this order, it is clear that the roots go back to the covenant tradition, which set before Israel the two possibilities of salvation or disaster, blessing or curse. That is also emphasized by related vocabulary. In the case that Israel is obedient, the people can eat off the land until they are well satisfied (Lev. 26:5, 10; cf. on this, 26:16, 26; Deut. 28:31, 33, among other passages). Deut. 6:11 shows that טוב (good gifts) also comes from the same context; this word is used to summarize the good gifts which, in other contexts, are mentioned individually when the promises which accompany the blessing are mentioned. And finally, the threat of the "sword" belongs primarily to the vocabulary connected with this tradition (Lev. 26:25, 33; Deut. 28:22, and often elsewhere).

It was the intention that the "lawsuit" would make very clear to Israel the alternatives which were offered it in its covenant with Yahweh; any kind of cheap alternative which would allow Israel to "wash away" its guilt was not part of the package. When he uses מרה (resist) (cf. 3:8), Isaiah uses an expression for Israel's breach of faith which, very much like סרה (revolt) (see 1:5), can describe the conflict between father and son (Deut. 21:18, 20; cf. also Hos. 14:1); the rebellion of Israel against its God can be compared with the "stubbornness" of a son against his father. מרה (resist) helps to further clarify the מאן (refuse) which precedes it. It is customary that this latter word is followed by an infinitive. Thus, Hosea says (11:5): מאן לשוב (he refused to return) (so also Jer. 5:3; 8:5), and Jeremiah, who uses the verb surprisingly often, says: "They refused to take correction" (מוסר, 5:3). One must ask oneself whether it is plausible that an infinitive should also be read in the present Isaiah passage, possibly something like לשמע (to obey), corresponding to the שמעתם (you are obedient) in v. 19; cf. 1 Sam. 8:19; Jer. 11:10; 13:10; in such cases, "hearing" would undoubtedly refer to hearing *and* observing the basic demands of the covenant stipulations. However, both אבה (be willing) and מאן (refuse) are consciously used by Isaiah without the infinitive which would seem to be necessary after the verb. Israel stands between the two possible choices. Either they are ready, deep down, to do everything for their Lord, or they are just as ready, deep down, to "barricade themselves" against him. In this light, מאן (refuse) has to do with the phenomenon of the "hardening" which is so clearly predicted to Isaiah at the time of his call (6:10ff.). This does not refer to a hardening which is imposed upon Israel by Yahweh, but rather, to the inability to stay faithful to Yahweh, an obligation which Israel had imposed upon itself.

Purpose and Thrust

Does it not seem clear that Israel had already lost this "lawsuit" to which it was summoned, even before it began? What else would be the result of it except its complete collapse, and what else ought one anticipate, except the judgment that the people no longer had any future open for themselves? Verse 18b helps one to see the utter seriousness of Israel's situation. Every avenue of escape is cut off as they look for a way to sweep aside the consequences of unfaithfulness. And yet: the judgment which would mandate complete destruction is not handed down. Even if it is not mentioned, there is still the very real hope that Israel would acknowledge its guilt and see the threatening consequences of its obstinacy if it would appear before Yahweh in this "lawsuit." Yahweh, the God of Israel, would have no joy in bringing on condemnation and obliteration. Even at this point, he hoped to engage Israel in a conversation, in which one could achieve a breakthrough to get insight and understanding. At that point, the offer of grace would still be in force. Thus, the faithfulness and patience of the God of the covenant illumine this passage. But no false impression should be left about the fact that this offer of grace calls for a fundamental and absolute reorientation. "One would falsely understand Isaiah if one would take the call for the people to repent, so necessary if they were to be saved, or take a decision to repent as if it were some type of action which was to be completed so that salvation could be obtained or one could have something to present in order to demand help. On the contrary, it is a possibility which is offered solely by God, and indeed, something he wishes to see actually happen, but it is something which must be freely received and in this way take effect. . . . The willingness of the human being and the readiness of God to forgive belong together; finally, they are two aspects or parts of a single process: the deliverance from an existence which is sinful through and through and bound to result in death" (G. Fohrer, *ZAW* 74 [1962] 264).

Jerusalem in a
Purifying Judgment

Literature

H. Jahnow, *Das hebräische Leichenlied im Rahmen der Völkerdichtung,* BZAW 36 (1923). L. Köhler, "Sig Sīgīm = Bleiglätte," *TZ* 3 (1947) 232–234. N. W. Porteous, "Jerusalem-Zion: The Growth of a Symbol," FS W. Rudolph (1961) 235–252. H. W. Hertzberg, "Die Nachgeschichte alttestamentlicher Texte innerhalb des Alten Testaments," BZAW 66 (1936) 110–121 = *Beiträge zur Traditionsgeschichte und Theologie des Alten Testaments* (1962) 69–80.

[**Literature update through 1979:** R. D. Honeycutt, "The Root Ṣ-D-Ḳ in Prophetic Literature," diss., Edinburgh (1970/71). M. Dahood, "'Weaker than Water': Comparative *beth* in Isaiah," *Bib* 59 (1978) 91–92.]

Text

1:21 How the faithful[a] city
  has become a prostitute,
filled[b] with justice,
  righteousness dwelt in her midst [but now, murders].[c]
22 Your silver has become burnished lead,
  your beer has [by means of water][a] been adulterated![b]
23 Your rulers are unruly[a]
  and partners with thieves!
Every one[b] loves graft
  and chases after gifts.
They do not help the orphan to get justice,
  the concerns of the widow do not come before them.
24 Therefore this is the verdict of the Lord,[a] Yahweh of Hosts,
  the Strong One of Israel:
Woe, I want to revive my activity against my adversaries
  and want to avenge myself against my enemies
25 [and I want to turn my hand against you]
  and I want to purify your burnished lead with potash[a]
  and want to remove all your slag.
26 I want to make your judges as at the earliest time
  and your counselors as at the very beginning.
At that time one will call you
  "stronghold of justice, faithful city."

* * * *

27 [Zion is to be ransomed by justice
   and its returnees[a] by righteousness;
28 however, above all else, the rebellious and sinners are to be
   crushed,[a]
   and those who forsake the Lord shall be brought down.]

21a After נאמנה (faithful) the Gk reads Σιων (Zion). It is not likely that it is meant to be in apposition to "faithful city" (which is how the Gk understands it). On the other hand, one ought to consider the possibility that the word could be taken as the accusative object of מלאתי (I have filled), which would then be pointed as מִלֵּאתִי: "I have filled Zion with justice"; cf. 33:5 (מָלֵא צִיּוֹן מִשְׁפָּט, he will fill Zion with justice), but see also 1:27, where Zion is also mentioned. However, it would be strange to have a speech of Yahweh at the beginning of a section which has the form of a lament for the dead, which means that the MT is best left as it is. "Zion" somehow got into the text of the Gk from v. 27.

21b Concerning the *ḥireq compagnis* (used to link two words together) in מלאתי (filled with), cf. Joüon, *Gr* §93m and Beer-Meyer I §45, 3d.

21c ועתה מרצחים (but now, murders) is rightly considered by many recent commentators (Duhm, Procksch, Fohrer, Kaiser) to be an addition. Metrically, both of the words are unnecessary. In terms of content, they provide no real antithesis to the sketch which has already been developed to portray the earlier condition, in addition to which, the specific reproaches leveled in vv. 22f. have a different style.

22a במים (by means of water) looks suspiciously like an addition to many commentators, since it articulates the obvious. This in itself is not enough of a reason for convincing one to remove it as a gloss, but the meter seems to suggest that this ought to be removed.

22b מהל (adulterated) has been explained as a less commonly used form of מול (circumcise), by means of which one would come up with a meaning something like "dilute, mix, water down." KBL makes reference to the Arabic *mahîn* (spoil, with reference to milk); others connect the word with the Arabic *muhl* and the Neo-Hebraic word מוהל (derived from the Arabic), meaning "fruit juice"; see Th. Nöldeke, *ZDMG* 40 (1886) 741. Gk reads here μίσγουσιν (mix); Targ reads מערב (mixed); Vulg reads *mistum* (mixed). In an analogous way, there are also other Semitic and Indo-Germanic languages which speak of adulterated liquids as being "cut": e.g., Arabic *'udah maqtū'ah* (cut aloes oil), Latin *castrare vinum* (cut wine), French *couper du vin, du lait* (dilute wine, milk), Spanish *traseqar* (to cut) (= Latin *transsecare,* to cut); see Marti, ad loc. It is recommended that one refrain from a textual emendation and just stay with the meaning "adulterated, cut."

23a This translation has been chosen to bring out the alliteration of the שָׂרַיִךְ סוֹרְרִים (*śārayik, sôr^erîm*) (*śārayik, sôrerîm*). The exact reading of the Hebrew text is: "your officials are obstinate."

23b The suffix in כֻּלּוֹ carries with it a vague sense of something like "its totality" = "each one"; cf. Joüon, *Gr* §146j.

24a It is possible that האדון (the Lord) serves as a doublet for יהוה (Yahweh). But since Isaiah also uses הָאָדוֹן (the Lord) as a title for Yahweh in other places (cf. 10:16 and 19:4) and the versions also read האדון, one should refrain from removing it.

25a בֹּר means "potash, lye"; Gk. (εἰς καθαρόν, clear of admixture) has certainly taken this to mean "purity," as has Vulg (*ad purum,* until unadulterated). But many commentators are not even satisfied with the translation "lye" and they emend this, reading בַּכֻּר (in a smelting pot), whereas Eichrodt actually reads both words together: "(I want to) purify you with lye in a smelting furnace." But this change is unnecessary, since salts of lye play a role as a flux when silver is being extracted (see Köhler, op. cit., 232f.).

27a וְשָׁבֶיהָ (its returnees) has caused much discussion, not only concerning how it is to be translated, but also as to whether it is part of the ancient text. Both questions are aspects of the question about whether vv. 27f. are from Isaiah. Gk reads ἡ αἰχμαλωσία αὐτῆς (her captivity), Syr *wašbîtāh* (and captivity), which is based on the Hebrew וְשִׁבְיָה ("its captivity, its captives"). One would then have to assume that it originated in the exilic-postexilic era, which is exactly the case when one translates the MT with "and its returnees." Tur-Sinai (op. cit. [in literature for 1:1] 157), with reference to 10:21, chooses to read וְשָׁבָה ("and will return"). However, Döderlein had already suggested reading וְיֹשְׁבֶיהָ (and its inhabitants), which could be based on 10:24 (יֹשֵׁב צִיּוֹן, who dwell in Zion; cf. also 30:19). But since v. 27 stands in a negative relationship to v. 28, one can hardly avoid the meaning "his (to Yahweh) returning ones," which is needed for the contrast with פֹּשְׁעִים (rebellious) and חַטָּאִים (sinners) in v. 28.

28a The substantive שֶׁבֶר (crashing) at the beginning of the verse sounds awkward, especially since no עַל (upon) follows. J. Huesman (*Bib* 37, [1956] 286) wants to read this as an infinitive absolute וְשָׁבֹר and translates it: "shall be destroyed"; yet, this suggestion runs into trouble when one notes that שׁבר (break in pieces) is always causative in the *qal*. The versions (Gk καὶ συντριβήσονται [and they are crushed], Targ וְיִתַּבְּרוּן [and they were broken], and Vulg *et conteret* [and it is ground down]) are all presumably based upon a form of the verb such as וְשֻׁבְּרוּ (and they are crushed) or, since the *pu'al* is never used elsewhere, possibly a form of the *niph'al*, וְנִשְׁבְּרוּ (they are to be crushed) or else יִשָּׁבְרוּ (they are to be crushed).

Form

A new section begins with v. 21; it consists of a prophetic reproach, or one might say accusation (vv. 21–23), followed by the accompanying threat or announcement of judgment (vv. 24ff.) which begins with הוֹי (woe), right after the introduction in v. 24a. This linkage of reproach with threat is characteristic of the prophetic proclamation since the announcement of judgment cannot, by its very nature, take effect unless the reason for it is given. Clearly, this message comes to its conclusion in v. 26 with עִיר הַצֶּדֶק (stronghold of righteous justice) and קִרְיָה נֶאֱמָנָה (faithful city), since these terms, which at the beginning of this message (v. 21) were used so ingeniously as predicates of Jerusalem, are now used once again. Verses 27 and 28 are a later addition (on this, see Hertzberg, op. cit., 75). However, v. 27 is closely connected with the content of v. 26b, and both of these verses have the obvious purpose of getting to a deeper level about what has already been said and modifying it in a particular way. One must wonder whether this "later interpretation" could be attributed to Isaiah himself. The fact that it is in the form of a promise cannot be used to argue against its authenticity. One must admit that there is no evidence for Isaiah making use of the word פָּדָה (ransom) elsewhere, but since both Hosea (7:13; 13:14) and Micah (6:4) use it, it is not impossible that he would have used it as well. The issue could be decided for sure if שָׁבֶיהָ (its returnees) could be used to describe only those who were returning from the exile, but there is no firm evidence for this being the only meaning (see above, textual notes). שׁבר (crush) is also used elsewhere by Isaiah and is also used by Amos (6:6); the other expressions cannot be rejected out of hand, since they are words which Isaiah might possibly have used. There is, therefore, nothing to suggest that this is dependent upon Deutero- or Trito-Isaiah (as does B. Duhm, for example, with reference to Isa. 52:3ff.; 59:17–20; 61:8). But it is highly unlikely that Isaiah himself would have inserted a later addition in order to expand an earlier message which he himself had spoken, which means that one should consider both of these verses to be the work of a disciple of Isaiah, particularly since the addition clearly inserts a new accent to that which had been stated just before this (see below for the exposition of both verses).

Thus, vv. 21–26 are to be attributed to Isaiah. The reproach in the first part is unique on formal grounds because it is clothed, by and large, in the dress of a lament for the dead. That is already made obvious when it uses אַיכָה (how), the characteristic opening word for this genre. Of course, it is a unique type of lament for the dead. The book of Lamentations, with its laments for the destroyed city of Jerusalem, demonstrates that it is possible for such a song to be used to refer to the whole city. However, what is noteworthy about this present lament is that it is not sung about a destroyed and therefore "dead" city, but rather that it laments a city which is corrupted in terms of its morals and system of justice. It is part of this genre that the characterization of the present deplorable downfall of the one who has died is compared with that person's former magnificence and honorable qualities (see Jahnow, op. cit., esp. 99 and 253f.). Whereas the "splendor" is mentioned only in v. 21aβb, in a short but pregnant expression, the "description of the miserable conditions" is given, by comparison, much more space (vv. 22f.). It has the form of a reproach, which is spoken by the prophet himself, whereas the announcement of judgment—having been furnished with a corresponding introduction—appears as a message from Yahweh. The prophetic speech and the message from Yahweh are connected to one another in chiastic correspondence: v. 24b corresponds to v. 23, v. 25 to v. 22, v. 26a to v. 21b, v. 26b to v. 21a (see R. Fey, *Amos and Isaiah*, WMANT 12 [1963] 64). The announcement of judgment changes into a message of promise in v. 26, which ought not come as a surprise, since the judgment is characterized as a smelting process, which serves as a means for purifying.

Meter: In vv. 21, 22, and 23aβ, after the glosses have been removed, one finds *Qina* verses (lament, 3 + 2), exactly what one would expect for this genre (see above, textual notes); in v. 21b מָלֵאתִי (filled) receives a double stress. Verse 23aα is a two-stress bicolon. Considering the inconsistency which is to be found in the number of stresses in each colon, which one observes again and again, one ought not insert הָיוּ (they were) between the first two words, by analogy with vv. 21 and 22, as is done by K. Budde (*ZAW* 49 [1931] 33). In the same way, the irregular length of the verse in v. 23b (2 + 4) is not sufficient grounds for eliminating this verse (as does Budde, op. cit., 33, followed in recent times by Fey, op. cit., 64). Switching the two halves of the verse (see Duhm, ad loc.) misses the point that it is undoubtedly by design that the first half of this message is brought to a conclusion with a colon which has more stresses than is usual. The introduction in v. 24a is not counted in the meter. Verse 24b is once again a *Qina* verse (3 + 2). Verse 25 has also been the subject of discussion on metrical grounds. The verse has three parts, which has resulted in attempts to make it normal, like the others, so that it would have two parts, sometimes by removing one of the cola and sometimes by adding a fourth colon (see Marti, Fohrer, and Budde, op. cit., 33). Actually, v. 25aα should be removed as a gloss, as Fohrer has suggested, which also eliminates the awkward repetition of וְאָשִׁיבָה (and I want to turn). Verse 26a is a *Qina* verse (3 + 2); v. 26b is once again problematic. J. Ley ("Metrische Analyse von Jesaja Kp. 1," *ZAW* 22 [1902] 229–237) considers קִרְיָה נֶאֱמָנָה (faithful city) to be a gloss and, after it is removed, identifies this verse as a five-stress colon;

however, it is this very expression which consciously makes reference to the beginning of the message. Budde (op. cit., 34) suggests replacing the "superfluous" אחרי־כן (at that time, after this) with a simple ו (and) and inserts, before עיר (stronghold, city), the word עוד (yet). But אחרי־כן is not "superfluous"; instead, it has the important function of making it very clear that the new era will be able to emerge only after the harsh judgment is complete. This verse is to be taken as a six-stress colon (2 + 2 + 2). Verse 27 is 3 + 2; v. 28 is 4 + 3.

Setting

An assured dating of this speech is impossible. It is certain that the city has not yet been through the catastrophe of 701, since specific dangers connected with war are not mentioned. The content in v. 23 includes the types of details which are also found in 3:12–15; 5:22–24, and 10:1–4, which belong in Isaiah's early period, when the primary interests of the prophet dealt with the degeneration of justice and the public breakdown of basic order. It seems quite likely that the prophet could have proclaimed this message at the "royal festival of Zion," the original setting in life for the Psalms of Zion, at which time Zion/Jerusalem was praised as the securely established city, full of justice, and righteousness. It must have caused a great stir when Isaiah uttered this macabre lament for the dead city which had just been praised in the liturgy as a city which could justifiably celebrate its being the city of God, with an accompanying euphoria which was characteristic of such a festival.

Commentary

[1:21] The city which is accused in a song for the dead is first addressed as קריה נאמנה (faithful city). The word קריה is used only rarely in the OT and no doubt would impress one as an archaic and festive term. In a lament for the dead, one would naturally choose the type of magnanimous words which would describe what the dead person had been at one time (see Jahnow, op. cit., 96ff.). It is also to be noted that this word is also found in the songs of Zion (Ps. 48:3, קרית מלך רב, the city of the great king), which might be the reason behind Isaiah's frequent use of the word (22:2; 29:1; 32:13). And yet, the attribute נאמן (faithful) is not used in the Psalms of Zion as an attribute for the city of God. However, the OT does refer to a בית נאמן (a sure house) for David (1 Sam. 25:28; see also 2 Sam. 7:16; 1 Kings 11:38, and Isa. 55:3), so that the word would have been recognized as a familiar expression when it was heard by those who visited Jerusalem at the time of the festivals. In addition, אמן (confirm, support) is a synonym for כון (firmly established), and various derived terms are found in the songs of praise for the city of God (Pss. 48:9; 87:5; see also נכון, firm foundation, in Isa. 2:2). Isaiah uses this synonym נאמן because of the double meaning which this root conveys: "firmly established" and "trustworthy, faithful." In this way he reinterprets the ancient tradition. The "firmly established" city of God can have confidence in its future and stability only if it is also the city of faithfulness, only if its king "remains" a believer (האמן, 7:9) and if the new community of Zion continues to be made up of believers (מאמין, he who believes, 28:16) and thus would have no need to be afraid. These parallels show that the Isaianic concept of belief is already intimated in the use of נאמנה (faithful) (cf. also אמת, faithfulness, in Isa. 10:20).

"Faithfulness" cannot, however, be separated from the way it is preserved by acting according to משפט (justice) and צדק (righteousness) (אמונה, faithfulness, and צדק, righteousness, are also parallel in 11:5). That is a characteristic of the Hebrew concept of righteousness, which cannot be separated from the faithfulness on which a person can rely. There is no need to furnish any examples which show Israel being praised in the traditions of Zion as the city of justice and righteousness (see Porteous, op. cit.). It could not be otherwise, since it is there that Yahweh, the protector of justice and guardian of righteousness, sits enthroned (צדק ומשפט מכון כסאו, righteousness and justice are the foundation of his throne, Ps. 97:2), but also because it is in that same place that the earthly vizier of God, the Davidic king, rules, about whom the same phrases can be used: צדק ומשפט מכון כסאך (righteousness and justice are the foundation of thy throne) (Ps. 89:15; cf. Isa. 9:6; 11:4). It is from that place that Yahweh sends forth judgment over Israel as well as over all the nations (Pss. 48:11; 97; 98; 99; see also 50:4); there "thrones for judgment were set, the thrones of the house of David" (Ps. 122:5; cf. 72:1ff., and others as well). The last Davidic king to rule from the throne in Jerusalem had the name צדקיהו (Zedekiah) and the branch promised by Jeremiah was to be called יהוה צדקנו (the Lord is our righteousness) (Jer. 23:6). Finally, the close connection between Jerusalem and "righteousness" is based upon the fact that the divine epithet צדק (Zedek) was connected with the city even before the time of the Israelites, as names like Melchizedek and Adoni-zedek would seem to suggest (see Porteous, op. cit., 239; in addition, see TDNT IV, 568). And yet, this concept makes sense just from the very fact that Yahweh was enthroned and ruling over Jerusalem. As happens frequently, משפט (justice) and צדק (righteousness) are expanded: if the first term basically refers to the extrinsic activities connected with administration of justice, the second term deals with the intrinsic relationships which are commanded for those who relate to others within a particular community. "Justice" corresponds to the demands which are imposed upon those who interact within a community. צדק (righteousness) is thus in no way simply a forensic term, even though it is obvious that, first and foremost, righteousness is evident when one is involved in a judgment setting, as the continuation of our message clearly demonstrates.

However, the city of Jerusalem, identified and praised with such high and lofty predicates, has now become a זונה (prostitute). Isaiah uses this imagery only here; he did not actually create it, for Hosea had already made much use of the term (1:2; 2:7; 3:3; 4:12–15; 9:1). With utter clarity, that prophet used the accusation of "whoring" to pass judgment on those who fell away from Yahweh by going to the Canaanite deities with their sexual cults. But Isaiah does not accuse Jerusalem of "whoring" in this sense. The point of comparison for him is rather that of the faithlessness (concerning this, cf. Ps. 73:27) and the fact that the inhabitants of the city had put themselves up for sale, so that זונה (whoring) and נאמנה (faithfulness) correspond to one another in an adverse relationship. Amos sang a similar lament for the dead concerning the fall, that is, the death, of the virgin Israel (5:1f.), and the song in Lamentations 1, which has similarities in several different respects to this present passage, speaks about the fully inhabited city which has now become a "widow." But with Isaiah, the genre is so radically recast that death is no longer the point of comparison. And yet, "the aura of death, which lurks in the background, gives the poem a sinister tone" (Jahnow, op. cit., 255).

The gloss "but now murders" is to be understood as the reactualization of Isaiah's message for what was considered a particularly appropriate situation. One could possibly think about the time of Manasseh (2 Kings 21:16; cf. Hos. 6:9). רצח refers to killing that is "inimical to community," to "the malicious manslaughter," to murder (see J. J. Stamm, "Sprachliche Erwägungen zum Gebot 'Du sollst nicht töten'," *TZ* 1 [1945] 81–90).

[1:22] Two examples follow now, using imagery which describes the inner degeneracy within the city, both examples typical of Isaiah: "Your silver has become burnished lead, your beer has been adulterated." The word סיג (burnished lead, lead oxide), derived from the root סוג, "detach from" (L. Köhler, *TZ* 3 [1947] 232ff.), has given both ancient and modern translators many problems, which has resulted in a variety of suggested meanings. It is a technical term, used to describe the refining of silver. In order to accomplish this refining, in ancient times one would begin with a type of lead sulfide (PbS) which contained some silver; then, to describe just one method, "one would heat it along with iron, which would combine with the sulfur to make iron sulfide; then silver plus lead would be left; that would be placed into suitable ovens and a suitable extraction technique would be used to stir it and oxidize it, forming lead oxide, that is, burnished lead (= PbO), also called foliated silver. . . . The extraction technique was painstaking and difficult, and if it was not done right, . . . then [the silver] would remain mixed in, to a certain extent, with the lead oxide slag, and this 'slag' would obviously reduce the amount of silver which was extracted and would cause great losses" (quoted by Köhler, op. cit., 232f., from a letter written by E. von Lippmann). With this interpretation, not only the exact meaning of סיג has been clarified in detail, but the imagery which Isaiah has in mind is also clearly explained. The original plan was to extract silver, but only a burnished lead is retrieved because of not paying close enough attention; the smelting process had gone awry. The meaning of סבא is explained by J. J. Hess (*MGWJ* 78 [1934] 6–9). It belongs with the Akkadian root *sabū* (make beer) or *sîbu* (beer), which designates a particular drink, and with the Arabic *sūbjeh,* which means "beer." These two images are very apt for describing what one sees when orderly life has fallen apart and justice has disintegrated. The first image shows how these good things are wrecked by not paying close attention; the second points out that they were wrecked with malice aforethought.

[1:23] While v. 22 dealt with the city and with its population, v. 23 goes on to highlight the responsibilities of the שרים (rulers). The שרים are the "lifelong and chief professional officials installed by, and thus answerable to, the monarchy" (so R. Knierim, "Exodus 18 und die Neuordnung der mosaischen Gerichtsbarkeit," *ZAW* 73 [1961] 146–171, p. 159). The שר (ruler) had responsibilities to fulfill as judge, but he could also be further encumbered with military and administrative duties (see 3:3). It is difficult to determine the extent to which these various functions were under the control of one individual, or to what extent that would even have been possible. The description of the proceedings against Jeremiah (chap. 26) gives one a close-up view of the judicial functions of the "princes" in Jerusalem (see also Isa. 32:1). These שרים (rulers) are סוררים (rebels), apparently a commonly used term (see Hos. 9:15; on סרר, rebel, cf. above, v. 5). There are times when officials could be "stubborn" toward their immediate lord, the king, but here they are described in this way over against the one who indirectly lays upon them their obligations, God. Even more shocking is the next rebuke: חברי גנבים (partners with thieves) (on חבר, companion, see Prov. 28:24). According to Ps. 50:18, contact with thieves is one of the denunciations which would have been raised in an accusation at the covenant festival. What is most unique about the present passage is that highly respected officials are put into this category of evildoers when Isaiah assesses the situation. They are bribed with money, and they permit thieves to go free. Isaiah also censures the abominable practice of bribery in 5:23 and stands in a united front with Micah on this point (3:11). The law expressly forbids the taking of a שחד (bribe) (Exod. 23:8; Deut. 16:19; see also 10:17). A curse is uttered against one who allows himself to be bribed to kill someone who is innocent (Deut. 27:25). שׁחֵד (from the root שׁחד, "give a gift") originally meant simply "gift"; the *hapax legomenon* שׁלמנים (from שׁלֵם, "recompense") is the repayment for the "service" of a judge. The two verbs אהב (love) and רדף (chase after) disclose the greed with which the pieces of money are snatched up. Those who are legally without defenses, including the orphans and widows mentioned as examples in v. 17, are thereby at the mercy of every imaginable reckless action (concerning the societal relationships which are behind the refusal to provide due process, cf. A. Alt, "Der Anteil des Königtums an der sozialen Entwicklung in den Reichen Israel und Juda," *Kleine Schriften III* [1959] 348–372; concerning the disorder within the system of justice, see L. Köhler, *Die hebräische Rechtsgemeinde,* Jahresbericht der Univ. Zürich, 1930/31, 15ff. = *Der hebräische Mensch* [1953] Supplement, 143ff.).

[1:24a] As happens so often, reproach and threat are linked by לכן (therefore). The announcement of judgment is cast in the form of an "utterance" of the Lord, Yahweh of Hosts. It is at this point that the actual message begins. What was proclaimed in the format of prophetic speech up to this point would be very obvious to anyone who knows the will of God; there is no question that Israel knows exactly what it has been commanded. And yet, the "reproach" is not unnecessary baggage, since it calls attention to the fact that Yahweh's actions in bringing about this judgment are not capricious, but are necessary when considered in light of the commands of the covenant. For Israel, this action will be beneficial in the end, since it will bring to an end the "wretchedness" resulting from its present faithlessness. The message of Yahweh is not introduced here with the frequently used messenger formula "thus says Yahweh" or something similar, but with נאם יהוה (verdict of Yahweh, utterance of Yahweh). Isaiah does not use this expression very often, but one must remember that he rarely uses formulas which introduce or bring to a conclusion a message of Yahweh (see, beyond this, 3:15, at the conclusion of an accusation; 17:3, 6, and 19:4, at the conclusion of an announcement of judgment; 30:1, inserted at the beginning of a woe-oracle; finally,

31:9, at the end of a word of promise for Israel, which functions at the same time as an announcement of judgment for Assyria). Thus, the formula is not used with any consistency, either with respect to the genre and content or in light of the way it is placed within the message from Yahweh. The observation of F. Baumgärtel ("Die Formel *ne'um jahwe*," *ZAW* 73 [1961] 277–290) still holds true, also for the Isaianic passages: "Wherever a message from God contains נ ''י [utterance of Yahweh], . . . its content is never a concrete command." נ ''י "has nothing to do with commands and directives" (p. 285). The only other place where יהוה נאם is at the very beginning of a message from God is in Ps. 110:1 (but see also Num. 24:3, 4, 15, 16, and 2 Sam. 23:1). Because of this usage, it is possible that this introduction was typical of oracles which were addressed to the king, so that Isaiah would have adapted it from that original setting. The etymology of the word is not clear, but it has often been compared with and related to the Arabic *na'ama* (whisper), so that one would be led to think it referred to a secretive communication from the deity. According to Baumgärtel (op. cit., 287ff.), the formula has its original roots in *Nabitum* (prophecy), whereas the formula יהוה אמר כה צבאות (thus says Yahweh of Hosts) has its roots in the cultic rituals. In any case, יהוה נאם, "so long as it has not yet lost its distinctive meaning, is a *signum* [sign, marker] for prophetic speech stimulated directly by God" (Baumgärtel, op. cit., 283).

It is also worth noting that, in this formula, נאם is not simply followed, as is typical in most cases, by יהוה (Yahweh) in the genitive relationship, but by the extensive list of titles ישראל אביר צבאות יהוה האדון (The Lord, Yahweh of Hosts, the Strong One of Israel). Except for the final element ישראל אביר, this formula is also found in 19:4. Isaiah uses the divine epithet אדין (Lord) relatively often in comparison to its use in the rest of the OT writings (see *TDNT* III, 1058ff.). The word is possibly connected to the Ugaritic word *'ad,* "father" (on this, see A. Herdner, in *GLECS* VI, 64; for other possible derivations, see F. Zimmermann, *VT* 12 [1962] 194f.). In contrast to "occupant," this refers more to the lord as the one who rules as master over everything which he had acquired (see Ps. 105:21), so that an important point is made if one renders this as בעל "overlord," as it is often translated. The word is commonly used as a divine epithet in the region of Phoenicia (see W. W. Graf Baudissin, *Kyrios als Gottesname im Judentum und seine Stellung in der Religionsgeschichte* II and III [1929]); thus, we find *Adon-Esmun, Adon-Palaṭ, Adon-Baal;* in cuneiform texts, *Adūni-iḫa, Adūni-ṭūri,* among others (see W. W. Graf Baudissin, *Adonis und Esmun* [1911] 66ff.). There is no doubt that Isaiah's frequent use of this epithet can be connected with the fact that this was an ancient predicate referring to God, being used even back in the Jebusite era, as the names Adonibezek (Judg. 1:5–7) and Adonizedek (Josh. 10:1, 3) demonstrate (for the Israelite era, see Adoniram in 1 Kings 4:6, and often elsewhere, and Adonijah or Adoniyahu in 2 Sam. 3:4; 1 Kings 1:8, and often elsewhere). It is precisely because of this derivation of the name that it was used in a more limited sense in ancient times in Israel; there was a desire to avoid using the divine epithets with Canaanite roots, as is very obviously the case as regards the synonym בעל ("Baal=Lord"). In and of itself, this designation is most apt as a description for Yahweh's essence; Isaiah had enough freedom to use this title, as he also made use of the related title מלך (king) (see 6:1ff.), though there must have been a similar hesitation about using it as well, as is demonstrated by its infrequent use in the other OT writings.

As in 10:16, 33, the epithet האדון (the Lord) is combined with the divine name יהוה צבאות (Yahweh Sebaoth) (אדני [Lord] is found with יהוה צבאות [Yahweh Sebaoth] in 3:15; 10:23, 24; 22:5, 12, 14, 15; 28:22). The relatively high frequency with which these two names are found together must be connected with their common background in cultic tradition, which once again must have had a special place and roots in Jerusalem (cf. its appearance in the doxology of Amos 9:5). The transfer of the designation of God as Yahweh Sebaoth, which had its roots in Shiloh and was closely connected with the ark, to become a cultic name for the God of Jerusalem formed a close bond, linking the Jerusalem traditions with the genuine articles of the faith of ancient Israel. The God of Jerusalem is the same God as the one who once was worshiped in Shiloh at the former center of the amphictyony.

But Isaiah wants this introductory formula to bring even more aspects of Yahweh to the attention of his audience and adds to this: אביר ישראל (the Strong One of Israel). The name "the Strong One of Israel" is only found in this one place in the OT. But there is no doubt that it is to be taken as a variant of אביר יעקב (Mighty One of Jacob) (see Gen. 49:24; Isa. 49:26; 60:16; Ps. 132:2, 5), and this latter phrase, in turn, is itself obviously the older form of the term אלהי יעקב (God of Jacob), which is commonly used elsewhere (Exod. 3:6, 15, 16; 4:5; 2 Sam. 23:1; Isa. 2:3; Mic. 4:2; Pss. 20:2; 24:6 [Gk]; 46:8, 12; 75:10; 76:7; 81:2, 5; 84:9; 94:7; we have already noticed [in 1:4] that קדוש ישראל [Holy One of Israel] seems to be still another variation of this name of God). In addition, these forms of the names are not found in all the layers of the OT. That this formula should have found its way into the specific circles responsible for the Jerusalem traditions is very surprising; neither in the theology about Zion nor in Isaiah is there anything which shows contact with the traditions which are concerned with portraying Jacob. Besides this, the "God of Abraham" and the "Fear of Isaac," honored in various regions of southern Judah, are passed over in the Jerusalem traditions, as well as by Isaiah, with a complete and absolute silence. There is no path which could be tracked with absolute certainty to show just how this designation for God would have come to the city ruled by the Davidic kings and how it would have been integrated into the traditions about Zion. Based on the evidence of the Psalms about the ark (Psalms 132 and 24), this designation also seems to have been attached to the ark traditions. (Concerning the gods of the fathers, cf. A. Alt, *Der Gott der Väter,* BWANT III/12 [1929] = *KlSchr* I [1953] 1–78, and V. Maag, *Der Hirte Israels, STU* 28 [1958] 2–28; in addition, see B. Gemser, *Vragen rondom de Patriarchenreligie* [1958]; J. Hoftijzer, *Die Verheissungen an die drei Erzväter* [1956] [on this, see M. Noth, *VT* 7 (1957) 430ff.]; L. Rost, "Die Gottesverehrung der Patriarchen im Lichte der Pentateuchquellen," VTSup 7 [1960] 346–359; F. M. Cross, "Yahwe and the God of the Patriarchs," *HTR* 55 [1962] 225ff.)

A unique assemblage of a variety of names for God is brought together here. This combination hints at a lively history for the religion of Israel and shows to what an extent Jerusalem brought together various types of traditions which were distinct up to that point and by which, up to that point, Israel had given witness to its faith. Yet, it is of utmost importance to realize that, within those traditions specifically tied to the Jerusalem cult, it is not the God of Jerusalem who finally begins to speak here (though Yahweh is so designated in 2 Chron. 32:19; see also Ezra 7:19, and the inscription from a burial cave found east of Lachish, *IEJ* 13 [1963] 84), but rather, he is the "Holy One of Israel." Israel's faith does not negate the magnificent expectations which are connected with Jerusalem as the "city of God" and Zion as the "mount of God." But no one can question the fact that the realization of all of these hopes is tied to placing oneself under the will of Yahweh, the God of Israel.

[1:24b] The first of the two verbs which announce Yahweh's lawsuit in v. 24b, the *niph'al* of נחם (console oneself), is used only here with the meaning "refresh oneself." The basic meaning of the Hebrew word, according to KBL, is "provide for oneself a (spiritual) refreshment" (cf. the Arabic *naḥama,* "breathe heavily"). Just as with the *niph'al* of נקם (avenge oneself) which follows, a very graphic anthropomorphism is used by the prophet. It is important for Isaiah to portray, in a stunning way, the deep inner involvement of Yahweh, his holy aggravation over against the breakdown of the chosen city, an emotional state which can be understood only when one considers the deep divine love of God for his people. "There is sorrow in God's anger. God's affection for Israel rings even in the denunciations . . ." (A. J. Heschel, *The Prophets* [1962] 82). Both verbs belong to the vocabulary used to characterize the Day of Yahweh. In the Song of Moses, in an announcement of the Day of Yahweh, next to נָקָם (avenge oneself), one finds the *hithpa'el* form התנחם (have compassion) (Deut. 32:35f.), which seems to be used just like the *niph'al.* But, in that text, the day of wrath poses a threat to Israel's enemies, and the *hithpa'el* has the meaning "have compassion" (toward Israel). The root נקם (avenge) also appears frequently in other passages which refer to the Day of Yahweh (Deut. 32:41, 43; Isa. 34:8; 35:4; Nah. 1:2, and often elsewhere). That means that Isaiah announces, in a matter-of-fact way, that a Day of Yahweh is coming, which is explicitly described in 2:12; however, the enemies of Yahweh, against whom he will bring his wrath, are the people of Jerusalem! Once again, that is Yahweh's "strange work, his alien work" (28:21; cf., concerning this, Amos 5:18–20; concerning the Day of Yahweh, see L. Černý, *The Day of Yahweh and Some Relevant Problems* [1948]; S. Mowinckel, "Jahves Dag," *NTT* 59 [1958] 1–56, 209–229; and, above all, G. von Rad, "The Origin of the Concept of the Day of Yahweh," *JSS* 4 [1959] 97–108). The specific details of the intervention of Yahweh are not mentioned. Yahweh is no fortune-teller who is able to describe the future down to the smallest details.

[1:25] The addition at the beginning of v. 25, "I want to turn my hand against you," nails down just exactly who is meant in v. 24 by the "oppressors" and the "enemies" of Yahweh. But that is followed up by a reference once again to the imagery of silver which has become nothing but burnished lead. If the process of smelting, which is to result in the extraction of pure silver, goes awry (see above, v. 22; cf. Jer. 6:29f.), then another attempt must be made to find a new extraction technique to separate out the silver. בֹּר, "alkaline salts," is made of potassium carbonate and sodium (potash and soda). "These salts serve as a flux, with many common applications even today" (E. von Lippmann, according to L. Köhler, *TZ* 3 [1947] 233). Isaiah clearly has in mind a judgment which is supposed to refine. He does not announce a complete obliteration of Israel, but says very plainly that Yahweh wants to remove the "slag." Thus, there is still hope for the future. The idea of a remnant, which many refuse to attribute to Isaiah himself (see the suggestions of G. Fohrer, *TLZ* 87 [1962] 748, but also the great hesitation concerning whether "remnant" was important for Isaiah, as expressed by von Rad, *OTTheol* II, 165), fits in very well with Isaiah's announcement of judgment.

[1:26] The new community, formed into a holy remnant as a result of the process of separation—and this is the decisive point in this context—will give plenty of room for righteousness and faithfulness in its midst. But that means that judges who are worthy of their office will be in charge of justice in the city of God. The text reads כבראשׁנה (at the earliest time), which corresponds to the כבתחלה (as at the beginning) in the second colon. Jeremiah (2:2) makes reference to an ideal epoch in the past, which established the norm by which the present is assessed, the "honeymoon" period of wilderness wandering. A similar concept is used here by Isaiah; however, his high point in the past, by means of which the present must be measured, is the history of Jerusalem. Without a doubt, this looked back to the time when David (and Solomon?) were kings. For Isaiah, Jerusalem is "the city where David encamped" (29:1). There must have been traditions already at the time of Isaiah which contained references to the onset of the reign of the first kings, references which would have furnished an idealized portrayal of that early era and which could have provided the conceptual framework for shaping the present and future (cf. Ps. 122:5). These traditions could have had their roots in what really happened in history. From the very beginning, one would presume that David, after he had conquered the city and had assumed the rights and duties of the Jebusite king, would have installed judges, since he was the supreme individual in matters of justice and also the one who established legal guidelines. For this reason, since this former Canaanite city would have had the political status of being the "royal domain" of the Davidic kings, there would have been unique regulations which would not apply to the ancient Israelite cities, where justice would have been in the hands of the elders of the clans who carried out justice "in the gate." However, according to v. 23, the judges in Jerusalem were the שׂרים (rulers, princes), royal officials, and such officials were also apparently installed, as time went on, in some other cities as well (cf. Deut. 16:18–20 and 19:16–18; 2 Chron. 19:4–11; see R. de Vaux, *Ancient Israel* I, 152ff., and Knierim, op. cit., 151). Surprisingly, the second colon mentions, parallel to the "judges," "the counselors." These also appear in the list in 3:3, among the dignitaries of the city. Without a doubt, the advisers of the king are meant here. Ahithophel is identified in 2 Sam. 15:12 as David's "counselor" (cf., in addition, 2 Sam. 15:31; 16:23; 1 Chron. 27:32–33; 2 Chron. 25:16; Ezra 4:5; 7:28; 8:25). Apparently in this passage it also refers to a royal position, indeed, one which Isaiah considers to be of utmost importance for order and the well-being of the state. The ideal time in the past is held up so a comparison can be made אחרי־כן (at that time, afterwards) with the time of salvation in the future. After the crisis, it will all come together again. אחרי־כן (at that time) in our text corresponds to באחרית הימים (in future days) in 2:2; עת אחרון (the future, the latter time) in 8:23 (in contrast to עת ראשון [an earlier time]); and יום אחרון (time to come) in 30:8. Neither the end of the entire era of history nor the breaking in of the transcendent into the immanent historical world is meant in these examples. Rather, a future time is in mind which will see a decisive turn of events unfold, and a new beginning will be set in motion. Thus far— but only within these parameters—can one speak about Isaiah's eschatology (concerning "eschatology" in Isaiah, cf. T. C. Vriezen, "Prophecy and Eschatology," VTSup 1 [1953] 199–229). According to our present passage, as Jerusalem moves into the coming age of salvation, it will not be any more than what it already had been in the ideal age in the past, and then it would once again be true to its original nature as the city of God. "The time of salvation" and "the very distant past" are corresponding eras. But this time of salvation would not come, of course, as something which would unfold by a natural sequence of events, but, as v. 25aα correctly interprets it, would happen only when Yahweh laid his hand once again upon Jerusalem.

[1:27] The interpretive comment which follows in vv. 27f. employs the theological term for "redemption," פדה. In secular usage, פדה is a neutral term in common legal parlance, with the meaning "release" (e.g., a member of one's own clan who had been reduced to slavery; see J. J. Stamm, *Erlösen und Vergeben im Alten Testament,* n.d. [1940] 7ff.). In the terminology of the cult, the verb is a technical term for the redemption of a being which, by rights, belongs under the control of Yahweh (Exod. 13:11–16, and also elsewhere). The term is commonly used in the Psalms when the deliverance of the individual from some distress is mentioned (69:19; 26:11; 31:6; 71:23, and also elsewhere). In Jer. 15:21, Yahweh promises the prophet deliverance out of the distress caused by his enemies. But, naturally, deliverance is also sought in the communal psalms of lament (see Ps. 44:27). As in Hosea (7:13; 13:14), so also here, the author of the present passage would have adapted this mental image from the cultic lyric poetry. There is no mention of that from which Zion was to be redeemed or bought back. But the OT often chooses to speak about the deliverance (of the individual) from death or from the underworld, which means deliverance from a life-threatening situation (Ps. 49:8, 16; Job 5:20; 33:28; Sir. 51:1f.; but see also Hos. 13:14). Ps. 25:22 pleads for deliverance from all troubles. Finally, in Ps. 130:8, the one who prays demonstrates a confidence that Yahweh can deliver Israel from all its iniquities. This present passage can hardly be interpreted by referring to these two late psalms. As in Hosea, one is made to think of a liberation from enemies who are threatening, essentially, a threat to one's physical existence. Oppression by foreigners can certainly also be described by using imagery of being oppressed by death and Sheol. This particular meaning is also demanded by the antithesis in v. 28, which threatens annihilation (כלה, be brought down). If this could be clearly demonstrated as coming from the exilic-postexilic era, then one could be more sure that deliverance from foreign powers was meant (see Isa. 35:10;

51:11), but v. 28 does not provide evidence which favors this interpretation.

The deliverance takes place במשפט (by justice) and בצדקה (by righteousness). The בְּ after פדה (ransom) is a בְּ *pretii (beth* of price, value); see Exod. 13:13, 15; 34:20; Lev. 27:27. One must question whether Zion's own righteousness or God's righteousness is meant here. This question is related to another one, how one is to understand שביה. If it means "returnees" (see above, textual notes), then it could refer only to the justice and righteousness of the new people of Zion. That does not mean that they would have freed themselves, as if done by means of their own righteousness; the logical subject could only be Yahweh. But the one who has added this here wants to stress the fact that justice could achieve and maintain its proper role only after deliverance had completely been realized. However, it must be noted that, according to the present context surrounding vv. 27 and 28, Yahweh himself—by means of purifying his people when he prosecutes them and gives them "judges" and "counselors" as "at the earliest time"—creates the circumstances which will make "this better righteousness" a reality.

[1:28] The returnees are contrasted with the פשעים (rebellious) and the חטאים (sinners); for such there is no longer any hope. "Sinners" describes all of them, in actuality, even the "returnees." Here it refers to the ones who persist in their resistance (concerning פשע, rebel, see 1:2; concerning חטא, sin, see 1:4). That they are persistent in sinning is made clear by the use of the intensive form חַטָּאִים = *pi'el* (in contrast to חֹטֵא = *qal* in 1:4) (see Ges-K §84be). Once again, the sin is that Yahweh has been forsaken (concerning עזב, forsake, see 1:4; concerning נשבר, be broken up, see 8:15; 14:29; and 28:13; concerning כלה, cease, see 29:20; 31:3; 32:10).

Purpose and Thrust

The section vv. 21–26 (and it is no different in the addition in vv. 27f.) represents an interchange with the Zion tradition, that is, with one of the traditions that recounted the election of Israel (see E. Rohland, "Die Bedeutung der Erwählungstraditionen Israels für die Eschatologie der alttestamentlichen Propheten," diss. theol., Heidelberg, n.d. [1956] 114ff.). Isaiah does not give any indication that he is aware that the people were chosen at the time of the exodus or that the patriarchs had been chosen. His message is apparently to be interpreted primarily on the basis of the presuppositions of the theology about Jerusalem, most easily accessible to us in the Songs of Zion. Using concepts which are connected with Jerusalem, the city of God, he is determined to single out the concept of righteousness, pointing out how the inviolability of the city, a related motif, cannot be expected to remain in force without faithfulness. There is absolutely no doubt that he modifies the concept of belief in God from the way it was understood in ancient Israel and by the amphictyony, doing so by using concepts which were unique to Jerusalem. The *Adon* (Lord) of Jerusalem is Yahweh Sebaoth, the Strong One of Jacob. But another point is even more significant: Isaiah also is not working with a concept that Jerusalem was chosen unconditionally and/or had a beginning explained by a myth. Therefore, there was also no absolute security for Jerusalem which could be guaranteed by means of cultic acts. He works only with an election which continues because of a continual faithfulness on the part of those who had been chosen. *Electio* (election) was integrally related to the opposite alternative, *reprobatio* (rejection). In light of Jerusalem's faithlessness, was not the election of Jerusalem declared no longer in force? Would judgment have the final word? In light of the faithfulness of God, such a conclusion cannot even be considered. It is true that the present community in Zion had fallen under a condemning judgment, but a remnant would make it through and be saved (return, as v. 27 correctly interprets what precedes), and they would get leaders whose most pressing concern would be the preservation of justice. The Holy One of Israel accomplishes this by means of establishing his own righteousness.

Decadent Cult

Literature

[**Literature update through 1979:** M. Tsevat, "Isaiah I 31," *VT* 19 (1969) 261–263. S. E. Loewenstamm, "Isaiah I 31," *VT* 22 (1972) 246–248.]

Text

1:29 Truly, 'you'[a] will bring shame upon 'yourselves' because of
     the trees,[b]
         your desires for them remain,
     and will turn red in humiliation on account of the gardens,
         which you have chosen for yourselves.
  30 Yes, you will become like a terebinth,
         which has leaves[a] which are shriveling,
     and as a garden, which
         has no water.[b]
  31 At that time the strong one[a] will become a broken fiber,
         and what he has made[b] will become tiny bits,
     and both will burn at the same time,
         and there is no one who can put it out.

29a The use of the third person in יֵבֹשׁוּ (they will be ashamed) is impossible next to the use of the second person in vv. 29bf. Gk and Syr read the third person throughout, which may have been influenced by v. 28. It should be read as תֵּבֹשׁוּ (you will bring shame upon yourselves), based on some MSS and the Targ.

29b Qᵃ reads אלים here instead of אֵילִים (terebinth) (see also Isa. 57:5). Is this only an orthographic variation, or is the plural of אֵל, "God," intended here? Gk reads ἐπὶ τοῖς εἰδώλοις (concerning the idols) and seems to presume the reading אֵילִים (terebinth), as is pointed out by P. Wernberg-Møller ("Studies in the Defective Spellings in the Isaiah-Scroll of St. Mark's Monastery," *JSS* 3 [1958] 244–264; see 254); H. M. Orlinsky ("The Textual Criticism of the Old Testament," FS W. F. Albright [1961] 122) in fact considers εἴδωλον to be a translation of אֵילָה, terebinths = idol. According to KBL, אֵילִים is the plural of (a never attested) singular אַיִל, "large, strong tree" and, in that sense, it is identical to אֵלָה (root אול, "be in front, be strong"). If this is the case, the spelling is correct in the MT. Whether אֵל, "God," is also connected to the same root as this אֵיל continues to be a controversial issue (concerning a discussion of this, see W. F. Albright, VTSup 4 [1957] 255: אלה actually means "female deity" and/or Eloth; F. Zimmermann, "'El and Adonai," *VT* 12 [1962] 190–195: אל is derived from אלל, אלה, "a tree god").

30a Many MSS read עליה (leaf), which is also possible in a root with a weak third root letter and is the most likely reading; cf. Beer-Meyer I §53.

30b Qᵃ reads this the other way around: אין מים (there is no water), which is an effort to make a smoother reading. Concerning the order of the words in the MT, see Ges-K §152o.

31a Instead of החסן (the strong one), the Qᵃ reads החסנכם (the strong one of yours), Gk reads ἡ ἰσχὺς αὐτῶν (their strength) and Vulg *fortitudo vestra* (your strength). All of these are to be judged as readings which try to smooth out the text, when compared with the MT.

31b Qᵃ: פעלכם (your deeds). Gk reads the third person also here: αἱ ἐργασίαι αὐτῶν (their deeds); Vulg *opus vestrum* (your deed). There is no reason to change the MT, and the vocalization need not be emended to read פָּעֳלוֹ (his deed); cf. Joüon, Gr §96Aj.

Form

The three verses before us present an announcement of judgment. They begin with כִּי, "therefore"; thus, they appear to be connected with the verses which immediately precede and thus there are some commentators who choose to take these verses as a unit along with vv. 27f. But v. 29 starts a completely new theme. For that reason, כי (therefore) might simply be a redactional bracket. Of course, it has often been thought that a corresponding word of reproach originally preceded the announcement of judgment. It seems very likely that this was the case, since it is difficult to make good sense of the passage as it now stands and it leaves the impression that it is in fragmentary form. But the redactor who put these two sections together wanted vv. 29ff. to clarify and further expand v. 28.

Meter: Verses 29 and 30a: 3 two-stress bicola; v. 30b also ought to be read as a two-stress bicolon. Verse 31 closes the section very effectively with 2 five-stress cola.

Setting

Marti, who takes vv. 29–31 together with vv. 27f. as a single unit, thinks that this cannot possibly be genuine, since Isaiah never speaks anywhere else of אילים (terebinths) and גנות (gardens) as cultic objects, whereas, on the other hand, "terebinths" and "gardens" were particularly favorite places which were frequented by the rebellious Jews who are the subject of the final chapters of the book of Isaiah (57:5; 65:3; 66:17). But there had always been sacred trees and gardens in Palestine, just as they still exist today; in a slightly altered form they are still used by Islam in modern times. Marti's second argument possibly carries more weight when he notes that בחר (choose) is never used by Isaiah himself for describing devotion to heathen cults, but that it is used, once again, in the third part of the book of Isaiah (65:12; 66:3f.), whereas the verb is actually found in 7:15f., with a different meaning. That could be just by chance; see the discussion about בחר (choose) below. And yet, a definite uncertainty still remains, which cannot be eliminated by the effusive statement of Procksch: "the fragment shows itself plain as day to be genuine." In spite of everything to the contrary, we think that Marti's reasons for denying the genuineness of the passage do not carry sufficient weight.

When did Isaiah speak this message, and who are the "you" (pl.) being addressed? It has often been suggested that this refers to the inhabitants of the Northern Kingdom before 722. Factually, that could be possible; see how Hosea engages in polemics against the nature cults (4:13, where the אֵלוֹן, oak, and the אלה, terebinth, are mentioned together). One cannot achieve a complete certainty about this, however, since cults of this type were also tolerated in the Southern Kingdom, an assertion that is supported by evidence that Josiah took measures against these when he sought to reform the cult. Since there are other sections in which Isaiah speaks about idolatry and magic, 2:6, 8; 8:19(?), which come from Isaiah's early period, this particular fragment might also come from this same time.

Commentary

One must arrive at some clearer picture of the entire section before one can move on to the detailed exegesis. Fohrer (commentary, ad loc.) has expressed the view that the verbs (בחר, choose, and חמד, desire) are descriptive of the types of intrigues which are denounced in 5:8 and Mic. 2:2; חמד would not only describe the craving desires but also the actions which would lead the person who was coveting something to obtain what was wanted. If this were true, this would be an accusation against an economic power which sought a way to bring groves of trees and gardens under its control. חמד is actually used with this meaning which Fohrer postulates for it here (see J. Herrmann, "Das zehnte Gebot," FS E. Sellin [1927] 69–82), but the special sense which Herrmann finds for this word when it is used in the Decalog need not be imposed upon our text. The main passage which can help determine the meaning of בחר is found in 65:12 and 66:3f., showing very clearly that this word is used in a cultic sense, that is, in connection with the cult that practiced rites under "green trees" in "sacred groves." This usage is clear enough to cause one also to reject Hertzberg's suggestion that this refers to cultivation of particularly beautiful "gardens" and "trees," about which a person could be justifiably proud and in which a person could have confidence. It is true that Isaiah does speak out against the hubris which leads a person to find one's security in one's own accomplishments instead of surrendering one's self to God in faith. But he would have certainly had nothing against a person simply planting trees and setting out gardens.

[1:29] אילים refers to large trees, oaks, or terebinths (concerning oaks in present-day Palestine, see Dalman *AuS* I 1, 65ff., and illuss. 3–9). It is true that the word is to be derived from the root אול II, as is done by KBL, meaning "be in front, be strong" (see above, textual note). But there was a certain meaning attached to it by the Israelites because of the similarity between the sounds of אֵלָה, "female deity," and those of אֵיל/אֵלָה, "tree." אילים are therefore "the trees of the deity," which are on holy ground or, as the case may be, refer to a place (אילים, Elim, and אילת, Eloth, are also place names) which can bestow holiness. Humans consummated sensuous fertility rites under these trees, symbolic of a very powerful vitality which was thought to be inside them, even considered to be sources of the power of life (Isa. 57:5; see also Hos. 4:13; Jer. 2:20, 23–27; 3:6). The sacred trees were located on a piece of property that was separated from the surrounding land, which was used for common activities; that separation was effected by means of a hedge (which is what גַּנָּה actually means). According to 65:3, sacrifices were offered in such gardens. One would consecrate and purify oneself in preparation for this, that is, in order to take part in the cultic activities there (66:17). In this passage, the verb חמד means "regard as desirable, consider to be worthwhile" (cf. Gen. 2:9; 3:6; and Ps. 68:17, where חמד [desire] is used in the same sense as בחר [choose] is used elsewhere). This brings into sharp focus the ability of the heathen cults to lead astray. Just as it is used, on the one hand, as a technical term for being chosen by God, בחר can also be used to describe the disposition of a person to turn toward a deity or to a particular cult (Josh. 24:15; Isa. 65:12 and 66:3f.; cf. also Judg. 10:14; Ps. 119:30, 173; Prov. 1:29).

One would expect that taking part in such cultic activities would result in security and life getting better. If nothing more, one would at least expect that fertility would increase. But, according to Isaiah, participating in this would lead to one's "shameful ruin." Here the prophet makes use of an expression which is common in the cultic songs of the Psalter, where one makes the request: "I trust in you, let me not be put to shame" (25:2; see also v. 20; 22:6; 69:7), or where one gives expression to the confidence that one will not be shamefully ruined, because one trusts confidently in Yahweh (25:3; cf. 31:18, among other passages), or even when one makes the request that one's enemies might be put to shame (6:11, and often elsewhere). One is put to shame when one is bitterly deceived by that in which one has trusted. Isaiah uses the verb in other situations, when he warns about placing trust in help from foreign powers (20:5; 30:5). But Hosea had already spoken about Israel coming to shame because it had been devoted to foreign cults (4:19; cf. 10:6, where the reading should be וִיבוֹשׁ יִשְׂרָאֵל מֵעֲצָבּוֹ, "and Israel will be put to shame because of its idol images"; cf. also 13:15). The word does not only include the objective situation when expectations fail to materialize as anticipated, but also, at the same time, the subjective sense of shame and humiliation; one would have to be ashamed of oneself, stand before the eyes of the world in disgrace and dishonor and would not have to work hard to earn scorn and mockery, which was so detestable to the ancient Israelite.

[1:30] The prophet uses two images in vv. 30f. to illustrate points already made in v. 29. "The final destiny for these decorated cultic trees, along with the immediate surroundings (גנה [garden]), furnish the model for describing the final destiny of those who serve the idols" (Procksch). The oak is symbolic of might (the only other time in the OT where חסן appears is Amos 2:9, where it is used to compare the Amorites to אלונים, oaks [אילם, terebinths]). But instead of getting more life power, those who take part in the cultic activities will have to discover that they are more like the oak which loses its leaves. This should not be taken as a reference to trees which lose their leaves during the course of the seasons (the Palestinian oak, *quercus aegilops* or *ilex* [cf. Dalman, *AuS* I 1, 66; see also Ps. 1:3], is an evergreen, though the terebinth, of course, does lose its leaves), but rather, "the garden" is brought to mind, completely dried out during the time of a drought (Pss. 52:10; 90:5ff.; 92:13f.; Isa. 40:6; and elsewhere). It is in this way that Israel shrivels up when it abandons "the fountain of life" (Ps. 36:10; cf. Jer. 2:13; Isa. 8:6).

[1:31] The participants in this nature rite of Canaan fancy themselves to be filled with powers, like an oak—and then become, when they finally have to show what they are made of, "a loose fiber" (נערת is from נער, "shake off violently"; the "fuzz from the flax" which is shaken off by swingling and combing the flax is a clump of very short and thin fibers which are worthless when weaving a sturdy piece of cloth; yet, this clump was very combustible and could therefore be used to get a good fire going). Their "work" would become nothing more than sparks flaming momentarily. If the text has been correctly transmitted and if v. 31 is actually originally a continuation of v. 30, neither of which can be said with absolute certainty, then פעלו (what he has made, done) must mean the activities taking place in the gardens under the sacred trees. Then we have a very understandable and most graphic scene. The one who has a fertile imagination must finally discover the decadence of the scene; even though the participants are promised security and help from cultic activity among the trees, their worship of idols will turn into sparks which blaze for an instant and destroy them, and all their efforts, at the same time. ואין מכבה (and there is no one who can put it out) is a common formula (Amos 5:6; Jer. 4:4; 21:12). The two passages in Jeremiah show that this is used when an attempt is made to describe the way God's wrath operates.

Purpose and Thrust

The present passage is the only passage in which Isaiah makes mention of the "tree-cult" of Canaan. But the prophet does deal with "serving idols" in other passages, and thus, he stands within the mainstream of the prophetic movement, which has such an intense interest in preserving the teaching about the absolutely unique position held by Yahweh. And thus, this section does not simply deal with a fanatical battle waged by one whose allegiance was to Yahweh alone, battling other forms of religious life; instead, it deals with the unmasking which would show the illusory character of the foreign cult, whose participants would have paid lip-service to Yahweh as well. Human beings seek ways to guarantee stability in life and to overcome the challenges of existence, but those who serve the idols bring themselves to ruin in the process. Yahweh does not need to interact with them by initiating a special judicial process. He can simply leave the people to the consequences of their own "efforts" at serving idols. Therefore, it is not at all necessary, as might be expected, to mention the consuming fire of the wrath of Yahweh. Falling away from the God who provides for all the things of life brings its own judgment along with it.

Purpose and Thrust (1:1–31)

When one considers the six originally separate entities which, apart from the superscription in 1:1, make up the first chapter of the book of Isaiah, only the second one can be dated with relative certainty; it is one of the last words of Isaiah which has been preserved for us, which he must have spoken not long after 701. The other sections seem more likely to have originated in Isaiah's early period. There can hardly be any doubt that chronology was not considered when these individual sections were brought together. And yet, the present arrangement is not simply the result of chance. The first four sections are connected to one another by means of certain catchwords. One cannot fail to see that there is a thematic connection. Verses 2–3 give evidence for the apostasy; vv. 4–9 speak about the judgment which has come upon Jerusalem because of its apostasy, and also about Yahweh's grace—they show that the city has not completely been destroyed even though great problems have resulted from the afflictions which were imposed. If the admonition to return is implicit in this section, it is explicit in the following section, showing plainly that an increase in cultic piety involving changes in external activities cannot serve as a replacement for a real turning to Yahweh as the God of righteousness. Finally, vv. 18–20 confront the people of God with the decision between life and death. These four sections are connected with one another insofar as they coherently present steps of developing thought. Verses 19f. apparently sound strong enough to suggest that the climax has been reached. In addition, these four individual sections also belong together in the way they present the reenactment of individual elements of the covenant tradition. Even when Rignell was writing, he felt that he had to point out the great similarities between the message of Isaiah 1 and that of Deuteronomy (op. cit. [in literature for 1:1] 157), especially based on evidence from Deuteronomy 28 and 32. The composition presumes that the readers were familiar with the traditions of the covenant. For such people, the inner connections among the individual sections would have been immediately apparent. Verses 19f. serve a function similar to that of the promises of blessing and threats of curses which conclude the OT legal corpus. The entire composition has the character of an extensive *rīb,* a judicial proceeding of Yahweh with his covenant partner; therefore, it is very logical that it is introduced with the call to the witnesses in v. 2. One might almost suspect that there was a very conscious effort to use selected words from Isaiah at a covenant festival, particularly since beyond this there is no other larger section in the book of Isaiah where the covenant tradition is dealt with in such clarity and intensity (cf. also Marshall, op. cit., in literature for 1:1). The final two sections of the chapter stand in a looser relationship with what precedes, also seen in the fact that they have a different traditio-historical background than what is found in vv. 21–26. The addition found in vv. 27f. takes up the alternatives suggested in vv. 19f. and thematically restates a part of what is in v. 17 as well. Finally, vv. 29f. apparently are supposed to further illustrate what is in v. 28.

Does this collection go back to Isaiah himself? It is entirely within the realm of possibility that at least the section vv. 2–20 could have been put together by Isaiah himself at the time when vv. 4–9 were being written down as a final appeal to the city which had been mightily tested. This would be similar to Jeremiah writing down, in the fourth year of Jehoiakim, the words which had come to him in earlier times (36:2). Both of the final sections could have been additions to this original composition, as the work of a disciple, the one who composed vv. 27f. and maybe also the superscription in 1:1. But the accuracy of such suggestions cannot be guaranteed by the mere mention of the possibility that it happened this way.

The Pilgrimage
of the Peoples to Zion

Literature

W. Staerk, "Der Gebrauch der Wendung באחרית הימים im at. Kanon," *ZAW* 11 (1891) 247–253. A. Bertholet, *Die Stellung der Israeliten und der Juden zu den Fremden* (1896). J. Jeremias, *Der Gottesberg* (1919). W. Eichrodt, "Die Hoffnung des ewigen Friedens im alten Israel," BFT 25/3 (1920) 36–38, 69–74. K. Budde, "Verfasser und Stelle von Mi. 4:1–4 (Jes 2:2–4)," *ZDMG* 81 (1927) 152–158. F. James, "Is There Pacifism in the Old Testament?," *ATR* 11 (1928/29) 224–232. T. J. Meek, "Some Emendations in the Old Testament," *JBL* 48 (1929) 162–168. W. Cannon, "The Disarmament Passage in Isaiah II and Micah IV," *Theology* 24 (1930) 2–8. A. Causse, "Le mythe de la nouvelle Jérusalem," *RHPR* 18 (1938) 377–414. G. von Rad, "Die Stadt auf dem Berge," *EvT* 8 (1948/49) 439–447 = *GesStud* 214–224. H. Gross, *Die Idee des ewigen und allgemeinen Weltfriedens im Alten Orient und im Alten Testament* TTS 7 (1956). E. Rohland, "Die Bedeutung der Erwählungstraditionen Israels für die Eschatologie der alttestamentlichen Propheten," diss. theol. Heidelberg, n.d. (1956). H. Wildberger, "Die Völkerwallfahrt zum Zion. Jes II:1–5," *VT* 7 (1957) 62–81. Idem, "Jesaja 2:2–5," in G. Eichholz, *Herr, tue meine Lippen auf,* vol. V (1961²) 97–105. J. J. Stamm, "Der Weltfriede im Alten Testament," in J. J. Stamm/H. Bietenhard, eds., *Der Weltfriede im Lichte der Bibel* (1959) 7–63. G. W. Buchanan, "Eschatology and the 'End of Days'," *JNES* 20 (1961) 188–193. A. S. Kapelrud, "Eschatology in the Book of Micah," *VT* 11 (1961) 392–405. W. Müller, *Die Heilige Stadt. Roma quadrata, himmlisches Jerusalem und die Mythe vom Weltnabel* (1961). H. Junker, *Sancta Civitas, Jerusalem Nova. Eine formkritische und überlieferungsgeschichtliche Studie zu Is 2,* TTS 15 (1962) 17–33. Th. C. Vriezen, *Jahwe en zijn stad* (1962). J. Schreiner, *Sion-Jerusalem, Jahwes Königssitz. Theologie der Heiligen Stadt im Alten Testament,* (1963). E. Cannawurf, "The Authenticity of Micah IV 1–4," *VT* 13 (1963) 26–33. P. R. Ackroyd, "A Note on Isaiah 2, 1," *ZAW* 75 (1963) 320f. H. Kosmala, "At the End of the Days," *ASTI* 2 (1963) 27–37.

[Literature update through 1979: K. Deller, "Zu את III Jes 2,4 = akkad. ma"uttu," *Or* 33 (1964) 260, note 1. R. Martin-Achard, "Israël, peuple sacerdotal," *VC* 18 (1964) 11–28. J. Schreiner, "Das Ende der Tage," *BibLeb* 5 (1964) 180–94. G. Rinaldi, "Nota (aharît e qes)," *BibOr* 7 (1965) 60. M. Delcor, "Sion, centre universel, Is 2,1–5," *ASeign* 2/5 (1960) 6–11. A. Deissler, "Die Völkerwallfahrt zum Zion, Meditation über Jesaja 2,2–4," *BibLeb* 11 (1970) 295–299.

H. H. Schmid, *Šalom, Frieden im Alten Orient und im Alten Testament*, SBS 51 (1971). O. H. Steck, *Friedensvorstellungen im alten Jerusalem: Psalmen, Jesaja, Deuterojesaja, TS* 111 (1972). J. S. Kselman, "A Note on Is 2:2 (lege בראש ההרים ‹רם› ונשא מגבעות) 'Higher than the top of the mountains')," *VT* 25 (1975) 225–227. Z. Shazar, "The Direction and Purpose of Time; Isaiah's Vision of the 'End of Days'," *Dor leDor* 3/3 (1975) 7–9.]

Text

2:1 [The message, which Isaiah, the son of Amoz, saw concerning
Judah and Jerusalem:]

2 It will happen[a] as day follows day:
There will be a firm base established[b]
for the mount of the house of Yahweh[c]
on the highest peak of the mountains
and it will be exalted above all hills.
Then to it[d] [all][e] peoples will stream,

3 and many nations will travel in that direction
and will say:[a]
"Rise up! let us go up to the mount of Yahweh,[b]
to[c] the house of the God of Jacob!
so that he might instruct[d] us concerning his ways
and we will travel along his paths!"
For instruction goes forth from Zion
and the word of Yahweh from Jerusalem.

4 And he will dispense justice among the peoples[a]
and will install himself as mediator for many nations.[ab]
Then they will forge their swords[c] into plowshares
and their spears into pruning knives.
No longer will a people lift up sword against a people,
neither will they any longer learn the warfare trade.[d]

* * * *

5 [House of Jacob, rise up! Let us travel about in Yahweh's light!]

2a Concerning the introductory formula והיה (and it will happen), cf. Joüon, Gr §119c.
2b נכון (established) must have been read in the Syr before בראש (as the highest, at the top), as is also read in Mic. 4:1. Gk translates ἐμφανές (visible to the naked eye), which is certainly incorrect here. Meek's suggestion (op. cit., 162f.) to alter יהיה (it will be) to read יֵרָאֶה, "shall be seen," is to be rejected.
2c בית (house) is missing in the Gk, which reads, in its place, after τὸ ὄρος τοῦ κυρίου (= הר יהוה, mount of Yahweh): καὶ ὁ οἶκος τοῦ θεοῦ (and the house of God). This is a secondary expansion (contra Eichrodt), since, at first, mention is made about only the height of the mountain. Wherever the establishment or the reestablishment of the temple is mentioned, the verb יסד (establish, found, fix), not כון (be firmly established, stable), is used (see 1 Kings 5:31; Isa. 28:16; 44:28; among other passages), and it makes sense to say that only the *mount* of Yahweh towers over all hills.
2d אליו (to it) is the preferred reading, even though Mic. 4:1 reads עליו (upon it). The Qᵃ reading of עלוהי, influenced by the Aramaic, is still less likely the original reading.
2e Instead of כל־הגוים (all the foreign peoples), Mic. 4:1 reads עמים (all the peoples), but then reads in 4:2 גוים (foreign peoples) instead of עמים (peoples), as read in Isa. 2:3a; כל (all) is a later expansion (see below). The reverse order of the words גוים (foreign peoples) and עמים (peoples) is also found in Mic. 4:3 (compared with Isa. 2:4).
3a Metrically, ואמרו (and they will say) is an extra word, but absolutely necessary,

as is possibly also the case with לכו (come), which follows; it might not be considered as part of the meter of the verse, but ought not be eliminated.

3b אל־הר־יהוה (to the mount of Yahweh) is missing in Q^a on account of haplography.

3c Instead of אל (to), many MSS and the versions read ואל (and to).

3d For ירנו (he might instruct us, defectively written), Mic. 4:2 reads יורנו (he might instruct us, fully written).

4a Instead of הגוים (foreign peoples) (the article is most likely secondary), Mic. 4:3 reads עמים רבים (many peoples, nations), but in what follows, it reads, instead of לעמים רבים (for many nations) rather לגוים עצמים (for strong nations); see above, note 2e.

4b At the end of the verse, the Micah passage adds: עד־רחוק (afar off), which the Syr also reads as the Isaianic form of the text. It is a gloss, which overloads the meter of the verse.

4c Instead of חרבותם (their swords), Mic. 4:3 reads חרבתיהם (their swords, longer form of the suffix).

4d For ילמדו (they shall learn), Mic. 4:3 reads the archaic form ילמדון (they shall learn); for ישא (a [foreign people] will lift up) it reads the plural ישאו (they will lift up).

Form

Isaiah 2:2–4 has a parallel in Micah 4:1–3. There is no corresponding verse for Isa. 2:1; the message is not quoted word for word by Micah. Instead of Isa. 2:5, Mic. 4:4 has a completely different ending: "They shall sit every man under his vine and under his fig tree, and none shall make them afraid; for the mouth of the Lord of hosts has spoken." But the essential character of Isa. 2:2–4 is, in effect, identical with Mic. 4:1–3.

The discrepancies which were noted above in the textual discussion are too insignificant for one to explain the duplicate form of the tradition by suggesting that two authors formulated this completely on their own or had come up with such similar formulations solely on the basis of a common fund of traditions. There must be a direct dependence, no matter how that finally might be explained. It has been frequently mentioned that the text in Micah 4 is better preserved (e.g., Naegelsbach and, more recently, Fohrer as well: the Micah text gives "the impression that it is, rhythmically, more tightly constructed and the content is more rounded out"). That is a subjective judgment and cannot be used as an argument for suggesting that the passage comes from Micah. Without a doubt, neither the Isaiah text nor that in the book of Micah preserves the exact form of the original prophecy. Taking into account the variants within both forms of the text and the different endings for each, one is furnished with an instructive example to show how the original text underwent both minor and major changes during the process of transmission and that text-critical study cannot set for itself the goal of reproducing the "original text" (on this, see A. Jepsen, "Von den Aufgaben der alttestamentlichen Textkritik," VTSup 9 [1963] 332–341).

Verse 1 is not part of the original form of the passage. It corresponds to the superscription at the beginning of a collection of prophetic words (see above, 1:1) and thus cannot serve simply as the introduction to the passage which immediately follows it. Ackroyd (op. cit.) offered a theory which suggested that chaps. 2–3 ought not be separated from chap. 1, since their content is very similar to chap. 1; thus, 2:1 would not actually be a "title" at all, but would have been inserted by a redactor who was aware of the problem of the double transmission of Isa. 2:2–4 and would have used the interpolation of v. 1 to express his conviction that this section indeed originated with Isaiah. But there is no doubt that this "literary critic" could have expressed his opinion still more clearly and would hardly have had to introduce Isaiah once again by using his father's name. The connections with the content of chap. 1 are not significant, since the "Zion" theme is heard again and again in Isaiah.

But it is just as true that neither conclusion, either as found in Isa. 2:5 or as it is in Mic. 4:4, is original. Isa. 2:5 clearly departs from the main point dealt with in the rest of the section, concerning "the pilgrimage of the peoples to Zion," and is to be taken as a special application intended for Israel. The reason for the addition might be clarified by positing the use of this text in a worship setting. Mic. 4:4a reminds one of 1 Kings 5:4b, 5: "And he [Solomon] had peace on all sides round about him. And Judah and Israel dwelt in safety, from Dan even to Beersheba, every man under his vine and under his fig tree." According to this, it seems "sitting undisturbed under each one's vine and fig tree" would have been part of the terminology of the kingdom (cf. also Zech. 3:10 and 2 Kings 18:31 = Isa. 36:16). In any case, this closing sentence departs radically from the train of thought in that which precedes. The addition changes the character of the message about peace for the peoples so that it becomes a promise for a peaceful life for the individual Israelite; one would no longer have to fear the foreigners who would come to Jerusalem, since they would no longer bring the terror of a quickly spreading war into the land.

The closing formula in Mic. 4:4b is found elsewhere only in the book of Isaiah (1:20; 40:5; 58:14). It is possible that it is the original conclusion of the message, now having dropped out from Isaiah 2, since someone might have wanted to use this new concluding sentence to achieve a smooth, unbroken transition to 2:6.

The actual, original introduction for 2:2–4 is at the beginning of v. 2: והיה באחרית הימים (it will happen as day follows day, at the end of the days). As in other places (Gen. 49:1; Num. 24:14; Deut. 4:30; 31:29; Jer. 23:20; 30:24; 48:47; 49:39; Ezek. 38:16; Hos. 3:5), באחרית הימים (at the end of the days) serves to introduce a prediction about the future, here very clearly a message of promise.

Meter: The introductory formula והיה באחרית הימים (and it will happen as day follows day) stands outside of the metrical pattern. Then, following this, there are 2 two-stress bicola in v. 2αβ. Verse 2b, after removing the suggested material and putting ואמרו (and will say) in parentheses, is united with the beginning of v. 3 to form a three-stress bicolon. A seven-stress colon follows (or, if לכו, rise up, is outside the metrical structure of the verse, a three-stress bicolon), and then another three-stress bicolon (with a double stress on both מדרכיו, his ways, and בארחתיו, his paths), and finally a four-stress bicolon (with a double stress on מירושלם, from Jerusalem); in v. 4, there are 2 additional three-stress bicola and an eight-stress colon to bring it to a close. In terms of meter, the poem is artfully constructed; it begins with short four-stress cola, getting one anxious about what is to come, describing the peoples who are streaming to the mount of God with six-stress cola which tell about the divine guidance to be found upon Zion, reaching the first high point with an eight-stress colon. Some more six-stress cola describe Yahweh's rule as a powerful arbitrator, making it possible for weapons to be resmelted to become tools for use in peacetime. Finally, the eight-stress colon in the final line brings one to the mighty finale: There will be no more war.

Setting

In light of the double transmission, but also because of the content, a lively discussion has taken place concerning the origin of Isa. 2:2–4, one which has not yet been settled.

Up to the middle of the eighteenth century, the traditional interpretation was held without serious objection, considering this passage to be authentic both in Isaiah and in Micah. Subsequently, it was thought that the prediction came from Isaiah and was borrowed by Micah from Isaiah's book (e.g., Beckhaus and Umbreit). In the next phase of the critical study of the prophets, a favorite solution suggested that the section came from what a third individual had produced, later borrowed by both Isaiah and Micah. Hitzig and Ewald presumed it was possible that this third person was Joel (Budde, op. cit., still championed this thesis, thinking that this section was originally located right after Joel 4:21; in reality, the seeming connection between Isaiah 2 and Joel 4 can be explained by the fact that both use elements from the tradition about Zion which were used in the prophetic proclamation). Naegelsbach vehemently defends the view (commentary, ad loc.) that this message stems from the man from Moresheth; the text in the book of Isaiah is to be taken as a citation, recreated as closely as possible from memory. The previous verse would have been the cause for this section to be written into the book of Micah, rounded off nicely by 4:5ff.; finally, "several different aspects of Micah's characteristic speech patterns" are to be found here. However, the first argument is not convincing, since one cannot make inferences about the authenticity of a text by assessing the present state of that text, and the third argument already runs into trouble because Naegelsbach does not differentiate between authentic and inauthentic parts of the book of Micah (besides which, the aspects of the speech in Isa. 2:2ff. are actually not uncharacteristic of Isaiah; on this, see Wildberger, op. cit., 72–76). Certainly, there is a connection between Mic. 3:12 and 4:1ff., but only in the form of two opposite positions which cannot be bridged; a promise of salvation such as Mic. 4:1ff. is unthinkable when it immediately follows Mic. 3:12. The man from Moresheth stands diametrically opposed to Jerusalem (see A. Alt, "Micha 2:1–5 ΓΗΣ ΑΝΑΔΑΣΜΟΣ in Juda," FS S. Mowinckel [1955] 13–23 = *KlSchr* III [1959] 373–381). It is hard to comprehend how the contemporaries of Jeremiah, who remembered very clearly the message concerning disaster in Mic. 3:12, could have also known this most significant message of promise as having come from Micah. Even though Mic. 4:1ff. does not have a parallel in the book of Isaiah, one must reject the possibility that this message comes directly from Micah. The thesis that it is an utterance of a prophet who was active before Isaiah and Micah is only rarely still mentioned today (but see Kapelrud, op. cit., 395, who considers this passage to be an old cultic oracle from the Fall–New Year's Festival; for a similar view, see J. Gray, *VT* 11 [1961] 15) and should not ever be considered again, in light of the picture which scholarship has painted concerning the development of the religious history of Israel. For this reason, one ought not have to decide between the view that the passage comes from Isaiah and the position first developed by B. Stade, who suggested that it comes from a postexilic individual who remains anonymous (see *ZAW* 1 [1881] 165–167, and *ZAW* 4 [1884] 292). Stade found a good number of later supporters, among whom Delitzsch, and especially Marti, went to the trouble of providing detailed support for the position; more recently, Kaiser and Fohrer have both come out in favor of a postexilic derivation. Cannawurf (op. cit.) has come out in opposition to the more recent efforts which argue that this is an authentic passage from Isaiah himself; Cannawurf does this by once again gathering together all the old arguments which seem to speak against this notion: The eschatological introduction and the unrestrained universalism presume a universal type of faith as is found in Deutero-Isaiah; תורה (torah) (v. 3), used without clarifying it any further, in the same sense in which it is used in Psalms 2, 19B, and 119, is a term commonly used in the postexilic era; in the older prophetic books, the promises of comfort and salvation were, according to E. Auerbach (see VTSup 1 [1953] 8), part and parcel of the "great reworking"; the parallel use of "Jerusalem-Zion" would also be typical of usage in the postexilic era, since the central position held by Zion would have come about only as a result of the reform of Josiah; the concept of the physical elevation of the mount of God would have come from the paradise myth, as also the "streaming" (נהר, v. 2), which would remind one of the stream of paradise; pilgrimages to Jerusalem would first have had a real importance in the postexilic era, since Jerusalem would not have been the singular center of the cult of Yahweh before this time. Whether one would consider these reasons to be sufficient as proof depends on exegesis of the individual passages, on the one hand, and one's conception of the overall development of the spiritual history of Israel, on the other, which the exegete recognizes as part of the task. Of course, there is no justification for taking אחרית הימים (as day follows day) in the sense used by the Gk, as an eschatological-apocalyptic term, which would have made sense only in the postexilic era (on this, cf. Kapelrud, op. cit., 395), and it is a blunder to interpret תורה (torah) with Cannawurf on the basis of the late psalms mentioned above (see more on this below). Besides this, one cannot deny that the passage sets forth a new interpretation of the ancient cultic tradition about Zion, the mount of God (on this, see von Rad, op. cit., and Wildberger, op. cit., but also Kaiser, ad loc.). That this tradition has preexilic roots is no longer disputed, even if there are individual psalms within the Psalter which might not have originated until after the exile, just as there can be no question, on the other hand, that Isaiah knew the tradition about Zion and is to be interpreted, essentially, in light of this tradition (Rohland, op. cit., 119ff., and von Rad, *OTTheol* II 155ff.). The great importance attached to Zion, for the faith of Israel, is not a consequence of the reform of Josiah but it is actually one of the presuppositions which called for that action (contra Fohrer, ad loc.). When considering all of the objections which have been raised against taking this message of promise to be an authentic word from Isaiah, as far as I can see, there are only two which remain: First, in this section, the motif of the battles between peoples is used in a different way than in the sections which can be clearly attributed to Isaiah within his book (Kaiser, ad loc.); second, the idea that the universalism which is mentioned here would have to be dependent upon Deutero-Isaiah. But no different use is made of the motif of battles between peoples at this point; rather, a different motif from the complex of traditions about Zion is readapted, namely, that of the pilgrimage of all nations. The Psalms of Zion speak very clearly about the meaning which the mount of God has for the honor accorded to Yahweh among the peoples of the inhabited world: "Surely, violent 'Edom' shall praise thee, the rest 'of the peoples shall hold festivals for thee.' Make your vows to the Lord and perform them '. . .,' let all around him bring gifts to 'him who is to be feared'" (Ps. 76:11f., emended text; see also Ps. 48:3, 11). Junker is quite right when he refers to the petition in 1 Kings 8:41–43, that Yahweh might hear, "when a foreigner (נכרי) who is not of thy people Israel, comes from a far country . . . and prays toward this house . . . in order that all the peoples of the earth may know thy name and fear thee, as do thy people Israel." Obviously, the "dedicatory prayer of Solomon" comes from a later era, but it is also certain that, when judged on the basis of its content, it "has developed out of the tradition of the temple." The second objection does not hold up either. If one refrains from interpreting the present passage solely in light of Deutero-Isaiah, the universalism which is found here is easily attributable to the first Isaiah.

There are, therefore, no adequate objections which can be marshalled which decisively speak against this passage coming from Isaiah, and, unless one is misled without knowing it, Isa. 2:2–4 comes from the prophet from Jerusalem, who knows that Yahweh is "the Lord, whose fire is in Zion, and whose furnace is in Jerusalem" (31:9; on this, see Bertholet, op. cit., esp. 99f., Causse, von Rad, Stamm, Junker, each op. cit., and, in addition, the commentaries of Duhm, Procksch, Hertzberg, Eichrodt, among others).

Junker presumes that the historical setting of this message of Isaiah is the reform of Hezekiah, which would have provided the necessary impetus for the renewal and acknowledgment of an old promise about the temple, going back to the time of Solomon; Junker also presumes that the message was actually spoken by Isaiah (op. cit., 29). Ignoring, for the moment, the fact that this reform is difficult to describe in detail historically, this text gives no indication that it was supposed to be used in connection with an event taking place within the cult itself. It is hardly possible that 2:2ff. could have come from Isaiah's early period, even though it will be shown that 2:6ff. does come from that time; instead, it is more likely the ripened fruit growing out of an extended period of activity. "Maybe it was his swan song" (Duhm, ad loc., and idem, *Israels Propheten* [1916] 190). Since the section makes use of elements from the tradition about Zion, this message may have been proclaimed in Jerusalem at the occasion of a festival, at which the meaning of the temple and Zion was articulated. Duhm (ad loc.) has offered the opinion that Isaiah meant this, along with 11:1–8; 32:1–5; and 32:15–20, "not for the wider public, but rather, for the disciples and believers, not as a prophet who had been sent, but formulated as a prophetic poet." It is possible that it was a legacy for a circle of confidants. But it was certainly not simply intended as a private poem, without any intention of its ever being made public; it was quite obviously meant to be made public, as the formula כי פי יהוה צבאות דבר (for the mouth of the Lord of Hosts has spoken) in Mic. 4:4 makes clear.

Commentary

[2:1] In contrast to 1:1, the content of the collection which begins with 2:1 is not characterized as a "vision" but as a "message," which the prophet "saw." The use of the word דָּבָר (message) as an absolute is not typical. Yet, Isaiah can also, from time to time, use the shorthand "message" when we would have expected "message of Yahweh" (9:7). But, in a case like that, a specific message is in mind, which "came upon" Israel at a particular hour in its history, whereas here, one gets the impression that the designation "message" refers to a timelessly valid and generalized address from the prophet.

The formula furnishes evidence which shows that the present book of Isaiah has been put together by uniting sections which at one time circulated independently.

There is no way to be sure how far the collection of the messages of Isaiah, introduced by 2:1, actually extends. The message of promise in 4:2–6 could have served as the conclusion for this collection; it is also possible that it continues in chap. 5 and, after the inserted material in 6:1—9:6, which seems to form a separate section on its own, could continue in 9:7ff. The only thing that is certain is that a new collection begins with chap. 13.

[2:2a] The way the introductory formula והיה באחרית הימים (it will happen as day follows day) was understood is apparent in the way it is translated in the Gk: ὅτι ἔσται ἐν ταῖς ἐσχάταις ἡμέραις (for it will be at the end of days) (in Targ, it is actually ויהי בסוף יומיא [and it will be at the conclusion of days]; Syr and Vulg are similar). The versions make it very clear that the expression is to be interpreted as "a technical eschatological term" (KBL).

W. Staerk devoted a special study to the formula באחרית הימים (at the end of the days) and came to the conclusion that it "cannot be shown to occur with certainty in even a single passage in the pre-exilic literature" and makes its first appearance in Ezekiel, in the sense of the "breaking in of the messianic kingdom" (op. cit., 251f.). But it is already found in the introduction to the Blessing of Jacob (Gen. 49:1; see also Num. 24:14), and Gunkel was already on the right track in his commentary on Gen. 49:1 when he voiced strong opposition to Staerk's viewpoint. In Hos. 3:5, באחרית הימים (at the end of the days) could be postexilic (see H. W. Wolff, *Hosea,* BK XIV/1, ad loc. [Engl: *Hosea,* 62f.]), and the passages in Jer. 30:24; 48:47; and 49:39 should be attributed to a postexilic redactor of the book of Jeremiah. But, on the other hand, there is no reason for doubting the authenticity of Jer. 23:20 (see Rudolph, commentary, contra Volz, commentary). The formula is thus already used before the exile, but there can be no doubt that its meaning changed over time, until it becomes distinctly a technical apocalyptic term in Dan. 2:28 and 10:14. E. Schrader (KAT² 153) has already called attention to *ina aḥrât ūmi,* or similar formulations meaning "for the future days," as a parallel from the Akkadian literature. There is no reason, with respect to the passages noted above, to interpret a Hebrew formula on the basis of a later meaning, that is, as a specifically apocalyptic term. Even the Septuagint does not always use a form of ἔσχατος (the last) when it translates this (cf. G. W. Buchanan, op. cit., and H. Kosmala, op. cit.).

Even if one does not find an apocalyptic sense for באחרית הימים (as day follows day) in our passage, the term is not intended as a description of a vague time period yet to come. It corresponds to אחרי־כן (at that time) in 1:26, which is contrasted with בראשנה (at the earliest time) and בתחלה (at the very beginning) (cf. also 8:23 and 30:8), which means that it refers to an altered future, resulting from God's entering into history, envisioning the coming time of salvation. As long as this intervention by Yahweh in history is designated "eschatological" and is clearly differentiated from "apocalyptic," one can say that באחרית הימים (as day follows day, at the end of days) is used to introduce an eschatological prediction. The promise itself makes use of many of the terms common to the tradition about Zion.

"The mount of the house of Yahweh" obviously refers to Zion, upon which the temple was standing. In the songs about Zion, the community of worshipers at the temple in Jerusalem confessed that the city of Yahweh had been accorded status that it would endure forever (יכוננה, establishes, Ps. 48:9; cf. 87:5) and that Zion was firmly established (יסודה, founded) on the top of holy mountains (Ps. 87:1). Since the city of God was established so solidly, it would not be moved (Ps. 46:6; cf. 24:2; 93:1; 96:10; 1 Chron. 16:30).

It is quite obvious that the overarching height of the temple mount is mentioned very seldom in the OT (but see Pss. 48:3; 78:69; cf. also Ezek. 40:2), which is only to be expected, since Zion is not even as high in elevation as the surrounding hills. But, in the ancient Near East, the temple mount was equated with the mountain of the gods. The ziggurat of the temple of Marduk in Babylon is called Etemenanki, "foundation of heaven and earth" (on this, see G. E. Wright, *Biblical Archaeology* [1958] 108f.). In Gudea's hymn about the construction of the temple one reads: "The lofty house surrounds the heavens. . . . The house was allowed to grow up like a mountain range, like a cloud which floats up into the midst of Heaven" (as found in A. Falkenstein/W. von Soden, *Sumerische und Akkadische Hymnen und Gebete* [1953] 158; see also 134f., 137, 159–162, 178–182). Without a doubt, the motif of the overarching height of the temple mount is just as much a part of the tradition about Zion as the idea that it was located in the far north (Ps. 48:3; cf. Isa. 14:13f.; Ezek. 40:2; Zech. 14:10; and see on this also H. J. Kraus, *Psalmen,* BK XV/1, excursus on Psalm 46 [Engl: *Psalms 1–59,* 89ff.]). The house of the deity had to be that big and/or had to be located on such a high mountain, since that is the place where the earthly world comes into contact with the heavenly realm. It is because Israel generally refrained from using the mythological terminology of its neighbors that one cannot learn more from the OT about this concept (and yet, see Gen. 28:17). The closest parallels also show the same type of caution; Israel was very circumspect about what it took and adapted from the ancient Near Eastern "kingship ideology." But, as happens in other cases as well (see, for example, below, 9:1ff.), Isaiah made use of mythological concepts to sketch out his expectations for the future, but uses the elements which were at his disposal in an eschatological way. That does not yet justify speaking about this as apocalyptic; we are rather to see here, as also in the ancient Near Eastern parallels, that the mythological terminology is used simply to put the very great importance attached to the sanctuary into a proper perspective. There is a long-standing controversy about whether the elevation of the temple mount ought to be interpreted in a "physical" or "spiritual" sense. While someone like Orelli (commentary, ad loc.) seeks a middle ground when he says that "the prophet sees physical and spiritual mixed together; everything external has a spiritual meaning and everything spiritual is also manifested visually," others maintain that a most wonderful transformation of nature will take place here. But, for Isaiah, the actual height of the mount does not play any central role. Kerygmatically, he employs this concept only to characterize the great importance of the sanctuary on Zion as a place where Yahweh will reveal himself to the nations of the world.

[2:2b, 3] In a sense, there will be something to be seen, since peoples and many nations will be streaming to this mount of God which towers over the entire world. The text-critical observation, that all the nations were originally not mentioned—most probably that the nations were not mentioned at all—is significant. It is a later, theologically motivated extension of Isaiah's line of thought to say that all nations will come. Much earlier, Gudea had said about the house of Ningirsu: "Around his name all the foreign lands, from the far reaches of the heavens, gather together; Magan and Meluhha come there from their own distant lands" (Falkenstein/von Soden, op. cit., 147; see also 152; *ANET³* 268). However, Isaiah himself speaks only about עמים רבים (many nations). One can see how radically he has reinterpreted the mythological elements of the tradition about the sacred mountain (in complete contrast to the postexilic era, in which one could actually speak about a "remythologizing") when one considers how he speaks about the "streaming" of the nations to Zion: The verb נהר I (stream), with the exception of Mic. 4:1, is used elsewhere only in Jer. 51:44. It is possible that Isaiah chose it because it would bring to mind, for him and his hearers, the concept of the "river (נָהָר), whose streams make glad the city of God, the holy habitation of the Most High" (Ps. 46:5; cf. also Ps. 65:10; Isa. 33:21). Finally, the background of this concept also includes the idea about the mount of God as the dwelling place of the Most High (cf. Gen. 2:10–14; on the other hand, see the similar formulation in the eschatological sense in Ezekiel 47; Joel 4:18; Zech. 14:8; concerning this, see H. J. Kraus, *Psalmen,* BK XV/1, 343 [Engl: *Psalms 1–59,* 89ff.]). The imagery visualizes the great power of attraction which is deep within Zion, serving as the dwelling place of Yahweh. The parallelism of גוי (*gôi,* nation, people) and עם (*'am,* people) is certainly from Isaiah himself; cf. Isa. 1:4; 10:6; 18:2, and (in the plural) 30:28 (concerning inauthentic passages, see 11:10 and 18:7, which also speak of the coming of the nations to Zion, but the reverse order of the Hebrew terms is used). The peoples encourage one another to go up to the "mount of Yahweh," to "the house of the God of Jacob." עלה (go up) is a technical term for the pilgrimage to the sanctuary; cf. the pilgrimage Psalm 122 (v. 4), and often elsewhere. One would declare to others, with a tone of great joy and expectation, just before leaving on the pilgrimage: בֵּית יהוה נֵלֵךְ (let us go to the house of Yahweh) (v. 1; on this, see Kraus, op. cit., ad loc.). But pilgrims do not make an effort to visit the sanctuary only so that they can bring the divinity gifts (Isa. 18:7; 60:11; Hag. 2:7f.; Ps. 96:8) or to fulfill a vow (Ps. 76:12 and, much later, Acts 21:23, 26) or just to celebrate festivals (Ps. 76:11, text emended) or even simply to praise Yahweh there (Pss. 96:7f.; 122:4), but also in order to "inquire of God" (1 Sam. 9:9) or to permit oneself the chance to receive an authoritative decision about some legal matter. This can be deduced from the "prayers of one who is accused," with requests to "deal with me justly" (Ps. 7:9; similar expressions are throughout the Psalter); Deut. 17:8ff. and 1 Kings 8:31f. presume the same circumstances (on this, see H. Schmidt, *Das Gebet der Angeklagten im Alten Testament,* BZAW 49 [1928]). In the sanctuary in Lagash, one could find the "throne for deciding fate" (Falkenstein/von Soden, op. cit., 170; cf., on this, Ps. 122:5). Gudea's temple, the "elevated dwelling place of the holy way," is called "the place for deciding cases of justice" (Falkenstein/von Soden, op. cit., 160). It seems likely that the amphictyonic sanctuary served as the place where legal differences between the tribes would have been settled. 2 Sam. 20:18f. ("Let one ask in Abel and in Dan, whether what the faithful ones of Israel once determined is still valid"; text emended as suggested by BHK³) demonstrates how complex political questions were dealt with at other Israelite sanctuaries (on this, see Bertholet, op. cit., esp. p. 92). But even the expectation that peoples and nations would be willing to receive an oracle from the God of Jacob or would be willing to be given a torah (instruction) is, without a doubt, connected to the actual practice in antiquity. The Romans are supposed to have had their twelve tables of law validated at Delphi (Duhm, ad loc.), and Herodotus tells about a visit from the Eleans of Greece to Pharaoh Psammetichus, who pointed out that unfair principles were used in setting up the Olympic Games (II 160), and Croesus went to receive an oracle from the Pythian Oracle (I 53–55). In fact, it seems that an attempt had been made in Delphi to create an international code of justice for war (Aeschines, *De falsa legatione* 115), and it was a significant issue for the priesthood there "that they had made the effort to at least make the wars, which were fought between groups which both worshiped the same god, wars which they could not prevent, at least more humane wars" (Pauly-W 35 [1939] 843). Finally, Isaiah himself offered instruction to the foreign peoples, that is, to their messengers, who had shown up in Jerusalem: the Philistines in 14:28ff.; Cush in 18:1ff.; and (if it is authentic) Egypt in 19:1ff. Jeremiah, in fact, was virtually designated a "prophet to the nations" in 1:5. What Isaiah announced was well within the parameters of what was conceivable in his own time. This passage has been repeatedly interpreted as proclaiming a return of the peoples to faith in Yahweh (which is mentioned in the late Psalm 102 [vv. 16 and 23] and Zech. 14:16). According to Kaiser (ad loc.), the peoples go up to Zion because they think that "a massive shaking and remaking of the earth" is occurring (though 2:2ff. does not mention this) and because they know that "only there will they be able to find guidance for a lifestyle which will allow them to survive the judgment of God." With such an interpretation, more is read into the text than is actually there. As far as involvement with the peoples goes, there is nothing about general guidance in living a life which will please God, but rather there is the assertion that actual conflicts will be set aside, as demanded by the authoritative judgment offered by a widely renowned sanctuary. תורה (torah) does not mean "God's system of justice" in Isaiah, but rather "instruction" in the sense found in Deut. 17:11, where the term is used parallel to משפט ("a decision which is pronounced") (on תורה, torah, as used by Isaiah, see above, on the form of 1:10–17). The second half of the verse in our passage shows that this interpretation is correct, using the corresponding term דבר־יהוה (word of Yahweh). The passage just cited from Deuteronomy makes it clear that the verb הורה (direct, teach, instruct) is also to be interpreted in the sense of instruction about what is legally right, not just in the general sense of religious instruction. Marti observes (ad loc.): "God is initially characterized as 'teacher,' but when there were 'scribes,'" his role diminished in importance. The terms ארה (way) and דרך (path) also need not be assigned a meaning like "the lifestyle desired by God" (Marti) on the basis of late passages such as Prov. 2:8 or Ps. 1:6, and they certainly need not have the sense of ὁδός (way) in some passages of the book of Acts (19:9, and often elsewhere; cf. also 2 Peter 2:2) or even as used in post-New Testament writings (Apoc. Pet. 22; see *TDNT* V, 93ff.). The דרך is more commonly used, for example, to describe the "way" which Yahweh opens up in the "oracle of salvation" for one who was accused, though innocent, or was in some way oppressed (Pss. 25:8, 12; 27:11; 32:8; 86:11, and often elsewhere; in other cases, it is used in the later sense, just like תורה, torah, Pss. 1:6; 119:33; cf. 119:102). In just the same way, the דרכים (ways) and ארחות (paths) which the peoples will want to follow are those exact paths which Yahweh shows them, then and there, when he utters his oracle. As elsewhere, Zion and Jerusalem are used as synonymous terms here (in the first part of the book of Isaiah, see also 4:3, 4; 10:12, 32; 24:23; 31:4f., 9; 37:22, 32).

Yahweh, the God to whom the people turn when up on the temple mount, is called here "the God of Jacob." The Lord of Zion is not addressed as (רב)מלך (great king), which is what Pss. 48:3 and 95:3 use when addressing the lord of the city and is also what Isaiah himself uses when describing his vision of Yahweh in the temple; nor is the Lord of Zion addressed as (El) Elyon, as Jerusalem's god had been known from ancient times (Gen. 14:18–22; Pss. 46:5; 78:17, 35, 36, and often elsewhere). Those are epithets of Canaanite derivation, which could be misunderstood in the present context. The people hurry toward Jerusalem, not simply because there is a famous cultic site there, which had been considered sacred from ancient times, but because they seek an encounter with the God who had made his glory known in Israel. In an analogous way, the ancient Israelite who came to visit the temple did not confess that the mount of God was his "refuge," but rather that Yahweh, the God of Jacob, was his "refuge" (Ps. 46:1, 8, 12). Even though it seems a bit clumsy, Ps. 48:2 says: "Great is *Yahweh* and greatly to be praised in the city of our God" and not, as present-day text critics would "improve" the text: "Great and highly to be praised is our God's city." Isaiah does not use the name "God of Jacob" anywhere else, but when one remembers that he speaks of the "Strong One of Israel" and of the "Holy One of Israel" (see 1:24), the use of אלהי יעקב (God of Jacob) cannot be used to argue against Isaianic authorship, especially since the less frequently used epithets of Yahweh, with the exception of Exodus 3f., are found exclusively in the OT strata which deal with the theology about Jerusalem (2 Sam. 23:1; Pss. 20:2; 46:8, 12; 75:10; 76:7; 81:2, 5; 84:9; 94:7; in addition to this, the emended text of Ps. 24:6). Of course, it is most surprising that this particular title found a home right in Jerusalem. Maybe the reason was a need to point out that what was once the city of the Jebusites had become the legitimate sanctuary of the Yahweh community, a faithful preserver of the relationship which had been inherited from the era of the ancient amphictyony.

[2:4a] Verse 4a describes the actual instruction which the peoples seek from Yahweh: שפט בין (justice among) points out that an arbitrator's decisions are meant. Just as in our passage, שפט (judge) and הוכיח (decide) are parallel in 11:3, 4, and there, הוכיח ל can only mean "set right for the benefit of," and thus, it means the same thing here, in contrast to its use in Prov. 9:8; 15:12; 19:25; it definitely does not mean "give someone instruction" (*Zürcher Bibel*) or something like that. That Yahweh also governs among the nations in this sense as a מוכיח (arbitrator) (on this, see above, commentary on 1:18, and V. Maag, *Text, Wortschatz und Begriffswelt des Buches Amos* [1951] 152f.) corresponds exactly to what Israel confesses about its God and to what is most illuminating about Isaiah's own concept of God. It is no contradiction for the passage mentioned in chap. 11 to use the same terminology to describe the decisive control wielded by the shoot from the stump of Jesse which is also used in this passage to describe the God of Zion himself. The Davidic king represents the divine king Yahweh in the midst of Yahweh's people. But it is to be noted that, while the function may be the same, the extent of the kingdom is not; the kingdom of God and the Davidic kingdom would not be one and the same, even in the future time of salvation, even though, in the OT, kingship psalms make a bold leap beyond political realities when they attribute the control of the "ends of the earth" to the king who reigns in Jerusalem (Pss. 2:8; 72:8; see also Zech. 9:10, where it is specifically stated that he would create peace for the peoples by issuing a command).

[2:4b] Submitting oneself to the decision issued by the arbitrator, Yahweh, would result in a cessation of war so that the actual armaments used in battle, in fact also even learning about how to engage in battle, could fall by the wayside. The *pi'el* of כתת is normally translated "recast," meaning, according to 2 Kings 18:4; Zech. 11:6; and 2 Chron. 34:7, "batter into pieces." The breaking of the weapons into pieces is also mentioned again within the context of the Songs of Zion; cf. Ps. 46:10: "He controls wars even to the end of the earth; he breaks the bow and shatters the spear; he burns the shields in the fire" (emended text, see BHK³; cf. also Ps. 76:4 and Zech. 9:10). But the whole idea itself is recast at a very critical point; Yahweh does not shatter the weapons which belong to the enemies who are storming the city of God, but the peoples do it themselves, after they have been confronted by God up on Zion. The exact meaning of the rare word את is unclear. Instead of plowshare, it can also mean mattock, two-pronged fork (so KBL). But the related Akkadian term *ittû* refers to the plow beam; Gk translates את with ἄροτρον (plow), 'Aquila with εχεγλη (plow handle), Targ with סיכין (spade), Syr with *sekkaj paddānâ* (plowshares), and Vulg with *vomer* (plowshare), so that, at least for our passage, the commonly accepted translation of "plowshare" is certainly justified. The vintner's knife is not used to cut off the grapes, but rather for pruning, that is, for removing the extra leaves and young shoots (see Dalman, *AuS* III, 23f., and IV, 312; for illustrations of swords, see *BRL* 473f.; for plows, *BRL* 428, and Dalman *AuS* II, illuss. 18–38; for spears, *BRL* 354; for vintner's knives, *BRL* 476, and Dalman, *AuS* II, illus. 44, and III, illus. 16). In place of the weapons, instruments of peaceful agriculture are fashioned; instead of fear of war, the peoples are filled with a feeling of security, in which there is no longer any place for a spirit among them which seeks war. In an absolute contrast to this mind-set, Joel 4:10 addresses the peoples at a time when the final judgment is expected very soon: "Beat your plowshares into swords, and your pruning hooks into spears." One might think of this as a proverb (see R. Bach, *Die Aufforderung zum Kampf und zur Flucht im alttestamentlichen Prophetenspruch*, WMANT 9 [1962] 72, note 1), which might have been formulated at a time when war threatened the farm people in Israel who did not have war on their mind. It does not talk about piling up an arsenal of weapons, but encourages people who had been summoned for battle to grab whatever they had at hand which could be used as a weapon. Isaiah would have thus taken this common quotation and used it in the opposite sense, while Joel preserved its original sense. But we have established the fact that Isaiah is also dependent upon the Songs of Zion for this motif. On the other hand, Joel takes over individual sentences or groups of words, by and large, as they were passed on from his predecessors, and recasts the material from this tradition in a way which suited him, even to the point of reversing the original meaning. In this way, the passage in Joel serves as a consciously used antithesis to Isaiah's vision of the future (see H. W. Wolff, *Joel,* BK XIV/2, 10 [Engl: *Joel and Amos,* 11]).

[2:5] Verse 5 calls for the Israelite cultic community to become fully aware of the salvation which is promised to them as the people of God, in light of the fact that the peoples will "seek" Yahweh. When they are referred to as the "house of Jacob," it is intended as a way to show the correlation between themselves and the "God of Jacob." They are reminded of what has been promised to Israel as the people chosen by Yahweh. This designation, which is not used very often, is used with surprising frequency in the various parts of the book of Isaiah (2:6; 8:17; 10:20; 14:1; 29:22; 46:3; 48:1; 58:1; that is, nine of the twenty-one occurrences in the OT). Isaiah's contemporaries, Amos and Micah, also know this term. It is not accidental that its only use in the Pentateuch, besides Gen. 46:27, is in the Sinai pericope, in Exod. 19:3. Israel, as the "house of Jacob," had experienced Yahweh's wonderful help during the exodus from Egypt. The expression אור יהוה (Yahweh's light) is unique in our passage. But in the cult of Jerusalem, "light" played a very important role as a symbol for the saving, gracious presence of Yahweh. From Yahweh, "a light streams forth (read זרח) for the righteous" (Ps. 97:11); "He lets righteousness (צדקה) come forth as the light" (Ps. 37:6; cf. Ps. 112:4); the thankful one who is praying confesses: "Yahweh is my light and my salvation" (יְשַׁע, Ps. 27:1; cf. Mic. 7:8). According to Isa. 10:17 and 60:1, אור ישראל (light of Israel) was used in Jerusalem virtually as a designation for Yahweh. The "light" which was emanating from Yahweh and experienced over and over again in new ways in the cult demands the corresponding response, namely, that one would "walk in light" (see Ps. 56:14). The gift of grace is thus followed by the imperative, that one should also live within it. In later times, the light which emanates from Yahweh is actually the equivalent of the תּוֹרָה (torah) (cf. Prov. 6:23, and J. Hempel, *Die Lichtsymbolik im Alten Testament,* Stud Gen 13 [1960] 352–368, see 366).

Purpose and Thrust

Fortunately, commentators are in agreement about the very important role this section plays. Words like those in Isa. 2:2–4 "carry their value within themselves, quite independently of the period or the author from which they derive" (O. Eissfeldt, *The Old Testament, An Introduction,* [1965] 318). But making this assertion does not alter the fact that the interpretation of these most important concepts is affected by a prior decision about whether the passage is genuine or not. In addition, the character of the prophet and his message is affected in a significant way if one believes that such an important section is to be removed from the material attributed to him. It cannot be denied that the message of a promise to the nations seems like an intrusion into the material which gives us a general picture of Isaiah's overall message, as is clear even when based on careful exegetical work which does not involve the way the terms were used in postexilic theology. Since Yahweh is the lord of history (on this, see H. Wildberger, "Jesajas Verständnis der Geschichte," VTSup 9 [1963] 83–117), he has the nations in view from the very outset of his proclamation. Yahweh sets his own decrees in motion, in direct opposition to the plans of the allied kings of Aram and Israel (7:7; cf. 7:24), and there is no reason to doubt that none of them can annul the "purpose that is purposed concerning the whole earth" or turn back "the hand that is stretched out over all the nations" (14:26f.). Assyria is the "rod" of God's anger, the "staff" of his fury (10:5), which means that that world power is a tool being used by Yahweh within the scope of world history. Assyria does not have access to any other power than that which is given to it by Yahweh (10:15); it must therefore also allow itself to be brought forth to give an account to this lord of the nations as soon as it oversteps the limited authority which has been granted to it. However, since crossing over the limits of authority occurs repeatedly (cf. 10:13ff.), Isaiah is forced to announce disaster also to the nations—and within this group specifically to Assyria, even though it is the one which has been carrying out the judgment sentence for Yahweh. But are threats of judgment the last words which Isaiah can speak to the nations? When one considers the ambivalence concerning judgment and salvation in his proclamation and his deep interest in the nations, one would expect a positive word about their future as well. As a messenger for Yahweh, the prophet naturally can envision what will happen to the nations—"as day follows day"—only in relation to Israel, Yahweh's own special people. Since Zion's election will continue to be in force in the future, in fact, since the results of that election are yet to come to fruition, the relationship between the nations and Yahweh has to be explained on the basis of their relationship with Zion. But that just deals with what is obvious at first glance; the exegesis has shown how far Isaiah pushes the notion that being bound to Jerusalem and the temple is to be understood as being bound to the God of Israel. No great importance is attached to all of Israel's dreams about supremacy throughout the world, which could be supported by the traditional motif that Zion would be elevated over all the mountains, or the idea that the holy city was the "navel of the earth, that is, the center of the world (Ezek. 38:12; cf. Judg. 9:37; Jub. 8:19; and see Müller, op. cit., 179f., and Jeremias, op. cit., 40, 92f.). The ideology of kingship, with the Davidic king becoming the ruler over the entire world, is given just as little emphasis. The nations place themselves under the guidance offered by the God of Jacob when they come to Jerusalem on their pilgrimage. From the wealth of available material which could be used to expand on the concept of what this type of pilgrimage of the nations to the city of God would involve, the only element to be chosen describes the function of Yahweh as an arbitrator who works for the benefit of oppressed peoples (concerning this, see Stamm, op. cit., 46f.). The uniqueness of this passage, measured against all similar passages in the OT, which take up and apply the traditions about Zion in an eschatological sense (especially in Isaiah 60 and Hag. 2:6–9; in addition, Zechariah 14; Isa. 25:6ff.; Tob. 13:9ff.; 14:5–7), can be found in the way Isaiah brings together disparate materials to dynamically portray a scene which is central to his concerns elsewhere, namely, that the justice of God is in force among the nations (on this, see Fey, *Amos and Isaiah,* WMANT 12 [1963] 77). Narrowing the focus to this exact point can be explained by noting how Isaiah sees Jerusalem as a stronghold for justice (see above,

1:21–28). The most that he can expect from his city is that judges and advisers would carry out the duties of their office in the city as they had in previous times. Just as realistically as the prophet speaks elsewhere about the future role of Jerusalem for Israel, here he is moderate in describing the importance of Zion for the future of the nations. He presumes that there would continue to be conflicts among the nations, even in the coming time of salvation, but that these conflicts would no longer be settled by the use of force, with weapons. One is almost tempted to say that he gives a rationale for the motif which describes Yahweh shattering the instruments of warfare (Ps. 46:10). "The vision stays very close to what will happen within history and stays away from mythological elements" (von Rad, op. cit., 440 = op. cit., 216). But it is presupposed that, before the weapons are "recast," there will be a submission under the divine דבר (word), which one presumes will be imparted through the mediation of a priest or a prophet. "Its coming into being [that is, the new order among the nations] is no longer dependent on chance happenings, under the influence of earthly-human events, but the word of God functions to create obedience. The reception of this new teaching means nothing less than new life" (ibid.). Isaiah's expectation is moderate, but it is also daring: there will be peace. "Peace" belongs, with "righteousness," to the group of symbolic expressions which show up whenever one hears something about Jerusalem (see, for example, Ps. 122:7ff.; and cf. N. W. Porteous, "Jerusalem-Zion: The Growth of a Symbol," FS W. Rudolph [1961] 235–252). Even the name of the city itself brings to mind the concept of שלום, "peace." Peace without end, supported by justice and righteousness, is also the highest good which would come to Israel under the Davidic kings at the end of time (9:6). The longing for peace went very deep, as is demonstrated by the addition to this passage in Micah: "But they shall sit every man under his vine and under his fig tree, and none shall make them afraid" (4:4). That is certainly a reasonable expectation for the one who expanded this promise to the nations. But the sentence provides remarkable evidence for how realistic the OT is; the salvation which is announced will have consequences which reach right down to the most common events of everyday life for the Israelite farmers, whose hearts were yearning with eager anticipation to celebrate the yield which their land had provided, without having to be caught up even once in terror and dread about having it taken away.

Even though there have been numerous changes in the global political situation since the days of Isaiah, the promise which is proclaimed here still remains in force. The message about "peace among the nations" cannot be silenced. But Isaiah's promise also reminds one that the peace among all peoples can be an ongoing reality only if it is a "fruit of righteousness" (32:17), but remember that "righteousness" also means recognizing the legal claims of the downtrodden. Wherever this becomes a reality, as a consequence of the pilgrimage of the nations to Zion, it will be because those who have come have submitted themselves to the will of the God of Jacob. Here one sets out on a path which will eventually lead to much more specific statements about the participation of all peoples in the coming salvation (Isa. 45:22–25; Phil. 2:10ff.). That is where the βασιλεία τοῦ θεοῦ (kingdom of God) actually draws near and becomes fully real.

Isaiah 2:6–22

A Day of Yahweh

Literature

H. Junker, *Sancta Civitas, Jerusalem Nova. Eine formkritische und überliefer-ungsgeschichtliche Studie zu Is 2,* TTS 15 (1962) 17–33. G. Bertram, "'Hochmut' und verwandte Begriffe im griechischen und hebräischen Alten Testament," *WO* 3 (1964) 32–43. G. Pettinato, "Is. 2,7 e il culto del sole in Giuda nel sec. VIII av. Cr.," *OrAnt* 4 (1965) 1–30. R. Davidson, "The Interpretation of Isaiah II 6ff.," *VT* 16 (1966) 1–7.

[**Literature update through 1979:** J. Milgrom, "Did Isaiah Prophesy during the Reign of Uzziah?" *VT* 14 (1964) 164–182. G. Garbini, "Tarsis e Gen 10,4," *BibOr* 7 (1965) 13–19. P. J. Garrido Roiz, "El problema de Tartessos en relación con la región onobense," Hom. à F. Benoit, *I Riv. di Studi Liguri* 33 (1967) 354–360. M. Koch, "Untersuchungen zu Taršiš. Die historisch-geographischen Tar-siserwähnungen in den Quellen aus vorchristlicher Zeit," diss., Tübingen (1973). H. W. Hoffmann, *Die Intention der Verkündigung Jesajas,* BZAW 136 (1974) 105ff. U. Täckholm, "Neue Studien zum Taršiš-Tartessusproblem," *Opusc. Romana* 10/3 (1974) 41–58. K. Seybold, "Die anthropologischen Beiträge aus Jesaja 2," *ZTK* 74 (1977) 401–415.]

Concerning the "Day of Yahweh": L. Černý, *The Day of Yahweh and Some Relevant Problems* (1948). A. Gelin, "Jours de Yahvé et jour de Yahvé," *LumVie* 11 (1953) 39–52. S. Mowinckel, "Jahves Dag," *NorTT* 59 (1958) 1–56, 209–229. G. von Rad, "The Origin of the Concept of the Day of Yahweh," *JSS* 4 (1959) 97–108. Idem, *OTTheol* II (1965) 119–125. J. Bourke, "Le Jour de Yahvé dans Joël," *RB* 66 (1959) 5–31, 191–212. E. Kutsch, "Heuschreckenplage und Tag Jahwes in Joel 1 und 2," *TZ* 18 (1962) 81–94. K. D. Schunck, "Strukturlinien in der Entwicklung der Vorstellung vom 'Tag Jahwes'," *VT* 14 (1964) 319–330.

[**Literature update through 1979:** M. Weiss, "The Origin of the 'Day of the Lord'—Reconsidered," *HUCA* 37 (1966) 29–60. E. Galbiati, "'Il giorno di Jahve'," *VP* 53 (1970) 611–620.]

Concerning the concept ביום ההוא: P. A. Munch, *The Expression bajjôm hāhū', Is It an Eschatological Terminus Technicus?* ANVAO 2 (1936). A. Lefèvre, "L'expression 'En ce jour-là' dans le livre d'Isaïe," FS A. Robert (1957) 174–179.

Text

2:6 Truly, you have abandoned your people,[a]
    Jacob's house.
    Because they are full of 'soothsayers'[b] from the east
    and of enchanters, as it is among the Philistines,

[c]and with a strange mob they clap each other's hands.[c]

* * * *

7 His land was full of silver and gold,
     and there is no end of his treasures.
   And his land was full of horses,
     and there is no end of his war chariots.
8 And his land was full of idols
   . . . .[a]
   In front of the workmanship of his own hands each one falls
     down,[b]
     in front of that which one's own finger has made.
9 Then the human being was bowed down and the man[a] was
     brought low . . .
   [b][and do not forgive them].[b]

* * * *

10 [a][Get into the rocks
     and hide yourself in dust
   before the terror of Yahweh
     and the splendor of his grandeur.[abc]
11 The haughty appearance of the human being 'must be brought
     low,'[a]
     and the pride of humanity will be subdued,
   and Yahweh alone will be exalted
     on that day.]

* * * *

12 Truly, a day comes for Yahweh of Hosts,
     over all which is haughty and lifted up
     [a]and over all elevated and 'high.'[a]
13 And over all the cedars of Lebanon [a][the ones elevated and lifted
     up very high][a]
     and over all the oaks of Bashan.
14 And over all the high mountains
     and over all the lofty hills.
15 And over every high tower
     and over every sheer wall.
16 And over all Tarshish transports[a]
     and all luxury ships.[b]
17 And the arrogance of humanity will be[a] brought down
     and human pride will be brought low,
   and Yahweh alone will be elevated
     on that day.

* * * *

18 And the idols 'disappear'[a] one and all.

* * * *

19 'Go on in'[a] into the crevices of the rocks
     and into the holes in the earth
   before the terror of Yahweh
     and the splendor of his majesty,
     when he rouses himself, so that the earth is terrified.
20 [On that day each man will cast away his silver idols[a] and his
   golden idols, which 'he had made for himself,'[b] so that he might do
21 obeisance before them, 'to the shrews'[c] and the bats, • in order to
   escape into the rock caves and the crevices of the crags
   before the terror of Yahweh
     and the splendor of his majesty
     when he rouses himself, so that the earth is terrified.]

22 a[Leave the human being alone, in whose nostrils there is just breath, for 'to what purpose'b is he to hold on?]a

6a If one presumes that there was originally a connection between v. 6 and vv. 7ff., the form of v. 6 in the MT is hardly satisfactory. In v. 6, Yahweh is addressed, while in vv. 7f., the prophet observes the danger inherent in economic, military, and cultic expansionistic activities throughout the country. Obviously, the transmission of the text is not uniform. Gk reads the third person in v. 6a instead of the second person: ἀνῆκε γὰρ τὸν λαὸν αὐτοῦ τὸν οἶκον τοῦ Ισραηλ (for he has come to his people, the house of Israel); Targ (ארי שבקתון דחלת תקיפא דהוה פריק לכון דבית יעקב) (Truly, you have abandoned the Strong One who has delivered you, O House of Jacob) uses the second person plural and the people are directly addressed. Syr and Vulg follow the MT. The variant readings in Gk and Targ are not persuasive, Gk because the subject, that is Yahweh, should still have been mentioned, even if the third person is used, the Targ because it translates too freely, so that one cannot be sure what the original text read. Duhm, followed by Procksch and Eichrodt, suggests reading נטש יהוה עמו (Yahweh abandoned his people). Gray places v. 19 before v. 6, accepting Duhm's suggested reading, but this is too arbitrary. If one stays with reading the second person singular, it would seem likely that בית יעקב (house of Jacob) ought to be taken as a vocative. But the idea that the house of Jacob has rejected "its people," possibly meaning that it had given equal protection to foreign practices which had come on the scene, stretches the imagination. For this reason, some would rather read אלהיך (your God) instead of עמך (your people) or have suggested that עמך (your people) ought to be replaced by עזך (your strength), based on evidence from the Targ reading. Since these suggested emendations are questionable at best, one does well to stay with the MT reading. Maybe v. 6a is an isolated fragment, which would explain why its stylistic form is at odds with what follows.

6b כי מלאו מקדם (for they fill from the east) does not make any acceptable sense. G. B. Gray (*ZAW* 31 [1911] 111–117) believes that he can reconstruct the original ancient text of v. 6b, partially on the basis of Gk: כי־מלאה ארצו ענגים ובילדי נכרים ישפיק (for his land is filled with enchanters and with children of strangers he claps hands). But that simply adjusts the text to read like v. 7, which does not explain how the present wording came to be. Instead of מקדם (from the east), D. W. Thomas (*JTS* 13 [1962] 323f.) suggests reading מְעַקְדִּים, which is supposed to mean "conjurer," on the basis of the Arabic. But since this meaning is only a secondary one in the Arabic, it is too risky to postulate this as the meaning for the Hebrew word. Changing מקדם (from the east) into the abstract מִקְסָם (divination), as suggested again recently by Kaiser, is unacceptable because the latter term is not likely to be used at the same time as ענגים (soothsayers). But the presupposition that a form of the word קסם (practice divination) actually ought to be read instead of מקדם (from the east) is undoubtedly correct. It could be that קֹסְמִים, "fortune-teller," or, better yet, קסמים מקדם (diviners from the east) ought to be read (so Koppe); cf. also Targ: אתמליאת ארעכון מטען כיד מלקדמין, "your land is full of images of idols, like those which come from the east." This would give us an excellent complement to the next part of the verse: ועננים כפלשתים (and of enchanters, as it is among the Philistines).

6c–c It does not seem possible that one will ever be able to arrive at a satisfactory meaning for the last part of this verse; the reason for this is possibly not because of a corruption of the text, but because we cannot be sure of the meaning of the word שפק (slap, clap, BDB) and the corresponding ritual to which reference is made. With the exception of Targ, the ancient versions take this passage as a reprimand for sexual aberrations (see Hos. 5:7; Gk; and cf. Naegelsbach on this point). Since the time of Hitzig, בילדי (with the children of) has been commonly altered to read בידי (with the hands of), which would postulate that v. 6b means: "and they exchange handshakes with foreigners," which would have been apparently a common way to seal a financial transaction. We know very little about that (Prov. 6:1 refers to the practice but uses different phraseology), but, more crucial to the argument, the suggested meaning for שׂפק in this passage cannot be documented elsewhere. J. A. Bewer (*JBL* 27 [1908] 163f.) changes the reading to וּכְילְדֵי נָכְרִים יְכַשֵּׁפוּ (and like children of foreigners they practice sorcery); it is just as doubtful that this is the correct reading. D. W. Thomas (*ZAW* 75 [1963] 88–90), who would rather completely remove ובילדי נכרים (and with the children of foreigners) from the text, reads וענגים ישפיקו and translates it: "and soothsayers abound." But we hardly have the right simply to remove the difficult וּבילדי נכרים (and with the children of foreigners) from the text. KBL explains שׂפק in this passage on the basis of 1 Kings 20:10 (cf. rabbinic Hebrew ספק, "suffice") and assigns to the *hiph'il* the meaning "have an overflow," so that this would furnish a parallel to מלא (fill) (so that Kaiser reads: "and have an overabundance of the foreign born"). The Gk understood the verb in a similar way: τέκνα πολλὰ ἀλλόφυλα ἐγενήθη αὐτοῖς (many foreign children have been born to them). But then, the rebuke in v. 6b would contrast markedly with the accusation which immediately precedes it; here also, it is best to stay with the MT and to understand שׂפק (= ספק, see Job 27:23) to mean "clap each other's hands." The rather unique use of the construct clause ילדי נכרים (strange mob) has been explained in BrSynt §76a; see also §70d. ילד (child) is meant in a deprecatory sense, as in a passage like 1 Kings 12:8: untrustworthy people, with whom no one ought to have anything to do.

8a The second colon has been lost; it might have been said something like: "and there is no end to their pictures."

8b The plural ישתחוו (fall down) attracts one's attention; commentators generally lean in the direction of reading it as a singular, whether or not the consonantal text is changed. But the plural can also have the sense of the generic "anyone."

9a On the collective use of איש (man), see Joüon, Gr §135c.

9b–b Verse 9b can hardly be translated in any other way, but it does not fit into the context, either in terms of form or content. With reference to Gen. 4:7; Job 13:11; 31:23, Duhm suggested reading וְאֵין שְׂאֵת לָהֶם, which is translated: "and there will be no bringing them up," a conjecture which is hardly convincing. The little phrase is missing in the Qᵃ (the same is true in v. 10), but it is already known in the Gk, though that text presumes a reading which uses the first person: καὶ οὐ μὴ ἀνήσω αὐτούς (and I will not let them go unpunished). It may just be a marginal gloss, which was inserted into the text.

10a–a The entire verse is missing in Qᵃ. This might be an indication that it is a doublet, with v. 19 inserted incorrectly here as a result of a copying error.

10b Concerning הדר גאנו (splendor of his grandeur), cf. Joüon, Gr §141m: Two synonymous nouns sometimes have *"une nuance superlative"* (the force of one superlative) when one is in a genitive relationship to the other. For Ps. 29:2, H. J. Kraus translates בהדרת־קדשו (emended), according to the Ugaritic (I K 155), as "at his holy appearance" (*Psalmen*, BK XV/1 [*Psalms 1–59*, 344]). One wonders whether, in our passage, the masculine הדר can also mean "revelation, appearance." In fact, the Ugaritic *hdrt* means "vision, dream" (cf. Aistleitner, *Wört.*² no. 817).

10c Gk adds at the end of this: ὅταν ἀναστῇ θραῦσαι τὴν γῆν = בקומו לערץ הארץ (when he rouses himself, so that the earth is terrified) as in v. 19, which is probably the source of the expansion in the text.

11a שׂפל (be brought low) does not agree with its subject עיני גבהות (haughty appearance). It seems to have something to do with a mistaken attempt to match the form with the use of שׂפל (be brought down) in v. 12 or 17. It has been suggested that one read שָׁפְלוּ (they have brought down); it is probably better to read תשפלנה (will be brought down) on the basis of Qᵃ (cf. Gk: ὑψηλοί, lofty; Targ: ימאכון, they will be humbled; Vulg: *humiliati sunt*, they are humiliated). The suggestion of J. Huesman (*Bib* 37 [1956] 287) is also worth mentioning, that one should read, instead of the perfect שָׁפֵל, the infinitive absolute שָׁפֹל ("shall be brought low").

12a–a For וְעַל כָּל־נִשָּׂא וְשָׁפֵל (over all elevated and low), Gk offers the reading καὶ ἐπὶ πάντα ὑψηλὸν καὶ μετέωρον, καὶ ταπεινωθήσονται (and over all which is high and raised, and they will be brought down). One actually expects another parallel term will follow נִשָּׂא (lifted up). Gk seems to have read וְגָבֹהַּ (and raised), which is to be read instead of שָׁפֵל (low) (not *in addition to* it, as in the Gk). The suggestion from Tur-Sinai ("A Contribution to the Understanding of Isaiah I–XII," *ScrHier* 8 [1961] 159) that one ought to read וְשָׁקוּף, "looking down from above," since that is closer to the MT, has little to commend it, since there is no evidence that such a reading can be found anywhere.

13a–a One comes across הָרָמִים וְהַנִּשָּׂאִים (the ones elevated and lifted up very high) once again, in a similar form, in v. 14. Since v. 13 is metrically too weighed down, both of these words must have been secondarily inserted from their places in v. 14.

16a Gk translates v. 16a: καὶ ἐπὶ πᾶν πλοῖον θαλάσσης (and upon all ships of the sea), which says little more than that the translator no longer understood the meaning of תַרְשִׁישׁ ("Tarshish").

16b In earlier times, שְׂכִיּוֹת (luxury ships) was considered to have come from שׂכה and understood to mean "object for viewing, thing to be looked at" (see Ges-Buhl). Since this does not fit in and balance with אֳנִיּוֹת תַרְשִׁישׁ (ships of Tarshish), it has been conjectured that one should read סְפִינוֹת = שְׂפִינוֹת, "ships." But instead, it seems that the source of the word שְׂכִיּוֹת is the Egyptian word *šk.tj,* "ship," which would make a textual correction unnecessary, except for the question about the vocalization (cf. K. Budde, *ZAW* 49 [1931] 198; G. R. Driver, FS Th. H. Robinson [1950] 52). This is even more likely because the same Egyptian word is presumed to be the basis for the Ugaritic *tkt* (see W. F. Albright, FS A. Bertholet [1950] 4f., note 3; and Aistleitner, *Wört.*² no. 2862). In addition to this, Driver (op. cit.) would like to vocalize הַחֶמְדָּה (beautiful) as הַחֲמֻדָה (preciousness), taking it to mean (Arabic) precious thing. This would offer a good parallel to תַרְשִׁישׁ (Tarshish), but this is highly unlikely conjecture.

17a Concerning the incongruence between a predicate and a subject, when the predicate precedes, see Joüon, Gr §150j.

18a Instead of יַחֲלֹף (it will disappear), the Qᵃ reads יחלופו (they will disappear), which is also attested in the versions and is probably original (caused by haplography, with the ו = and, before ובאו = and they have gone, at the beginning of v. 19). N. J. Tromp (*VD* 41 [1963] 301f.) believes that one must distinguish between חלף I (*succedere,* move to a position below) and II (*esse acutum, succidere,* be cut off so as to give way). In Isa. 2:18, חלף II would be in use and the Vulg (*conterentur,* be destroyed) would have correctly caught the sense of the word. He would suggest vocalizing יחלף as a *qal* passive (or as a *niph'al*) and translates it with *abscindi* (be torn away). Because this interpretation is tenuous at best, it is better to stay with the traditional translation.

19a Based on a comparison with v. 10 (see the previous note), בֹּא (go on in) ought to be read.

20a In genitive constructions like אֱלִילֵי כַסְפּוֹ (silver idols), the suffix refers back to the entire construction, not just to the immediately preceding word to which it has been connected; cf. Joüon, Gr §140b, and J. Weingreen, "The Construct-Genitive Relation in Hebrew Syntax," *VT* 4 (1954) 50–59.

20b Instead of עָשׂוּ (they had made), עָשָׂה (he had made) is to be read, on the basis of the Gkᴬ and other texts. This change would not be necessary, of course, if the text should be expanded on the basis of Qᵃ (after לוֹ, for himself, or עָשׂוּ, they had made?, the text shows evidence of a gap) so that one would read אצבע[עתיו] (his fingers).

20c לַחְפֹּר פֵּרוֹת makes no sense at all. Theod reads φαρφαρωθ, on the basis of which

Isaiah 2:6–22

the text is emended to read לחפרפרות (moles, feminine plural), and Q^a reads לחפרפרים (moles, masculine plural).

22a–a This is lacking in the Gk (except in Gk^h, 'Aquila, Sym, Theod; see Ziegler). Without a doubt, it is a very late addition.

22b M. Dahood (*Bib* 44 [1963] 302) suggests vocalizing this as בָּמָה and translates it "beast": "Turn away from man in whose nostrils is divine breath, but who must be considered a beast," but the Ugaritic *bmt,* upon which Dahood bases this reading, though it does have the meaning "back," does not mean "beast." One must consider the supposition offered by S. Talmon just as unlikely, when he suggests (*Textus* 4 [1964] 127) that במה (to what purpose) had been misread from the original רמה (high) (even though the Vulg translates it *excelsus reputatus est ipse,* he himself has been thought to be most eminent). Syr (*'ajk,* as; see also the Targ וכלמא חשיב הוא, and like what is he considered?) seems to have read כמה (like what), which would seem to be correct, supported by Isa. 5:28; 29:16, and often elsewhere.

Form

Analysis: Verse 6a (with 6b providing the reason) falls stylistically outside the framework of what follows, as has already been demonstrated above (see textual note 6a), unless one feels compelled to impose some questionable alterations in order to restore the supposed original text. Also, when one considers the content, the concept of "soothsaying" can stand by itself. With כי (truly, because) at the beginning of v. 6, the verse is linked to the message of salvation which precedes it, even though the content of the two verses is not at all related. The ותמלא (was full) in vv. 7 and 8 seems to pick up on the מלאו (they are full) in v. 6a, but vv. 7a, 7b, and 8b are constructed very differently from v. 6aβb. Even if מלא (be full) does occur in vv. 7 and 8, it indicates that the arrangement of sections was the result of linking catchwords. Thus, v. 6 ought to be separated from that which follows. The verse is a fragment, which has been removed from a much larger section to provide what follows with an introduction which would forcefully get one's attention.

Verses 7–21 seem to have been woven together because of the phrases which sound somewhat like a refrain in vv. 9a, 11, and 17, and also because v. 11 sounds very much like vv. 19 and 21, and finally, because כסף (silver), זהב (gold), and ישתחוו (each one falls down), as used in vv. 7f., are used again in v. 20: כספו (his silver idols), זהבו (his golden idols), and להשתחות (so as to do obeisance), binding the verses closely together. The "refrain" is also to be found in 5:15f., and there are some commentators such as Procksch and, more recently, Kaiser and Eichrodt who seek to insert both of those verses into our section (Kaiser, after v. 21; Eichrodt, after v. 9). In reality, it is more probably a familiar quotation (see below, commentary on 2:9a), which Isaiah has brought into his prophetic speech, modifying it as is most appropriate in the context. Proof that the refrains were not part of what had been originally a single poem can be given when one notes the use of the imperfect consecutive in v. 9 while the perfect consecutive was used in vv. 11 and 17; besides this, the humiliation of the human beings in vv. 11b and 17b results from a confrontation, when the "exalted nature of Yahweh" is made manifest. Now we can come to a conclusion: The present linkage between these verses is not original. Just as vv. 7–9a are connected to what precedes them on the basis of the catchword מלא (be full), the final line caused them to be connected with and placed before the section which follows. These verses also took shape as an individual unit (now preserved in only a fragmentary form). One sees how much this particular section has been affected by the activity of those who came later. Note how the demand in v. 9b seems to have displaced the original conclusion of the text (see above, textual note 9b–b and below, commentary on 2:18).

Verse 10, which, like v. 9b, is missing in Qᵃ, provides a variant reading of v. 19, mistakenly inserted into the text at this point. Verse 11 presents us with the same type of variant reading for v. 17, which, intentionally or unintentionally, has been placed in the text here also. Verses 12–17 form one complete unit, which can be clearly removed from its context. On the other hand, v. 18 does not provide the conclusion to vv. 12–17, whether one considers its form or its content, and even if the catchword אלילים (idols) links the verse to v. 20, it cannot originally have belonged with vv. 19ff. For, if the idols have disappeared altogether, then there is no reason why they would have to be thrown to the shrews and the bats. At one time, the verse might have been the conclusion of vv. 7–9a.

With v. 19, we are once again dealing with a fragment. A reflective comment was appended to this, introduced by the popular formula ביום ההוא (on that day); v. 21b thus refers back to v. 19b, but its prosaic form shows that it is a later interpretation. Finally, v. 22 is also an addition, inserted by a later writer.

The section vv. 6–22 presents one with a very complex unit. Within it, four originally separate units have been woven together: 6; 7–9a (18); 12–17; and 19. Verses 10 and 11 are variants of other verses within the text, and vv. 20f. offer a later interpretation for v. 19. Verses 9b and 22 are additions which put into words the sentiments of those who read this at a later time. However, the entire section is to be taken as a single unit in its present context. The individual elements are linked to one another in a variety of ways, based on the use of catchwords. The entire complex presents a threat in a sermonlike form, with the compiler's central theme being a polemic against soothsaying and worship of idols. This corresponds to the thought-world of Deuteronomy.

Meter: The meter of such a complex section cannot follow the same pattern throughout. (1) v. 6aα: 2 + 2; v. 6aβb (taking into account the emendation mentioned above): 3 + 3 + 3. (2) Except for the damaged first line, vv. 7 and 8 are three-stress bicola. The section concludes very effectively with a four-stress colon (v. 9a) and a three-stress colon (v. 18). (3) The section from vv. 12–17, except for the introductory line 12aα and the closing 17b (3 + 2), is made up of 6 three-stress bicola. (4) Finally, v. 19 is made up of 2 five-stress cola and a final closing three-stress colon. The analysis of the form which has been presented seems to be supported by the results of the metrical analysis.

Setting

According to H. Junker, vv. 2–4 and 6–21 belong together thematically, in spite of the variety of literary types, the result of "the very lively way in which Isaiah characterizes the majesty and sacred holiness of Zion as the place where Yahweh is enthroned" (op. cit., 33). Both parts of the chapter would have been a response to the cultic reform of Hezekiah. The main event which occasioned vv. 6–21 would have been the contamination which forced its way into the "house of Jacob," culminating in Ahaz's construction of an Assyrian altar (2 Kings 16:10–20). But the history of the development of chap. 2 is certainly more complicated than Junker imagines. The same point can be made in rejecting Davidson (op. cit.), who takes "house of Jacob" to refer to the Northern Kingdom and concludes from this that the entire section vv. 6–22 was composed during the Syro-Ephraimitic War. Since God is addressed in vv. 6a and 9b, but the people are addressed in v. 10, Kaiser surmises that the prophet delivered this address at a festival gathering in the Jerusalem temple, "where he could address both God and the festival community at the same time." At least this much is clear: One must distinguish the "setting" of the present complex of texts, which reflects the deuteronomic preaching against soothsaying and idols and shows how Isaiah's message was reshaped to help later writers with their concerns, from the original "setting" of the individual units or fragments which have been identified above.

Research which seeks to clarify the individual elements brought together to form 2:6–22 naturally also involves the question about the genuineness of the individual elements of the composition; both problems can be solved only within the context of detailed exegesis (concerning this analysis, see also R. B. Y. Scott, FS Th. H. Robinson [1950] 184).

Form

[2:6] Since v. 6 addresses God, it must be a fragment of a prayer. In a song of lament, Yahweh is addressed in such a way, being accused of abandoning his people, in fact, handing them over to the enemy; cf. passages such as Ps. 27:9 (an individual song of lament): אל־תטשני ואל־תעזבני אלהי ישעי ("Cast me not off, forsake me not, O God of my salvation!"); in addition, see 1 Kings 8:57; Pss. 60:3, 5, 12; 74:1; Lam. 2:7, and often elsewhere. In those cases, such a statement has the characteristics of a challenge, actually of an accusation against God, indicated by the "why" which immediately precedes it. But here, the rejection of the house of Jacob, corresponding to prophetic thought in general, is seen as wholly justified, since it is rooted in Israel's behavior. In this case, the lament usually directed against God becomes an accusation against the people. As happens so many other times, a form of speech used in the cult is taken up by one of the prophets and decisively reshaped to serve the completely opposite purpose.

Setting

[2:6] Since the message is so short, it is hardly possible to decide whether this comes from Isaiah or from the pen of a commentator who was using it to introduce vv. 7ff. in order to establish a proper focus for what follows. נטש (abandon) is not found again in Isaiah, but is used in the books of Jeremiah and Ezekiel (Jer. 7:29; 12:7; 15:6; 23:33, 39; Ezek. 29:5; 31:12; 32:4). But why could Isaiah himself not also be aware of this verb, used in songs of the cult, with which he was certainly familiar? The polemic against soothsaying is admittedly not a central theme for him. But he does also mention soothsayers in 3:2 and his contemporary Micah clearly distances himself from the קסמים (diviners) (3:7) and threatens the

104

מעוננים (soothsayers) that they will be no more (5:11). The one who expands this text also used the designation בית יעקב (house of Jacob) for Israel in 2:5. But Isaiah himself also knows of this term, even though it appears particularly often in the secondary passages of the book of Isaiah (see above, commentary on 2:5). There is no compelling reason to deny the verse to Isaiah, even if one cannot exclude the possibility that v. 6 is being used here to give new meaning to the following verses, in which case Isaiah's own words would have been used to further the deuteronomistic program.

Commentary

[2:6] נטש (abandon), as the parallels from the cultic speech which are mentioned above demonstrate, does not have the primary meaning of the theological term "reject," though it is normally translated that way. The verb means "leave one to one's own devices, give up on, not to take time to care for something any more" (see KBL). If Yahweh gives up on his people, then they are powerless when given over to their enemies. It is not said that their status as the elect would be abrogated by that action. Israel remains the people of Yahweh, even when he allows them to be on their own, which means: allows them to experience the consequences of their faithlessness. The "judgment" does not mean that Yahweh himself has to intrude directly so as to punish them; it is enough just for Yahweh to take away his guidance and protection from his people.

Concerning the designation of Israel as the "house of Jacob," see the general treatment above, in the commentary on 2:5. The perspective of the history of salvation functions as a backdrop when this term is used, reminding the people of Israel of their obligation to be faithful to their God. But they had unilaterally renounced this relationship when they permitted the קסמים (soothsayers) and ענגים (enchanters) to function in their midst.

The Arabic word *qasama,* which corresponds to קסם, means "divide, separate, give a portion," but also: "ascertain" (either by God or by fate); in the tenth root form it means: "seek an oracle from the divinity, eavesdrop," used particularly when one spoke oracles which involved the shooting of arrows (belomancy) (see J. Wellhausen, *Reste arabischen Heidentums* [1897²] 132f.). According to KBL, קסם means, as corresponding meanings in Ethiopic and Palmyric also would attest, "inquire of an oracle by means of lot," the substantive קסם means "oracle by lot," and the related term used here, מקסם, would mean "inquiring of an oracle by means of a lot." But this would narrow the definition of the term too drastically, so it could refer only to a special type of mantic; on this, see A. R. Johnson, *The Cultic Prophet in Ancient Israel* (1962²) 31ff., who refers not only to an oracle connected with the shooting of arrows but also to inquiring of teraphim and liver examination; see Ezek. 21:26, and refer to the model of a liver which was found in Hazor (B. Landsberger/H. Tadmor, *IEJ* 14 [1964] 201–218). In Josh. 13:22, Balaam is called a הקוסם (soothsayer), and 1 Sam. 6:2 mentions not only the priests but also the קסמים (diviners) of the Philistines. According to 1 Sam. 28:8, divining can also be carried out by consulting spirits of the dead (אוב). In Isa. 44:25, the Babylonian קסמים (diviners) are mentioned, without it being possible to understand their actual function more specifically. Mic. 3:7 mentions them along with the חזים (seers), and, in 3:11, the prophet says that the נביאים (prophets) carry out the activity of קסם (divining). Finally, in Jer. 27:9, the קסמים (diviners) are mentioned together with the נביאים (prophets), the

חלמים (dreamers) (emended text), the כשפים (soothsayers), and, as in Isa. 2:6, with the ענגים (sorcerers); see also Jer. 29:8.

One can hardly make precise distinctions between these varieties of mantics who are involved in divination. But the passages just cited show that קסם (divining) was not always assessed in a negative way in Israel. Divining can be mentioned in connection with the נביא (prophet), and also with the elder, the judge, and others who held positions of honor within the sphere of public life (Isa. 3:2). And yet, there is the other side: Israel also viewed the mantic with skepticism, sometimes taking the hard line of absolute rejection; cf., in an earlier time period, Num. 23:33; 1 Sam. 28:3; and then, particularly, Deut. 18:10f., which brands all the various types of divination by mantics, along with the practice whereby "one makes his son or his daughter pass through the fire," as heathen misconduct and "an abomination to Yahweh." This interpretation has a bearing on this present passage also, as is demonstrated by the use of כפלשתים (as the Philistines) in the second part and the נכרים (strange mob) in the third part of the verse. If מקדם (from the east) was also originally used with קסמים (soothsayers), then קסם (soothsaying) is very specifically designated as a foreign activity. קסם (soothsaying) is often used with ענן (Deut. 18:10, 14: מעונן, soothsaying, enchanting) in parallel. The Arabic 'anna means "stand up, appear," and the Hebrew pi'el עגן means "bring about an appearance," so that "charm" is the basic meaning of the po'el. There are times when it seems actually to be a synonym of קסם (soothsaying). And yet, from the very beginning of the OT, it is treated in a negative way. However, its frequent appearance in parallel with various forms of the root נחש, "divination of portents," shows on the other hand that there is no sharp dividing line between magic and divination.

Some have questioned the comparison "like the Philistines" because it is not known that such practices were particularly common in the Philistine territory. But we know virtually nothing of the religious practices of the Philistines and, in any case, it must be noted that, even though 1 Sam. 6:2 does not mention the ענגים (soothsayers), it does still mention their קסמים (enchanters).

The interpretation and translation of the text, as presented above, is to be preferred not only because the MT need not be altered, but it also explains the text in a way which is consistent with the verses which follow. The discussion must involve participating in a foreign cultic practice. The only other time where the OT uses שפק I (clap hands) is Job 27:23, where the original meaning is watered down so that "clap hand to hand" seems simply to imply gloating over misfortune and derision. But שפק I (clap hands) is identical with ספק (clap hands) (on this, see G. Fohrer, *Das Buch Hiob*, KAT XVI [1963] ad loc.). One claps hands together to ward off something unpleasant (Num. 24:10) or if one is going through deserted regions (Lam. 2:15), apparently to frighten away the fiends and demons. This background would suggest that the present passage makes reference to a rite for warding off demonic powers.

Purpose and Thrust

[2:6] By rejecting mantic techniques and adjurations, Israel drew a sharp line to separate itself from Canaan and that environment. As with many other elements of pagan religious life, Israel would have tried to integrate these practices into its own faith in Yahweh. The oracle of Urim and Thummim shows that these practices were not completely unknown to Israel. But finally, Israel still came to the point of a decisive No! to them, since they stood in direct contradiction to its understanding of Yahweh. Divination and magic do not respect the boundaries which Yahweh set for human freedom and thoughtful action. Everyone in the ancient Near East understood that one would use magic to ward off wicked powers and would try to use the arts of divination to figure out how one could use magic for one's benefit. Israel's No! to these attempts, so commonly accepted everywhere else as the way to manipulate the future, furnishes evidence for the lively power of its faith in God, who had been experienced by them as the Holy One.

Form

[2:7–9] In v. 9, at the end of this section, there is a confirmation that "the human being" has been brought low; in vv. 7 and 8 the explanation is provided which shows why this has to take place. The passage refers back to a humiliation which Israel/Judah must have experienced, but which we cannot verify historically, and then explains why it happened. It has a rough parallel in the section 9:7ff., which closes with the refrain: "In all this his wrath did not turn away, and his hand is still stretched out." The section is very much like a prophetic reproach or judgment speech, one which has been transposed back into past time. One might best characterize it as a prophetic interpretation of history.

Setting

[2:7–9] Its authenticity is hardly ever brought into question. As no other prophet, Isaiah stands out in opposition to anyone who places trust in stockpiling armaments for war (31:1ff.). It makes good sense that he also voices opposition to stockpiling treasures because one expects to go to war in the future. It is most surprising that Isaiah mentions idolatry in this very connection. Worship of idols is not a central theme in his proclamation. "In front of the workmanship of one's own hands each one falls down, in front of that which one's own finger has made" sounds very much like a stock phrase; cf., for example, 17:8 (not Isaianic); Mic. 5:12; and Jer. 1:16. One wonders whether someone is reworking the text here. Although Isaiah also uses אלילים elsewhere to mean idols (see below, commentary on 2:8), the genuineness of v. 8b remains questionable.

There were some years within the period of Isaiah's activity when preparations for war were actively pursued, and idol worship is a recurring theme in prophetic criticism. And yet, it is most likely that the message of Isaiah focuses on the situation during the time of Jeroboam II in Israel and Uzziah in Judah (cf. 2 Kings 14:25; 2 Chron. 26:7ff.; 27:3ff.), so that the message was most likely delivered during the time of Jotham. (There is no doubt that the picture of the economic situation painted by Pettinato [op. cit.] for the eighth century is too pessimistic.) During that era, both kingdoms were in the midst of one last golden age, which must have seemed like the splendor of the Solomonic era and during which conscious decisions would have been made to pattern economic policy and military decisions according to what Solomon had done.

Commentary

[2:7] Silver and gold would have been gathered throughout the land, chiefly as subjugated peoples paid tribute and as various business activities were carried out. We are told about how Uzziah assembled an army, supplied with "army shields, spears, helmets, coats of mail, bows and stones for slinging," in addition to which he had catapults built (2 Chron. 26:14f.). We are also told about how Hezekiah opened up his treasure-house for inspection by the emissaries of Merodach-Baladan, who was obviously interested in determining how well prepared Judah was for war; thus, they were shown the silver and gold, along with the rest of the valuables which he had amassed (2 Kings 20:12f.). Horses were kept in the ancient Near East solely for the purposes of war; in fact, even up to the late Assyrian era, they were not used to establish a cavalry, but for pulling war chariots. Riders were used only to deliver important messages (see 2 Kings 9:18, and often elsewhere, and cf. the article "Pferd," *BRL* 419ff.; J. Wiesner, "Fahren und Reiten in Alteuropa und im Alten Orient," AO 38/2–4 [1939]; and S. Mowinckel, "Drive and/or Ride in the O.T.," *VT* 12 [1962] 278–299). For this reason, the charioteer corps is often mentioned along with horses (Exod. 15:19; Deut. 20:1; Josh. 11:4; 1 Kings 20:1; Ps. 20:8, and often elsewhere; normally they are called רֶכֶב [chariotry], though, in our passage, as in Exod. 14:25; 2 Sam. 15:1; Mic. 5:9, and often elsewhere, the collective noun מרכבה [chariot] is used). Concerning the chariots themselves, two horses were harnessed together and were manned by three individuals (driver, shield-bearer, archer) (see for illuss.: *AOB*² nos. 106, 118f., and 137; *ANEP* nos. 165f., 172, 327f., among others). In the Near East, war chariots were known from the time of the Hyksos on; sociologically, their existence presumes that there was a military aristocracy, since maintaining horses and chariots was an expensive operation. In ancient Israel, a charioteer corps did not play any great role; the hilly countryside of Palestine did not provide very favorable conditions for the use of a charioteer corps in a battle. Solomon had been able to establish such a troop and had developed his famous chariot cities (1 Kings 9:19ff.; 10:26). According to 1 Kings 10:29, a war chariot cost 600 shekels and a horse 150 shekels of silver, an exorbitant price when one considers the fact that one could buy a ram then for two shekels of silver or a bushel of wheat for the same price (see *BRL* 177f.). The charioteer corps was apparently used more for prestige than as a useful weapon in that terrain; see 2 Sam. 15:1 (Absalom) and 1 Kings 1:5 (Adonijah). Steeds and chariots are symbols of honor accorded those in power. Ashurbanipal praises himself in the Rassam cylinder: "chariots, horses, mules were all part of my gift to him for majestic travel" (*ana rukub bēlūtišu,* Rm II, 14, quoted from M. Streck, "Asshurbanipal," VAB VII, vol. 2 [1916] 15; see also Rm III, 73f.). Chariots and steeds are frequently mentioned in lists of spoils of war. It is significant that the deuteronomic laws about the king state that he is not to have a lot of horses (Deut. 17:16). In North-Syrian Sam'al, a god named *rkb-'l* was known, from whom the reigning dynasty expected crucial help in battle; see Donner-Röllig, *KAI* no. 24:16; 25:4, 5f.; 214:2, 3, 11, 18, and often elsewhere. In Israel, the believing community confessed, concerning the time when the king had to go against an enemy: "Some boast of chariots, and some of horses; but we boast of the name of Yahweh, our God" (Ps. 20:8; cf. also Pss. 33:17; 76:7; 147:10). "The chariots of Israel and its horsemen" is the name of honor given to Elisha, which was secondarily also applied to Elijah (2 Kings 13:14 [Elisha]; 2:12 [Elijah]). In 2 Kings 6, the visionary sees fiery steeds surrounding Elisha. The enemy who trusts in his chariots or in the chariots of his god opposes the Israelite who trusts in his God or opposes the prophet who is entrusted with the message of Yahweh (on this, see K. Galling, "Der Ehrenname Elisas und die Entrückung Elias," *ZTK* 53 [1956] 129–148). Thus, in Israel, it was a tenet of the faith to say that one ought not place one's trust in chariots. Yahweh proclaims, concerning the time of salvation: "I will cut off your horses from among you and will destroy your chariots . . ." (Mic. 5:9). It is not luxurious living, in and of itself, against which Isaiah stands in opposition; he does not consider the outlay to pay for armaments to be primarily a sociological problem—even though the burden of payment was regularly imposed upon the little people; instead, he is left unsettled by the question about whether or not Israel was ready to stay true and act in accordance with its faith—the very same question which is addressed to Ahaz in chap. 7.

[2:8] For this reason, the transition to the new theme of idol worship is no real μετάβασις εἰς ἄλλο γένος (transition to a different topic); war chariots and other gods stand on the same level. The rarely used designation for them, אלילים (idols), appears exactly ten times in the book of Isaiah, with only six other occurrences in the OT. As an adjective, the word means "nothing, null"; see Job 13:4; Sir. 11:3. With this term, the gods of the other peoples are designated as "nothings."

As one would expect, the etymology of the word is disputed. On the basis of the adjective, some consider it a derivation of אל (not), Akkadian *ul(a)*, thus, KBL Suppl.; others refer to the Akkadian *ulālu*, "weak," and the Syriac *'alîl*, "miserable, weak, unimposing." Still others refer (as also KBL), along with Th. Nöldeke ("Elohim, El," SAB 54 [1882] 1191), to the old South Arabian אלאלת, "gods." The derivation from אל is unlikely; the connection made with the old South Arabian word does not help, except to show that it is derived from the name of the chief Babylonian god Ellil, a view taken by A. T. Clay (*AJSL* 23 [1906/07] 277); further, that connection does not help even if the special meaning "idols" might very easily have been derived from this, since אלילים (idols) would have sounded so much like אלהים (God). Thus, the meaning "weak" seems most likely. Ps. 96:5 = 1 Chron. 16:26 (כל־אלהי העמים אלילים, all the gods of the peoples are idols) and Ps. 97:7 show how the word could take on the meaning "idols."

In terms of content, Isaiah's designation for the idols is very close to Jeremiah's use of הבל (vapor, breath). The prophet does not say that the gods do not exist at all, but rather that they are weak, powerless. The use of this designation in the two God-king-psalms shows that it has its roots in the Jerusalem cult tradition, which is how Isaiah would have come to know it. It is not just by chance that this designation is used elsewhere only in the Holiness Code (Lev. 19:4; 26:1) and Habakkuk (2:18). As to the rest of the verse: it is very common for the OT to say that the idols are just a "clumsy attempt," made by one's own hands; this saying is chiefly found in the deuteronomic writings (Deut. 4:28; 27:15;

31:29; 1 Kings 16:7; 2 Kings 19:18 = Isa. 37:19; 2 Kings 22:17), but it is also found in Hosea (14:2; cf. also 13:2) and Jeremiah (1:16) (see also Isa. 17:8; Mic. 5:12; Jer. 25:6f.; 32:30; 44:8). Very obviously, those who lived near Israel knew how to distinguish between a god and its image (cf. H. Wildberger, *TZ* 21 [1965] 494f.). It thus seems to be a gross oversimplification to portray the gods as human fabrications. But this is not entirely inappropriate, since it is an inherent danger in all religious activity that one adores the clumsy efforts of one's own hands, the ideas produced by one's own spirit, the idols of one's own power. The question about whether השׁתחוה is derived from the root שׁחה and is thus a derived form of שׁוח and שׁחח (bow) (KBL) or is an Št-form from a root חוה (KBL Suppl.) is to be decided in favor of the second possibility, on the basis of the Ugaritic (see W. F. Albright, *The Old Testament and Modern Study*, ed. H. H. Rowley [1951] 33; Aistleitner, *Wört.*[2] no. 912; S. Moscati, *An Introduction to the Comparative Grammar of the Semitic Languages* [1964] 128). That does not alter the fact that one is undoubtedly supposed to catch a play on words between השׁתחוה (fall down) in v. 8b and שׁחח (bow down) in v. 9. In and of itself, the verb refers to a "gesture of respectful greeting shown to those whom one would or should honor as masters and therefore especially, though not exclusively, [to] a gesture to rulers" (J. Herrmann, *TDNT* II, 788); thus, it is admirably appropriate for describing the very reverent action of prostrating oneself in holy places. In the Aramaic sections of the book of Daniel, סגד (do homage) is used, having the same exact meaning; it is used as far back as Deutero-Isaiah, parallel to השׁתחוה (bow down) (Dan. 2:46; 3 passim; Isa. 44:15, 17, 19; 46:6). The gesture corresponds to the *suğûd* in Islam, which E. W. Lane describes in the following way: "He (that is, the Moslem) next drops gently upon his knees, . . . places his hands upon the ground, a little before his knees, and puts his nose and forehead also to the ground (the former first) between his two hands" (cited according to D. R. Ap-Thomas, *VT* 6 [1956] 229); see also above, commentary on 1:15.

[2:9a] First of all, one bows down before the idols and then, in a very different sense, has to bow down in submission as a consequence of the first act. Verse 9a is noteworthy in more than one way: The discussion does not deal with the people as a whole, but rather with the אדם (human being) *and* אישׁ (man); the description of the submission makes use of two verbs, שׁחח (bow down) and שׁפל (bring low), neither of which is commonly used in the prophet literature; in addition, the divine lord who is judging is not mentioned, even though apparently it is the judgment of Yahweh which is being described. That has to be explained by referring to the traditio-historical origin of the acts being described. Since it is not Israel but human beings in general who are mentioned (אדם, human being, and אישׁ, man, are parallel), this points back to an origin in wisdom (cf. Prov. 12:14; 19:22; 24:30; 30:2; in addition, see Psalm 49 [v. 3], a wisdom psalm). On the other hand, one who is praying, in the individual song of lament, mentions being bowed down (Pss. 35:14; 38:7; cf. also 107:39; Lam. 3:20), and, in the song of thanksgiving, there is an admission that Yahweh brings the proud down (השׁפיל, bring down; see Pss. 18:28; 75:8; 147:6, but also 1 Sam. 2:7). However, in the song of lament, being bowed down is viewed as an undeserved lot in life and, in the song of thanks, the humiliation of the proud enemies is praised as something which Yahweh helps bring about. The way Isaiah characterizes what happens sounds more like the way the verbs are used in wisdom, as in Prov. 14:19: "The evil have to bow down before the good" (שׁחח *qal*) and 29:23: "A man's pride will bring him low" (שׁפל *hiph'il*); see also 25:7. Without a doubt, Isaiah is quoting a wisdom saying, which he puts in the form of an imperfect consecutive in v. 9, but he also uses it in its original form in 2:17. In such sayings, bowing down and being brought low are seen as the consequences of prideful arrogance; it is an important concern for wisdom to show how the arrogant will fall, according to the established order in the world, and how the humble one will eventually receive honor. Naturally, as Isaiah understands history, there is no automatic, built-in corrective which redirects whatever goes off course against established order; for him, Yahweh is the actual subject, the one who brings about such corrections. But when Isaiah makes use of wisdom terminology, without modifying the basic sense too radically, then it is because what wisdom teaches has been confirmed by his own observations.

[2:9b] The author of the addition in v. 9b knows that Yahweh has the power to intervene in the events which would soon take place in history, as the action-consequences relationship takes its natural course. But he requests that God not act. There are times when the righteousness of God, built into the unfolding events of history, should be allowed to take its course.

[2:18] As explained earlier (see p. 103), v. 18 might have been the original conclusion to vv. 7–9a. This is possible even if the verb is in the imperfect: When the human beings were humiliated, the idols showed themselves to be exactly what their name says—worthless beings without any staying-power. One could say: time goes by (Sir. 11:19), so does the wind (Hab. 1:11; Job 4:15), and so also the grass (Ps. 90:5f.), symbolic of the transitory nature of earthly things, and this is also the final fate for idols.

Purpose and Thrust

[2:7–9, 18] Isaiah learned from wisdom that the pride of humans is dashed to pieces when it comes up against harsh reality, and saw how this insight was aptly demonstrated in Israel's own destiny. But he interpreted the wisdom teaching theologically, insofar as he saw that rather than placing confidence in power and money and offering reverence to worthless gods, one ought to place one's trust in Yahweh. This assessment is not simply a prophetic commentary about past events; also, it is not simply meant to lead the people to recognize that they themselves were responsible for events leading up to their humiliation; rather, Isaiah's purpose was to warn the people, though not in so many words, to avoid doing in the future what had caused them such misfortune in the past.

Form

[2:12–17] Concerning vv. 10 and 11, see above, p. 103. Verse 10 is a variant of v. 19, and v. 11 is an expansion on v. 9, which itself is modeled after and provides the transition for vv. 12ff., using the words גבהות (haughty appearance), שׁפל (bring low), and רום (subdue). A new section begins with v. 12, describing the Day of Yahweh, introduced secondarily, as is often the case, with כי (truly, for), which connects it with what has already been mentioned. In terms of content, it is not a clumsy transition from the preceding section, since reference is made in both passages to the pride of human beings, a pride which lacks any real power. In the earlier section, the prophet looks to the past, here, into the future. Here it is a threat, even though it is not formulated in the style of a speech of Yahweh; yet it provides the details about what is going to happen.

Setting

[2:12–17] There is no question that this passage originated with Isaiah. It is characteristic of Isaiah to make mention of the reprehensible nature of pride, and terms such as גאה (haughty), רם (lifted up), and נשא (elevated) are also commonly used by him. Concerning איש (man) and אדם (human being), cf. not only v. 9 but also 5:15 and 31:8. Since this is the same theme as is discussed in vv. 7–9, it is possible that this passage also belongs to the beginning of Isaiah's activity.

Commentary

[2:12aα] Isaiah does not actually speak of a "Yahweh-Day," but of *a day for Yahweh* (as also Ezek. 30:3). With this descriptive term, he wants immediately to make it clear that he has his own concept of what is involved in such a day, differing from what the Yahweh-Day normally meant. However, his formulation is possible only because the Day of Yahweh in his own time did not yet carry the weight which it would in the NT era, which used either ἡμέρα θεοῦ (Day of God) or ἡμέρα κυρίου (Day of the Lord): the eschatological day of judgment, which at the same time would be the day when Christ would appear in glory (concerning this, see *TDNT* II, 951f.).

There are various "days" on which Yahweh reaches into the affairs of history in an extraordinary way, and they do not all have the same exact characteristics. The actions of God on the Day of Yahweh can be directed against Israel (Amos 5:18), against the nations (e.g., Ezek. 30:3ff.; Isa. 13:6ff.), or simply against all the presumptuous transgressors on earth, with Israel as the head of the group (e.g., Zeph. 1:14ff.; cf. Bourke, op. cit., 16; H. W. Wolff, *Joel*, BK XIV/2, 39 [Engl: *Joel and Amos*, 34]). Joel still makes a clear distinction between the Day for Judah and the Day for the heathen: the first takes place within history, the second is eschatological (Bourke, op. cit., 16, 22; cf. also von Rad, *OTTheol* II, 119–125). Amos had already spoken of the Day of Yahweh (יום יהוה); (concerning the use of יום יהוה and related terms, see Wolff, op. cit., 38f. [Engl, 33f.]; Bourke, op. cit., 18, note 1; von Rad, op. cit. ["Origin"], 97, note 2). However, that does not mean that Isaiah was dependent upon Amos. The prophet Amos also uses this concept as one which is well known already, since he contrasts his own conceptualization with that which was widely accepted by the people of the day. Ignoring those passages which are secondary, we encounter the same general viewpoint once again in Isaiah's own message in 22:5. The designation יום יהוה (Day of Yahweh) is not actually mentioned in that passage, but the terms which are used there leave no doubt that a Day of Yahweh is also being announced in that passage: יום מהומה ומבוסה לאדני יהוה צבאות (for Yahweh God of Hosts has a day of tumult and trampling). Right after that, the specific details follow which focus in on the actual historical time period, at which time all the commonly used terms disappear. This demonstrates how Isaiah felt completely free to change the traditional material which he adapts. In the present passage, 2:12–17, he speaks much more generally—there is no specific historical time period which can be discerned, to which this message actually would have been addressed—even though his own style of speaking can be easily discerned. From Isaiah himself, one cannot really discover the typical, one might say, the orthodox viewpoint about the Day of Yahweh. What was involved with this concept would be easier to discover in the secondary parts of the book of Isaiah, which would have been formulated by the prophets of salvation and which, although they came later than Isaiah, would have represented a more ancient stage in the history of the transmission of the concept of salvation. This is what takes place in the oracle about the downfall of Babylon in chap. 13, clearly fashioned from a great number of elements which are all part of the concept of the Day of Yahweh: Yahweh has commanded his consecrated ones, summoned his mighty ones for a day of wrath. He musters out an army for the battle. For: "Behold, the Day of Yahweh comes, cruel, with wrath and fierce anger" (v. 9). He wants to bring the haughtiness of the proud (גאון זדים) to a final end and wants to bring down the arrogance of the tyrants (גאות עריצים) (v. 11). After this takes place, specific details follow immediately: The downfall of Babylon through the intervention of the Medes will make it possible for Israel to return and be reestablished. The Day of Yahweh will impose a horrible sentence upon the wickedness of the world, concentrated in the city of Babylon; however, for Israel it would be the day on which the necessary breach would be opened so that salvation could break forth. In a similar way, reference is made to the Day of Yahweh in chap. 34; this time it is called יום נקם ליהוה (a day of vengeance for Yahweh) (v. 8). The section begins with the announcement of the tremendous wrath which will come upon Edom, so that the annihilation of this people will be accomplished by the sword of Yahweh, which will drip with blood, and the complete devastation of the land is described. Jer. 46:10 also describes a day of vindication, יום נקמה לאדני יהוה צבאות (the Day of the Lord, Yahweh of Hosts, a day of vengeance), using well-known and most likely the actual words of the prophet spoken against Egypt on the occasion of the battle of Carchemish. In the same way, the word of Ezekiel in 30:1–19 is directed against Egypt: "For the day is near, the Day of Yahweh is near; it will be a day of clouds, a time of doom for the nations" (v. 3). In the threat of judgment in Ezekiel 7, on the other hand, the Day of Yahweh is a day of judgment for Israel. In Zephaniah, both groups, Israel and the peoples, are dealt with at the same time. In addition, cf. Joel 1:15; 2:1, 11; 3:4; 4:14; Obad. 15; Zech. 14:1.

Thus, there are references to the Day of Yahweh or to a Day of Yahweh, יום יהוה, which can be traced back to a time before that of Amos and which continue to be found in the latest sections of the OT. Within this time frame, one can clearly recognize the way this concept develops historically: the Day of Yahweh goes from being an event which would take place within a historical time frame, against a specific enemy of Israel, to being a day of judgment taking place at the end of time and directed against all the peoples. This is not the proper place to deal with the concept any further; see primarily Černý, Bourke, and Schunck, op. cit. There can be no doubt that this concept has developed within the traditions which are associated with holy war (contra Mowinckel, op. cit., following von Rad, op. cit.), and there also can be no doubt that those traditions are implicit, even if the technical term יום יהוה (Day of Yahweh) is not mentioned.

In more than one way, Isa. 2:12–17 occupies a unique position in the history of this concept and the several terms associated with it. In the first place: It is clear that the day for Yahweh of Hosts is a day of judgment upon Israel/Judah. The storm of God (most commentators think immediately that this is an earthquake; concerning this, see J. Milgrom, *VT* 14 [1964] 178ff.) begins in Lebanon and wreaks havoc as far as the Gulf of Aqaba. The mountains and hills, towers and walls, through which it travels, are those of Palestine. But within this threat of judgment, Isaiah speaks about אדם (human being) and איש (man), just as he does in v. 9 and also in v. 17. For this, there is no parallel in any of the passages mentioned above in the discussion about the Day of Yahweh. The pride of humanity in general is being considered. According to 10:12ff., the storm of God, which is bringing down the pride of Israel here, will also bring down that of Assyria, in the same way. Second: The judgment upon Israel is not the actual goal of Yahweh's actions but rather the demonstration of the majesty of God: "and Yahweh alone will be elevated on that day." Finally: The description of a theophany of Yahweh is contained within the announcement of the day itself; the mythological pictures are either avoided or else made much less obvious when used in combination with the portrayal of a powerful storm. With a sure hand, however, Isaiah has highlighted one particular motif from the traditional material: Yahweh, on his Day, shatters the arrogance of the proud (cf. גָּאוֹן, pride, and גַּאֲוָה, haughtiness, 13:11); unless it was Isaiah himself who was the one who, for the first time, set forth the Day of Yahweh as essentially a judgment against pride. And here it is important to mention that it is obvious that the motifs in vv. 12–17 have points of contact with those in Psalm 29. This psalm also portrays the manifestation of the overarching, majestic power of Yahweh, his הדרת־קדש (holy array) (v. 2). In this case, Yahweh does not, of course, appear in battle and judgment, which would correspond to elements of the Day of Yahweh, but rather as the lord over the cosmic powers which are manifested in storms. Indeed, his coming strikes fear as well, but one still expects from him strength, blessing, and salvation (v. 11). Even though the psalm describes a completely different type of theophany than one in which the God of history acts on the day of wrath, there are still striking points of contact concerning certain specific details: One might compare v. 5 ("The voice of Yahweh breaks the cedars, Yahweh breaks the cedars of Lebanon") with Isa. 2:13aα, or compare v. 9a ("The voice of Yahweh makes the oaks to whirl") with Isa. 2:13b. In addition, according to the psalm, the thunderstorm goes from the north toward the south, until it reaches the wilderness of Kadesh (v. 8). There are other specific motifs in this psalm which are similar to those found elsewhere in Isaiah; cf. v. 9b ("in his temple all cry, 'Glory!'") with Isa. 6:3. Psalm 29 is constructed on the basis of a Canaanite pattern, presumably a hymn to Baal, which was first pointed out by H. L. Ginsberg, "A Phoenician Hymn in the Psalter," *Atti del XIX Congr. Int. d. Oriental* (1935) 472–476. In fact, a parallel from Ugarit (II AB VII 27a–41) also mentions how the cedars sink down, utterly helpless, before the judgment of Baal (*tġd . 'arz . bymnh,* line 41); cf. Th. H. Gaster, "Psalm 29," *JQR* 37 (1946/47) 55–65; F. M. Cross, "Notes on a Canaanite Psalm in the Old Testament," *BASOR* 117 (1950) 19–21. Thus, Isaiah has combined elements from the poetry of the Jerusalem cult, which have their source in the pre-Israelite history of the city, with the tradition about the Day of Yahweh. But, of course, the transformation is radical: The ancient motifs from the theophany, which describe how the storm god brings fruitfulness to the land, are now recast to serve the purpose of proclaiming how the Holy One of Israel has control over history. Since the whole complex of ideas which describes the Day of Yahweh had its source in the concept of holy war, it is not surprising that, when the Day of Yahweh is mentioned here, as elsewhere (13:4, 13; Jer. 46:10), the epithet Sebaoth (of Hosts) is appended to the divine name; see above, commentary on 1:8–9.

[2:12aβ, b] In v. 12aβ, b the adjectives גאה (haughty), רם (lifted up), נשא (elevated), and גבה (high) are used in parallel (see textual note 12a–a) and are used again, in a slightly different way, in vv. 13ff. What is really at issue, throughout this section, as later also with the use of the imagery of the cedars of Lebanon, oaks of Bashan, high mountains and towering hills, the towers and walls, travel to Tarshish and luxury ships, is the hubris of human beings which puts trust in God far from one's own mind, indeed installs the individual in God's own place. The *eritis sicut deus* (you will be like God) in Gen. 3:5 is here, even though no traditio-historical connection can be detected which would link this to the account of the fall into sin. The related substantives גָּאוֹן (majesty) (Exod. 15:7; Isa. 2:10, 19, 21; 24:14; Mic. 5:3; Job 40:10; cf. Isa. 14:11), גֵּאוּת (majesty) (Isa. 26:10; Ps. 93:1), שְׂאֵת (majesty) (Job 31:23), גֹבַהּ (majesty) (Job 40:10), and similar terms describe the divine attributes, which the human being can appropriate as one's own only by sacrilegious arrogance. Yahweh himself sits on a high and lofty throne (Isa. 6:2). From the midst of the whirlwind, he suggests that Job ponder this: "Have you an arm like God, and can you thunder with a voice, like his? Then, deck yourself with גאון (majesty) and גבה (dignity), clothe yourself with glory and splendor! Pour forth the overflowings of your anger, and look on every one that is proud, and abase him!" (Job 40:9–11). "Job is thus challenged: Put on God's royal robes!" (G. Fohrer, *Das Buch Hiob,* KAT XVI [1963] ad loc.). It is an important concern for wisdom that humans are made aware of their limitations, calling for moderation to be observed, calling for self-imposed restrictions. The idea μηδὲν ἄγαν (nothing in excess) belongs to the standard admonitions which are also found in Israelite wisdom (cf. O. Plöger, "Wahre die richtige Mitte; solch Mass ist in allem das Beste!" FS H. W. Hertzberg [1965] 159–173). For this reason, wisdom proclaims: "Yahweh tears down the house of the proud" (גֵּאִים, Prov. 15:25) and "Pride (גאון) goes before destruction, and a haughty spirit (גֹבַהּ רוּחַ) before a fall. It is better to be of a lowly spirit (שְׁפַל־רוּחַ) with the poor than to divide the spoil with the proud" (גֵּאִים, Prov. 16:18f.). עֵינַיִם רָמוֹת (haughty eyes) belong to the list of six things which Yahweh hates (Prov. 6:17; see, in addition, 21:4; 30:13). "Every one who is arrogant is an abomination to Yahweh" (16:5; see, in addition, Song of Sol. 5:7; 7:8). When peering into the mirror which reflects upon his kingly rule, in Psalm 101, the king says that he cannot endure the גְּבַהּ־עֵינַיִם (haughty looks) and the רְחַב לֵבָב (arrogant heart) (v. 5); cf. also Pss. 18:28; 131:1, and often elsewhere. Isaiah sounds one of the chief notes of wisdom, but then completely transforms it by transplanting it into the conceptual framework of the Day of Yahweh. Isaiah does not speak, as wisdom does, about what is good or better, but rather about what Yahweh Sebaoth opposes with his whole being, because of his claim to be the only one who is "high," the only one who is lord and king.

[2:13] The cedars of Lebanon portray, first of all in the cultic lyrics of the OT, a living power (Pss. 29:5; 92:13; cf. also 104:16; 148:9; Ezek. 17:23; 31:3, and often elsewhere). Therefore, in Ps. 80:11, they are actually called ארזי־אל, "cedars of God" = mighty cedars (concerning the use of this "superlative," cf. D. W. Thomas, "A Consideration of Some Unusual Ways of Expressing the Superlative in Hebrew," *VT* 3 [1953] 209–224). Significant objections have been raised which call into question whether ארז (cedar) really refers to the well-known cedars of Lebanon (*Cedrus Libani Barell;* see L. Köhler, *ZAW* 55 [1937] 163–165, and W. Helck, "Die Beziehungen Äegyptens zu Vorderasien im 3. und 2. Jahrtausend v. Chr.," *ÄA* 5 [1962] 29f.). But, since ארז (cedar) probably ought not be taken as a specific botanical term, but rather in a general sense which refers to majestic trees, such as those which grow in Lebanon, we will stay with the standard translation; concerning this, see M. Noth, *Könige* BK IX, 90f. In Ps. 37:35, the cedars of Lebanon are used for painting a picture of human arrogance: "I have seen a wicked man overbearing, and towering like a cedar of Lebanon" (emended according to Gk; see BHK³). Since Psalm 37 is a relatively late psalm (see H. J. Kraus, *Psalmen,* BK XV/1 [Engl: *Psalms 1–59*]), one should probably conclude that Isaiah himself took this ancient picture describing majestic power and reshaped it so that it became an allusion to someone's own arrogance. Lebanon is already mentioned in the texts from Ras Shamra as the supplier of the coveted cedarwood mentioned in connection with the construction of the palace for Baal (II AB VI: 18–21). Since cedarwood was also used in Jerusalem (1 Kings 5:20ff.), everyone who lived in that area had a first-hand impression of the magnificence of these trees. For more on Lebanon, see *BHHW* II, 1080f., with reference there to other literature. *Bashan,* "the flat ground," generally refers to "the very fruitful plain, 500–600 m. in elevation, which is situated on both sides of the middle and upper Yarmuk" (*BHHW* I, 203; see reference there to other literature). In Isa. 2:13, there is apparently a much more general and broader use of the term, since here, as in Ps. 68:16 (mountain of Bashan), Ezek. 27:6 (also oaks of Bashan), and often elsewhere, it must refer to what is at the western edge of this high plain, including the forest region and pasture area, known today as *dschōlān* (Golan). The oaks of Bashan are also mentioned, along with the cedars of Lebanon, in Zech. 11:2, enjoying also in that passage a similar type of proverbial notoriety (see Amos 2:9 and cf. Ps. 29:9 and "cows of Bashan" in Amos 4:1). Concerning the types of oaks in Palestine today, see above, commentary on 1:30; Noth, *The Old Testament World,* 63; and *BHHW* I, 374.

[2:14–16] More images are used in vv. 14f., and these are appropriate when characterizing how Yahweh goes into action against the pride of humans: First of all, there is the image of the mountains and hills. In Deut. 12:2, and often elsewhere, they are mentioned as places used by the Baal cult, but Isaiah would hardly refer to them in this sense. One would probably be closer to the truth if one recognizes that Palestinian cities were built on hills and occasionally on mountains and that a whole host of places are named גבעה (Gibeah) or something similar (cf. "a city set on a hill," Matt. 5:14).

In v. 15, high towers and sheer walls are also mentioned. A מגדל

can be a watchtower out in the open country (Isa. 5:2), but as a rule, it is a fortification tower, whether it is a single tower out in the open country (e.g., 2 Chron. 26:10) or is one part of the wall which encircles a city (e.g., 2 Chron. 26:15), chiefly used to protect the city gate and the places where the wall changes direction (2 Chron. 26:9). But a מגדל could also be erected as a fortress in the middle of a city (Judg. 9:46ff.; see E. F. Campbell/J. F. Ross, *BA* 26 [1963] 16, and, in addition, G. E. Wright, *Shechem* [1964] 94f., 124f.). In Judges 9, it refers to a fortification temple, and one could find one of these also in Thebez (v. 51). Further, the passive participle בָּצוּר means "solid," in the sense of "impenetrable"; for this reason, it is used as a description for strongly fortified cities; e.g., עיר בצורה (fortified city) (27:10) or קריה בצורה (fortified city) (25:2; cf. 36:1; 37:26, but also ערים בצרות חומה גבהה, cities fortified with high walls, Deut. 3:5); indeed, the cities could be "fortified up to heaven" (Deut. 9:1, and often elsewhere). Such cities or towers are considered the work of human arrogance (Gen. 11:1ff.).

The proud ships which sail the seas are assessed in the same way. Israel was not a seafaring people, and whenever it did happen, in opportune moments of its history, to be involved in maritime commerce, it was with considerable assistance from the Phoenicians. The foreign word שכיות (luxury ships) (see above, textual note 16b) is thus easily understood. But the vocalization of the word makes it seem likely that the Hebrews used it according to the meaning which it had in earlier times, that of "lavish spectacle." The actual, specific type of ship has not yet been determined. It would have attracted attention because of its splendor, while the ships traveling to Tarshish would have gotten attention because of their size, since they would have had to be able to transverse the expansive sea all the way to Tarshish. אניות תרשיש (Tarshish transports) is a set expression, as is demonstrated in various passages in which it is used (1 Kings 22:49; Isa. 23:1, 14; 60:9; Ezek. 27:25; Ps. 48:8). Tarshish was a commercial city (Ezek. 38:13; Jer. 10:9) which had close contact with the Phoenicians; i.e., most probably it was established by the Phoenicians (23:1, 6, 10; Ezek. 27:12). In Gen. 10:4, the city is mentioned along with Elishah (= Cyprus) and Javan. In Ezek. 27:12, Gk reads for it Καρχηδόνιοι *(Karchēdonioi),* Vulg, *Carthaginenses.* The OT associates this city with the idea of being as far away as one could go (66:19; Jonah 1:3; Ps. 72:10). In spite of recent attempts to locate it in Tunis (thus, A. Herrmann, "Die Tartessosfrage und Weissafrika," *Petermanns Geogr. Mitt.* 88 [1942] 353–366) or on Sardinia (W. F. Albright, *BASOR* 83 [1941] 21f.), it still seems most likely, especially on the basis of grammatical considerations, to identify it with Tartessos, at the mouth of the Baetis River, known today as the Rio Guadalquivir, in southwestern Spain (a region presently known as Mesa de Asta, north of Jérez de la Frontera and Cadiz; see W. Auer, "Das biblische Tharschisch," *BK* 14 [1959] 112–114; cf. W. Zimmerli, *Ezechiel,* BK XIII, 652 [Engl: *Ezekiel 2,* 65]). It was known to the Greeks, since the seventh century, by the name Ταρτησσός *(Tartēssos).* It is also mentioned in an inscription of Esarhaddon: "All kings, who dwell in the midst of the sea, from Cyprus and Javan even as far as Tarshish *(Tar-si-si),* subjugated themselves under my feet" (see R. Borger, *Die Inschriften Asarhaddons,* BAfO 9 [1956] 86). Even though תרשיש seems to mean "refinery" (according to

Albright, op. cit., who takes it as an Akkadian loanword, derived from *rašāšu*, "smelt"), that does not exclude the possibility that there were various ports with this name. Like the German word "Indienfahrer," "a Tarshish transport" eventually described any commercial ship which sailed upon the high seas, in spite of its storms. In a similar vein, the Egyptians had "Keftiu ships" which sailed to Crete (H. Th. Bossert, *Altkreta* [1937³] 55, note 2). This interpretation has an advantage over that suggested by Albright, who wants to explain אני תרשיש (Tarshish ships), on the basis of the meaning of תרשיש, as "refinery fleet": What is rather meant is a fleet which brought refined metal home from the colonies. Jehoshaphat commissioned such ships to be built in the port of Elath (1 Kings 22:49). Uzziah, about whom it is mentioned that he won Elath back and fortified it (2 Kings 14:22; 2 Chron. 26:2), did the same thing. While engaged in this type of activity with commercial ships, the people of Judah, who knew little about sailing the seas, probably had many catastrophes like the one mentioned in 1 Kings 22:49. According to the description in the present passage, the storm of God would rage out of the north (Lebanon), across the land, and on into the deepest southern regions. Only there, at the Gulf of Aqaba, could Judah have had ships. Whether the direction of the storm has to do with the mount of God being located in the north, as Fohrer and Kaiser maintain, is doubtful at best. If Yahweh would appear in a theophany, he would come from Sinai or from the land of Seir (Deut. 33:2; Judg. 5:4; Ps. 68:9, 18). Isaiah is formulating this independently, on the basis of what he himself envisions is on the way: The disaster threatens Judah from the north.

[2:17] Verse 17a refers back to the terms used in v. 12b to announce the decisive threat. For the sources of the terminology, refer to the extensive commentary on v. 9a, above. The basic difference between this passage and v. 9a is not that גבהות (arrogance) and רום (pride) are inserted, but that the verse is to be taken in a future sense rather than a preterite sense. The striking conclusion is completely new: ונשגב יהוה לבדו ביום ההוא (and Yahweh alone will be elevated on that day). Generally, נשגב has been translated as "elevated." But the basic meaning of the root שגב is "be solid, be impenetrable," and is generally chosen when one is describing walls (e.g., 30:13, but also 25:12). A משגב is a mound, which offers refuge. In the OT, the term is used almost solely in the vocabulary of the Psalms, in a metaphoric way, to describe God: 2 Sam. 22:3 (= Ps. 18:3, in parallel with מנוס, refuge); Pss. 9:10; 46:8, 12; 48:4; 94:22, and often elsewhere. This imagery has its roots in the theology of Zion, is based on the concept of the mount of God, and is also the source used by Isaiah in our passage: In the storm, which comes on the Day of Yahweh, the only refuge to be found will be with God. The same idea is behind the post-Isaianic passage 33:5; cf. also 12:4 and Ps. 148:13. The use of the formula ביום ההוא (on that day) is related once again to יום ליהוה (a day for Yahweh) in v. 12. According to Munch (op. cit.), it is to be understood as an adverb of time, which either lays stress on two events happening simultaneously or emphasizes the particular day on which the anticipated events take place. However, in many cases, it is simply an overused expression which does little more than connect two sections. It is in this way that it is used quite often in the book of Isaiah, to introduce additions which are being inserted (2:20; 3:18; 4:2; 11:10, 11; 12:1, 4; 17:7; 19:16; 23:15; 28:5; 29:18; 31:7, and often elsewhere). And since the יום ליהוה (day for Yahweh), which is described here, ought not be interpreted as referring to the final day of judgment for the entire world (see above, commentary on 2:12a), the closing formula cannot be used to suggest that the previous section has an eschatological character; cf., concerning this problem, Munch and Lefèvre, op. cit.; in addition, see H. Wildberger, VTSup 9 (1963) 113.

Purpose and Thrust

[2:12–17] Isaiah's final thought, coming from the world of wisdom, which maintains that all human pride will be brought low, is placed into a new setting by Isaiah when he takes what originally was a wisdom saying and incorporates it into his description of the Day of Yahweh. The picture is painted with many different hues, reminiscent of the ways in which the storm-god raged on through the land; this threat is rounded out by making use of the motifs connected with fleeing to Yahweh on the sacred mountain. The section, when considered from a traditio-historical point of view, has a very complex structure, an example of the richness and variety of the traditions which were passed on about Jerusalem, but also providing evidence for the complete freedom with which Isaiah takes the material at hand and creates a well-rounded composition with his own stamp on it. The poem is at once both a work of art and a prophetic message. The prophet continues on relentlessly, passing judgment on all arrogance. In the end, however, he places human beings before the majesty of Yahweh, who is a mighty fortress at all times, even when all walls are being broken down and towers are falling. The "if you do not believe, then you will not remain" has echoes here as well; concerning 18, see above, p. 111.

Form and Setting

[2:19] Verse 19, which is preserved only in fragmentary form (cf. the variants in vv. 10 and 21b), is also a threat, based on the way it sounds after making the suggested change, reading וּבָאוּ (and they will come) as an imperative. Based on the evidence provided by the way the vocabulary is used, it should be taken as an authentic message from Isaiah. Since it also speaks about a theophany of Yahweh, it is not completely out of place when it is connected with the preceding message in vv. 12–17.

Commentary

[2:19] Yahweh appears in royal majesty in the הדר גאונו (splendor of his majesty). In a way similar to that of כבוד *(kābôd)*, הדר is used to describe the glory of either the earthly or the heavenly king; cf., among other passages, Pss. 21:6; 29:2, 4; 45:4; 104:1; 145:5, 12; Job 40:10 (on this, see H. Wildberger, *TZ* 21 [1965] 482; on גאון = majesty as an attribute of the king, see above, commentary on 2:12aβ,b). But if Yahweh appears in his majesty, then the inhabitants of the earth are gripped with fear; their solid foundation quakes beneath them; indeed it splits asunder (Isa. 24:14, 17–20). The ideology of holy war is behind this, to which this concept also belongs, since Yahweh brings terror and fear to the peoples (Deut. 2:25; 11:25, and often elsewhere; concerning this, cf. G. von Rad, *Der Heilige Krieg im alten Israel,* 1965⁴, 10f.). One can plead with God: "Arise (קומה) O Yahweh, and let thy enemies be scattered" (Num. 10:35; cf. Ps. 132:8), or: "Arise, O God, plead thy cause" (Ps. 74:22), or even: "Arise, O God, judge the earth" (Ps. 82:8). The plea to Yahweh to rouse himself is also an important element within the individual song of lament (Pss. 3:8; 7:7; 9:20, and often elsewhere). But, in every case, the request is accompanied by the expectation that Yahweh, if he does rouse himself, will come forth as the judge who establishes justice. Thus, the earth has reason to be afraid when Yahweh stands up, and all human beings have good reason for sneaking into caves in fear; cf. Rev. 6:15.

[2:20, 21] Verses 20f. offer a later interpretation, providing a commentary on v. 8. Following v. 18, where it has already been established that the gods will disappear, it really does not fit into its present context, providing us with evidence that the entire complex is not one smooth-flowing unit. For a discussion of the introductory ביום ההוא (on that day), see above, commentary on v. 17. The glossator speaks about אלילי כספו (silver idols) and אלילי זהבו (golden idols). He thus makes use of Isaiah's expression for "idols." He speaks about silver and gold, since Isaiah made mention of silver and gold in v. 7, even though that was in a different context. Naturally, he cannot let that pass, without repeating once again that idols are things which humans themselves have made (see v. 8b). Finally, in v. 21, using his own style, he brings v. 19 to a conclusion. Since Isaiah spoke about אדם (human beings), he now makes use of the word, so that it is the individual, אדם, who is responsible for casting out the idols. The imagery seems to be an attempt at depicting someone who flees in fear when Yahweh makes his appearance, first dragging the beloved idols along, but then finally tossing them away, so that they will no longer be a heavy burden, but also because one would finally be utterly disgusted that they were not able to offer any real protection. That is hardly surprising, the glossator mockingly points out, since human beings themselves made them in the first place. With great mockery, he adds as well: "to the shrews and the bats." According to Y. Aharoni (*Osiris* 5 [1938] 463f.), חפרפרה is *crocidura religiosa,* an insect-eater, which was treated as sacred in Egypt and was often even mummified. עטלף is normally translated "bat." According to N. H. Tur-Sinai it is the *roussettus aegyptiacus,* a type of bat with an elongated, doglike snout (*Leshonenu* 26 [1961/62] 77–92, quoted from *IZBG* 10 [1963/64] no. 363). "The bankruptcy brought on by worshiping idols is clearly seen in the absolute disdain which the one who has been betrayed shows when he tosses away that which had previously been such a precious fixture in a sanctuary, when that individual attempts to flee from judgment before the real lord of all the earth" (Eichrodt, ad loc.).

[2:22] The entire section vv. 6–21 now comes to a conclusion with this puzzling v. 22, which can hardly be explained with any confidence in one's interpretation. Dillmann, and more recently, once again, A. Bruno,

Jesaja (1953) 60, 247, take this verse along with 3:1ff., which is not at all impossible, since. v. 22 does not fit well with the message about setting aside the idols; and yet, it really ought to be taken as a gloss to vv. 6–21. Marti is of the opinion that the verse attempts to bring one to a fitting conclusion, based on what has been described up to this point concerning the judgment, saying: "Stop it now, this trusting in humans, who are so transitory!" (Kaiser and Eichrodt analyze it in a similar way). According to J. Fichtner (*TLZ* 74 [1949] 78), the verse belongs to "sayings" which have the stamp of Isaiah on them, which are very close to a Chokma-type of proverb, whereas Steinmann, 369, attributes the verse to a redactor who belongs to the circle of the wise. Job 7:16b, 17 can demonstrate how this relates to wisdom. In that passage, Job makes a demand of God: חֲדַל מִמֶּנִּי כִּי־הֶבֶל יָמָי מָה־אֱנוֹשׁ כִּי תְגַדְּלֶנּוּ וְכִי־תָשִׁית אֵלָיו לִבֶּךָ (Let me alone, for my days are a breath. What is man, that thou dost make so much of him, and that thou dost set thy mind upon him?) (10:20 and 14:6 are similar). It is not stated in this passage, in so many words, that a human being is to be considered as nothing, but the content is similar. The use of חדל in this passage, "leave alone, not bother oneself with," tending toward the meaning "forget" (cf. Exod. 14:12), would most likely come from the vocabulary of prayer, more specifically, from the song of lament. In this, one bases the petition for consideration on the relatively limited importance of the one about whom one prays. Thus Amos says, "חדל־נא (Cease, I beseech thee!) How can Jacob stand? He is so small!" (7:5); see, in addition, Pss. 79:8; 89:48f.; Song of Azariah 14 (Dan. 3:37 Gk). Concerning the "sufficient reasons for divine intervention" in the individual song of lament, in addition to noting the fact that human life is so short (Pss. 39:5–7; 89:48; 102:12; 109:23; 144:3f.; cf. Sir. 18:8ff.), mention is also made of the weakness of human beings (Ps. 103:14–16; cf. H. Gunkel/J. Begrich, *Einleitung in die Psalmen* [1933] 130, 231f.). Contradicting the interpretation of the text which was cited above, the verse is rather, as Duhm explains it, "a heartfelt sigh, which a reader wrote in the margin," meaning: Let this weak human, who must endure so much which comes along anyway, finally have a little peace! But this interpretation brings with it the following difficulty: the sense of the plural of חדלו (leave alone); according to the parallels which have been consulted, one would expect that Yahweh would be the one addressed. Procksch is correct in noting: "One does not know for sure which powers are addressed with the words חדלו לכם (leave alone)." It is possible that one should read this word as a singular. Since the verse is missing in the Gk, meaning that it is a late addition, it might also suggest that demonic powers are intended. Further, the word נשמה (breath) is used here in a special way. According to Gen. 2:7, Yahweh breathed the נשמת חיים (breath of life) into the nostril of the human being, which in that case means that the gift of the divine breath of life is given; cf. Job 32:8; 33:4; Isa. 42:5, and often elsewhere. T. C. Mitchell, "The Old Testament Usage of *nešāmâ*," *VT* 11 (1961) 177–187, comes to the conclusion that נשמה is, in actual fact, always used to describe the breath of God, which, insofar as this gives humans a special relationship with God, distinguishes humans from animals (186). However, in this present passage, נשמה (breath) is used with the same sense as הבל (breath, vapor, vanity), found in the passage cited from Job (7:16b) or as עפר (dust) is used in Ps. 103:14, and often elsewhere. Concerning 22b, cf. Job 18:3, but also Sir. 18:8.

Purpose and Thrust

[2:6–22] Duhm offered the following assessment of 2:6–22: "This section is in the worst state of preservation in the entire book. The beginning is not there; toward the end we have only the scanty remains of the original text; along with this, there are prosaic expansions; gaps and additions are numerous." This judgment has proven to be the correct one according to our analysis, in spite of many recent attempts to deal with this section as a single, integral unit (e.g., Junker and Davidson, op. cit.). But those who hold this differing viewpoint about this section are right when they maintain that vv. 6–21 actually could be taken as a single unit (v. 22 is a unique gloss regardless). Its central theme is the Day of Yahweh, and the compiler no doubt took this to be the eschatological judgment day. In this latter sense, it is referred to, because of certain elements within this complex unit, in Rev. 6:15; 9:20, and in 2 Thess. 1:9f. Just as the phrase יום ליהוה (day for Yahweh) was understood by the reviser to be a special eschatological term, he also used his own favorite phrase ביום ההוא (on that day) in the same way. Since Isaiah himself speaks about judgment coming upon human beings, to expand the interpretation to include an eschatological judgment of the world would not be all that difficult. When considered in the light of the work done by the reviser, Fohrer is right when he says: "It is also clear that the harsh No to Israel's claim to be the chosen and to its own importance shows that this does not apply to an isolated, living 'people of God,' but applies to 'humanity' in general. Israel is simply the concrete example of what actually applies to the whole world."

The main interest of the redactor is in the unmasking and in the final downfall of the gods; both events would take place when the images of the gods would be set aside. "With the final theophany of Yahweh the end of the gods would be sealed" (von Rad, *TheolAT* I[4], 226). The arrogance of human beings, which Isaiah so powerfully proclaims is about to be smashed, is portrayed by the compiler by focusing in on the way humans pray to the gods, which are nothing else but what they themselves have made. But, thanks to the fact that the short passages of Isaiah have been preserved, in contrast to the abolition of the gods, there is a positive side which recognizes that Yahweh alone actually reigns in majesty. He is the only one who offers the protection of a real sanctuary, which human beings can find for all the storms and quakes of life—something the reviser sees as protection which comes at the end of time.

Isaiah 3:1–11

A Threat of Anarchy

Literature

H. M. Weil, "Exégèse d'Isaïe III, 1–15," *RB* 49 (1940) 76–85. R. de Vaux, *Ancient Israel. Its Life and Institutions* (1961). J. L. McKenzie, "The Elders in the Old Testament," *Bib* 40 (1959) 522–540. J. van der Ploeg, "Les anciens dans l'Ancien Testament," FS H. Junker (1961) 175–191. S. Bahbout, "Sull' interpretazione dei vv. 10–11 del cap. III di Isaia," *AnnStEbr* 1 (1963/64) 23–26.

[Literature update through 1979: L. Köhler, "Der Stab des Brotes," *Kleine Lichter* (1945) 25–27. F. Stegmüller, "Prudentem eloquii mystici. Zur Geschichte der Auslegung von Is 3,3," in *Wahrheit und Verkündigung*, FS M. Schmaus, I (1967) 599–618. W. L. Holladay, "Isa. III 10–11: An Archaic Wisdom Passage," *VT* 18 (1968) 481–487. W. Borowski, "Ciemiężcy zostaną ukarani (Iz 3,1–15) [Les oppresseurs seront punis]," *Ruch Biblijny i Liturgiczny* 25 (1972) 242–248. C. Schedl, "Rufer des Heils in heilloser Zeit (Is 3,1–12)," *TGl* 16 (1972) 92–98. H. W. Hoffmann, *Die Intention der Verkündigung Jesajas*, BZAW 136 (1974) 90ff.]

Text

3:1 [For] behold, the Lord, Yahweh of Hosts,
    takes away from Jerusalem and Judah
    support and staff: [a][every support of bread and every staff of
        water],[a]
2   the champion and man of war,
    judge and prophet,
        fortuneteller and elder,
3 captain[a]
    and dignitary,
    counselor, conjurer,[b]
        and those who are proclaimers of incantations.
4 Then I will make lads their princes,[a]
    and mischievousness shall rule over them.
5 And the people shall be its own tyrant, man against man
    and each one against the other.
    [a]The youngster will let loose against the oldster
    and the rascal against the honored man.[a]
6 Then one will pounce on his brother
    in his father's house:[a]

123

"You have a robe,
   you shall be our leader,
and this heap of rubble[b] over here
   is to be under your hand."[c]
7 Yet, he will cry out on that day:
"I do not want to be a doctor for wounds,
   and in my house there's no bread [a][and no robe].[a]
Do not make me become
   the leader of the people."

         *   *   *   *

8 Yes, Jerusalem is a heap of rubble,
   and Judah is fallen,[a]
for their tongues and their deeds are 'against'[b] Yahweh,
   to defy[c] [the eyes of][d] his majesty.
9 [a]Their regard of the person[a] witnesses against them,
   their own sins[b] they publicize out in the open [like Sodom],[c]
they do not conceal them.

         *   *   *   *

[Woe to them,[d] they prepare their destruction for themselves.[e]]

         *   *   *   *

10 ['Salvation'[a] to the righteous one, for it goes well with him,[b]
   truly, he will enjoy the fruit[c] of his deeds.
11 Woe to the transgressor, 'truly'[a] it will go badly for him,
   [b]truly, the work of his hands will be 'paid back'[b] to him.]

1a–a כל משען־לחם וכל משען־מים (every support of bread and every staff of water) is an addition, as is generally acknowledged (see B. Stade, *ZAW* 26 [1906] 129f.).
3a It has been suggested (see *TLZ* 19 [1894] 68) that, instead of חֲמִשִּׁים ("fifty"), חֲמֻשִׁים ("armed") ought rather to be read here (see Exod. 13:18; Josh. 1:14; 4:12; Judg. 7:11). But, in reality, חֲמֻשִׁים means "arranged in companies for battle" (actually: "separated into five companies of troops"); one never sees any mention of a שַׂר־חֲמֻשִׁים (captain of armed ones), but does find a שַׂר־חֲמִשִּׁים (captain of fifty men) (2 Kings 1:9; cf. the Neo-Assyrian officer's title *rab-ḫanšā* = captain of fifty, so that the Masoretic pointing is to be left as it is.
3b חֲכַם חֲרָשִׁים has been taken to mean "practiced in an art, skilled at handwork" or something similar, understood in such a way already in the Gk: σοφὸν ἀρχιτέκτονα (skilled) and Vulg: *sapientem de architectis* (proficiency in constructing) (in the latter case reading חרשים from חרש I, "engrave, manufacture," from which חָרָשׁ, "one who works with his hands," is also a derived from). Such a meaning does not fit very well in the context, which speaks about the deterioration of authority. Instead, חרשים ought to be understood in light of the Aramaic חֲרָשָׁא (Syr *heršê*), "sorcery"; cf. also the Ethiopic *ḥaras*, "magic." Of course, it is not impossible that Isaiah, in conjunction with יועץ (counselor), simply mentioned חכם (wise one), (cf. the meter); i.e., it is not impossible that חרשים (sorcery) should be removed from the text.
4a On the use of the double accusative with נתן (make, give), cf. Joüon, Gr §125w.
5a–a This translation follows Fohrer.
6a On the local use of the accusative, frequently in conjunction with בית (house), when it is followed by a genitive, cf. Joüon, Gr §126h.
6b For והמכשלה הזאת, Gk reads καὶ τὸ βρῶμα τὸ ἐμόν (= ומאכלתי = and my food), but this has to have been caused by a mistake in reading, possibly influenced by 3:7 and 4:1 (J. Ziegler, *Untersuchungen zur Septuaginta des Buches Isaias*, AA XII/3 [1934] 136).
6c Some MSS and Q[a] read ידיך (your hands), but this is hardly correct.
7a–a One already knows from v. 6 that the man possesses a robe, but he is making it up when he says that there is no more bread in his house. ואין שמלה (and no robe)

is thus a silly addition, which is evident just by looking at the meter of the verse.

8a Instead of נפל (fallen), Qᵃ reads the feminine נפלה (fallen). However, יהודה (Judah), when it refers to the people, is masculine (see, for example, Hos. 5:13; 8:14), but when it refers to the land, it is feminine (Jer. 13:19; 14:2; Lam. 1:3).

8b Qᵃ reads על (against) instead of אל (to), which is most likely the more original reading.

8c לַמְרוֹת (to defy) is a *hiph'il* infinitive with ל, a shortened form of לְהַמְרוֹת; cf. Ps. 78:17 and בְּהַמְרוֹתָם (on their provocation), Job 17:2.

8d Instead of this surprising example of the defectively written עֲנֵי (the eyes of), many MSS and Qᵃ have the normal form עיני. But the way עני is written, certainly more ancient than עיני, leads one to suspect a textual error. It is too easy a solution to simply eliminate the word from the text, as is usually suggested. It is worth mentioning that some suggest it originally read פְּנֵי (face of); one might compare this with the formula הִמְרָה אֶת־פִּי, "show oneself to be rebellious against a command" (e.g., Deut. 1:26, 43). Gk (διότι νῦν ἐταπεινώθη ἡ δόξα αὐτῶν, wherefore now their glory has been brought low) obviously was reading it as a form of the verb ענה (be bowed down, afflicted) (Dillmann, Ziegler, op. cit., 137). But it is possible that עני was misread from an original עם so that המרה עם could mean the same as ב המרה (defy, rebel against).

9a–a Concerning הכרה (regard): ה as a preformative is used rarely, but it is not impossible; see Joüon, Gr §88Lb. The form is derived from the *hiph'il*. The etymology and meaning of the word remain a matter of dispute: Gk paraphrases it with καὶ ἡ αἰσχύνη τοῦ προσώπου αὐτῶν (and the disgrace on their face). Syr, Vulg (*agnitio*, recognition) seem to have taken the word as a form of הכּיר, "inspect, recognize, know." F. Zimmermann (*JBL* 55 [1936] 307f.) postulates that this means "deceit," on the basis of the Arabic. As is so often the case with supposed meanings for OT words which are based on the Arabic, this suggestion is too unreliable. הכּיר פנים means "carefully observe a person = be prejudiced" (Deut. 1:17; 16:19; Prov. 24:23; 28:21), so that הכּיר פנים should be understood to mean something like "bias" and not, as it is usually translated, "appearance of the face." The Targ already understood the text in this way: אשתמודעות אפיהון, "their respecting of persons" (Stenning). Logically, the suffix on the genitive does not just govern this word, but refers to the entire clause in the construct state; cf. Joüon, Gr §140b; in addition, see J. Weingreen, "The Construct-Genitive Relation in Hebrew Syntax," *VT* 4 (1954) 50–59.

9b Syr, Targ read, for חַטָּאתָם (their sin), the plural. However, Isaiah always uses the singular (6:7; 27:9; 30:1 [bis]). The plural would, of course, be necessary if one wants to read חטאותם (their sins) as the subject of the sentence, following H. L. Ginsberg (*JBL* 69 [1950] 52): "And their sins have told everything."

9c Qᵃ: כסדום (like Sodom); see above, textual notes on 1:9, 10. The word is to be taken as a gloss (cf. 1:7).

9d On לנפשם (for them, for their *nephesh*), see BrSynt §11c.

9e להם (for themselves) is reflexive; see Joüon, Gr §146k. G. R. Driver (*Textus* 1 [1960] 120) would actually rather read, instead of להם, לאלהים (for their God), as in 1 Sam. 3:13 (Gk) (Tiq. soph.), which does not seem to be correct.

10a אמרו (say) is impossible and does not provide a word which follows the pattern of אוי (woe) at the beginning of v. 11, a verse which is connected with v. 10. Years ago Roorda (see Dillmann, ad loc.) suggested אַשְׁרֵי (blessings of), which has become the generally accepted reading. This emendation is supported by the reading in Gk, δήσωμεν (τὸν δίκαιον) (we will bind [the righteous]), which presumes that the original verb was אשר = אסר, meaning that it misread אַשְׁרֵי (εἰπόντες = saying, which precedes δήσωμεν = we will bind, in Gk, is most likely an alternate reading; cf. Ziegler, op. cit., 61).

10b After טוב (well, good), some want to insert לו (for him), so that it would be translated: "for it goes well with him," but טוב לו does not mean: "it is going well with him" but: "it is good for him, it is a gain for him" (Exod. 14:12; Num. 14:3;

Ps. 119:71). On the other hand, טוב, standing by itself, can mean "fortunate" (Jer. 44:17; Lam. 3:26; Ps. 112:5), so that the text is not to be changed, though it still could be translated: "For it goes well with him."

10c It has been suggested, for example, by Procksch, that one should read, instead of כי־פרי (for the fruit of), rather just one word כִּפְרִי (like fruit), and then, v. 10 would be translated: "Salvation for the righteous one! For he will enjoy good things according to the fruit of his deeds" (Eissfeldt also reads it this way). That is impossible: One can enjoy good things in proportion to one's deeds or could even enjoy the fruit of one's deeds, but not good things according to the fruit of one's deeds. The text is to be left exactly as it is, unchanged, which would also make sense because it has a parallel in v. 11.

11a Before רע (badly), as the parallel in v. 10 shows, the text should be expanded by adding כִּי (truly).

11b–b Instead of יעשה (will be made), Qᵃ reads ישוב (will return). That makes sense, since עשה (make) never, in any other place, means "recompense, repay something," which is the connotation which it must have here, but even more so because of the great frequency with which גמול (dealing, recompense, benefit) appears in the OT along with some form of the verbal root שוב (return) (Joel 4:4, 7; Obad. 15; Pss. 28:4; 94:2; Lam. 3:64). Our verse is very similar to Prov. 12:14b: וּגְמוּל יְדֵי־אָדָם יָשׁוּב לוֹ (and the work of a man's hands comes back to him) (which is to be read according to the Ketib יָשׁוּב = come back; cf. v. 14a with Isa. 3:10b). On the basis of this, the emendation which has been suggested on the basis of Gk (κατὰ τὰ ἔργα = according to the works of), to change כי־גמול (truly, the work of) to כגמול (as the work of) (Procksch, Eichrodt), is just as wrong as the change from כי־פרי into כפרי in v. 10a (see textual note 10c).

Form

The analysis of 3:1–15 does not yield the type of results in which one can place confidence. It is quite obvious that v. 1 begins a new section, both in terms of form and theme, and it is also clear that a new section begins with v. 16. But it is highly unlikely that vv. 1–15 were a unified section from the time of their composition. Kaiser divides it: vv. 1–9a (vv. 9b–11, an addition) and vv. 12–15; Fohrer does much the same. Eichrodt thinks that he can recognize three originally separate units in vv. 1–15: vv. 1–9 (vv. 10f. are not genuine); v. 12; and vv. 13–15. On the other hand, Duhm takes vv. 1–12 (again, after removing vv. 10f.) as one unit, while Marti includes vv. 13–15 in this unit, but still removes vv. 9b and 15b. Gray divides it: vv. 1–12 (vv. 2f. are not genuine) and vv. 13–15; Mauchline considers it actually to be four distinct sections: vv. 1–5; vv. 6–8; vv. 9–12; and vv. 13–15; others divide it in still other ways. The reason for this uncertainty rests, as elsewhere, in the fact that individual sections are joined together which fit together thematically and are thus not easy to separate from one another. In much the same way as chap. 2, one must reckon with the possibility that comments have been added to the text, but also that some of the original may have been lost. Verses 1–9a seem to contain a single threat: vv. 1–5 contain the general threat; vv. 6–7 compose a single scene, which demonstrates what will happen after the threatened dissolution of all authority takes place. With v. 8 comes a change of tense: after the future imperfects, perfects follow at this point, describing what has happened and what will continue to be repeated, or, one might say, how past activity would affect the present. One could interpret these verses as an independent description of the deterioration, but they are more likely, from the time they were composed, intended to provide the proof for the preceding threat. In the discussion which follows, we thus take vv. 1–9a as a single unit. The prediction of the disaster is, as a whole, not written in the style of a speech of Yahweh; the prophet takes responsibility for what he himself says, as we also noticed in chap. 2. Only in v. 4, surprisingly, the divine "I" comes into view; the prophet thus knows, at this point as well, that he is speaking as Yahweh's representative.

Both vv. 9b and 10f. are to be taken as additions. They do not differ all that much from the content of Isaiah's messages. Since Isaiah frequently uses the woe-oracle, vv. 9b and 10f. might very likely come from the narrow circle of Isaiah's disciples.

If one skips over vv. 9b–11, v. 12 could be taken, as Marti and others do, as a continuation of v. 9a. But the suffix on עַמִּי (my people) would speak against this. It is not impossible that both of these lines provide the introduction to the judgment speech in vv. 13–15. And yet, it is more likely that they are a fragment, completely separate from the rest of this context, originally part of a much larger context.

Meter: If 3:1b (כל משען־לחם וכל משען־מים), every support of bread and every staff of water) is eliminated (see above, textual note 1a–a), one reads, first of all, one seven-stress colon in the important introductory sentence v. 1aα; then 4 two-stress bicola follow in vv. 1aβ and 2a, in v. 2b, in v. 3a, and in v. 3b. In this way, the enumeration of the dignitaries is also shown, on the basis of the meter, to be a single unit in and of itself. Verses 4, 5a, 5b, and 6aα are joined to the preceding by the use of five-stress cola, unless one simply takes v. 6aα as prose. The excited, hurried speech in v. 6aβb is formed by using 2 four-stress cola. After the introductory formula in v. 7, presuming also that ואין שמלה (and no robe) has been removed, the response is to be understood as having the form of a five-stress colon and a four-stress colon, with syncope (the elimination of a letter, here the article) on the final word, which helps to mark the end of a section. In vv. 8 and 9aα (after eliminating כסדם, like Sodom, in 9), there are 3 more five-stress cola, after which v. 9aβ ends with a two-stress colon to bring this section to a close, reckoning, of course, with the possibility that the original ending might have been lost. The meter of the verses corresponds logically, once again, to the division of the section based on its content. Verse 9b: an inverted five-stress colon? Verses 10f., as is common in wisdom sayings, are composed of three-stress bicola.

Setting

There is no basis for Kaiser's conjecture that Isaiah spoke this message to an assembly of upper-level advisers in the king's palace or else at an opportune moment at an assembly gathering devoted to worship. There is virtually no evidence to support the contention that the message is specifically addressed to the senior advisers. According to v. 5, it is more likely that all levels of the society are equally culpable, most particularly those who see deliverance coming through revolution. They have to realize that casting off the present authorities will not lead to better national order, but rather to a nationwide chaos.

It is also not possible to determine the actual historical situation. We do not learn about the precise way in which Yahweh will remove "support and staff" from Judah and Jerusalem. It is highly unlikely that Isaiah is thinking of a foreign enemy (thus Fohrer, among others), since wherever the Assyrians vigorously seized control—and they are the only ones who could be meant in such a situation—there was no chaos as a result, but rather there was a *pax Assyria,* with iron-fisted control, and thus there was absolutely no chance while under them to initiate a rebellion. Therefore, Isaiah must be announcing an overthrow being plotted internally. That would probably have been during a time when the Assyrian threat was not yet acute. Probably the most likely time period would be during the reign of the weakling Ahaz.

Except for the additions and glosses which have been mentioned, the message is from Isaiah himself. That assessment also applies to the enumeration of the various honored leaders in vv. 2f. (contra Gray); cf. similar listings in 2:7, 8a or 3:13–16. Finally, Isaiah is fond of sketching out little scenes, like the one in vv. 6f., to illustrate the point he is trying to make; cf. passages like 4:1. "With this illustration, full of potent power, sketched out in broad strokes, one has once again an early example of the efforts of the young prophet, which indicates already then that a master is at work" (Procksch, ad loc.).

Commentary

[3:1] כִּי (for) provides the redactional connection which links this new section to chap. 2, most specifically to v. 22aβb, which speaks of the powerlessness of human beings. The attention-getting presentative interjection הנה (behold) is often used to introduce threats (see J. Blau, *VT* 9 [1959] 130–137); the designation "prediction with a presentative" has been suggested (K. Koch, *The Growth of the Biblical Tradition, The Form-Critical Method* [1969] 212). Normally one would use the first person for this: הנני (Behold, I), but Isaiah likes to use the third person; see 8:7: הנה אדני (Behold, the Lord); 10:33, as 3:1, uses הנה האדון יהוה צבאות (Behold, the Lord, Yahweh of Hosts), and 28:2 uses הנה חזק ואמץ לאדני (Behold, the Lord has one who is mighty and strong) (or, according to some other MSS, ליהוה [Yahweh]). The use of the presentative is very effective: The listener is supposed to see clearly what is coming, as if it were happening at that very moment. Concerning האדון יהוה צבאות (the Lord, Yahweh of Hosts), see above, commentary on 1:24a; concerning the word pair in the order "Jerusalem and Judah," see above, on the setting of 1:1. The bland term מסיר (take away) does not give any indication about the way in which the disintegration of the "supports" will take place. But that is inconsequential: No matter who swings into action, the actual main character in this history is Yahweh. One ought not think that God will interfere directly in historical events in some sort of miraculous way, since, according to Isaiah's understanding of history, Yahweh makes use of earthly powers when seeking to achieve his purposes. מַשְׁעֵן (support) is found only here in the OT, along with two instances of מִשְׁעָן (support) in a metaphorical sense (about Yahweh). The feminine form מַשְׁעֵנָה (support) is used only in the combination found here; it is, in fact, constructed solely to make this pair of words (P. Saydon, *Bib* 36 [1955] 38f.). Otherwise, only the מִשְׁעֶנֶת form of the feminine is used, which refers to the actual staff upon which one leans (Exod. 21:19; 2 Kings 18:21 = Isa. 36:6; Ezek. 29:6). It can serve as the emblem of honor accorded a leader (Num. 21:18), does serve shepherds who lean on it as they watch over their flocks (Ps. 23:4), and can be of help to the invalid and to the old man, who leans on it for help when it is harder for him to get around

128

(Zech. 8:4). The adjutant of the king actually carries the title "the captain on whose hand the king leans" (2 Kings 7:2, 17; cf. 5:18). In Israel, there was a belief that one could receive all the support one needed from the political powers (Isa. 10:20) or from military aid (31:1, and often elsewhere), whereas one ought to have been relying only on God (Mic. 3:11; Isa. 50:10, and often elsewhere). נשען על יהוה (support oneself on Yahweh) is virtually a parallel term for האמין (believe) (Isa. 10:20). This word usage is to be kept in mind when one seeks to explain the full meaning of the phraseology which Isaiah uses: Instead of letting Yahweh be the "support," security is sought in the protection offered by human authorities.

[3:2, 3] As these "supports" are enumerated, one quickly notices that the king and the priest are not mentioned, which cannot be accidental, since the passage seems to be an attempt to give a comprehensive listing, not just selected examples. For Isaiah, it is certain that God legitimatized the king and that kingship had a definite role to play in Yahweh's plan for history, even if some of those filling that position failed to live up to expectations. In the same way, Micah (see 3:9ff.) and Zephaniah (see 1:4ff.; 3:1ff.) do not directly attack the king in Jerusalem. Along with other prophets, Isaiah was able, of course, to issue a sharp condemnation of the priests (28:7). As to the persons mentioned in the list, one might pose the question whether the enumeration of these honored leaders suggests that they held clearly defined offices and/or functioned in specific positions or whether they were men who were able to have a certain influence because of the way they personally appeared to others or because of a special charisma which they possessed. Apparently, in this list, there is room for some who would fit each category.

Concerning the parallel use of גבור (champion) and איש מלחמה (man of war), cf. Ezek. 39:20; Joel 2:7; 4:9. Are these two terms exact synonyms? גבור is clearly a technical term here, used when describing a mercenary force, whose chief function was to serve as a bodyguard for the king; see 2 Sam. 23:8f., and, on this point, de Vaux, op. cit., 220. איש מלחמה seems, in some places, to apply to those who are part of the conscripted troops (Judg. 20:17; cf., in addition, Num. 31:28, 49; Deut. 2:14–16, and often elsewhere), but in other situations it refers to men who were trained for hand-to-hand combat in war (1 Sam. 16:18; 17:33; 2 Sam. 8:10; 17:8). Concerning שופט (judge), one can consult what was said above, p. 70, on 1:26 (see also de Vaux, op. cit., 152ff.); concerning נביא (prophet), see above, p. 6. Even though the שופט (judge) was indeed an official, it is still a disputed matter whether the נביא (prophet) is also named as the holder of an office. Along with many others, Fohrer (ad loc.) agrees that it is an official post, citing 1 Kings 22. One must certainly take that passage into account; on this, see A. R. Johnson, *The Cultic Prophet in Ancient Israel* (1962²); for a different view, de Vaux, op. cit., 454ff.; in addition, see the very judicious study by O. Plöger, "Priester und Prophet," *ZAW* 63 (1951) 157–192. That does not mean, in fact it likely excludes the possibility, that Isaiah had been a cultic official. When assessing the function of the נביא (prophet), one notes that the קסם (conjurer) is mentioned immediately afterwards; see above, pp. 105f., on 2:6, and cf., in addition, Mic. 3:6f. and most importantly, 3:11, where the נביא (prophet) is assigned the tasks normally ascribed to the קסם (conjurer) (see also Deut. 18:14f.; Ezek. 13:9, 23; 21:26, 28, 34; 22:28). One can purchase the services of a קֹסֵם (conjurer) by offering remuneration, which is what happens, for example, in the case of Balaam, who is designated a קוֹסֵם (soothsayer) in Josh. 13:22. Prophets were also accused of doing what they did so that they could make money (Mic. 3:11; Amos 7:12). Even if the נביא (prophet) was originally an ecstatic and the קסם (conjurer) was a person skilled in interpreting oracles, it is still true that both of these functions blended together, thus becoming interchangeable as designations for persons and functions.

Next comes the mention of the elder of the clan, the זקן; on this, see de Vaux, op. cit., 138, and McKenzie and van der Ploeg, both op. cit. The word order is most interesting: van der Ploeg (op. cit., 181) suspects the terms are arranged this way because a chiasm is intended, in the sense that judges and elders, prophet and diviner would each be linked. There is no doubt about the change in the meaning of the term "elder," originally a designation for the leader of the clan. During the era when kings were ruling, when the people of Israel, by and large, lived in cities, there was a change in usage, certainly also in the capital city Jerusalem. The social structure of the clans fell apart, *"les anciens deviennent les hommes importants."* One would seek out their advice. On the basis of their achievements and their influence, they could expect to be treated with deference as a respectable, moral authority (van der Ploeg, op. cit., 185, 190f.). On the other hand, frequent complaints about matters of justice show that the elders did not always function at the level of maturity which their position demanded. They became rich landowners and, as such, are themselves mentioned in the laments which complain about the mistreatment of very unimportant people. They are no longer the representatives of the people, but rather, they have become advocates of their own private interests (cf. McKenzie, op. cit., 538f.).

שר־חמשים (captain) also designated a military grade in the Northern Kingdom, as is seen in 2 Kings 1:9. The "captain over fifty" serves as a general designation for anyone in the officer's corps (cf. 1 Sam. 8:12; שר הצבא, commander of the army, in 1 Sam. 17:55; שר־האלף, commander of the thousand, in 1 Sam. 17:18; שרי אלפים, ruler of thousands, as well as מאות, of hundreds, חמשים, of fifties, עשרת, of tens, in Exod. 18:21), a person who, by the very nature of his position, needed to keep in close touch with the palace. Kaiser thinks it is possible that one of the duties of the שר חמשים (captain) involved judicial decisions, which would explain why he was mentioned as one of the civilian dignitaries. The נשוא פנים, "the favorite friends," were just as closely tied to the king as the officers. In fact, Fohrer translates the term here as "court official" (cf. 2 Kings 5:1, where Naaman, the שר־צבא [commander of the army], is described as נשא פנים [in high favor]). In Isa. 9:14, such a person is mentioned along with the elders; in Job 22:8, the favored man is named in parallel with איש זרוע (man with power). Concerning the term יועץ (counselor), see above, p. 71, on 1:26. After these honored ones, the חכם (wise one) could be mentioned all alone, without any words following. One would obviously seek out advisers among the circles of the wise; cf. Isa. 19:11: פרעה חכמי יעצי (wise counselors of Pharaoh). Because of this fact, "conjurer" (see textual note, 3b) is a very fitting parallel to נבון לחש, "those who are proclaimers of incantations." In fact, these two terms are synonyms. Of course, this does not refer here to personnel who served in an official capacity. These are men, just like the "soothsayers" and "enchanters" in 2:6, who were very influential, even though they were treated as suspect by those who served in official religious capacities, men who would not have always performed their ritual activities out in the open. Just like the Hebrew לחש, the Akkadian *luḫḫušu* essentially means "whisper," but it later took on the connotation of "conjure"; see A. van den Branden, "La tavoletta magica di Arslan Tash," *BeO* 3 (1961) 41–47, and B. Meissner, *Babylonien und Assyrien,* II (1925) 208; see, in addition, for example, the great Shamash-Hymn, line 131 (Falkenstein-von Soden, *Sumerische und Akkadische Hymnen und Gebete* [1953] 245); H. Zimmern, *Akkadische Fremdwörter* (1917²) 67. Jer. 8:17; Ps. 58:6; Qoh. 10:11; and Sir. 12:13 demonstrate that there was snake-charming, so that the מלחשים (charmers) are mentioned in the passage from the Psalms parallel to the חובר חברים מחכם (cunning one, enchanter); he is the one who is being taught how to put people under a spell. Charming snakes was a well-known activity everywhere in the region around Israel. Ps. 58:5 helps us recognize that one would go directly against one's enemies with powerful curse-formulas and/or curse-words (see H. J. Kraus, *Psalmen,* BK XV/1, ad loc. [Engl: *Psalms 1–59,* 536]), and "enemies" in the Psalms seem occasionally to have been this type of "enchanter" (Pss. 10:7ff.; 41:8; 59:13).

It is a rather attractive list of "supports" presented by Isaiah: officials and "charismatics," governmental and religious functionaries, those who held necessary and recognized positions of responsibility in the state and the society, along with those who used outlawed practices. Legitimate functions could also be mishandled, in which case those responsible would themselves be undermining their own position.

[3:4] The punishment which Yahweh is ordaining for his people involves God delivering Jerusalem/Judah up to political and social chaos, and this is characteristic of Isaiah's viewpoint that justice would take place within history. Whenever one does not take one's authority seriously while functioning in an office or while using a charismatic gift, or when someone seizes authority without having been legally assigned such responsibility, the unavoidable consequence would be anarchy, leading to destruction. Lads (נערים) would become princes (concerning שרים, see above, pp. 65f., on 1:23). נער (lad, young boy) is a comprehensive term and thus has many meanings. H. W. Weil (op. cit., 78) tries to use Gen. 14:24; 18:7; 37:2; Exod. 33:11, and often elsewhere, to arrive at the meaning "serfs, gens" (bondman, servant), which would, at this point, be in direct contrast to the שרים (princes). But, in v. 5b, youngster is used opposite זקן (oldster), and there is no doubt that it should be taken in v. 4 in the same way: The נער (lad) is one who does not yet have the strength and experience of a mature man (see Judg. 8:20; 1 Sam. 17:33; 1 Kings 3:7; Jer. 1:6f.). In Isa. 66:4, the parallel word תעלולים means "mistreatment," but that meaning would not fit here. On the basis of the *hithpaʿel* of עלל I, which means "force his mischievousness on someone, deal in an evil way with someone," it ought to be translated with a word like "mischievousness." It is possibly used as an adverbial accusative; however, based on the parallelism, it is more likely a subject, in this case taken as an *abstractum pro concreto* (Ges-K §83c): mischievous, raw types, who will deal in an evil way with their fellow citizens. But the "hoods" are only exposing the basic attitude about life which has taken hold of all the people: Everyone wants to rule over everyone else.

[3:5] The נֹגֵשׂ is a tyrant and taskmaster (Isa. 14:2, 4; Exod. 3:7; 5:6, and often elsewhere), but נגשׂ also means "exact payment" (2 Kings 23:35, and often elsewhere), "put pressure on a debtor." Even in this passage one should keep in mind that the word can have a great variety of meanings: Reckless use of power takes many different forms (for another view, Weil, op. cit., 79, who translates: "*la nation sera corveable*," a nation will be subject to forced labor). When battles are described, mention is sometimes made of the enemies being so utterly mixed up when attacked by surprise that they themselves kill each other (Judg. 7:22; 1 Sam. 14:20). In a similar way, those who belong to Israel shove each other into this judgment scene before God. The tension between generations is even more acute when every level of authority breaks down, leading up to a rebellion by the younger ones (v. 5bα), when tensions between various classes lead to a rebellion by the have-nots (v. 5bβ). קלה in the *niph'al* is normally translated "be scornful." And yet, in 1 Sam. 18:23, נקלה (of no repute) is used with רשׁ, "poor man" (cf. also Prov. 12:9). In the same way, with נכבד (honored), one must consider that, among the possibilities, כָּבוֹד can also mean "possessions" and "riches," and, with reference to ירהבו (let loose against), the chaos monster in the OT is frequently called רהב (Rahab) (cf. 30:7, and often elsewhere): If the "supports" for order fall away, the powers of chaos find room to operate.

[3:6] A unique description follows in v. 6 to clarify the desperate situation. The rabble, shocked by the deterioration of order, seeks someone who would be available to reestablish the order that has broken down. In their perplexity, they put pressure on someone, who at least still has a cloak, to take the job. The chosen one is seized in his father's house; this means that order in one's own family group is still intact; at the very least, such a person would find strength for the task in having "authority in one's own home." Even to this day in the Near East, it is a hopeless situation, if one wants to be involved in political leadership, if one does not have the backing of one's own clan. Marti wants to take שׂמלה (robe) as a reference to an "official cloak," a garment passed down in one's own family. But שׂמלה (robe) is never used in this special sense in the OT; it means (just as שׁלמה) simply "overgarment, covering." During the hubbub of the revolt, virtually everything would have been lost and there is an advantage in at least still owning a coat. Part of being installed into an office involves having a corresponding garment, so the wrap does symbolize the robe of a ruler. It might be visualized as decorated with braiding and fringes (see H. W. Hönig, "Die Bekleidung des Hebräers," diss., Zurich [1957] passim; in addition, *AOB²* illus. no. 125; *BRL* 335; G. E. Wright, *Biblical Archaeology* [1962] 190ff.). The indicative קצין תהיה־לנו (you shall be our leader) is stronger than either an imperative or a jussive: It is a categorical command, symbolic of how precarious the situation had become no matter where one went. Concerning קצין (leader), see above, commentary on 1:10. The irony in the offer, "This heap of rubble over here is to be under your hand," is a stylistic trait which Isaiah likes to use (see H. W. Wolff, *Das Zitat im Prophetenspruch* [1937] 60ff. = *GesStud* 83ff.). מכשלה (heap of rubble) is used here metaphorically: "over this political debacle, in the middle of this general confusion."

[3:7] The response is just as categorical: "I do not want to be a doctor for wounds." נשׂא (raise, lift) is used as a pregnant expression for נשׂא קול (cry out, raise one's voice), as also in 42:2 and Num. 14:1 (there next to נתן קול, raise one's voice). The verb reflects the agitation of the moment: One shouts something out, the other one, who has been singled out, shouts back vehemently in a verbal defense of himself. חבש can mean "bind"; cf. 1:6; 30:26 (חבש את־שׁבר עמו, bind up the hurt of his people, is parallel to רפא מחץ מכתו, heal the wounds inflicted by his blow); 61:1; Hos. 6:1; Job 5:18; Ezek. 30:21; 34:4, 16; the last passage cited shows that "bind" is part of a shepherd's responsibility and thus, it can describe the way in which the leader would act symbolically as a shepherd. It is not possible, based on Exod. 29:9, that it means here: "to bind on a turban" (so Kaiser, according to Gk: חֹבֵשׁ = ἀρχηγός, founder, chief; on this, see Ziegler, op. cit., 137), since, in this case, the object being bound on cannot be left unmentioned. Concerning the duties of the doctor, see above, p. 27, on 1:6. It might appear strange in this context that the unwilling candidate would add: "In my house there's no bread," but this is quite understandable under the circumstances: The masses expect, more than anything else, in the condition in which they find themselves as they demand a leader, that he will be able to guarantee them the basic necessities of life. Concerning ביום ההוא (on that day), see above, pp. 118f., on 2:17.

[3:8, 9a] When stating the reason for the threat, Isaiah uses כשׁל (heaps of rubble), connecting it with the just-mentioned מכשלה (heaps of rubble), which explains our rather free translation. Jerusalem/Judah is actually just like a pile of rubble, even if its condition is very different from what the thronging masses in the streets—who are truly in trouble—might imagine; in truth, Jerusalem/Judah is in its present condition because the people are in revolt against Yahweh. Not only do the people act (on מעלל, deeds, see above, commentary on 1:16f.), but also, and primarily, they use their tongues to speak against Yahweh; cf. Jer. 9:7; Mic. 6:12; Zeph. 3:13; Isa. 59:3, and often elsewhere. All of these passages condemn lies, whereas, in the present verse, one must consider that reference is being made to ways of speaking which undermine confidence in Yahweh. Verse 8bβ describes the negative tone explicitly: "they defy [the eyes of] his majesty." Concerning מרה (defy), see above, commentary on 1:19f. (the *hiph'il* has the same meaning). In deuteronomic speech, המרה (rebel) is virtually a technical term used to describe the rebelliousness of Israel, even in light of God's saving deeds (see also Ps. 78:17, 40, 56, and often elsewhere). But Isaiah does not make use of the formula המרה את־פי יהוה (rebel against the command of Yahweh), so common in that literature (Deut. 1:26, 43, and often elsewhere); here it involves—if the textual correction is right—not a refusal to fulfill a command or the commandments (משׁפטים, ordinances, Ezek. 5:6), but rather a removal of one's trust in God (ב המרה, rebel against, is used explicitly about going against

Yahweh in Ezek. 20:8, 13, 21; cf. also Ezekiel's oft-used formula בית מרי, rebellious house). The name of God used in v. 8bα is used parallel to כבודו (his majesty) in 8bβ. Of course, these are two variations of the same idea: Defiance of Yahweh's כבוד (majesty) is defiance of Yahweh himself. And yet, the use of this expression in the present context is not by chance: "כָּבוֹד is, by and large, that asset which makes peoples or individuals, and even objects, impressive, and usually this is understood as something that can be perceived or expressed" (von Rad, *OTTheol* I, 239). The word is practically a technical term in descriptions of theophanies; cf. its use already in Pss. 29:9; 97:1ff. Even if Yahweh himself remains hidden, his כבוד (majesty, glory) is still recognizable; in fact, the whole earth is filled with his "glory" (see 6:3). But defiance of Yahweh is immediately realized in one's relationship with others in the community. To give a concrete example, Isaiah mentions הכרת פניהם, the people's "sizing up a person," which means, their choosing up sides, what the NT calls προσωπολημψία (partiality); see above, textual note 9a–a. Deut. 1:17 makes it very clear what is condemned when using the phrase הכיר פנים (regard of the person) (as is also the case with נשא פ״, lift the face): "you shall hear the small and the great alike (in judgment); you shall not be afraid of the face of man; for the judgment is God's"; cf. also 16:18ff. The admonition to be totally impartial has its roots in the arena of the paranesis to be found in wisdom teaching (cf. Prov. 24:23ff.; 28:21, but also 18:5; 17:15, and also Isa. 5:23, and often elsewhere). Concerning wisdom outside the context of Israel, see F. W. von Bissing, *Altägyptische Lebensweisheit* (1955) 54f., 87.

The second specific accusation is about the way the people shamelessly call public attention to their sins (sing.!; see textual note 9b and above, commentary on 1:4), which are committed out in the open, an absolutely unique observation within the entire OT, showing Isaiah as a reflective observer. By means of לא כחד (they do not conceal them), it is noted that they are completely unrestrained when it comes to hanging out their own dirty linen. כסדם (like Sodom) is a marginal note, written by someone reading this, who felt compelled to put into words how this phrase of Isaiah's reminded that person of "the shameless way in which the Sodomites had the urge to overpower outsiders" (Duhm).

[3:9b] The woe-oracle in v. 9b fits in rather well as a closing comment to what has just been described in detail. Evil comes back upon the one who perpetrates it. Just as woe-oracles have their original setting in life in the wisdom passed down in the ethic of the clan (see E. Gerstenberger, "The Woe-Oracles of the Prophets," *JBL* 81 [1962] 249–263), so also, it is part of the special teaching of wisdom that evil comes back to get the one who committed the evil: "A man who is kind benefits himself (גמל נפשו איש חסד), but a cruel man hurts himself" (Prov. 11:17).

[3:10, 11] It is just as clear that vv. 10f. come from a wisdom context. The woe-oracle is the reverse of the salvation oracle, introduced by אשרי (blessed), having developed in the pedagogy of the clans along with the הוי (woe) or אוי (woe) sayings (H. W. Wolff, *Amos' geistige Heimat*, WMANT 18 [1964] 18ff.). More importantly, the content of the saying—that it goes well for the righteous, but goes badly for the wicked—points back to a wisdom context. Each reaps what each has sown; there is a close connection between a particular action and one's destiny (cf. U. Skladny, *Die ältesten Spruchsammlungen in Israel* [1962] 41: "action-consequences connections"). This corresponds to the order in the world as God established it. But it is significant that such sayings do not speak of a retribution which will be set in motion by the action of Yahweh; instead, it happens by means of a basic system built into the ethical structure of the world. Based on its content, v. 10 is very similar to Ps. 128:2, where it is said, not to the righteous, but to those who fear Yahweh: יְגִיעַ כַּפֶּיךָ כִּי תֹאכֵל אַשְׁרֶיךָ וְטוֹב לָךְ (You shall eat the fruit of the labor of your hands; you shall be happy, and it shall be well with you); cf., in addition, Prov. 16:20; 28:14. Moreover, v. 11 has just as close a parallel in Prov. 12:14: מִפְּרִי פִי־ אִישׁ יִשְׂבַּע גְּמוּל יְדֵי־אָדָם יָשׁוּב לוֹ (From the fruit of his words a man is satisfied with good, and the work of a man's hand comes back to him) (emended text, see BHK³). The contrasting characterizations of the צדיק (righteous) and the רשע (wicked) can be explained by the wisdom teacher using typical examples of human life experience in his pedagogy, without going into the gray areas of actual life (on this, see Skladny again, op. cit., 7ff.). In terms of content, vv. 10f. fit well with v. 9b, and linking the catchwords (גמול–גמלו, pay back) provides a formal connection.

Purpose and Thrust

The breakdown of every form of authority in Jerusalem is announced in 3:1–7. This section makes its greatest impact when it describes the chaotic lack of order resulting from reckless mob rule. One ought not draw the conclusion that Isaiah comes from an allegedly conservative position and wants simply to get agreement that the revolution will finally turn against the very ones who started it. He is neither a conservative nor a revolutionary, but rather, he announces divine judgment. The central point of the kerygma of this section is made already in v. 1: Yahweh is removing support and staff. It is not anarchists who are behind it all, seeking to bring down legitimate order, but it is Yahweh who is at work, bringing down those in power, those who have swung away from a position of reliance upon him to serve "gods"; the section then is about a people which has raised up its own "idols." The people stumble when they place trust in a human system of offices and authorities, when all the time they should have been relying on God alone. Therefore, Yahweh has to set aside all of these alleged "supports for society" so that the people will then once again be forced to rely on him alone. It is not surprising that war heroes and soldiers are mentioned first, since military strength holds the greatest promise for guaranteeing one's security. And it is not by chance that conjurers and those who speak incantations come at the end of the list of authorities. Wherever the official leaders who are to keep order fail at their task, practices surface which would otherwise shun the light of day. But judges, prophets, and honored people are also mentioned, the leading individuals, who could indeed serve the best interests of the people if they would carry out the responsibilities of their office, if they would let themselves be guided by Yahweh's will. Wherever Yahweh's rule is not acknowledged, wherever one defies his majestic presence (v. 8), even if it happens in the offices of those responsible for the city, where one finds those who are supposed to preserve justice and are supposed to be concerned about freedom (in the full sense of the Hebrew

שָׁלוֹם, *shalom,* wholeness, peace), where one finds those who have the ability to act to bring blessing, it is precisely there that these offices would be destroyed from within and finally would disappear completely, so that even the formal offices themselves would cease to exist. The chaotic downfall is thus God's judgment; the situation cannot be saved by a last-ditch effort, in the final hours, with an attempt to establish some provisional government; rather, what is called for is essentially a brand new orientation, going back toward Yahweh.

The additions seek to provide a deeper basis for the prophet's threats by reference to the basic viewpoints already found in wisdom. They point out the way in which the messages of the prophets were taken to be concrete examples of the insights of wisdom and that such messages were to be passed along, to teach a lesson. But in doing this, of course, the careful observations which Isaiah made, with such attention to detail, were now laid into a Procrustean bed of dogmatic theory. The prophet himself did not want to report some general experiences about life; instead, he was speaking about what was to happen to those who were in power at that very time, based on his judgment that a complete break-down had to take place. Although it would have been entirely possible for Isaiah to make use of the insights from wisdom to aid in his prophetic proclamation, that does not happen here; rather, here, the prophetic message has been further substantiated with proof-texts someone else inserted from wisdom. On the other hand, the section does rework some material from wisdom: The "righteous one" in a wisdom context is defined by this present context as the one who relies upon Yahweh, just as the "wicked one" is one whose speech and actions are against Yahweh (v. 8). This means that, instead of the general concept of order, as in wisdom, a living relationship is described—a relationship with the one who is the sovereign lord who maintains all order.

Isaiah 3:12

Lament for the People of God

Literature

[**Literature update through 1979:** C. H. Yalon, "Zu Jes 3,12 und 4,5," *BetM* 12 (1966/67) 3–5.]

Text

3:12 O, my people! [a]Its tyrants are 'people fleecers,'
    and 'extortioners'[a] rule over it.
O, my people! Your leaders are misleaders,
    and the path on which you ought to go, they mess it up.

12a–a The main reason for the uncertainty about the meaning of this verse is the word מְעוֹלֵל. Some derive this word from עול II and base the meaning of the passage on a connection with עוֹלֵל, "child." Others refer to עלל I, to which they assign the meaning "play," which could also lead to the translation "kid, rogue." And yet, the meaning of the *po'lel* participle of this root is closer to something like "do evil to someone." Based on תעלולים (mischievousness) in v. 4, this would seem to be the most likely meaning. G. R. Driver (*JTS* 38 [1937] 38) tries to establish the meaning using the Arabic *'âla*, "inclined to one side, deviated from justice" (cf. עול I in the *pi'el*, "handle unfairly"). Since the singular מְעוֹלֵל (people fleecer) is not actually congruent with נגשיו (its tyrants), the plural ought to be read. On this same point, one ought not alter נגשיו (its tyrants) to read נגשיך (your tyrants) in order to have an exact correspondence with the suffixes in v. 12b, since the third person is shown to be correct by the use of בו (it) at the end of the line. נָשִׁים, "women, wives," would be no problem if one would translate מְעוֹלֵל with "kid, rogue" or something similar. But if one translates this word with "oppressor" or a word close to that, then one ought to consider whether the word ought to be pointed נֹשִׁים, "creditor, profiteer." This emendation is supported by the Gk: καὶ οἱ ἀπαιτοῦντες κυριεύουσιν ὑμῶν: "and the creditors will rule over you" ('Aquila also reads ἀπαιτουντες, demanding payment; Theod reads a nearly synonymous word: δανεισται, lend money at interest). An assured solution is not possible. When one takes all the possibilities into account, it seems best to read: נֹגְשָׂיו מְעוֹלְלִים (or עוֹלְלוּ) וְנֹשִׁים מָשְׁלוּ בוֹ (its tyrants are people fleecers [or, fleece people], and extortioners rule over it), a reading which has support from Gk and Targ (מרי חובא, creditors).

Form

Verse 12 is a fragment; as is obvious from the difference in the suffixes in vv. 12a and 12b, it is composed from two originally independent sentences. One runs into a problem in trying to connect this with either what immediately precedes or what immediately follows, because it is clear that Yahweh himself speaks here, and yet he does not raise an accusation, as in vv. 14f. Instead, he laments about the people. Thematically, this section fits very well into the context of chap. 3, and the connecting links formed by the use of key words are to be found here once again (נגשׂיו [its tyrants] in v. 12a and ונגשׂ [tyrant] in v. 5; מעולל [people fleecers] and משׂלו [rule over] in v. 12a with תעלולים [mischievousness] and משׂל [rule over] in v. 4b; עמי [my people] in vv. 12a,b and 15). This shows how the redactor arranged this, but ought not lead one to the false conclusion that vv. 1–15 are to be considered one unit. In the present context, this message is intended to provide the reason for the judgment proceedings which follow (vv. 13–15).

Meter: 2 three-stress bicola.

Setting

It is generally presumed that Isaiah is responsible for this verse. Its theme matches up with Isaiah's early period. If one dates this passage in this way, one would have difficulty translating מעולל as "child," seeking to interpret it with reference to the king. Neither Jotham nor Ahaz was a child when he ascended the throne, which would mean one would have to consider that the word might refer to Hezekiah. But one must note, in addition, that נגשׂ (tyrant) is never used to describe any of the kings of Israel or Judah, another reason for staying with this present interpretation of the text (contra Fohrer).

Commentary

[3:12a] Yahweh's lamenting about the people proves that he considers himself bound to them in spite of everything. Whereas Isaiah often speaks in other places about "this people," in the present lament he refers to them, just as in the accusation which he raises up against their oppressors, as "my people" (cf. also "his people" in vv. 13f.). In spite of all the faithlessness of Israel, the cord which binds Yahweh to his people is not severed. נגשׂ (tyrant), which can describe many different aspects of life under a brutal ruler or authority, is used again in the parallel colon, along with נשׂים (extortioners). A creditor is consistently viewed in a negative way in the OT, which means such a person is considered a profiteer (see Exod. 22:24; Ps. 109:11), insofar as he demands interest from someone who owes him money, contrary to Israelite law; in that situation the people who had very little came more and more to be at the mercy of the powerful moneylenders.

[3:12b] Concerning אשׂר (leader), see above, p. 36, on 1:17. This saying is quoted here because it also speaks about the downfall of the leaders. A מאשׂר is, of course, a leader in a different sense than that of a political ruler or an economic magnate. He knows the way (cf. ארח, path, and דרך, way you should go, as used with אשר, leader; see also Prov. 4:14; 23:19, and cf. Sir. 4:18); this means that the מאשרים are the learned, the teachers, the advisers, those upon whom one would normally rely for guidance. But they have become the ones who have led others astray. One leads others astray (התעה) when one quits acting in a disciplined manner (Prov. 10:17; cf. 12:26) or when one takes away the "heart" of another (Job 12:24f.). The prophets can also lead the people astray (Mic. 3:5; Jer. 23:13, 32; cf. Hos. 4:12, and often elsewhere).

The rare word בלע III (mess it up, confuse) is used in a similar way on four occasions (see, besides this, 9:15; 19:3; 28:7). One can confuse advice (19:3), the tongue (Ps. 55:10), wisdom (Ps. 107:27). According to Isa. 28:7, the priests and prophets allow themselves to be confused with wine and intoxicating drinks (parallel to תעה [mislead, stagger], also there). It is likely also here that spiritual leaders are being accused of not fulfilling their duties; this is not a sufficient reason for denying that this passage comes from Isaiah (contra Marti). And yet, the content of v. 12b also indicates that this half-verse was combined with v. 12a only at a later time. One realizes that such secondary combinations must be taken into account when one notes that this verse is found, almost verbatim, in 9:15. Concerning דרך (way) and ארח (path), see above, p. 91, on 2:3.

Purpose and Thrust

These two lines show, in a new way, that Isaiah is a harsh critic of those who are in leadership positions, whether they be leaders in economic or spiritual-religious matters. What is new here, when compared with the preceding passage, is how clearly the message comes through that Yahweh suffers with this confused and misguided people, which must suffer because of the unscrupulousness of its leaders.

Yahweh's Accusation

Literature

For literature on the Rîb-pattern, see above, pp. 8, 10f.

[**Literature update through 1979:** H. W. Hoffmann, *Die Intention der Verkündigung Jesajas*, BZAW 136 (1974) 82ff. H. W. F. Saggs, "'External Souls' in the OT," *JSS* 19 (1974) 1–12.]

Text

3:13 Yahweh takes his place for a lawsuit,
   stands there, in order to pronounce judgment upon 'his
      people.'[a]
14 Yahweh comes to the judgment proceedings
   with the elders and leaders of his people:
Truly, *you* have grazed the vineyard bare,
   filled your houses with what you have robbed from the poor!
15 What will happen to you![a] You mercilessly destroy my people,
   and you crush the face of the poor!
[b]it is [from the Lord], Yahweh of Hosts, an utterance.[b]

13a For עמים (peoples), Gk reads τὸν λαὸν αὐτοῦ (his people), Syr *le'ammeh* (to his people). H. D. Hummel (*JBL* 76 [1957] 100) suggests reading עמו־ם (his people) (with an enclitic *mem;* see above, p. 19, on 1:6), which is possible but very difficult to substantiate. If one leaves the MT as is, this would have to be translated "tribes," and evidence for such a meaning for עם can hardly be found; the text of Deut. 33:3 is not reliable and does not provide conclusive evidence for such a meaning. עמים can indeed mean "companions within a tribal unit," but not "tribes" (contra Gesenius, Ewald, Duhm, and others; see also Eichrodt). In addition to this, v. 14 uses the singular of עם (people). Tur-Sinai's suggestion (op. cit. [in literature on 1:1] 162) that one point this as עִמָּם (with them) is hardly likely, since then the suffix would be left hanging in the air without any referent. F. Hesse (*ZAW* 65 [1953] 48) thinks that Isaiah speaks here in the same way as one of the cultic prophets, among whose duties was the responsibility for uttering accusations against other peoples in the name of Yahweh. One would have expected that Isaiah was going to speak out against Israel's enemies and would have been most surprised when it was noticed that Isaiah was departing from the usual pattern.

140

But Isaiah also uses the format of a judgment speech of Yahweh against Israel in another accusation (see above, pp. 9ff.), so that the easiest solution is found by reading עַמּוֹ (his people) on the basis of the Gk and Syr.

15a Concerning the asyndetic connection which links מלכם (Qere: מה־לכם, what will happen to you) with the following sentence, see BrSynt §133d.

15b–b This is missing in the Gk. Since Isaiah also uses the concluding formula נאם יהוה (utterance of Yahweh) (17:3, 6; 31:9; see also 30:1), there is no reason to remove it here. On the other hand, אדני (Lord), which is only secondarily inserted in Qᵃ above the word יהוה (Yahweh), ought to be removed.

Form

Verses 14b and 15 are a message from Yahweh, formulated as an accusation speech before a court of justice. It is said very explicitly in vv. 13 and 14a that Yahweh plans to hold a court session. ריב, usually translated "lawsuit," describes the entire judicial proceedings; דין, in this case, means "hold court, hold someone accountable," not as in 1:17, "help someone get justice," as is shown by the parallel in Ps. 50:4. משפט refers to the judgment proceedings, the "judicial action" (in 2 Sam. 15:4, the term means the same as ריב, lawsuit; see H. W. Hertzberg, *ZAW* 40 [1922] 269).

Meter: 4 three-stress bicola, brought to a conclusion with the closing formula (a three-stress colon).

Setting

There is no doubt that this comes from Isaiah. Concerning the question about the roots of the judgment speech in the cult, see above, pp. 10f., 54. Kaiser (ad loc.) presumes that Isaiah spoke this message at a covenant festival. But we know too little to say anything certain about that.

Commentary

[3:13] Yahweh has come forward so that he can hold court proceedings. The participants are seated (see L. Köhler, *Die hebräische Rechtsgemeinde,* Rektoratsrede, Zürich [1931] = *Der hebräische Mensch* [1953] 149), but when someone speaks, that person stands. Cf. the similar introduction in Ps. 82:1: אֱלֹהִים נִצָּב בַּעֲדַת־אֵל בְּקֶרֶב אֱלֹהִים יִשְׁפֹּט (God has taken his place in the divine council; in the midst of the gods he holds judgment), and also the frequent challenge to Yahweh to rise up and judge (Pss. 74:22; 82:8, and often elsewhere).

[3:14a] Concerning עמו (his people), cf. עמי (my people) in v. 12. A parallel for לדין עמו (in order to pronounce judgment upon his people) can already be found in Psalm 50, the "covenant festival psalm." Most importantly, Psalm 50 also speaks about the coming of Yahweh (v. 3); cf. also Job 9:32; Ps. 143:2. In 50:3 בוא, "the coming," is paraphrased as "shining forth" (הופיע), which is the technical term for a theophany of Yahweh (see Deut. 33:2 and cf. Pss. 80:2; 94:1, where the texts speak about Yahweh's coming to judge the peoples; cf. also Pss. 96:13; 98:9). One can clearly see that the traditio-historical background of vv. 13 and 14a is rooted in a cultic tradition which included speaking about Yahweh's appearance in judgment. The extent to which the tradition recorded here represents actual cultic activity can remain an open question at this point. It is enough simply to recognize that Isaiah makes use of a conceptual construct with which the people were familiar. Those listening to Isaiah were completely aware of the idea that Yahweh would act in judgment against Israel also, and not just against foreign nations. The general term עמו (his people), which is used in v. 13 in its traditional sense, is given further clarity in the paraphrase in v. 14, as זקני עמו ושריו (the elders and leaders of his people): Yahweh goes into judicial proceedings with those who have been entrusted, in a special way, with insuring the stability of the people. Concerning זקן (elders), see above, p. 130, on 3:2. The שרים (leaders) are practically identical with the זקנים (elders). The elders and leaders were charged with guiding the people, but were also in charge of judicial affairs; see above, pp. 65f., on 1:23; they are being brought under indictment because of the way they have handled these judicial affairs.

[3:14b, 15] Without any transition at all, Yahweh's accusation speech commences in v. 14b. The אתם (you), who are addressed, are members of that group which is assigned responsibility for judicial decisions. The ו (and) before אתם (you) also sharpens the point; here it means "truly, (you) ..." The way it is formulated suggests that the real cause for the threatening circumstances had been sought elsewhere: in the economic conditions, in natural catastrophes, in the disorder caused by wars, or some other such cause, maybe even God himself. This means that Isaiah presents the accusation speech of Yahweh in the form of a countersuit.

Only Israel, as the people of Yahweh, could be meant when he speaks of the "vineyard." Isaiah states this explicitly in the "song of the vineyard": "For the vineyard of Yahweh of Hosts is the house of Israel, and the men of Judah are the pleasant planting of his delight" (5:7). Even if this imagery is unique to Isaiah, it must still have been well-known to his contemporaries, since it can be used here without further clarification. Verses 5:1ff. illustrate the great amount of care which had to be provided for a vineyard in Palestine. Instead of the leaders of the people carefully cultivating the vineyard, Israel, they have "stripped it bare," earning the assessment that they were terrible shepherds (see Jer. 12:10).

The meaning of the *pi'el* בער, which is also used in 5:5 (cf. also 4:4 and 6:13), is still disputed. KBL suggests "burn down" for all four occurrences, but Ges-Buhl offers the meaning "devastate (strip bare?)." The Greek translators are also split: Gk: ἐνεπυρίσατε (you set on fire) (but in 5:5: לבער = εἰς διαρπαγήν, for plunder), 'Aquila: κατενεμήσασθε (you had assigned as pasture land), Sym: κατεβοσκήσατε (you have fed flocks); cf. Syr: 'awqedtûn (you have burned up), Targ: אנסתון ית עמי (you have oppressed my people), Vulg: *depasti estis* (it is eaten up, consumed). It is no surprise that most recent commentaries offer a variety of solutions. Procksch thinks that בער means "the vineyard has been picked clean, down to the very last grape, so that it is completely plundered." Hertzberg, Herntrich, Kaiser, Eichrodt: "strip bare"; Fohrer: "burn down"; Leslie: "devour"; Steinmann: "*dévaster*" (lay waste)! The similar expression in Jer. 12:10 (רעים רבים שחתו כרמי, many shepherds have destroyed my vineyard), and also in Exod. 22:4, clearly demands "strip bare" as the meaning.

The terrible "shepherds" rob the poor until there is nothing left.

What that means in concrete terms can be seen in passages like the invectives found in the contemporary prophet Micah (e.g., 2:1ff.; cf. also Isa. 5:8; the accusation about robbery is also found in Mic. 3:2; cf. Isa. 10:2). During the era when kings were ruling, an upper-level power structure gradually developed in the capital city, formed by officials who were capable of concentrating more and more economic control in their own group; at the same time the number of free and independent farmers continued to dwindle, which caused the growth of a lower-level of society made up of people who had no land holdings or who were indebted to and dependent upon these "lords" (cf., on this matter, A. Alt, "Der Anteil des Königtums an der sozialen Entwicklung in den Reichen Israel und Juda," *KlSchr* III [1959] 348–372; H. Donner, "Die soziale Botschaft der Propheten im Lichte der Gesellschaftsordnung in Israel," *OrAnt* 2 [1963] 229–245). The law expressly forbids that one should find a legal way to rob fellow citizens (Lev. 19:13; cf. Lev. 5:23, but also Ezek. 18:7ff.). Of course, even closer to Isaiah's formulation, there is an admonition in Prov. 22:22f.: אַל־תִּגְזָל־דָּל כִּי דַל־הוּא וְאַל־תְּדַכֵּא עָנִי בַשָּׁעַר: כִּי־יְהוָה יָרִיב רִיבָם (do not rob the poor, because he is poor, or crush the afflicted at the gate; for the Lord will plead their cause); it is exactly this same issue about which Amenemope also speaks (IV 4f., 18f.). The similarity in the way it is formulated leaves no room for doubt; the close agreement between these passages is not just by chance: When he speaks, Isaiah makes specific use of the exact wording of the teachings which were taught to the officials when they themselves were instructed in wisdom. In addition, this passage confirms that the elders and princes are addressed most magnificently as those whose function was to be guardians of justice. But the wisdom teaching has been recast into the form of a judicial accusation. For this type of accusation, a question introduced by מלכם (what will happen to you) or מה־לכם (what will happen to you) is typical (cf. Ps. 50:16). טחן, "grind," is not ever used again in this transferred sense, but it is characteristic of Isaiah's powerful and graphic style (on this, see A. Scheiber, *VT* 11 [1961] 455). It has the same meaning as דכא, "dash to pieces." Duhm (ad loc.) paraphrases as follows: "You grind up the downtrodden, as if between two millstones, with your powerful tactics and your judicial strategies." It is the responsibility of the king—and this would naturally apply to the elders and leaders—"to give deliverance to the needy and crush the oppressor" (Ps. 72:4), but in the lament song raised to Yahweh, to whom an appeal is made as the judge of the world to "shine forth" in judgment (see above), one hears the following reproach: "They [the godless] crush thy people" (Ps. 94:5). Concerning the concluding formula נאם־אדני יהוה צבאות (it is from the Lord, Yahweh of Hosts, an utterance), see above, pp. 66f.

The section closes with the accusation, just as the judgment speech in 1:2f. But it has correctly been pointed out that the way the accusation speech is put together, here as well as in similar cases, it is presumed that the accuser functions also as the judge. That was not impossible in ancient Israel, even in the secular realm, such as when the king, who was the accuser, also had the final word in the settlement of a judicial matter (1 Sam. 22:6–19; concerning this, see Boecker, *Redeformen des Rechtslebens im Alten Testament,* WMANT 14 [1964] 87ff.). There can be no further doubt about what Yahweh's judgment will be; the stolen belongings, which are now in the houses of those who are guilty, make it impossible to find a way to elude detection and culpability.

Purpose and Thrust

Judicial accusations are brought on the basis of clearly established, widely recognized norms. As it is, we have not discovered as much "the law" in this section, but rather, admonitions from wisdom teaching. It is worth noting that this very passage gives evidence that Israel had specific knowledge about the wisdom teachers who taught peoples who lived nearby and that insights from those teachers were adopted and used. Isaiah agreed with using this wisdom to set the standards for judging Israel's own actions, but he is not himself a wisdom teacher. He makes it abundantly clear that he has set the admonitions of wisdom into a theological framework. The poor person whom he defends is a member of the people of God. "Not breaking regulations as such, but violation of the demands of God would best describe the actual offense of the upper levels of the society" (Fey, *Amos and Isaiah,* WMANT 12 [1963], 63). Along with this, one ought to note that the people of God are almost identified, by use of the term, as the דלים (poor).

Against the Pride
of the Daughters of Zion

Literature

Concerning the list of jewelry and toiletry articles: S. Daiches, "Der Schmuck der Töchter Zions und die Tracht Ištars," *OLZ* 14 (1911) 390–391. J. P. Peters, "A Hebrew Folksong," *JBL* 33 (1914) 158–159. H. F. B. Compston, "Ladies' Finery in Isaiah III 18–23," *CQR* 103 (1926/27) 316–330. J. Ziegler, *Untersuchungen zur Septuaginta des Buches Isaias,* ATA XII/3 (1934) 203–212. H. W. Hönig, "Die Bekleidung des Hebräers," diss., Zürich (1957). A. van den Branden, "I gioielli delle donne di Gerusalemme secondo Isaia 3, 18–21," *BeO* 5 (1963) 87–94.

[**Literature update through 1979:** C. H. Yalon, "Erklärung einiger Schriftstellen," *BetM* 11 (1965/66) 17–20 (concerning 3:16 and 15:15). O. Loretz, "Kj 'Brandmal' in Jes 3,24," *UF* 8 (1976) 448.]

Text

3:16   [And Yahweh said:]
Because the daughters of Zion
   are so haughty
and come out forth[a] with neck outstretched[b]
   and send out[c] enticing looks with their eyes,
tripping pitter-patteringly back and forth[d]
   and jingling with their[e] foot bracelets,

17   therefore 'Yahweh'[a] will strip the crown of the head of the daughters of Zion,
and Yahweh will uncover their forehead.[b]

18   [On that day, 'Yahweh'[a] will take away the jewelry: the foot
19   bracelets, the little suns[b] and the little moons, • the lockets and the
20   arm bands and the veils, • the head bindings[a] and the little foot chains[b] and the breast wrappings[c] and the bosom coverings and
21,22   the magic amulets, • the finger rings and the nose rings, • the festival garments and the coats and the cloaks and the handbags,
23   • and the outer garments[a] and the vests and the turbans and the wrap-around shawls.
24   and so it will be:]

> Instead of salve, it will be rottenness
> > and instead of a belt, a rope
> and instead of artistically braided hair,[a] a bald head
> > and instead of a majestic robe,[b] a wrap-around sack.[c]
> [d]Truly, instead of beauty, 'humiliation.'[d]

16a Concerning the use of the imperfect consecutive, cf. Joüon, *Gr* §118p.

16b נטוות (outstretched): The Qere נטויות (outstretched) is most likely a secondary correction which adjusts the original form to the form which later became normative.

16c Some MSS and B are wrong when they read ומשקרות (deceiving; שׂ for שׁ).

16d Concerning the construction with two infinitive absolutes, see Ges-K §113s and u; its meaning: "they unceasingly go pitter-pattering back and forth."

16e Concerning the masculine suffix with the feminine meaning, cf. BrSynt §124b; Ges-K §135o.

17a Instead of אדני (Lord), many MSS read the original יהוה (Yahweh); in Qᵃ, יהוה is written in as a correction above אדני (Lord).

17b Concerning the suffix on פתהן (forehead), see Beer-Meyer §46, 2c.

18a Instead of אדני (Lord), יהוה (Yahweh) should be read here, a reading supported by many MSS. In Qᵃ, above יהוה (Yahweh), which is certainly correct, אדני (Lord) has been written in secondarily right above it.

18b Qᵃ reads: והשביסים (and the little suns), which is nothing more than a variant spelling style; cf. the Ugaritic *špš*, "sun."

20abc The vocables follow the order of the alphabet (Tur-Sinai, "A Contribution to the Understanding of Isaiah I–XII," *ScrHier* 8 [1961] 163); no discernible pattern can be found in the list of the decorative articles.

23a Read גְּלֹמִים (outer garments); for the reason behind this change, see below, pp. 154f.

24a The Syr did not take מעשה (artistically fashioned, done, made) into account, but this is not a sufficient reason for removing it.

24b פְּתִיגִיל (majestic robe) is certainly a loanword from an unknown source; attempts to translate it are thus based on the ancient translations, rendering it with "splendorous robe" or something similar. The emendation suggested by Tur-Sinai (op. cit., 163; see also *VT* 1 [1951] 307), which reads תֻּפֵּי גִיל as "joyous drums," fits very poorly into the context.

24c Literally: "wrapped around with a sack."

24d–d כִּי־תַחַת יפי (truly, instead of beauty) is missing in the Gk. If one wants to stay with the text as is, then כי must be taken to be a substantive and, according to the sense of the passage, assigned the same meaning as כְּוִיָה, "brand" (Exod. 21:25), resulting in a reading "brand instead of beauty." But this meaning for כי is not very likely, and the pattern of the parallels which precede it leads in a different direction than that of the final sentence. Qᵃ, with its reading, offers the solution: כי תחת יפי בשת (truly, instead of beauty, humiliation). כי (truly) remains a particle (see J. T. Milik, *Bib* 31 [1950] 216; F. Nötscher, *VT* 1 [1951] 300; see, for the opposite viewpoint, G. R. Driver, *JTS* 2 [1951] 25).

Form

The section is a threat. The introduction in v. 16, ויאמר יהוה (and Yahweh said), is not appropriate, since Yahweh is mentioned later in the third person (a different situation here than in 29:13 or when יאמר יהוה, says Yahweh, is used in 1:11, 18). This formula is not used in this way anywhere else in the entire book of Isaiah; it is a redactional element, as was noted already by Cheyne. In other places, the reason for a threat is often given as a reproach, either preceding or following it, but here it is preceded by a causal clause introduced by יען כי (because) (just as in 8:6;

29:13; in the latter case, in v. 14, the threat is introduced by לכן [there-fore], which one would expect in our section, at the beginning of v. 17; however, it is missing there). Cf. C. Westermann, *Basic Forms of Pro-phetic Speech* (1967) 148, chart on pp. 174f.; K. Koch, *The Growth of the Biblical Tradition. The Form-Critical Method* (1969) 211f.

The announcement of judgment which follows in vv. 17 and 24 is interrupted by an enumeration of types of jewelry and clothing in vv. 18–23. As is often the case with such redactional material (see above, p. 118, on 2:17), the interpolated material is introduced by ביום ההוא (on that day), whereas והיה (and so it will be), at the beginning of v. 24, provides the transition for the continuation of the word of judgment. For an explanation of why vv. 25ff. are treated separately, see below, pp. 157f.

Meter: If one removes the introduction in v. 16, 3 five-stress cola remain, furnishing the reason for the judgment. The threat itself, in v. 17, should be read as a seven-stress colon. There are 2 seven-stress cola in v. 24, with a three-stress colon at the conclusion (unless the ending has not been completely preserved). There is no need to discover a metrical pattern in the inserted material, in spite of Budde's suggestion (*ZAW* 50 [1932] 39) and that of Peters (op. cit.), who thinks that the verses might originally have been a popular song, composed to mock a woman's finery.

Setting

Except for the interpolation in vv. 18–23, the authenticity has not been disputed (at most, v. 24b might be an addition).

The view that vv. 18–23 do not come from Isaiah has found greater consensus as time goes on, ever since the time of Duhm. To be sure, Budde still argued vehemently for the authenticity of the passage. The section supposedly would have offered an example of Isaiah's great love for the type of rhetorical method which seeks to assemble a compre-hensive list: "Which interpolator would have been so daring as to add in such a list, as if it came from the prophet himself, when all interpolations actually tend in the direction of making something more spiritual! It remains a fact that this section is as authentic as one could find. . . . It is definitely not correct to say that Isaiah is indignant about clothing cus-toms as such, . . . since one presumes that Isaiah would certainly have been able to find all these effects in his wife's wardrobe" (op. cit., 38f.; similarly Feldmann, Fischer, Herntrich, Ziegler, ad loc.). It is true that Isaiah also assembles comprehensive lists and uses them, as a rhetorical technique (see 1:10ff. and 3:2ff.), but heaping up words, as it is done here, is simply not necessarily a rhetorical technique. Concerning whether Isaiah could have become indignant enough about clothing (whether the passage is accepted as authentic would not matter—he distances himself in enough places from the Jerusalem fashion plates), it is also most unlikely that he would have put in the time and effort to assemble such a list. If Budde thinks that such a catalog is rhythmically completely accu-rate, that shows, more than anything else, only that one can designate every list Hebrew poetry, if one does not impose any more narrow defini-tion on poetry than that it has alternating accented and unaccented syllables. It is simply not true that all interpolations tend toward spiri-tualizing. What is decisive for designating this an interpolation is the use of the connecting formulas at the beginning of vv. 18 and 24. S. Daiches (op. cit.) believes that he can prove that the pieces of jewelry and clothing Ishtar owned, as listed in "The Descent of Ishtar to the Nether World" (*AOT²* 206ff.; *ANET²* 106ff.), are practically identical to those owned by the daughters of Zion in the present passage. It is certainly plausible that pieces of jewelry belonging to goddesses were similar to those owned by prominent women, even though a detailed comparison is made more difficult by problems with identifying not only the individual Hebrew terms but also the terms in the Assyrian "counterpart." However, Daiches's opinion contributes nothing, one way or the other, to determining whether the passage is authentic.

Concerning the time when Isaiah spoke this message about the proud daughters of Zion, nothing can be said for sure. And yet, it would seem that when there were times of great political tension, other concerns would have held his attention. Since the actual theme is that of human pride, one ought to presume that this section also comes from the early period of the prophet's activity.

Commentary

[3:16] The causative clause which furnishes the reason for the judgment message is introduced by כִּי יַעַן (because). KBL, just as Ges-Buhl had already suggested, places the substantive יַעַן under ענה III, "be troubled with," or something similar; it means "cause" and, having become a conjunction (which is often used with אֲשֶׁר, less often with כִּי), furnishes the reason. It is stronger and more distinct than simply כִּי (because) or אֲשֶׁר (that) (see Joüon, Gr §170f.). Since the reproach and the threat are paired, a dependent with an independent clause, forming one complex sentence, the strict correspondence between the two parts of a message of judgment are very clear, also on a formal level. The prophets basically never speak of the coming intervention of God without providing the reason. Yahweh is a God whose actions are not capricious, but are always to be understood on the basis of faith in Yahweh. Specifically with Isaiah, who does not always present the announcement of judgment in the form of a message from Yahweh, it is still clear that the prophet did not try to find the reasons for his increasing conviction that a catastrophic judgment was on the horizon; it was just the other way around. His assessment of the inner disposition of the people of God would have led to a certainty that the coming judgment of God was unavoidable. An assertion we noted above would agree with this, that assertion being that introductory formulas, like the one in our present passage, which identify a message as coming from Yahweh, would have been inserted secondarily. That does not mean Isaiah would have been unaware of his status as one sent by Yahweh when speaking such words. But he does not proclaim his message on the basis of a special inspiration which dealt with a specific case, but rather in fulfillment of his general task, being one who is sent by Yahweh.

The Jerusalem women are addressed as the בְּנוֹת צִיּוֹן (daughters of Zion) (except in v. 17, this is found elsewhere only in 4:4 and Song of Sol. 3:11), which certainly does not refer to young girls but to the society women. If Isaiah speaks here about "Zion" and not "Jerusalem," he reminds one that בַּת צִיּוֹן (Zion's daughter) is a designation for Jerusalem (see above, p. 30, on 1:8) with the full theological force which that carried. To be a "daughter of Zion" included placing oneself under the God who revealed himself there. Instead of that, the women of Jerusalem were proud (concerning גבה, be haughty, see above, p. 115, on 2:12). That can be demonstrated in the way they make their appearance: they walk back and forth נטוות גרון (with neck outstretched) (גרון actually means "throat"; that is where their jewelry is; cf. Ezek. 16:11). The common translation "with outstretched neck" (Gk: ὑψηλῷ τραχήλῳ, high raised neck) is more a makeshift translation than an exact rendering: נטה does not mean "upwards," but "turn to the side, stretch sidewards," which means that the women glance flirtatiously to one side, to see if those who meet them have noticed and been taken with their beauty. Understood in this way, the first colon provides a close parallel to the second. For the *hapax leg.* שקר *pi'el*, KBL gives the meaning "cast seductive glances"; J. Hempel (*Hebräisches Wörterbuch zu Jesaja* [1965³]) suggests "wink," but it is possible that it ought to be understood on the basis of the Syriac *s^eqar* and the Late Hebrew סקר as "color red," *pi'el* "put on make-up" (cf. also the Arabic *šaqira* and *šaqura,* "having a light complexion, have a fair complexion"). טפף, another *hapax leg.,* is also uncertain. Some take it as a denominative from טף and translate it with "trip pitter-patteringly," while Gk reads σύρουσαι τοὺς χιτῶνας, "with skirts gliding," but this can be attributed to translator's guesswork, not accurate knowledge. As they pitter-patter along, the women make jingling sounds with their foot bracelets (עכסים, see below, on v. 18), which they wear around their ankles. At least this is the usual explanation. However, based on the parallel טפף (pitter-patter), one would more logically expect, here as well, a description of the way they moved along. Possibly G. R. Driver is right; he claims that the ancient versions and the Arabic *ta'akkasa fi mišyatihi,* "as one goes along, one moves by leaps and bounds," leads to the meaning "hop, jump" (*VT* 1 [1951] 241).

[3:17] There are also many difficulties with understanding the exact meaning of the threat in v. 17. Ges-Buhl, Hempel, and KBL suggest for the *pi'el* שפח, according to the Jewish tradition, the meaning "make scabby," since they associate this word with the word מספחת, "scratches" (KBL: "scales"). On the other hand, Driver (op. cit., 241f.) refers to the Akkadian *suppuḫu/šuppuḫu,* "open up, loosen" (see the Arabic *'asfaḫu,* "bald on the front of the head"). He may be right, since Vulg reads *decalvabit* (will make bald), so that one should translate this something like "lay bare." In v. 17b, פת does not mean, as had been thought in the past, "feminine private parts"; the word is also not derived, following Origen, from פאה (side, corner) (on this, see B. Stade, *ZAW* 26 [1906] 130–133), but from the Akkadian *pūtu,* "forehead" (see G. R. Driver, *JTS* 38 [1937] 38, who refers to the Akkadian phrase *muttutam gullubu,* "shave off the hair of the forehead," a humiliating punishment known among the Babylonians; cf. also the Vulg: *dominus crinem earum nudabit,* the Lord will make it bare where their hair is). This provides a fine parallel expression in v. 17b to match v. 17a. It does not deal specifically with a sickness—that is impossible, according to v. 24—but rather with a degrading spectacle concocted by the victorious enemies: the spectacle of displaying the women of Jerusalem.

[3:24a] One cannot be completely sure about all the aspects of v. 24a either, as the threat continues. בשם (Greek: βάλσαμον, balsam) is oil from the balsam bush; it was expensive, imported from Sheba and Raamah (Ezek. 27:22; 2 Chron. 9:1), and therefore, it was stored in the king's treasure house (Isa. 39:2). It was used in cultic activity (Exod. 25:6, and often elsewhere), but was also used as a cosmetic (Esther 2:12; Song of Sol. 4:10, 14, and often elsewhere). A time would come when none of it would be left; instead of its wonderful fragrance, מק, "the smell of decay," would come from "the daughters of Zion" (see 5:24). According to Ps. 38:6 (מקק, fester), מק can describe the smell which comes from festering wounds. The girdle (חגורה) also belongs to the articles of finery. Indeed, something like this is mentioned, as part of the feminine finery in the OT, at most only in Prov. 31:24; Gen. 3:7 (cf. also Prov. 31:17); in all the other cases, it is descriptive of something worn by a man who is fit out for warfare (1 Sam. 18:4, and often elsewhere; but cf. קשרים, attire, in Jer. 2:32). In its place, there will be a rope, "the most primitive means which can be used for fastening an article of clothing" (Kaiser). As to the care given to hairstyling, those who lived in the ancient Near East attached great importance to that as well. Combs made of wood or ivory have been found in archaeological excavations, and metal mirrors are also mentioned in the OT (Exod. 38:8; Job 37:18; Sir. 12:11; cf. *BRL* 255). "Hair curlers and hair clamps or hair pins, made of metal, copied from Egyptian patterns, were not unknown" (F. Nötscher, *Biblische Altertumskunde* [1940] 64). Since מִקְשָׁה means "twisted, fashioned work," the *hapax leg.* מִקְשָׁה can hardly mean "curled hair," as KBL translates it, but rather "artistically woven hair" (cf. ἐμπλοκή, braiding of hair, in 1 Peter 3:3, and πλέγματα, braided hair, in 1 Tim. 2:9; see I. Benzinger, *Hebräische Archäologie* [1927³] illus. 78; A. Jirku, *Die Welt der Bibel* [1957] illus. 61 [ivories from Megiddo]). Instead of that, the daughters of Zion will have to have a bald head. Along with crying, lamenting, and wearing sackcloth, having a bald head is part of the rite connected with mourning (e.g., when in a hard-pressed political situation, 22:12; 15:2; Mic. 1:16; Amos 8:10, and often elsewhere). The very next colon refers to binding around oneself the garment of mourning, שק (sack). Here one must presume that reference is made to a cloth, wrapped around the loins. One would wear this right over bare skin (Job 16:15, and often elsewhere); it would not be taken off at night (1 Kings 21:27, and often elsewhere). It was made of black goats' hair. It could be worn as the only article of clothing or beneath an outer garment (see Dalman *AuS* V, 202f.; Benzinger, op. cit., 72ff.; Nötscher, op. cit., 60; Hönig, op. cit., 102ff.; H. W. Wolff, *Joel* BK XIV/2, 34 [Engl: *Joel and Amos,* 29]). A שק (sack) such as this would be worn instead of the פתיגיל (majestic robe). One gathers from the context that the latter would have been a very luxurious and magnificent dress. But we do not know how it looked or how it would have differed from other similar festival garments.

[3:24b] Verse 24b brings it all together: "Instead of beauty, 'humiliation.'" The story about Jezebel (2 Kings 9:30) describes how women, in wartime, came to meet the enemy, provocatively dressed, but also points out that such a dubious attempt to save one's skin could also very easily go awry. A Hebrew could say that one ought to cloth oneself in shame and dishonor (Pss. 35:26; 132:18; Job 8:22) and would hope that an enemy would be wrapped up in shame as one is wrapped up in a coat (Ps. 109:29). In no way does v. 24b go beyond the bounds of what has preceded; rather, it repeats, at the end, what has already been said.

[3:18–23] The interpolation in vv. 18–23 speaks about setting aside תפארת (jewelry, glory), about which those in Jerusalem are so proud. In the following enumeration, jewelry, in the narrow sense, is mentioned first, followed by a description of luxurious articles of clothing. תפארת (jewelry, glory) is, of course, a general term, and includes everything which might bring pleasure and might provide one with a reason to be proud (cf. Isa. 10:12, but also 28:1, 4, 5). The expander went to a lot of trouble to provide a comprehensive list of fashionable articles which would have given the women a cause to be proud; this would not suggest that each woman owned all of these trinkets. In addition to the items already mentioned by Isaiah, this catalog shows (cf. also Ezek. 16:10–13, 17, 39; 23:26, 42) that ancient Israel was very much aware of luxury and trinkets and that the fashionable members of society ambitiously kept up with the elegance which one would find in foreign palaces of kings and princes. The terms which are used in vv. 18–23 cannot, by and large, be identified with any certitude, and a precise identification cannot be made even with the help of archaeology, though archaeology has provided a wealth of information about the pieces of jewelry and the toiletry articles used by the women of the ancient Near East. Already in 1745, the following appeared: N. W. Schroeders, *Commentarius philologo-criticus de vestitu mulierum Hebraearum ad Jesai. III. vs 16–24* (A philological-critical commentary about a woman's clothing in Isaiah 3:16–24); indeed, a three-volume work comes from 1809/10, by A. Th. Hartmann: *Die Hebräerin am Putztisch und als Braut. Vorbereitet durch eine Übersicht der wichtigsten Erfindungen in dem Reiche der Moden bei den Hebräerinnen von den rohesten Anfängen bis zur üppigsten Pracht* (The Hebrew woman at the dressing table and as a bride. Prepared by a review of the most important finds in the area of fashion among the Hebrew women from the earliest beginnings up to most luxurious magnificence). But there has been little success in providing a real clarification of all of the individual items, either by these earlier attempts or by the efforts of modern scholars. Unfortunately, the Gk is also not much help here. Ziegler (op. cit., 203f.) has shown that when the translator came to vocables which were difficult and not easily understood at his time, he chose terminology which would have been appropriate for fashion items in his day, "without going to too much trouble to find the exact equivalent terminology." Thus, to a point, it is unclear which terms belong together, so that one cannot really speak about a real translation into Greek. Because of this, 3:18–23, in its Greek format, can be described as a "piece of Alexandrine Egypt cultural history" (ibid., 211).

[3:18a] The redactor makes use of Isaiah's own terminology when he employs סור (take away) *hiph'il* (1:16, 25; 3:1; 5:5). The verb is often used to describe getting rid of idols (Gen. 35:2; Josh. 24:14, 23; Judg. 10:16; 1 Sam. 7:3, 4, and often elsewhere). For the author, luxury in jewelry and toiletry articles is on the same level as idol worship—from a religio-historical point of view, some of these enumerated items actually had their origin in the cult or in magic.

[3:18b] עכסים, which begin the listing of items, are foot bracelets or ankle rings, made of bronze, worn by both husbands and wives (see Dalman, op. cit., 250; *BRL* 168; cf. the Arabic *'akasa* "pedem collumque cameli fune colligavit" [fastened by a rope on the foot and neck of a camel]). According to Compston (op. cit., 321), they would have been worn to draw attention to the women who were wearing them, often having been equipped with bells; illuss. in Benzinger, op. cit., nos. 104, 106.

שביסים is traditionally translated with "bands on the forehead" (so even Hempel, *Wört.,* KBL, Fohrer, Kaiser). Based on the Ugaritic, which verifies the existence of the word *špš* = Hebrew שֶׁמֶשׁ (sun) (Aistleitner, *Wört.*[2] no. 2667; cf. also the Akkadian personal names *Šapši* and *Šapša*), there can no longer be any doubt that the meaning suggested already by Schroeder (op. cit., 23ff., with reference to the Arabic *šabîsa* and Pliny, *Nat. Hist.* XII, 14 §63, who mentions the Arabic deity *Sabis*) is the most likely; that meaning is "little sun," which is especially likely since, immediately following this, there is a reference to a "little moon." Possibly van den Branden is correct when he suggests that שביס is an Arabic loanword (in West Semitic, the sun is *šmš* and/or *špš;* in South Semitic, it is *šms* and/or, dialectically, *šbs,* op. cit., 88f.; see, in addition, J. W. Jack, *ExpTim* 45 [1933/34] 501, and J. Gray, *The Legacy of Canaan,* VTSup 5 [1957] 191); illuss. are in Jirku, op. cit., illus. 57; Nötscher, op. cit., no. 68a; *AOB*[2], no. 218, 221, 224. There is no doubt that שהרונים means "little moon"; cf. שהר as a name for the moon god on the *zkr* stele of *Āfis* (Donner-Röllig, *KAI* no. 202 B 24), and often elsewhere in the Aramaic inscriptions, with cognates also in other Semitic languages; illuss. in Benzinger, no. 101; Nötscher, no. 68a; *BRL* 27, no. 15. Moon crescents are also mentioned in Judg. 8:21, 26 as spoils of war which Gideon had taken from the Midianites; according to the first passage, they were also hung around the necks of camels. The women who wore them would probably not even have known that these articles of jewelry were originally symbols of the sun- and moon-deity and, as such, had a religious meaning (as amulets or as a guarantee of fertility).

[3:19] נטיפות are named, using good Hebrew word formation, because of the shape which they have: נטף, "drip"; נֵטֶף, "drop." It has been customary to translate this as "ear pendants" or something similar. But, according to Dalman (op. cit., 350), it has been determined that נטיפות does not refer only to earrings, but, as is also true of the moon crescents (one would have to also add: the little suns), it also refers to something on a necklace. According to its form, it is likely that it was generally made of pearls (Ges-Buhl); illuss.: *BRL* 27, no. 17 and 399, nos. 11–14, possibly also nos. 7–9; cf., in addition, Benzinger, no. 101. The שירות are arm bands or arm bracelets (see *BRL* 30ff.). The word goes back to the Akkadian *sewiru* (H. Zimmern, *Akkadische Fremdwörter* [1917²] 38; cf. also the Arabic *siwar,* pl. *'asāwir;* Syriac *ši'râ;* Aramaic שֵׁירָא), which once again demonstrates the cultural influence which came from foreign lands. Illuss.: *BRL* 31, nos. 1–9; Nötscher, no. 68b; *AOB*[2], no. 636, 3.

Following the decorative pieces, made of metal, articles of clothing are listed. First comes the רעלות, usually translated "veil." But C. Rabin (*The Zadokite Documents* [1954] 51) noted that this meaning first appeared during the late Middle Ages and that, previously, the word had been understood as meaning "small bell, little bell": *ğalāğil* "ring a bell," according to Dalman (op. cit., 331); evidence can also be furnished for this meaning by consulting רעל, which in the *hoph'al* means "be shaken." Van den Branden (op. cit., 90) suggests the translation "neck band," saying that the other items in the list are still referring to articles of jewelry, not clothing. But the Arabic *ra'l* "is a two-part cloth for the head, the upper half placed above the eyes and thrown over the top of the head, while the lower half goes under the eyes and hangs down to the breast" (Dalman, op. cit., 331). Thus, one does well to stay with the generally accepted rendering, "veil." Concerning the varieties of veils, see Benzinger, 84f., and the representations shown there.

[3:20] פאר seems to be an Egyptian loanword (*pjr*) which means "headband, turban." Even though van den Branden pleads his case for the translation "diadem" or "crown," it seems best, here also, that one stay with the commonly accepted rendering. The priest wears the פאר (turban) (Exod. 39:28); the bridegroom puts it on (Isa. 61:10); if one is in mourning, it is set aside (Ezek. 24:17, 23; Isa. 61:3); illuss. in Benzinger, nos. 84–87; Jirku, charts 61 and 63, top.

צעדה means "stride"; the plural צעדות is usually understood as "short stride chain"; KBL suggests this means "jingling rings on one's ankles." However, according to Dalman (op. cit., 350f.), these little chains on the feet prohibited one from taking long strides; they "helped the women to take flirtatious little pattering steps" (Kaiser; cf. Nötscher, 67f.).

For קשרים, a wide divergence of opinion is once again to be noted. Traditionally, it has been translated "girdle" (as is still the case in Hempel, *Wört.*). But קשר hardly means "put on one's belt"; rather, it means "tie on." According to Jer. 2:32, the bride wears קשרים. Saadia thinks this refers to a "neck chain" (Dalman, op. cit., 350), but Gk translates Jer. 2:32 with στηθοδεσμίς (chest binding), so that KBL translates this as "breast binding" (Fohrer: "breast bands"). Much controversy also surrounds בית הנפש. Gk omits the word altogether; Sym translates it with τα σκευα της εμπνοιας (the vessels of inhalation), Vulg with *olfactoriola* (little smelling bottles); therefore, most recently commentators suggest "little scent bottles, little perfume bottles." But נפש never means perfume in the OT and the perfume bottles which have been found by archaeologists hardly seem the type which would have been worn as jewelry (see the little ivory perfume bottle found at *tell ed-duwēr*, in Jirku, chart 65). It is not certain that the Akkadian *nipšu* really means "perfume" and one cannot verify that the Ugaritic *npš* is to be translated with "perfume" (contra Gray, op. cit., 191). J. G. Frazer (*Folk-Lore in the Old Testament*, II [1919] 514) had already thought this referred to amulets, as suggested again by D. Lys ("Nèphèsh": *EHPR* 50 [1959] 147). Van den Branden (op. cit., 91ff.) would like to explain the meaning of בתי הנפש on the basis of צרור החיים (bundle of the living) (1 Sam. 25:29), which he suggests is a "container," which was supposed to protect the "soul" of the person who wore it.

In other places, לחש means "conjuring," see above, p. 131, on 3:3. Here, and possibly also in 26:16, some material means for conjuring is intended, that is, an amulet. Van den Branden thinks it refers to small tablets, upon which a magic formula would have been written, and which one would have then worn around the neck. However, KBL suggests "humming mussel shells" (as already suggested by S. Fraenkel, *Die aramäischen Fremdwörter im Arabischen* [1886] 59). לחש means, in its basic sense, "whisper," but that alone is not enough to justify this supposed meaning. It might be that such amulets were also tied on to arm bands and necklaces; illuss.: *AOB*², nos. 555ff.; *BRL,* pp. 25ff.; *BHHW,* p. 90.

[3:21] טבעות belongs to the same root as the Akkadian *ṭimbu'u* or *ṭimbūtu* and the Arabic *ṭābi'*; cf. also the Egyptian *db'.t,* "seal"; it is thus a loanword in Hebrew. The seal ring belongs to the equipment issued to someone holding an official post (Gen. 41:42; Esther 3:10, and often elsewhere). A טבעת can also be, as δακτύλιος (rings) in Jdt. 10:4, a finger ring; illuss.: Benzinger, no. 98; Nötscher, no. 80; *AOB*², nos. 574, 613, 627. One could also wear rings in the nose: נזמי האף. נֶזֶם, in and of itself, is simply a general term for ring, as shown in Judg. 8:24–26, and can also be used specifically for earrings (Gen. 35:4). But it can also be used by itself, meaning specifically "nose ring" (Gen. 24:22, and often elsewhere); illuss.: Benzinger, no. 103; see also *AOB*², no. 144. Among archaeological finds, one can hardly distinguish between nose rings and earrings; see *BRL* 399f.

[3:22] The word מחלצות must have some connection with the Akkadian *ḫalṣu,* "clean," and the Arabic *ḫalaṣa,* "clean, be white" (contra Dalman, op. cit., 209, who suggests deriving the word from חלץ *hiph'il,* "furnish"). It is plain that clean, white clothing is meant, as evident when comparing it with its opposite, the "filthy garments" of Zech. 3:4 (see Hönig, op. cit., 115). It is easy to see how the transferred meaning "festival garments" developed. In the same way, there is no doubt that מעטפות is derived from עטף, "wrap oneself up, wrap around oneself"; the word must mean "wrap up," referring to something like "outside clothing" (Ges-Buhl, KBL), "outer garments" (Hönig, op. cit., 118), "clothes with long arms" (Compston, op. cit., 326; cf. the Arabic *'iṭāf* and *mi'ṭaf,* "coat"). Might one think that this could be similar to the article of clothing worn by a young girl on one of the Megiddo ivories (see Wright, op. cit., illus. no. 136, and Jirku, plate 60; see also Benzinger, illus. no. 79)? The מטפחות would have possibly looked about the same. Deriving the word from טפח I, "spread out," the word must mean "shawl, cloak"; this article of clothing would have simply been made out of a piece of cloth (cf. Ruth 3:15). Also for חריט Hempel (*Wört.*) assigns the meaning "shawl," even though it is normally taken to mean "money bag, purse" or something similar, close to the meaning in 2 Kings 5:23 (Gk: θύλακος, "sack"; cf. the Arabic *ḫariṭa,* "leather bag"), in which case it may have been such a "purse," simply made out of a piece of cloth.

[3:23] Once again with גלינים, the suggested solutions are far apart. For 8:1, "papyrus sheet" (K. Galling, *ZDPV* 56 [1933] 211ff.) and "placard" (G. R. Driver, *Semitic Writing* [1954²] 80, 229) or "writing tablet" (KBL) have been suggested. In our passage, the attempt has been made to translate this, on the basis of the Targ and Vulg, as "mirror." But since reference is made, both preceding it and following it, to articles of clothing, this suggestion should be dealt with using due caution. Gk translates it as διαφανῆ Λακωνικά, which means "clothing which is transparent." F. E. Peiser (*ZAW* 17 [1897] 348) utilized the Arabic *galwa,* "fine, silky raiment," to help clarify the meaning and made reference to the Akkadian *gulīnu,* "outer garment"; on the other hand, the Akkadian *gulīnu* is itself comparable to the Hebrew גְּלוֹם, "coat, wrap" (see *AHW* 296f.). Possibly גלמים (wrap) was miscopied as גלינים and then vocalized as גִּלָּיוֹן, "mirror."

סדינים = *saddinu,* or something similar, is an Akkadian word (Zimmern, op. cit., 36f.). Once again, one cannot be certain of its exact meaning, especially because it is not certain that the word is connected with the Greek word σινδών, "fine Indian linen garment." Some have tried translating this as "undergarment, shirt," or something similar. Prov. 31:24 shows that סדין does not just refer to a type of material, but is that which is produced by the diligent work of a homemaker, and Judg. 14:12 points out that this article of clothing was very valuable; illuss.: Benzinger, nos. 58ff.

A צניף is a headband or turban, and since the term belongs to the root צנף, "wrap around, bind around," it must be connected with some type of head covering "in which the cloth is wrapped around several times" (Dalman, op. cit., 258). It was worn by kings (Isa. 62:3; Sir. 11:5; 47:6), but was also used, along with the similar term מצנפת (turban), as a designation for the head covering of the high priest (Zech. 3:5; Sir. 40:4). It was probably hardly distinguishable from a פאר (turban) (see above, p. 153, on v. 20), especially since that term is also used when mentioning the head covering of the priest. The final article of clothing is called the רדיד; that is also some sort of garment which is wrapped around (Gk: θέριστρον κατάκλι(σ)τον, "light, flowing summer dress"), as Song of Sol. 5:7 makes quite clear, possibly a cloth which one would place upon one's head.

The impressive variety of designations, in the final analysis derived from foreign sources, remind one of Zephaniah's complaints about "the officials and the king's sons and all who array themselves in foreign attire" (1:8). In any case, this particular list betrays the influence which the palace had on the lifestyle of the leading citizens of the capital city. Without intending to do so, it indicates how intensely Israel allowed itself to be influenced by foreign customs. But it is simply impossible to determine how large a group was able to live in such luxury. One has the impression that the expander wanted only to underscore the message of Isaiah, but actually distorted the evidence instead. And yet, in this passage one can hear distant echoes of those laments of the prophets that described the way those in control were exploiting the commoners. One cannot be sure about the time period from which this list comes, but it is clear that the primary foreign influence came from Babylonian cultural circles. One might thus consider this to have come from the time toward the end of the era when kings still ruled.

Purpose and Thrust

A simple comparison with the interpolation in vv. 18–23 shows the uniqueness of Isaiah's polemic. The prophet does not rail against luxury as such. He also does not zero in on the antisocial behavior of the women (which makes his theme different from that in Amos 4:1–3), but he speaks against the pride of the women of Jerusalem. In and of itself, beautiful clothes, with the accompanying decorative touches, could give expression to the naive, natural joy of an Oriental wife who wanted to adorn herself. But the style of life shown by the "daughters of Zion" is a symptom of the drive to be important, a drive which leads one to ignore those around whom one lives; that lifestyle reveals a haughtiness in which one is so wrapped up in human affairs that there is no time left to bow down before God. It is against such a mental attitude that the onrushing storm of God must come, so that everything high and mighty will be crushed to pieces.

Isaiah 3:25—4:1

Women in Need
in the City Devastated by War

Literature

K. Galling, "Die Ausrufung des Namens als Rechtsakt in Israel," *TLZ* 81 (1956) 65–70.

Text

3:25 Your men fall by the sword
and your heroes in battle.
26 Thus your gates[a] will lament and mourn,
and she will sit all alone on the ground.
4:1 And then, seven women will take hold of
one man [a][on that day][a]
and will say: We will eat *our* (own) bread
and will clothe ourselves in *our* (own) garment,[b]
if only your name will be spoken over us;
take away our humiliation!

26a Gk reads, for פְּתָחֶיהָ (her gates), θῆκαι (graves, tombs). But this is a mistake within the Greek textual transmission, a mistaken reading of the word θύραι (gates) (Sym reads it thus).
4:1a–a ביום ההוא (on that day) is not in the Gk and is probably a secondary addition, as is often the case with this formula.
4:1b The plural שׂמְלֹתֵינוּ (our garments), read by some MSS and the versions, can hardly be original.

Form

There is no agreement about the boundaries of this section, a problem related to the question about its authenticity. Since judgment is proclaimed against the women in this passage as well, some have taken these verses to be a continuation of the preceding section. But the suffixes in v. 25 are in the second person feminine singular. It must be a city, indeed almost certainly Jerusalem, which is addressed here. It might be sup-

157

posed that the beginning of this section was eliminated when it was combined with the preceding section. In fact, in v. 26, the person also changes to the third feminine singular. It is possible that the suffix on פתחיה ought to be adjusted to agree with the second singular of v. 25, but one should probably presume that the traditional material employed here was simply not adjusted grammatically. Other solutions have also been suggested. Duhm, followed by Marti, suggests linking 4:1 with 3:16f., 24, taking v. 25 as nongenuine. But 4:1 would not follow directly after v. 24 without a rough sound to it, and the half-line in v. 24b provides a formal indicator that the section is at an end. Indeed, Duhm thinks that the portrayal of the destiny of the unnamed city is too elegant in v. 26 for the verse to have possibly come from Isaiah. But, in this matter of judgment, he trusts his own subjective inclinations more than he has a right to do.

The reason for the announcement of disaster is lacking. Possibly the compiler removed it apparently in order to bring together various words about the women of Jerusalem. It is typical of Isaiah's style that he would first present the situation in very general, more or less traditional, terms (vv. 25f.) and then illustrate it vividly with a very lively, very realistic little concluding section (4:1).

Meter: In v. 25, we have a five-stress colon; in 4:1, 3 five-stress cola; in v. 26, a six-stress colon.

Setting

Based on what has been explained above, there seems to be no over-arching reason against this being from Isaiah himself. Further, in terms of its chronological point of view, this section is justifiably attached to the previous sections of the chapter.

Commentary

[3:25] The tradition about holy war mentions that the enemy "will fall by the sword" (normally לפי־חרב) or that Israel will smite its enemy "with the edge of the sword" (Josh. 8:24, and often elsewhere). But this motif is also found in the promises of blessings in the covenant tradition (Lev. 26:6ff.). On the other hand, one can also discover that, already at a very early time in Israel's history, the exact opposite could be said; from within this tradition threats of disaster could be made in which the enemies or Yahweh himself would strike Israel down with the sword (Deut. 28:22; see also Lev. 26:25, 33, 36f.). The prophets made use of the negative aspect of this motif (2 Kings 8:12; Amos 4:10; 7:9, 11, 17; 9:1, 10; Hos. 7:16; 11:6; 14:1; Mic. 6:14; see also Isa. 1:20). It is not just by chance that Isaiah mentions מתים (men) in this context (see also 5:13). This rather rare word is chosen wherever reference is made to the ban being carried out (Deut. 2:34; 3:6) or where it is announced in the covenant tradition that only a few will survive the catastrophe (Deut. 4:27; 28:62). Isaiah refers to these מתים (men) in conjunction with the גבורה (hero) mentioned in the second colon. The word which is used in a unique way in this passage, used in place of the more concrete term גּבּוֹרִים (men of valor), certainly does not have the narrow sense of "bodyguard" (see above, p. 129, on 3:2), but the more general meaning "soldier"; cf. the common expression גבורי החיל (men of valor) (Josh. 1:14; 6:2, and often elsewhere). To translate this as "younger forces," meaning "unmarried young men"—in contrast to the מתים who are married—has no justification (contra Fohrer). These two terms are, in essence, synonymous.

[3:26] The transmission-historical connections, from which v. 25 comes, make it immediately clear to the hearer that Isaiah wants to speak about the judgment of Yahweh in a very comprehensive sense. Of course, he does not direct his words against all of Israel, but against Jerusalem, underscoring the weighty import of the coming disaster in v. 26, which speaks of the mourning of the city, even "its gates." Instead of the usual שערים (gates), the word פתחים, "entrances," is used, as in Josh. 8:29; 1 Kings 17:10. More often, one would refer to the פתח השער (entrance of the gate) or something similar; e.g., Judg. 9:35 (concerning the פתחים, openings, cf. also Ps. 24:7, 9). The rare term אנה I (mourn) (elsewhere only in 19:8) is one of the verbs used to describe mourning for one who has died, as is shown by the use of the substantive אנים, "time for mourning," and אֲנִיָה, "lament" (always together with תַּאֲנִיָה, mourning, Isa. 29:2 and Lam. 2:5). As in this present passage, 19:8 also uses this verb parallel to the common synonym אבל I (mourn, lament). The Israelite can refer to the mourning of the earth and/or the land (Hos. 4:3; Isa. 24:4; 33:9; Joel 1:10) or mourning of something like the pastures of the shepherds (Amos 1:2). But Yahweh can also cause the bulwarks and walls of a city to mourn (Lam. 2:8). Or, as the paths to Zion mourn (Lam. 1:4), so here the "entrances" into the city could. The second colon is more difficult to understand, specifically because the exact meaning of נקה is unclear. Gk reads καὶ καταλειφθήσῃ μόνη (and she will be left alone); KBL suggests, but only for our passage, the meaning "to be deprived (of one's men)." Hempel (*Wört.*) wants to change the text to read נֶחָתָּה (press down, cause to descend) and Ges-Buhl suggests the translation "cleared out, devastated," which apparently is the suggested meaning only for the present passage. Since the basic meaning of the verb is "bare, clean, be pure," it is more likely this means that the city is described as a mourning woman, a childless widow sitting all alone on the bare ground; cf. Lam. 1:1: יָשְׁבָה בָדָד הָעִיר רַבָּתִי עָם הָיְתָה כְּאַלְמָנָה רַבָּתִי בַגּוֹיִם (How lonely sits the city that was full of people! How like a widow she has become, she that was great among the nations!). Cf. also 2:10 and Isa. 27:10. נקתה must have a meaning similar to בָּדָד (lonely) or שַׁכּוּל, "deprived of children" (2 Sam. 17:8 = Hos. 13:8 = Prov. 17:12; Jer. 18:21; cf. Isa. 49:21). Therefore, KBL is basically on the right track, but the mourning is not only because one's husband has been lost, but just as much because of the loss of one's sons and other relatives from one's clan. Sitting on the ground was part of the mourning rites (cf. Gen. 23:2f.; 2 Sam. 12:17; 13:31; Ezek. 26:16; Lam. 2:10; Esther 4:3). This practice was also known among the ancient Egyptians and Babylonians (on this, see H. Jahnow, *Das hebräische Leichenlied,* BZAW 36 [1923] 7).

[4:1] The mourning does not come so much because of their strong attachment to the dead as it does because their own situation has become so precarious. Having no husband and no sons any longer means being completely unprotected, which was precisely what made existence so precarious for a wife in time of war. And so, "seven women" all throw themselves at one man, hoping to convince him to accept them as his wives. The number seven is not to be taken literally; one must take into account that Isaiah intends to show how such a situation would lead to drastic measures. Naturally, the sentence presumes polygamy: Even a married man could take concubines in addition to his wife. Polygamy was not the norm in ancient Israel (cf. de Vaux, *Ancient Israel. Its Life and Institutions* [1961] 24–26, and W. Plautz, "Monogamie und Polygynie im Alten Testament," *ZAW* 75 [1963] 3–27). After the male population had been decimated in time of war, polygamy would provide a natural safety valve to deal with having many more women than men; in normal times, on the other hand, having many wives would have caused a financial burden, not to be discounted as an insignificant problem: The מֹהַר (purchase price) was to be paid, which, according to Deut. 22:29, was fifty shekels of silver. The husband was then obligated to provide for his wives' food (שְׁאֵר) and clothing (כְּסוּת) and was not to abstain from sexual intercourse (עֹנָה) (Exod. 21:10). But the normal order in society did not apply any longer during wartime. One could not even bring up the issue of the מֹהַר (purchase price). In fact, the wives would have even been willing to provide food and clothing, summarized here in a general way with the words לחם (bread) and שׂמלה (garment); they could afford to do this as well, since, in some cases, they were the only ones left from their entire family. They had just one desire: that the name of a man would be "proclaimed" upon them. That does not mean: "if we could only have your name," or something like that, as it is often translated; after the marriage the wife often kept the name she had had before it. קרא שם פ׳ עלפ׳, "speak someone's name over someone or something," describes a very specific legal action; the sentence functions as a legal formula, used whenever property was transferred (Galling, op. cit., 67; see also Köhler, *OTTheol,* 33). It points back to an ancient custom which was practiced also when one participated in marriage rites, which formally were handled like a purchase: the announcing of the name was the last action, declaring the marriage transaction had been finalized (H. J. Boecker, *Redeformen des Rechtslebens im Alten Testament,* WMANT 14 [1964] 167f.). One ought not attempt to draw conclusions about actual marriage practices in Isaiah's day just because the ancient formula is being used. The very passage before us shows that the legal action which finalized the marriage was no longer the purchase, but placing the wife under the care and responsibility of the husband (on this, see W. Plautz, "Die Form der Eheschliessung im Alten Testament," *ZAW* 76 [1964] 298–318). It was important for the wives that their "humiliation" would be taken away from them. Duhm thinks that the beginning of 4:1 "was strangely enough echoed" in Zech. 8:23 (similarly, Marti, among others). One must question whether that is true; yet, that verse does show how those who were looking for help would attempt to gain some security for themselves by being attached to men of importance and power.

"Rape" (2 Sam. 13:13) and childlessness counted among the things which would have been called humiliating by an Israelite. When Rachel, after a long wait, gave birth to a son, she said, "God has taken away my reproach" (אסף אלהים את־חרפתי, Gen. 30:23). Zion, portrayed as a lonely wife in Isa. 54:4, is promised: בֹּשֶׁת עֲלוּמַיִךְ תִּשְׁכָּחִי וְחֶרְפַּת אַלְמְנוּתַיִךְ לֹא תִזְכְּרִי־עוֹד (for you will forget the shame of your youth, and the reproach of your widowhood you will remember no more). Widowhood was also considered to be a humiliation. Unfortunately, we cannot be sure of the exact meaning of the parallel expression בשׁת עלומיך (reproach of your widowhood). עלומים, in and of itself, means something like "strength of youth," but the expression seems to be making some reference to the humiliation which a woman would feel if she had not been able to find a husband (cf. Jer. 31:19). The חרפה (humiliation), from which all the women of Jerusalem, according to Isa. 4:1, would like to escape under any circumstances, consists of being a widow and unmarried, and possibly also in having no children and living under the threat of being raped (on this, cf. the first inscription of *sefire,* Donner-Röllig, *KAI* no. 222 A, 40–43).

Purpose and Thrust

Whether one takes 4:1 by itself or takes the verse as a conclusion to 3:16f., 24, one still comes to the conclusion that the aim is to unmask the pride of the Jerusalem women, which is really utterly despicable. "Proud of their high and secure position at the present time, at that time they will be brought to desperate straits, hoping to get rid of their feeling of humiliation by throwing themselves around the neck of the first good man they can find, . . . so that, by just being a wife or concubine, they could get some protection from the most vulgar insults" (Duhm). But if one looks at the passage in the way we suggest, in connection with 3:25f., then 4:1 is also a polemic against the women, but this verse illustrates the frightening collapse of all order: After the men have fallen in battle, the women would see themselves exposed to the deepest degradation, so that they would employ doubtful techniques in order to provide themselves some type of existence which could at least somewhat protect their worth as women. Therefore, this message is also an announcement of judgment. But what is also detected in this message is the violent emotional reaction of the prophet and his God; they react strongly because the situation had to come to this, and there is a hint of compassion for the unfortunate wife, Jerusalem, which is portrayed so clearly in Second Isaiah (54:1ff.). It is worth noting that Isaiah, who so severely criticized the pride of the daughters of Zion, is now capable of using such a very short description to bring out the depth of the calamity which would be in store for the wife.

161

Isaiah 4:2–6

The Holy Remnant
on Devastated Zion

Literature

J. Búda, "*Semah Jahweh*," *Bib* 20 (1939) 10–26. G. Fohrer, "Article: Σιών," *TDNT* VII, 292–319. J. G. Baldwin, "*Semah* as a Technical Term in the Prophets," *VT* 14 (1964) 93–97.

[**Literature update through 1979:** M. Prager, "Durch Gericht zum Heil—durch Tod zum Leben (Is 4,2–6)," *BibLeb* 38 (1964/65) 250–253. E. Lipiński, "De la réforme d'Esdras au règne eschatologique de Dieu (Is 4,3–5a)," *Bib* 51 (1970) 533–537. W. Herrmann, "Das Buch des Lebens," *Das Altertum* 20 (1974) 3–10.]

Text

4:2 On that day,
>   whatever Yahweh allows to sprout,
>   will be for decoration and honor
>   and the fruit of the land
>   will be for splendor and for adornment
>   for the escapees of Israel.[a]

*　　*　　*　　*

3 And whatever remains in Zion and what is still left in Jerusalem
4 shall be called holy, all written down for life in Jerusalem. • When the Lord[a] has washed away the filth of the daughters[b] of Zion and has rinsed away the bloodguilt of Jerusalem out of its midst through the spirit of judgment and the spirit of cleansing,[c]
5 • Yahweh will create[a] over every part of the mountain of Zion and over its gathering places a cloud by day and smoke and the glow of a blazing fire by night.

*　　*　　*　　*

6 [b]For there will be a protective roof over all the magnificence, • and a leafy canopy will serve to give shade [during the day] from the heat[a] and a place of refuge and shelter from downpour and torrential rain.

2a Q[a] inserts, in addition, ויהודה (and Judah), which is unnecessary, since Judah is naturally included when Israel is mentioned.

4a Targ reads for אדני (Lord): יהוה (Yahweh).

4b Gk: τῶν υίῶν καὶ τῶν θυγατέρων (of the sons and of the daughters), a most understandable expansion: Why should the filth of the daughters, but not also that of the sons, have to be washed away? However, the expression בנות ציון (daughters of Zion) is unique; except for 3:16f., where it makes good sense, it is found elsewhere only in Song of Sol. 3:11 (cf. also בנות ירושלם, daughters of Jerusalem, in 1:5, and often elsewhere). בנות (daughters), because the daughters of Zion were mentioned in 3:16f., might have been substituted for a more original בת (daughter) (so Procksch, and more recently once again, Fohrer). But it is more likely that 4:2ff. was, from its very beginning, considered an expansion on 3:16ff., so that בנות ציון (daughters of Zion) was consciously taken from 3:16.

4c Gk translates ברוח בער (spirit of cleansing) with πνεύματι καύσεως (spirit of burning); thus Fohrer, among others, reads "spirit of burning down," or something similar. But it is more likely in this context that the other meaning of בער *pi'el* is intended: "take away, cleanse, purify" (see above, p. 131, on 3:4). It should be noted that Qᵃ reads, instead of בער (cleansing): סער, "stormwind." That is hardly the result of influence from 2:12ff. (so Kaiser), since the term סער (storm-wind) is not even used there. The term רוח סערה (stormy wind) is a fixed term (Ezek. 1:4; 13:11, 13; Pss. 107:25; 148:8). It may well be that a copyist let his pen write סער (stormwind) in place of the more difficult בער (cleansing). Tur-Sinai's suggestion is hardly acceptable ("A Contribution to the Understanding of Isaiah I–XII," *ScrHier* 8 [1961] 164), replacing both occurrences of רוח (spirit) with דוח, "to purge," and משפט (judgment) with משטף, "ablution."

5a The expression that says Yahweh "creates" a cloud and smoke is unique; normally, the announcement proclaims that he "comes" or "comes down" when he "appears" or "shows himself" in clouds and smoke and other similar media; see F. Schnutenhaus, "Das Kommen und Erscheinen Gottes im Alten Testament," *ZAW* 76 (1964) 1–22. Therefore, it is misleading to follow the Gk, which reads ובא (καὶ ἥξει, and he will come) instead of וברא (and he will create). But then one would expect a ב before ענן (cloud), עשן (smoke), and נגה (glow). This leads to the conclusion that the present passage apparently does not intend to speak of an appearance by Yahweh, but about the protection which Yahweh will bestow upon Zion after the judgment. Actually, the OT does speak of the same thing elsewhere, saying that Yahweh stretches out cloud and fire for Israel's protection: פרש ענן למסך ואש להאיר לילה (He spread a cloud for covering, and fire to give light by night) (Ps. 105:39; מסך, covering, comes from the same root as סכה, canopy, in v. 6). One does well to stay with the MT here also.

5b–6a With vv. 5b and 6a, difficulties in understanding the text are presented which simply cannot be solved, most likely because of a major disruption to the text itself. It is possible that כבוד יהוה (glory of Yahweh) has to be read instead of simply כבוד (magnificence), that the preceding כל (all) is not in the construct state but is an independent substantive, that v. 5 does not come to an end until one comes to סכה (canopy) at the beginning of v. 6, or that this word has to be eliminated as in the Gk, so that v. 6 begins with והיה (and it will be). But none of these suggested emendations is any more convincing than any other; it is much more prudent to stay with the text as given—even though one recognizes that it can hardly be original. The יומם (during the day), after לצל (to give shade), which has no corresponding word in the Gk, indeed ought to be removed; the word was originally in v. 5.

Form

The section 4:2–6 is clearly a separate unit. Without any doubt, this section is intended to be an appendage to the announcement of judgment in chap. 3 and contrasts that with a message of hope. This section also deals with the destiny of Zion and its daughters. In contrast to the preceding description of the disastrous events which would befall the city of God, this sets forth the expectation that, some day, everything which is left there would be made holy, that the threatening circumstances for the inhabitants of the holy city there would be dealt with by the announcement of coming protection and shelter. But even if these verses betray an awareness of the preceding proclamation of Isaiah, those preceding verses in no way call for this particular continuation of what was sketched out there. Even if one would maintain that these verses are from Isaiah (on this matter, see below), one would have to admit that this is an independent addition, composed by Isaiah in a very different time period and in different circumstances, in a completely different frame of mind. "The style is slow-moving, long-winded and clumsy, in a way not duplicated in any other pre-exilic prophetic book" (Duhm).

It is also not an easy task to determine whether the section is one single unit. There is no doubt that it is set forth as one kerygmatic unit. But even this does not preclude the fact that this short section has its own history about how it took shape. Formal considerations show that v. 2 has a *meter* (two lines, each with 3 two-stress cola). Even more clearly, the parallel lines, 2a and 2b, correspond to one another, showing that one ought not read the verse as prose. But the rest of it is clearly prosaic (contra Procksch, who thinks that he can at least establish a metrical pattern in v. 3). In addition to this, v. 2 speaks about the fruitfulness of the land, provided by God, but vv. 3f. deal with the purity and holiness of the remnant which remains in Zion. והיה (it shall be) formally starts a new section. In vv. 5b and 6, a still later glossator can be seen at work. It seems that it was an important matter for that expander that the future salvation in Jerusalem would also furnish protection from every form of inclement weather. Since the transmission of the text itself raises so many questions, it is simply not possible that one could be confident about any solution to the problem of composition for this section. It remains most likely that the message of promise in the two poetic lines in v. 2 is the original unit, being expanded first of all by vv. 3–5a and then later, once again, by vv. 5b, 6.

Setting

The question of authenticity, which is also closely connected to the question about the unity of the section, continues to be a matter of dispute. On a purely formal basis, the following would speak against it: the introduction ביום ההוא (on that day) (see above, p. 118, on 2:17), the prosaic form in vv. 3ff., and finally, the observation that even though these three chapters, 2–4, are part of a collection of messages from Isaiah, it is common to find secondary messages of salvation at the conclusion of each. Since the character of this section is so complex, it is possible that at least a core of these words could have come from Isaiah himself. Mauchline presumes that vv. 5f. come from a different situation than vv. 2–4 and that it is questionable whether they, like vv. 2–4, could come from Isaiah. In a similar way, both B. Stade (*ZAW* 4 [1884] 149–151) and K. Budde (*ZAW* 50 [1932] 44ff.) maintain that vv. 2–4 are authentic, even though they both reverse the order, so that, after v. 1, the order is 4, 3, 2, denying vv. 5f. to Isaiah. Dillmann pleads his case that vv. 2–5a are authentic, and Procksch takes at least vv. 2f. to be from Isaiah himself. Finally, one could attempt to preserve, at the very least, the poetic v. 2 as Isaiah's own (see O. Eissfeldt, *The Old Testament. An Introduction* [1964] 317). But there has been general consensus, particularly since the time of Duhm, that the entire section is to be considered a secondary addition (Marti, Kaiser, Fohrer, Eichrodt, Leslie, 203f., A. Weiser, *Introduction to the Old Testament* [1961] 188; R. H. Pfeiffer, *Introduction to the Old Testament* [1953] 439, C. Kuhl, *Die Entstehung des Alten Testaments* [1953] 183). "Ch. 4 is a mosaic of *clichées* from different sources, bearing the mark of epigonism" (A. Bentzen, *Introduction to the Old Testament,* II [1952²] 108). Of course, this judgment is based on exegetical study, which must reexamine Duhm's own conclusion that "the concepts of 'holiness' and 'the escapees of Israel,' the spirit of judgment and the 'rinsing away' of the uncleanness by Yahweh, the physical presence which is assumed to be over the festival assembly, and the allusion to his analogous, original presence above the Mosaic tabernacle are all post-exilic elements." Kaiser's opinion that "it would not be impossible that this first came into existence in the third or early second century before Christ" is connected with an overall conceptualization of the history of the development of the book of Isaiah which is just not acceptable. We will have to let it go with a general statement that it is "postexilic."

The eventual shaping of the book of Isaiah, including such additions which announce salvation, and thereby set all of the harshness of the preceding words of judgment into the framework of Yahweh's eventual goal for history and for his people, apparently was not the learned work of someone sitting at a writing desk, but developed instead in the liturgical use of the prophetic writings in the assemblies of the community during the era of the second temple (cf. chap. 12). Such sections provide evidence for the tension within Judaism in the time after the exile, as it dealt with the message of the prophets, which at that time was already achieving a canonical character and being treated as a source of revelation.

Commentary

[4:2] The correct interpretation of צמח יהוה (whatever Yahweh allows to sprout) is absolutely essential if one is to make any sense of this passage. Gk renders it ἐπιλάμψει ὁ θεός (thereupon God shined) and seems to have had a text with some form of the root צחח (be dazzling) or to have understood צמח on the basis of the Aramaic צמחא, "brightness" (Ziegler, op. cit., 107; cf. Gray, *The Legacy of Canaan,* VTSup 5 [1957]), unless it is simply the result of a rather free translation of the text. 'Aquila, Sym, Theod read ανατολη κυριος (rising of the Lord); Vulg reads *germen Domini* (bud of the Lord); Syr reads *denḥeh dᵉmārjâ* (manifestation, brightness of the Lord). This ought not undermine the MT. The Targ, which surely had the reading צמח (sprout), translates it with משיחא דיהוה (the messiah of Yahweh), which means that it took the phrase to be a messianic title. The commentators of the Middle Ages (Kimchi, Lyra, et al.), but also more modern exegetes like Hengstenberg, Delitzsch, de Lagarde, et al., also treated it in a messianic sense, which explains why E. Sellin maintained that Zerubbabel, from the Davidic family, was meant (*Serubbabel* [1898] 35f.). צמח (sprout) is, in fact, used in the OT when reference is made to the king who would rule when salvation would arrive (see Jer. 23:5: צמח צדיק, a righteous branch; 33:15: צמח צדקה, a righteous branch; Zech. 3:8: עבדי צמח, my servant, the Branch; and 6:12: איש צמח שמו, the man whose name is the Branch; cf. also Ps. 132:17). And yet, the term, as used in the book of Jeremiah, has not yet become a messianic title, but simply refers to "those who come after"; an explicit reference is added to both of the Jeremiah passages: לדוד (for David). But the passages in Zechariah do not make any other point than that they point to Zerubbabel as the descendant of David promised by Jeremiah. However, in Isa. 4:2, the reference is not to a "sprout" for David but rather, a "sprout of Yahweh." In 11:1, Isaiah speaks about a "shoot from the stump of Jesse," a "sprig from his roots." This shows that he also was able to speak about a צמח (sprout) from the family line of David, but hardly about a צמח יהוה (sprout of Yahweh). But since 4:2 is not Isaianic, this line of reasoning does not apply when interpreting this passage. And yet, a most compelling argument against taking this passage in a messianic sense can be found in the parallel in v. 2b: פרי הארץ (fruit of the land). There is no possible way that could be understood as a designation for the Messiah. Vitringa's opinion, that the sprouts from Yahweh and the fruit from the earth pointed to the divine and human nature of the Messiah, certainly cannot be read in between the lines of this particular text. Interpreting "fruit of the earth" as referring to the pious ones in Israel (Raschi), and possibly seeing in the offspring of Yahweh a reference to the holy remnant (Mauchline) falter as an explanation, since "the fruit of the land" is supposed to be provided *for* the redeemed of Israel. There is no other explanation left, except the one which is closest at hand, that the פרי הארץ refers to the fruits which the land will bring forth (Deut. 1:25, and often elsewhere). The expression has the same meaning as what is otherwise referred to in the expression טוב הארץ (good gifts of the land) (1:19; Jer. 2:7) but most explicitly means the same as פרי האדמה (fruit of the ground) (Gen. 4:3, and often elsewhere, especially in the promises of blessing in Deuteronomy, e.g., 28:4, 11, and often elsewhere). In an analogous way, the OT can make reference to the צמח האדמה (what grew on the ground) (Gen. 19:25; cf. Isa. 61:11; Ps. 65:11). Since Yahweh causes the fruit trees to come forth from the ground (צמח *hiph'il,* Gen. 2:9), it should not come as a surprise that one would find reference to יהוה צמח (what Yahweh allows to sprout), even if this expression cannot be found anywhere else in the OT. This phrase emphasizes that every good gift of the land comes from Yahweh (cf. Hos. 2:10). Verse 2 speaks unpretentiously about the expected fruitfulness of the land, just as it is found in the promises of blessing in Leviticus 26 and Deuteronomy 28 (see mention already in Exod. 23:25) and in the prospects for the salvation, as predicted in the prophetic books (Amos 9:13ff.; Isa. 30:23ff.; Jer. 31:12; Isa. 41:17–20; Ezek. 34:29; Zech. 9:16f.; Mal. 3:11, and often elsewhere). It would finally happen "on that day," long expected but not yet come, when Yahweh would allow his salvation to come upon Israel. Since this passage comes from the postexilic era, judgment is already in the distant past; what Isaiah had proclaimed about disaster had already come to pass. Only a remnant, from all Israel, was still left, called here the פליטה (escapees). Yahweh's actions to bring salvation for "those who were still left" was still awaiting its fulfillment. But since the storm which brought the judgment had already passed through Judah and gone on from there, one could speak unguardedly, as if it were Isaiah himself speaking, about the expected eschatological salvation. Of course, this was not yet in the sense which expected that the end of time was near and a transcendent world was soon to follow, but rather in the sense of an unending era when all would be completely restored. This expectation would be realistic for "the escapees of Israel." פליטה (escapees) is expanded upon in v. 3, with נשאר (whatever remains) and נותר (what is still left) (see above, p. 28, on 1:9). The פליטה (escapees) are characteristically referred to as *the remnant,* those who are able to escape during a wartime catastrophe (Gen. 32:9; 2 Sam. 15:14; Isa. 15:9, and often elsewhere). This word apparently does not belong, as do various derivations from the root שאר (remain), to the typical vocabulary used when discussing holy war. But it has theological importance in other secondary passages of the book of Isaiah; see 10:20 and 37:31f. The escapees of Israel constitute the holy community of the postexilic era, who have hopes that the fulfillment of all their present needs will be brought about by the action of Yahweh, one which would provide a lasting change in meeting the challenges of staying alive (though the *verb* פלט, escape, is never used when discussing the eschatological actions by which Yahweh brings salvation).

What Yahweh permits to grow in the time of salvation will provide such an abundance that "decoration and honor" will be bestowed upon the future assembly. Isaiah himself uses צבי (decoration) in a completely secular sense (28:1, 4, 5). But Jeremiah speaks about the land which Yahweh had given to Israel as the נחלת צבי (heritage most beauteous) (3:19), by means of which Israel is accorded special honor in the presence of all the peoples, and the same is true for Ezek. 20:6, 15, which says that the "land flowing with milk and honey" is called the צבי (decorated one) throughout all the countries. In Daniel, the land of Israel is called the ארץ־הצבי (glorious land) (11:16, 41); in fact, it can even be simply designated the צבי (glorious) (8:9), and Zion is the הר־צבי־קדש (the glorious holy mountain) (11:45). צבי (decoration) is thus the preferred term used in the song of praise to describe the land, bestowed upon Israel as a gift, part of the salvation provided by Yahweh. However, according to the present passage, in the coming time of salvation, the fruits which are to be produced in this land will be a "decoration" for the eschatological community, serving to make that community stand out among the "heathen." This צבי (decoration) of the new Israel also constitutes its כבוד (honor). As happens frequently, כבוד is difficult to translate with a single English word. The term includes everything which could describe the future community, calls attention to its importance, and accords it honor (see above, pp. 133f.). In the second half of the verse, these two terms are highlighted still more, with mention of גאון (splendor, majesty) and תפארת (adornment). For the pre-exilic prophets, גאון (splendor) is used only when referring to Yahweh. Every גאון (splendor) which Israel confers arrogantly upon itself will have to be stripped away, showing that it is nothing (Amos 6:8; Hos. 5:5; 7:10, and often elsewhere). On the other hand, according to other passages (Ps. 47:5; Nah. 2:3), the land is Israel's גאון (pride), just as it can be called its צבי (decoration, beauty). For the Chaldeans, their צבי (glory) and תפארת גאון (splendor and pride) are Babylon (Isa. 13:19). In its basic sense, Israel's תפארת (adornment) is

Yahweh himself (Ps. 89:18; see also Isa. 60:19 and 63:15). It might just be by chance that the land is never called Israel's תפארת (adornment). If, according to this present passage, the "fruit of the land" is called Israel's גאון (splendor) and תפארת (adornment), this might be a reflection on the very precarious nature of the economy in the postexilic era (cf. Hag. 1:6, 10f.), at which time the community considered material goods to be a most welcome gift from Yahweh.

[4:3] The one-sided portrayal of the future has been enlarged by a first expander. The different terminology used for the "remnant," נשאר (whatever remains) and נותר (what is still left), does not actually convey any difference in meaning. To show how both פליטה (escapee) and words derived from the root שאר (remain) have been found to mean the same thing, one need only compare the use of פליטה (those who fled) and שאר (the remnant) used together in 10:20 and שארית (remnant) and פליטה (band of survivors) in 37:32. In 37:31, specific mention is made of the פליטה בית יהודה הנשארה (surviving remnant of the house of Judah). No evidence even needs to be provided to show that נשאר (whatever remains) and נותר (what is still left) are thus synonymous.

Whereas v. 2 mentions the remnant of Israel, v. 3 speaks of those in Zion/Jerusalem (see above, on 1:8). The expander was simply not conscious of the unevenness which resulted. As far as he was concerned, there was no problem in seeing those from Israel who escaped as being identical with the remnant in Jerusalem. Not even once is there mention of Judah along with Jerusalem. Those who could still lay claim to represent Israel had assembled in and around the holy city of God and had been waiting there for the promised fulfillment of the deliverance for Israel. That matches the situation which is known from the writings of Haggai and Zechariah, but is also presumably true for the time of Nehemiah and Ezra. The historical developments during the Persian era led to the situation that Jerusalem functioned as the cultic center after the loss of the political sovereignty of Judah, having been accorded far-reaching religious privileges, so that the city became more and more the place where Judaism took shape and where all the important religious decisions were handed down. In addition, in Judaism's expectations for salvation, the city, with its sanctuary, was right in the center of the action. It is there that the eschatological events would originate. From there, salvation would stream forth upon all of Judaism; cf., among other examples, Zech. 1:14–17.

The remnant in Zion was to be called "holy." Isaiah himself never speaks of Israel/Judah or the inhabitants of Zion/Jerusalem as a holy community; he is interested only in proclaiming the holiness of *Yahweh* (see above, pp. 24ff.). גוי קדוש (a holy nation) or עם קדוש (a holy people) is an ancient name of honor for Israel, referring to Israel's election (on this, see H. Wildberger, *Jahwes Eigentumsvolk*, ATANT 37 [1960] 95ff.). In connection with this ancient tradition, Israel is holy because it is the possession of Yahweh and therefore, Israel's enemies ought to watch out so they do not lay a hand on them. According to this present passage, Zion/Jerusalem will be called holy when the Lord—it is certainly not just by chance that Yahweh is not mentioned here—will have completed the action which will effect an eschatological purification.

This holy remnant is defined more explicitly as כל־הכתוב לחיים (all written down for life). There is disagreement about the exact meaning of the formulation as well as the origin of the concept. Normally, it is explained something like this: A remnant of Israelites has been spared at the time of judgment because their names were found in the heavenly book of life. God would have previously decided that they would remain alive. Specific mention is made of this, using the exact words *book of the living,* in the OT in Ps. 69:29. There, the psalmist pleads that his opponents should be stricken from the ספר חיים (book of the living); they are not to be listed any longer among the righteous. (Based on Isa. 4:3, the translation "book of life" is shown to be more correct than "book of the living"; cf. Gk: βίβλος ζώντων, book of the living, but in Phil. 4:3; Rev. 3:5; 13:8 [P⁴⁷א*]; 20:15: βίβλος τῆς ζωῆς, book of life; Rev. 13:8; 17:8; 20:12; 21:27: βίβλιον τῆς ζωῆς, book of life.) In terms of its content, Ps. 69:29 is connected, without a doubt, to Exod. 32:32 ("thy book, which thou hast written") and, finally, also with the book in Dan. 12:1, in which each one who is to be redeemed at the end of time is identified (cf. also "bundle of the living" in 1 Sam. 25:29). It is clear that Israel is familiar with the concept of a heavenly book, in which Yahweh either writes, or causes to be written, all the names of the righteous who are to remain alive. If the name of any one of them is erased, that one must die. There is no thought of an eternal life in the OT passages. It also ought not to be presumed that virtually everyone who is alive has been recorded in this book before God. Only select individuals or the group of those who are to survive the catastrophe are registered. Therefore, חיים (life) must be understood here, as elsewhere, in a qualified sense: living under the protection of God and helped along by his blessing (concerning the understanding of "life" in the OT, see Ch. Barth, *Die Errettung vom Tode in den individuellen Klage- und Dankliedern des Alten Testaments* [1947] 21–51; cf. also G. von Rad, "'Gerechtigkeit' und 'Leben' in der Kultsprache der Psalmen," FS A. Bertholet [1950] 418–437 = GesSt, TBü 8, 225–247; W. Zimmerli, "'Leben' und 'Tod' im Buche des Propheten Ezechiel," *TZ* 13 [1957] 494–508 = GesAufs 178–191). The MT's understanding of the βίβλος τῆς ζωῆς (book of life) is not as far removed from that of the OT as it might at first appear. The OT, of course, also speaks of such a book before God in another sense. Ps. 56:9 mentions a book of Yahweh in which all the tears of those who are distressed are recorded; Ps. 139:16 mentions a book in which all the deeds of the one who is praying (read גְּמָלָי, my deeds) are written; Mal. 3:16 speaks of a ספר זכרון (book of remembrance); cf. also Isa. 65:6; Dan. 7:10; see, in addition, Ethiopic Enoch 81:4; 89:61–64, and often elsewhere, and also Rev. 20:12. Kaiser points out that a similar expression is used in Yasna 31:14. The original source of the figure of speech "book of life" is most generally connected with the list of the citizens of Jerusalem, using Jer. 22:30 as a prime reference (Dillmann, Duhm, Procksch, et al.); see also Ezek. 13:9, where mention is made of כתב בית־ישראל (enrolled in the register of the house of Israel), and Ezra 2:62; Neh. 7:5, 64; 12:22f., and cf. Ps. 87:6. But since God himself writes the names in the book of life and, therefore, is the only one able to remove them once again, and since those who are written into the book are not simply the living, but rather those designated as the ones who are to live a full life, the origin of this metaphor is

169

problematic. Because of this, others have suggested that the royal "book of memorable deeds," the ספר הזכרנות, serves as the model for the book of life. This concept could actually be behind those passages which speak of the book in which human achievements are listed. But, in the book of life, names, not deeds, are recorded. For this reason, still others have made comparisons with the destiny tablets which are mentioned in connection with Babylon (see B. Meissner, *Babylonien und Assyrien,* II [1925] 125, and *TDNT* I, 619f.). *Nabû,* the god of writing, is called the "one who carries the gods' destiny tablet." One can beseech *Nabû,* the one who writes on the tablet at Esagila, to "inscribe on his tablet a long existence" for someone's lifetime. One acknowledges: "My life is written in your presence" and requests: "Upon your tablet which cannot be altered . . . proclaim length of days for me, write down offspring!" (see KAT³ 401 and SAHG 286). If one can interpret Isa. 4:3 on the basis of this concept, then the remnant in Zion could be the assembly of those designated by God, in an act of election, to receive eschatological salvation. The salvation is dependent upon predestination.

[4:4] The eschatological community is prepared by means of an act of purification. This comes about through the Spirit, called in this passage רוח משפט (spirit of judgment) (see also Isa. 28:6) and רוח בער (spirit of cleansing). משפט means many things; it is unlikely that it means simply "justice," since it is used with בער (cleansing); it must be referring to a purifying judgment, not one which happens during a catastrophe within history (although it is possible that Isaiah himself did refer to such a catastrophe in history), but rather one carried out through the Spirit of God. הדיח (rinse away) belongs to the cultic language of Jerusalem (Ezek. 40:38; 2 Chron. 4:6), but here it is used to describe an eschatological activity of God. One might think of Zech. 4:6: "Not by might, nor by power, but by my Spirit," and naturally also of the baptism through the Holy Spirit (Mark 1:8, and often elsewhere): The רוח יהוה (Spirit of Yahweh) is God's power which judges and brings salvation (see *TDNT* VI, 362f.). In case בער ought to be taken to mean "burn completely"—see above, textual note 4c—one might also connect this with the "baptism of fire" referred to in the NT (Matt. 3:11f./Luke 3:16f.; see *TDNT* VI, 376f., 943). Thus, the holiness of the future community depends upon a "baptism," which is not effected through water but through the Spirit. The Qumran documents also refer to a cleansing through the Spirit: "[God] cleanses [טהר *pi'el*] the community, through the Holy Spirit, from all godless deeds, and he will let the spirit of truth be poured out upon all the members, just like water used for purification [מי נדה], to get rid of all the abominations of lies" (I Q S IV, 21; cf. III, 6ff.).

The "filth of the daughters of Zion" and the "bloodguilt of Jerusalem" will be "washed away." צאה means, in its basic sense, human excrement (see Isa. 36:12 Qere = 2 Kings 18:27 Qere). The text does not answer the question about whether the uncleanness was a result of cultic or ethical offenses and which would have been judged worse than the other by the author of the section. The plural דמים actually means "bloodguilt" (Exod. 22:1; 1 Sam. 25:26, and often elsewhere), but the אנשי דמים (bloodthirsty men) (Ps. 26:9, and often elsewhere) are plainly not all murderers in the literal sense; see above, p. 48, on 1:15, and, in addition,

Prov. 29:10. Nineveh is a עיר דמים (bloody city) (Nah. 3:1), but not simply in the sense that it is a city populated by murderers, but because it is full of lying and oppression and there is no end to robbery in sight. Jerusalem is similarly described by Ezekiel as a bloody city (22:2; 24:6, 9). Blood-guilt can also be brought upon oneself by violating the regulations for making offerings (Lev. 17:4); in the same way, it could come because of worshiping idols (see Exod. 22:3ff.). According to priestly understanding, which must be presumed as the background for this present passage, bloodguilt is connected with every single offense which disregards the taboos ordained by God, departing from the order which God established. Using דמים (bloodguilt) serves to characterize the offense in its full depth, not to be overcome by any rational actions, not to be removed through any counteracting of the wrong by doing good works.

[4:5, 6] Verses 5f., which are difficult to understand in their specific details, speak about the protection which the community will find upon Zion. The concept that Yahweh creates a cloud by day and smoke by night and the glow of a flaming fire over every single dwelling upon the mountain of Zion and over all of its assemblies (on מקראים, festival days, see above, p. 45, on 1:13) is quite unique (see above, textual note 5a; for another view, see H. W. Hertzberg, BZAW 66 [1936] 117, who considers the Septuagint text to be more original, whereas the change suggested by the MT would "make allowances for a conceptualization of God as one who was more transcendent." But the concept of an eschatological appearance of God above Zion, hidden by clouds and smoke, would not have been offensive in a later era either).

It was a fixed element in the ancient traditions concerning the exodus from Egypt that Yahweh was out ahead, pulling Israel along ולילה ... יומם בעמוד ענן בעמוד אש (by day in a pillar of cloud . . . and by night in a pillar of fire) (Exod. 13:21f.; see 14:19, 24; Deut. 1:33; Ps. 78:14, and often elsewhere). "Leading Israel" thus refers to Yahweh being in charge. But in the traditions about Sinai, the discussion centers around theophanies in a cloud: הנה אנכי בא אליך בעב הענן (Lo, I am coming to you in a thick cloud) (Exod. 19:9), but there is also mention of Yahweh's appearance in fire, along with thunder and lightning, and hidden in smoke (19:18), after which God begins to speak. Here Yahweh reveals himself in order to make his will known (cf. 34:5; Deut. 4:11ff.; 5:22). In such circumstances, concepts are used which apparently are connected with the storm god, an idea which is still exercising some influence (see Ps. 18:9ff. = 2 Sam. 22:9ff.; Psalm 29; Ps. 97:2ff.). It is hardly surprising that the two complexes of traditions blended together, e.g., when it is reported that the *pillars* of cloud took their places at the entrance to the tent every time Yahweh conversed there with Moses (Exod. 33:9f.; Deut. 31:15, and often elsewhere). Even Ezekiel sees Yahweh's coming, in his call vision, according to the pattern of the ancient storm theophany (1:4, here as in Ps. 18:13 = 2 Sam. 22:13, using נגה [brightness], which is also used in Isa. 4:5, along with ענן [cloud], עשן [smoke], and אש [blazing fire]; concerning the general concept of theophany, see H. J. Kraus, BK XV/1, 144f. [Engl: *Psalms 1–59*, 261] and J. Jeremias, *Theophanie*, WMANT 10 [1965]). In the later stages of its development, as can be seen most clearly in the priestly writings, Yahweh does not himself actually appear, but his כָּבוֹד (glory) is seen in the cloud (Ezek. 1:28; Exod. 16:10, and often elsewhere). The motif of the cloud, in which Yahweh makes an appearance, attached itself over a matter of time to the Jerusalem temple ideology. If one knew that pillars of cloud had come down upon the tent of meeting, so that Yahweh could appear, one could now describe the "cloud," and the כָּבוֹד (glory) of Yahweh along with it, filling the temple (1 Kings 8:10f.; cf. Isa. 6:4; Ezek. 10:4; Exod. 40:34f.).

One must bear in mind that the concept of the revelation of Yahweh in the clouds and in fire was subjected to quite a variety of modifications as the religious history of Israel unfolded, and only then will one be able to assess correctly the connections with traditions *and* the unique alterations of the ancient idea as it is interpreted in Isa. 4:5f. As far as the juxtaposition of עָנָן יוֹמָם (cloud by day) and אֵשׁ לַיְלָה (blazing fire by night) is concerned, it is easy to recognize that the author has in mind the ancient concept of the God who led Israel during the wilderness period. On the other hand, he uses the concepts after they have already been united with concepts about Zion. But he boldly proclaims, using the term ברא (create), which has its roots in the description of Yahweh's creative activity, that Yahweh will begin by creating cloud and glowing fire. It was only with Deutero-Isaiah that ברא, the technical term for creating, was transposed to be used to describe the coming time of salvation and, furthermore, to see this as a new creation. Yahweh re-creates, in the eschatological future, that which he had once provided for Israel in the former act of salvation in the past. And yet, cloud and glowing fire would have a new meaning above Zion, since the people have already been in the land a long time and do not have any further need to be guided on a journey. Above the כָּבוֹד (magnificence, glory), for which the cloud and glowing fire simply serve as a vehicle, a protective roof would be stretched out. The decisive element in this new act of salvation is found in the absolute protective security, about which the community of Zion could rejoice in the future (see above, textual note 5a, concerning Ps. 105:39). חָפָּה (חפה, "wrap up") is used elsewhere in the OT to describe the bridal chamber (Ps. 19:6; Joel 2:16; see also m. Yeb. 3:10, and often elsewhere, and cf. Dalman, *AuS* VI, 35, and A. G. Barrois, *Manuel d'archéologie biblique,* II [1935] 18), but in this case its exact meaning is determined by the parallel term סֻכָּה (leafy canopy). The cultic songs about Jerusalem announce that Yahweh has a shelter (סכה or סֹךְ) or a place of residence upon Zion, and the pious person who prays confesses that God hides that person in his shelter (Ps. 27:5; 31:21; see above, pp. 30f.). No more need be said about the function of the sanctuary as a place of protection and asylum. Yahweh's shelter or tent is the place of refuge for the pious (סֵתֶר, cover, Ps. 27:5; 31:21a; cf. מסתור, shelter, in Isa. 4:6b, and מחסה, refuge, next to סתר, shelter, in 28:17), protecting one who is hidden within the deepest confines of the shelter. But what comes as a great surprise is the fact that the protection anticipated for the eschatological era when salvation, which the believers already had to some extent upon Zion, would acquire new and deeper dimensions with provision for protection from heat, downpours, and rain. The glossator, in vv. 5b, 6, seems to have taken the least common denominator to explain what cloud, smoke, and fire would mean for Zion and its assemblies. But it is possible that he considered heat and rain as images of powers which were able to disrupt the peace and contentedness within the community of the Holy One. Isa. 25:4abα uses what seems to be a very close parallel to this passage: "For thou hast been a stronghold to the poor, a stronghold to the needy in his distress, a shelter from the storm and a shade from the heat" (מחסה מזרם צל מחרב). Commentary is furnished for this statement in 4bβ, 5: "For the blast of the ruthless was like a 'wintry' downpour, like heat in a dry place...." But one must also remember that hail, floods of water, storm, and downpour all accompany or serve as symbolic images of the wrath of God (28:17; 30:30). No matter how that might be related, it is, in any case, the main purpose of the text to show plainly that in the time of salvation the believing community upon Zion would have no reason to be terrified of any dominions and powers that would hold sway over them. In a way which would far outstrip both times past, when God had led the people in that ancient great time of the wandering in the wilderness, and the present, when the believers were sheltered by the sanctuary of Yahweh, absolute, secure protection would be provided in the future.

Purpose and Thrust

The various authors who made their contribution to this section apparently paid scant attention to preserving the unique aspects of the elements of tradition which came before their own time. At a relatively late time, the transmitted materials were used in a new way, even a rather loose way, so as to give a definite shape to hopes for the future. As this section now stands, vv. 3f. provide the theological center: the proclamation of a new Israel which can be called holy. The action of the divine grace for the escapees of Israel could reach its goal only when the Spirit of God had finished his cleansing and purifying activity. The economically oppressive conditions in postexilic Israel are sufficient to explain why the richness of the gifts of the land, as rich as paradise itself, were not carried still further to develop a spiritualized adaptation of the traditions. On the other hand, the requirement for security which can be detected in the text is the result of confronting the difficulties which made things increasingly unstable, an instability which Israel could not control simply with its own resources. The portrayal of the future offered in this section developed out of the question about which promises of God might still be applicable to those living in the gloom of the postexilic era, those promises having been made in the great era now past. The faith of Israel made an effort here to keep hold of the ancient promises at a time when the new situation brought marked changes. This faith had acknowledged the validity of the judgment which had been imposed since it considered itself, the community of the present age, to be the "holy remnant." It is part and parcel of the limitations placed on the expectations of salvation in the OT, plainly visible in so many different situations, that hope for all the peoples does not come up for consideration in the message (see, on the other hand, 2:2–4). What is still more significant is that the proclamation of salvation is made without Isaiah's call to believe. It seems that promises are made here without any demand for human response toward God. In this way, the section is in obvious tension with Isaiah's own proclamation. But it is not fair to say that the glossators leave the impression that they are minimizing the threats from the past (Fohrer). One must rather understand this on the basis of the deep unrest which Israel experienced after the collapse of the ancient orders. The people's radical loss of orientation is answered in this section by a proclamation of the grace of God which would take effect only because it was rooted in the divine election. The section gives witness to Israel's condition, having made a sober appraisal of its external and internal circumstances, without mistaking the inadequacy of Israel's own faith and obedience in times past; but yet the section shows that Israel desired to keep on acknowledging God's faithfulness and, therefore, to stay true to the goal of walking on the path upon which God was leading it.

Isaiah 5:1–7

The Song of the Vineyard

Literature

M. Cersoy, "L'apologue de la vigne au chapitre V[e] d'Isaïe (versets 1–7)," *RB* 8 (1899) 40–49. P. Haupt, "Isaiah's Parable of the Vineyard," *AJSL* 19 (1902/03) 193–202. A. Bentzen, "Zur Erläuterung von Jes 5:1–7," *AfO* 4 (1927) 209–210. W. C. Graham, "Notes on the Interpretation of Isaiah 5:1–14," *AJSL* 45 (1928/29) 167–178. Dalman, *AuS* IV, 291–468. H. Junker, "Die literarische Art von Is 5:1–7," *Bib* 40 (1959) 259–266. S. Pezzella, "La parabola della vigna Is 5:1–7," *BeO* 5 (1963) 5–8. H. Kosmala, "Form and Structure in Ancient Hebrew Poetry (continued)," *VT* 16 (1966) 152–180 (see esp. 167f.).

[**Literature update through 1979**: P. Buis, "Notification de jugement et confession nationale," *BZ* NF 11 (1967) 193–205. P. R. Berger, "Ein unerklärtes Wort in dem Weinberglied Jesajas (Jes 5,6)," *ZAW* 82 (1970) 116f. W. Schottroff, "Das Weinberglied Jesajas (Jes 5,1–7)," *ZAW* 82 (1970) 68–91. K. Beyer, "Althebräische Syntax in Prosa und Poesie," FS K. G. Kuhn (1971) 76–96 (see esp. 92–96). W. E. Rast, "Disappointed Expectation in the Old Testament," *Perspectiva* 12 (1971) 135–152. M. Har'el, "כרם היה לידידי בקרן בן־שמן (Is. 5,1–2)," in B. Uffenheimer, ed., *HaMiḳra' weToledot Yiśra'el* (1972). H. J. Krause, "hôj als prophetische Leichenklage über das eigene Volk im 8. Jahrhundert," *ZAW* 85 (1973) 15–46. D. Lys, "La vigne et le double je. Exercice de style sur Esaie V 1–7," *VTSup* 26 (1974) 1–16. O. Loretz, "Weinberglied und prophetische Deutung im Protest-Song Jes 5,1–7," *UF* 7 (1975) 573–576. J. T. Willis, "The Genre of Isaiah 5:1–7," *JBL* 96 (1977) 337–362.]

Text

5:1 Let me sing[a] about my friend,
    the song of my beloved[b] about his vineyard.
My friend owned a vineyard
    up on a fertile headland.[c]
2 He dug around it and removed its stones,[a]
    he planted it with excellent vines,[b]
built a tower within it
    and even[c] constructed a winepress in it.
Then he expected that it would produce[d] grapes for him,
    but in fact it produced nothing but rotten berries.
3 And now, inhabitants[a] of Jerusalem
    and men of Judah!

175

> Go ahead, judge between me
> and my vineyard!
> 4 What was yet to be done[a] for my vineyard,
> which I would not have done for[b] it?
> Why did I hope that it would bring forth grape clusters,
> and it bore[c] nothing but rotten berries?
> 5 Well, I want to announce to you,
> what I am going to do to my vineyard!
> Remove[a] its hedge,[c]
> so that it will be grazed bare,
> tear down[b] its wall,
> so that it will be given over to be trampled.
> 6 [a]I will let it be given over for destruction,[a]
> it shall not be pruned
> and not hoed; it is going to become
> thorns and thistles.
> And I will command the clouds,
> not[b] to moisten it with rain.
> 7 For the vineyard of Yahweh of Hosts
> is the house of Israel,
> and the men of Judah
> are the planting of his delight.[a]
> He hoped for judging in justice,
> but look there: destroying through injustice,
> for covenant faithfulness,
> but look there: cries of helplessness!

1a Concerning the cohortative with נא (I pray, now), see Joüon, Gr §114d; see also אודיעה־נא, well, I want to announce, in v. 5.

1b It is not necessary to change דודי (my beloved) to read דודים (my beloved ones) (Lowth, et al.) or to דודי (my beloved ones) (Cersoy, et al.; see B. Stade, *ZAW* 26 [1906] 134f.).

1c Procksch would rather read בן־שמש (son of the sun) instead of בן־שמן (fertile, lit.: son of fatness), since "the sun is necessary for the vineyard." That may indeed be the most important matter to which attention must be given in a German vineyard, but for a Palestinian vineyard, the most important concern is the nature of the soil (see Dalman, *AuS* IV, 308).

2a The *pi'el* סקל (remove stones) has a privative meaning; see Joüon, Gr §52d.

2b Concerning the double accusative with נטע (plant), cf. BrSynt §94b.

2c The suggestion made by K. Budde (*ZAW* 50 [1932] 55) to read וְגַת וַיֶּקֶב, "winepress and vat," instead of וגם יקב (and even a winepress) destroys the intentional effort which heightens awareness about the extraordinary attention which was given to laying out the vineyard.

2d G. R. Driver (FS Th. H. Robinson [1950] 53f.) suggests that one ought to interpret עשה (produce) in light of the Arabic, meaning "press out," in which case Yahweh would remain the logical subject of the infinitive, an interpretation which is too speculative for one to be inclined to follow it; cf. also the similar expression עשה פרי (bear fruit upward) (2 Kings 19:30, and often elsewhere).

3a Qᵃ: יושבי (inhabitants), instead of the singular, but איש (men) is also a singular collective.

4a Concerning the use of ל with the construct infinitive, to express a necessary activity, cf. BrSynt §47.

4b Some MSS read, instead of בו (in it), rather לו (for it) (Gk: αὐτῷ, to it; Targ: להון, to them; Syr: *leh*, to him; Vulg: *ei*, to it); possibly this is more correct. Qᵃ reads, in the first colon, בכרמי (in my vineyard), instead of לכרמי (for my vineyard). Both of these alterations were the result of the copyists not understanding that "vineyard" is a metaphor for a wife.

4c For וישע (it bore), Qᵃ reads וישה (and it lifted up). Is that nothing more than a copying mistake (in v. 2, Qᵃ reads וישה, but it produced)? Possibly Qᵃ had in mind a derivation of the verb נשא (lift, bear, carry) (cf. Ezek. 17:8: נשא פרי, bear fruit, mentioned in connection with a grape vine; in addition, see 36:8; Ps. 72:3).

5ab Here we have infinitive absolutes with a future sense; the imperfect in v. 6 continues the thought of the infinitive (cf. Joüon, Gr §119p and 123w).

5c The vocalization מְשׂוּכָּתוֹ leaves open the question about whether it is to be read מְשְׂכָּתוֹ (its covering) (from שׂכך, overshadow, screen, cover) or מְשׂוּכָתוֹ (its hedge) (sometimes written מסוכתו, from שׂוּךְ or סוּךְ, hedge, fence about, shut in; cf. Mic. 7:4; Prov. 15:19). The two roots of the verb are related, so that there is no change in meaning in either case.

6a–a It has been suggested, following Perles, that ואשׁביתהו should be read: "and I want to plan for its demise," but that just avoids the difficulty inherent in בתה (destruction). It is just as unacceptable simply to eliminate ואשׁיתהו בתה (I will let it be given over to destruction), following Buhl and Fohrer. Many identify בתה (destruction) with the (just as uncertain) word בַּתָּה, in 7:19, for which "precipice, ravine," or something similar has been suggested as a translation (cf. the Arabic *batta,* "cut off"), but this can also mean "decline, utter ruin," or something similar (Eichrodt: "I will make it an utter ruin"). We follow G. R. Driver (*JTS* 38 [1937] 38), who refers to the Akkadian *batû,* "demolish," and postulates, for בתה, the meaning "ruin," or something similar; he also consults the Targ (רטישׁין, abandoned), Syr (*nehrab,* he will be destroyed), and Vulg (*desertam,* deserted).

6b Concerning the negating function of מן (from), see BrSynt §111f.

7a Note the chiasmus which is found in the first two lines of v. 7!

Form

This section, which is generally recognized as a unit, is identified in v. 1 as a שׁירת דודי, "Song of My Beloved"; if one changes the text to read שׁירת דוֹדִי (see above, textual note 1b), then it would be translated "Love Song." Cersoy, who advocated this solution, certainly has a "Friend's Song" in mind, by means of which the prophet would try to comfort his friend and let him know that he is also deeply affected, as a friend, by the latter's disappointment with the vineyard. Presumably, the prophet quotes, in vv. 1b, 2, the beginning of a short little popular song. It is frequently suggested that Isaiah wanted to get the attention of his listeners by playing the part of a popular singer, which has led to the song being interpreted sometimes as the song of the vineyard, sometimes as a love song. To interpret it as a love song is initially based on the textual correction which has been mentioned already, but can also be substantiated by the frequent comparison which is made, in descriptions about love in the ancient world, between the bride and a "vineyard" (see below, p. 182, and G. Gerleman, *Ruth/Das Hohelied,* BK XVIII, 100f.), and for this reason this interpretation has been accepted by some. But if one tries to use this approach consistently through the whole text, then one runs into all sorts of problems. Who is the דוד/ידיד (beloved) in v. 1, about whom Isaiah sings the song? H. Schmidt is of the opinion, also advocated by Budde, op. cit., 53, and Fohrer, that the bride is speaking of her bridegroom; this is not feasible, not only because the bride would certainly never say, in a love song, that she bore bitter fruit, but it is even more clearly incorrect because the one speaking in the first person in vv.

3f. is not the "vineyard," but the owner of the vineyard. Bentzen (op. cit.) has gone a step further by advocating an interpretation which states that the prophet attempts to keep alive the illusion, all the way to v. 7, that he is presenting the melancholy lament of a friend, who viewed himself as having been betrayed in his love. For example, v. 6 would mean that the faithless beloved one was not going to be given the chance to have any children in her marriage. According to Bentzen, Isaiah carries through, to the very end, a double pseudonymity: He speaks about his friend so that the audience will not figure out that Yahweh is the one being referred to, and he also speaks about an unthankful lover, without giving the audience a chance to recognize that he is really referring to the people, until the beloved would have spoken its own judgment sentence to itself, based on the presumed verdict passed down by the lover. Bentzen's interpretation is basically correct, but needs to be modified in certain details. It does not explain why Isaiah speaks about Yahweh as *his own* יָדִיד/דוד (beloved), and thus, not as the beloved of the bride. No evidence needs to be provided to show that Isaiah is not using the language of a mystic. But Junker (op. cit.) has recently provided a further clarification, referring to the designation ὁ φίλος τοῦ νυμφίου (the friend of the bridegroom) (John 3:29), a technical term for the one who arranges the marriage, identical to what the rabbis called שׁוֹשְׁבִין, "best man at a wedding." Since, according to custom, there was to be no direct contact between the groom and bride before the wedding took place, the "friend of the bridegroom" assumed the role of go-between and spokesman for the bridegroom. In addition, he was to represent the bridegroom when the husband had occasion to accuse the bride of something. According to Ex R 46 (101a), he is the one who is authorized to tear up the official wedding certificate if the bride has acquired an evil reputation, using the words: "It is better that she is judged as a single person than as a married woman." In regard to similar circumstances and for a summary of the overall function of the one who brings forth the bride, see Str-B I, 500ff. If, therefore, Isaiah speaks of Yahweh as his יָדִיד/דוד (beloved), that does not suggest any special intimacy which he had with God, which would seem very odd in his case, but rather, it means that he wants to leave the impression that he is serving as the "friend" of the bridegroom who is bringing an accusation about the indecent behavior of the bride.

But yet, Duhm is correct: "Isaiah does not want to sing a love song, or even his own love song . . . , and one ought not try to conjecture how one might make all of this fit aesthetically." One might indeed speak about a "song of the vineyard" or a "parable of the vineyard," based on its content, but that does not yet get at the real essence of the form. The "friend of the bridegroom" stands up as an accuser. According to its formal characteristics, what we have here is a judgment speech, more correctly an accusation speech, spoken in the name of a disappointed lover who sees himself as having been cheated. In marked contrast to the speeches of judgment in 1:2f.; 1:18ff., and 3:13ff., which point back to the covenant with God, the present accusation is set within the framework of the jurisdiction of the civil justice system. An accusation speech includes "establishing the fact that there is a mutual relation which binds the accuser and the accused, demonstration on the part of the accuser that his own obligations have been fulfilled, the accusation about the shortcomings in the one who is accused, who has failed to fulfill obligations, and the summons to those in the community responsible for justice to come together to pass judgment" (Fohrer). All of these elements are to be found in vv. 1–4. The passage goes beyond the basic form in vv. 5f. when the speaker functions no longer solely as the accuser, but also as the judge, who announces the punishment; further, vv. 5f. give the impression that this accuser, now functioning also as judge, is in fact Yahweh himself.

Meter: Haupt (op. cit.) believed that it was possible to establish a text which has four strophes, each with 4 two-stress bicola, a uniformity which he is able to achieve only after numerous alterations to the text. All too often, others have proposed alterations in order to establish a meter which is as consistent as possible. In vv. 1–3, 7 five-stress cola can be found (שירת דודי, song of my beloved, in v. 1aβ, is *one* stress; ויסקלהו, and removed its stones, in v. 2aα, has two stresses. Since Isaiah undoubtedly did not pronounce it שפטו [judge], but rather שָׁפְטוּ [judge], in v. 3bα, it also has three separate enunciated syllables). Verse 4 is constructed with 2 six-stress cola (2 + 2 + 2), by means of which the indignation detected in these questions is given expression. The announcement of punishment follows in v. 5a, using a very heavy four-stress bicolon; the judgment in vv. 5b, 6a follows with four harsh-sounding two-stress bicola (v. 6aβ is most likely to be read: ולא יעדר ועלה שמיר ושית, and not hoed; it is going to become thorns and thistles). In v. 6b, the announcement of punishment comes to an end with a three-stress bicolon (the article on העבים, the clouds, may be a "prosaicising element." Verse 7, giving the meaning of the allegory, is composed by using a five-stress colon (v. 7aα) and 3 two-stress bicola (vv. 7aβ, ba, and bβ, with לצדקה, for justice, thus having two stresses, which gives it the strongest emphasis of all). The change in the pattern of the stresses in the verses apparently corresponds to the content; see Kosmala (op. cit.).

Setting

The authenticity has not been questioned. Nothing more specific can be said, here either, about the exact circumstances behind this. In general, it is assumed that Isaiah presented this message at a fall, or vintage, festival. That is possible, not so much because the imagery of the vineyard is used, but rather because Israel's relationship to Yahweh was carefully examined at the time of the Fall Festival. There is also general agreement that the song belongs to Isaiah's early period of activity. There is nothing to suggest that any of the terrible catastrophes of war have as yet come upon the land. The place of the song in the book of Isaiah also speaks in favor of this dating, since the woe-oracles which follow are without a doubt from the first period of Isaiah's activity. A point made by Duhm is also well taken; he says Isaiah "was so well known in the later period of his activity, even among the people of the land, that any attempted disguise would not have worked very well then."

Commentary

[5:1a] Reflections upon the form of 5:1–7 have led to the conclusion that the דוד/ידיד (beloved) is the bridegroom, by whose authority the prophet claims to speak. The OT uses ידיד almost solely when referring to the "beloved" *of God* (Deut. 33:12; Jer. 11:15; Pss. 60:7; 108:7; 127:2). In Ugarit, *ydd* or *mdd 'il* "Beloved of El" is a standard epithet of Mot (I* AB I 8, and often elsewhere) and Yamm (II AB II 34, and often elsewhere; cf.

also the personal name *mdd-b'l*). As the Arabic cognates show, the factor of friendship is most central in the verbal root ידד. Unfortunately, there is no way to determine whether Yahweh is known as the ידיד (beloved) of Israel (concerning the name ידידיה, Jedidah, 2 Sam. 12:25, see M. Noth, *Die israelitischen Personnennamen,* BWANT III/10 [1928] no. 577). It is likely that this is the case with the parallel term דוד. This word means "relative, friend" (see Amos 6:10; 1 Chron. 27:32), but also "uncle," in the sense of a father's brother (Lev. 10:4, and often elsewhere), and "loved one, beloved" (Song of Sol. 1:13ff., and often elsewhere). Akkadian uses divine names such as *Dadi-ilu* (G. W. Ahlström, *Psalm 89* [1959] 164) and personal names such as *Abu-dadi, Dadija, Dadanu* (see *AHW* 149). In line 12 of the Mesha-inscription, which unfortunately is not very easy to understand in that aspect, דוד (beloved) seems to be an epithet of Yahweh (on this, see S. Segert, *ArOr* 29 [1961] 241), and for Amos 8:14 a conjecture which makes some sense has been suggested, reading, parallel to אלהיך (thy god), not דרך (the way), but rather דּדְךָ (your beloved). Ahlström (op. cit., 167) has defended the thesis "that Dwd is the form which a 'vegetation deity' takes and is the way in which it is worshiped in the Jerusalem temple" (a similar view had already been advocated by Th. J. Meek, "Canticles and the Tammuz Cult," *AJSL* 39 [1922/23] 1–14). But the available material is too limited to guarantee that such conclusions are valid. Yet, it does give some support to the notion that Isaiah's audience, insofar as they were paying close attention, could have gotten the idea that the "friend" or "beloved" of Isaiah had to be Yahweh. According to what has been determined about the form of 5:1–7, it is most surprising that this section of Isaiah's material is called a שירה (song). But the prophet does not lay all his cards on the table; he describes it as a harmless שירה (song), which quickly pops out of its cocoon to become a harsh accusation. In Ps. 45:1, the song of praise about the bridegroom and bride is designated a שיר ידידות (concerning such songs about the bride, see Str-B I, 513ff.). The question remains whether שיר ידידות actually means "song of love," which is how one generally sees it translated but which does not in any way fit the content of the psalm. Maybe it ought to be translated as "song about the female loved one," that is, the bride.

[5:1b] Isaiah's "friend" laid out his "vineyard" on a fertile "headland." It is not easy to say what קרן exactly means, since the word is used only this one time in a description of a geological formation. "Horn" is certainly not intended in the sense of a peak of a hill. KBL gives the meaning "slope of a hill" (so also A. W. Schwarzenbach, "Die geographische Terminologie im Hebräischen des Alten Testamentes," diss., Zurich [1954] 19f.). But it is hard to figure out why a slope of a hill would be called a "horn," and it is not absolutely necessary that a vineyard be set on a slope in Palestine. In Greek, κέρας (horn) can also refer to a branch of a river (cf. the "golden horn" of Constantinople) and the Latin *cornu* (horn) can refer to a spit of land. In German, "horn" designates the type of meadow found in a crooked and narrow valley. But all of these possibilities can be eliminated. The most likely explanation, following Budde, is that this refers to the "spur" of a mountain (op. cit., 55).

[5:2a] KBL renders the *hapax leg.* עזק as "hoe, weed," Ges-Buhl as "break up soil." Gk (φραγμὸν περιέθηκα, I placed a fence around it) and Vulg (*saepivit,* surround it with a hedge) did not understand the original sense correctly. The Arabic *'azaqa* means "hoe up, dig up" and the rabbinic Hebrew עזק is used to describe the "most basic activity of working up a field" (Dalman, *AuS* IV, 323f.; cf. rabbinic Hebrew עֲזִיקָה, "broken up soil"). Thus, the word simply does not refer to ongoing hoeing or weeding, but rather to deeper digging up of the ground which is necessary to prepare the soil so that it is ready for planting the grape vines. It is also part of the original preparation, when one set up a new vineyard, that the ground had to have the stones removed (סקל). One would either throw all the stones onto the path or pile them up in layers along the entire border of the plot, to form a protective wall, and one could also use them to set up a retaining wall to prevent erosion (Dalman, op. cit., 309; cf. Isa. 62:10). After the ground is prepared in this way, the vines are planted; in this case, they are vines of highest quality. In Jer. 2:21, one comes across the idea that Yahweh planted Israel in the land as a שׂרק (choice vine of the highest quality), זֶרַע אֱמֶת (wholly of pure seed). There it is said that they had become "stinking, rotten vines" (סוּרִיָה, text emended) and had become a "wild vine." According to the root meaning of שׂרק, this must refer to a bright red type of grape (cf. R. Gradwohl, *Die Farben im Alten Testament,* BZAW 83 [1963] 21f.). Judg. 16:4 mentions the נחל שׂרק (valley of Sorek), which had been as famous as משׂרקה (Masrekah) in Edom (Gen. 36:36; 1 Chron. 1:47) because of the high quality of grapes which flourished there.

Thus, the owner of the vineyard wanted to provide a wonderful example of what a vineyard could be and built a tower in the middle of his property. Normally, one would have been content with just having a hut in the vineyard (see above, p. 31, on 1:8). But a מגדל (tower) offers much better accommodations for the one who protects the vineyard (see Dalman, op. cit., 317 and 333; illus. no. 94 shows a round tower built up with layers of unhewn stones). It is certainly obvious that someone would also install a winepress. יקב (winepress) (cf. the Arabic *waqb* "depression"; rabbinic Hebrew יקב *pi'el* "hollow out") seems more specifically to refer to the trough of a winepress, the vat, whereas גת is used when describing the entire winepress. Yet, the two terms are not easy to distinguish. A winepress can be manufactured by using wood, clay, or stone; in all of these varieties, it would have to be made watertight. It is constructed by hollowing out an upper and a lower pit, the upper serving as the place for treading (see Amos 9:13; Isa. 63:2, and often elsewhere), while the lower one, into which the grape juice would flow through a groove, called a צָנּוּר, would serve as a temporary holding tank (illuss.: Dalman, op. cit., nos. 95f., 99–111; in addition, G. E. Wright, *Biblical Archaeology* [1957] no. 133).

[5:2b] It is easy to understand why one who owned such property, and had paid so much attention to all the details, going to such great expense to set it up, would have high hopes for a high-quality harvest (cf. Song of Sol. 8:11). But at this very point Isaiah can say: "He expected that it would produce grapes for him," which means that he anticipated nothing more than that it would produce a decent yield. But the vineyard produced nothing but באשים (rotten berries). This word also, which is found only here and in the verses which follow in this same section, cannot be defined exactly. Gk reads ἀκάνθας (thistles), Vulg *labruscas* (fruit of wild vines). Ges-Buhl refers to the Coptic *bees,* "unripe fruit," and also notes the Vulg rendering, suggesting the reading "grapes with a tart, sour taste"; G. R. Driver (FS Th. H. Robinson [1950] 53, note 6) says it means "spoiled by antracnosa" (cf. 'Aquila: σαπριας, rottenness, putridity). KBL, noting the meaning of the verb באש (stink), reads: "stinking, spoiled berries," which is preferable to the other suggestions.

[5:1b, 2] According to v. 1a, one would expect a song about a bride, but now, the singer seems to be singing about a vineyard. Yet, there are elements of symbolic language in the description of the vineyard which one could use to describe a beloved young girl. Verse 1b has a striking formal parallel in Song of Sol. 8:11: כרם היה לשלמה בבעל המון (Solomon had a vineyard at Baalhamon) (see also 8:12 and cf. 1:6, 14; 2:15). But it is unclear as to just how far one can go in explaining expressions such as עזק (dig about) or יקב (wine vat) as having sexual overtones. The lack of certainty about the exact interpretation is not surprising, since the double meaning of many expressions is intentional. But it is already apparent in v. 2b that a complaint is being raised; praise is not being proclaimed.

There are also well-known examples beyond the OT which compare a wife or maiden with a piece of ground. In the wisdom teaching of *Ptah-hotep,* the husband is admonished: "Make her heart rejoice, as long as she is there; she is a good field for her lord" (von Bissing, *Altägyptische Lebensweisheit* [1953], 48). From the other side, a young maiden describes herself in an ancient Egyptian song as a piece of property which belongs to her beloved, and adds at the end: "Lovely is the canal within it, which your hand has dug out" (S. Schott, *Altägyptische Liebeslieder* [1950] 56). W. F. Albright (VTSup 3 [1955] 7) calls attention to a proverb which is cited four different times by the ruler of Byblos in the Amarna letters: "My field (territory) is likened (*mašil*) to a woman without a husband, because it is not plowed" (J. A. Knudtzon, *Die El-Amarna Tafeln,* VAB II/1 [1915] nos. 74:17ff.; 75:15ff.; 81:37f.; 90:42ff.). But an Assyrian bridegroom makes it clear that he would make his bride as fruitful as the fruit of an orchard (*kīma inib kirî;* see Th. G. Pinches, "Notes upon Some Recent Discoveries in the Realm of Assyriology," *JTVI* 26 [1893] 154).

[5:3] In v. 3, the listeners are encouraged to give their attention, as those who had legal responsibilities, to their function as judges. ועתה (and now), with which this verse is introduced, "always identifies the turning point in the discussion"; see H. A. Brongers, "Bemerkungen zum Gebrauch des adverbialen *wᵉ'attāh* im Alten Testament," *VT* 15 (1965) 289–299, see 299; cf., for something similar, the transition to the announcement of the judgment in Amos 7:16. Concerning the word order Jerusalem/Judah, see above, p. 3. One would expect that Isaiah would now say: Judge between my friend and his vineyard! But the bridegroom and his friend, that is, God and his prophet, are seen as one and the same individual in vv. 3–6, whereas, in v. 7, the "he" once again refers to God. The fact that the audience is supposed to call the "vineyard" to account indicates that an enigmatic address is being delivered.

[5:4] The accuser makes it clear that he fulfilled his responsibilities in every possible way and gives the reasons why expecting a corresponding yield is not unreasonable. He expects grapes. "Grapes" also belong to sexual imagery, as in Song of Sol. 7:8f.: "This your stature is as a palm tree, and your breasts are like its clusters (אשכלות). I say I will climb the palm tree. . . . Oh, may your breasts be like clusters of the vine." מדוע (why) does not look for the reason for hope, but for the cause of the disappointment. It is a favorite stylistic technique to couch an accusation in the form of a question (cf. passages like Judg. 11:25ff.; Ps. 39:8); the same is true for the assertion that someone has trusted or hoped in vain (cf. Ps. 69:21; Job 6:19f.; 30:26, and often elsewhere; Jer. 8:15, and often elsewhere; Lam. 3:18; Isa. 59:9, 11).

[5:5] Introduced once again by ועתה (well, and now) (see v. 3), v. 5 begins the proclamation of judgment. It must be assumed that the accuser has found a sympathetic audience, as the reasons for his disappointment are explained. He would tear down the hedges and walls which surround the vineyard, which guarded against its being decimated by grazing cows or wild animals. A משוכה (hedge) would have been constructed with thorns, similar to what is commonly done in Palestine today, made by planting cactus hedges along the outside border of the property; in any case, one ought not think that this could describe a fence made with closely placed wooden stakes in a land like Palestine, with its scarcity of wood. A גדר is a stone wall. Walls and hedges could have easily been used in combination; see Dalman, op. cit., 316, illus. no. 92. Concerning בער (graze bare), see above, p. 142, on 3:14. In contrast to the normal way animals would graze on a piece of ground, this verb speaks of the destructive consumption of cultivated plants, or even trees, done by animals which had forced their way into a restricted area (cf. Exod. 22:4). מרמס (trample) is basically used in the OT in two particular types of circumstances (see 7:25; 10:6; 28:18; Mic. 7:10; Ezek. 34:18f.): when ground is being trampled by livestock and when a people is being trampled by an enemy, with the first usage sometimes functioning as a simile which describes the second problem.

[5:6] Regular care for a vineyard includes pruning and trimming. According to Lev. 25:3, pruning the vines is just as important for a good harvest as sowing seed in a field. It takes place in two stages: The first comes in the very early part of the year, when the sprigs which are not expected to bear any fruit are cut off; the second comes after the fruit begins to form, as the surplus sprouts are removed (in John 15:2, this is called καθαίρειν, prune, clear), so that the greatest amount of juice flows into the berries (see 18:5, where the מזמרות, pruning hooks, are mentioned; cf. also 2:4). Trimming (עדר *pi'el*), according to Dalman (*AuS* II, 328), would be completed sometimes between sowing and harvesting or right after plowing and sowing. Weeding (pulling out/cutting off) and hoeing in the field are activities which go hand in hand. If one does not hoe, "thorns and thistles" would overrun the grape vines, which, unlike the common practice in Northern Europe, were not supported with racks or stands which lifted the vines up off the ground; they were stretched out on ground level. As is true in English, which reads "thorns and thistles," the combination שמיר ושית is chosen because of alliteration (7:23–25; 9:17; 10:17; 27:4). According to

Saadia (see Dalman, *AuS* II, 321), שמיר is the wild carrot, *daucus aureus;* according to I. Löw (*Die Flora der Juden* III [1924] 133) and G. E. Post (*The Flora of Syria, Palestine and Sinai* [1932] 203), it is the prickly thorn, *paliurus aculeatus.* Based on the previous word, the שית is an *achillea* (a type of strong-scented Eurasian herb known as a yarrow; Arabic *qeiṣum,* according to Löw (op. cit., IV [1934] 33); it is a general term for thorny undergrowth. The exact botanical identification is, as in similar cases, impossible to determine; cf. A. E. Rüthy, "Die Pflanze und ihre Teile im biblisch-hebräischen Sprachgebrauch," diss., Basel (1942) 19ff. What is announced in vv. 5b, 6a is well within the power of the owner of the vineyard. But the threat in v. 6b, that rain would be withheld, already anticipates what will be further clarified in v. 7: Only God has control over the clouds. Bentzen (op. cit., 210) is of the opinion that Isaiah has still not shown his hand to indicate that he is speaking about God, suggesting that this is more of a wish, as in 2 Sam. 1:21, but cf. the negation, אל (not), in that passage. It is just as hard to justify the viewpoint that vv. 5f. are still to be explained allegorically in reference to the beloved, possibly in the sense that v. 6 says that the faithless beloved should not be able to have any children in her future marriages (so Bentzen, op. cit., 210).

[5:7a] According to some hints already dropped in v. 6b, the audience was confronted bruskly with the real message in v. 7: "For the vineyard of Yahweh of Hosts is the house of Israel, and the men of Judah are the planting of his delight." Finally, one can see it all clearly: Isaiah's friend is God; in fact, it is the Lord of Hosts (see above, on 1:9), the God connected with the ark in Jerusalem, concerning whom all the traditions about his relationship with Israel are immediately brought to mind for the audience.

In the same way as the epithet of God (Sebaoth), בית ישראל (house of God) is used initially in connection with the ark (1 Sam. 7:2; 2 Sam. 6:5, 15). In 2 Sam. 12:8; 16:3; 1 Kings 12:21; 20:31, the expression is used clearly as a designation for the inhabitants of the Northern Kingdom. The term is used frequently by Jeremiah: 2:4 (the families of the house of Israel parallel to the house of Jacob); 2:26; 3:20; 5:15; 9:25, and often elsewhere. Here the expression refers to Israel as the people of God, even though, in the secondary passages in the book of Jeremiah, it refers to the Northern Kingdom to distinguish it from the "house of Judah" (see passages like 3:18; cf. also the addition ובית יהודה, house of Judah, in 5:11), a usage also found in Hosea (1:6; 12:1) and Amos (5:1, 3, and often elsewhere). With Ezekiel (3:1, 4f., and often elsewhere), we encounter the religio-cultic usage again. In the present passage, בית ישראל (house of Israel) is, without a doubt, parallel to, not contrasted with, איש יהודה (men of Judah). Of course, this modifies the more common political meaning of איש יהודה (men of Judah), so that the religious aspect is highlighted. However, in the final analysis, both terms are identical to the terms יושב ירושלם (inhabitants of Jerusalem) and איש יהודה (men of Judah) in v. 3, which means: the exact same group of listeners who were called upon to serve as judges are now confronted with guilt and punishment, in a way similar to Nathan's famous parable in 2 Samuel 12, in which he first turns to David as the judge and then he himself speaks a judgment against David.

"Vineyard of Yahweh" is not a common metaphor for Israel. The imagery of the grapevine which Yahweh plants in the land and allows to prosper abundantly (Ps. 80:9–12; cf. Jer. 2:21) is different. But 3:14 shows that it was entirely possible for Isaiah to speak of the people as Yahweh's כרם (vineyard). And yet, one ought to note the ambivalence between 3:14 and 5:7: In the first passage, the leaders of the people are accused of having grazed the vineyard bare; in this verse, the people themselves must acknowledge that "being grazed bare" is certainly deserved.

Parallel to כרם יהוה (vineyard of Yahweh), one finds נטע שעשועיו (the planting of his delight). The *pilpel* of שעע II means "play, handle affectionately" (cf. 11:8); therefore, the substantive means "circumstances surrounding play, amusement, delight." In Jer. 31:20, Yahweh calls Ephraim יֶלֶד שַׁעֲשֻׁעִים, which does not mean, as generally translated, "beloved child" but rather, "son, in whom the father delights" (cf. Prov. 8:30f.). Presumably, the word was also used in erotic songs, but no examples of this have been found.

[5:7b] Yahweh expected from his people משפט (justice) and צדקה (covenant faithfulness, righteousness). One can refer to the discussion of "justice and righteousness" above, p. 64, on 1:21–26. The specific point Isaiah was making was possibly spelled out in detail by the redactor who appended the woe-oracles of 8–24 to the song of the vineyard. But, in light of 1:21–26, we would have to think primarily about a refusal to deal justly when handing down verdicts; cf. 5:23. So that something sounding similar to משפט (*MISHPAT*) and צדקה (*TSEDAQA*), but meaning the exact opposite, could be used, the two terms משפח (*MISPACH*) and צעקה (*TSE'AQA*) are selected. The attempts to replicate the wordplay in German—all at the expense of the precise meaning—are numerous, e.g.: Zürcher Bibel: *Guttat, Bluttat—Rechtsspruch, Rechtsbruch;* Duhm: *Gut Regiment, Blutregiment—Rechtsprechung, Rechtsbrechung;* Fohrer: *Rechtsspruch, Rechtsbruch—Gerechtigkeit, Schlechtigkeit.* The meaning of the *hapax leg.* משפח is not known for sure. Some have connected it with the root ספח (for which the spelling שפח would have been used here), which has been connected with the Arabic *safaḥa,* "pour out, spill (blood)" (see Koran 6:146; cf. also *saffāḥ,* "one who spills blood, murderer"). Marti, Gray, Procksch take this to be the meaning, while Duhm is more cautious; Buhl thinks there is a connection with the Arabic *mušaffah,* "hindered from an accomplishment," which is not very plausible; KBL uses the Arabic *fašaḥa,* "divert," and thus arrives at the meaning "aberration, violation of justice," in which case one must accept the view that there was a metathesis of the letters שׁ and ס. Since the versions are not able to furnish any help (Gk: ἀνομία, lawlessness; Vulg: *iniquitas,* iniquity), it is best to stay with the meaning "bloodshed." צעקה is the cry of woe coming from someone who is politically and socially oppressed (e.g., Gen. 27:34; Exod. 3:7, 9; 11:6, and often elsewhere); Ps. 9:13 says that Yahweh never forgets the outcry of such a person. With this, the song concludes with a sharply worded accusation, which must have sounded even harsher in the ears of those in the audience, since the prophet had used the vehicle of a parable to bring them to the point where they would have had to agree with the announced threat of punishment.

Purpose and Thrust

This section—which at first leaves the audience unsure about whether Isaiah, as a "friend of the bridegroom," will praise his bride or whether he wants to praise his friend for the great care with which he set up a vineyard—seems to be hiding something as Isaiah raises an accusation against the bride or, as the case may be, a lament about the vineyard; finally, he exposes everything with an accusation against Israel/Judah. One ought not try to match up the details of the specific precautions taken by the generous owner of the vineyard with specific events in the story of salvation, so that, for example, the "horn" would be seen as referring to the mountainous area west of the Jordan or the building of the tower would refer to the establishment of the Davidic dynasty (on this, see Kaiser). The point of comparison, on a surface level, is identified with the triple repetition (vv. 2, 4, 7) of קוה (expect): disappointment concerning what Yahweh could justifiably expect, caused by the unthankfulness of his people. The reason Isaiah brings across this simple truth with the ambiguous song of the vineyard, as in the similar case of Nathan's parable in 2 Samuel 12, can be explained by his intention to convince his audience that Yahweh was right in expecting something, that he was justified in his disappointment, and that his wrath was certainly understandable.

Even if it is not fitting to give this an allegorical interpretation, seeking historically to link all the provisions for the vineyard, the question still remains about what Isaiah did have in mind, according to this present section, concerning the benevolent actions of Yahweh for Israel. Since he chose the imagery of the vineyard, one might think of the third major element of the exodus tradition, the giving of the land; cf. Exod. 15:17: "Thou wilt bring them in, and plant them on thy own mountain. . . ." But Isaiah does not ever mention that Yahweh gave to Israel field and vineyard as an inheritance, as one finds elsewhere in the OT (Deut. 6:11), but rather, that Israel/Judah itself *is* the vineyard, from which the good fruit is expected. There is no "little historical creed" behind Isa. 5:1–7. On the contrary, we have seen that, not only Sebaoth as a divine name for Yahweh, but also "house of Israel" as a designation for the people of God, would connect this with the ark traditions. This would mean that Yahweh was seen as the God who acted with his favor on behalf of Israel ever and again during times when it was under duress, had guaranteed Israel protection, and had offered assurance that it would be prosperous. One would hardly go wrong if one would paraphrase Yahweh's care, as it is intimated here, by using the terminology of Psalm 98 (1–3). The watchtower in the vineyard, the hedge, and stone wall surrounding it surely indicate the way Yahweh provided help against the enemies who wanted to trample Yahweh's inheritance. Yahweh was a mighty fortress for his people. And yet, Yahweh is seen in v. 6b as Lord over processes within nature. He demonstrates his goodness to his people by giving them rain for their land in due season. That is also mentioned over and over again in the covenant tradition (Deut. 11:11, 14; 28:12). On the other hand, it is proclaimed that punishment for breaking the covenant would come as rain would be withheld (Deut. 11:17; 28:24; cf. also Lev. 26:4; Amos 4:7; Isa. 30:23, and often elsewhere). From this, one would conclude that Isaiah had in mind the general blessings which Yahweh provided Israel as well as the specific protection from enemies. These were known to the people as the promises of the covenant, and it is well-known that those promises had not remained unfulfilled.

Yahweh's goodness toward the house of Israel is seen as a systematic, deliberate activity, carried out over a long period of time (see von Rad, *OTTheol* II, 177). Whoever plots out a vineyard must be able to wait for a while until the "investment" begins to pay dividends. So it was that Yahweh had the long view in mind, planning to gradually help Israel to grow up. Yahweh is no "impetuous lover" who tries to overpower the beloved like a whirlwind, but rather one who patiently surrounds her with care and continuously tries to show new evidence of his affection. It is an image which, in the end, gives clear insight into Yahweh's relationship with his people, as well as what God himself is really like. At the same time, it points out the completely preposterous nature of Israel's relationship with God; they were unthankful toward their Lord, and most clearly that resulted in the deep, deep disappointment of the God who had loved them and given himself so completely in his care for them. Yahweh suffers immensely because his gracious reaching out to his people had not met with the type of response which he had anticipated. Therefore, Isaiah is not too audacious when he uses the parable of the disappointed, unsuccessful lover, Yahweh.

The owner of the vineyard announces what he will do with his property, protected by the hedge, as he tells the parable. But the interpretation of the parable breaks off sharply, after Yahweh's horrible disappointment in his people has been revealed in the carefully chosen words in v. 7b, words fashioned like the facets of a diamond. The NT used the parable of Isaiah in the allegory of the evil vine-dresser (Mark 12:1–12, par.). There, rejection by the people of God is pushed still further, to the point that the son, who has come to receive the produce from the vineyard, is murdered. The fellowship of believers, from which the allegory undoubtedly received its present form, gives witness to the fact that God's will to bring about redemption had to come to completion, in spite of and precisely because of Israel's No! But Isaiah takes leave of his audience with the worrisome question about whether there would be any kind of future for the people of God following Israel's rejection.

Isaiah 5:8–24; 10:1–4

Woes on the Callous
and Irresponsible

Literature

J. Fichtner, "Jahwes Plan in der Botschaft des Jesaja," *ZAW* 63 (1951) 16–33 = *GesStud* (1965) 27–43. S. Speier, "Zu drei Jesajastellen (1:7; 5:24; 10:7)," *TZ* 21 (1965) 310–313. G. von Rad, "Das Werk Jahwes," FS Th. C. Vriezen (1966) 290–298. J. A. Emerton, "The Textual Problems of Isaiah V 14," *VT* 17 (1967) 135–142.

   Concerning the woe-oracles: C. Westermann, *Basic Forms of Prophetic Speech* (1967) 189ff. E. Gerstenberger, "The Woe-Oracles of the Prophets," *JBL* 81 (1962) 249–263. H. W. Wolff, *Amos' geistige Heimat,* WMANT 18 (1964) 12–23, G. Wanke, "אוי und הוי," *ZAW* 78 (1966) 215–218. R. J. Clifford, "The Use of HOY in the Prophets," *CBQ* 28 (1966) 458–464.

   [**Literature update through 1979:** A. Mirsky, "The Third Benediction of the 'Amida and the Passage 'The Lord of Hosts is Exalted' (Is 5,16)," *Tarb* XXXVIII/3 (1969) 297–300. H. Bardtke, "Die Latifundien in Juda während der zweiten Hälfte des achten Jahrhunderts v. Chr.," FS A. Dupont-Sommer (1971) 235–254 (concerning an understanding of Isa. 5:8–10). H. W. Hoffmann, *Die Intention der Verkündigung Jesajas,* BZAW 136 (1974) 105ff. P. W. van der Horst, "A Classical Parallel to Isaiah 5:8," *ExpTim* 89 (1977/78) 119–120.

   Concerning the woe-oracles: W. Janzen, *Mourning Cry and Woe Oracle,* BZAW 125 (1972). C. Hardmeier, *Texttheorie und biblische Exegese. Zur rhetorischen Funktion der Trauermetaphorik in der Prophetie,* BEvT 79 (1978).]

Text

5:8 Woe to those who join house to house,
   who unite field with field,
   until there is no more[a] room and you alone are
      settled in[b] as full citizens in the midst of the land.
9 [a]'Truly,' Yahweh of Hosts 'has made an oath'[a] in my hearing:
   Indeed, many houses, large and beautiful,
      will become deserted, to be without[b] inhabitant.
10 For ten yoke[a] of a vineyard will not produce *any more* than *a single*[b]
      bath,
   and a homer of seed-corn[c] will not produce *any more* than *a
      single* ephah.
11 Woe to those who hunt for intoxicating drinks early[a] in the morn-
      ing

188

who stretch the evening out until it's very late, when wine
    inflames them.[b]

12 Then there are box-lyres and yoke-lyres, hand-held drums and
    flutes
    [a]'during' their lying down,[a]
but they do not pay attention to the activity of Yahweh,
    and they do not observe the work of his hands.

13 Therefore my people must go into exile,
    since it has no insight,
and its nobles are 'robbed of strength'[a] by hunger,
    and its populace is dried up completely by thirst.

14 For this reason Sheol opens wide its gullet,
    expands its jaws without limit,
so that their[a] majesty[b] and their[a] tumult[b] go down there
    and their[a] uproar[b] and whoever rejoices[b] in that.[a]

15 [Then the human being was[a] bowed down and the man was
    brought low,
    and then, the haughty glance had to be brought low;

16 yet, Yahweh of Hosts showed himself majestic in judgment,
    and the holy God showed himself holy[a] through righteousness.]

17 And lambs will graze, as[a] upon their own pasture land,
    [b]and the fat sheep ['little rams'] will consume the ruined area.[b]

18 Woe to those who draw along guilt with cords of deception[a]
    and, as[b] with a wagon rope,[c] payment[d] for their sins,

19 who say, "May it hasten,[a] may his work come quickly,
    so that we may see it;
may it draw near, may the judgment of the Holy One of Israel take
    place,
    so that we will recognize him!"

21 Woe to those who are wise in their own eyes,
    and think themselves to be understanding.

22 Woe to the heroes—in drinking wine
    and to the men, who are so well qualified—when mixing intoxi-
    cating drinks.

20 Woe to those who call the evil good
    and the good evil,
who make darkness into light
    and light into darkness,
who make bitter into sweet
    and sweet into bitter,

23 who decide in favor of the wrongdoer in return for a gift of a bribe,
    but, 'for'[a] the guiltless, deny him his justice.[b]

24 Therefore, as the licking flames consume[a] stubble
    [b]and withered grass sinks down in a blaze,[b]
their root will be like dry-rot[c]
    and their blooms will rise up as dust.
For they have despised the instruction of Yahweh of Hosts
    and rejected the word of the Holy One of Israel.

10:1 Woe to those who draw up[b] statutes,[a] which are plainly evil,
    and eagerly establish[d] 'decrees'[c] which are full of affliction,

189

2   so as to bend the 'case'ᵃ of the small one
        and to rob the poor of my people of their rights,ᵇ
    so that widows become their booty
        and they are ableᵈ to plunder the orphans.ᶜ
3   What will you do then duringᵃ the day of affliction
        and at the time ofᵃ a violent storm,ᵇ which comes from a dis-
        tance?
    To whom will you flee for help
        and ᶜwhere will your riches 'flee'?ᶜ
4   ᵃ[All in vain! As captives, one must bow oneself down,
        and as one struck, one will fall down.]ᵃ
    [For all this his anger has not turned away
        and his hand is still stretched out.]

8a Concerning אפס (no more), see Joüon, Gr §160n.
8b The rendering in the Gk (μὴ οἰκήσετε μόνοι, you shall not dwell alone) and the Vulg (*nunquid habitatis vos soli,* you will not dwell alone) would suggest that the reading is based on an original הֲיֵשַׁבְתֶּם (shall you dwell?); Syr (*wᵉtettebûn,* and you will dwell), and most likely also Targ (יתבון, you will dwell), presume the *qal* form. Qᵃ reads, in fact, וישתם (and he will place them), but that is obviously nothing more than a copying mistake for וישבתם (you shall dwell). The *lectio difficilior* in the MT is preferred as the more likely reading (concerning הוּשַׁב, shall be inhab-ited, see Isa. 44:26).
9a–a It is hardly possible to take באזני יהוה צבאות ("in my ears is Yahweh Sebaoth") as if it is a correct sentence. Gk reads ἠκούσθη γάρ, for it was heard = וְנִשְׁמַע (Latin: *audita sunt,* they are heard; cf. also Targ: הוית שמע, they heard, and Syr: *'eštᵉma',* it was heard). Since an oath clause follows right after this, introduced by אִם־לֹא (indeed, if it is not true that), some commentators presume that this נשמע (will be heard) was a corruption from an original נִשְׁבַּע, "he had sworn." For parallel expressions, one can compare Amos 4:2; 6:8, and 8:7, but also Isa. 14:2, where נשבע (has sworn) is a part of an introductory formula. In addition, one notes that נשמע (it was heard) is never used in the OT with the presumed meaning "express one's opinion." Since v. 9 begins with a threat, maybe a כי (truly) (or possibly לכן, therefore) was read before this נשבע (he made an oath). Therefore, v. 9a would read: כי נשבע באזני, truly, he has made an oath in my hearing.
9b Concerning the double negative מאין (without), see Joüon, Gr §160p.
10a Concerning the *dagesh* in the ד of צִמְדֵּי (measure), cf. Joüon, Gr §96d.
10b Instead of אחת (a single, feminine form), Qᵃ reads אחד (a single, masculine form); since בת (bath) is masculine in Ezek. 45:10, 11, 14, Qᵃ might be right.
10c Procksch translates literally: "the seed of a shovel," but here חמר (homer) is a "general term" and זרע (seed-corn) is a "descriptive term" (on this, see Gen. 43:12; Dan. 8:17; 11:35, 40, and often elsewhere; cf. A. Schulz, *BZ* 21 [1933] 150f.).
11a Concerning the asyndetic connection between the participle משכימי (those who rise early) and the imperfect ירדפו (they hunt for), cf. BrSynt §139a; con-cerning the construct state being used with a participle before a preposition, see Joüon, Gr §129m.
11b Kissane (ad loc.) changes ידליקם (inflames them) to read יַדְלִיקוּן and translates: "that they may pursue wine," reasoning that this rendering is called for by the parallel expressions (cf. שכר ירדפו, they hunt for intoxicating drinks early, in v. 11a; a similar suggestion is made by H. L. Ginsberg, *JBL* 69 [1950] 52f.). But the term, with the meaning which these exegetes postulate for דלק, is not used in this way in the *hiph'il.*
12a–a משתיהם (their drinking feasts) is considered by some commentators to be either unnecessary or impossible. W. Caspari, "Hebräisch בין temporal," *OLZ* 16 (1913) 337–341, suggests changing ויין משתיהם (and wine of their drinking feasts) to read בֵּין משתיהם instead, translating it "during their carousing." Procksch elimi-

nates וְיֵין מִשְׁתֵּיהֶם (and wine of their drinking feasts) altogether; many remove at least וְיֵין (and wine) (as, for example, Eichrodt: "and have their drinking bouts . . ."). Others suggest reading מְזִמָּתָם, "their scheming" (as, recently once again, Fohrer), and Ginsberg (op. cit.) would similarly read מַשָּׁעְתָם, "their interest(s)," since Isaiah could not have had in mind the forbidding of alcoholic beverages and instrumental music from all the festivals. From among these various suggestions, it is most likely that Caspari is correct.

13a מְתֵי רָעָב, "men of hunger" (Kaiser: "hunger sufferers"; Eichrodt: "in agony because of hunger"), is not impossible. In addition to this reading, one also finds מֵתֵי רעב, "having died because of hunger" (as apparently also Gk, Syr, Vulg, Targ). But "dead" does not correspond, as an exact parallel, to צחה (dried up completely) in the second half of the verse. On the basis of Deut. 32:24, מזה/מזי, "exhausted," has been suggested, which would offer a better parallel, also deserving attention since there are other terms from Deuteronomy 32 which are used elsewhere in Isaiah.

14a There is no referent for the feminine suffixes. In Targ, they are masculine plural. Since the suffixes are masculine singular in v. 13, many try to have these suffixes also read in v. 14. But לכן (for this reason, therefore), at the beginning of v. 14, shows that this verse cannot be a continuation of v. 13, which also begins with לכן (therefore). In reality, the threat in v. 14 which begins with לכן (for this reason) cannot originally belong with either vv. 11–13 or with vv. 15f.; the suffixes refer to a city, actually, to Jerusalem itself (see Emerton, op. cit., 136).

14b G. R. Driver (BZAW 77 [1958] 42f.) considers the substantives המון, הדר, and שאון to be abstract terms used for concrete terms, translating it: "and their splendid ones, their multitude and noisy throng shall go down and suffer pangs therein (namely, in Sheol)," concerning which, in his translation, he makes reference to עלז, in Arabic *'aliza,* which, besides meaning "was jubilant," also means "was restless, had colic." But there is no justifiable reason for not taking עלז in the sense which it is used everywhere else in the OT; the translation "rejoicing, exuberant," is also the preferred rendering in 22:2 (see, in addition, 13:3; 23:7; 24:8; 32:13). Emerton's suggested textual emendation (op. cit., 137ff.), reading וְעֹז לִבָּהּ (her courage) for ועלז בה (whoever rejoices), is much too uncertain for one to forego using the transmitted text in favor of this.

15a For וַיִּשַּׁח (and he was bowed down), Qᵃ reads only ישח (he will be bowed down), which means it is to be translated in the future sense. But then, one must also read וְשָׁפֵל (and he will be brought low). Since the text as it now stands is within a threat, this alteration to the MT text seems necessary. But vv. 15f. may very well have been inserted here from a different context (cf. the uncertainty concerning the tense for the same phrase in 2:9, 11, 17).

16a The Cairo geniza text and other MSS point נִקְדַּשׁ (showed himself majestic) as a perfect, whereas the Leningrad text, the Aleppo codex, et al. (also the Bomberg text), read it as a participle נִקְדָּשׁ (showing himself majestic). Since we read an imperfect consecutive in v. 16a, with the MT, the perfect is the preferred reading.

17a כדברם, "as upon their own pasture land," makes good sense and is not to be altered, on the basis of Syr, to read כדברם (in their own pasture land).

17b–b If one does not want to alter the MT, this has to be translated: "and commoners who are standing guard eat small scraps from fatted sheep," which would not be expected at this point. It is too easy for one just to go along with Steinmann (56) and simply remove the entire verse as a gloss. It has been suggested to point מחים as a passive participle of מחה (מְחִים, wiped out), and to explain גרים on the basis of the Akkadian *gurū* (or as *(a)gurratu,* "mother sheep," *AHW* 299; cf. Syriac *gurjâ,* whelp, cub, Arabic *ğarw,* whelp, cub; see G. R. Driver, *JTS* 38 [1937] 38f.), but this meaning of גר is not found in Hebrew at all and "devourer of ruined places" does not seem to be quite right, but see Kaiser. Gk (καὶ τὰς ἐρήμους τῶν ἀπειλημμένων ἄρνες φάγονται, and sheep graze the deserted parts which had been taken) can give more help. It must have read גְּדָיִם (little rams) instead of גרים (sojourners) (cf. the parallel כבשים, lambs) which, in this instance, was probably inserted in an attempt to clarify the מֵחִים, "fat sheep," which no longer made any sense (see Ps. 66:15). (That גדים, little rams, was incorrectly read as גרים, sojourners, can possibly be explained as "later history," since, in reality, it was "strangers" who came to graze upon the meadows of the people; see H. W. Hertzberg, BZAW 6 [1936] 112 = *Beiträge zur Traditionsgeschichte und Theologie des Alten Testaments* [1962] 71.) If one would remove גרים (sojourners)/גדים (little rams), then מחים (fat sheep) would become the subject and, instead of וְחָרְבוֹת (and swords of), one would have to read וְחָרְבוֹת (and ruins of). Even if these changes do not remove all doubts about what the original text read, these suggestions are still preferable to any other proposed emendations.

18a The OT speaks of "cords of sin" (Prov. 5:22), "of Sheol" (2 Sam. 22:6 = Ps. 18:6), "of death" (Pss. 18:5; 116:3), et al., and is familiar with expressions like חזון שוא (false vision) and מתי שוא (false men). Why would Isaiah not be able to speak of "cords of deception" (cf. Hos. 8:5)? And yet, there are numerous suggested emendations for this: Since Gk has taken עגלה in v. 18b to mean δάμαλις, "cow" (Hebrew עֶגְלָה), it has been suggested, in parallel to v. 18a, to read חבלי הַשּׁוֹר, "cords for bulls." M. J. Dahood (*CBQ* 22 [1960] 74f.), whom Kaiser follows, suspects that, behind the form שוא, there was an original *haššā'â* (for העגלה, cart, he reads *hā'egel,* the calf) and takes this *šā'â,* on the basis of the Ugaritic *t'at,* to mean "sheep." But it does not seem wise, on the basis of the questionable rendering of העגלה (cow) in the Gk, to change שוא (deception, emptiness, vanity) at the same time.

18b The reading of ובעבות (and with a wagon rope [not: and, *as* with]) in a few MSS is to be rejected; in the second half-verse, one is dealing with a comparison; however, in the first half-verse, in spite of Gk and Sym (ὡς σχοινίῳ, as with a small cord; cf. Syr: *aijk ḥablâ,* like a rope), if one does not change שוא (deception) to become שוֹר (a head of cattle), one ought to stay with בחבלי (with cords of).

18c One should stay with the reading עֲגָלָה (cart), rather than follow the Gk (see above, textual note 18a; cf. also Vulg: *plaustrum,* wagon, cart, and Targ: עגלתא, the cart). The parallelism between the two half-verses is not exact, as is often the case; this can be seen in the way the prefixes alternate between ב (in) and כ (as).

18d Read החמאה (*the* payment for their sins), as is found in Gk, 'Aquila, Sym, Theod (cf. העון, *the* deception, in v. 18a), a case of haplography.

19a Concerning the cohortative ending on יחישה (may it come quickly), cf. Joüon, Gr §45, note 2. Syr reads, for יחישה (may it come quickly), *nᵉsarheb marja* = יָחִישׁ יהוה (the Lord will hasten), but Yahweh is not the subject in v. 19b either, so that, in v. 19a, יחישה (may it come quickly) is to be taken as intransitive; the subject is מעשהו (his work).

23a Some MSS, and the versions, read the singular צדיק (the one who decides in favor of) which, since it is placed next to רשע (wrongdoer) (cf. also ממנו, [deny to] him), is most likely correct. Concerning the paronomasia in the genitive construction צדקת צדיק (righteousness of the righteous one), cf. BrSynt §79a; it is in the so-called *casus pendens* relationship (Joüon, Gr §156).

23b Concerning the continuation of the participle by means of the imperfect, cf. Joüon, Gr §121j). ממנו ([deny to] him) ought not be removed on metrical grounds, as is done by Procksch, Eichrodt, Kaiser.

24a קַשׁ (stubble) is the accusative object; לְשׁוֹן אֵשׁ (licking flames, tongues of fire) is the logical subject of the infinitive כאכל ([as the licking flames] consume); cf. Ges-K §115k.

24b–b Qᵃ reads ואש לוהבת (and burning fire) for וחשש להבה (and chaff blade); 'Aquila, Sym, Theod render חשש as θέρμη (with heat) (Vulg: *calor,* heat). As Speier (op. cit., 311f.) points out, many Jewish commentators understood חשש to mean "fire," or something similar. Qᵃ seems to be working already in this same tradition and, for that reason, replaced the חשש (chaff), which was no longer understood, with אש (fire). But Isa. 33:11 shows that the generally accepted translation "withered grass," or something similar (cf. the Arabic *ḥašša,* "dried out"), is correct (cf. an additional, most unlikely, suggested emendation for v. 24 which has been made by H. L. Ginsberg, FS G. R. Driver [1963] 72). להבה (blade, flame) is to be taken in the sense of an adverbial accusative, but it is also possible that, based on the Targ (בשלהביתא, in a flame), one ought to read בלהבה (in a blaze) here. It is clear that רפה (sink down) is used in a unique way, but there is no cause to replace the word with יִסְפֶּה, as suggested by Tur-Sinai (op. cit. [in literature for 1:1] 167): ". . . the flame consumeth the chaff."

24c Gk (χνοῦς, anything which is light of weight) possibly read כמץ (like chaff) here.

10:1a חקקי (statutes) is, according to Joüon, Gr §96Ap, derived from חֵק* and not from חֹק; cf. also Ges-K §93bb. Qᵃ reads (חוקקי) and has possibly preserved the original vocalization (see G. R. Driver, *JTS* 2 [1951] 21). חִקְקִי is also found in Judg. 5:15 (textually uncertain; RSV: searchings of). The way of writing this, which uses a doubled ק, is—contra L. Köhler, *HUCA* 23 (1950/51) 155—hardly just an older form of writing. The rarely used secondary form of חק (statutes) may have been chosen to make the alliteration with חקקים (statute, in its verbal form) even more distinctive.

1b Qᵃ: חוקקים (statutes) (without the article), but see below, p. 221, textual note 12a.

1c Targ reads וכתב (and a writing) for ומכתבים (and decrees), which presumes a Hebrew reading of וּמְכְתָּב (and decree). It is possible that ומכתבי-ם should be read here, that is, an enclitic מ should follow after the construct state. This would establish a parallelism with the first half of the verse (see H. L. Ginsberg, *JBL* 69 [1950] 54; H. D. Hummel, *JBL* 76 [1957] 94; and Kaiser).

1d If one does not accept the textual alteration suggested above, then one would translate "[woe] to the scribes, who constantly write distressing things" (Fohrer's rendering is similar), which means that one has a "bare" relative clause. The *pi'el* of כתב (write) is found only in this one place; it seeks to show how zealously the ones who write the laws are working, but this form is also chosen because of the alliteration with מכתבי (decrees, writings).

2a Some attempt to translate v. 2aα: "to push away little people from just proceedings," or something similar. But דין means "legal claim, legal action, verdict," so that it seems obvious that the מ ought to be removed, since it also does not seem likely that one would posit a substantive מדין (so Luzzato). Possibly this מ also ought to be read, as done by Ginsberg (see above, textual note 1c) and Kaiser, as another example of an enclitic *mem.* הַטֶּה דִין (bend the case) must have the same sense as the phrase הטה משפט (pervert justice), which is used repeatedly (Deut. 16:19; 24:17; 27:49).

2b Targ reads בדינא (in justice); yet, it does not seem necessary to change the MT to read במשפט (in their rights, in their seeking justice), since the parallelism in the first half of the verse demands the meaning "legal claim" for משפט.

2c Concerning the use of the particle which identifies the accusative, even though the substantive is indefinite, see Joüon, Gr §125h.

2d Concerning the use of the imperfect to continue a thought begun with the construct infinitive, cf. Joüon, Gr §124q.

3a ליום פקדה does not mean "*upon* the day of affliction" but "*during* the day . . .";
see לבקר, "every morning, with the morning," in Amos 4:4; Ps. 30:6. לשואה (during the time of stormy weather) is to be understood in the same way.

3b שואה comes from the root שוא (in *hiph'il* "handle roughly") and not from שאה, "lay desolate, wasted"; thus, it is not to be translated with "devastation."

3c–c Maybe a pregnant expression is used here: "To what place do you want to go, so that you can leave your wealth there?" But it is not out of the question that אנה could still be translated with "where"; cf. Ruth 2:19. However, the most likely solution is to change תָּעִיזּ (flee, seek refuge), since this is most likely, on the basis of the parallelism.

4a–a The text in v. 4a presents one with difficulties which may have been occasioned by damage to the text. P. de Lagarde (*Symmicta* I [1877] 105) suggested reading v. 4aα: בְּלְתִּי כָרַעַת חַת אֹסִיר, "Belthis is sinking, Osiris has been broken." This emendation, also adopted by Steinmann, Eichrodt, Leslie, and Fohrer, is a fascinating one, since it does not need to make any alteration in the consonantal text. But K. Budde (*ZAW* 50 [1932] 69) spoke out against it. Osiris is never mentioned in the OT and Beltis, which, when used parallel to Osiris, would have to be referring to Isis, is not mentioned either (H. Zimmern, FS P. Haupt [1926] 281–292, thinks this refers to Ṣarpanitu, the city goddess of Babylon). We have no basis for thinking that these two deities ever played any kind of role in Jerusalem. The versions give us no help at all; since v. 4aβ is not even in Gk (BS*Q), one obviously cannot get help from that source. Gray suggests reading: לְבִלְתִּי כָרֹעַ (or מִבִּלְתִּי) and translates: "to avoid crouching under(?) prisoners, and falling under the slain." C. J. Labuschagne (*VT* 14 [1964] 99) takes the י in בלתי (all in vain, except) as a prefix on the verb and reads: בֶּלֶת יִכְרַע, "No, he will crouch . . ." (cf. Ugaritic *blt* "no, indeed!"). I suggest taking בלתי by itself: "nothing [remains left over]," and כרע (to bow oneself), which seems to be incorrect when used with the imperfect plural יפלו (they will fall), ought to be pointed as an infinitive absolute כָּרֹעַ: "it is necessary to bend oneself down." Concerning this particular usage of בלתי (all in vain, except), see Num. 11:6. Finally, תחת אסיר does not mean "among the prisoners" or "under prisoners" but "at the place of prisoners"; see Exod. 16:29; 2 Sam. 7:10; 1 Chron. 17:9. It is possible, in light of all of this, that this line of the verse is a fragment from a different context, and that the difficulties in interpretation are a result of the context not having been preserved.

Form

In the present context, the woe-oracles, which have been assembled to form this section, serve to show, in very specific ways, why one has to raise a צעקה (cry of helplessness) over Israel (see v. 7). But originally, they had nothing to do with the song of the vineyard. The collection, as it now stands, does not actually represent an original kerygmatic unity, from the mouth of Isaiah. Every individual woe-oracle was directed by the prophet to a specific group of listeners in the context of unique, specific circumstances. That can be demonstrated just by comparing the very similar content in vv. 11 and 22; it is impossible that both of these oracles would have been delivered at the very same time. Therefore, the individual sayings were secondarily brought together to form a small collection, similar to the way in which the sayings-source of the synoptics collected the woe-oracles against the scribes and Pharisees (Matt. 23:13–36; Luke 11:37–52). One must therefore reckon with the possibility that individual oracles could have been expanded at a later time, and also with the possibility that the arrangement which the compiler had in mind was later disrupted.

Modern exegetes have attempted to work with 5:8–24 (or –25, occasionally including also 10:1–4, and other passages), until one is able to restore the woe-oracles from Isaiah to their original condition and original sequence. The most impressive effort is K. Budde's attempt (*ZAW* 50 [1932] 57ff.). He presumes that a fragment of an initial section is now in 1:29–31, which lost its introduction, along with its "woe." According to him, the second woe-oracle is now to be found in 5:8–10, 17, the third in 5:11–13. After switching the verses, he claims to find a fourth in 5:22, 14. Verses 15f., which have been considered an addition, dependent upon 2:9, 11, ever since the time of Eichhorn, are removed by Budde (see below, pp. 205f.). The fifth woe-oracle is preserved, according to Budde, in vv. 18f., the sixth in v. 20, the seventh in v. 21. He sees the beginning of the final original unit in this collection (as suggested, previous to his analysis, by G. Studer, *JPT* 7 [1881] 172ff., et al.) in 10:1. After 10:1, 5:23 would follow immediately, then 10:2–4a and then 5:24. Thus, Budde works on the premise that there were various transpositions. But many of these suggestions are shaky, at best, if not highly unlikely. That applies, more than anywhere else, to the attempt to place 1:29–31 at the head of the woe-oracles in chap. 5, which would still be the assessment even if one accepts Budde's interpretation of those verses, seeing them as directed against "the intensive exploitation of the soil for the purposes of sumptuous gratification" (op. cit., 60). On the other hand, a large number of other commentators (among others, Feldmann, Ziegler, Eichrodt, Fohrer, Kaiser, Leslie; see also S. Mowinckel, "Die Komposition des Jesajabuches Kap. 1–39," *AcOr* 11 [1933] 275, and O. Eissfeldt, *The Old Testament. An Introduction* [1965] 308) are of the opinion that 10:1ff. is a passage which somehow became separated from the group of woe-oracles in chap. 5. Justification for assuming that this passage was removed so far from the rest of the oracles comes, as will be shown below, by demonstrating that 9:7–20 itself precedes, and is continued by, 5:25ff. If one leaves 1:29–31 out of the discussion, seven individual units remain. The group of seven may be intentional.

Budde was also correct when he observed that v. 14 does not provide a continuation for v. 13, since the feminine suffixes seem to refer to a city and the לכן (for this reason, therefore) in v. 14 does not mesh with the לכן (therefore) which precedes it in v. 13. But precisely because of these suffixes, it is not clear how, as Budde would suggest, v. 14 provides the continuation of v. 22. On the other hand, v. 17 should be taken with v. 14; it is a well-known motif that animals graze where magnificent cities once stood. The two verses are apparently an isolated fragment, intended to add emphasis to the threat in v. 13.

The verses which come in between, vv. 15f., hardly belong with a collection of woe-oracles. Eichrodt, following others, placed these verses after 2:9, Kaiser after 2:21 (see above, p. 102), and Hertzberg after 5:21f., doing so by removing the הוי (woe) from v. 21 and expanding v. 15 by adding another לכן (therefore), which is hardly permissible. Even if one notes that one is dealing here with an insertion, the question about the authenticity of the passage is still not decided (on this, see below, pp. 205f.), but the variety and number of suggestions concerning where to place these verses show just how unsure exegetes are in their assessment of the passage.

There is also a question about the extent of the woe-oracle which begins with 5:20. There are new individual units in vv. 21 and 22. As will be shown below, p. 210, v. 23 is most likely a continuation of v. 20. Introduced by לכן (therefore), v. 24 is connected, as a threat, to the preceding woe-oracle, which leaves no question about how harsh things would become. But it is surprising that v. 24b, introduced by כי (for), furnishes still another reason for the message of judgment. In contrast to the other invectives in the woe-oracles, the accusation leveled here, about rejection of the law and having ignored the word of Yahweh, sounds quite general. Both of these lines appear to be a summary which would have been appended to the woe-oracles after 10:1ff. was removed. For this reason, the question is raised about the authenticity of v. 24b (on this, see below, p. 212).

After all these considerations, the following arrangement seems correct for 5:8ff.:

5:8–10   First woe-oracle, with threat
5:11–13   Second woe-oracle, with threat

5:14, 17	Fragment of a threat
5:15f.	Insertion: Yahweh's grandeur
5:18f.	Third woe-oracle
5:21	Fourth woe-oracle
5:22	Fifth woe-oracle
5:20, 23, 24a	Sixth woe-oracle, with threat
5:24b	Conclusion of the woe-oracles from chap. 5
10:1–3 (4)	Seventh woe-oracle

The woe-oracles are all introduced with הוי (*HÔY*) (not with אוי = *'ÔY*, as in 3:11; see also 1:4 and 24). See Wanke, op. cit., for an explanation of the difference between the two interjections. In five of the seven cases, a participle follows הוי (5:8, 11, 18, 20; 10:1; see also 31:1); in two cases, as in 1:4, a noun follows (5:21, 22; see also 10:5; 17:12; 18:1; 28:1; 29:1; 30:1). Wanke (op. cit., 217f.) might be right in holding to the view that הוי (*HÔY*) was originally a part of the lament for the dead. In most of the cases, this would be followed immediately by a substantive, which would describe how the one who had died was related to the person raising the lament (1 Kings 13:30; Jer. 22:18; 34:5; cf. הו = *HÔ* in Amos 5:16). If the prophets make use of this הוי (*HÔY*) from the lament for the dead as the introduction for their reproach, it is because their aim would have been to announce that the seeds of death were to be found within the wickedness which had been observed. The continued existence of basic orders within the community, established by God, and promises to provide blessing and prosperity, are now in doubt; in fact, they are destroyed, which means that the transgressor has already come under the power of death. In this way, the woe-oracle is not far removed from the curse: It complains about those who are already to be found in the realm of death. (In addition, it is also true about a curse, in this "synthetic thinking" in the ancient world, that this is not actually "cursing," but establishing the fact that one *is* under a curse.) According to this understanding, Westermann attempted to make sense of woe-oracles as being related to curses (op. cit.), while Gerstenberger and Wolff (each, op. cit.) see them as having their roots in the wisdom traditions.

It is certainly not just by chance that a participle often follows הוי (*HÔY*) in the prophetic woe-oracles. One does not complain about or reproach the individual as such, but the way in which someone acted in a specific case when that person violated the order which God had established.

No matter where one searches to find the original setting of a woe-oracle, in and of itself, it does not have to be expanded to include a threat. Whoever violated the established order would already be standing outside the sphere, inside which a full and secure life would be possible. "Coming disaster is already implicit in the mere mention of 'woe'" (Wolff, op. cit., 14). Therefore, the woe-oracles in vv. 20 and 21 are completely intact and not to be considered simply to be fragments, which, for some unknown reason, had been separated from the threats to which they would have been attached at one time. On the other hand, it is significant that, in the very cases where a participle follows right after הוי (*HÔY*), a threat of judgment also follows: In vv. 9f., this is introduced by an oath formula; in vv. 13 and 24, it is identified by לכן (therefore); cf. also 10:3. This means that the "synthetic thinking" somewhat minimizes the importance of the explicit knowledge that Yahweh is the Lord of history and that he sets the consequences of the evil deed in motion. It is only at this point that the woe-oracle becomes a specific prophetic genre.

Setting

The authenticity of the woe-oracles and the threats which are attached to them—except for later additions—is generally accepted. Concerning vv. 15f.; v. 24b, and 10:4a, b, see below, pp. 205f., 212, 215f. Since this section deals with a collection whose individual parts once existed separately, these could have been spoken in very different situations, and one must attempt to identify, as much as is possible, the setting of each originally distinct section. But there is simply a lack of evidence which could help to determine where and how they fit chronologically. One can presume, however, that all of these oracles were uttered before the Assyrian threat, with the menacing presence which that brought, had become a critical issue. Thus, these also belong to Isaiah's early period and are aimed at roughly the same situation in Jerusalem as that described in the song of the vineyard.

1. Woe-oracle [5:8–10]
Against Housing Speculators and Large Landowners

Literature

Literature concerning ancient Israelite rights for possession of land: G. von Rad, "Verheissenes Land und Jahwes Land im Hexateuch," *ZDPV* 66 (1943) 191–204 = *GesStud* TBü 8, 87–100. A. Alt, "Der Anteil des Königtums an der sozialen Entwicklung in den Reichen Israel und Juda," *KlSchr* III, 348–372. H. Wildberger, "Israel und sein Land," *EvT* 16 (1956) 404–422. F. Horst, "Das Eigentum nach dem Alten Testament," *Gottes Recht* TBü 12 (1961) 203–221. H. Donner, "Die soziale Botschaft der Propheten im Lichte der Gesellschaftsordnung in Israel," *OrAnt* 2 (1963) 229–245.

Form

Meter: Verse 8, the reproach: 2 three-stress bicola; vv. 9f., the threat, disregarding the introduction: a five-stress colon and 3 two-stress bicola. The short two-stress cola symbolize the biting harshness of the judgment.

Commentary

[5:8] One can accurately understand the accusation raised here by Isaiah only after careful consideration of the economic aspects of life in ancient Israel. The land was under the control of the individual clan, which endeavored to provide its members with a plot of ground sufficient to assure their continued survival. The story of Naboth, in 1 Kings 21, shows that even the king himself did not have any recognized and legal means to take control and expand his own landholdings at the expense of a simple farmer; concerning this, see the prohibition in Lev. 25:23 against selling off land לִצְמִתֻת (in perpetuity), which means that one could sell property only with the proviso that it could be repurchased later. Thus, owning land was not only a question of the economic condition in which an Israelite found himself, but it also identified his position as a citizen within the community. Whoever had to give up land and property became a simple day laborer or slave and thereby lost his ability to influence daily affairs (see L. Köhler, "Die hebräische Rechtsgemeinde," in *Der hebräische Mensch* [1953] 147). It is on the basis of these circumstances that one can understand the meaning of the formulation וְהוּשַׁבְתֶּם לבדכם בקרב הארץ (you alone are settled in as full citizens in the midst of the land). The translations in Gk and Vulg (cf. also Targ and Syr; see above, textual note 8b) render this accusation of Isaiah harmless. The *hoph'al* הוּשַׁב (be settled in) conveys the idea that one is settled in the land with all the obvious rights and duties pertaining thereunto.

One should note that the woe-oracle now changes its form to become a direct address, which means that it takes the form of a reproach in v. 8bβ (see Fey, *Amos and Isaiah,* WMANT 12 [1963] 59, note 1).

This means that the rich are so driven to possess more that they take away the rights of their fellow citizens. As Mic. 2:1ff. demonstrates, Isaiah did not stand alone when he became enraged because the ancient standards of justice were being distorted (see A. Alt, "Micah 2:1-5 ΓΗΣ ΑΝΑΔΑΣΜΟΣ in Juda," FS S. Mowinckel [1955] 13-23 = *KlSchr* III, 373-381). One ought to pay careful attention to the way Isaiah speaks, since he does not make the accusation that a sacred order has been destroyed, but that justice and freedom have been taken away from fellow citizens. לבד means more than our word "alone": Arabic *badda* means "divide" and the Hebrew בדד means "all alone, be all by oneself." The greed which drives one to possess more and more results in an isolation which comes for those who are successful at the expense of normal interaction with other human beings. When ארץ (land) is mentioned here, one must remember what the fulfillment of the promise concerning the land means for the Israelite. The land can be called the נחלה (inheritance) of *Israel,* but it is also *Yahweh's* נחלה (inheritance) (Jer. 2:7; 16:18; 50:11; Deut. 32:9). It is an attack against the central confessional statement of Israel when the land, the great gift of God, now rests under the control of just a few. One ought not press בקרב (in the midst) too much, and yet, the deeper meaning does not come out when using its original sense, "middle": Isaiah is thinking about a person who is in the "center" of the land, sitting in the very secure and prosperous capital city, adding to his holdings by buying land in out-of-the-way places, without having to bear the burdens and dangers of living in regions like that.

[5:9] Isaiah formulates the threat, as also in many other places, as an oath of Yahweh (see Amos 4:2; 6:8; 8:7; Jer. 22:5; 44:26; 49:13; cf. also the introduction to the promise message in Isa. 14:24). There is a preference, in an oath of this type, as elsewhere, to use terminology from the promise to David (Pss. 89:4, 36; 110:4; 132:11), and also, notably in the deuteronomistic formulations, to use terminology rooted in the promise to give land to the patriarchs (Deut. 1:8, and often elsewhere; concerning this, see F. Horst, "Der Eid im Alten Testament," *EvT* 17 [1957] 366-384 = *Gottes Recht* TBü 12, 292-314). One might suppose that Isaiah, in direct contrast to the oath of assurance concerning the land, was formulating the threat about the devastation of the land in the same exact form of an

oath from Yahweh. But Isaiah was not familiar with the typical deuteronomic phraseology, and the threat which follows this does not make use
of the terminology employed in the promise to the patriarchs. The
existence of the oath formula in Isa. 14:24, and the use in Ezekiel (16:8,
and cf. the phrase נשׂא יד, raise a hand, in 20:6, 15, 23, and often elsewhere) show that there are vastly different circumstances in which a
message from Yahweh can have the force of an oath which obligates
someone. It is striking how the oath was given "in the ears" of Isaiah.
There is a parallel expression in 22:14a: וְנִגְלָה בְאָזְנִי יְ׳ צ׳ (the Lord of Hosts
has revealed himself in my ears), which also functions as an introduction
to an oath. In this way, the prophet identifies himself as the recipient of a
secret revelation.

It is a commonly acknowledged way of thinking to expect that the
punishment will begin to take effect in the same arena where the wickedness began; therefore, in the present case, there is a threat that houses and
fields will become deserted (שׁמה). The announcement about שׁמה (become
deserted) has its roots within the covenant tradition (Deut. 28:37; 2
Kings 22:19; cf., in addition, שׁממה, a wilderness, in 1:7 [see above, p. 27];
6:11; 17:9, and the verb שׁמם, become desolate, in Lev. 26:22, 31f.). In the
same way, the stereotypical threats concerning the violation of the
covenant include the case where someone would build houses but not
have the chance to live in them (Deut. 28:30; see Lev. 26:32). This motif
is taken up here with מאין יושׁב (without inhabitant) (see 6:11; Jer. 4:7;
26:9; 33:10, and often elsewhere; Zeph. 2:5; 3:6). One might suspect that
an invasion could cause the dwellings to become deserted. The limited
fruitfulness of the fields would, of course, be brought about by natural
catastrophes.

[5:10] Ten yoke of vineyard, that is, a generally respectable piece of
property, which ten yoke of oxen should be capable of plowing in a single
day (on this, see *BHH* 1162, according to which a yoke is about 2000
square meters, about one half acre), would produce only one bath (concerning the use of עשׂה, in the sense of "bring forth fruit," see above, on
5:1–7, textual note 2d). A *bath* is a liquid measure; concerning the
various estimates, which are anywhere from 22 to 45 liters (roughly 4.5–
9.5 gallons), see *BHH* 1163. In terms of content, it is the same size as the
ephah, which is a measurement for grain. The "donkey load" (חֹמֶר is from
the same root as חֲמוֹר, "donkey"; the Akkadian calls them both *imēru*)
would be ten homers, according to Ezek. 45:11; in Assyria, one would
reckon an *imēru* at 134 liters (28 gallons), which would correspond to
about 90 kilograms (40 pounds) of barley (see *IDB* IV, 834; H. Lewy,
RSO 39 [1964] 181–197). Thus, the produce from the field is exactly one-
tenth of what was planted. The formulation is unique to this passage, but
the idea that the land would not give the wicked people the expected
produce is, once again, connected with the covenant threats; see Lev.
26:20: ". . . your land shall not yield its increase" or Deut. 28:38: "you
shall carry much seed into the field, and shall gather little in." These
traditio-historical relationships make it quite obvious that the activities
of the "housing speculators" and "owners of large estates" fell into the
category of what Isaiah considered violations against the covenant.

2. Woe-oracle [5:11–13]
Against Heavy Drinkers and Thieves of Days

Form

Meter: Woe-oracle: v. 11a is a five-stress colon; v. 11b is a two-stress bicolon. Based on the suggested emendation, we have 2 six-stress cola in v. 12. Threat: v. 13a (taking לכן, therefore, parenthetically): a two-stress bicolon, which, in its concise form, underscores the harshness of the threat. Verse 13b is, once again, a six-stress colon.

Commentary

[5:11] It is presumed in this message that there is a comfortable standard of living, but there is also evidence of the influence exerted by what was once a Canaanite way of life. In general, Israel was a temperate people, even though there were plenty of vineyards in its land. There are frequent references which speak against overindulgence in wine, one of the customs practiced among the Canaanites (cf. Num. 6:2ff., 20; Jer. 35:8f.; Deut. 29:5; Amos 2:12; 4:1; 6:5f.; Mic. 2:11). The texts from Ras Shamra point out that wine also played a very important role in the cult in Ugarit (I K 164, as an offering; II D I 32, as part of the cultic meal; II AB III 43; IV–V 37; VI 53–59, and often elsewhere, connected with the drinking-bouts of the gods). According to Isa. 28:7 and 29:9, the situation in Jerusalem at the time of Isaiah was no different (cf. also 1 Sam. 1:9, 13ff.). However, this passage refers to customs which are part of secular life. With a passion similar to what might seize someone if one was pursuing an enemy, and which could also be appropriate in more acceptable circumstances (cf. רדף צדקה, pursue righteousness, in Prov. 15:9; 21:21), *"they run,"* already early in the morning, to get intoxicating drinks; cf. Eccles. 10:16f.; Acts 2:13ff. And just as they are already sitting with their booze glass in front of them early in the morning, so it is that they stretch the evening out (נשׁף) as long as they can. The נֶשֶׁף is the time of day when a cooling wind blows (נָשַׁף), and one is happily refreshed after the heat and hard work of the day, but it is also the time when adulterers (Job 24:15) and prostitutes (Prov. 7:9) ply their trades. שׁכר (Akkadian *šikaru*) appears to be a beer which was produced using grain, particularly barley, into which various additives were mixed to spice it up (see *BRL* 110f.; concerning drinks and drinking customs, cf. also F. Nötscher, *Biblische Altertumskunde* [1940] 41).

[5:12a] There was also entertainment, in the form of music, in Isaiah's day, to accompany such amusement.

It is not easy to identify exactly the instruments which are mentioned here. כנור (box-lyre) is a word which appears in Akkadian as *kinnārum*, Hittite as *kinir*, Sanskrit as *kinari* (*kinnāra* in Tulugu, see KBL); the name of the instrument must have stayed with it as it went from one people to another, but this hardly means that it had the same shape at all times and in all places. To translate it as "harp" (Luther) or "zither" (KBL) is, by its very nature, only an approximation, since neither of these musical instruments has been found in archaeological excavations in Syro-Palestine. Of course, in spite of this, many still think that a

נבל is a harp (Zürcher Bibel; KBL; E. Kolari, "Musikinstrumente und ihre Verwendung im Alten Testament," diss., Helsinki [1947] 58–64). It would appear that the word is connected with נבל, "water bottle, jug," and might, according to *BRL* 391, designate the "bevelled lyre or yoke-lyre"; the sounding board for this was possibly shaped like a jug or covered with hide (*BHH* 648). Illuss.: *BRL* 393 (right) = *ANEP* no. 199 (right); *AOB* no. 151 = *ANEP* no. 205 = *BHH* 1259 no. 2. If this is the case, כנור would designate the "box-lyre" (see Kolari, op. cit., 64–72). Illuss.: *AOB* no. 51, 456f.; *BRL* 393 (middle) = *ANEP* no. 199 (middle) = *BHH* 1259 n. 1. Concerning the Egyptian stringed-instruments, see H. Hickmann, *Ägypten: Musikgeschichte in Bildern* II/1 (1961) 126–139. תף, on the other hand, without a doubt is the term used for the tambourine. Illuss.: *BRL* 393 (left) = *ANEP* no. 199 (left) = *BHH* 1259 no. 7; *ANEP* no. 211; Hickmann, op. cit., no. 71. Finally, חליל is a flute or shawm (an obsolete type of oboe); possibly what is meant here is a double-flute (for a different view, see Kolari, op. cit., 31ff., who opts for this being a "simple blowpipe"). The word belongs to the verbal root חלל II, "bore through"; the Akkadian *halālu* also means to "play the flute." Illuss.: *BRL* 391; *AOB* nos. 509, 654; *BHH* 1259 no. 6. These same four instruments are mentioned together in 1 Sam. 10:5, in the description of a band of prophets who have been brought into an ecstatic state. They are used to accompany songs; cf. 30:29 and the description of a drinking-bout in Amos 6:4–6.

When Isaiah criticizes these drinking-bouts, this is not so much connected with an ancient Israelite nomadic ideal (cf. the Rechabites in Jer. 35:6f.), but rather with precepts of wisdom concerning the way one is to live. "Wine is a mocker, strong drink a brawler [הֹמֶה; cf. המון, its populace, in Isa. 5:13]; and whoever is led astray by it is not wise," Prov. 20:1; cf., in addition, 21:17; 23:20f.; 31:4f.; but, most of all, the "sermon" against the wine drinker in 23:29–35; see מאחרים על־היין (those who tarry long over wine) in v. 30 and בל־ידעתי (I did not feel it) in v. 35. Prov. 23:29ff. belongs to a section of the book of Proverbs which is extracted from the wisdom of Amenemope. It is certainly not surprising that Egyptian wisdom also contains warnings about the evil effects of drunkenness: "Whoever satiates himself with too much wine has to go to bed with a hangover" (Pap. Insinger, quoted by F. W. von Bissing, *Altägyptische Lebensweisheit* [1953] 95; see, in that same work, also 62f., 65, 89, and 31 [foreword]). In the teaching of Ani one can read: "Do not start anything which comes as a result of beer which was most enjoyable; if you do so, words which have two meanings—even though you are not aware of it— will come out of your mouth. If, because of it, you fall down and break your limbs, there will be no one there who will reach out a hand to you. Your drinking buddies will stand up and say: 'Out with the drunk!'" (von Bissing, op. cit., 74).

[5:13] The carousers who always have drinking on their minds are threatened with exile. Amos, already at an earlier time, had uttered this threat, and indeed, he was also fully aware of the Assyrian danger (5:5, 27; 6:7; 7:11, 17). The Assyrians were the first ones to use resettlement, to any great extent, as a means of bringing to a quick end the power of any group of people who were hostile toward them. Without a doubt, even in Jerusalem, there was general knowledge that these events were taking place, but confidence was placed in the protection offered by weaponry—and the protection offered by the God of Zion. Isaiah saw all that confidence as an illusion; the Assyrian threat was to be taken seriously. But he does not sketch out the exact details of what the future order of events would be. That is shown by v. 13b: "and its nobles are: robbed of strength by hunger, and its populace is: dried up completely by thirst!" There can be various reasons for this happening. Here is another case where the type of judgment corresponds to the wicked deed: Those who cannot curb their drinking (cf. 22:13; 28:7ff.) would end up being destroyed by hunger and thirst.

Even if this threat did belong originally with this woe-oracle, one notices how the people of importance (כבוד, glory, abstract term for a concrete one) are particularly singled out from among the larger masses of people (המון, populace; cf. Amos 5:23), even though both of these groups are to be overrun by the same judgment. The preceding mention of the details of the carousing which took place at drinking-bouts is only symptomatic, for Isaiah, of a far larger problem which had taken hold of all of the people, high *and* low, who were very comfortable with the wild customs and carefree life or, as Isaiah himself said it, were held by what resulted from "lack of insight." מבלי־דעת is translated, in the Zürcher Bibel, among other places, as "unintentionally" or, by Fohrer, as "without noticing it." In Deut. 4:42, and often elsewhere, the similar term בבלי־דעת actually means "without noticing it, unpremeditated," but this expression can also mean "without insight" (Job 35:16). In the parallel cited above, Prov. 20:1, מבלי־דעת (no insight) is similar to the phrase לא יחכם (is not wise) and, in a setting which has a similar traditio-historical background, in Hos. 4:6, the meaning "without insight" is clearly demonstrated as an accurate rendering. One must note that it says nothing about knowledge of Yahweh, but speaks of insight in a general way. This absolute usage of ידע (know) has its primary roots in wisdom (see above, p. 15, on 1:3). But Isaiah immediately clarifies this wisdom terminology on the basis of his prophetic understanding of history.

[5:12b] Actually, the accusation in v. 13, that there is a lack of insight, is identical to that in v. 12b: "but they do not pay attention to the activity of Yahweh, and they do not observe the work of his hands."

Just as Isaiah uses פעל יהוה (activity of Yahweh) and מעשה ידיו (work of his hands) in parallel here, מעשהו (his work) and עצת קדוש ישראל (the judgment of the Holy One of Israel) are used together in 5:19. More than anything else, v. 19 shows that this terminology is a way to paraphrase Yahweh's exercise of lordship within the arena of history. In 28:21, a synonym for מעשה (deed, work) is עבדה (labor); in 28:29, next to עצה (counsel), one finds the typical wisdom term תושׁיה (wisdom), and Isaiah also speaks, in other places, about Yahweh's plans, his decrees (14:24–27; see also 10:12). Naturally there are also earthly powers who attempt to carry out their plans; thus, the inhabitants of Jerusalem had a plan, according to 30:1, but it was one "which did not come from me [Yahweh]," and the enemies of Ahaz threatened Jerusalem (7:5), but Yahweh uttered his own decree directly against their decrees: לא תקום ולא תהיה (it will not happen and will not succeed) (v. 7), because *his* plan, and not the nations' plans, would finally come to fruition (cf. 14:24). One should note that מעשה (work), פעל (activity), עבדה (deed), and עצה (decree) are always used in the singular: At issue are not individual actions or plans of Yahweh, but rather the unique power of the one God, acting according to the plan which he determined beforehand. "This work of Jahweh thus enfolds the whole realm of world history . . . ; and the way in which the great world empires who were proudly strutting about on this very stage of history came into collision with God's plan is one of the great themes to which Isaiah returned again and again" (G. von Rad, *OTTheol* II, 162).

With this background, it might seem that history is deterministically fixed according to Yahweh's plan. But this very passage, 5:12, shows that this inference does not square with reality: It is worthwhile to look at the work of Yahweh and to observe the deeds of his hands, specifically because history could take a different direction. Yahweh handles himself in a way that is "wonderful and marvelous, so that the wisdom of their wise men shall perish" (29:14), which means, according to the parable of the farmers who had been taught by God (28:23–29), that Yahweh does everything when the time is right. It is definitely not a matter of indifference, for the history of the Davidic kingdom, whether Ahaz believes or not. Just because history proceeds according to the plan of God, and all human desires which are opposed to him must finally fall by the wayside, there is still no reason to conclude that human beings are not answerable for their actions. For Isaiah himself, for one who speaks so passionately about the עצה (decree, plan) of God, the way humans are and the way they act take on a decisive significance, seldom portrayed elsewhere in such a clear way. One is almost tempted to state the case as follows: History is viewed as the result of human actions. But such a statement has validity only when it is considered along with its dialectical opposite: Yahweh is the absolute lord of history, and he alone gives history its shape. Of course, prophets who came before Isaiah or lived when he did knew that as well. But Isaiah alone uses עצה (plan), פעל (activity), etc. as terms which specifically described God's activity within history. From which arena did Isaiah get this? He is conversant with the traditions of holy war. But this terminology does not come from that source. The parable in 28:23–29, which seeks to explain the way in which God makes decisions, comes from the arena of wisdom. But the most prominent person who is responsible for wisdom is the king. It is the prerogative of the king, and also the obligation of the king, to formulate strategy (יעץ עצה, plan a plan) (see Jer. 49:30; and cf. 49:20; 50:45). For this reason, the messianic king is also equipped with the spirit of עצה (planning) (Isa. 11:2); in fact, he is plainly called פלא יועץ (planner of wonders) (9:5). Isaiah speaks so forcefully about Yahweh's counsel because he had seen the vision of Yahweh as king upon a high and lofty throne (6:3): Yahweh's planning is seen as analogous to the planning done by an earthly ruler, though the analogy is used here in a way which goes beyond what would be done in the earthly sphere: תפליא עצה (wonderful in counsel) is the way it is said in 28:29. This does not lay as much stress, as one might normally suppose, on פלא as the wonderful, but rather on the surprising, since this refers to the gradually unfolding actions of God. Thus, it is not surprising that the work of God is described as strange in 28:21, his actions as unusual.

Beyond the book of Isaiah, Yahweh's work (מעשה, work; פעל, activity; מעלל, practice; עלילה, deed; עבדה, labor, is unique) is almost only mentioned in the Psalms (for the list of occurrences, see H. Wildberger, *Jesajas Verständnis der Geschichte,* VTSup 9 [1963] 95), chiefly in the creation hymns; see Pss. 74:12ff.; 77:12ff., but the terms are also found in the so-called historical psalms (e.g., Ps. 87:7, 11). But in these hymns, the deeds of Yahweh, in contrast to the way the terminology is used by Isaiah, always refer to his deeds (note the plural!) done in the very ancient times (but cf. Ps. 44:2), unless reference is made to how God took control in the life of an individual. The unique way in which Isaiah uses these terms provides impressive evidence for his ability to come up with a means of describing Israel's experiences in its faith relationship, using terminology which was completely appropriate.

Purpose and Thrust

According to this present passage, after one took a careful look at Yahweh's activity, one would have to gain דעת (insight). But this searching evaluation of historical events simply never happened; they were given nothing more than a careless once-over. For Isaiah, this was evidence for how deep the delusion went, how hard the heart, about which he speaks in 6:9ff. The threat of an exile is formulated on the basis of current historical realities. But the announcement that there would be hunger and thirst, in v. 13b, actualizes once again a reality rooted in the covenant tradition (see Deut. 28:48). Amos makes use of this same motif, though in a more refined form (8:11).

Threat [5:14, 17]
The End of Glory

Form

Meter: (apart from לכן, therefore), 2 three-stress bicola; 17: after the elimination of גדים, little rams, once again a three-stress bicolon.

Setting

This passage seems to fit in very well with that which immediately precedes it, since the downfall of the המון (populace) is also mentioned there. There is also a correspondence between כבודו (its nobles) in v. 13 and הדרה (majesty) in v. 14b. But the connection is more apparent than real: In v. 13, כבוד and המון mean "high" and "low," thus designating various levels of society, whereas הדר (majesty) and המון (tumult) (further defined by שאון, uproar) point to the haughty, boisterous nature of the inhabitants of the city.

Commentary

[5:14] המון (tumult) and שאון (uproar) are terms which are used to describe human bragging (see 13:4; 17:12f.). עלז (rejoice) is also used when this topic is being discussed (cf. עיר המיה, tumultuous city, along with קריה עליזת, exultant town, in 22:2). עלז/עליז (exultant, jubilant) lay particular stress on the aspect that one is proudly self-assured; see Zeph. 2:15; Zeph. 3:11 and Isa. 13:3 very specifically mention עליזי גאוה (proudly exultant ones). It is in this light that הדר (majesty) is to be interpreted in our passage: Unlike the use of כבוד (nobles) in v. 13, it does not refer to a particular level of society, namely the nobility, but describes the pride found among all the people as they are showing off. In v. 14, Isaiah mentions, once again, one of his favorite themes: the judgment concerning the pride of human beings; cf. 2:12ff. The description uses the mythological imagery of Sheol, portrayed as greedily gobbling up whatever is offered, still being thought of as a real creature which is in control of the deep; cf. ירד (go down) and see how this same concept is used in Num. 16:30ff. and Hab. 2:5: כשאול נפשו הרחיב (his greed is as wide as

Sheol). פער (expands) conveys the idea of insatiable greed; cf. Job 16:10; Ps. 119:131. The texts from Ras Shamra use the same terminology to explain that Baal must go down into the yawning abyss of Mot, the son of El; see I*AB I 7f. and cf. I AB II 17f. and I*AB II 2ff.

[5:17] The motif is now expanded and indicates that cities, upon which the judgment of God has come, will become "pasture" (see 17:2; 27:10; 32:14; Zeph. 2:6, 14; cf. Mic. 3:12; Lam. 5:18). "The imagery of the flocks being pastured in a place where rubble is all that is left of a major city, having now gone down into the underworld, characterizes, in a very striking way, the realization that this self-confident pride in human glory has been completely extinguished" (Eichrodt, ad loc.).

Insertion [5:15f.]
The Holy God

Form

Meter: Verse 15: a seven-stress colon; v. 16: a four-stress + four-stress bicolon.

Setting

According to the Masoretic pointing, both of these verses are to be translated as preterites, since it is unlikely that simple imperfects would have been altered, coming between vv. 14 and 17, to be read as imperfect consecutives. Since 2:9, a verse very similar to v. 15, uses the imperfect consecutive, vv. 15f. might come from a context in which Isaiah looks back upon judgment which has already taken place. And yet, it is more likely that an expander, having read the threat of judgment in v. 14, wanted to show that the announced judgment had actually taken place. For this, he would have used Isaiah's way of speaking when he composed v. 15 (on this, see above, pp. 102f.; 111, on 2:9, 11, 17).

Commentary

[5:16] The expander of the text chiefly uses his own words in v. 16. The preciseness of the phrase attracts attention and is characteristic of the way the OT understands God. Certainly, this verse is not meant to offer "instruction" about the nature of God: It speaks about how God, as Yahweh of Hosts, "showed himself." Yahweh is a God who can be recognized only on the basis of his interaction with human beings within history. But it is noteworthy, nonetheless, that "Yahweh of Hosts" is used, in *parallelismus membrorum,* with האל הקדוש (the holy God). In its present form, this expression is unique; Isaiah himself uses the term קדוש ישראל (holy one of Israel), which is tied more specifically to acts within history (see above, p. 24). Of course, there are similar expressions elsewhere in the OT: אֵל קַנָּא (jealous God), Exod. 20:5, and often elsewhere; קַנּוֹא (jealous God), Josh. 24:19; Nah. 1:2; אֵל־חַנּוּן וְרַחוּם (a gracious God and merciful), Jonah 4:2, and often elsewhere; אֵל גָּדוֹל (a great God), Deut. 7:21, and often elsewhere; אֵל חַי (living God), Josh. 3:10, and often elsewhere. According to this, the short form אל (*EL*) is customarily used when an attributive adjective is to be used, and not all of these are ancient, well-established formulas. One notes that אל (*EL*) is chosen when the might of God is to be contrasted with the weakness of human beings (31:3; Ezek. 28:9). But what is actually meant by the divine designation האל הקדוש? In Josh. 24:19, Yahweh is described as אלהים קדושים (holy God), used there parallel to אל־קנוא (jealous God), as the one who punishes transgressions. 1 Sam. 6:20 speaks about God as האלהים הקדוש (this holy God), the one before whom no one is able to stand, which suggests, according to the context, that his holiness is experienced as something completely awful, powerful enough to bring about one's death. It is in a completely different sense that the one who prays in Hab. 1:12 addresses Yahweh as אלהי קְדֹשִׁי (my God, my Holy One) (text emended), namely, as the God who will not deliver the speaker over to death, no matter what else happens. But one ought to note carefully how this expression is modified. Thus, one must presume that, also for this present passage, designating Yahweh as the האל הקדוש (holy God) is meant to show that this God will not allow those who act in opposition to him to go unpunished.

It is very common in Ezekiel for Yahweh to be described as the one who "shows himself as holy," נקדש (20:41; 28:22, 25; 36:23; 38:16; 39:27; see also Lev. 10:3; 22:32, and Num. 20:13). But in these passages, Yahweh demonstrates his holiness by acting mercifully toward his people: He shows himself to be holy "toward" his people (נקדש ב, I will show myself holy among those, Lev. 10:3; parallel to נכבד על־פני, before [all the people] I will be glorified). This priestly usage must be differentiated from that in Isa. 5:16, since ב is used in our text to identify the means which Yahweh uses to manifest his glory. This forces one to examine more carefully what specific meaning is attached to משפט (*MISHPAT*) and צדקה (*TSEDAQA*) in the present context. In 5:7, Isaiah used the two terms together to paraphrase the orderly, and therefore, caring manner of life in relation to one's fellow citizens (see also 1:21 and 28:17). In 9:6, "justice and righteousness" describe the activity of the future king who will establish peace and salvation (cf., on this, 11:5; 16:5; 32:1, 16f.). In all these examples, a righteousness is implicit which brings with it and guarantees שלום (peace) and ברכה (blessing). "Justice" and "righteousness," insofar as these proceed from God, being divine gifts of salvation (see Fey, op. cit., 75f.), can, therefore, be used in 33:5 as general terms for the gifts which will be installed upon Zion in the eschatological time of salvation; cf. also 30:18. Isaiah never speaks of צדקה (*TSEDAQA*) as righteous punishment (10:22 would seem, like 5:15f., to be a later addition by another hand; cf. Fey, op. cit., 76, note 1). However, in light of this very passage, 5:16, one cannot agree with the generalizing conclusion of K. Koch (*ZTK* 52 [1955] 29 [Engl: *Theodicy in the Old Testament,* Issues in Religion and Theology 4, 77]; similarly G. von Rad, *OTTheol* I, 377, and F. Horst, *RGG*³ II, 1404) that צדק (*TSEDEQ*) and צדקה (*TSEDAQA*) are never used to refer to a punishing action, but only to actions which bring benefit, even if this is used in a judicial setting. Wherever the saving order, which is what is meant by צדק (*TSEDEQ*), is damaged, then Yahweh must step in; then, the punishment of the wicked person would also be part of Yahweh's acting in a righteous way. If that would not take place, then the holy God would not be preserving his holiness. It is noteworthy that someone who followed afterwards felt compelled to add a confessional statement to Isaiah's threat of punishment, pointing out that the righteousness of the holy God was shown most clearly in Yahweh's judgment upon human pride.

3. Woe-oracle [5:18f.]
Against Those Who Mock the Plans of Yahweh

Form

Meter: The metrical analysis presents difficulties. Verse 18: a seven-stress colon; v. 19: 2 six-stress cola (2 + 2 + 2), with the last word, ונדעה (so that we will recognize him), being given two accents.

Commentary

[5:18f.] This passage presupposes that Isaiah has run into opposition because of his message of the coming disaster and that his opponents sought to employ mockery in an attempt to get rid of this irksome admonisher. The opponents of the prophets are often characterized by the latter as having said some words which they could not possibly have spoken (see H. W. Wolff, "Das Zitat im Prophetenspruch," *BEvT* 4 [1937] = *GesStud,* TBü 22, 36–129). But there is little room for doubt in this case; the אנשי לצון (scoffers), as Isaiah calls them in 28:14, actually spoke in this or in quite a similar way. One can conclude from v. 12b that Isaiah wanted to bring his listeners to the point that they would pay attention to Yahweh's "work" within history. Here, along with מעשה (work), he uses עצה (judgment), which is actually the *terminus technicus* for his understanding of history (on this, see the excursus, p. 203). It is most appropriate, in the present context, that Isaiah mentions the plan of the Holy One of Israel at this very point, bringing up the issue of the history of Yahweh with his people. Actually, "plan of the Holy One of Israel," in this case, means Yahweh's complete control of history, even up to the point of bringing his judgment upon the people. One might justifiably infer that mockers who would have pointed out, in a haughty way, that the judgment had not appeared would have had to quit talking if this had been during or after the Syro-Ephraimitic War or, at the very least, would have had to put the time for making their case on hold; see 28:14ff.

Jeremiah was also subjected to a similar type of mockery (17:15; 20:8) and complained about this treatment to God, from whom he knew he had received his commission to announce threats of disaster. Isaiah speaks this woe against the opponents without any indication that he felt himself to have been personally attacked: They pull along עון (guilt) and חטאה (sins) as if attached with ropes. One can make sense of this passage only if one keeps clearly in mind that the overall sense of the two words עון and חטאה is broader than our words "guilt" and "sin" (concerning the so-called "synthetic view of existence," see above, pp. 22f.). Sins and guilt already have the punishment latently built right in. Yahweh's patience can hold off the virulent power of the evil deed, which will assuredly bring disaster, but the disaster can also be accelerated by the carelessness of human beings. This means that the disaster, which is hanging over Israel like the sword of Damocles, will not automatically take its course, but that it is still under the overall control exercised by Yahweh.

S. Mowinckel points out that the חבלי השוא (cords of deception) (*Psalmenstudien* I [1921] 51f.) remind one of the cords which were tied into knots and used in various magical practices in the ancient Near East (e.g., Maqlû II, 148ff.; on this, see also M. Jastrow, *Die Religion Babyloniens und Assyriens* I [1905] 285, 288, and B. Meissner, *Babylonien und Assyrien* II [1925] 230). Presumably, Isaiah knew of such practices, by means of which someone would try to use ropes or strings to set in motion a particular event, for which one had high hopes, such as harming one's enemy. This first image leads to another: As one pulls a wagon on ahead by means of ropes, the opponents are pulling punishment for their sins right along as well. An עגלה is a farmer's wagon, normally pulled by cows (in Isa. 28:27, the term for threshing sledges is used). According to Amos 2:13, this is what is used when one brings in a harvest (illus.: *BRL* 532 = *BHH* 2129, where there is a portrayal of the way the inhabitants of the conquered city of Lachish were taking away their possessions; see also *ANEP* no. 367). Often enough, people would have had to pull wagons like this by themselves, with ropes (see M. A. Beek, *Bildatlas der assyrisch-babylonischen Kultur* [1961] no. 42). How ridiculous it was that such manual labor would be expended on dragging punishment for sin along, instead of something which had some value.

4. Woe-oracle [5:21]
Against the Pride of the "Wise"

Form

Meter: a three-stress bicolon.

Commentary

[5:21] To be called חכם (wise) and נבון (understanding) is highest praise in the world of wisdom. Joseph is praised as a man who is understanding and wise, as no other. That is not surprising, since the spirit of God is within him (Gen. 41:38f.; concerning this, see G. von Rad, "Josephgeschichte und ältere Chokma," VTSup 1 [1953] 120–127 = *GesStud,* TBü 8, 272–280). David is נבון דבר (prudent in speech) and an איש תאר (man of good presence) and, once again, it is mentioned that Yahweh is with him, 1 Sam. 16:18; concerning Solomon, cf. 1 Kings 3:12. Moses sought out wise, understanding, and insightful men to install as pre-eminent among the people, Deut. 1:13, 15. Finally, the king who would come at the end of time would be most remarkable, because he would have the רוח חכמה ובינה (spirit of wisdom and insight), and also because the Spirit of God would rest upon him, Isa. 11:2. Wisdom and insight thus provide the measuring stick by which one initially assesses a ruler or some other type of leader. However, in the proverbial literature, wisdom and insight are set forth as the ideal for everyone (see also Deut. 4:6). The passages just mentioned show that wisdom was considered, in Israel, to be a gift of God and that the ideals set forth by the wisdom teachers were known to be highly prized by many different groups. It is also true that Isaiah is not opposed to wisdom, in and of itself, but rather, is opposed to the "wise" who proudly praise their own wisdom. An important aspect of a correct understanding of wisdom is being aware of the danger of arrogance; see above, commentary on 2:9a, and commentary on 2:12. This is not an observation initially set forth by Isaiah; rather, wisdom had already distanced itself very pointedly from a conceited wise man: "Do you see a man חכם בעיניו (who is wise in his own eyes)—there is more hope for a fool than for him" (Prov. 26:12; see, in addition, 26:5, 16; 28:11). Wisdom states point-blank: "Be not wise in your own eyes; fear the Lord, and turn from evil" (Prov. 3:7). We come across similar formulations within the Egyptian wisdom teachings. Ptah-hotep admonishes his son: "Do not be proud of your own learning and do not trust the fact that you are knowledgeable" (von Bissing, op. cit., 45). Thus, Isaiah is not contending, as a prophet, against wisdom itself, as our passage is usually explained, but rather assesses those who think themselves wise, measuring themselves by their own standards. He incorporates a much deeper understanding of wisdom in his proclamation.

Presumably, Isaiah has his eye on politicians when he mentions the arrogance of the wise, those who believe that they can adequately handle the responsibilities of their office by using their own insight, without having to pay attention to Yahweh and/or his prophets. The battle front is not correctly identified by Marti and Kaiser (ad loc.), who interpret the passage to say that "religion," in the eyes of these men, is considered as something for women and children. Just as Isaiah employs the correct understanding of wisdom when battling against a caricature of it, he also goes forth in the name of Yahweh against a religiosity which refuses to recognize Yahweh's might and seriousness in being active within the historical arena.

5. Woe-oracle [5:22]
Against the Boasting of "Champions"

Form
Meter: a three-stress bicolon.

Setting
In spite of a thematic connection with vv. 11–13, v. 22 is still a distinct unit. Here, being intoxicated is not assailed; rather, what is assailed is the desire to boast among those who pass themselves off as "champions" and "top of the line among the skillful."

Commentary
[5:22] גבורים (heroes) can be used to designate the members of the king's bodyguard (see above, commentary, on 3:2). The term איש חיל (men who are so well-qualified) can also be used as a technical term, namely, to describe the "controlling and influential landowner, who is fit, and thus ready, to be called up for battle and is gallant" (KBL). These are the people whom one would put in charge (Gen. 47:6), the judges (Exod. 18:21), and the officers (2 Sam. 23:20 Q). Thus, Fohrer interprets this: "They serve as a guard—but much less a king's bodyguard than a guard of

drunks. Yes, they are fit men—but . . . they would more likely fit in as followers of a prince in a circus than as the militia for a king who is answerable to God." But, what is true for גבור (heroes) is also true for איש חיל (men who are so well-qualified); that is, one is not so locked in to a special sense of the phrase that it could not be used in a general way. Isaiah makes use of this term to describe praising oneself, and employs it within incisive mocking observation: Yes, champions—but when drinking wine; truly, top of the line among the skillful—but only when mixing alcoholic drinks. Herbs and honey were mixed into the שכר (intoxicating drinks) (see above, on 5:11; cf. 19:14; Prov. 9:2, 5; Song of Sol. 8:2). It was a special art, even in ancient times, to be able to add just the right herbs to make a tasty mixed drink.

6. Woe-oracle [5:20, 23, 24a]
Against the Perversion of Truth

Form

Meter: 20: 3 five-stress cola; 23: a three-stress bicolon (וצדקת צדיק, justice of the guiltless [or: the just one], gets *one* stress); 24a (after setting לכן, therefore, off from the rest): 2 three-stress bicola.

Setting

According to Fohrer, among others, the woe-oracle in v. 20 is directed "against those who intend to 'revalue all values' and who live 'on the other side of good and evil,' who rearrange the standards of the day to mesh with their own opinion and construct their own personal new world view" (ad loc.). But these are modern ideas, which one ought not use to reconstruct one's own interpretation of Isaiah, just because one does not consider vv. 23f. to be the continuation of v. 20. However, this connection is very likely. Using the same phraseology, Amos demands that evil be hated, good loved, *and* justice established in the gate (5:15; cf., on this, 5:7). Fey is just not convincing when he maintains that Isaiah attempts "to set forth a sharp antithesis to the content of the woe-oracle in Amos 5:7, 10, 12b" (op. cit., 58), but the comparison with the "parallels" found in Amos still shows that specific circumstances are meant when Isaiah makes this authoritative statement.

Commentary

[5:20] It is characteristic of prophetic thought that the good is so strongly identified with justice and evil with injustice, more specifically: with the denial of justice. One must keep in mind that, for the Hebrew individual, טוב (good) and רע (evil) were not originally descriptions of ethical norms, but identified salvation or disaster; they were not primarily ethical terms, but rather, religious and aesthetic terms. In the present context, this meaning is highlighted by using the antonyms light-darkness and sweet-bitter as word-pairs in v. 20b. Where there is light, there is salvation, blessing, happiness (cf. Amos 5:18, 20; Isa. 9:1; Pss. 27:1; 36:10). One can actually speak of the light of life (Pss. 56:14; 112:4; cf. Isa. 2:5; see also Ps. 107:10, 14, and cf. S. Aalen, " Die Begriffe 'Licht' und 'Finsternis' im Alten Testament, im Spätjudentum und im Rabbinismus," *SNVAO*

[1951] 1). Since that which is good brings salvation, the paraphrase "sweet" can be used; the same is true for evil as "bitter." In a similar way, Amos contrasts justice with "gall" (5:7; cf. also Deut. 32:32; Lam. 3:15; Prov. 5:4). Isaiah works within an overall framework in which moral + good, light + saving, and sweet + pleasant are various aspects of the same reality.

[5:23] Concerning the system of justice being ruined, see above, pp. 65f., on 1:23. צדיק (guiltless) and רשע (wrongdoer) are both used here in a forensic sense: The רשע is the guilty party, who must be condemned and, for this reason, the צדיק (guiltless) cannot be the "righteous one," in an absolute sense, but rather, the one who is the innocent party in a particular indictment. Amos, who speaks out against bribery in the parallel passage 5:12, mentions כֹּפֶר, "hush money." Isaiah condemns (as in 1:23) the reception of a שֹׁחַד, that is, a present used to bribe someone. The various terms which are used are most likely tied to specific circumstances. Amos thinks that justice is to be protected by the just community at the city gate. If there is no plaintiff on hand, possibly because the silence of a potential plaintiff has been bought with כֹּפֶר (hush money), then the injustice which has taken place will never even come out in the open. But in Isaiah's case, on the other hand, as in 1:23, the focus is on official judges within the capital city. These are the שׂרים (officials) who are appointed by the king; they are supposed to be those to whom one could turn when making appeal in official proceedings. In carrying out this function, the judges in the capital city would have to distinguish themselves as possessing a high degree of integrity. But they let themselves be influenced by pay-offs: "Its [Jerusalem's] heads give judgment for a שֹׁחַד [bribe]" is the way that Micah accuses those who are in charge of justice within the capital city (3:11).

[5:24a] The threat in v. 24a does not follow directly from the woe-oracle which precedes it. And yet, it is highly unlikely that v. 24 ever existed independently (contra Fohrer); לכן (therefore), at the beginning of the verse, is itself an argument against that interpretation. In v. 24a, we have one of the magnificent images which Isaiah has at his disposal. קשׁ is the stubble, more specifically, the dried out stalks of the cereal grains, which are left lying on the ground after the heads of grain have been cut off (concerning present practices, cf. Dalman, *AuS* III, 37). The OT is fond of making reference to קשׁ (stubble), since it is so easily blown about by the wind (Isa. 40:24; Jer. 13:24, and often elsewhere), but even more so because it catches fire so quickly (Exod. 15:7; Isa. 33:11; 47:14; Nah. 1:10, and often elsewhere; cf. Dalman, *AuS* III, 137). Fields which had already been harvested were often set on fire on purpose; cf. Judg. 15:4f.; 2 Sam. 14:30. In the teaching of Amenemope, the same imagery is used, even though in a different context: "Be well rested before you speak; otherwise, a storm will break forth like fire in straw" (according to von Bissing, op. cit., 81). As is shown in Exod. 15:7, stubble being consumed by fire is an ancient and well-known image, which serves to describe the consuming passion of God's wrath. Isaiah developed the metaphor further: Just as stubble and hay sink down in the fire, all opposition to God's powerful judgment will become powerless in an instant: a striking illustration of the destiny which awaits those who have set themselves outside the divine order and have thus descended into the realm of nothingness; Isaiah used a similar image in 1:31.

As is typical of Isaiah, he goes on in v. 24aβ to use quite a different image: Whoever wreaks havoc with the order which God established will be like a plant which has rotting (see 3:24) or decaying roots (cf. מקק, pine away, in Lev. 26:39; Ezek. 4:17, and often elsewhere). If the root is decaying, the blooms will also wither and will be blown away by the wind (see 29:5). אבק is the dust which hangs in the air, Deut. 28:24, or the dust on the street, which one kicks up with one's feet, Nah. 1:3; cf. Ezek. 26:10. In a way similar to the mention of root and bloom, Isa. 14:29 speaks of root and fruit (cf. 37:31; Amos 2:9; Mal. 3:19; see also Isa. 9:13, and often elsewhere; on this, see H. L. Ginsberg, "'Roots Below and Fruit Above' and Related Matters," FS G. R. Driver [1963] 72–76). In all of these cases, what is meant is complete destruction.

Conclusion of the Woe-oracles from Chapter 5   [5:24b]
The Repudiation of the Instruction from Yahweh

Form
Meter: a four-stress bicolon.

Setting
The reasons for taking v. 24b by itself are noted above, p. 195. The question remains about whether this is from Isaiah himself. Duhm is of the opinion that the poetic term אמרה (word) does not have the "taste" of Isaiah's style. Marti is even more sure that v. 24b (as also 1:4b) is the formulation of a later collector, using a typical deuteronomistic style. Procksch adds to this the problems connected with the use of a different meter; yet, he admits that the terminology is typical of Isaiah. מאס (reject) is actually used by Isaiah in 8:6 and 30:12 (cf. also 7:15 and Amos 5:21). As is true for נאץ (scorn) (on this, see above, pp. 23f., on 1:4), this verb belongs to the vocabulary of the covenant tradition; cf. Lev. 26:15, 43; but neither of the verbs is uniquely deuteronomic terminology. A correct understanding of the passage depends on the meaning of תורה (instruction); on this, see above, pp. 38f., on 1:10, and p. 91, on 2:3. It is a matter of one's personal opinion as to whether אמרה (word) "tastes" like an Isaianic passage, but Isaiah does use the word in 28:23 and 29:4. The very use of this rare term by Isaiah gives evidence for its authenticity; the Deuteronomist does not use it (but see Deut. 32:2 and, above all, 33:9: שמר אמרה, they observed thy word, parallel to נצר ברית, they kept thy covenant). Words completely typical of Isaiah come first with the designations for God: Yahweh of Hosts and Holy One of Israel. It is not just by chance that קדוש ישראל (Holy One of Israel) is used in the same way as in the very similar context of 1:4. As stated above, this still does not prove that v. 24b should not be separated from what precedes it. It seems much more likely that in v. 24b a redactor used a passage which originated with Isaiah, and used it in order to draw to a conclusion this collection of woe-oracles, as they are presently found in chap. 5.

Commentary

[5:24b] The accusation which is raised by this closing verse points to a complete break with Yahweh, as is suggested by the specific terminology which is used. (Concerning 5:25–30, see below).

7. Woe-oracle [10:1–3 (4)]
Against the Zeal of the Lawgivers

Form

Meter: 1–3: 5 three-stress bicola; in the secondary passages 4a, b, each is also a three-stress bicolon.

Commentary

[10:1] Circumstances connected with Jerusalem are also at issue in this section. The חֹקְקִים (those who draw up statutes) are the royal officials, who are looking for ways to adjust legislation to fit in with new political and economic realities.

It is worth noting that the issue here deals with the authorities who do not work with מִשְׁפָּט (*MISHPAT*), the system of justice transmitted from a previous era, but with *statute* (חֻקִּים). Whoever has complete power can at any particular time proclaim such regulations at will; cf. the formula שִׂים לְחֹק (he made it a statute) in 1 Sam. 30:25, where David ad hoc establishes a regulation for the way to divide the spoils of war, thereafter becoming an acceptable custom, a just solution from then on (מִשְׁפָּט, an ordinance). In this same way, Joseph establishes a חֹק (statute) concerning the tillable land in Egypt (Gen. 47:26; see also 22). The heads, who are able to implement what is thus authorized, are known as מְחֹקְקִים (those who draw up statutes) (Judg. 5:9, 14; see also Isa. 33:22). As God provided nature with its own orderliness (Ps. 148:6; Job 28:26; 38:10; Jer. 5:22; Prov. 8:29), a king could also establish certain regulations. But inherent within such a power is the danger of either being arbitrary or misusing it for one's own interests. In this regard, Israel was most susceptible; it is not just by chance that the king never really had a lot of influence when it came to passing legislation (M. Noth, "Die Gesetze im Pentateuch," *Schr. der Königsberger Gel. Ges.* 17/2 [1940] 10 = *GesStud,* TBü 6, 25).

If the suggested textual emendation which has been mentioned is correct, מְכַתְּבִים עָמָל (decrees which are full of affliction) stands parallel to חִקְקֵי־אָוֶן (statutes which are plainly evil). As in 2 Chron. 35:4 (see also 36:22 = Ezra 1:1), מְכַתְּבִים refer to written regulations. The *pi'el* of כתב (write), used only in this present passage, is chosen deliberately, since it highlights the suspicious zeal which is behind the drafting of new legislation. One would not be off the mark if one would, for example, think of the types of laws which would legitimate practices mentioned in 5:8. The upper levels of society would want to give themselves a legal foundation to justify their efforts to expand their property. That which the people would have simply called a timely adaptation of justice, to meet present needs, is what Isaiah calls אָוֶן (evil) (on this, see above, pp. 45f., on 1:13); the "regulations" are the result of an inner drive which would bring disaster upon fellow citizens. Parallel to און (evil) is עמל (affliction) (cf. Num. 23:21; Pss. 10:7; 90:10, and often elsewhere). The full meaning of the term is not rendered by the usual translation "affliction," as is shown by the parallel word און (evil) in this very passage (in Ps. 7:17, עמל, mischief, is parallel to חמס, violence; in 10:7, along with און, iniquity, מרמה, deceit, and תך, treachery, are used; in Prov. 24:2, it is parallel to שד, violence; in Job 7:3, it is parallel to שוא, emptiness; etc.). In עמל, the exact moment when someone overpowered another and cheated another is at issue.

[10:2] Among those who are sacrificed, in the name of giving new laws, one finds the "humble" and the "poor," among whom the widows and orphans are singled out for special mention. This corresponds to what Isaiah says in 11:4, when he identifies the most pressing task for the king, in the time of salvation, that he be involved with giving legal protection to the humble and poor (text emended), just as he calls elsewhere for legal help for the orphans and widows (1:17; see the commentary, above, on 1:17). Just as the עניים (poor) are clearly identified in 3:15 as the people of God, so in this passage they are called the עניי עמי (poor among my people). The poor of Israel are the chosen people κατ᾽ ἐξοχήν (the chief ones, preeminently). Concerning the accusation that the laws were distorted in such a way that the poor were short-changed, see 3:14; Amos 2:7; Deut. 16:19; Prov. 17:23; 18:5; Lam. 3:35; for a different side of this, see Exod. 23:3; Lev. 19:15. This present passage is unique in that it does not only make the accusation that the insignificant people have been virtually denied their legal rights, but that even the chance to lay claim to such rights had been violently torn away from them. Similar to regulations concerning one's enemies in battle (cf. גזל, tear away, and שלל, plunder), one of the most ancient obligations of a king was to be responsible for providing protection for the helpless, and the same would hold true for all who were responsible to him in matters of justice (see above, commentary on 1:17).

[10:3a] The threat is stated in the form of a question: "What will you do then during the day of affliction?" It is obvious that the day of affliction (יום פקדה, Gk: ἡ ἡμέρα τῆς ἐπισκοπῆς) will be the day of judgment, even though פקד can also be used in the positive sense, "take an interest in someone." Hosea already knows of this concept (9:7, with ימי השלם days of recompense, read in parallel; see, in addition, the use of the verb פקד, punish, in 1:4; 2:15; 4:14; 8:13). Amos, within the framework of a message from Yahweh, speaks of יום פקדי (on that day, I will punish) (3:14; cf. also 3:2), and the verb is a favorite one in the book of Isaiah when divine judgment is discussed. It is striking that the substantive, in the sense of "visiting affliction," is virtually confined, in its usage, to the prophetic literature (on this, see H. W. Wolff, *Hosea* BK XIV/1, 1:4 [Engl: *Hosea,* 17ff.], and J. Scharbert, *BZ* 4 [1960] 221f.). The פקיד is the official, in the sense of an overseer; correspondingly, פקדה refers to the "scrutiny which one applies, as part of one's duty, to oversee what happens in one's own area of responsibility: making one accountable and going after the one who is responsible for neglect and mistakes" (F. Horst, *EvT* 16 [1956] 73 = *Gottes Recht,* TBü 12, 289). Thus, the word comes from a completely different background than a word such as עון (evil), which can also refer to punishment, but meaning, by that, punishment which takes effect within the action-consequences relationship. It is very close to "vengeance" (see 1:24), which indeed also presupposes there is someone to bring about the "punishment." But, whereas the avenger is a private person, the פקיד (punisher) carries out this action as part of his official responsibilities. One would presume that יום פקדה (day of recompense) refers to a fixed time, at which subordinates would be summoned to give an account of their actions to their superiors. Ps. 89:33 shows how someone would carry out the punishment by hitting another with a rod. According to its meaning, the "day of recompense" can hardly be anything else than what is meant by "the Day of Yahweh" (see above, pp. 112f., on 2:10ff.), but the original source of the expression is completely different. In its original sense, there is even less of an eschatological aspect to יום פקדה (day of recompense) than there is in the יום יהוה (Day of Yahweh), though this is quite different for late Judaism; cf. מועד פקודה (appointed time of recompense) in 1 QS III, 18 and עת פקדת הארץ (time for recompense for the earth) in 4QpJs^b II 2, and often elsewhere.

There is at least a general hint in v. 3aβ about what Yahweh will use to carry out the punishment for the actions which have already occurred: He will act by means of a שואה (violent storm), which comes from afar. This word is often chosen as an image for disaster, that which overtakes someone suddenly (Isa. 47:11; Prov. 1:27; 3:25; in a special sense, this describes the approach of an enemy, Ezek. 38:9). Zeph. 1:15 explicitly describes the Day of Yahweh as יום שאה (a day of rain). Certainly, Isaiah also has an enemy in mind, one who comes suddenly, as would a thunderstorm; just as he announces a שואה ממרחק (violent storm which comes from a distance) in this passage, he also mentions a גוי ממרחק (a people from afar) (text emended) in 5:26; cf. 13:5; 30:27. According to Kaiser (see also Fohrer), the "storm from afar" is an ambiguous metaphor, since the prophet is thinking not only of just a human enemy who comes to do battle, but also of Yahweh, who is himself coming in a storm for a day of judgment (see 2:12ff.; 59:19; 1 Kings 19:11). But no more is mentioned at this time, beyond the fact that the enemy comes quickly and with power, as if a storm were breaking. Isaiah would have the Assyrians in mind, and 5:26ff. portrays for us how he assessed their proficiency in war. But it is Isaiah's strong conviction that the enemy could carry out its task only because it was being used as the tool of the wrath of God (see 10:5).

[10:3b] When facing an enemy such as this, resistance would be unthinkable. One would not even be able to grab a few of one's belongings to take along (see 2:20f.); one would not know where to find a safe place to hide whatever could be stowed away, since one would have no chance to gradually grow accustomed to what would happen on that day (cf. 5:12b). The wrath of God is a reality from which one cannot escape.

[10:4a] Apparently, v. 4a seeks to answer the question posed in v. 3, the answer to which, according to the way the woe-oracle is framed, ought to be self-explanatory. The expander took כבודכם (your riches), at the end of v. 3b, just as in 5:13, to be a reference to the upper level of society (cf.

כבוד, honor, riches, importance, as a polite reference in modern Hebrew). His answer is the sharpest No! בלתי (all in vain) is actually a substantive, with the meaning "to be no longer"; see KBL and Job 14:12. There is no chance to be saved; all that remains is imprisonment or death. Those who have been taken as prisoners would have to bow down to show submission before the one whose victory had to be acknowledged. For that reason, they would run for their lives (2 Kings 1:13; cf. 2 Sam. 22:40 = Ps. 18:40; Pss. 17:13; 78:31 [כרע *hiph'il,* lay low, is used parallel to הרג, slay]; illus.: *AOB* no. 123 = *ANEP* no. 355; Jehu submits himself before Shalmaneser III). תחת (underneath) still carries a definite substantive sense; see 2 Sam. 2:23; Job 40:12, and often elsewhere, and cf. J. C. Greenfield, "The Prepositions B . . .Taḥat. . . in Jes. 57:5," *ZAW* 73 (1961) 226–228. Thus: At the very place where prisoners have to bow down before the victors, the victors themselves will also have to bow down, and at the place where the executions take place, they will also fall.

[10:4b] Verse 4b uses the same refrain as is found in 9:11, 16, 20; 5:25. It cannot be originally part of this passage because it presumes that the goal of bringing about repentance by mentioning an act of judgment has not yet been attained, and that a more severe punishment than the one which had already taken place had to be announced. This sentence probably came from the same redactor who separated 10:1–3 (and possibly v. 4a) from the grouping of the woe-oracles in chap. 5. He would seemingly have taken v. 4a as a reference to an actual judgment activity, which had already taken place. But one does well to admit that it is so difficult to comprehend the various relationships within the overall composition of Isaiah that one cannot be positive about the attempts to understand the development of passages such as the present one. Concerning the meaning of this sentence, see below, pp. 232f.

(Concerning 10:5ff., see below, following 9:6).

Purpose and Thrust

The broad range of Isaiah's interests are mirrored in the collection of woe-oracles. The disastrous economic development, which led to the degradation of the weaker members of society, reducing them to the level of outcasts, roused him to indignation, just as did the failure of the officials who were responsible for preserving justice. He saw the frivolous nature of those who wanted to live a pleasure-filled life, to the accompaniment of wine and music. He was shocked by the arrogance of the mockers and the self-conceit of the wise. He was most deeply upset that there were leaders, in responsible positions, who misused their abilities by changing the laws in a way which would benefit them.

However, the expander who inserted vv. 15f. interpreted this correctly when he pointed to the pride of human beings as the mainspring of this antisocial behavior, about which Isaiah had issued such a harsh judgment in 2:12ff. Destructive arrogance is not only behind the greed of the large landowners, but also behind the boasting of the carouser, the self-love of the wise, the sneers of those who mocked Isaiah's announcement that judgment was close at hand, behind the corruptibility of the judges and the arrogance of those who proposed changes in the laws.

Here and there, one can easily recognize how Isaiah uses covenant tradition, with the accompanying threats, or how he uses wisdom traditions as the source of his criticisms. However, in the final analysis, Israel's sins were not simply disregard for the letter of the law or the teachings of wisdom; they were also not due to a lack of social sensitivity or to failing to recognize that there was danger inherent in the *dolce vita;* rather, Israel's sins were rooted in its pride, which caused it to fail to see the plan and work of the Holy One of Israel and possibly to fail to take the meaning and seriousness of that plan and work to heart. The knowledge of Yahweh, the Holy One of Israel, was alive for neither the leadership nor the people.

The term for "observing" the deeds of Yahweh carries with it a theological accent; in fact, it is almost a synonym for "belief; in any case, like the term 'being still,' it describes a very important aspect of what Isaiah calls 'faith'" (G. von Rad, *OTTheol* II, 161). Occasionally, some have given the impression that Isaiah is an advocate for a certain viewpoint about what constitutes order and, as such, does little more than point out the evil results which are to follow a destruction of order in the world, an order which, in and of itself, could bring about prosperity and peace. In reality, he is a theologian, passionately so, continually and singularly speaking about the obligations which Israel has toward its God. The threats, which are frequently attached to the woe-oracles, make it abundantly clear that Isaiah is not merely announcing the consequences of a way of life which goes against established order, but rather that he is speaking about the intervention of the Holy One of Israel who, as the interpolator points out, makes himself holy by executing his function of judging with righteousness. The closing sentence in 5:24b has it right: What has finally come to a head, becoming clear in the various woe-oracles, is contempt, the rejection of the God who entered into a relationship of rock-solid faithfulness with Israel. That means, as the verbs מאס (despise) and נאץ (reject) help one to see, that, if this was not the complete end of all fellowship with Yahweh, it was definitely the end of any right to seek his help and protection (cf., on this, J. Fichtner, "Die 'Umkehrung' in der prophetischen Botschaft. Eine Studie zu dem Verhältnis von Schuld und Gericht in der Verkündigung Jesajas," *TLZ* 78 [1953] 459–466).

Isaiah 9:7–20; 5:25–30

Yahweh's Outstretched Hand

Literature

H. Donner, "Israel unter den Völkern," VTSup 11 (1964), esp. pp. 64–75. A. M. Honeyman, "An Unnoticed Euphemism in Isaiah IX 19–20?" *VT* 1 (1951) 221–223.

Concerning "message": O. Grether, *Name und Wort Gottes im Alten Testament*, BZAW 64 (1934). L. Dürr, *Die Wertung des göttlichen Wortes im Alten Testament und im antiken Orient*, MVAAG 42/1 (1938). K. Koch, "Wort und Einheit des Schöpfergottes in Memphis und Jerusalem," *ZTK* 62 (1965) 251–293.

Concerning שוב *(return)*: H. W. Wolff, "Das Thema 'Umkehr' in der alttestamentlichen Prophetie," *ZTK* 48 (1951) 129–148 = *GesStud* TBü 22 130–150. W. L. Holladay, *The Root Šûbh in the Old Testament* (1958). [Literature update through 1979 (on 9:7–20): M. Wallenstein, "An Unnoticed Euphemism in Isaiah IX 19–20?" *VT* 2 (1952) 179–180. H. Wohlmann, "'The Bricks Are Fallen, But We Will Build with Hewn Stones; . . .,'" *BetM* 1 (1956) 37–43. J. L. Crenshaw, "A Liturgy of Wasted Opportunity (Am 4,6–12; Isa 9,7—10,4; 5:25–29)," *Semitics* 1 (1970) 27–37. M. H. Goshen-Gottstein, "Hebrew Syntax and the History of the Bible Text," *Textus* 8 (1973) 100–106.]

Text

9:7 'Yahweh'[b] sent a message[a] against Jacob,
and it fell down upon Israel.

8 And the whole nation learned of it,[a]
Ephraim and the inhabitants of Samaria.
[b]'Yet they boasted about themselves'[b] in arrogance,
and they spoke with a haughty disposition:

9 "Brick walls are fallen down, we will rebuild with squared stones;
sycamore rafters are smashed, we will install cedarwood in their place."[a]

10 Then Yahweh allowed 'its oppressors' [Rezin][a] to come up[b]
and spurred on its enemies against it:[c]

11 Aram from the east[a] and Philistia from the west,[a]
and they devoured Israel with a full mouth.
In all this his wrath did not turn away,
and his hand is still stretched out.

12 And the people did not turn back to him, who struck it,[a]
    and it did not seek out Yahweh of Hosts.[b]
15 The leaders of this people were misleaders
    and the misled ones, a deluded crowd.[a]
16aα Therefore Yahweh[b] did not spare[a] its young warriors
    and was not merciful to its widows and orphans,
13 [a][Yahweh of Israel]:[a] he removed head and tail,
    branch of the rod[b] and bulrush stem, on one day.
14 [a][The elder and honored one, that is the head,
    and the prophet, who teaches lies,[b] that is the tail.][a]
16aβb Godless and scoundrels, that is what they all are,
    and every mouth speaks what is foolish.
In all this his wrath did not turn away,
    and his hand is still stretched out.

17 Truly, the evil burned like a fire,
    which consumes thorns and thistles.
It sets the thicket of the forest on fire,
    so that it curls upward[a] like a pillar of smoke.
18 On account of the fury of Yahweh [of Hosts][a] the land is
        scorched,[b]
    and it has gone for the people as if it had been consumed by
        fire.[c]
No one takes care of anyone else,[d]
19b   everyone consumes his 'neighbor's'[a] flesh.
19a One foraged on the right—and remained hungry,
    and devoured on the left—and was not satisfied.[b]
20 Manasseh Ephraim and Ephraim Manasseh,
    yet both of them (fall upon) Judah.
In all this his wrath did not turn away,
    and his hand is still stretched out.

  . . . .

5:25 Therefore, Yahweh's wrath was kindled against his people,
    and he stretched out his hand against them and struck them,
so that the [a]mountains quaked[a] and their dead bodies lay
    in the middle of the narrow streets just like dung.
In all this his wrath did not turn away,
    and his hand is still stretched out.

26 For he will raise up a signal [a]for a people from afar[a]
    and whistle for them from the end of the earth.
And behold, hurriedly, he draws them quickly closer!
27   No exhausted one[a] and no stumbler is among them,
    [b][no one sleeps or slumbers].[b]
No one's loincloth comes loose,
    and no one's shoe strap tears apart.
28 Its arrows are sharpened
    and all its bows are bent.
Its horses' hoofs are like flint[a]
    and its wagon wheels are like[b] the stormwind.
29 It lets out a roar like a lion
    and like a young lion it howls.[a]
It snarls and packs up the spoil
    and hauls it away, and none can get anything back from it.

30 [And it will thunder above it on that day
　　like the thundering of the sea.
　　And one will look to the earth, and behold, oppressive[a] [b]darkness
　　and light,[a] which is obscured by its clouds.][c]

9:7a Gk reads θάνατον (death), which means that it read רבר as דֶּבֶר, "pestilence," which is translated as θάνατος in quite a number of OT passages (Exod. 5:3; 9:3, 15; Lev. 26:25; Num. 14:12; Deut. 28:21, and often elsewhere).

7b For אדני (Adonai, Lord), Qᵃ reads יהוה (Yahweh), which is preferable.

8a D. W. Thomas (*JTS* 41 [1940] 43f.) does not wish to translate ידע according to the meaning "know"; instead, he takes it from the Arabic *wadu'a,* which means "be humiliated" ("And all the people, even Ephraim and the inhabitant of Samaria, shall be humiliated"; cf. G. R. Driver, *JTS* 41 [1940] 162: "shall be subdued"). But since this meaning is not used anywhere in Hebrew, one does well to disregard this suggestion.

A basic problem for the interpretation of this chapter involves determining whether the prophet speaks about the future or the past. The perfect consecutive וידעו (and they will know) seems to look at that which is yet to come, in which case the perfects in vv. 7 and 9 would have to be interpreted as prophetic perfects. But according to what follows afterwards, there is no doubt that Isaiah wants to re-create for his audience what has already taken place. It is thus possible that one ought to point it וַיֵּדְעוּ (and they learned), though it is certainly possible that one ought to leave the vocalization as it is in the MT, but translate it as a preterite, just as was done with ונפל (it fell down) which precedes it.

8b–b Verse 8b seems to have suffered damage. Procksch suggests reading הַמִּתְגָּאֶוה בגאוה (the arrogant who act arrogantly); Duhm and Donner, op. cit., 68, expand it somewhat blandly: כִּי יֹאמְרוּ (for they say) or הָאֹמְרִים (those who say). However, it is more likely that a different verb, now lost, ought to be read here, most certainly an imperfect consecutive with the meaning "boast about oneself."

9a G. R. Driver (*JTS* 34 [1933] 381f.) would like to use the Syriac ḥālûftâ, "knife," and the Arabic *maḫlûf* (see R. Dozy, *Supplément aux dictionnaires Arabes* I [1927²] 398) to give evidence for the existence of a verb חלף (possibly vocalized as *qal* or *pi'el*) with the meaning "dress, chisel, carve," whereas F. Wutz (*BZ* 21 [1933] 18) renders חלף *hiph'il* as "fell" (cf. also above, textual note on 2:18). Gk translates this very freely and adds, in addition, based on Gen. 11:3f.: οἰκοδομήσωμεν ἑαυτοῖς πύργον (let us build for ourselves a tower); see Ziegler, op. cit., 63, 109. But the generally accepted meaning of חלף *hiph'il,* "allow someone to take another's place" (see KBL), is not so unlikely that one would have sufficient reason for objecting to its use here.

10a צרי רצין (adversaries of Rezin) cannot be right. A great number of MSS attempted to correct the damaged text by reading שָׂרֵי רְצִין (Rezin's princes). But why only "Rezin's princes" and not Rezin himself? רצין must be removed altogether, which is also suggested by metrical considerations, and צרי (adversaries of) should be changed, based on the parallel with איביו (its enemies), to read צָרָיו (its oppressors, adversaries) or, as is even more likely, with K. Budde and Kaiser, to read צֹרְרָיו (its oppressors, adversaries). רצין (Rezin) would originally have been a marginal note, put there by a reader who shared his own thoughts about which specific enemy might have been in the author's mind.

10b Gk reads καὶ ῥάξει (and he shall strike). Because of this, Driver (*JTS* 34 [1933] 278f.) and Wutz (op. cit.; see above, textual note 9a) would like to read שׂגב as having the meaning "pull," on the basis of the Arabic *šaǧaba,* but in this instance also, there is no justification for finding a substitute for the generally accepted meaning.

10c The imperfect יסכסך (spur on) does not refer to a further development of the action, but describes something which is taking place at the same time as that which has just been mentioned. Therefore, there is no need to change it to read a perfect סִכְסֵךְ (he spurred on) (B. Stade, *ZAW* 26 [1906] 141). The mark of the direct object, את and ואת, may suggest some effort to make this more like prose, and עליו (against it) is to be taken along with the second colon.

11a קדם refers to the front side, אחור to the back side. Since one would orient oneself in any particular place by facing toward the sun, קדם is the east, אחור is the west.

12a One MS reads הַמַּכֶּה (the one who struck); Qᵃ inserted the article ה afterwards, above the line. Grammatically, the MT is fine as it is; the accusative suffix on the participle does not make this definite; see BrSynt §73b; yet, maybe the article should be removed on metrical grounds. The Hebrew participle can also refer back to past time; see ibid., §99a.

12b צבאות (of Hosts) is missing in Gk, but is found in Sym, Theod, and the Hexaplaric recension (※); there is no good reason to remove it (but see Marti, Procksch, Donner, op. cit., 68, et al.). On the other hand, את, which is the mark of the accusative, before יהוה (Yahweh) is not original.

13a–a Copies of the Lucianic recension read Ἰερουσαλημ (Jerusalem) instead of ישראל (Israel), but the word is intended as a reference to Israel as the Northern Kingdom. Maybe יהוה מישראל (Yahweh from Israel) (as suggested by Duhm, Fohrer, Kaiser, et al.) ought to be removed, since the two words disturb the meter and according to the suggested rearrangement (see below, p. 226) are thus superfluous.

13b כִּפָּה (feminine form of כַּף) is generally translated "palm branch," but see KBL and I. Löw, *Die Flora der Juden* I (1928) 666f.

14a–a Verse 14 looks very much like an ancient addition which sought to furnish a detailed listing of those alluded to in v. 13 (Marti, Gray, Duhm, Kaiser, Donner, op. cit., 68, et al.). One must consider the possibility that it could still have come from Isaiah if הוא הראש (that is the head) and הוא הזנב (that is the tail) would be eliminated (thus, Procksch and Fohrer; see also M. A. Klopfenstein, *Die Lüge nach dem Alten Testament* [1964] 111f.). However, according to v. 13, one would need to refer to the people from the lower levels of society and not only to the leadership.

14b Instead of מורה (one who teaches), three Gk-MSS (41, 106, 233) and Cyril read καὶ διδάσκοντα (and one who teaches). If this reading is correct, v. 14b would also have two parts.

15a Literally, "deluded." Of course, it is not certain whether מבלעים is derived from בלע III, "deluded, confounded," or from בלע I, "entangle, annihilate" (בלע I in 28:4; בלע II *pi'el* in 3:12; *niph'al* in 28:7). It is preferable, since מתעים (misleaders) is used in close proximity, to adopt the meaning "deluded."

16a לא־ישמח, "he was not delighted," is not a very good parallel for לא ירחם, "he was not merciful," which is certainly correct. Therefore, some have suggested reading יפסח (= יפסח) (he will limp) for the rather bland ישמח (be delighted) or, based on the Arabic *samuha,* "be gracious, magnanimous," having changed the word so it reads יִשְׁמַח* (Perles, *JQR* 11 [1899] 689). Qᵃ reads יחמול (take care, have compassion), which possibly comes from v. 18. But possibly this verb was used with the intention of clarifying the word ישמח, which was no longer understood and which finally was inserted into the text at this point. Indirectly, the Qᵃ would attest to the correctness of Perles's conjecture.

16b There is no good reason for eliminating אדני (Lord) (Procksch); on the contrary, this word is likely a replacement for יהוה (Yahweh), as is true in so many other cases, even though in this particular case there is no textual evidence anywhere for this adjustment (Gk: ὁ θεός, God).

17a One cannot be completely sure about the exact meaning of אבך (curls upward) *hithpa'el.* Gk interpreted this difficult passage in light of Jer. 21:14; 27 (50):32: συγκαταφάγεται τὰ κύκλῳ τῶν βουνῶν πάντα (It will devour all the hills round about) (Ziegler, op. cit., 109f.). It has been common for אבך to be treated as related to הפך (overturn) and to the Akkadian *abāku,* "carry away, carry forth," which is completely permissible on linguistic grounds. Concerning הֹפֵךְ, "turn," one might consider the meaning here to be "turn itself into."

18a צבאות (of Hosts) is missing in Gk (with the exception of the Lucianic recension) and—also in light of the metrical pattern of the verse—possibly should be removed.

18b The meaning of נעתם *niph'al* is simply not clear. Gk: συγκέκαυται (is burned up); Targ: חרובת, "is devastated"; Syr: *zā'at,* "is shaken"; Vulg: *conturbata est* (is thrown into confusion). KBL furnishes no translation, choosing instead to suggest an alternate word which would read נִתְעָה (strayed, lost), while others read נִצְּתָה (fallen into ruins) on the basis of Gk, Targ (Cheyne, Procksch, Donner, op. cit., 68f.). W. L. Moran (*CBQ* 12 [1950] 153f.) takes the word to be a third feminine singular perfect *qal* from נוט (totter) with an enclitic *Mem;* this is also the conclusion of H. D. Hummel (*JBL* 76 [1957] 94: "at the wrath of Yahweh the earth reeled") and Kaiser, and it may be that the rendering in the Syr also has this meaning in mind. And yet, the parallelism with the second colon shows that the Gk basically got the right sense, without which we would not be able to reconstruct the Hebrew original. As a result of haplography, it would seem that the article may have been lost from the following word, ארץ (land) (pay careful attention to the meter!).

18c כמאכלת אש (as if consumed by fire) is considered an unsatisfactory reading by many commentators. It would seem "impossible to explain why the people would not actually be, but would only be like (כְּ) food for the fire and to explain how those who were consumed as if by a fire would still be able to consume themselves" (Marti). For this reason, Duhm suggested reading כְּמוֹ אֹכְלֵי אִישׁ, "like those who consume human beings," an interesting notion, but not really very likely. More worthy of discussion is the conjecture כְּמוֹ אֵשׁ אֹכְלָת (just as fire consumes), and yet, the transmitted text (see also 9:4) would seem to be correct as it is, namely in the sense that the people were so wasted away that they were like the individual sticks on a burning wood pile which catch on fire at the same time; this means that כמאכלת (as [fire] consumes) is there in the text but what is actually meant is כבמאכלת (as consumed by); see Joüon, Gr §133h.

18d Verse 19b is to be inserted after v. 18, as suggested on the basis of both meter and content.

19a "Every one of them eats up the flesh of his arm" (זְרֹעוֹ) neither makes any sense nor fits into the context. The Alexandrine group of Gk transmitted texts (see also the Boharic and Syp texts) add the words τοῦ ἀδελφοῦ (of the brother) and Targ reads קְרִיבֵיהּ (his relative), which would suggest an original Hebrew word רֵעוֹ (his neighbor). Of course, one also ought to mention pointing this זְרֹעוֹ (his arm) (see Honeyman, op. cit., 222), but the text does not flow smoothly if this is inserted.

19b One notices that the plural שבעו (they are not satisfied) is used; it is to be read as שָׂבֵעַ (he is not satisfied), since the ו (*Waw*) in שבעו should be taken as part of the following word.

5:25a–a Some have had problems with the MT because the suffix on נבלתם (their dead bodies), in its present context, seems to refer to הרים (the mountains); thus, it has been suggested that ויהרגו השרים (and they killed the princes) be read (BHK³; Steinmann). But the suffix on נבלתם (their dead bodies) can very easily refer farther back than הרים (mountains), so that עמו (his people) is its referent.

26a–a Since the time of Roorda, instead of לגוים מרחוק, "the peoples from afar," Jer. 5:15 has been used when suggesting the following reading: לְגוֹי מִמֶּרְחָק (for a people from afar), with good reason since, in what follows, the discussion is about only one people.

27a Instead of עיף (be exhausted), the Qᵃ text reads יעף, which has the same meaning; see also 40:29 and 50:4.

27b–b This is eliminated by Duhm. His reasoning does not hold up, saying that Isaiah, even though he idealizes the Assyrians, could never use the exact same words which the poet uses in Ps. 121:4 about God; yet, the similarity of the terminology certainly catches one's attention. The best reason for removing this passage is that the colon in v. 26b is expanded upon in v. 27aα (treated thus by all modern exegetes except Schmidt, Fischer, and Kissane).

28a For כצר (like flint), Qᵃ reads כצור (like rock); cf. Gk: ὡς στερεὰ πέτρα (like hard rock). It is likely that the MT ought to be pointed כַּצֻּר. If that is the case, it is no longer necessary to posit the meaning "meteor" for צר (G. R. Driver, *JTS* 45 [1944] 13; see also FS Th. H. Robinson [1950] 55). Tur-Sinai's suggestion (op. cit. [in literature on 1:1] 168) to read כַּצִּנּוֹר instead of כצר, meaning "God's flash of lightning," would also no longer be necessary; cf. the Greek κέραυνος (thunderbolt).

28b The poem is composed of surprisingly regular three-stress bicola. Because of this, Procksch places נחשבו (they are thought to be) as a predicate after כסופה (like the stormwind). It would be simpler to remove the ו (*Waw*) before גלגליו (and its wagon wheels) as a dittography and to move the Zaḳēp qāṭôn from נחשבו (they are thought to be) and place it on כצר (like flint).

29a Qere: יִשָּׂא (it will let out a roar; Kethib: וְשָׂאג (it let out a roar). By analogy with the verb which follows, וַיִּשְׁאַג (and it let out a roar) ought to be read. But the word does not coordinate well with שׁאגה (it lets out a roar) at the beginning of the verse; in addition, the colon is too short. ושאג (and it let out a roar) may have been used as a replacement for a more original יתן קולו (he sounded forth his voice), or something similar (cf. Amos 1:2). However, Ziegler (op. cit., 16) might be more correct when he supposes that behind the Gk παρέστηκαν (he set before the mind, presented) there might be the Hebrew phrase וַיִּשָּׂא קוֹל (and he raised his voice), which might have been read as וַיִּשְׁקֹל (and he weighed).

30a The Zaḳēp qāṭôn should be moved from חשׁך (darkness) to the next word, צר (oppressive); the one over ואור (light) should be eliminated altogether; this means that צר (oppressive) is an adjective or a substantive in a genitive relationship, connected with חשׁך (darkness).

30b E. Zolli (*TZ* 6 [1950] 231f.) would like to read, instead of this, rather צח צר, meaning "flickering, shining, bright, clear," so that Kaiser arrives at the following translation for v. 30b: "Brightness and light are darkened in a downpour." But since צח is never used as a substantive elsewhere in the OT, this suggested emendation ought to be disregarded.

30c The suffix on עריפיה (by its clouds) seems to refer back to ארץ (earth), but what this means is not intelligible. Should it be read in the absolute state? Or is the *hapax legomenon* עריפים possibly nothing more than the result of a textual corruption? Gk (ἐν τῇ ἀπορίᾳ αὐτῶν, in their difficult straits) does not give much help, since that translation seems to be nothing more than an attempt to make some sense of a text which could not correctly be understood (coming here from 8:22?). Since v. 30 is an addition to the text, which could have come here from some other original setting, one cannot come to any definite conclusions, and it is best not to attempt any textual emendations. The exact meaning is uncertain at best. KBL derives the word from ערף I, "trickle," and suggests translating it with "drizzle." But since the word cannot be interpreted without taking into account the Akkadian *erēpu/arāpu,* "become overcast," and *erpetu* or *urpu* (and Ugaritic *'rpt*), "cloud," one is best advised to stay with the common translation "cloud cover."

Form

[9:7–20] Because of the refrain, "In all this his wrath did not turn away, and his hand is still stretched out" (11, 16, 20), one can recognize that 9:7–20 is to be treated as a single unit. But the sentence is found at two other places in the book of Isaiah: 5:25 and 10:4. When discussing 10:4, we came to the conclusion above, on pp. 215f., that it was to be attributed to the hand of a redactor who thought 10:1–4 was a continuation of 9:7–

20. Actually, that cannot be correct, since 10:1ff. is a woe-oracle which looks ahead into the future, whereas 9:7–20, as will now be explained in greater detail, speaks about judgments of God which have already broken out upon Israel, but which will not lead to the repentance for which Yahweh had hoped.

[5:25] Verse 25 is to be evaluated in a different way. It is clear that a conclusion has been reached with 5:24b and, in addition, the threat of judgment which is introduced by לכן (therefore) does not seem to antic- ipate any additional threat with a similar introduction. Since, on the other hand, v. 25a (as also the individual sections in 9:7–20) speaks about a harsh intervention by Yahweh, in his wrath, and v. 25b makes the point once again that the wrath of God was still threatening the people, it seems very possible that this verse should be considered (as already had been suggested by Ewald and G. Studer, *JPT* 7 [1881] 172) as belonging to the same context as 9:7ff. In recent scholarship, a wide-ranging consensus has been established on this point.

There is less of a consensus concerning the original placement of 5:25 within the context of 9:7ff. That only stands to reason: An independent unit cannot begin with על־כן (therefore); it must have been preceded by mention of the reasons for the judgment which would result (see 9:15, 16). That is what moti- vated W. Staerk (*Das assyrische Weltreich im Urteil der Propheten* [1908] 48) to insert the verse right after 9:9 (as is also done by Schmidt and Eichrodt). It is also possible that 5:25 is a fragment from a section which at one time spoke of an earlier phase of judgment, which would have preceded that mentioned in 9:7. Possibly the best solution is the one adopted by those who follow Budde, Duhm, et al., taking v. 25 as a continuation of 9:20, seeing this verse as a further escalation of the pouring out of God's wrath. But, even in this case, without a doubt we have nothing more than a fragment, which appears to have been removed from its original context by someone who damaged the text in the process. In its present position, 5:25 brings the previous woe-oracle to a close and apparently serves to accent, as is shown by the use of the imperfect consecutive, the fact that the disaster which had been previously threatened had become a present reality, but had not yet reached its final conclusion. In such a context, the reason for the "kindling" of the wrath of Yahweh had to be omitted.

A definite uncertainty remains about the original setting of 5:25. But no matter how one may make a decision about that verse, there is still the question about where the conclusion to 9:7ff. is to be found. The refrain, which hammers home the point that Yahweh's hand is still stretched out, demands that something will happen. One might conclude that Isaiah called for some definite steps to demonstrate a real repen- tance, in light of all the problems brought on by the wrath of God which continued to threaten Israel. But it is more likely that he proclaimed that another blow would be struck, due to the wrath of Yahweh, which would be even more severe than the acts of judgment which had occurred up to that point. There is much to recommend the interpretation—scholarship has reached a general consensus on this point also—that the next step which one would expect to take place is to be found in 5:26ff. One would indeed expect a short notation just before v. 26, saying that the final decisive judgment would now be the subject of the discussion. But apparently, without rambling on, Isaiah wanted to confront his hearers simply by mentioning the harsh reality of what was ahead. In any case, it is unlikely that 5:26 begins a new, independent section. It certainly does not do so on formal grounds: וְנָשָׂא (for he will raise up), at the beginning of v. 26, has to be connected with something already mentioned. And not on grounds of content either: Taking vv. 26ff. as an isolated unit would make them simply a prediction of the invasion of an awesome enemy. Then there would be nothing about this enemy being one which would bring on the wrath of God and nothing about Yahweh having good reasons for punishing in this way. But that is not the manner of the prophets when they speak about future events. However, the strongest argument in favor of taking 5:26ff. as connected with 9:7ff. is made by comparing this with the structure of the closest parallel to this passage, another one which shows the way prophets viewed history in the OT: Amos 4:6–12. Also in that passage, there is mention of a series of blows struck in judgment, but after each one of them it had to be stated: "Yet you did not return to me, says the Lord." Yet, that series does not conclude with the simple portrayal of the act of judgment and the repetition of the refrain, but rather with the announcement of another intervention of Yahweh, which was still to come, calling for preparations to be made for it. This same way of looking at history is also found in Leviticus 26; cf. v. 21: "Then . . . I will bring more plagues upon you, sevenfold as many as your sins," and v. 27: "And if in spite of this you will not hearken to me. . . ." This means that one blow would come after another, becoming more and more severe, until finally, at the end, the people would actually return (vv. 40ff.). The reflection upon historical events which is found in the prophets, which looks back upon a series of harsh blows, has as its pattern the threats of judgment which are found in the context of the covenant tradition. Just as Amos calls upon Israel, at the end of his series of threats, to get itself ready for the final blow, so it is that Isaiah also brings his observations to a conclusion in 5:26 with the announcement of the harshest blow. He is more restrained than Amos, since he seems content just to mention what is going to come. Since he is making use of a specific form of historical paranesis, the purpose of which would have been clear to everyone, he can leave it to his hearers to consider for themselves the consequences which would follow after the disaster which he announced.

This literary-critical assessment is tied closely to the answer to the question posed above (see textual note 8a) about whether actual reference is made to the past in the individual sections which begin with 9:7ff. Some exegetes (Gesenius, Meinhold, Driver, Marti, Gray, Duhm, Procksch, Herntrich, et al.) presume that Isaiah is speaking about future events from the very beginning; Isaiah did not wish to present "some sort of school assignment," as if he had nothing better to do (Duhm). But the imperfect consecutives in vv. 10, 11, 13, 15, 17, 19; 5:25 (and, based on the emendation suggested above, also at the beginning of v. 8) show that it is impossible to understand this as referring exclusively to the future. Naturally, it is different in the case of 5:26ff., since everything else in the section leads up to that prediction.

The observations about the historical past which precede the threat of judgment serve the same function as a reproach, which would normally be used to provide the reason for a threat. On purely formal grounds, this is seen in 9:9 where, as is completely typical of a reproach, the character of Israel, which is to "be reproached," is brought out by using a quotation.

Meter: Donner (op. cit., 68) maintains that the message, to which 10:1–4 would also belong, can be divided into six strophes, each with 7 three-stress bicola. As the refrain shows, these are actually strophes. But even if three-stress bicola predominate, the only way to arrive at a completely smooth textual reading is by means of adjustments to the text and forced changes in the metrical reading. And it remains uncertain whether each strophe is made up of seven lines. One simply cannot deal with this text without some textual emendations, but these ought not be determined solely on the basis of a pattern of strophes and verses.

1. *Strophe:* 9:7–11: seven lines. Verse 7: a seven-stress colon (4 + 3); בישראל (upon Israel) is given two stresses. The beginning of the strophe is indicated by an extra long line. Verse 8: (see above, textual note 8b–b): 2 three-stress bicola. Verse 9: 2 two-stress bicola, which portray the animated way in which the hearers object to what is said. Verse 10: a three-stress bicolon (presuming that one accepts the suggested way of settling the textual problem). Verse 11a: a seven-stress colon, just as at the beginning of the strophe. Verse 11b, the refrain: a three-stress bicolon.

2. *Strophe:* 9:12–16: This section also seems to be seven lines in length. But v. 14 is an interpretive comment about v. 13. In addition, there seems to have been some displacement of individual verses: v. 13 already speaks about judgment, which means that v. 15 cannot speak about the way in which guilt was incurred, using imperfect consecutives. On the other hand, one would expect a reason to follow v. 12 to explain why the punishment would have to continue. These difficulties can be eliminated if we place v. 15 along with v. 16aα right after v. 12. Then v. 13 follows with a description of the judgment, which is buttressed with still more evidence in the כי-clause in v. 16aβ. Thus, what remains was originally only six lines, but the many disruptions to this text certainly make it possible that it was also composed with seven lines at one time.

3. *Strophe:* 9:17–20: seven lines. Verse 17: 2 three-stress bicola. Verse 18abα seems to be a four-stress bicolon, but one ought to proceed here with great caution in light of the numerous points of uncertainty in the text. Verses 18bβ and 19b: a three-stress bicolon, just as in v. 19a. In v. 20a, the line just before the refrain also portrays the events with a seven-stress colon.

4. *Strophe:* 5:25 (fragment): three lines, namely v. 25aα: a four-stress bicolon; v. 25aβ, once again, before the refrain, a seven-stress colon. The meter of the fragment shows that, at least on formal grounds, it fits well into the framework of 9:7–20.

5. *Strophe:* 5:26–29: After removing v. 27aβ, and after taking into account the comments made concerning the text of v. 29bα which were noted above, this is also made up of 7 three-stress bicola.

The entire poem has a type of metrical and strophic structure which is much more consistent than in the rest of the OT, which seldom has this type of strophic format.

Setting

The presentation of the prophetic view of history in 9:7ff., and that of the haughty mind-set of Israel, which did not see that Yahweh was in control of history and did not permit itself to be warned, is definitely from Isaiah himself. In addition to this, because the section has identifiable connections which link it to the history of Isaiah's day, its authenticity is generally recognized. The message, according to 9:7, is addressed to Israel/

Judah. It could be that this refers to Israel as the people of Yahweh. But v. 11a, which speaks about the oppression of Israel by Aram and the Philistines, suggests that it is most likely referring to the Northern Kingdom. Above all else, Israel, as mentioned in v. 7, is apparently identical with Ephraim and the inhabitants of Samaria, referred to in v. 8. It is true that Procksch believes that the message is addressed to the entire people of God, "which does not only refer to the Northern Kingdom but is also meant to include Judah (9,20)." But L. Rost (*Israel bei den Propheten,* BWANT IV/19 [1937] 44ff.) sees in 9:20 the key which can help to interpret the entire passage in the exact opposite way: "The reference here is to the battle waged between the two tribes Ephraim and Manasseh, interrupted only when it was advantageous for them to join together to attack Judah. Judah is not on the same level with these two Israelite tribes" (p. 44).

To determine more exactly the time when this was composed, one must begin with 5:26–29. It is very obvious that the "people from afar" in v. 26 are the Assyrians. This message must therefore come from a time period when Assyria posed an acute threat for the Northern Kingdom. Isaiah's way of portraying the battle readiness of the enemy's army, which is a thoroughly believable description (see J. Hunger, *Heerwesen und Kriegführung der Assyrer auf der Höhe ihrer Macht,* AO XII/4 [1911]), presumes that those who live in Jerusalem were already very well aware of the specific details about the characteristics of the Assyrians. There are some, such as Donner, who has made the suggestion once again (op. cit., 71; see also Fohrer and Kaiser), who believe this refers to the time right after the Syro-Ephraimitic War, at the time when Assyria had already seized from the Northern Kingdom the territory of Galilee, the land east of the Jordan, and the coastal region (2 Kings 15:29). The main reason which he gives for assigning this passage this date comes from connecting 9:13 with the actions of Tiglath-Pileser after he defeated Damascus in 732, when he also reduced Israel to a rump state, with Ephraim alone remaining as the main part of the country. But this interpretation is by no means the only possibility (see below, pp. 235f.). One gets the impression from 5:26–29 that a harsh military conflict had not as yet taken place between Assyria and Israel; that could hardly square with the situation of Israel after it experienced harsh defeat at the hands of Assyrian might in 732. "A people from afar" would simply not do justice to describe Assyria at a time when it was already on Israelite soil and had already established its provincial authority. This same reason can be used to refute Leslie, who takes 5:25–30 as a single unit and believes that Isaiah is portraying, "with sensitive picturesqueness, but in great solemnity," the advance of the military might of Assyria against Judah in 701 (p. 109). Instead of adopting this viewpoint, we do better to identify the section with the first period of Isaiah's activity, which means at the time shortly before the Syro-Ephraimitic War. Because of the insertion of the so-called memoir of Isaiah, covering the complex of passages stretching from 6:1—9:6, 9:7ff. was wrongly separated from chaps. 1–5, in which one finds material which by and large comes from the first period of Isaiah's activity. The poem "stands no longer *in situ"*; "it belongs rather, like chapter 5, to the *early period of the prophet* (so Gunkel, Duhm, Schmidt) and fits in naturally as the continuation of chapter five" (Procksch, 102; similarly, Eichrodt). It is not wrong to discover that these passages are interwoven with the woe-oracles, since they belong to roughly the same era.

There is general agreement among scholars when it comes to concluding that 5:30 does not come from Isaiah himself.

Commentary

The First Blow: Aramean and Philistine Wars (9:7–11)

[9:10, 11a] The second half of this address, vv. 10, 11a, gives the actual details about what has taken place: Israel came under extreme pressure (צָרִים) because of enemies. צר (oppressor) and איב (enemy) are synonyms, but they describe the "enemy" from two different vantage points: איב highlights mental attitude and behavior; צר describes the one who brings trouble and death. Verse 11a shows that Isaiah has specific events in mind: As history took its course, Israel had to suffer immensely at the hands of both the Arameans in the east and the Philistines in the west (cf. 2:6, another passage where peoples of the east are matched up with the Philistines). The Arameans were actually hereditary foes of Israel, often bringing them to the brink of destruction (see M. Noth, *The History of Israel* [1960²] 240–250). The worst of the battles were fought between them during the ninth century. But Israel also frequently felt the pressure from the might of the Philistines (see Noth, op. cit., 238–240). Amos 1:3–8 shows how real these events still were for the general population at the time of Isaiah. Procksch considers this to be taking place at the time "between Menahem's paying tribute (738) and Pekah's accession to the throne"; the latter broke with Assyria and looked for ways to form closer ties with the Arameans and the Philistines. Menahem would have just recently caused hard feelings with these two powers when he became a vassal of Assyria, an action which, according to this passage, would not have been allowed to pass without the Northern Kingdom suffering frequent invasions as a result. However, according to the Assyrian sources (*AOT²* 346; *ANET²* 283), Rezin of Damascus also paid tribute so that when Isaiah says that these enemies had devoured Israel "with a full mouth," we ought to have found some reference to these events in the OT. The prophet peers still farther back into the past. He still wanted to remind his hearers about the way in which Yahweh had raised his hand to chastise them, over a long period of time, as would a παιδαγωγός (pedagogue), having still hoped that Yahweh's wrath could be diverted.

Yahweh himself had allowed the enemies of his people to rise up, had in fact goaded them on. The basic meaning of the root שגב is "be high," but the verb has a secondary meaning, "inaccessible, impossible to reach" (see above, p. 118, on 2:17). That fits right in with the fact that Israel, to its chagrin, could never once and for all defeat these two neighboring countries which at one time had been part of the Davidic kingdom; at least they could never subjugate them for any extended period. Yahweh had not simply given these states the power, but he had actually "spurred them on" against Israel, his people. The *pilpel* סכסך (spur on) (from סוך, hedge, fence about; see משוכה, hedge, 5:5) is used again in 19:2; it is related to the Arabic *šawk* and the Ethiopic *šōk,* "thorns," conveying the idea of getting poked by sharp spurs.

The Hebrew often uses, as a paraphrase for a crushing defeat in battle, the description that one would "be devoured" (אכל, eat; see 1:20; in addition, see Jer. 10:25; 30:16; 51:34; Ps. 79:7). The imagery compares the enemy to a wild animal which falls voraciously upon its kill (cf. v. 19; 5:29; Hos. 13:7f.; Jer. 2:15; 4:7; 5:6; see also Hab. 1:8).

[9:7] What happens cannot be explained as bad luck or a harsh, inexplicable fate, but rather must be understood as the judgment of God. Isaiah is by no means the first one to develop the idea that Israel's enemies were the tools which Yahweh used in punishment; one might compare the traditions about both Elijah and Elisha, 1 Kings 19:16; 2 Kings 8:12, et al. In v. 7 Isaiah describes the activity of earlier prophets whom he considers to be his predecessors. The message, which goes forth from Yahweh, comes to Isaiah in this passage as a reality in and of itself, not as a word which is to be conveyed as a message to someone else; it is not something which is to be heard but is an actual event about which one becomes aware, a word which makes history happen and gives a particular shape to the future. It is significant that the Gk can translate this: θάνατον ἀπέστειλεν ὁ κύριος (the Lord sent death). The word דבר (message) is understood as having a particular content which actually brings with it the ability to bring about an action of God; it is "just like an accumulation of latent energy, which could not be held back much longer" (Grether, op. cit., 104). Just as the דבר (message) is simply not described as the דבר יהוה (message of Yahweh), in the same way, the prophet is not designated here as the one who carries the message. But—against Grether —one does not have to be under the impression that the prophet is to disappear completely into the background as these events unfold, so that nothing more is remembered than that someone "had been sent" to proclaim the word (op. cit., 105). On the other hand, the "message" from Isaiah has also not just become a hypostasis, taking effect whether it was spoken or not; even if he does not say it in so many words, Isaiah also considers this to be a prophetic message. One might consider Elisha, who receives instructions to go to Damascus to anoint Hazael as king, a man who would wreak so much havoc upon Israel. This same concept is close to the passages in Jeremiah which have often been mentioned by those trying to understand this present passage. In 23:29, the דבר (message) of Yahweh, compared to fire or to a hammer which smashes rocks, is identified as a message which Jeremiah himself shapes (cf. also 5:14); in Hos. 6:5, נביאים (prophets) and אמרי־פי (words of my mouth) are actually parallel to one another. Thus, the prophets prepared the way for the deuteronomistic theory that the דבר (message) is the means by which Yahweh controls history (cf. also Isa. 55:10f. and Deut. 32:47: הוּא לֹא־דָבָר רֵק, for the word is no trifle for you). In contrast to the widely held concept found in all parts of the ancient Near East, which views the word of the deity as a physical-cosmic power, remnants of which are still to be found throughout the OT (e.g., Ps. 147:15, 18), the word of Yahweh which is laid upon the prophets is, generally speaking, a power which sets historical events in motion (cf. Dürr, op. cit., and see also Koch, op. cit., 278). Normally, it is said that Yahweh sends his messengers, servants, or prophets to deliver his message (see Isa. 6:8; Judg. 6:8; Jer. 26:12; Ps.

103:20). Not much is changed when Isaiah uses a shorthand expression to describe the sending of the message. It "has fallen" upon Israel, just as a warring people would fall upon the enemy (Josh. 11:7).

We have already determined above, p. 227, that in this particular passage "Israel" is a designation for the Northern Kingdom. In the same way, we arrive at a meaning for "Jacob." Just as certainly as the name Jacob can be used to identify the entire tribal league, it still has a particular affinity with the term Israel as a designation for the Northern Kingdom (cf. Hos. 10:11; 12:3; Amos 6:8; 7:2, 5; Mic. 1:5). The reason for this can be found in the special attention which was given to the Jacob traditions in the Northern Kingdom, since those groups who considered Jacob to be their hero were brought into the tribal system in that part of the land. But yet, there is a marked difference between these two designations, since "Jacob" does not identify the people according to its status as a state but on the basis of its past as recorded in its salvation history, shared with Judah (cf. also the numerous parallels "Jacob-Israel" in Deutero-Isaiah 40:27; 41:8, 14, and often elsewhere). What Isaiah proclaims from Jerusalem in the direction of Israel is not spoken by him as a citizen of Jerusalem or as a Judean who addresses the citizens of a neighboring state, but as someone who belongs to the same fellowship of believers, to which the citizens of the Northern Kingdom would also confess allegiance. This presupposes that there was still an intimate group of inhabitants from both states who were bound together because they identified themselves with a common religious heritage, which made an even greater impact when Amos of Tekoa knew that he himself had been called to action in the Northern Kingdom.

[9:8a] The designation "Ephraim and the inhabitants of Samaria" is actually just another way to refer to "Israel." In 9:20, Isaiah speaks of "Ephraim" in its basic meaning, referring to the tribe as it is contrasted with "Manasseh." But in 7:2, 5, 8f.; 17:3 (see also 11:13), "Ephraim" clearly refers to the entire Northern Kingdom. In the light of this passage and similar ones, it simply is not correct to suggest that "Ephraim" serves as a designation for the rump state which was all that remained after Tiglath-Pileser's invasion in the year 732 (contra Donner, op. cit., 71, and A. Alt, *KlSchr* II, 319, note 1). Ephraim is the tribe which laid claim to a leadership position in Israel and generally functioned in that capacity. Gen. 49:26 already mentions Joseph as the designated leader among his brothers; see also Deut. 33:13–17. For this reason, his name could be used, because it held a pre-eminent position, to designate the whole of Israel (see also Hos. 4:17; 5:3, 5; 11:8, though Amos never speaks of Ephraim). Because Isaiah begins by speaking of the "people as a whole," this interpretation of the present passage proves to be correct. The capital city of the land, Samaria, does not of course actually lie within the territory of Ephraim, but is rather in Manasseh. But the reason for mentioning the inhabitants of Samaria is not because it is within Ephraim but especially because it had the special legitimate status which belonged, from its very beginning, to the capital city. Omri, who established the capital there, had originally bought the land and thus, the city was originally royal property (see A. Alt, *Der Stadtstaat Samaria,* BAL 101/5 [1954] = *KlSchr* III, 258–302).

Even though we cannot agree with translating ידע as "be brought low" (see above, textual note 8a), it must still be admitted that there are real difficulties for understanding וידעו. Some translate the verb with "perceive" (Eichrodt, Fohrer, et al.). One would certainly have to take it this way if one maintains, as Grether does, that sending forth the message was in itself a demonstration of the power of Yahweh. But if this refers to a prophetic message, then וידעו העם כלו must mean "and the entire people learned about it and was aware of it." It was not a message which stayed hidden, so that Ephraim could issue a disclaimer that it had never heard the message. No one could deny having been warned. One is reminded here of the prophetic "office of being a watchman" (Jer. 6:17; Ezek. 3:17; 33:6f.). If, at this point, Ephraim and the inhabitants of Samaria are mentioned, in addition to the people as a whole, that would make good sense. No one can get away without guilt, but the responsibility is twice as heavy at the place where leadership is to be forthcoming.

[9:8b, 9] And yet, it is pride which gets in the way of considering the consequences of what one has come to know. The same can be said about גאוה (boasting, being high) as about all of its synonyms (see above, p. 115): only God could claim it as a proper designation (Deut. 33:26; Ps. 68:35); if a human being tried to be like that, such a person would end up being destroyed (Prov. 16:18). גדל לבב (big of heart), an expression which is found elsewhere only in 10:12, seems to be an expression coined by Isaiah himself, but the formulation really reminds one of language used by wisdom, a similarity which is noted whenever Isaiah speaks about haughtiness; one is reminded of expressions such as גבה רוח (haughty spirit) and שפל רוח (lowly spirit) in Prov. 16:18; רחב לבב (arrogant heart) in Ps. 101:5 (see Prov. 21:4); and גבה־לב (arrogant [of heart]) in Prov. 16:5. Isaiah quotes, as an illustration of this type of haughty attitude, a defiant proverb, one which might be quoted by someone who was trying to minimize for oneself the severity of a hard blow; see H. W. Wolff, *Das Zitat im Prophetenspruch*, BEvT 4 (1937) = *GesStud* TBü 22, 36–129. When it comes out of the mouth of the people, who are being called to pay attention to the blows which Yahweh sends in order that they might repent, it demonstrates that they had misread the actual situation in which they found themselves; indeed, they were under the spell of a most dangerous delusion. Normally, buildings were made with mud brick, using the wood from a sycamore tree for beams (cf. Amos 7:14). Bricks which had not been fired but had just been dried in the air, sometimes strengthened with straw, provided a very inexpensive building material (see Exod. 5:7, 16, 18; and B. Meissner, *Babylonien und Assyrien* I [1920] 275; Dalman, *AuS* VII, 18; illustrations of how bricks were made in Egypt: *AOB* no. 176 = *ANEP* no. 115 = *BHH* 2239f.). In present-day Palestine, according to T. Cana'an, one might say: "The air-dried brick (when it falls) only hits the one who is suffering already" (Dalman, op. cit., 19). Sycamore trees are cultivated in great numbers in the Shephelah (1 Kings 10:27 = 2 Chron. 1:15; 1 Chron. 27:28; 2 Chron. 9:27; illuss.: Dalman, *AuS* I/2, illuss. nos. 6, 8). Its wood is inexpensive, which one can surmise when it is contrasted with cedarwood (concerning the difficulties involved with translating ארז as "cedar," see above, pp. 115f., on 2:13, and cf. H. Mayer, *BZ* 11 [1967] 53–66; illus.: *BHH* 2207). In business transactions, sycamore wood and cedar would not be mistaken one for the other (Tos. BM VIII 32). In contrast, dressed stones (גזית) are a much more durable building material; these are very expensive stones dressed to a specific size (1 Kings 7:9). Procksch, Fohrer, Kaiser, et al. suggest that the sycamore trees are mentioned because the enemy had cut them down out in the field (2 Kings 3:25; 19:23) and had now planted cedars in their place (so also the Zürcher Bibel: "we are planting cedars"). This explanation is contradicted by the fact that cedars and squared stones are also mentioned in conjunction with one another in other places as being most expensive building materials (1 Kings 6:36; 7:11; see A. Alt, *KlSchr* III, 317), but also because cedars are not "planted" in Palestine (*BHH* 2207). גדע does not only mean "cut down" (concerning felling trees, see 10:33), but it also means to "hew into pieces" (cf. Zech. 11:10, 14; Ezek. 6:6). Thus, what is meant is that precious cedarwood will be used in construction instead of the cheap sycamore wood. It is possible that what is presumed is that events during battles caused simple residences to fall down. Of course, there were also frequent earthquakes which brought whole villages down, since the building materials were not very substantial (so Eichrodt).

[9:11b] The stylized phrase used in this refrain . . . לא־שׁב אפו (his wrath did not turn away) must be considered along with the one used in 5:25a: חרה אף־יהוה . . . ויט ידו עליו . . . (Yahweh's wrath was kindled . . . and he stretched out his hand against them).

In a way similar to the message which is delivered, wrath also exists independently in a most remarkable way, going into motion whenever it is "kindled." One can say that Yahweh has turned away from the heat of his wrath: וישׁב יהוה מחרון אפו (the Lord turned from his burning anger) (Josh. 7:26; cf. also Deut. 13:18; 2 Kings 23:26; Jonah 3:9); one can also plead with God that he would turn away from it, Exod. 32:12. But one might also say that God does turn his wrath away (שׁוב = *hiph'il*, Ps. 78:38; cf. Job 9:13; Prov. 24:18; Ezra 10:14) or that individual human beings are able to turn away his wrath (Num. 25:11; Jer. 18:20; Ps. 106:23). Finally, there are still many passages where the wrath of Yahweh is the subject of a sentence (besides the present passage and its parallels in vv. 16, 20; 5:25; 10:4; see also 12:1; Num. 25:4; Jer. 2:35; Hos. 14:5; Job 14:13; Dan. 9:16; 2 Chron. 12:12; 29:10; 30:8). Even Jeremiah had to admit that the heat of Yahweh's wrath had not turned away from Israel, 4:8; 23:20; 30:24. (In light of these passages, the suffix on לא אשׁיבנו, I will not cause it to return, in the refrain in Amos 1, 2, may well also be referring to the wrath of Yahweh [Holladay, op. cit., 102, thinks this just means punishment in general]).

The wrath of Yahweh is kindled wherever a taboo has been violated. A typical example of this occurs in the story in Num. 25:1–4, a story in which this concept is deeply imbedded. Yahweh's wrath is kindled because Israel has taken part in the Baal Peor festival. It is turned away because Moses impales the guilty ones (25:4; cf. Josh. 7:26). It is only after the full consequences of the ban are carried out that the heat of the divine wrath can be subdued (Deut. 13:18), since whoever violates a taboo has committed a mortal sin (Exod. 22:23; 32:10f.; Num. 11:1, 33; 12:9). Therefore one can indeed pray that Yahweh might lessen the consequences of his wrath or one might seek a way to atone for one's sins

(Exod. 32:12, 30), but Moses did not achieve this even by offering his own life (32). Restoring wholeness, after order had been destroyed, could be achieved only by the death of the guilty party. It is with this background in mind that one can understand the refrain which Isaiah uses: The wrath of Yahweh is a power which comes to rest once again only after the evildoer has been destroyed. Even though, in this present construction, the subject of the sentence is "wrath," this is not really an objective, independent power, since Yahweh is the lord of history and the destiny of his people is completely under his control.

"And his hand is still stretched out." Already in the song of the sea in Exodus 15, there is mention of Yahweh having raised his right hand at the time of the exodus of his people (12). The phraseology, that Yahweh brought Israel out "by a mighty hand and an outstretched arm," belongs to the deuteronomistic theology as a basic element of the confession of Israel (Deut. 4:34; 5:15; 7:19; 11:2; 26:8; Jer. 32:21; Ps. 136:12; cf. Ezek. 20:33f.; 1 Kings 8:42 = 2 Chron. 6:32). In the priestly account of the Egyptian plagues, one also finds the deeply imbedded motif of the raised hand of Moses or Aaron, as well as the motif of the raised hand of Yahweh (Exod. 7:5; see also 6:6). Isaiah himself speaks about the hand of Yahweh in 14:26f., which he stretched out over the people because he purposed to do it, and in that same context a strong point is also made about the immutability of his plans within history. It would thus seem that the imagery of Yahweh's outstretched hand was used originally when someone wanted to talk about the protection which Yahweh gave to Israel in the time of salvation (see also Zeph. 2:13). However, in this refrain, it is put to use as part of an announcement of punishment (see also Jer. 21:5; Ezek. 6:14; Zeph. 1:4, and often elsewhere).

The Second Blow: The Jehu Revolution
(9:12, 15, 16aα, 13, [14], 16aβb)

[9:12] The first point made here is that the initial blow did not accomplish its purpose. The wrath of Yahweh had not been turned back, since the people had not turned around to go back to its God; see Wolff, op. cit., 133 (TBü 22, 134); Holladay, op. cit., 116–157. As was mentioned above, this judgment is not something which automatically goes into action when it is set off by Israel's offenses. The wrath of God which hovered over Israel could have been turned away if repentance had occurred.

The second half-verse explains what is meant by repentance, using the phrase: דרש את־יהוה צבאות (seek out Yahweh of Hosts). Isaiah uses this phrase once again in 31:1b, in fact, in a paraphrase which discusses the way in which faith ought to be expected to function as Israel related to God (cf. the parallel, "look to the Holy One of Israel"). Passages all the way from Gen. 25:22; 1 Kings 22:5ff.; 2 Kings 3:11; Jer. 37:7; Ezek. 14:7 up to 2 Chron. 1:5 show that דרש את־יהוה (seek out Yahweh) referred originally to obtaining a decisive response from God in a time of need, when one was sick or when war threatened. Such a response could be obtained only through a go-between, a prophet or a cultic official (see C. Westermann, "Die Begriffe für Fragen und Suchen im Alten Testament," *KuD* 6 [1960] 2–30, see p. 20). But, as is the case in Amos (5:4, 6), Hosea (10:12), and Zephaniah (1:6), this formula also has a more general sense in Isaiah, so that it should not be translated "consult" but "ask about, seek out." Consulting Yahweh (and not, for example, the spirits of the dead, 8:19) had become, like swearing by Yahweh (Jer. 12:16), a shibboleth which tested the authenticity of those who were true believers in Yahweh.

[9:15] Happy is a people which, in the critical moments of its history, has leaders who call for a time of careful deliberation. In Israel, the responsible groups had failed to live up to expectations (concerning אשׁר, do right, see above, commentary on 1:17, and commentary on 3:12b). מאשׁרים (leaders) is intended as a reference to the spiritual leaders who were supposed to have been able to lead the people in such an hour of need to reorient itself. Instead of that, they were misleaders, מתעים (see, once again, above, on 3:12b). One cannot be more specific about what Isaiah has in mind about the exact type of leaders and what their actual misleadings entailed. One must bear in mind that Isaiah charges, in other passages, that the priests and prophets "stagger" (תעה) when having a vision just as they would after having too much to drink (28:7), and that Micah makes an accusation that the prophets lead the people astray (תעה hiph'il), since they "cry 'Peace' when they have something to eat" (3:5). But the concept connected with "misleading" is also rooted deeply within wisdom and Isaiah may be thinking of those "wise ones" who are only "wise in their own eyes" (5:21), but who do not hold high the eternally valid norms of justice and truth. No wonder, then, that those who lead are "confused"! Whoever observes the deeds of Yahweh must take time to reflect upon them. However, the spiritual leaders of the people choked off any desire to move in that direction.

[9:16aα] This in no way makes it possible for those who were "misled" to be excused from any responsibility. Yahweh knows no mercy. This is articulated here with an unheard-of severity. The בחורים (chosen) are the proud ones, the elite from among the people (1 Sam. 9:2; Jer. 48:15; Isa. 40:30, and often elsewhere). They are the ones who make up Israel's fighting force and, therefore, are particularly exposed to dangers (Jer. 11:22; 49:26, and often elsewhere). But not even the widows and orphans are to be spared, those weak ones who are under the special protecting care of Yahweh and for whom Isaiah otherwise speaks with such intense passion (see the discussion at 1:17 and 10:2). One cannot smooth over this "contradiction" with a psychological explanation, as Duhm does: "One senses the difference between the fire of the youthful man and the circumspection of the mature man." It is rather part of the bitter experience of life to see that the defenseless and unimportant ones are also unable to avoid being counted as guilty and that they are also pulled down, along with those who oppress them, into the abyss of destruction. Isaiah had certainly spoken out vehemently elsewhere in favor of the weak receiving favorable justice, but the concern of this present passage is to portray, in the sight of the people, in its true severity, the consequences of its stubbornness when viewed in the light of Yahweh's call to repentance (see the similar threats in Jer. 6:11; 15:8; 18:21).

[9:13] Isaiah paraphrases the totality of the judgment in v. 13 by using a proverbial expression concerning extermination: "head and tail, branch of the rod and bulrush stem"; cf. 19:15. Donner tries to relate the metaphor to the "territorial relationships which resulted after Assyria asserted itself so mightily when it invaded" (op. cit., 72). In Egypt, *tp,* meaning "head," is used frequently to describe the geographical "beginning of a land," and *ph.wj* could describe the "rear part," the "farthest border of a region." Additionally, Donner attempts to use כפה (branch of the rod) and אגמון (bulrush stem) in an Egyptian sense, taking the terms as descriptive of parts of the insignia of kingly dominion. So interpreted, the image would suggest that there was a "shrinking of the kingdom: The tokens of sovereignty have been knocked out of his hand, the kingdom has become nothing more than a vassal kingdom" (op. cit., 73). But this ingenious suggestion attributes to Isaiah and his hearers too much knowledge about Egyptian symbolism. In addition, even though the basic meaning of כרת is actually "hew down, cut off," the *hiph'il* הכרית is never used in the sense of "cut off" and the *qal* is also never used to describe partitioning a country. One will thus do well to take "head and tail" simply as a proverbial expression for "high and low" (Duhm; see Deut. 28:13, 44). The second image, כפה (branch of the rod) and אגמון (bulrush stem), does not really fit well with "head and tail" if one translates it, as is normally done, as "palm branch and rush" (as is still done by Eichrodt and Kaiser). Gk paraphrases this expression, according to its basic meaning, by translating μέγαν καὶ μικρόν (large and small). But the translation used above helps the sharpness of the image to come out clearly: Just as one might cut off the stem of the plant as soon as it sprouts, in the same way the destructive activity would come to its end; then there would no longer be any hope (Job 15:32).

[9:14] As is also often true elsewhere, it is easy to find mistaken interpretations for such sketchy portrayals. Someone who was reading this added his own explanation in v. 14. Concerning זקן (elder), see above, commentary on 3:2, 3; concerning נשוא־פנים (dignitary), see above, commentary on 3:2, 3; concerning נביא (prophet), see above, commentary on 3:2, 3. The glossator has made use of the vocabulary found in chap. 3. In that passage, Isaiah himself had simply included the נביא (prophet) when he listed the authorities who had failed to come up to what was expected; cf. 28:7. The commentator zeroes in more specifically on one aspect: the נביא (prophet), insofar as he is a מורה־שקר (one who teaches lies) (here one must follow those Gk-MSS which read καὶ διδάσκοντα, and the teacher). In Hab. 2:18, where this phrase is used once more, מורה שקר is used in the sense of the heathen oracles which furnish lies (parallel to מסכה, idol, and פסל, metal image). The "oracle at the terebinth" (אלון מורה) in Shechem was widely known as a cultic center (Gen. 12:6; Deut. 11:30; in Judg. 9:37, it is called אלון מעוננים, Diviner's Oak; see Gen. 35:4; Josh. 24:26; cf. also the "oracle hill," גבעת המורה, in Judg. 7:1). If we stay with the MT, this would refer to prophets who furnish oracles which are nothing but lies. Fohrer thinks this means "the priests who furnish oracles," Procksch that it refers to the priestly teachers who impart torah (see 2 Kings 17:28; 2 Chron. 15:3). Isaiah himself uses the verb ירה *hiph'il* (teach) with a wisdom nuance (2:3; 28:9, 26; cf. 30:20 [inauthentic]). Those who provide false oracles would have contributed in no small way to the misleading of the people.

Which specific events does Isaiah have in mind concerning the Northern Kingdom when he mentions this attack? Procksch thinks that Isaiah is referring to the time when Pekah murdered Pekahiah (2 Kings 15:25). But that was a purely political matter, whereas our text seems to suggest that we should be looking for spiritual authorities. If it is true, as we suggested above, that references to the Aramean and Philistine battles in the ninth century furnish the background for the comments immediately preceding this section (v. 10), then it is possible that Isaiah is also looking relatively far into the past once again. Eichrodt, Fohrer, Kaiser, et al. are correct when they interpret this passage with reference to the revolution of Jehu (2 Kings 9f.). Hos. 1:4 shows how much the events of that era were still clearly in mind at the time of Isaiah.

[9:16aβ] The sentence in v. 16aβ, which provides corroborating evidence, connects very well with what precedes it. The judgment is all-inclusive because "all of them" have gone astray, all are "alienated from God," which is how KBL renders חָנֵף; cf. Jer. 23:11. According to Prov. 11:9, the חָנֵף (godless man) destroys his neighbor with his mouth. The second half-verse, וכל־פה דבר נבלה (and every mouth speaks what is foolish), expresses the very same idea; cf. Ezek. 13:3. נבלה (foolish) can be used as an antonym for חכמה (wise), as is done in Deut. 32:6; yet, this very passage shows that the foolishness of the fool is that he is not in the right relationship with God. A נבלה (foolishness) happens whenever one of the basic aspects of order, which has been established by Yahweh, is broken within Israel (Gen. 34:7; Deut. 22:21, and often elsewhere).

[9:16b] The refrain points out once again that Yahweh's wrath continues to hang over Israel like a sword of Damocles. The revolution set in motion by Jehu had not eliminated the abuses, and the dynasty of the son of Nimshi "showed itself to be almost more incompetent and worse than the one it replaced" (Fohrer).

The Third Blow: The Lacerations Inflicted by the Tribes upon Their Own Brothers (9:17–20)

[9:17] As someone who uses good style, Isaiah does not repeat the statements from v. 12 one more time. In v. 17, we come once again to the concept which has been seen many times, that evil gives birth to its own punishment; see 1:31 or Prov. 13:6: The evil (רִשְׁעָה) causes the sinner's ruin. It is thought of as a consuming fire which burns up "thorns and thistles" (concerning שָׁמִיר וָשַׁיִת, thorns and thistles, see above, commentary on 5:6) and engulfs the "thickets of the forest" (see 10:34; Gen. 22:13; concerning the Palestinian shrub woodlands, with their thick undergrowth, see Dalman, AuS I/1, 73–89, 254–261, and BHH 2133f.). Isaiah is fond of using the imagery of a consuming fire (1:31; 5:24; 10:17; 30:33). When one speaks of wrath, one is also close to imagery of "burning" or "glowing" (see 30:27; Jer. 4:8, and often elsewhere). We translated somewhat freely above when rendering גאות עשן as a "pillar of smoke." Isaiah also uses גאות (majesty, lifting up) in 28:1, 3, but with the transferred meaning "arrogance," the same meaning the vocable has elsewhere, 12:5; 26:10. He certainly chose this word because he was aware that it can have two meanings, also describing "haughty arrogance," Ps.

17:10; yet, he describes the judgment which is due for such arrogance (see גאוה, boast in arrogance, used with גדל לבב, haughty disposition, in v. 8), just as, on the other hand, "undergrowth of the forest" can be used to describe the nature of the people, characterizing "those led astray and confused." The "undergrowth," which goes up in smoke as if it wanted to demonstrate its kingly majesty (Ps. 89:10; 93:1), disappears into nothingness.

[9:18] In all this, Yahweh is at work. According to its basic sense, עברה (fury) can hardly be differentiated from אף (wrath). But it is worth noting that Isaiah, in this passage also, does not formulate it as follows: Yahweh scorches the land by means of his wrath, but rather: the land is scorched —as if by means of an independently existing power—on account of his wrath. Yahweh does not even need to interfere; Israel lacerates itself all by itself. God needs only to leave the people to their own devices (see above, commentary on 2:6).

[9:19] The imagery used in v. 19b has a counterpart in Mic. 3:3, where there is even more detail: The flesh is torn off the poor people and their bones are broken. This comes originally from a coarse proverb, used by the common people. And yet, it is used by Micah to portray the force which is used to overpower the ordinary people; here it is used to describe the power struggle between leading groups; v. 18bβ leaves one with the impression that such descriptions could apply to all of the petty disagreements which crop up in daily life as human beings fight for status and influence. Times which witness power struggles in the larger arena only serve to accentuate the ruthless harshness (see לא יחמלו, no one takes care of anyone else) which characterizes the relationships between individuals. Verse 19b alludes to the quarrels and bloody battles which took place again and again within Israel, between various leaders, continually giving witness to some regional interests or political parties which took advantage of opportune moments. KBL places גזר in our passage into the category גזר II, separating it from the commonly used גזר I, "cut," and assigns it the meaning "eat up" on the basis of the Arabic *ǧaraza* (note the metathesis!), as had already been suggested by Hitzig. The exact meaning of the imagery is not easy to establish. The verb seems to suggest that the attempt to enlarge one's own territory or the territory of one's tribe was carried out at the expense of the others, accompanied, of course, by an increase in power.

[9:20a] In v. 20a, Isaiah gets specific: Manasseh and Ephraim, which together made up the "house of Joseph," engaged in a continual rivalry during the entire history of the Northern Kingdom. Donner thinks this refers to tribal conflicts about the time of 732/31, "as the confusion which surrounded the usurper Hoshea's seizure of the throne threatened the structure which held together the rump state" (op. cit., 73). But neither 2 Kings 15:30 nor the Assyrian annals (*AOT* 348; *ANET*² 284) tells us anything about any tribal conflicts which were taking place at that time. It is more likely that Procksch has hit upon the right idea, that this refers to conflict between the followers of Pekah and Pekahiah, with "Manasseh" being the land east of the Jordan (cf. Num. 32:39ff.), from whence Pekah came (2 Kings 15:25), whereas "Ephraim" would represent the western territory of the tribe of Joseph. In this case, v. 20a would allude to the beginning of the Syro-Ephraimitic War (cf. 2 Kings 15:37, and Isa. 7:1ff.). Chronologically, however, this causes serious difficulties, beginning with the fact that this is already part of a backward glance at the events. One would probably be more on the mark to take v. 20a with reference to the battle between Amaziah of Judah and Jehoahaz of Israel, at which time the Judeans were defeated (2 Kings 14:8ff.), an event which resulted in severe trauma for Jerusalem. Even though a political stance of good neighborly relations had been pursued between Judah and Israel during the time of the Omri dynasty, after Jehu massacred the members of the Davidic family (2 Kings 9:27; 10:12–14), the relations between them were most strained. When looking at the future for both of these small countries—a future which by their own admission should have suggested that they work together—it was clear that this enmity was sufficient to practically cause them to self-destruct, as the Syro-Ephraimitic War, with its eventual consequences, pointed out so clearly. Concerning the individual tensions which existed between Ephraim and Manasseh (Kaiser refers to Gen. 48:14ff.; Judg. 6:35; 8:1), we do not have enough specific information to identify actual events which might have been at issue.

[9:20b] Once again, it is said that the wrath of Yahweh continues to threaten Israel.

(Concerning 10:1–4, see above, pp. 213f.)

The Fourth Blow: The Mountains Quake (5:25)

[5:25] Since this verse is preserved only in fragmentary form (see above, on the form of 5:25), there is simply no way to identify how it is connected to other passages. Apparently, Isaiah connects the kindling of the wrath of God with a theophany. The mountains quake (cf. Ps. 18:8; Hab. 3:6; 1 Sam. 14:15). It would seem natural to consider this as a reference to an actual earthquake, but it is certainly very possible that the "quaking of the hills" is to be understood figuratively and one should rather presume that this is about distress caused by warfare. When the wrath of God interferes, the result can be nothing but gruesome destruction. There is not enough time, in the midst of so much death, to bury all the dead; cf. Amos 8:3. To leave a corpse unburied was a wish uttered in maledictions, following a pattern widely used not only in Israel but in the entire ancient Near East, whenever one spoke of one's hopes for the demise of evildoers; on this, see D. R. Hillers, *Treaty Curses and the Old Testament Prophets* (1964) 68f. (no. 15). In the Kudurru-inscriptions, the wish is expressed that the gods would step in to hinder any attempt to bury the corpses of scoundrels (e.g., L. W. King, *Babylonian Boundary-Stones* [1912] 127 [VI 54f.]: "May his corpse drop and have no one to bury it"). According to the succession-treaty of Esarhaddon, lines 425–427, Ninurta is supposed to fill the plain with corpses and give their flesh over for the eagles and jackals to consume (D. J. Wiseman, "The Vassal-Treaties of Esarhaddon," *Iraq* 20 [1958] 61f.; cf. Deut. 28:26 and see the additional examples furnished by Hillers, op. cit., and F. C. Fensham, *ZAW* 75 [1963] 161ff.).

It is obvious that in 5:25 a catastrophe is being discussed which is more intense than the previous judgment actions. If Yahweh's wrath cannot "turn away" this time, a final settlement of the account is due to be paid. It is clear that the final end of Israel must now come into full view.

The Fifth Blow: The People from Afar (5:26–29[30])

The verbs which are used in vv. 26–29 point clearly to the future; note, in addition to the imperfect and perfect consecutives, how the "presentative" הִנֵּה (behold) is used (v. 26b), which "describes the sudden intervention by God, by which the untenable present state of things described in the diatribe will be radically altered" (K. Koch, *The Growth of the Biblical Tradition* [1969] 211). The perfects in v. 27b carry the sense of the present-perfect (Beer-Meyer, Gr §101.2b).

[5:26] The subject of נשא (raise up) is not an unidentified "someone" but Yahweh, as is shown by the word שרק (whistle), which follows soon after; this also becomes clear when one compares 5:26 with 7:18. But it is to be noted that Yahweh is not specifically identified. Also, הנה (behold), as is usually the case in threats, is not linked with the first person "I," Yahweh (cf. Jer. 5:15: הנני מביא עליכם גוי ממרחק, Behold, I am bringing upon you a nation from afar, and see also Koch, op. cit.). Yahweh is in fact the lord of history, but he remains hidden in the midst of its events.

נס is a standard which is erected so as to identify the particular place where troops are to gather together (cf. 11:10, 12; 18:3). One would place a standard on a clearly visible high place, 13:2; 20:17; more than anyone else, the leaders were to stay right there with it, 31:9. According to G. Schumacher (*ZDPV* 9 [1886] 232), at the time when those leaders were still in office, there was still a practice in Hauran and the Golan region that a flag would be erected on the summit of a mountain located in the grazing lands of a particular clan which would serve to call that clan to take up arms. Standards were carried out in front of the Assyrian army; they displayed a variety of emblems on the end of long poles (birds with outspread wings or a circular disk with representations of gods, e.g., with the national god Ashur shooting with a bow; see *BRL* 160–163; *BHH* 194–196). The name of the people is not mentioned, though only the Assyrians could be meant. That is part of the prophetic style: No specific reference is made in advance of the actual experience. In fact, this corresponds to what actually happens in history, that the foe comes from afar (cf. 39:3), but it is, at the same time, a recurring motif which is commonly found in such announcements concerning enemies (10:3; cf. 30:27; in Jer. 4:16; 5:15, it refers most likely to the Scythians; in 6:22, מארץ צפון, from the north country, is parallel to מירכתי־ארץ, from the farthest part of the earth; cf. Ezek. 38:6, 15). When Isaiah speaks in this passage about the "end of the earth" (cf. Ps. 72:8; Zech. 9:10; Sir. 44:21), one does not need to check the veracity of the text; גוי מרחוק (a nation from afar) and הארץ מקצה (from the end of the earth) are also found next to each other in Deut. 28:49. The greater the distance from which the enemy comes, the less one would know anything about him and therefore, his appearance is all the more sinister. Based on the very realistic manner which is used in the description which follows, one would have to suppose: an enemy which can cover so much ground could not be driven back very easily. שרק seems originally to refer to the "whistle" of the bee-keeper which is used to entice a swarm of bees (see below, 7:18, and cf. Zech. 10:8).

The enemy comes from an immense distance, but also comes with surprising speed. The speed of the Assyrian army was one major reason for its success. Tiglath-Pileser I boasted that he had been able to march from Suhi-land to Carchemish in a single day and Ashurbanipal conquered Elam in a month (B. Meissner, *Babylonien und Assyrien* I [1920] 109). The warrior's speed was also highly valued in Israel; Amos 2:1, 4f.; Jer. 46:6.

[5:27] The physical condition of the army is excellent (on עיף, exhausted, cf. 29:8; Judg. 8:4f.; 2 Sam. 16:14; 17:29). If someone is tired, then one stumbles easily; cf. Isa. 40:30; soldiers who stumble and fall are lost in the battle (cf. Jer. 46:6, 12, 16; Nah. 2:6; Lev. 26:37). The discipline is faultless: no loincloth is loose, no shoe strap is torn. The אזור (loincloth) could be made of leather (2 Kings 1:8) or from the pelt of some other animal (cf. Mark 1:6; Matt. 3:4), but would more likely have been manufactured from linen (Jer. 13:1f.; illuss.: *BHH* 924; 963, 1). One would have worn it on one's hips (11:5, and often elsewhere). The loin-cloth is often held on by means of a belt or even just by means of a knot, which would have been made by tying together the ends of the material (see H. W. Hönig, "Die Bekleidung des Hebräers," diss., Zurich [1957] 22f.). נעל refers to sandals which are tied on with laces; see Gen. 14:23. The nimble Assyrian archers went barefoot when marching; in battle they were protected by means of boots which went up as far as their ankles and stockings or else by means of simple sandals with a protective piece for the top of the foot (Meissner, op. cit., 96; illuss.: ibid., 258, nos. 70a, b; *BRL* 359, 3 and 4; Dalman, *AuS* V, nos. 77f.; *BHH* 809f., 1738, no. 1).

[5:28] Just as the personal equipment is in perfect order, the weapons are also ready for battle.

The largest contingent of the Assyrian army consisted of archers, who were particularly adept at using the tactic of the surprise attack.

"That the bow and arrow were the weapons which were prized because of their use in the first attack and that the archers were the most important of the troops in Assyria can be surmised from the very fact that the deity Ashur was frequently portrayed shooting a bow. The bas-reliefs from Ashurbanipal's campaign against Elam brings out in a very real way that the archery troops were fleet of foot and marched at a brisk pace" (H. Schmökel, *Kulturgeschichte des Alten Orient* [1961] 114; illuss.: Meissner, op. cit., tablet illustration 57 = M. A. Beek, *Bildatlas der assyrisch-babylonischen Kultur* [1961] no. 212). The tips of the arrows, made of horn, bone, fired clay, bronze, or iron, are sharpened (see Pss. 45:6; 120:4; Prov. 25:18; cf. Jer. 51:11; illuss.: *BRL* 418; *BHH* 1437f.); the bows are bent and are therefore ready to shoot at any moment. Based on the evidence in the artistic representations, the composite bow was used in Mesopotamia, indeed in its angular form (H. Bonnet, *Die Waffen der Völker des Alten Orients* [1926] 135–145; see illuss. no. 64 and *BRL* 115 = *BHH* 264; ANEP no. 185, and often elsewhere). When one is at rest in camp, only one end of the bowstring remains tied on; before use, the bow has to be "stepped on" (דרך), which means that one would make use of one's foot to bend the bow further so that one could attach the other end of the string to the bow with a loop (illuss.: Bonnet, op. cit., no. 58; F. Rienecker, *Lexikon zur Bibel* [1960] 239). In addition to the troops on foot, the chariots are also mentioned (see above, commentary on 2:7).

The hoofs of the horses were not fitted with shoes, so that stony ground was not particularly pleasant for them; see Amos 6:12. But it seems that the Assyrians had horses which had hoofs as hard as flint. The wheels of the chariots roll along as fast as the wind (cf. also 17:13; 29:6). They had either six or eight spokes and, in the late Assyrian era, the wheels were as big in diameter as a man is tall.

The approach of a stormwind causes one to sense that disaster is close at hand; when one sees the stormwind coming, then one cries out already: "Woe to us, for we are ruined" (Jer. 4:13).

[5:29] Using a different approach, v. 29 describes the enemy by using the imagery of the lion. It is natural to compare a wild warrior to a lion. B. Mazar (*VT* 13 [1963] 132) suspects that לבאים (lions) might refer to a military division, which had as its emblem a lion goddess. Possibly these troops are the same identical ones famed for their unique method of shooting arrows, known from inscriptions on arrows which were found at *el-hadr* in the vicinity of Bethlehem. These have the following wording: חץ עבד לבית ("the arrow of the servant of the lion goddess"; cf. also the Ugaritic personal name *'bd-lb'it*, 130, III 38).

Just as his predecessors, Esarhaddon also compared himself to a raging lion (*AOT²* 356 = R. Borger, *Die Inschriften Asarhaddons,* BAfO 9 [1956] 43; see also 96f.). שאג (roar) and שאגה (howl) are the favorite words used when referring to lions, Judg. 14:5; Job 4:10, and often elsewhere. The cry shouted out in battle when one begins the attack plays an important role also in Israel; cf. Josh. 6:16, 20; Jer. 50:15. It also creates quite a stir: The enemy is panic-stricken with fear as soon as it hears the sound (Jer. 4:19).

Everyone shudders when hearing the roar of a lion (Amos 3:8). One knows: It will pounce upon its prey right away and haul it off so that it can swallow it down in a safe place. It is most effective that this poem ends with ואין מציל (and none can get anything back from it). Who would dare venture to retrieve the prey from the lion once it is taken?

Usually, Isaiah uses the words לביא and כפיר to designate the lion. According to L. Köhler (KBL and *ZDPV* 62 [1939] 124) לביא (*panthera leo persica*) is an "Asiatic" word (cf. Akkadian *lābu;* Ugaritic *lb'u/lb'it;* Old South Arabic *lb';* Egyptian *rw;* λέων; *leo*), whereas אַרְיֵה (sometimes אֲרִי) basically refers to African lions. כפיר, on the other hand, designates young lions (see Judg. 14:5), which are, of course, old enough to seek their own prey. (In addition, the OT uses as a fourth word for lion: לַיִשׁ; see 30:6.) The differentiation which has been reported here for the various terms has been disputed by McCullough/Bodenheimer (art. "Lion": *IDB* III, 136f.), who maintain that the normal word for a lion is ארי and all the other designations are simply poetic terms. If nothing else, the variety of designations points out what a significant role the lion played in Israel's imagination in ancient times. There were certainly still lions in Palestine in the time of Isaiah, coming from the southern regions (30:6); they were known to jump out of a thicket (Jer. 4:7) or from the thick growth along the Jordan (Jer. 49:19; 50:44; Zech. 11:3). The last lions were slain in Palestine about 1300 at Megiddo and

Beth-shan and they were not exterminated in Iraq until the beginning of this century (*IDB,* op. cit.).

[5:26–29] The poem ends without any comment. Except for v. 26a, where Yahweh appears to be the subject, no theological interpretation is offered. In short but very precise expressions, the imagery of a raging enemy is presented in a simple way; against this enemy any type of resistance would be unthinkable. One can hardly say that Isaiah idealizes Assyria (so Duhm); rather, he chiefly uses Assyria to confront his hearers with a very harsh reality. The enemy comes "from the end of the earth"; that heightens his mysterious nature, but is not to be interpreted in a mythological way (see, on the contrary, the "end of the heavens" in 13:5). Those who were listening would not have been ignorant of the fact that Yahweh himself came forth in storm and tempest (Nah. 1:3; cf. also Amos 1:14), yes, even that Yahweh could roar like a lion when he appeared in judgment, Amos 1:2. But this does not refer to a theophany of Yahweh himself; throughout the portrayal, this is an earthly, human power, through which Yahweh was carrying out his judgment, and the events which were predicted could all be carried out within the realm of historical realities which could take place in the world of that day. The historical picture which Isaiah presents is completely free of mythological elements.

[5:30] Verse 30 is a different story. It is characteristic of the book of Isaiah, with its prophetic message, that short additions offer new interpretations of the text, within the framework of a far-reaching world judgment. The glossator betrays himself by the use of ביום ההוא (on that day), which is obviously not to be removed, as Procksch suggests, just because it is "not put together very well and is unnecessary" (see above, commentary on 2:17). The "roaring of the lion," coming from the Assyrians, is not enough for the glossator. He wants to take the verb נהם (snarl, thunder) in v. 29 to describe the roars which are yelled out by supernatural powers (cf. עליו, above it) which roar like the sea (cf. passages such as 13:4). Isaiah himself also speaks about the roaring of the mighty sea when he wants to describe the advance of the masses of peoples, but of course he does not use the verb נהם (thunder, snarl) at that point, but rather the related term המה (thunder) (17:12). It seems that the idea of the battle of the creator God against the sea or against mighty waters representing the aboriginal chaos has been completely removed (see Ps. 46:4, 7; it would seem that the root המה [הום, המם], thunder, might be connected with תהום, deep, abyss). But this ancient mythological concept is useful to Isaiah only for demonstrating the force used by the historical enemies. In the addition in v. 30, an attempt is actually made to say that the chaotic conditions are coming back once again. Darkness, חשך, is also part of this; see Gen. 1:2. The word is often used without an article, even where one would be expected (Ges-K §126n), which would show that it originated as a term used in a mythological way. The vocabulary in v. 30b is not, in and of itself, completely foreign to Isaiah; see 8:22. But the glossator remythologized the concepts; he thinks that the creative activity will now go in a reverse direction: The light will be swallowed up by darkness. Unfortunately, no clear meaning can be determined for the ending, בעריפיה (by its clouds), possibly because the word is damaged beyond recognition. In any case, we do not find out what will set this world catastrophe in motion.

Purpose and Thrust

The section which includes 9:7–20 and 5:25–29 is not made up of originally independent units, even though it is quite long; instead, from the very beginning, it flows like water toward the mouth of a river, toward the threat in 5:25–29. The threat is tied closely to a very extensive historical overview. If we have understood the historical allusions correctly, Isaiah looks back over several centuries, back to the beginning of the era when Israel became a state. The entire epoch is characterized as a time when Yahweh intervened within the history of Israel, with one new blow after another. What is in mind here relates to the harsh struggle for existence and space for living, the continual struggle which Israel endured with its neighbors. There is no doubt that Isaiah saw that Israel's enemies were functioning, at the same time, as Yahweh's tools. But this viewpoint in no way constitutes a mythologizing of history. The enemies of Israel were not aware of a deeper purpose being served by their actions. Not only the difficulties in the past, but also the perils which would bring on the final blow in the future were events which played themselves out in the daily occurrences within the historical realm. But that does not mean that Israel's history took place in a closed system, with no access to the meaning of the events for the people. The message was delivered against Jacob as it was proclaimed and interpreted; it fell upon Israel in such a way that everyone would have some knowledge of it, 9:7. Israel did not face a puzzling destiny without any key to interpret what was happening.

According to this section, the purpose for these attacks, which came as part of Israel's destiny, and which were not only allowed but provoked by Yahweh (9:10), was not simply to bring about judgment, but rather, this was Yahweh's way hopefully to lead Israel to repentance (v. 12). The prophetic message provided the means whereby the people would recognize that Yahweh was present in history. But it had the capability of helping them escape from their destiny. Yahweh does not put pressure on Israel by means of some physical power. In a strange, yet continually growing defiance, Israel had continued to opt for going against Yahweh of Hosts. Even if the actual terminology is not used, Israel's history in the presence of its God is a history of its stubbornness, which is hammered home every time the refrain is used, showing that Israel's relationship with Yahweh did not change even a little, in spite of new judgments being piled upon old judgments. This section reminds one of the plagues of Egypt, which caused Pharaoh to become even more hardened in his heart, opposing Yahweh's will.

The reason for the "stubbornness" is Israel's original sin, pride (vv. 8f.). It was a hindrance which kept the people from seeing the seriousness of its situation. No one could be delivered from his or her offenses, all of them spoke foolishly, all of them were alienated from God by their high-minded attitude. But it is still clear that the prophet found fault chiefly with the spiritual leaders, the prophets and the wise, and certainly also with the political leadership. They had all led the people astray, even though those who had gone astray were also to be held

243

accountable for their disorientation. The specific reasons for Yahweh's wrath having to break forth are not spelled out in detail. The redactor actually gave his own answer in his own way, and the unique way this section was placed in conjunction with the woe-oracles reveals that the redactor was certainly aware of what was happening. This section speaks quite generally about "evil" (v. 17): It is the breakdown of the solidarity and community among fellow citizens: "Everyone consumes his neighbor's flesh." Isaiah begins by considering the relationships within the political realm, those unmentioned, unseen, confused actions which had hindered Israel from actually making the necessary strides to put together and develop its society.

As is true for the OT prophetic movement in general, one must also note the seriousness with which Isaiah mentions the wrath of Yahweh. "Here there is no room for a carefree trust in a merciful God; a real harshness is used to bring the terrible consequences into focus, showing the results of historical offenses, making efforts to calm oneself down . . . just a worthless exercise" (Eichrodt, 118). There is no mention of Israel being just a little state, without sufficient resources to protect itself, sacrificed to its neighbors' drives to expand; nor is there mention of the politics of world domination which motivated the major powers. The need to settle accounts with Assyria, which follows in 10:5f., right after the refrain concerning wrath upon Israel, shows that Isaiah had asked the question about how God would dispose of the enemy. One must, of necessity, be very careful when asserting that Assyria is treated in a completely different manner in 10:5f. than in 5:26ff., as if the true nature of Assyria were something which Isaiah would have come to recognize only after bitter experiences. One should also be careful not to draw the conclusion from 9:20 that Isaiah considered Judah to be an innocent party, sacrificed by the actions of its more powerful brother. In 9:7ff. he speaks neither to Israel's neighbors nor to Assyria, but to Israel itself. No possible escape route was left for Israel; no way was left open which could allow it to evade the message of impending judgment.

The wrath of Yahweh which was about to break out upon Israel would be different from all of the damage which Isaiah had pointed out as having already taken place in the past. An hour of unexpected darkness was anticipated, the likes of which they had never before experienced. It is only in this sense that one can justifiably use the term *eschatological* to describe the final blow yet to come.

Is this time also to be a judgment which is intended to bring about a purification? Or is this יום פקדה (cf. 10:3) the day of destruction? Will Yahweh's wrath "turn back" only after there is no more Israel, when the complete final end has come for the history of God with Israel? This section does not make any comment to answer that; one ought not make too much of the phrase ואין מציל (and none can get anything back from it), which closes this whole section in an utterly serious way. In the final analysis, the prophet is silent about what the assault by Assyria would mean for Israel's existence. He does that on purpose, since he is no predictor who knows about everything which is yet to come. Rather, his task is to show, as clearly as possible, the great threat in this καιρός (kairological moment in time). What would actually happen when the Assyrians came would remain part of the עצה (plan) of God. But that was not a horrible predetermined fate; rather, it would become clear according to the way Israel answered the wrathful judgment of Yahweh.

The glossator in 5:30 indeed seems to have wanted to make it clear that Israel would end up having to go down into the chaos of the divine darkness, since the eschatological end had come and the cosmos would sink once again into chaos.

Isaiah 6:1–13

Theophany and Commissioning

Literature

K. Marti, *Der jesajanische Kern in Jes 6:1–9:6,* BZAW 34 (1920) 113–121. M. M. Kaplan, "Isaiah 6:1–11," *JBL* 45 (1926) 251–259. A. Vaccari, "Visio Isaiae (6)," *VD* 10 (1930) 100–106. K. Fruhstorfer, "Isaias' Berufungsvision," *TPQ* 91 (1938) 414–424. V. Herntrich, "Die Berufung des Jesajas," *MPT* 35 (1939) 158–178. I. Engnell, *The Call of Isaiah,* UUÅ 1949, 4 (1949). V. Laridon, "Isaiae ad munus propheticum vocatio," *Collationes Brugenses* 45 (1949) 3–8, 29–33. P. Béguerie, "La vocation d'Isaïe," *LD* 14 (1954) 11–51. L. J. Liebreich, "The Position of Chapter Six in the Book of Isaiah," *HUCA* 25 (1954) 37–40. J. P. Love, "The Call of Isaiah," *Int* 11 (1957) 282–296. E. Jenni, "Jesajas Berufung in der neueren Forschung," *TZ* 15 (1959) 321–339. C. F. Whitley, "The Call and Mission of Isaiah," *JNES* 18 (1959) 38–48. H. Wildberger, "Jesaja 6:1–8," in G. Eichholz, *Herr, tue meine Lippen auf,* V (1961²) 346–355. F. Montagnini, "La vocazione di Isaia," *BeO* 6 (1964) 163–172.

Concerning the text: P. Ruben, "A Proposed New Method of Textual Criticism in the Old Testament," (Isa. 6:11–13) *AJSL* 51 (1934) 30–45. W. H. Brownlee, "The Text of Isaiah VI 13 in the Light of DSIa," *VT* 1 (1951) 296–298. F. Hvidberg, "The Masseba and the Holy Seed," *NorTT* 56 (1955) 97–99. S. Iwry, "*Maṣṣēbāh* and *Bāmāh* in 1Q Isaiah^A 6:13," *JBL* 76 (1957) 225–232. N. Walker, "The Origin of the 'Trice-Holy'," *NTS* 5 (1958/59) 132–133. B. M. Leiser, "The Trisagion of Isaiah's Vision," *NTS* 6 (1959/60) 261–263. N. Walker, "Disagion versus Trisagion. A Copyist Defended," *NTS* 7 (1960/61) 170–171. J. Sawyer, "The Qumran Reading of Isaiah 6:13," *ASTI* 3 (1964) 111–113.

Concerning the descriptions of prophetic calls: A. E. Rüthy, "Das prophetische Berufungserlebnis," *IKZ* 31 (1941) 97–114. S. Mowinckel, *Die Erkenntnis Gottes bei den alttestamentlichen Propheten,* BNTT (1941). I. P. Seierstad, *Die Offenbarungserlebnisse der Propheten Amos, Jesaja und Jeremia,* SNVAO 1946, 2 (1946). F. Horst, "Die Visionsschilderungen der alttestamentlichen Propheten," *EvT* 20 (1960) 193–205. T. T. Crabtree, "The Prophetic Call—A Dialogue with God," *SWJT* 4 (1961) 33–35. N. Habel, "The Form and Significance of the Call Narratives," *ZAW* 77 (1965) 297–323.

Concerning individual motifs: W. Schmidt, "Jerusalemer El-Traditionen bei Jesaja," *ZRGG* 16 (1964) 302–313. H. Schmidt, "Kerubenthron und Lade," FS H. Gunkel I (1923) 120–144. R. de Vaux, "Les chérubins et l'arche d'alliance, les sphinx gardiens et les thrones divins dans l'ancien Orient," *MUB* 37 (1961) 93–124. H. P. Müller, "Die himmlische Ratsversammlung," *ZNW* 54 (1963)

254–267. E. C. Kingsbury, "The Prophets and the Council of Yahweh," *JBL* 83 (1964) 279–286. W. Caspari, "Um ein vorhellenistisches Verständnis des Trisagion," *TBl* 4 (1925) 86–89. M. Garcia, "Cordero, El Santo de Israel," FS A. Robert (1957) 165–173. W. Schmidt, "Wo hat die Aussage: Jahwe 'der Heilige' ihren Ursprung?" *ZAW* 74 (1962) 62–66. O. Eissfeldt, "Jahwe als König," *ZAW* 46 (1928) 81–105. A. Alt, "Gedanken über das Königtum Jahwes," *KlSchr* I, 345–357. V. Maag, *Malkût JHWH,* VTSup 7 (1960) 129–153. J. Gray, "The Kingship of God in the Prophets and Psalms," *VT* 11 (1961) 1–29.

Concerning the hardening: F. Hesse, *Das Verstockungsproblem im Alten Testament,* BZAW 74 (1955). J. A. Diaz, "La ceguera del pueblo en Is 6:9–10 en relación con la acción de Dios," *EstEcl* 34 (1960) 733–739. J. Gnilka, *Die Verstockung Israels. Isaias 6:9–10 in der Theologie der Synoptiker,* SANT 3 (1961).

[Literature listed in first edition, read only after study on 6:1–13 was completed: A. F. Key, "The Magical Background of Isaiah 6:1–13," *JBL* 86 (1967) 198–204. K. R. Joines, "Winged Serpents in Isaiah's Inaugural Vision," *JBL* 86 (1967) 410–415. R. Kilian, "Die prophetischen Berufungsberichte," *Theologie im Wandel* (1967) 356–376. R. Knierim, "The Vocation of Isaiah," *VT* 18 (1968) 47–68. K. Baltzer, "Considerations Regarding the Office and Calling of the Prophet," *HTR* 61 (1968) 567–581.]

[Literature update through 1979. *Concerning the 'memorial record' (6:1—9:6):* T. Lescow, "Jesajas Denkschrift aus der Zeit des syrisch-ephraimitischen Krieges," *ZAW* 85 (1973) 315–331. H. P. Müller, *Glauben und Bleiben. Zur Denkschrift Jesajas Kapitel VI 1—VIII 18,* VTSup 26 (1974) 25–54.

Concerning 6:1–13: B. Uffenheimer, "הקדשת ישעיהו וגלגוליה במסורה הזיייל," *HaMikra' weToledot Yiśra'el* (1972); Engl: "The Consecration of Is. in Rabbinic Exegesis," *ScrHier* 22 (1977) 233–246. O. H. Steck, "Bemerkungen zu Jesaja 6," *BZ* NF 16 (1972) 188–206. M. Tsevat, "ו' ישעיה (Is 6)," FS Z. Shazar (1973) 161–172. A. Zeron, "Die Anmassung des Königs Usia im Lichte von Jesajas Berufung," *TZ* 33 (1977) 65–68.

Concerning the text: G. R. Driver, "Isaiah 6:1: 'His Train Filled the Temple,'" *Near Eastern Studies in Honor of W. F. Albright* (1971) 87–96. P. H. Vaughan, *The Meaning of bamâ in the OT. A Study of Etymological Evidence,* SOTSMS 3 (1974). U. F. C. Worschech, "The Problem of Isaiah 6:13," *AUSS* XII/2 (1974) 126–138. J. Schreiner, "Zur Textgestalt von Jes 6 und 7,1–17," *BZ* NF 22 (1978) 92–97.

Concerning the descriptions of prophetic calls: R. Knierim, "The Vocation of Isaiah," *VT* 18 (1968) 47–68. K. Gouders, "Zu einer Theologie der prophetischen Berufung," *BibLeb* 12 (1971) 79–93. Idem, "Die Berufung des Propheten Jesaja (Jes 6,1–13)," *BibLeb* 13 (1972) 89–106, 172–184. G. del Olmo Lete, *La vocación del lider en el antiguo Israel. Morfologia de los relatos bíblicos de vocación,* Bibliotheca Salmanticensis III, Studia 2 (1973). W. Vogels, "Les récits de vocation des prophètes," *NRT* 95 (1973) 3–24. H. Cazelles, "La vocation d'Isaïe (ch. 6) et les rites royaux," FS J. Prado, edited by L. Alvarez Verdes (1975) 89–108. B. O. Long, "Reports of Visions among the Prophets," *JBL* 95 (1976) 353–365. G. G. Nicol, "Isaiah's Vision and the Visions of Daniel," *VT* 29 (1979) 501–504.

Concerning individual motifs: H. Krüger, "Die Kerubim," diss., Halle-Wittenberg (1968/69). E. Lacheman, "The Seraphim of Isaiah 6," *JQR* 59 (1968/69) 71–72. J. de Savignac, "Les 'Seraphim'," *VT* 22 (1972) 320–325. D. Flusser, "Jewish Roots of the Liturgical Trishagion (Is 6:3; Yannai's piyyuṭim)," *Imm* 3 (1973s) 37–43. K. R. Joines, *Serpent Symbolism in the OT. A Linguistical, Archaeological and Literary Study* (1974). J. Sperna Weiland, "Analyse du mot קדוש," *Le Sacré, études et recherches* (1974) 225–242. J. Edwards, "Prophetic Paradox: Isaiah 6:9–10," *Studia Biblica et Theologica* 6 (1976) 48–61. O. Keel, *Jahwe-Vision und Siegelkunst. Eine neue Deutung der Majestätsschilderungen in Jes 6, Ez 1 und Sach 5* (1977). M. Görg, "Die Funktion der Serafen bei Jesaja," *BN* 5 (1978) 28–39.

Concerning the hardening: J. H. Schmidt, "Gedanken zum Verstockungsauftrag Jesajas (Is 6)," *VT* 21 (1971) 68–90. A. Cohen, "השמן, הכבד והשע (Is 6:10)," diss., South East Asia Graduate School of Theology (1974). R. Kilian, "Der Verstockungsauftrag Jesajas," FS G. J. Botterweck (1977).]

Isaiah 6:1–13

Text

6:1 In the year of king Uzziah's death, I saw[a] 'Yahweh':[b] He sat upon a
high and lofty throne, and [c]the hems (of his robe) filled the palace.[c]

2 Over[a] him stood seraphim. Each one had[b] six wings: With two
they[c] covered their face, with two they covered their feet, and
with two they flew.

3 And one called[a] to the other and said:
"Holy, holy, holy[b] is Yahweh of Hosts!
His glory shouts out, that which (always) fills[c] the earth."

4 Because of the (loud) voices of those who called, the door pivots[a]
trembled violently in the door sills, and the house was filled[b] up

5 with smoke. • Then I said:
"Woe is me, I must be silent,[a]
for I am a human being with unclean lips
and I dwell among a people which has unclean lips.
For my eyes have seen the king, Yahweh of Hosts!"

6 Then one of the seraphim flew to me with a red-hot coal[a] in his

7 hand, which he had taken from the altar with a pair of tongs. • With
this, he touched[a] my mouth and said:
"Behold, this has touched your lips,
[b]thus your guilt withdraws and your sin is covered."[b]

8 Then I heard the voice of 'Yahweh'[a] saying:
"Whom shall I send; who will go for us?"[b]
I answered: "Here am I! Send me!"

9 Then he said: "Go and speak to this people:
'Hear continually,[a] yet gain no insight,[b]
and see unceasingly,[a] but do not achieve understanding!'[b]

10 [a]Make the heart of this people fat
so that its ears harden and its eyes stick shut,[a]
so that it cannot see with its eyes and cannot hear with its ears
and its heart[b] does not gain insight [c]and then it would return and
be saved."[c]

11 Then I asked: "How long, Lord?" He answered:
"Until the cities lie deserted,
without inhabitant
and the houses are without any human beings
and the field 'remains, yet'[a] (only) as desert."

[12 And Yahweh will carry off the human beings
and the devastation[a] will be massive in the midst of the land.]

[13 And if there is still a tenth there,
it will serve as pasture until grazed bare[a]
as the oaks and terebinths,
which, [b]if someone fells them, shoots[c] are still there.[b]
[d][The shoots[c] upon it are holy seed.][d]

1a Q[a] reads only אראה (I saw [without *Waw*]); however, cf. the use of ו (*Waw*) after
a designation for time, BrSynt §123f.
1b Instead of אדני (Lord), a large number of MSS read יהוה (Yahweh), which is
probably the original reading. The tendency to replace יהוה (Yahweh) with אדני
(Lord) can be observed in several different passages in the book of Isaiah.
1c–c Gk reads καὶ πλήρος ὁ οἶκος τῆς δόξης αὐτοῦ (and the house was full of his
glory). Without a doubt, this is the Hebrew text which was available; this "translation" is a dogmatic corrective, based on a viewpoint which could not tolerate

anthropomorphisms. The Greek translator of the book of Isaiah had an obvious preference for the term δόξα (glory) (concerning this, see L. H. Brockington, "The Greek Translator of Isaiah and His Interest in ΔΟΞΑ," *VT* 1 [1951] 23–32). The שׁוּלִים are the hems of a coat; the word is related to the Arabic *sawila,* "hang down loosely" (see J. Hehn, *BZ* 14 [1917] 15–24).

2a Gk reads, instead of מִמַּעַל לוֹ (over him), κύκλῳ αὐτοῦ (around him). It is very possible that this is also an intentional alteration, since it would not set well with the translator that the seraphim should be standing *over* their divine Lord. However, according to יְעוֹפֵף (they flew), which comes at the end of the sentence, they are indeed soaring *over* him.

2b In Qᵃ, the second שֵׁשׁ כְּנָפַיִם (six wings) is lacking, most likely due to haplography. Using the phrase twice serves a distributive function; BrSynt §87.

2c Because of the sense of the passage, we use the plural, though the Hebrew uses the singular here and in the following verses, since אֶחָד (each one) is the subject.

3a Qᵃ reads וקראים (and calling [plural]). That is not original, as can be seen by the use of the singular verbs in v. 2 (וְאָמַר, and said, is missing from the end of 3aα in Qᵃ). But the plural קֹרְאִים, calling, shows that Qᵃ presumes that there is a multitude of seraphim. MT could, at best, be interpreted as speaking about just two of them. Then one would translate: "and the one called to the other"; on this, see Engnell, op. cit., 34f., and see below, pp. 263f.

3b Qᵃ reads קָדוֹשׁ (holy) only two times, but is hardly correct (contra Walker, op. cit.). The triple "holy" corresponds to liturgical style; Psalm 99, a kingship of God psalm, has a threefold repetition of the formula "holy is he"/"holy is Yahweh, our God"; cf. also Jer. 7:4; 22:29; Ezek. 21:32.

3c Instead of מְלֹא (fills), it would seem that Gk, which translates it with πλήρης (has filled), must have read מָלְאָה (Vulg: *plena,* full of; Targ: מְלִיא, filled; Syr: *dᵉmaljâ,* of fullness), in addition to which one ought to consult Pss. 33:5; 72:19, and 104:24. But Psalm 24, which has concepts which sound very similar to Isaiah 6, mentions "the earth and the fulness thereof" in v. 1 (הָאָרֶץ וּמְלוֹאָהּ); cf. also Deut. 33:16; Pss. 50:12 and 89:12. One can see from 8:8 and 31:4 that Isaiah makes use of the term מְלֹא (fill). If one follows Gk, כָּל־הָאָרֶץ (all the earth) is the subject of the sentence; if it is a noun clause, as the MT reads it, then מְלֹא כָל־הָאָרֶץ (that which fills all the earth) would be the subject; see BrSynt §14bγ.

4a The meaning of the word אַמָּה (otherwise "forearm, ulna") is not clear for this passage. A meaning like "doorposts," "solid foundation," or something similar is usually presumed, so that אַמּוֹת הַסִּפִּים is usually translated "doorposts in their foundations" (Eichrodt); "sill of the threshold" (Duhm); "foundations of the threshold" (Engnell, Leslie), or something similar. But it is most likely that what is intended is rather the door pivots of the swinging doors which are set into the threshold (J. Halévy, *REJ* 14 [1887] 151f.). Therefore, the סִפִּים do not describe or at least do not exclusively refer to the upper crosspieces (Gk: ὑπέρ θυρον, lintel of a door) but at the very least also include the foundation sill at the entrance. Illuss.: *BRL* 525; *BHH* 2031.

4b One should note the imperfect יִמָּלֵא (filled up) and the word order which is used for this description, showing that v. 4b provides the accompanying circumstances for v. 4a.

5a נִדְמֵיתִי has usually been translated "I am lost" or "I am destroyed," or something similar. This makes good sense as it describes the reaction of the prophet, aware of his sinfulness in the presence of the majesty of God. Gk reads κατανένυγμαι, "I am stunned"; Syr: *tawîr 'nâ,* "I am startled"; however, 'Aquila, Sym, Theod read ἐσιώπησα (I remained silent); Vulg: *tacui,* I was silent. The rabbinic exegesis is closely allied with this interpretation, according to which Isaiah, in a sinful way, had said nothing in response to the wrongs which were described in 2 Chron. 26:16ff.; cf. Targ (חבית) "I have transgressed" (Stenning). Even though this interpretation is most unlikely, it still does presume that one could use דמה niph'al with the meaning "be silent, say nothing." This translation would also be possible on the basis of the context, since Isaiah spoke about the uncleanness of his *lips*. The Habakkuk commentary (1 QpHab V 9f.) uses the verb חרש *hiph'il* "be silent" in conjunction with the *niph'al* of דמה in Hab. 1:13. But what is decisive here is that the meaning "transgress," or something similar, for דמה II (and דמם), is hardly ever attested (see L. Köhler, *Kleine Lichter,* Zwingli-Bücherei 47 [1945] 32–34, and Jenni, op. cit., 322; the translation "be silent" is also adopted by Eichrodt, Fohrer, and Kaiser).

6a רצפה is not, as it is usually translated, a red-hot stone, but rather a "red-hot coal" (Gk: ἄνθραξ, charcoal; see Lev. 16:12).

7a Literally: "and he allowed my mouth to be touched."

7b–b Note the chiastic word order in the Hebrew. The imperfect describes the accompanying circumstances; see Engnell, op. cit., 17, who translates: "thy guilt certainly departs, thy sin being expiated."

8a Instead of אדני (Lord), many MSS once again read the more original יהוה (Yahweh).

8b Instead of לנו (for us), Gk reads πρὸς τὸν λαὸν τοῦτον (for this people), a reading which has been inserted here from its original place in v. 9 (לעם הזה, to this people), unless לנו (for us) was misread as לְגוי (for a people).

9a The infinite absolute, placed after the verb, stresses the continuation of an activity, the persistence with which something is carried on (Joüon, Gr §123l).

9b After an initial imperative, a second one in Hebrew will often be used in a consecutive manner (cf. Joüon, Gr §116f 3), which is also true in this case, with the jussive being negated.

10a–a Gk reads v. 10a: ἐπαχύνθη γὰρ ἡ καρδία τοῦ λαοῦ τούτου, καὶ τοῖς ὠσὶν αὐτῶν βαρέως ἤκουσαν καὶ τοὺς ὀφθαλμοὺς αὐτῶν ἐκάμμυσαν (for the heart of this people exalted itself, and they heard with their heavy ears, and they shut their eyes), which means that, instead of saying that Isaiah is to bring about a hardening, it is said that *the people* has already hardened itself. Whether this was done intentionally or not, it completely removes the theological problem posed in the Hebrew, whether the prophet himself was actually supposed to cause the hardening.

10b Qᵃ reads בלבבו (in its heart), by analogy with the substantive which immediately precedes it; the versions also seem to presume that this is the original reading, so that Eichrodt translates: "and in its heart." The adjustment seems an obvious one to accept, which is exactly why it is suspect.

10c–c When translating ושב ורפא לו (and then it would return and be saved) (concerning the pointing וָשָׁב, see Joüon, Gr §104d), the suggestions from the commentators are quite diverse. In the first place, there is the question about whether שוב (return) ought not be taken, as in v. 13, as a so-called modal verb and translated "happen once again." Then, of course, one would expect the pointing to be וְשָׁב (see Procksch). But that Israel, if it returned (שוב), would find salvation was more likely the contemporary viewpoint of the official cult theology (cf. Hos. 6:1). The subject of ושב (it would return) actually seems to be the people (Gk: καὶ ἐπιστρέψωσι, and it will turn around). But who is the subject of the following רפא (be saved, heal): God, the heart, or an indefinite "someone"? If the people are the subject of שב (return), then, at the same time, they should be considered the subject of רפא (be saved, heal), which follows immediately. In this case, לו (for itself) would have to be understood in the reflexive sense (see KBL), literally: "and find salvation for itself."

11a The *niph'al* תִּשָּׁאֶה (be brought to ruin) does not seem to fit well with the *qal* שאו (lie deserted). The root שאה I (crash into ruins) is not otherwise found in the *niph'al* (in 17:12, the *niph'al* of the root שאה II [roar] is used). The translation "the sown ground will be laid waste, becoming barren land," or something similar, is not an impossible rendering, but the reading in Gk (καὶ ἡ γῆ καταλειφθήσεται ἔρημος, and the land shall be left behind, deserted), which presumes an original reading תִּשָּׁאֵר (remain, be left), is to be preferred (cf. 24:12; concerning the construction, see Jer. 42:2).

12a עזובה means literally something like "abandoned, undeveloped land"; cf. Syr: šᵉbîqûtâ (forsaken). Gk translates v. 12: καὶ μετὰ ταῦτα μακρυνεῖ ὁ θεὸς τοὺς ἀνθρώ-πους, καὶ οἱ καταλειφθέντες πληθυνθήσονται ἐπὶ τῆς γῆς (and after these things, God will remove the human beings far away, and those who remain will be multiplied in the land). This does not automatically presume that there was a different Hebrew text besides the MT version, since μακρυνεῖ could possibly translate רחק (become far, distant) and καταλειφθέντες could be a translation of עזובה (leave, loose). If this is the case, the harsh threat of judgment has been recast to become a prediction of salvation (see Engnell, op. cit., 14).

13a Based on its usage in Isaiah, in 3:14 and 5:5, בער in the *pi'el* means "graze until bare" (contra KBL, Eichrodt, Fohrer, but in agreement with Hertzberg, Kaiser, et al.; see K. Budde, *ZAW* 41 [1923] 167), in which case the grazing of a herd of small animals could mean the complete destruction of all the vegetation (Dalman, *AuS* I/1, 87; VI, 209, 212; cf. Zeph. 2:6).

13b–b The text is uncertain; שלכת (felling) is a *hapax legomenon;* Qᵃ reads משלכת (cause to fall) for בשלכת (if someone fells) (concerning this, cf. Sym: αποβαλουσα, throwing away; Vulg: *quae expandit ramos suos,* which stretches out its branches) and במה (heights) for בם (them). These variations come at the initial stage of a radical reinterpretation of this very difficult passage: Iwry suggests reading כאלה וכאלון (ו)אשר(ה) (ה)(מ)שלכת(מ)מצבת במה and translates: "Like a terebinth, or an oak, or an Asherah, when flung down from the sacred column of an high place" (op. cit.; cf. also W. F. Albright, VTSup 4 [1957] 254f., Brownlee, op. cit., and Leslie). But that would be a most strange comparison. Just as questionable is the attempted reconstruction which has been suggested by Sawyer, who is quite free with 13bα, reading אשר משלכת מצבת (which sends forth shoots) and, since there is a space after מצבת (shoot) in Qᵃ, takes במה (vocalized as בַּמֶּה, wherein) with what follows and consequently translates 13bβ: "Wherein is the holy seed? Its stump!" (op. cit., 112). As a result of all this, that which has the most to commend it, in spite of the acknowledged difficulties, is the MT as it stands (thus also Hertzberg, Steinmann, Fohrer, Eichrodt, Kaiser, who does in fact read מְשַׁלֶּכֶת, from sending forth).

13c מצבת is found only one other time, in 2 Sam. 18:18, where it means "monument stone," just as מצבה does in so many places; however, in this passage, the meaning generally suggested is "stump of a tree." At the very least, the addition at the conclusion of this section, זרע קדוש מצבתה (the shoots upon it are holy seed), shows that מצבת is not understood to be a *maṣṣebah.* It is still most doubtful that it actually refers to the "stump of a tree." Tur-Sinai's suggested solution has much to commend it (op. cit. [in literature on 1:1] 169), taking מצבת to mean "new planting" (Syr reads in 13bβ nesbᵉteh, his planting; נצב means "plant" in both Aramaic and Syriac), thus resulting in the reading: "the new growth to come forth after the trees have been entirely denuded of foliage and fruit."

13d–d It would seem that Gk (A, Q, B, Syh) L did not have this phrase in its text at all, but some of the Hexaplaric and Lucianic recensions read, with Theod, σπέρμα ἅγιον τὸ στήλωμα αὐτῆς, holy seed is its pillar ('Aquila has a similar reading). Sym translates v. 13bβ as σπερμα αγιον η αντιστασις (holy seed is the opposing party). Some exegetes would suggest removing the short phrase as a late gloss. But if one finds that necessary, one ought not rely on the Gk to supply the conclusive evidence: In the Gk, the chapter comes to a close with ἀπὸ τῆς θήκης αὐτῆς (from its memorial grave), which means that it concludes with (מ)מצבתה (from its monument stone) and not with מצבת בם (shoots upon it) at the end of v. 13bα. It is simply the result of an *aberratio oculi* (diversion of the eyes) that v. 13bβ is missing (K. Budde, *ZAW* 41 [1923] 167).

Form

Chap. 6 is a kerygmatic unity: v. 1 begins anew with its very precise date and v. 13 concludes with a short but very meaningful glimpse into a time of salvation which is yet to come, bringing the section to a close.

The chapter is placed at the very beginning of the "memorial record" which comes from the time of the Syro-Ephraimitic War, and includes the material all the way to 9:6 (see K. Budde, *ZAW* 41 [1923] 165 and, above all, idem, *Jesajas Erleben* [1928] 1–5; cf. O. Eissfeldt, *The Old Testament. An Introduction* [1965] 310; E. Sellin-G. Fohrer, *Introduction to the Old Testament* [1968] 363ff.). This generally is designated Isaiah's call narrative, even though this interpretation is not without its detractors; see below, p. 256f.

We begin by addressing the question of the traditio-historical background of the account. When Isaiah portrays the experience connected with his vision, a portrayal which belongs to the general category of autobiographical descriptions in the first person form, he employs a pre-existent pattern which had been used for prophetic descriptions about being commissioned. This means that he describes his vision within the framework of the pattern which was generally used in Israel when speaking about such experiences.

The closest parallels to details from Isaiah 6 are to be found in 1 Kings 22, in the story about Micaiah ben Imlah. A comparison results in the following picture:

	1 Kings 22		Isaiah 6	
19.	ראיתי את־יהוה		ואראה את־יהוה	1.
	ישב על־כסאו		ישב על־כסא רם ונשא	
	וכל־צבא השמים		שרפים	2.
	עמד עליו מימינו ומשמאלו		עמדים ממעל לו ...	
20.	ויאמר יהוה		ואשמע את־קול יהוה אמר	8.
	מי יפתה את־אחאב ...		את־מי אשלח ומי ילך־לנו	
21.	... ויאמר אני אפתנו		ואמר הנני שלחני	

The points of contact are even more significant than one might perceive at first glance: Micaiah sees *the host* of the heavens; Isaiah had seen Yahweh *of Hosts.* Isaiah identifies Yahweh as *king,* and the Micaiah story also depicts Yahweh as king, even though the actual term מלך (king) is not there. The זה אל־זה (one to another) in Isa. 6:3 corresponds to זה בכה וזה... בכה (one said one thing, and another said another) in 1 Kings 22:20. In Isaiah, as in Kings, the commissioning does not take place only by means of a divine message going from God to the person being called, that is, through a bluntly worded command, but is rather in the form of a conversation: In 1 Kings 22:21, Yahweh asks the "spirit" about what way he will find for his mandate to be carried out. In Isa. 6:11, the prophet wants to know about how long he will have to perform his difficult service, work which goes far beyond what one could expect any human to complete. As the "spirit" is to delude Ahab, Isaiah is to "harden" the people.

W. Zimmerli, in his study of the transmission-historical background for Ezekiel 1–3 (BK XIII, 16–21 [Engl: *Ezekiel 1,* 97–100]), differentiated between two types of call narratives: The first type is identified by the characteristic that all the motifs are subordinate to the message of Yahweh which goes forth. Included in this type, one finds hesitation and denial on the part of the *vocandus* (the one called), both of which have to be overcome by persuasion and assurance through the offer of signs. One would include in this group the call and commission of Moses according to J, E, and P; some of the elements of this pattern are found in the stories of Gideon and Saul (cf. Zimmerli, op. cit., 17 [Engl: 97]), and the classical development of this type is found in Jeremiah. It would seem that this first pattern received its unique shape in the description of the call of a charismatic type of leader (on this, see H. Graf Reventlow, *Liturgie und prophetisches Ich bei Jeremia* [1963] 24–77). That seems to be the case when one observes that it is presented in a similar fashion in the OT in the traditions about Moses, Gideon, and Saul. Some particular elements also lead us to this conclusion: The encouraging word ("have no fear!") comes to the prophet and has parallels in the oracle of salvation addressed to the one chosen as a leader for a holy war; cf. Deut. 20:3f. and, on this point, see below, on Isa. 7:4. The sign which is given serves to provide a confirmation for the people who will have the leader out in front of them. When using this particular pattern, the prophet is characterized as one from a long line of savior figures, stretching back to the early period of Israel.

The second pattern is very different. In 1 Kings 22 the account begins with ראיתי את־יהוה (I saw the Lord); the recounting in Isaiah 6 begins with ואראה (I saw): The *visio* aspect has much greater importance here. In both of these cases, the prophet is presented with a vision of the divine king who is in the midst of his court, which itself has the task of proclaiming the majesty of its Lord. The one who is called is ready to accomplish the will of his Lord in the earthly realm of his overall dominion. He is thus just like the ministering spirits who are there to carry out Yahweh's commands; cf. Ps. 103:20f. It is for this reason that the question is asked: את־מי אשלח (מי ילך לנו) (Whom shall I send; who will go for us?)/מי יפתה (who will entice?); the messenger is brought in on the planning being done by the divine king. In Isaiah 6, of course, the response does not come from one of the divine beings who surround the throne of the world's ruler, but comes from the prophet himself. But he is taken into the inner circles of God's council just as if he were one of the heavenly beings. A very different image of a prophet is presented by this pattern when compared with the first type. The prophet functions as *a divine messenger.* As such, he was present at the heavenly *meeting of the full council,* for "surely Yahweh God does nothing without revealing his secret [סוד] to his servants the prophets" (Amos 3:7). The same is true for Jeremiah, for whom this concept was not unknown, even though the descriptive narrative about his call has other traditio-historical roots; like Isaiah, Jeremiah is also given his legitimacy by having stood (עמד) in Yahweh's "meeting of the full council" (once again סוד) which afforded him a glimpse (ראה) into what was really happening at that time when he heard the message, 23:18, 22. This type of narration, modified substantially, is also found in Ezekiel. Heaven also opens up above this prophet. The four living creatures which, according to the way they are portrayed, encircle the throne of God, are in reality nothing more than accessories (on this, see Zimmerli, op. cit., 36 [Engl: 109]). The form is not strictly followed at this point, since there is no glimpse into the heavenly meeting of the full council. Therefore, Ezekiel does not really depict an actual סוד

(meeting of the full council), since the awesome magnitude of the divine majesty demands in his case that his description uniquely concentrate on the manifestation of God. But the form had still been intact at the time of Isaiah. According to what has been said, this can be designated a vision of the council around the throne.

Fey notes points of contact between Isaiah 6 and Amos 9:1–4 and suggests that Isaiah had this "borderline statement from the sayings of Amos" in front of him when he put the narrative of his call into writing (op. cit., 114); in fact, he wonders whether the first words of the Amos passage were taken by Isaiah as a description of a call narrative (op. cit., 109f.). However, in that passage, there is no description of a heavenly council around the throne and there is nothing which suggests clearly that this is a description of the initial call of a prophet. Zimmerli comes more to the point when he refers to the narrative about Paul's call (Acts 9:3ff.; 22:6ff.; 26:12ff.; op. cit., 20f. [Engl: 100]). Also in that passage, the connection is made to link a manifestation of majesty, though not of God but of Christ, with a commissioning to carry out the divine task. One might also refer to the vision of the seer in Revelation 4 and 5, replete with scenes reminiscent both of Ezekiel and of Isaiah. The four beings which surround the throne simply fulfill the function of offering adoration in that passage; they are the prototype for the adoration offered by the worshiping community, represented by the 24 elders. In the place of the prophet, the seer comes to praise the glory of the "lamb," but is also to publicize God's decisions concerning the whole earth (cf. Müller, op. cit., and his dissertation "Formgeschichtliche Untersuchungen zu Apc. 4f.," Heidelberg, 1963). And finally, Horst (op. cit., 198) draws connections with Zech. 1:7–15; 6:1–8, and, above all, 3:1–7. "In all these cases where the prophet, within the context of a visionary experience, is present for discussions or decisions made before the throne of God . . . and by this means is able to 'know the knowledge of the Most High,' he is then required to proclaim this, and strengthened for the task, whether it be a message which is unusual, one which will alienate him from others because it is so harsh, or whether it is a message which leads to very high expectations" (ibid.).

There are also other places in the OT which refer to the motif of the assembly of the gods or, as the case may be, the heavenly council. This presumes a polytheism, with a king of the gods ruling as head of the pantheon. It is not difficult to identify similar concepts being used in the nearer and more distant regions surrounding Israel.

This motif is found in Ps. 89:6–8, where the assembly is called a סוד־קדשים (council of the holy ones) in v. 8a and קהל קדשים (assembly of the holy ones) in v. 6b. The בני אלים (sons of gods) in v. 7 and סביביו (all that are round about him) in v. 8b and the צבאות (hosts) in v. 9a are one and the same group. In v. 6a, a simple שמים (heavens) is used to convey the same idea. When the name for God appears as אל (El) in v. 8, that betrays the source of this general concept as being rooted in Canaanite mythology. It cannot be simply an accident that the motif happens to be used in a kingship psalm, since the heavenly council furnishes the original pattern from which the earthly one is patterned. Ps. 25:14 (סוד יהוה ליראיו, the assembly [RSV: friendship] of the Lord is for those who fear him) might very likely provide a final faint echo of the ancient mythology, given such a radically "democratic" shape that those who are the God-fearers are even able to take part in Yahweh's סוד (heavenly council), shrouded as always in mystery; see also Job 15:8: סוד אלוה (council of God) (in Job 29:4, the reading סוד is probably the result of a textual error). But this concept is not limited to the term סוד (heavenly council). In addition to 1 Kings 22:19, Job 1:6 (בני האלהים, sons of God; see also

2:1) also speaks about Yahweh's court advisers. In Job 5:1 קְדֹשִׁים (holy ones) is used, as is also the case in 15:15 (there once again parallel to שָׁמַיִם, heavens). בְּנֵי הָאֱלֹהִים/בְּנֵי אֵלִים (sons of God) is also to be found in Gen. 6:2, 4; Deut. 32:8 (text emended on the basis of Gk, Lucian, Sym, and Qᵃ; see O. Eissfeldt, BAL 104, 5 [1958] 9, 15–25); 32:43a (Gk); Ps. 29:1; Job 38:7; see W. Herrmann, "Die Göttersöhne," *ZRGG* 12 (1960) 242–251. Ps. 82:1 speaks of the עֲדַת־אֵל (divine council), at which the בְּנֵי אֱלֹהִים (sons of God) or the בְּנֵי עֶלְיוֹן (sons of the Most High) (v. 6) assemble. Beyond this, there are passages such as Pss. 97:7, 9; 103:19, 21, and Sir. 24:2 (ἐκκλησία ὑψίστου, assembly of the Most High) which can be consulted. It has frequently been articulated that Gen. 1:26 is another passage which can only be interpreted by presuming that a divine assembly scene is being depicted (see W. H. Schmidt, *Die Schöpfungsgeschichte der Priesterschrift,* WMANT 17 [1964] 129f.).

The OT passages here noted clearly betray some relationship with concepts known in the lands surrounding Israel. Evidence for their use in the Canaanite world is furnished by the Ugaritic texts: "assembly of the sons of El" (*phr bn 'ilm*) II AB III 14; "assembled host" (*phr m'd*) III AB, B 14, 20, 31; "assembly of El" (*phr 'ilm*) 17:7 and 21:2; and "place of assembly for the sons of El" (*mphrt bn 'il*) 2:17, 34; 53:3, and the like. The closest parallel to Isaiah 6 is found in the Keret-legend (II K V 10–30), to which attention has been drawn by Müller, op. cit., 260ff. In addition, one can compare this with מפחרת אל גבל קדשם (Assembly of the Holy Gods of Byblos) in the Yehimilk inscription from Byblos, dated to the tenth century (Donner-Röllig, *KAI* no. 4, 4–5; [*ANET* 653]) and to דר בן אלם (Group of the Children of the Gods) on the stele of Azitawadda (*KAI* no. 26 A III, 19 [*ANET* 654]). Müller (op. cit., 262ff.) has also gathered Babylonian material together. It is particularly noteworthy that, in one of the series of Maqlû incantations, a man functions as a messenger for the deity (see G. Meier, *Die assyrische Beschwörungssammlung Maqlû,* BAfO 2 [1937] 9).

Since Jerusalem is the place where many Canaanite mythological elements were integrated into the faith and since Isaiah is more closely tied to the Jerusalem traditions than any other prophet, it is not surprising that these concepts have also been employed by Isaiah in his proclamation. On the other hand, the use of this same pattern in the narrative about Micaiah ben Imlah, which must have taken shape in the Northern Kingdom, shows that what we are dealing with here is a widely known "pattern."

The traditio-historical connections which have been set forth here point to the path which one must follow when arriving at a basic understanding of Isaiah 6. H. Schmidt could still write in his commentary: "This is a literary-historical event which is taking shape here, as is true for similar passages in Amos and Hosea; a literary category known as *autobiography* is being joined with other literary genres which were in use in ancient Israel and Judah" (p. 26). But Isaiah's account of his experiences is not intended to preserve a report of "the inner, spiritual experiences" of the next world (op. cit.), but instead, it provides an account of Isaiah's right and duty to serve as a spokesman for Yahweh. For this reason, the exact "official" dating is included at the beginning of the chapter: The prophet chronicles the precise circumstances of his commissioning. This is also the reason for the comprehensive manner used by Isaiah to describe the hardening; in light of the lack of success, indeed the senselessness of his proclamation, it was important to underscore the specific factors involved with his assignment. The biographical and psychological value, which has occupied the attention of so many, must be studied with due caution, since the narrative does not have the purpose of providing an answer to questions which so many put to it. Jenni, expanding on an idea from H. W. Wolff, calls this ἀπομνημόνευμα, *memorabile* (memorial record) (op. cit., 328). It would be still more correct to say: Isaiah 6 provides Isaiah's prophetic credentials of legitimacy.

Meter: The Trisagion (holy, holy, holy) in v. 3 is composed by using a five-stress colon and a three-stress colon. Concerning Isaiah's personal cry of woe at the beginning of v. 5, one might note the introductory אוי־לי כי־נדמיתי (Woe is me, I must be silent). Following this, there are 3 five-stress cola (the first כי, I, receives two stresses and the article on מלך [king] is to be eliminated as an attempt to turn poetry into prose). The message of the seraphim in v. 7 should be taken as two short two-stress bicola. The message which Isaiah is to deliver to the people, according to v. 9, is a three-stress bicolon, whereas the command addressed to Isaiah himself in v. 10 is accented as 2 four-stress bicola. Yahweh's answer to the prophet's question in v. 11 ought to be read once again as 2 three-stress bicola (the first מאן receives two stresses, which attaches greater significance to it). One would do well not to look for a metrical pattern in vv. 12f.

Setting

The problem of "authenticity": As a first person report, this section claims to come from Isaiah himself. There should be no question about this since, in general, this is a correct assessment, even though there is no doubt that the report has been forcefully shaped by traditional elements which describe such visions (for another view, see Whitley, op. cit., 38–42). No prophet has ever taken on the responsibilities of such an office in a way which was not consistent with the traditions of his people. If Isaiah wanted to find a way to demonstrate that he was a legitimate prophet of Yahweh, he had to show that the message of Yahweh by which he was issued a call was just like what had been experienced by other, recognized prophets of Yahweh. The detailed exegesis will show that there are many places where the concepts in this chapter are intertwined with those from other examples of Isaiah's proclamation. It is not just by chance that it is precisely this Isaiah from Jerusalem—whom we are to thank for the "messianic" predictions and who so passionately attacks the pride of human beings, since "Yahweh alone will be exalted on that day"—who saw God as the king on his "high and lofty throne." Isaiah 6 bears all the marks of authenticity; it is a report about a genuine experience and must have been composed or dictated by Isaiah himself.

The biographical arrangement of Isaiah 6: In order to determine whether this passage represents an account of Isaiah's initial call, it is necessary to sketch the content of other relevant OT passages. We have already sketched out a description of Jeremiah 1 as an example of the pattern for the call of a charismatic leader, and there can be no question that it provides us with the inaugural vision of the prophet. But in 1 Kings 22, the event described is not the first call of Micaiah, but rather his commissioning for a specific task, that of "deluding" Ahab. On the other hand, there is no doubt that Ezekiel 1–3 recounts the call vision of the prophet, but there both types of narratives for commissioning are meshed together. In addition, the visions in Amos 7, 8, and 9, in spite of efforts in this direction (H. Graf Reventlow, *Das Amt des Propheten bei*

Amos, FRLANT 80 [1962]), are not to be interpreted as inaugural visions. M. M. Kaplan has revived a very old thesis (see C. P. Caspari, *Commentar til de tolv føste Capitler of Propheten Jesaia* [1867] 240–245, and S. Mowinckel, *Profeten Jesaja* [1925] 16, 20ff., quoted by Seierstad, op. cit., 43) which states that chap. 6 ought not be interpreted as an account of Isaiah's initial call. If that really were the case, according to him, there would have to have been a direct address to the prophet. But that does not happen; Isaiah freely offers himself; he must have already considered himself to have been called. Further, in Kaplan's view, the command about the hardening is the main reason for rejecting the traditional interpretation which sees Isaiah 6 as an initial call: "In my opinion, such unqualified and irredeemable destruction could not have constituted the burden of an inaugural message." Similar to the proclamation of the destruction of Israel in Amos 9:1–4, this vision could only be understood "as a result of the failure of the people to heed the repeated call to repentance" (op. cit., 253). Thus, Isaiah 6 would take it for granted that Isaiah had already been active as a prophet for an extended time period. In the course of his activity, he would have been suddenly overcome by the awareness that his efforts were all for naught; the theory about the hardening of the people would have offered itself to him as the explanation.

There are many important questions which need to be raised about this thesis. The reference to 1 Kings 22 and similar passages is not conclusive, since one must allow Isaiah the freedom to adapt a particular form of speech for a new situation. Concerning Kaplan's comments in connection with the hardening, one must ask whether we are in a position to gauge how one determines the exact boundaries which God established for what one of Israel's prophets was to do for him. But the most serious problem with Kaplan's interpretation is the dating which is now at the beginning of the chapter. It is unlikely that Isaiah had already been active for an extended period of time before Uzziah died, even if one admits working under the burden of uncertainty concerning the absolute chronology for the time of Isaiah. If Isaiah speaks about his unclean lips, that would be more of an argument against, rather than for, Kaplan's thesis: Every prophet considers himself an adaptable tool to be used by his lord, and it would completely contradict his prophetic consciousness for him to confess that he had made his lips unclean during the time he carried out the duties of his prophetic task. It seems that only one convincing argument against the traditional interpretation remains: A prophet of Yahweh is never called "one who is sent" (שָׁלִיחַ) by Yahweh. Wherever any reference is made to the "sending" of a prophet, it usually comes in the more ancient passages which consistently speak about commissioning for a specific task (2 Kings 2:2; Jer. 26:12, and often elsewhere). The verb is also not connected with the actual call in Judg. 6:14; Jer. 1:7; Ezek. 2:3f.; 3:6 (cf. also Judg. 6:8; 13:8; 1 Sam. 15:1; 2 Sam. 12:1). A clear delineation must be made between being called and being commissioned for a specific task. In spite of this, it is certainly possible that mention can be made of the commissioning within the context of the call. In contrast to the passages to which reference has been made, Isaiah uses the term in an absolute sense. In post-Isaianic passages, when one speaks of "commissioning," the basic actual call to prophetic service is meant (Isa. 48:16; 61:1; cf. also Jer. 14:14; 23:32; 27:15, and often elsewhere). Kaplan has not found a large following. Y. Kaufmann (*Toledot ha-Emunah ha-Yisraelit* III [1947] 206f., 176, note 4) does agree, as does J. Milgrom, who dates 1:10—6:13 entirely in the time of Uzziah (*VT* 14 [1964] 172f.), and Horst (op. cit., 198), who is inclined to agree with Milgrom's views. In the final analysis, the question will be answered on the basis of the way one understands the command concerning the hardening, which was decisive for Kaplan in arriving at his interpretation (on this, see below, pp. 272f.).

The question of integrity: The chapter is initially divided into two main sections: theophany (1–5) and commissioning (6–8). The command concerning hardening in v. 10 is inseparable from the commissioning. That is most strange, but Micaiah ben Imlah was given a similar assignment, being asked to deceive king Ahab. On formal grounds, v. 9, which immediately precedes this, already includes a message for the people. But, in reality, this message was to prepare Isaiah himself for the great difficulty which this task entailed. The follow-up question posed by the prophet and the response of Yahweh in v. 11 also belong to the original material of the chapter. It is not so with v. 12. The style alone keeps one from considering this verse a continuation of the speech of Yahweh in v. 11: Reference is made to Yahweh in the third person, whereas v. 11 is Yahweh's own message. The announcement that human beings will be carried off is at odds with the מאין יושב (without inhabitant) in v. 11. This verse must be a later interpretation inserted by a redactor. It is possible that vv. 13a, bα come from the same hand, but it is more likely that they are an addition from a still later time. Finally, v. 13bβ would be more recent yet, so that the original account was updated by use of glosses on three separate occasions, as circumstances changed. There are some commentators who maintain that vv. 12 and 13a, bα are from Isaiah himself, the prophet having expanded the account of his vision in a later period of his activity (Jenni, op. cit., 330); others believe it is possible that a redactor took an authentic message of Isaiah from a different context and inserted it here (Fohrer, Kaiser). The uncertainty within the textual transmission itself and the problem with translating v. 13 make a final decision all the more difficult. Because there are so many different passages where authentic words of Isaiah have been supplemented by additions, one ought to stay with the assessment that these are "post-Isaianic."

The fact that so many glosses are found in this section is indicative of how intensively readers involved themselves with the narrative of Isaiah's call. But it also shows that the authority of Isaiah was very great, so much so that some were willing to subsume their own insights under his words. It is worth noting that there are also other reports of visions which are expanded by additions of new threats (see Amos 7:9 in connection with 7:1–8 and 8:3 as a gloss to 8:1f.).

The date when this was given a fixed written form: According to v. 1, this experience which is being described in chap. 6 took place in the year in which King Uzziah/Azariah died, which means, according to the chronology established above, p. 4, that the year would be 739. But one cannot presume that Isaiah put this report into writing immediately afterwards. The central message of "Isaiah's memorial record," for which chap. 6 serves as the prelude, is found in chaps. 7 and 8, in the prophet's proclamation during the time period of the Syro-Ephraimitic War. The call narrative has been placed, quite intentionally, immediately before the recounting of these events: Isaiah identifies himself here as one commissioned by Yahweh. The concept of hardening takes on a concrete reality when Ahaz refuses to believe (7:12); the proclamation about the devastation in 6:11bff. comes clear in the threats that the land will be depopulated by the Assyrians (7:17ff.). It is thus a strong possibility that 6:1–11 was not put into a written form until a long time after the call, possibly not until after the events of 733/32. It is possible that the very mention of the date in 6:1 serves as an indicator that it was written down at a time quite far removed from the actual experience. It is also a possibility that there was an earlier attempt to write this down, being shaped in its present form only at this later date. In any case, this much is clear: Chap. 6 does not furnish us with the exact minutes which describe a conversation between God and Isaiah. "At least half of all narrated visions are artificially composed, but that does not mean they are untrue or just plain fiction" (Duhm). The exegetical study must keep in mind the question about whether the present formulations may have taken shape within the framework of the impressions which deepened over a long period of time, during which the prophet found little positive response (see Fohrer, 21f.).

Commentary

[6:1] Concerning dating based on the year of a king's death, see 14:28. "The way in which the prophets give the exact time at which they received certain revelations, dating them by events in the historical and political world, and thereby emphasizing their character as real historical events, has no parallel in any other religion" (von Rad, *OTTheol* II [1965] 363). Isaiah stands at a particular point in time in the development of the history of Israel, and his message is specifically for its own historical time frame. The year of Uzziah's death is not the same as the first year of the reign of his successor, Jotham, since the latter was a co-regent with his father already from 750/49 on (see above, p. 4). It may be precisely because of this complication (which misled the author of 2 Kings 15:32, so that he placed Jotham's accession to the throne in Pekah's second year) that it seemed preferable to Isaiah to date the event by the death of Uzziah instead of by the particular year of Jotham's reign. The death of this important person Uzziah, who had guided the destiny of Judah for such a long time, but who was afflicted with leprosy, was certainly an event which would not have quickly faded from the minds of the people. There is no way to tell whether the call took place before or after the death of the king. Officially, the year in which a king died was still fully reckoned as one of the years of his reign. One can find no apparent reason for this king being called Uzziah here and in some other places, but in still other places being known as Azariah. Concerning the name Uzziah, see above, pp. 2, 5. It is possible that Azariah is the king's official throne name (see H. Wildberger, "Die Thronnamen des Messias, Jes. 9:5b," *TZ* 16 [1960] 314–322). One chooses the best course if one does not look for some inner connection between the death of the king and the call, concluding possibly that the prophet's experience could be explained as having been occasioned by the impression which the death of the king made upon him (see also M. Buber, *Der Glaube der Propheten* [1950] 181f.). There were no particularly important events on the international political scene in 739. Tiglath-Pileser III (745–727) was already past the initial difficulties of his reign, but had not yet made his appearance at the border of Israel. The prophecies from Isaiah's early period of activity (chaps. 2, 3, 5) show that he was not particularly agitated because of any external political threat against either Israel or Judah; during the first period of his activity, he was most deeply upset by the pride and unbelief, the general degeneracy and the lack of accountability which was so apparent in the leaders. One ought not even raise the question about what could have caused this experience for Isaiah. For him, it had its source in the intervention of the hand of God into the normal course of events in his life (see 8:11), something which could be given no logical explanation.

⸢By using ראה (see), Isaiah has in mind a visionary type of event. The ראֶה is the seer and/or the vision itself (28:7; see 30:10 ראֹים, seers, parallel to חזים, prophets, visionaries). The verb ראה can certainly mean "see a vision" (1 Kings 22:19; Amos 7:8; 9:1; Jer. 1:11, 13; Zech. 1:8, and often elsewhere; cf. also the *hiph'il* in Amos 7:1, 4, 7, and often elsewhere). The fact that the narrative is composed using a long-established form and employing specific concepts and motifs, particularly from the Jerusalem cult theology, should in no way be used in an attempt to deny that the report describes something which was actually experienced.

⸸   ⸢Scholarship has expended a great deal of energy in trying to answer the question about what type of a visionary event the prophet saw, i.e., which category of religious psychology might possibly be used to explain what happened. As a result of such discussion, the following must be clearly said: The prophets were not ecstatics in the sense that they were somehow robbed of their normal state of consciousness (see G. Hölscher, *Die Propheten* [1914], and J. Lindblom, *Prophecy in Ancient Israel* [1963²]); they were also not actual mystics, in the sense that they experienced an *unio mystica* (mystical oneness) (cf. H. W. Hines, "The Prophet as a Mystic," *AJSL* 40 [1923] 37ff.)⸴ On still another front, one does not do them justice if one attempts to describe their experience by using the analogy that this was a poetic vision (as does J. Hänel, *Das Erkennen Gottes bei den Schriftpropheten* [1923] 96f., who speaks of the prophet experiencing an "inner seeing" and an "inner hearing," p. 86)! The term "ecstasy" is an inadequate one, since the prophet remains completely in a state of normal consciousness; for the same reason, "mystic" is inadequate, since the human being and God stand opposite to one another, a distinction which is not in any way blurred when the prophet experiences this; also, to categorize this as some type of poetic inspiration is inadequate, since the prophet experiences the vision not only in the sense of an inner conviction, but as a *visio externa* (an actual external vision), something which comes to him. It is very clear that it is not to be confused with something which happens in one's own psyche. "In no way can one do away with the actual content of what is presented by accenting the trans-subjective character, accenting that something comes from Yahweh; therefore, it is not correct to suggest that one's own personal conviction is simply being intertwined with divine thoughts and plans which are somehow being revealed" (Seierstad, op. cit., 221). If one thinks that the "seeing" might really refer to an *inner* seeing, one must recognize that v. 5 clearly maintains ("... for *my eyes* have seen the king, Yahweh of Hosts), that Isaiah is talking about a *visio corporalis* (an actual vision), no matter what approach we might use to try to explain what happened. Along with everything else, one must recognize that the "vision" of God is surely not an end in itself. Completely lacking is any description of what the prophet sees: The prophet does not provide a visual sketch of Yahweh; rather, he mentions nothing more than the hem of his royal robe. The seraphim are not described either; the only reason the three pairs of wings are mentioned is because covering face and feet with wings helps demonstrate the impressive nature of the divine holiness, so that one might find a way to say that they reflected the divine holiness. We find out so little about the היכל (palace, temple) that commentators cannot even agree about whether the divine presence, of which Isaiah gets a glimpse, is located in the earthly sanctuary or in the heavenly palace of the king (see below, pp. 271f.). There is, in fact, mention of the כבוד (glory), but not as one would actually expect during a vision, describing how glory streams forth from God and blinds the one who looks on. What Isaiah sees is only preparatory to his call, which is communicated to him in a clear message which sent him forth to serve.

Even though there is no attempt to describe Yahweh's appearance, yet his throne is mentioned. It is a throne with steps (cf. 1 Kings 10:18ff.; on this, see K. Galling, *JPOS* 12 [1932] 44f.; *BRL* 526f.; *BHH* 1976). It corresponds to Isaiah's concept of God, since it is high and lofty. (However, Baal, in Ugarit, also sits upon a majestic throne; see I AB I 31ff.) When Yahweh is depicted sitting upon such a throne, he is presented as king; cf. 40:22; in v. 5, he is actually called מלך (king), Yahweh of Hosts. It has often been maintained that Isaiah 6 is the oldest passage, which can be dated with certainty, which refers to Yahweh as king (A. von Gall, BZAW 27 [1914] 152, and Eissfeldt, op. cit., 104). Yet, both implicitly and explicitly, the concept about Yahweh's kingdom is much older. Already when mention is made of the ark, one basically deals with the concept of Yahweh's kingdom (see O. Eissfeldt, "Silo und Jerusalem," VTSup 4 [1957] 138–147; see 143f.; J. de Fraine, "La royauté de Yahvé dans les textes concernant l'arche," VTSup 15 [1966] 134–149). Concerning the age of the concept of God as king, cf. H. Wildberger, *Jahwes Eigentumsvolk*, ATANT 37 (1960) 20ff.; 80ff.

Basically, there are two separate series of concepts which must be distinguished when one speaks about how Yahweh functions as a king in the OT: The first way speaks about Yahweh exclusively as king of Israel (Exod. 19:6; Num. 23:21; Deut. 33:5; Ps. 114:2). As such, he is the leader of the people; he goes ahead, leading them into battle, and yet he also protects them as rear guard (Isa. 52:12). The second way considers Yahweh as the king of the gods (Pss. 95:3; 96:4f.; 97:9; see also Jer. 10:10), lord of the cosmos (Ps. 47:8f.; Psalm 93; Psalm 97; see also Ps. 29:10), ruler over the peoples (Pss. 47:3f.; 96:10; 99:1f.; see also Mal. 1:14), and as the great judge over the whole world (Pss. 96:13; 97:8; 98:9). As such, he established his throne in heaven, from which place he rules over absolutely everything (Ps. 103:19). Isaiah clearly follows this second pathway, which is not surprising, since the concept of the divine king who sits upon his throne and is surrounded by his heavenly counselors must have begun and been developed right in Jerusalem. Already in the words of dedication for the temple, 1 Kings 8:13, Solomon says that Yahweh had erected a dwelling which would serve as a place for his throne throughout eternity. Once again, it is in the "enthronement psalms" that one finds more about Yahweh's enthronement than anywhere else (47:9; 89:15; 93:2; 97:2). If not these exact songs, Isaiah certainly knew similar hymns which praised Yahweh as king. The מלך-title (king) is a very ancient one for the deity who was right in Jerusalem and goes back into the era before Israel came on the scene, as shown by the name Melchizedek. In the Ugaritic texts, *mlk* is primarily an attribute of El (cf. Schmidt, op. cit., 306f.), and it is not just by chance that, in Psalm 29, which has been recognized as having many Canaanite elements (see above, p. 114), mention is made of Yahweh being enthroned for- ever. Israel adopted from Canaan not only the general concept of an assembly of the gods but also most specifically the idea of a king ruling over all the gods, including particular details which are connected with this title. Psalm 24 provides evidence for this very significant process, where מלך הכבוד (King of glory) is explicitly used parallel with יהוה צבאות (Yahweh of Hosts). It fits right into the context of the general view within the ancient Near East that Yahweh's kingdom, in these texts, is always seen as one which does not change: God is enthroned from eternity to eternity, and the seraphim make it known that the entire earth is filled with Yahweh's glory. There is no hint of a suggestion that Yahweh's rule was to be understood as an eschatological dominion.

Even though this is an ancient concept, the OT uses it amazingly infrequently as a royal title for Yahweh. Isaiah's contemporaries Amos and Hosea do not use it at all, and the idea that Yahweh is king in Zion is found in Jeremiah only as a quote from the mouth of the complaining people, 8:19. Micaiah ben Imlah does speak of Yahweh's throne, but avoids using the royal titles. The reason for this astonishing reticence must be sought in the defensive attitude over against the Canaanite thought world and the cultic customs, particularly those connected with the מלך-concept (king), and especially those related to the Molech cult in Jerusalem. But Isaiah had the inner freedom to use this concept in spite of these drawbacks. This bold integration of the Canaanite, ancient Near Eastern concept of the kingdom of God showed itself to be a most impor- tant step for the future development of the description of faith in Yahweh within Israel (see Maag, op. cit.).

For Isaiah, Yahweh is elevated so high that just the hem of his royal mantle fills the entire היכל (palace). It is quite easy to understand how God, as king, would be clothed with a robe, which would serve to indicate that he was deemed worthy to rule (concerning the earthly king, see Jonah 3:6). According to Ps. 104:1, Yahweh is clothed with הוד (honor) and הדר (majesty) and wraps himself in light as if within a robe. According to Ps. 93:1, גאות (majesty) and עז (strength) are his garment. One can hardly say that Isaiah is simply using an anthropomorphism when he mentions Yahweh's "robe." The prophet sees Yahweh en- throned in the היכל (palace). It may be because there was a foreign source for the idea about the heavenly council that he does not speak of the בית יהוה (house of Yahweh) but rather uses the foreign term (Akkadian: ekallu, "palace"; Sumerian: é-gal, "big house"). In Hebrew, the word serves not only to designate the (royal) palace, as in Akkadian, but also the temple or, more precisely, its central chamber, which is more specif- ically called היכל קדשך (thy holy temple) in Pss. 5:8; 79:1; 138:2, and often elsewhere. But היכל (palace) can also mean the heavenly dwelling place of the deity. This is already the case in Ugarit; in their mythology, the construction of the palace for the deities plays a very important role (see J. Gray, *The Legacy of Canaan*, VTSup 5 [1965²] 48ff.; W. Schmidt, *Königtum Gottes in Ugarit und Israel*, BZAW 80 [1961] 56ff.), but it is also important in the "Canaanite" Psalm 29 (9), in Ps. 11:4 and Mic. 1:2f., and in Ps. 18:7 and Hab. 2:20 as well. The פתחי עולם (ancient doors), through which Ps. 24:7, 9 says the king of glory enters, may actually refer to the "gates of heaven" (H. J. Kraus, *Psalmen* BK XV/1 [Engl: *Psalms 1–59*]). The reason why היכל can refer to both the earthly sanctuary of God and also his heavenly royal palace can be explained by the fact that the temple is a copy of the heavenly original, Exod. 25:9, 40, and cf. Gen. 28:10–17. It is by no means clear, as is presumed by the majority of the exegetes, that Isaiah is speaking of the temple in Jerusalem. Based on the form-historical parallels in 1 Kings 22:19 and Ezek. 1:1 ("the heavens were opened, and I saw visions of God"), but also Genesis 28 and Psalm 29, it would seem much more likely that the heavenly dwelling place is meant (interpreted thus, among recent commentators, by Fischer, König, Fohrer, and Wright; cf. also Engnell, op. cit., 27f.). That would seem to mean that it is also necessary to conclude that Yahweh lives in heaven. Of course, most likely making use of a liturgical formula, Isaiah also speaks about Yahweh "whose fire is in Zion, and whose furnace is in Jerusalem" (31:9), which means, however, that he has control over a place there, which is used for offerings and living quarters; this employs the certainly much more ancient formulation: יהוה צבאות השכן בהר ציון (Yahweh of Hosts who dwells upon Mount Zion), 8:18; cf. 1 Kings 8:13. And yet, the heavenly and earthly dwelling places of God being mentioned next to one another (see G. von Rad, *TDNT* V, 502–509; for Ezekiel, see W. Zimmerli, BK XIII/1, 46 [Engl: *Ezekiel 1,* 116]) does not disprove the approach which interprets היכל as the heavenly palace of Yahweh the king; to try to distinguish between an earthly and a heavenly sanctuary attempts to make a distinction which the ancient person would never have attempted. God dwells in heaven, but he is also present in the sanctuary (see Habel, op. cit., 310, note 29). But the specific manner in which Isaiah depicts this scene yields evidence that would lead one to conclude that the prophet actually did experience this vision of his at the entrance to the temple in Jerusalem. He speaks about the shaking of the door pivots in the door sills and about the glowing coals from the altar of incense. But, within his vision, his view extends farther out into the heavenly realm.

[6:2] The ark is located within the holy of holies in the Jerusalem temple, the דביר, and upon it the two cherubim are situated. Whether the ark itself is the chair of Yahweh's throne, or whether Yahweh, one of whose titles is ישב הכרבים (enthroned on the cherubim) (1 Sam. 4:4; 2 Sam. 6:2 = 1 Chron. 13:6; Pss. 80:2; 99:1; 2 Kings 19:15 = Isa. 37:16; cf. 1 Chron. 28:2; Pss. 99:5; 132:7; Lam. 2:1), sits upon the cherubim (see de Vaux, op. cit.), he is enthroned, invisible, in the holy of holies. Should one get the idea that the doors of the דביר (holy of holies) swing open before Isaiah in his vision (1 Kings 6:31f.) and that he sees the otherwise invisible God enthroned? In this case, one would have expected that Isaiah would mention the *cherubim* on Yahweh's right and left but not that he would speak of a host of seraphim. Since the time of Origen, who interpreted the seraphim as the Logos and the Holy Spirit, the thesis has often been advanced that Isaiah speaks only about two "angels" (so also Vulg: *et clamabant alter ad alterum,* and they cried out, one to the other). It was very common in the ancient Near East for two beings to be put on the two sides of the king to serve as protecting deities (on this, see Engnell, op. cit., 34f.). And yet in his vision of the chariot throne, Ezekiel speaks about four living beings who look much like human beings. In 10:20, they are taken to be cherubim. But that only gives evidence that Ezekiel and his disciples were standing at a distance from the traditional motifs which are part of such a vision. We have understood Isaiah's vision to be a heavenly council of the divine king and to such belongs *a great number* of praising and serving beings. The seraphim are not protective deities, comparable to *Šēdu* and *Lamassu* positioned at the sides of a king's throne in the Babylonian region, but rather they serve the function of the "host of heaven," as in 1 Kings 22. They do not carry Yahweh's throne, as in Ezekiel, but they hover above him. One must distinguish, therefore, between cherubim and seraphim; we are not justified in presuming that the seraphim are nothing more than "*un-adjectif appliqué par Isaïe aux chérubins*" (one of the adjectives applied to the cherubim by Isaiah) (Steinmann, 38). That would not even work on the purely external level, since the cherubim in the דביר (holy of holies) have only *one* set of wings.

Of course, it is difficult to come up with an exact picture of the nature and appearance of the seraphim. Some have tried to derive their name from the verbal root שׂרף, "burn up," and to explain that they are fiery angels or purifying angels, in which case one can make reference to the act of purification in v. 6 (Delitzsch). Some have also suggested a connection with the Akkadian *Šarrabu* or *Šarrapu,* epithets of Nergal, the god of pestilence, but this should more likely be connected with the Hebrew שָׁרָב, "heat of the sun," Isa. 35:7; 49:10 (KAT³ 415). In the same way, one ought not attempt to discover the meaning by referring to the Arabic *šarif,* "noble," which supposedly refers to a member of the heavenly assembly (Koppe, Gesenius). It is more likely correct to connect it with the Egyptian *śfr,* "fabulous winged creature," as portrayed in a grave at Beni Hasan (*AOB* 392) (cf. the Demotic *serref* "griffin").

There are also other places where Isaiah mentions seraphim (14:29: שָׂרָף מְעוֹפֵף, flying serpent, parallel to נחש, serpent, and צפע, adder), so that one really ought not translate this as "serpent," as is done by KBL, but one ought to consider seraphim to be demons in the form of snakes, which carry on their activities in the desert. The same applies to 30:6, where the flying seraph is mentioned along with two types of lion and the otter and, as is also presumed in 14:29, this animal is even more sinister than the others which are mentioned. This same concept is also found in Num. 21:6 and Deut. 8:15; in both cases, the seraph is further identified as a נחש, serpent, and in Num. 21:8 Nehushtan is described as a seraph. Up to the time of Hezekiah, this emblem was found in the Jerusalem temple, 2 Kings 18:4. Isaiah must certainly have known about it and must have known that the "bronze serpent" was also called שׂרף (seraph). This may explain why the seraphim had become members of the heavenly host in his commissioning vision and why they served a completely different function than that found in the rest of the OT. No matter what the origin of Nehushtan in the history of religion had been, it had to be integrated into the Yahweh faith, after it found its proper home within the sanctuary in Jerusalem. That seems to have happened precisely because it was considered the representative of the heavenly host of Yahweh Sebaoth. From its origin as a sinister demon of the desert, it had become a heavenly being which proclaimed Yahweh's praise and stood ready to serve him.

Because of this transformation, its external shape may have also changed. According to Fohrer, the seraphim were a mixture of beings, with human heads and hands, but with the body of a serpent and a bird's wings; there would have been a merging of two very ancient concepts: the bird-human and the serpent-human (similar viewpoints are held by Procksch, Ziegler, Kaiser, et al.). They surely had wings, but that does not give one the right to conclude that the seraphim in our text also had the body form of animals (Kissane, H. Haag, *Bibellexikon* [1968²] 1580f.). Unfortunately, there are problems in verifying this archaeologically, since one must deal with the fact that there are several beings which are similar. The closest help for identifying Isaiah's description may come from a guardian angel found at Tell Halaf (*BRL* 384, 3 = *ANEP* no. 655 = *BHH* 1775; cf. also *ANEP* nos. 654, 656). It has three pairs of wings, but otherwise has the body of a human being. It holds a serpent with its two hands. As in similar cases, it seems that the human form becomes more pronounced and the animal form less so, although the symbolism connected with having an animal's body continues to play a role.

Though they have three pairs of wings, the seraphim need only one of the pairs for flight. With the second pair they cover their faces. At no time are the heavenly beings which surround Yahweh's throne to see his countenance, for whoever sees it must die. If that is true for the heavenly powers, it applies all the more to humans (cf. Exod. 33:20; Judg. 13:22). With the third pair of wings, the seraphim cover their feet. As in Exod. 4:25, Isa. 7:20 uses רגלים (feet) as a way to avoid mentioning the genital area (see גויה, bodies, Ezek. 1:11). "Covering up one's private parts brings one to the very ancient experience which linked sex with a feeling of guilt" (Kaiser). Originally, there must have been a completely different reason for them to have three pairs of wings, but now the motif is used to show that God had an exalted nature and thus possessed holiness, by means of which he clearly and fundamentally shows himself to be separate from all creatures: The way the seraphim act corresponds with the words in their song of praise.

[6:3] Without a doubt, the Trisagion was part of the liturgy in the Jerusalem cult. The adoration by the heavenly beings serve as a model for the adoration which the earthly community is to replicate, see Rev. 4:8; in the depiction of the adoration within the heavens there is also a call to the people of God on earth to follow suit. As in a responsive liturgy, the praise from one seraph (or seraph-choir) is passed on further by the next one. "Yahweh Sebaoth" is the cultic name applied to the god of Jerusalem (see above, commentary on 1:8–9 and, on this, cf. W. Kessler, *WZ* [Halle] 7 [1957/58] 767). "Sebaoth" makes particularly good sense in this acclamation scene, since the seraphim represent the צבא השמים (host of heaven) (for another view, see M. Liverani, *ZAW* 80 [1968] 99).

The heavenly beings proclaim Yahweh's exalted nature as they praise his holiness. As was noted above (commentary on 1:4), holiness, as a predicate referring to Yahweh, also has its origin in the adoration of El among the Canaanites. From there, it seems to have found an entrance into the cultic theology of Jerusalem, most obviously in the "enthronement psalms" (see Ps. 99:3, 5, 9, and cf. H. Ringgren, *The Prophetical Conception of Holiness,* UUÅ [1948] 12, 9ff.), whereas, in ancient Israel, the primary referent for holiness was Israel as the people of God (Exod. 19:6, and often elsewhere).

The attribute of the holiness of God is not mentioned nearly as often in the OT as one would expect when one considers the importance of this concept. Except for a very few passages (Hos. 11:9; Hab. 1:12; 3:3), God is never designated the Holy One by the pre-exilic prophets, and this does not even happen very often in the Psalms (22:4; 99:3, 5, 9; 1 Sam. 2:2, and see the passages mentioned above on p. 24 in connection with קדוש ישראל, Holy One of Israel; cf., in addition, 1 Sam. 6:20; Josh. 24:19). Isaiah also takes a risk here with this bold stroke, which some might have warned him not to take, suggesting instead that some other term might be used. In this way, he made a contribution to Israel's understanding of God which was not ever abandoned after that. Religious experience is, of course, everywhere and at all times a confrontation with the Holy One (see R. Otto, *The Idea of the Holy* [1917] [Engl: 1965⁸]). But even so, the question about what Yahweh's holiness actually meant for Isaiah cannot be avoided. Procksch says: "God's nature is set in opposition to the whole of created nature . . . , as the thrice holy [he] stands in an absolute tension with the world and all things worldly; because of the creaturely antithesis, the human being experiences fear, terror, dread, annihilation." One ought to be careful, first of all because of Hos. 11:9 ("holy, but not a destroyer"), not to take this concept of holiness from its use in a context of the history of religions and then simply apply it to Isaiah's understanding of God. Isaiah does not think, first and foremost, about the opposition between God and the world or between the creator and the creation. Israel is the people of Yahweh and his creatures have, as such, their own worth. Immediately after the thrice-holy is mentioned, it is made very clear that the "fullness of the earth" bears witness to Yahweh's honor. The seraphim who are uttering these praises and are certainly among those considered to be the creatures of Yahweh are not in any way shocked and filled with fear, but are rather deeply moved by the kingly majesty of their Lord. Isaiah does not tremble; this absence of trembling is not the result of his knowing how to keep his distance from God since he is a creature, but rather is the result of his having been moved to keep silent because of his "unclean lips." Yahweh's holiness is a completely dynamic reality, not a static "quality." It is seen in action when it destroys all the opposition which human beings set up over against God. It is his absolute will, his kingly majesty in the midst of his people, which will even cause him to be acknowledged by all the peoples of the world. This means that there is a very decisive modification of the concept of holiness over against what it was generally understood to mean by those who lived in the region around Israel and also in contrast to the way it is conceived in the history of religion studies, an alteration occasioned by Israel's understanding of God.

"If Yahweh Sebaoth is described, according to his inner nature, as קָדוֹשׁ (holy), then his 'glory' (כָּבוֹדוֹ) is the revealed side of his nature" (Procksch). The translation of כבוד is problematic. It is true that the word "glory" is meant in the sense of something which appears objectively, but, on the other hand, in passages such as the one before us, one cannot miss the point that it also means "honor," in fact, the honor which he appropriates for himself, the same as that which is offered to him by his creatures. One will not go wrong if one understands this passage in light of Ps. 19:1a, according to which the heavens tell of the honor of God— that is, give witness to his majesty. Since in that passage, according to v. 1b, the heavens which are the "work of his hands" proclaim the praise of God, naturally the earth and all which fills it can serve in the same way by functioning as witnesses. Ps. 29:1f. seconds this: Yahweh ought to receive "honor" since he reveals his "glory" in the thunderstorm; cf. Ps. 97:2–6. כבוד (glory, honor) belongs to the vocabulary which is used for both the earthly and heavenly kingdoms (see H. Wildberger, *TZ* 21 [1965] 481f.). For this very reason, Yahweh receives the designation מלך הכבוד (King of glory) in Ps. 24:8ff. (cf. אל הכבוד, God of glory, in Ps. 29:3). According to these passages, which all seem to be quite closely connected with Isa. 6:3, the concept about the כבוד (glory) of God also developed among the Canaanites. It is hardly just chance that the glory of El is mentioned in Ps. 19:1 (cf. Schmidt, op. cit., 308f.; R. Rendtorff, *Offenbarung als Geschichte*, BKuD 1 [1965³] 28ff.). But in Ps. 89:6a, in a single breath, mention is made of the "heavens" which declare the praise of Yahweh and the קהל קדשים (heavenly beings) and, according to Ps. 29:9, one of them calls out כבוד (glory!) in the היכל (temple), in the place where Yahweh is enthroned above the "flood." It is one of the main functions of the beings which surround Yahweh's throne that they proclaim his "glory." But we can recognize the way in which this has been recast here: According to Isaiah 6, the representatives of the host of the Holy One point out that everything which fills the earth is also involved in praising Yahweh's majesty. His כבוד (glory) can be seen in all the richness of its manifestations throughout the earth, all of which are the works of Yahweh. Ps. 97:6 says it in a similar way: "The heavens proclaim his righteousness; and all the peoples behold his glory"; cf. also Ps. 8:2, 10. Passages such as Deut. 33:16; Isa. 34:1; 42:10; Pss. 50:12; 96:11, and often elsewhere make it clear that "what fills the earth" is not only or even most specifically human beings or peoples; it is the living and nonliving cosmos, which speaks of the majesty of Yahweh, even though "there is no speech, nor are there words; their voice is not heard" (Ps. 19:4); cf. Rom. 1:20.

To a much greater extent than is true in Isaiah, Ezekiel used the occasion of the vision of the council surrounding the throne, speaking as it does about the KABOD of Yahweh, to set forth a new interpretation, in which the כבוד (glory) becomes the bodily form in which Yahweh appears (cf. Exod. 33:18, 22, but also 1 Kings 8:11). And, once again, in a very different way, Isa. 40:5 speaks—in recounting the vision which describes a call in a radically altered format—about the כבוד (glory) of Yahweh which is to be revealed. But, according to the context, this does not take place in the realm of nature, but in that of history; it is not visible at that very time but would make its appearance when the time of salvation broke upon the scene.

Therefore, in that example, the appearing of the כבוד (glory) of Yahweh is the main eschatological event. But even in liturgical texts, the appearance of the glory of Yahweh takes place within the context of future events (Pss. 57:6, 12; 72:19; see also Num. 14:21). One anticipates the time when the entire earth will be filled with the glory of God. That corresponds to the expectation that the kingdom of Yahweh, which according to the "enthronement psalms" is already somewhat present, would be completely visible in the time of salvation, which is still in the future; Isa. 52:7; 24:23. The "mythical-magical formula which was once part of the Canaanite thought world [was] completely transformed into historical-eschatological categories" (Maag, op. cit., 151).

[6:4] Because of the song of praise being sung by the seraphim, the door pivots of the door sills tremble violently and "the house" becomes filled with smoke. One must wonder about the source of the smoke; some think it is from the altar; Duhm, et al., think it is from the mouth of the seraphim, and Procksch has a still more detailed answer: The smoke is the condensed breath of those singing the praises. In reality, there is a mixture of elements from the "vision of the assembly around the throne" and from a depiction of a theophany (cf. 4:5 and see above, pp. 171ff.; in addition, see Ezek. 1:13f.; 10:4, and often elsewhere). The earth's shaking is part of a theophany. That is not specifically mentioned in the text, but the quaking of the door pivots in the door sill is most likely to be understood in this way. It is an open question whether "the entire aura of the Sinai-theophany" is still present in this passage (Maag, op. cit., 143; H. Schmid, *Judaica* 23 [1965] 250ff.).

[6:5] Isaiah feels himself being moved to join in the praise of the holiness of God and is also conscious of what a special privilege it is to be able to do that. But he also knows that he can only keep silent and senses that that is a most terrifying circumstance, uttering: "Woe is me!" Concerning אוי (woe), see above, p. 196. This terror is itself an element of the theophany (cf. Gen. 32:31; Exod. 3:6; Judg. 6:22; 13:22). Those who utter such a cry of woe about themselves are witnessing to the fact that their very existence is threatened, in fact, that the lament for one who has died can begin immediately for them (cf. Jer. 4:31; 45:3, and often elsewhere). It is therefore quite justified to use the traditional translation נדמיתי, "I am lost." The "woe is me" which Isaiah utters comes because of his thoughts about his guilt. He knows that he is "unclean as far as his lips are concerned" and sees that he suffers under the even heavier burden of dwelling in the midst of a people whose lips are not any less unclean. It was a widely accepted principle in the thought world of the ancients that the individual carried responsibility for the guilt of the collective whole and also felt personally accountable for that guilt. In other cases, טמא (unclean) is used to identify a cultic impurity. The one who was cultically impure was not allowed access to the sanctuary; in the most basic sense, someone with unclean lips was someone who had partaken of some unclean type of nourishment, so that such a person surely ought not be able to come into the presence of the deity in order to speak even a single word. But Isaiah uses the term in a transferred sense: His lips are unclean because they have spoken what is impure, untrue, possibly also because they have not spoken appropriately about God. One has to consider here the regulations which are part of the entrance liturgies (Psalms 15 and 24; Isa. 33:14b–16), which are, in some ways, formulated in a similar way: נקי כפים (clean hands) and בר־לבב (pure heart) in Ps. 24:4. They set the standard for who could gain access to the sanctuary, and it is worth noting that those coming to worship in the temple are to give evidence that they have fulfilled ethical demands. There is no mistaking the fact that the thought world of Psalm 24 is in the background as Isaiah formulates the description of how he experienced his call. One should note that v. 3 makes it very explicit that Zion is מקום קדשו (his holy place), that Ps. 15:1 calls it "Yahweh's holy hill," and that Isa. 33:14 even speaks of the devouring fire and the eternal flames which one must endure when coming before Yahweh. This at least provides the general background for making sense of the "unclean as far as his lips are concerned." The actual details which Isaiah has in mind in his confession must remain in the realm of speculation (cf. also H. J. Hermisson, *Sprache und Ritus im altisraelitischen Kult,* WMANT 19 [1965] 89f.). The parallel passages mentioned above make it clear that the "unclean lips" are not an allusion to offenses which the prophet himself committed. Just as the entrance liturgies remind one of just what type of God is to be encountered when one climbs the mount of Yahweh, it is also clear to Isaiah that he has seen, with his own eyes, not just any deity but the king, Yahweh of Hosts. The מלך הכבוד (king of glory) is the God of the ark of Israel and his holiness shows itself in his passionate zeal when dealing with all impurity. One must have an encounter with the Holy One of Israel in order to be able to measure the great weight of sin. Isaiah is not a preacher of morals, but rather a human being who speaks of judgment, based on his experience of being terrified when he was in the presence of the holy God, and therefore he is also aware that it is because of grace that he has been selected for service to this God, in spite of it all.

[6:6] This action of grace is portrayed by an action which removes the sinful condition. A seraph cleanses Isaiah's lips with a glowing coal. The tongs which it uses to take the coal from the altar are used in other cases to keep the fire going. Since the scene transpires within the היכל (holy place), this cannot refer to the altar of the whole burnt offering in the courtyard, but we have to presume it is the altar of incense in the main chamber of the sanctuary; cf. מזבח הקטרת, Exod. 30:27; 31:8, and often elsewhere. Our passage, of course, furnishes the first real evidence for this altar actually being within the Solomonic temple already at this time (see above, commentary on 1:13). It is true that, among the listed inventory for the sanctuary in 1 Kings 7:13–50, a מזבח הזהב (golden incense altar) is also listed (v. 48). Certainly there were glowing coals upon the altar of incense, upon which one could sprinkle incense at any time; cf. Lev. 16:12f. One could suppose that there were reconciliation acts being performed in the Jerusalem temple, in which the glowing coals from the altar of incense could have played a role as the means used to transmit cleansing power. Unfortunately, we know nothing about this; yet, one might refer to the similar rites which involved cleansing one from sin by using hyssop (Ps. 51:9; Num. 19:18) and the purifying of metal by means of fire (Num. 31:22f.). Whatever the seraphim or other beings who served might have to do in the heavenly temple as they surrounded the divine king, the service of the priests within the earthly temple included purification rites. If the seraphim were permitted to carry out the action of purifying Isaiah, then they did it as part of the responsibilities which they had been given by their lord. The act of removing sin (חטא *pi'el,* Ps. 51:9) is thus symbolic of divine forgiveness. As regards the removal of the sin, there was nothing the guilty prophet had to do in his own behalf.

[6:7] עון (guilt) and חטאת (sin) are often found together with one another (concerning this, see above, commentary on 1:4). The chiastic arrangement in v. 7b shows that the two terms are not completely synonymous. The singular חטאת (sin) designates, as the context makes clear, not simply an isolated, specific transgression but rather Isaiah's sinful nature as such. Individual sinful acts have created a permanent condition. In the same way, עון (guilt) is used in the singular, but refers to specific offenses which grow out of that condition and threaten the existence of the human being. This guilt is "softened" because the sins are "covered." The verb כפר (cover over) belongs to the vocabulary of the cult (see J. J. Stamm, *Erlösen und Vergeben im Alten Testament* [1940] 61ff.; cf. also G. R. Driver, *JTS* 34 [1933] 34–38), and it is used in this special sense for an act of expiation which is to remove bloodguilt (cf. O. Procksch, *TDNT* IV, 329, and J. Herrmann, *TDNT* III, 302ff.). The root meaning is "cover up," but this word is rarely used in secular settings (see the questionable passage Isa. 28:18). It is naturally not just by chance that Isaiah uses this exact verb in this place, since he is relating this to details of a well-known cultic rite. The *pi'el* of the verb is used when a human being or a priest is the subject, "making atonement"; on this, see Lev. 19:22. But one should also notice, that ונסלח לו (and shall be forgiven him) is added there, which means that the action of atonement, also in the priestly realm, is getting farther away from the context of magic and ritual, since here it requires divine forgiveness in order to become real. It can also be said that Yahweh himself brings about atonement, e.g. Deut. 32:43; 21:8. Wherever he acts in this way toward human beings, כפר can actually be translated "forgive," Isa. 22:14; Ezek. 16:63; Pss. 78:38; 65:4 (see J. Herrmann, *TDNT* III, 304); see also Ps. 79:9 and 2 Chron. 30:18. "Wherever God is the subject, there is no mention of any means; God's כִּפֶּר is pure grace, yet it has less to do with the forgiveness of a father than it does with a judicial deliverance from the punishment" (KBL). In any case, the glowing coal is no more important than are the seraphim as the means by which the grace is applied. But the fact that the atonement does not take place solely within the realm of the spoken word but, so to speak, takes place within a sacramental action serves to underscore the reality and authentic power inherent in this action.

[6:8] After Isaiah has been "atoned," he can become a tool for Yahweh, one who announces and carries out his will; out of *visio* proceeds *missio*. God's own voice is heard speaking: את־מי אשלח ומי ילך־לנו (Whom shall I send; who will go for us?). The formulation לנו (for us) presents difficulties and it cannot be just by chance that the Gk does not provide a word for word translation (πρὸς τὸν λαὸν τοῦτον, to this people). One must remain uncertain about whether it did this to avoid giving the impression that God was speaking with other beings around his throne. In any case, Yahweh never speaks about himself by using the plural of majesty and לנו (for us) is a remnant, left over from the concept that Yahweh was surrounded by a group of court advisers who served as ministering spirits, with whom he discussed matters of importance (cf. Gen. 1:26; 3:22; 11:7).

Naturally, God expects that Isaiah will declare himself ready to be sent. But one must understand that the history of traditions connected with the concept of the heavenly council dictated that this take the form of a question, not a direct command. The question is phrased exactly as the one mentioned above, on p. 255, in the Maqlû-text (*mannu lušpur*). God wants Isaiah freely to make a decision. Isaiah, unlike Jeremiah, has the impression that he is in no way being coerced or even forced into service. Just like a heavenly being, he freely declares his readiness to be sent out: "Here am I, send me!" But one must pay very careful attention when contrasting the narratives of Jeremiah's and Isaiah's calls, since the traditional material comes from different sources; one must take these factors into consideration before one draws conclusions about the psychological make-up of the prophets based on the disparity of their reactions (cf. Procksch: "The kingly, heroic elements show up already in his [Isaiah's] call"). But one also ought to recognize the different situation in which each prophet is confronted with the word of God which sent each of them forth: Isaiah has just viewed the imposing majesty of God and has been drawn up from the deep shock which had struck him down. Out of the deeply upsetting but at the same time freeing experience, Isaiah was able to declare his unconditional readiness.

[6:9] It should have been mentioned that Yahweh accepted Isaiah's offer. But that is obvious. The specifics of his commission are now given.

The commissioning is completed by using the short formula לך ואמרת (go and speak). It is used in this or some similar form also in the secular domain when a messenger is sent (cf. 2 Sam. 18:21; 1 Kings 18:8, 11, 14; 2 Kings 8:10), but it also is used when a prophet is commissioned (2 Sam. 7:5; 24:12; Isa. 20:2; 38:5; Jer. 2:2; 3:12, and often elsewhere). The question in v. 8, מי ילך־לנו (who will go for us?), already anticipates this formula for commissioning. The parallels, to which reference has been made, show that this is a very specific commission, which does not simply await some general statement about the goal of prophetic activity.

However, the content of the task which is to be completed, according to v. 9b, sounds utterly strange: "Hear continually, yet gain no insight, and see unceasingly, but do not achieve understanding!" First of all, it is astounding that the message would be directed toward "this people here." It is remarkable that Isaiah does not speak here about "Israel" or the "house of Jacob," or something similar. Jenni (op. cit., 337, note 32) points out that אמר (speak), in the prose of Isaiah, is always used elsewhere together with אל (to), insofar as it describes a direct conversation with another individual (7:3f.; 8:1, 3, 19), so that it is possible that the ל ought to be translated "against" or "concerning." But that is unlikely, since imperative address follows. Further, Isaiah certainly never spoke to the people in the way that Yahweh here speaks to Isaiah. In actual fact, this is not a threat, reproach, warning, or message of promise, but it is also not "a power-filled word, which works dynamically and takes effect, even if the people do not pay attention" (Jenni, op. cit., 337). The half-verse 9b more probably intends to characterize the people in the sense that they were lacking readiness to listen. Just as Isaiah is able to depict his opponents in other passages by placing words into their mouths which expose their innermost thoughts, here he formulates a message for the people which points out that Israel will respond with a harsh rejection of his message, even though it was never actually phrased quite that way. Essentially, v. 9b already serves to characterize the preceding העם הזה (this people); the direct address to the prophet begins already here, not first in v. 10a. Therefore, v. 10a can be directly linked with v. 9b, since the addressee changes only in a formal way. This makes clear once again that v. 9b is not to be construed as a final summary of the message of Isaiah. The ואמרת (speak) in v. 9a is there only because the narrative of the call of Isaiah is constructed on the basis of the pattern of a vision of the heavenly council, used to send a messenger out on a very specific task. The form, constructed in this way because it follows an established pattern, is replete with elements which describe an actual inaugural vision. What is most important is that the difficulty connected with this mission is clearly explained. Based on content, vv. 9f. are a very close parallel to Ezek. 3:4–9; cf. also Jer. 1:17–19.

Thus, Isaiah ought to know that he will have to be active among a people which indeed can "hear" and "see" but, as Ezekiel puts it into words, has a hard forehead and a stubborn heart and does not want to listen (3:6; cf. לא אבוא, would not hear, in Isa. 28:12; 30:9, 15). In the present passage, Isaiah of course says "not able to gain insight" and "not able to achieve understanding" (הבין and ידע). These two verbs are typical of the terminology he uses, both because of their basic meaning and because they are used together. In the final analysis, both terms are rooted in wisdom (see above, commentary on 1:2). The reproach is not simply that Israel does not pay attention to what the prophet says or does but rather that, in spite of all admonition which Yahweh delivers to Israel through his prophets, and in spite of all the deeds which take place in their midst, they do not find their way clear to basically live a "righteous" style of faith and life. It is important that the prophet does not only mention "hearing" but also "seeing"; it reminds one of 5:12b: "they do not pay attention to the activity of Yahweh and they do not observe the work of his hands."

[6:10a] In v. 10a, what follows is known as the "command for hardening." Since the discussion is about the ears hardening and the eyes sticking shut, this is linked to the parallelism of the "seeing" and "hearing" in v. 9b. Concerning the use of "eye" and "ear" together in the context of hardening, see Hesse, op. cit., 23ff. But, in the most important position, more important than either ear or eye, the heart is mentioned, לב, the "residence" of that insight and understanding which is identified as missing in v. 9b (concerning the relationship between ידע, learn, and בין, pay attention, with לב, heart, see, e.g., Prov. 8:5; see, in addition, F. Baumgärtel, *TDNT* III, 605–607; Köhler, *OTTheol,* 146; Eichrodt, *TheolOT,* 142ff.; Hesse, op. cit., 21f.). השמין לב (make the heart of this people fat) seems to be a phrase which Isaiah himself formulated (cf. Hesse, op. cit., 15f.). The meaning, which is given as "heart" in this passage, corresponds completely to the wisdom tradition, which is detected again and again in Isaiah. It is the highest goal of a pious Israelite to get a "*wise* heart" (Ps. 90:12; Prov. 16:23; 21:11, and often elsewhere).

The verb שעע (stick shut) is used only by Isaiah (see 29:9, and Hesse, op. cit., 14f.); the prophet seems to have had a sharp ear for detecting the phenomenon of hardening. But it was, of course, already noted by the Yahwist (Exodus 7ff.), who was not only able to say that the heart of the Pharaoh was hardened, but also that *Yahweh* had hardened it, 10:1 (J?). Other prophets, not just Isaiah, know very clearly that Israel is "hardened," even if they do not use this specific terminology for hardening. Such is the case, for example, in Amos 4:6–12, where the prophet asserts that after each blow which brought judgment Israel had not returned to Yahweh. It could easily be said here that the people "hardened their heart." But, because the judgment blows had not accomplished their purpose, Yahweh is still the one from whom the hardening comes. The hardening is not something which takes place in just one way: The expression that Israel's heart is "heavy" must be understood in a dialectical relationship with the statement that Yahweh has "made it heavy." It is very doubtful that Isaiah knew the tradition about the Egyptian plagues. But 9:7ff. shows that he was aware of historico-theological observations which contended that Israel became more and more entrenched in its opposition to God as a result of Yahweh's judgments. Yet, the harshness of the formulation in 6:10 is unique. However, as 9:7ff. shows, it would also be wrong for him not to recognize the polarity between Yahweh as the cause for hardening and Israel's own role in the hardening.

[6:10b] Even stranger than the command concerning the hardening, the continuation in v. 10b, which is introduced by פן (so that, lest), explains the purpose and goal for the commissioning which is to bring about the hardening. Israel is not to be able to see or hear; neither is it to gain insight. Isaiah must actually hinder them, so that they do not return and find salvation. There are other places where he reproaches the people for not paying attention to the deeds of Yahweh (5:12), and he calls upon the people to listen to Yahweh's word (1:10, and often elsewhere), certainly not intending that such a call to listen is supposed to simply hasten the hardening. He laments the fact that Israel does not want to listen (28:12, and often elsewhere). He certainly does hope for a return (30:15, and often elsewhere), even though he obviously knows that this return is simply never going to take place. The alternatives in 1:19f. are not only rhetorical, but are meant sincerely. Thus, basically, the actual results of Isaiah's activity would remain to be seen. But the actual behavior of Israel is such that the way to salvation is demonstrated over and over again to be an unreal possibility. It is for this reason that it is to be perfectly clear to the prophet that he would not be going in the wrong direction as he carried out his commission, even if his "success" is measured as nothing more than an ever-increasing hardening. Israel had to know that this result, which came after a period of prophetic proclamation, in no way had anything to do with whether Isaiah could legitimately claim that he was a messenger of Yahweh. Isaiah is not purely and simply a prophet of doom, but he had to learn that, things being what they were, there was nothing else to do but announce the judgment, making it publicly known that Israel was ripe for judgment, was indeed putting its own judgment into effect. Moreover, and precisely in this way, he would be a faithful servant of Yahweh.

[6:11] One can see that Isaiah did not consider himself, from the very beginning, to be a prophet of doom, since he raises the objection: "How long, Lord?" עד־מתי is an element in the song of lament and is frequently found in the communal laments. It is used especially in those cases when pressure from Israel's enemies is cause for lament (Pss. 74:10; 79:5; 90:13; 94:3, and often elsewhere). By means of the question, Isaiah brings out something about the dread which he faces as he ponders his task, that apparently also being an issue both for Jeremiah and Ezekiel (cf. S. H. Blank, *HUCA* 27 [1956] 81–92). But above all else: "In this question, one sees that there is a basic presupposition in Isaiah's faith up to this point, that the judgment imposed upon the people could not possibly be the final goal of God's journey with this people" (Jenni, op. cit., 339). But how else is Yahweh's answer to be understood? Does this simply invalidate Isaiah's basic understanding of the faith which he confessed up to that time? Does it say that nothing but complete destruction is to be expected (Fohrer)? In other words: Does עד אשר (until) focus upon the end of Israel or does it rather refer to the culminating point in time when total judgment would occur, at which time the salvation would also be set in motion? Since עד אשר (until) is an answer to the question עד־מתי (how long?), the second possibility must be presumed to be the correct one (see Jenni, op. cit., 331). And yet, the interpretation finally has much to do with an overall understanding of Isaiah, indeed of prophecy in general. Even though the cities are devastated and the countryside is deserted, this does not yet mean that there is no longer an Israel and that the election has become meaningless. Yet, one must keep in mind that God says absolutely nothing at this point about what would "follow after." The passage deals only with the fact that it is to be clear to Isaiah that he must persist until Yahweh's wrath had ceased its raging.

The answer provided to the prophet announced a catastrophe involving war, without saying it in so many words. In fact, the form has points of contact with 5:9, where it is said that "*many* houses" would be laid waste (on this, cf. also 1:7). Ancient threats within curses, scheduled to take effect in case the covenant was broken, resonate here as well. Isaiah would not be able to count on the people taking this seriously until the curse which had been threatened from ancient times, and which was recently activated once again by Isaiah, had taken its course. The downfall of Samaria made this proclamation real for Israel; when Sennacherib marched against Jerusalem, it became real for Judah.

[6:12] In the first addition, there is clear reference to a deportation. This message comes most likely from the time after 721, as the population in the Northern Kingdom suffered its most severe losses and the land itself was treated very harshly. One notices that the technical term for exile, גלה in the *hiph'il*, is not used here but rather the very general term רחק (carry off) *pi'el*. But the use of the *hiph'il* of רחק in Jer. 27:10 and Ezek. 11:16 shows that this also does refer to a deportation of the population. עזובה (forsaken) is used otherwise to describe an abandoned, divorced wife (60:15; 62:4), but can very easily be used, as these same passages demonstrate, metaphorically to refer to a city or a country.

[6:13a, bα] This is apparently intended as a warning, issued after Israel ceased to exist, to deny credence to the illusion that, because judgment had taken its effect upon Israel, Judah was a "remnant," at a safe distance from all the threats. This interpretation, of course, depends upon taking עשירה (tenth) as a play on words, referring to Judah. It is a widely held theory that Judah constituted one tenth of all of Israel; cf., for example, 1 Sam. 11:8: Saul musters his troops; there are 300,000 Israelites and 30,000 Judeans (see also 2 Sam. 19:44; 1 Kings 11:31; see Engnell, op. cit., 51). And yet it is possible, in light of Amos 5:3 and 6:9, that it simply describes a very severe decimation of the people.

There is wide disagreement about the interpretation of the details, being explained by many exegetes on the basis of textual emendations which are unsure at best. Since it is hardly feasible to explain this as having to do with the destruction of a cultic high place (see above, textual note 13b–b), one would do well to attempt an interpretation on the basis of the MT. What we have is imagery of a shoot from a root, which sprouts once again after a tree has been felled. Such a shoot from a root is a symbol of the indestructible life force; see Job 14:7–9. Judah certainly seemed to be such a "tree stump," after the catastrophe which befell its relatives or possibly even after the end of the rule of the Davidic dynasty, when there remained the hope that new shoots could sprout. The author of this section destroys such a confidence. After the one who felled the trees had finished his work, the pasturing animals which grazed would complete the destruction by nibbling all new growth down to the bare ground (see textual note 13a).

This sentence (13a, ba) does not leave any room for a time of salvation in the future. It has played a fatalistic role in exegesis, insofar as it has been used by those who suppose that this provides evidence for Isaiah being exclusively a preacher of destruction, finally expecting Israel's complete extermination. When even the new growth which sprouts from the root of a tree is destroyed, then the final end of that tree is plain to see. But vv. 12, 13a, ba, 13bβ are not from Isaiah, and the gloss in v. 13bβ is a conscious attempt to make a correction, a protest against an exegesis which seeks to characterize Isaiah as one who is to proclaim the absolute end of Israel.

[6:13bβ] The promise is along the same lines as 4:3, according to which those who remain upon Zion will be "holy." As in that passage, the final observation in Isaiah 6 leads one to think about the eschatological community. The presence of God, or at least that of his "glory," would reject any dimming of the prospects that salvation would finally come. The expression "seed of holiness" is certainly unique but, with other vocabulary and in different circumstances, the "idea of a remnant" is already incorporated into the call narrative. According to the ancient creed, Israel is an עם קדש (holy people) (see H. Wildberger, *Jahwes Eigentumsvolk,* ATANT 37 [1960] 95ff.). Here it is attested: The promises which had been given to them were not robbed of their power by the catastrophe of the judgment; they would still be fulfilled in the future time of salvation.

Purpose and Thrust

In Isaiah's call, his task is clearly described within the context of one commissioned by Yahweh. The events which accompany the depiction of the council which surrounds the throne of the heavenly divine king are most adaptable for bringing out the point that the prophet has complete authority. As a messenger of Yahweh, he had been given the opportunity to have access to the council of Yahweh and knew that he was not only sent to declare the will of his God on earth, but he was also able to set it in motion. The word which he was to proclaim would bring about what it was intended to accomplish—if not for life, then for death (cf. 2 Cor. 2:15f.). Just as the word of the Holy One of Israel manifested itself for him personally in the act of atonement and accomplished what was intended by the declaration of forgiveness, it would also be able to, and of necessity would have to, effect a hardening among the people who were no longer able to hear, leaving no room for hope. Any apparent breakdown in carrying out his task, even a manifest failure as one who called for repentance, would not be enough to call his ἐξουσία (authority) into question. Because of his commissioning, the prophet was able to stand in absolute freedom, in which he was completely unaffected, whether his message would find agreement from others or not, even if these human beings were the ones who so highly prized the Israelite traditions of salvation. Finally, he considered himself responsible only to the living God, Yahweh of Hosts, whom he had seen with his own eyes.

Therefore, at the beginning of his report, which gives an account of his activity, there is a description of how it came about that he was Yahweh's messenger. If someone does not pay attention to these indicators, which are at the beginning of the entire section recounting what the prophet has to say, then there will be little prospect for such a person to understand the prophetic message. It has been made clear that it is obviously not possible to take all the events about which Isaiah speaks and satisfactorily explain them psychologically. But even if that would be possible, the secret of the revelation of God would still remain, which the prophet does not seek to "explain" but only to attest. Even with his "proof of his legitimacy," the prophet is aware of the fact that whoever agrees with his claims will do so by bowing down before the reality of the holy God, a reality that has been demonstrated. It is a most amazing turn of events that a prophet like Isaiah could risk making the demand that people should acknowledge that he was sent at the very same time that he is proclaiming so bluntly that he would in no way try simply to be an advocate for that which his people held to be religiously adequate reverence toward God (see 8:11–15) or for what was generally considered to be acceptable truth concerning faith.

But just as Isaiah does not call attention to any office which could be used to establish his authority and which could have been connected with managing Israel's religiously prized faith traditions, just as clearly he is still a son of Jerusalem who in no way denies his own historical circumstances. What Israel had inherited, in which he also had a stake, had not only shaped the way he spoke, but had also—and certainly in a way even greater than he could anticipate—shaped his own experience. One would certainly be able to say that the deepest relationship, the context in which Isaiah lived, the decisive point at which one begins if one wants to understand him in relation to that which had been given to Israel—all that is also for him the world of the Yahweh amphictyony. At the beginning this is not patently clear. But the elements are already there which belong to the portrayal of a theophany (5), most clearly in the threat of judgment in v. 11, which brings into the present the curses of the ancient covenant tradition. No matter how much one can point out the elements of the Jerusalem cult tradition, as done above, which finally have their source in the Canaanite era of the city's history, it is still very clear that it is the God from Sinai whom Isaiah encounters.

Because he stood so firmly within the context of what was central to Israel's "knowledge of God," it was still possible for him, with great freedom, to adapt traditional elements within his description of God, even though the "foreign" origin can still be detected. The concept of the holiness of Yahweh is filled with new meaning when compared with the way the tribal league experienced God. This reinterpretation of the "transferred" concept about the holiness of God is apparently done by Isaiah with intentionality, since he also speaks elsewhere about Yahweh as the Holy One of *Israel.* Concerning the broader history of Israel's belief in God, in addition to the accent placed on the holiness of God, what is of chief importance is Isaiah's portrayal of the kingdom of the Most High God, well-known in the ancient Near East, which is used as he depicts the details of his call. Here a widely known representative of Israel attests to the existence of the βασιλεία τοῦ θεοῦ (kingdom of God) in a very important setting. In this way, an element was introduced into the way God was described, an element which could most exquisitely describe the nature and power of Yahweh. The reinterpretation is also most clear at this point: The מלך (king), Yahweh, is not the most high god for the region surrounding Israel, enthroned in far-removed majesty over the entire cosmos, praised in the abstract because of his nature. God reaches into the history of his people; however, even though he is the Holy One *of Israel,* it is not for the benefit of his people, but solely to deal in just measure because of what his holiness demanded. "Strange is his deed, alien is his work!" (28:21). Yahweh is not a deity like the other gods of the peoples or a projection of an earthly kingdom, predicated as existing in a transcendent realm. As the Holy One, he must also judge his people, precisely this people. The goal of history, whose lord is Yahweh, can be nothing less than the realization of the divine dominion. Though it is not obvious at the beginning, in the final sense this manifestation of the holiness of God also would result in salvation. In this way, the expander who added the final phrase was right when he said, in the short phrase in 13bβ, that the judgment would not bring about the final end. But since this conclusion is appended to vv. 12 and 13a, bα, which express in the harshest way possible that judgment has to be carried to its bitter end, one cannot miss the point in vv. 9–13 that the anticipated deliverance which would bring life out of death could be possible only if there would be a fresh action which would put the grace of God in force again. Isaiah himself would not have understood his own atonement any differently, as one can see in his "Woe is me, I must be silent."

It has been made clear for us that Ezekiel 1–3 formally has many points of contact which make it similar to our chapter. In spite of this, Ezekiel's description, detailing the visions of his call, is not dependent upon this passage. That which these two prophets have in common belongs to the structural elements in the genre. In Deutero-Isaiah (40:1–8), the elements are so pointedly modified that one would hardly think that it is dependent upon Isaiah. It is clear when one attempts to trace subsequent passages which could have been influenced by the vision of Isaiah that descriptions of call visions are anything but literary devices, intended to establish credence for the prophetic claim of being sent to proclaim the message of Yahweh. Instead, these are a written record of actual experiences which still permit one to detect individual traits of the personality of the person involved and the uniqueness of each one's historical experience.

That also applies even to the narrative of Paul's call, which in some ways reminds one of Isaiah 6 (see above, p. 253). But in the NT, the concept of God as enthroned, surrounded by beings, has been recast so that it is the community of the end time which sings God's praises (see Müller, op. cit., and his diss.). In this way, elements of traditional material originating with both Isaiah and Ezekiel have been fused together. The visions of the call of these two prophets both contain the imagery which deeply affected the way both synagogue and church conceptualized God as king in heaven, where his throne is located. On the other hand, one can also recognize from the NT that the young emerging church spent much time struggling with the theme of hardening. Isaiah 6 provided them an answer to the question about why their message did not gain acceptance, which they had seemingly hoped would occur (cf. Matt. 13:14f.; Mark 4:12; Luke 8:10; Acts 28:26f.; on this, see also Gnilka, op. cit.). They stayed with the rendering found in the Septuagint, which formulated the command for hardening as a statement about the hardness of heart. Only John 12:40 is aware of the fact that Isaiah saw God himself as the original source of the hardening. But in the very light of this NT use of the passage from Isa. 6:9f., one must be reminded that the prophet was not setting forth some general theory concerning hardness of heart; instead, within the context of his own call, he spoke about a particular historical situation for which Yahweh had brought him into his service to declare a harsh message which left no room for self-pity. It was for this situation that he had declared himself ready to serve.

Not Cowardice, but Faith!

Literature

Because of the abundance of the literature which has appeared concerning this section, no effort has been made to cite it in its entirety. Please consult the research summaries listed at the end of this section.

P. de Lagarde, "Kritische anmerkungen zum buche Isaias," *Semitica* I (1878) 1–23. H. Schmidt, *Der Mythos vom wiederkehrenden König im Alten Testament,* Schriften der Hessischen Hochschulen, Universität Giessen 1 (1925). J. Hempel, Chronik, *ZAW* 49 (1931) 151–154. E. G. Kraeling, "The Immanuel Prophecy," *JBL* 50 (1931) 277–297. K. Budde, "Das Immanuelzeichen und die Ahaz-Begegnung Jesaja 7," *JBL* 52 (1933) 22–54. W. C. Graham, "Isaiah's Part in the Syro-Ephraimitic Crisis," *AJSL* 50 (1934) 201–216. E. Hammershaimb, *The Immanuel Sign: Some Aspects of Old Testament Prophecy from Isaiah to Malachi* (1966) 9–28 (reprint from *ST* 3 [1951] 124–142). S. H. Blank, "Immanuel and Which Isaiah?" *JNES* 13 (1954) 83–86. J. J. Stamm, "Die Immanuel-weissagung," *VT* 4 (1954) 20–33. E. Würthwein, "Jesaja 7, 1–9. Ein Beitrag zu dem Thema: Prophetie und Politik," FS K. Heim (1954) 47–63. E. J. Young, "The Immanuel Prophecy. Isaiah 7:14–16," *Studies in Isaiah* (1955) 143–198. W. Vischer, "Die Immanuel-Botschaft im Rahmen des königlichen Zionsfestes," *TS Zürich* 45 (1955). E. Rohland, "Die Bedeutung der Erwählungstraditionen Israels für die Eschatologie der alttestamentlichen Propheten," diss. theol., Heidelberg (1956). J. Lindblom, *A Study on the Immanuel Section in Isaiah,* Scripta Minora Regiae Societatis Humaniorum Litterarum Lundensis 4 (1957–1958); see reviews of this in J. J. Stamm, *VT* 9 (1959) 331–333, and in W. Rudolph, *TLZ* 85 (1960) 916–918. H. W. Wolff, *Immanuel* (BibS(N) 23 (1959). M. Sæbø, "Formgeschichtliche Erwägungen zu Jes. 7:3–9," *ST* 14 (1960) 54–69. J. J. Stamm, "Die Immanuel-Weissagung und die Eschatologie des Jesaja," *TZ* 16 (1960) 439–455. M. McNamara, "The Emmanuel Prophecy and Its Context," *Scripture* 14 (1962) 118–125. H. W. Wolff, *Frieden ohne Ende,* BibS(N) 35 (1962). A. H. J. Gunneweg, "Heils- und Unheilsverkündigung in Jes VII," *VT* 15 (1965) 27–34. S. Herrmann, *Die prophetischen Heilserwartungen im Alten Testament,* BWANT 85 (1965). H. Kruse, "Alma Redemptoris Mater. Eine Auslegung der Immanuel-Weissagung Is 7:14," *Trierer TZ* 74 (1965) 15–36. J. Schildenberger, "Die jungfräuliche Mutter des Emmanuel," *Sein und Sendung* 30 (1965) 339–353. R. de Vaux, "Jérusalem et les prophètes," *RB* 73 (1966) 481–509. Th. Lescow, "Das Geburtsmotiv in den messianischen Weissagungen bei Jesaja und Micha," *ZAW* 79 (1967) 172–207. J. Becker, *Isaias—der Prophet und sein Buch,* Stuttgarter Bibelstudien 30 (1968) 30–32, and passim. J. J. Scullion, "An Approach to the Understanding of Isaiah 7:10–17," *JBL* 87 (1968) 288–300.

Concerning the text: K. Budde, "Isaiah vii. 1 and 2 Kings xvi. 5," *ExpTim* 11 (1899/1900) 327–330. O. H. Gates, "Notes on Isaiah 1, 18b and 7, 14b–16," *AJSL* 17 (1900) 16–21. E. Nestle, Miszelle, *ZAW* 25 (1905) 213–215. A. Brux, "Is 7,6," *AJSL* 39 (1922) 68–71. J. Fichtner, Mitteilung, *ZAW* 56 (1938) 176. J. Linder, "Zu Isaiah 7:8f. und 7:16," *ZKT* 64 (1940) 101–104. S. Speier, Notes, *JBL* 72 (1953) xiv. W. F. Albright, "The Son of Tabeel (Isaiah 7:6)," *BASOR* 140 (1955) 34–35. N. E. Wagner, "A Note on Isaiah vii 4," *VT* 8 (1958) 438.

Concerning the historical and topographical situation: J. Begrich, "Der syrisch-ephraimitische Krieg und seine weltpolitischen Zusammenhänge," *ZDMG* 83 (1929) 213–237 = *Gesammelte Studien zum Alten Testament,* TBü 21 (1964) 99–120. G. Dalman, *Jerusalem und sein Gelände,* BFCT 2/19 (1930). K. Budde, "Jesaja und Ahas," *ZDMG* 84 (1931) 125–138. H. J. Kraus, *Prophetie und Politik,* ThEx NF 36 (1952). E. Jenni, *Die politischen Voraussagen der Propheten,* ATANT 29 (1956). M. Burrows, "The Conduit of the Upper Pool," *ZAW* 70 (1958) 221–227. C. Schedl, "Textkritische Bemerkungen zu den Synchronismen der Könige von Israel und Juda," *VT* 12 (1962) 107–110. G. Brunet, "Le terrain aux foulons," *RB* 71 (1964) 230–239. J. McHugh, "The Date of Hezekiah's Birth," *VT* 14 (1964) 446–453. R. Martin-Achard, "Esaïe et Jérémie aux prises avec les problèmes politiques," *RHPR* 47 (1967) 208–224.

Concerning the topic of faith: A. Gamper, "La foi d'Esaïe," *RTP* NS 10 (1922) 263–291. J. Boehmer, "Der Glaube und Jesaja," *ZAW* 41 (1923) 84–93. S. Virgulin, "La 'fede' nel profeta Isaia," *Bib* 31 (1950) 346–364. C. A. Keller, "Das quietistische Element in der Botschaft des Jesaja," *TZ* 11 (1955) 81–97. S. Virgulin, *La 'Fede' nella Profezia d'Isaia* (1961) 27–49. R. Smend, "Zur Geschichte von האמין," in *Hebräische Wortforschung,* FS W. Baumgartner, VTSup 16 (1967) 284–290. H. Wildberger, "'Glauben', Erwägungen zu האמין," ibid., 372–386. Idem, "'Glauben' im Alten Testament," *ZTK* 65 (1968) 129–159.

Concerning the person of Immanuel and his mother: K. Thieme, "Vierzigjahrfeier der Eisenacher Erklärung und Jungfrauengeburt," *TBl* 11 (1932) 300–310, see 306ff. K. Budde, "Noch einmal, Dank an Karl Thieme," *TBl* 12 (1933) 36–38. A. E. Skemp, "'Immanuel' and 'The Suffering Servant of Jahweh'," *ExpTim* 44 (1932/33) 94–95. A. Schulz, "'Almā," *BZ* 23 (1935) 229–241. J. E. Steinmueller, "Etymology and Biblical Usage of 'Almah," *CBQ* 2 (1940) 28–43. J. Coppens, "La prophétie de la 'Almah," *ETL* 28 (1952) 648–678. B. Vawter, "The Ugaritic Use of GLMT," *CBQ* 14 (1952) 319–322. G. Delling, art., "παρθένος," B 1, *TDNT* V, 831–832. L. Köhler, "Zum Verständnis von Jes 7:14," *ZAW* 67 (1955) 249–258. G. Fohrer, "Zu Jes 7:14 im Zusammenhang von Jes 7:10–22," *ZAW* 68 (1956) 54–56 = BZAW 99 (1967) 167–169. H. Ringgren, *The Messiah in the Old Testament,* Studies in Biblical Theology 18 (1957). H. Junker, "Ursprung und Grundzüge des Messiasbildes bei Isajas," VTSup 4 (1957) 182–196. F. L. Moriarty, "The Emmanuel Prophecies," *CBQ* 19 (1957) 226–233. L. G. Rignell, "Das Immanuelszeichen," *ST* 11 (1957) 99–119. N. K. Gottwald, "Immanuel as the Prophet's Son," *VT* 8 (1958) 36–47. E. Jenni, art., "Immanuel," *RGG*³ III, 677–678. C. Vendrame, "Sentido Coletivo da Almāh (Is 7, 14)," *Revista de Cultura Biblica* 7/24 (1963) 10–16. G. Vella, "Isaia 7,14 e il parto verginale del Messia," *Il Messianismo,* Atti della XVIII Settimana Biblica (1966) 85–93. F. Montagnini, "L'interpretazione di Is 7,14 di J. L. Isenbiehl (1744–1818)," ibid., 95–104. F. Salvoni, "La Profezia di Isaia sulla 'Vergine' partoriente (Is 7,14)," *Ricerche Bibliche e Religiose* 1 (1966) 19–40. J. Coppens, "Le messianisme royal," *NRT* 90 (1968) 30–49, 225–251, 479–512, 622–650, 834–863, 936–975.

Concerning individual motifs: H. Guthe, "Zeichen und Weissagung in Jes 7:14–17," FS J. Wellhausen (1914) 177–190. A. Kaminka, "Die fünfundsechzig Jahre in der Weissagung über Ephraim Jes 7, 7–9," *MGWJ* 73 (1929) 471–472. T. E. Bird, "Who Is the Boy in Isaias 7:16?" *CBQ* 6 (1944) 435–443. S. H. Blank, "The Current Misinterpretation of Isaiah's She'ar Yashub," *JBL* 67 (1948) 211–215. M. Brunec, "De sensu 'signi' in Is 7,14," *VD* 33 (1955) 257–266, 321–330, and *VD* 34 (1956) 16–29. St. Porúbčan, "The Word *'OT* in Isaia 7, 14," *CBQ* 22 (1960) 144–159. K. H. Rengstorf, art., "σημεῖον," B 2, *TDNT* VII, 209–219. J. Scharbert, "Was versteht das Alte Testament unter Wunder?" *BK* 22 (1967) 37–42. S. Stern, "'The Knowledge of Good and Evil'," *VT* 8 (1958) 405–418. P. G. Duncker, "'Ut sciat reprobare malum et eligere bonum', Is VII 15b.," *Sacra*

Pagina 1 (1959) 408–412. H. D. Preuss, "'. . . ich will mit dir sein!'," *ZAW* 80 (1968) 139–173.

Summaries of research: A. von Bulmerincq, "Die Immanuelweissagung im Lichte der neueren Forschung," *Acta et Commentationes Universitatis Tartuensis (Dorpatensis)* B 37, 1 (1935) 1–17. J. J. Stamm, "La prophétie d'Emmanuel," *RTP* NS 32 (1944) 97–123. J. Coppens, "La prophétie d'Emmanuel," *L'attente du Messie* (1954) 39–50. J. J. Stamm, "Neuere Arbeiten zum Immanuel-Problem," *ZAW* 68 (1956) 46–53. J. Coppens, "L'interpretation d'Is., VII, 14, à la lumière des études les plus récentes," in *Lex tua Veritas,* FS H. Junker (1961) 31–45. J. Prado, "La Madre del Emmanuel: Is 7, 14 (Reseña del estado de las cuestiones)," *Sefarad* 21 (1961) 85–114. B. Kipper, "O Problema da Almâh nos Estudos Recentes," *Revista de Cultura Biblica* 7/25–26 (1963) 80–92, and NS 1 (1964) 180–195.

[Literature update through 1979: J. Bright, *The Authority of the Old Testament* (1967), 219–226. W. McKane, "The Interpretation of Is 7, 14–25," *VT* 17 (1967) 208–219. N. Lohfink, *Bibelauslegung im Wandel* (1967). J. Lust, "The Immanuel Figure: A Charismatic Judge-Leader. A Suggestion Towards the Understanding of Is 7,10–17 (8,23—9,6; 11,1–9)," *ETL* 47/3–4 (1971) 464–470. E. Bouzon, "A Mensagem Teoiógica do Immanuel (Is 7,1–17)," *REB* 32/128 (1972) 826–841. O. H. Steck, "Beiträge zum Verständnis von Jes 7,10–17 und 8,1–4," *TZ* 29 (1973) 161–178. Idem, "Rettung und Verstockung. Exegetische Bemerkungen zu Jesaja 7,3–9," *EvT* 33 (1973) 77–90. G. del Olmo Lete, "La profecía del Emmanuel (Is 7,10–17). Ensayo de interpretación," *EphMar* 23 (1973) 345–361. G. Barrois, "Critical Exegesis and Tradition Hermeneutics. A Methodological Inquiry on the Book of Isaiah (7; 40–55; 56–66)," *Eisegeseis Protou Orthodoxou Hermeneutikou Synedriou* (1973) 151–173. H. W. Hoffmann, *Die Intention der Verkündigung Jesajas,* BZAW 136 (1974) 59ff. G. Brunet, *Essai sur l'Isaïe de l'histoire: Études de quelques textes, notamment dans Is 7,8 et 22 (I. L'Emmanuel; II. Le Siloé)* (1975). E. Testa, "L'Emmanuele e la Santa Sion," *FrancLA* 25 (1975) 171–192. J. Homerski, *Piesni Izajasza o Emmanuelu,* Studia Theologica Varsaviensia 14/2 (1976) 13–46. F. Huber, *Jahwe, Juda und die anderen Völker beim Propheten Jesaja,* BZAW 137 (1976), see esp. 10–34. G. Rice, "The Interpretation of Isaiah 7:15–17," *JBL* 96 (1977) 363–369. Idem, "A Neglected Interpretation of the Immanuel Prophecy," *ZAW* 90 (1978) 220–227.

Concerning the text: W. Watson, "Shared Consonants in Northwest Semitic," *Bib* 50 (1969) 525–533.

Concerning the historical and topographical situation: S. Mittmann, "Das südliche Ostjordanland im Lichte eines neuassyrischen Keilschriftbriefes aus Nimrūd," *ZDPV* 89 (1973) 15–45 (concerning Tabeel). A. Vanel, "Ṭâbe'él en Is. VII 6 et le roi Tubail de Tyr," VTSup 26 (1974) 17–24.

Concerning the topic of faith: N. H. Ridderbos, "Enkele beschouwingen naar annleiding van ta'aminū in Jes 7,9," FS W. H. Gispen (1970) 167–178.

Concerning the person of Immanuel and his mother: N. Lohfink, "On interpreting the OT (Is 7:14)," *TD* 15 (1967) 228–229. B. E. Jones, "Immanuel: A Historical and Critical Study," diss., Univ. of Wales (1966/67). R. Kilian, *Die Verheissung Immanuels, Jes 7,14,* SBS 35 (1968). M. Rehm, *Der königliche Messias* (1968). J. N. Carreira, "Is 7,14: Da Exegese à Hermenéutica," *Theologica* 4/4 (1969) 399–414. R. Kilian, "Die Geburt des Immanuel aus der Jungfrau," *Jungfrauengeburt* (n.d.) 9–35. R. W. Neff, "The Announcement in Old Testament Birth Stories," diss., Yale (1969), *Diss.Abs.* 30 (1969/70). J. A. Motyer, "Context and Content in the Interpretation of Is 7:14," *TynBul* 21 (1970) 118–125. J. Sancho-Gili, "Sobre el sentido mesiánico de Is 7,14. Interpretaciones bíblicas y magisterales," *CB* 27 (1970) 67–89. H. Gese, "Natus ex virgine," FS G. von Rad (1971) 72–89. H. L. Ginsberg, "Immanuel (Is 7,14)," *EJ* 8 (1971) 1293–1295. R. Kilian, "Prolegomena zur Auslegung der Immanuelverheissung," FS J. Ziegler (1972), pt. 2, 207–215. H. M. Wolf, "A Solution to the Immanuel Prophecy in Isaiah 7:14—8:22," *JBL* 91 (1972) 449–456. G. L. Lawlor, *'Almah—Virgin or Young Woman?* (1973). D. Yubero, "El 'Emmanuel' o 'Dios con nosotros'," *CB* 252 (1973) 295–298. W. Abschlag, "Jungfrau oder junge Frau? Zu Jes. 7,14," *Anzeiger für die katholische Geistlichkeit* 83 (1974) 290–292. G. Brunet, "La vierge d'Isaïe," *Cahier Renan* 22/86 (1974) 1–16. H. Lehnhard, "'Jungfrau' oder 'junge Frau' in Jesaja 7,14–17?" *TBei* 7 (1976) 264–267. J. Coppens, "Un nouvel essai d'interprétation d'Is 7,14–17," *Salm* 23 (1976) 85–88.

Concerning individual motifs: G. F. Hasel, "Linguistic Considerations Regarding the Translation of Isaiah's Shear-Jashub: A Reassessment," *AUSS* 9 (1971) 36–46. W. D. Stacey, "Prophetic Signs: A Re-examination of the Symbolic Actions of the Prophets of the OT," diss., Bristol (1971/72). D. J. A. Clines, "X, X ben Y, ben Y: Personal Names in Hebrew Narrative Style," *VT* 22 (1972) 266–267. G. F. Hasel, *The Remnant. The History and Theology of the Remnant Idea from Genesis to Isaiah,* Andrews University Monographs 5 (1972). F. Stolz, "Zeichen und Wunder," *ZTK* 60 (1972) 125–144. P. Zerafa, "Il resto di Israele nei profeti preesilici," *Ang* 49 (1972) 3–29. E. Lipiński, "Le š'r yšwb d'Isaïe VII 3," *VT* 23 (1973) 245–246. R. Frankena, "'Dit zij u een teken'," Studies B. A. Brongers (1974), Theol Inst 28–36. H. Madel, "Die Gottesbefragung mit dem Verb שאל," *Bausteine biblischer Theologie,* FS G. J. Botterweck (1977) 37–70.

Summaries of research: J. J. Stamm, "Die Immanuel-Perikope im Lichte neuerer Veröffentlichungen," ZDMG Suppl. I/1 (1969) 281–290. G. del Olmo Lete, "La profecía del Emmanuel (Is 7,10–17). Estado actual de la interpretación," *EphMar* 22 (1972) 375–385. J. J. Stamm, "Die Immanuel-Perikope. Eine Nachlese," *TZ* 30 (1974) 11–22.]

[*An addition made at the time of proofreading:* P. Höffken, "Notizen zum Textcharakter von Jesaja 7,1–17," *TZ* 36 (1980) 321–337.]

Text

7:1 In the days of Ahaz, the son of Jotham, the son of Uzziah, the king of Judah,[a] [Rezin,[b] the king of Aram went forth, with Pekah, the son of Remaliah,[c] the king of Israel, against Jerusalem ⟨to wage

2 war against it[d]⟩, but he was not able[e] to conquer it].[a] • When it was announced to the house of David: Aram has settled itself down upon Ephraim,[a] then his heart and the heart of his people

3 shook, as the trees shake[b] in the wind. • Yahweh, however, spoke to Isaiah:[a] Go out to confront Ahaz, together with your son Shear-jashub, at the far end of the water conduit for the upper pool on

4 Fuller's Field Street • and say to him: Take care for yourself and remain calm, do not fear for yourself, and do not let your heart despair before these two smoking[a] stubs from burning sticks [b][before the furious rage[c] of Rezin and Aram and the son of

5 Remaliah][b]!, • because[a] Aram has determined to do evil to you

6 [Ephraim and the son of Remaliah][b] and says: • We will go up against Judah, strike[a] terror in it and force it open for our use, in

7 order to install the Tabelite[b] as king there. • Thus says the Lord Yahweh:
It will not happen and will not succeed,

8 for the head[a] of Aram is Damascus,
and the head[a] of Damascus is Rezin,
[b][and sixty-five years remain yet; then Ephraim is to be broken and will have ceased to be a people].[b]

9 And the head of Ephraim is Samaria,
and the head of Samaria is the son of Remaliah.
If you do not believe, then[a] you will not remain.[b]

10,11 And 'Isaiah'[a] set out, in order to speak with Ahaz, and said: • Request a sign from Yahweh, your God, deep 'within the under-

12 world'[a] or high above in the heights! • But Ahaz answered: I will not

13 make a request and will not test Yahweh. • Then he[a] said: Listen anyway, you from the house of David! Is it too little for you, to

14 weary human beings, that you also weary my God?[b] • Thus 'Yahweh'[a] himself will give you a sign: Behold,[b] the young woman[c] is[d] pregnant and will bear a son and will[e] give him the

15 name Immanuel.[f] [a][• He will eat butter[b] and honey, that he might

282

16 learn[c] to reject the evil and to choose the good.][a] • For before the
lad understands how to reject the evil and how to choose the
good, the land of both the kings who cause you to shudder will
17 become deserted. • However,[a] Yahweh will allow days to come
upon you and upon your people [b][and upon the house of your
father][b] the likes of which have not come since the days when
Ephraim separated itself from Judah, [c][the king of Assyria].[c]

1a–a In 2 Kings 16:5 we read: אז יעלה ר' מ'־א' ופ' בן־רר' מ'־י' ירושלם למלחמה ויצרו על־אחז
ולא יכלו להלחם (Then Rezin king of Syria and Pekah the son of Remaliah, king of
Israel, came up to wage war on Jerusalem, and they besieged Ahaz but could not
conquer him). It ought not be presumed that the text of Isa. 7:1, even though it
can no doubt be traced back to the book of Kings, at one time agreed word for
word with the text as it is cited here. One ought to give up on the attempt to use
critical tools to establish a text which finds complete agreement in both passages
(see also K. Budde, op. cit. [*ExpTim*]).
1b For רְצִין (Rezin), Gk reads Ραασσων; for this reason, some believe that the
name *raṣunnu,* which appears in the annals of Tiglath-Pileser, would suggest that
the Hebrew reading should be רְצוֹן (Rezon). However, according to B. Lands-
berger (*Sam'al* [1948] 66, note 169), the name of the last Aramean king in
Damascus should be transcribed from the Akkadian texts as *ra-ḫi-a-nu* (on this,
see W. von Soden, "Das akkadische Syllabar," *AnOr* 27 [1948] 108), so that he
suggests it would be read in Aramaic as *ra'jān* and in Hebrew as רַצְיָן. This would
mean "satisfaction," which makes better sense than the meaning "source," which
had been suggested as the meaning for רְצִין (see M. Noth, *Die israelitischen
Personennamen,* BWANT 46 [1928] 224; cf. also J. Lindblom, op. cit., 11).
1c Q[a]: רומליה, as also in vv. 5 and 9; in v. 4 it reads רמליהו; in vv. 1, 5, 9 Gk reads:
Ρομελίου; see *BASOR* 189 (1968) 42.
1d למלחמה עליה (to wage war against it) may be a dittography for להלחם עליה (to
conquer it).
1e יכל (he was not able) is no doubt more original than the plural in 2 Kings 16:5
(so also Q[a], Gk, Syr, Vulg); the driving force behind the undertaking was Rezin;
Pekah came along because the Arameans pressured him to do so (on this, see H.
M. Orlinsky, *JQR* 43 [1952/53] 331–333).
2a נחה, in the normal sense of "settle oneself down, rest," does not make good
sense, which has resulted in some suggestions for correcting the text, such as נֶאֶחָה,
"had become brothers with," or חָנָה, "had set up camp for themselves." G. R.
Driver (*JTS* 34 [1933] 377), on the basis of the Arabic *naḫā,* "lean oneself upon"
(IV "support oneself upon"), suggests reading נָחָה ("has inclined towards =
become allied with," on the basis of which KBL reads: נחה II, "support oneself").
In the L. Köhler festschrift (*STU* 20 [1950] 23–26), O. Eissfeldt points out that
the Akkadian *nāḫu,* from the inscription on the stele of Idrimi of Alalakh (*Tell
'Atšana*), means "become reconciled, enter into a treaty agreement," or something similar, and believes that the Hebrew נוח is to be interpreted in that exact
sense in the present passage. This view seems to be supported by the translation
of the Gk: συνεφώνησεν Αραμ πρὸς τὸν Εφραιμ (Aram entered into an agreement
with Ephraim) and by the rendering of the verb in the Syriac: 'est[e]wî, "bind
oneself, take an oath" (Targ: אתחבר, bind oneself). Nevertheless, the על (upon),
which is connected with נחה at this point, would speak against such an interpretation. More than anything else, however, a political agreement between these two
states would not explain the reason for such a panic in Jerusalem. On the other
hand, that would be very easy to understand if an Aramaic army had already
established its own base of operations in Israel. In the present passage, נוּחַ could
be used in the same way as in v. 19 or Exod. 10:4; 2 Sam. 17:12; 21:10, to mean
"allow oneself to settle down upon, fall down upon," which does away with the
need for any alterations to the text.

2b Concerning the infinitive construct form נוע (to shake) (instead of the standard form נוּעַ), see Joüon, Gr §80k.

3a Instead of אל ישעיהו (to Isaiah), it has been suggested that one read אֵלָי (to me); see Budde, op. cit. (*Jesajas Erleben*), 1. If this were correct, then it would be easier to understand the section as part of a report which justified Isaiah's activity during the time of the Syro-Ephraimitic War (chaps. 6:1—9:6). Text-critically, however, there is no basis for this change; rather, as it has been transmitted to us in its present form, it is the report of someone who is unknown to us.

4a Qᵃ: עושנים (smoking), which reads this as a participle instead of an adjective; this form is also used in Exod. 20:18.

4b–b Gk: ὅταν γὰρ ὀργὴ τοῦ θυμοῦ μου γένηται πάλιν ἰάσομαι (for whenever the rage of my wrath goes forth, I will heal again). Naturally, the Masoretic text is to be preferred, but it is not part of the original text either; it is probably intended as an explanation about what is meant by the reference to the smoking stubs from burning sticks.

4c For בחרי (before the furious rage), the Syr reads *men ḥemtâ,* suggesting that the reading should possibly be changed to מחרי (from the furious rage). Qᵃ reads בחורי. That is simply an orthographic variant; it is not to be treated as a construct plural participle (contra Wagner, op. cit.).

5a M. Sæbø (op. cit.) tried to demonstrate that vv. 5f. furnish the reason for v. 4; thus, it would not be interpreted as if connected with v. 7. But both of these verses intend to provide the reason for the message of Yahweh which follows, not that which precedes, and v. 7, with its assurance that "it will not happen, it will not succeed," refers to the plan of Rezin noted in v. 6 (cf. 14:24; 40:8; 46:10; Jer. 44:28f.; 51:29; Prov. 19:21).

5b The phrase אפרים ובן־רמליהו (Ephraim and the son of Remaliah) is to be taken as a gloss (correct in terms of content; see v. 4b).

6a Instead of ונקיצנה (we will strike terror), it has been suggested that the reading be ונציקנה ("and want to press down upon it," Gesenius) or וְנִתְצֶנָּה ("and want to set it on fire," de Lagarde, *Semitica* I [1878] 14), whereas Driver (*JSS* 13 [1968] 39) suggests translating it, based on Gk (συλλαλήσαντες, conversing with) and the Arabic *kāda* ("negotiated, bargained with [a person]"): "let us open negotiations with it." H. M. Orlinsky (*JQR* 28 [1937/38] 65ff.) presumes for Job 14:12 that there is a root קוץ II (= Arabic *kāṣa*) which has the meaning "tear apart," a suggestion which S. Speier (*JBL* 72 [1953] xiv) adopts to explain Isa. 7:6. Since the *hiph'il* of קוץ I (strike terror, cause a sickening dread) is not attested elsewhere, this solution is worth noting. And yet, קוץ II is not attested in Hebrew at all, so that we still consider it preferable to derive it from קוץ I; the opponents do not at all have it in mind to destroy Jerusalem, but only to put their own plans into effect.

6b The Masoretic pointing טָבְאַל is, in fact, a prejudiced alteration ("Good-for-Nothing"; see H. W. Wolff, op. cit. [BibS(N) 35], 9, note i). Gk reads Ταβεηλ and in Ezra 4:7 we actually encounter the name טָבְאֵל (Tabeel) ("El/God is good"; cf. [ו]טוֹבִיָה = Tobiah[u], Zech. 6:10, 14, and often elsewhere). The form of the name is not Aramaic just by chance; there must have actually been a man who was ready to carry out Aramaic political policy. W. F. Albright (op. cit., 35) has pointed out that there is a text from Calah which mentions a messenger named Ayanûr, the Tabelite (*Ṭa-ab-i-la-aja*): When *Ṭāb'el* or *Bêt Ṭāb'el* is used, it definitely refers to a region north of Gilead. (One might compare Judg. 3:31: Shamgar בן־ענת, which does not mean "son of Anath" but "from Beth-Anath.")

8a Instead of ראש (head), M. Scott (*ExpTim* 38 [1926/27] 525f.) has suggested reading ירוש ("trample, harry"), but this is hardly correct. E. Baumann (*ZAW* 21 [1901] 268–270) presumes that there is a wordplay when ראש (head) is used: It would not only be called "capital (city)" but also "poison (plant)." It may be that Isaiah's audience would have caught the double meaning for this word, but one certainly ought to stay with the traditional translation, "head."

8b–b This is a later insertion, easily noticed also because this line interrupts the flow of the material in an unacceptable way. Isaiah sees that the attacking enemies will come to an end in the very near future; thus, there cannot be any talk of something which would occur sixty-five years later. Kaminka's attempt to make some sense of the sixty-five years within the context is simply unconvincing (*MGWJ* 73 [1929] 471f.). The change suggested by Procksch and H. W. Wolff (op. cit., 22)—changing ששים וחמש שנה (sixty-five years) to read שש וחמש שנים (six or five years), or something similar—removes the difficulty, but this reading is also unlikely, since the pre-exilic prophets did not work with such exact dates and even if they did, the passage would still be an intrusion within this context. In addition to this, Isaiah uses חתת (cease to be) in a different sense (see 8:9).

9a Some have objected that כי (then [for, because]) would not be used to introduce the final clause in a conditional construction and have thus suggested replacing it with בי (with me) (see E. Nestle, op. cit.), which would then be linked with, and interpreted with, תאמינו (you will [not] believe). But Isaiah also uses האמין (he who believes) in the absolute sense in 28:16. כי ("thus, indeed") is, as the texts from Ugarit demonstrate, an archaic emphatic particle (see *ZAW* 77 [1965] 300); its use gives emphasis to the sentence; cf. Gen. 42:16 and Ges-K §159ee.

9b Gk translates v. 9b: καὶ ἐὰν μὴ πιστεύσητε, οὐδὲ μὴ συνῆτε (and if you do not believe, then you will not perceive) (Lat: *intelligetis,* understand thoroughly; Syr: *testaklûn,* you will perceive), which presumes that the Hebrew read תָּבִינוּ (you will perceive). That is, without a doubt, the result of damage to the text, which results in a distortion of Isaiah's wordplay. Vulg translates it according to the correct sense: *non permanebitis* (you will not remain).

10a It is often the case that יהוה (Yahweh) is changed to read ישעיה (Isaiah). But it is actually quite odd that Yahweh would speak directly to Ahaz, as if he were a prophet. If יהוה (Yahweh) were the correct reading, then in v. 11 it would have to read מֵעִמִּי (from me) instead of מעם יהוה (from Yahweh). The subject of ויאמר (then he said) in v. 13 is clearly Isaiah.

11a Concerning the two asyndetic imperatives העמק (make deep) and שאלה (ask), which follow directly after one another, the first is given an adverbial sense, see Joüon, Gr §123r; concerning the *hiph'il* העמק (make deep), see Ges-K §114n. But Gk reads, for שְׁאָלָה ("Go on, ask"), εἰς βάθος (into the deep), 'Aquila, Sym, Theod: εἰς αδην (into Hades), both of which readings presume an original שְׁאֹלָה (into Sheol). That is, without a doubt, the original textual reading, since in this case the repetition of שאל (ask) is avoided and למעלה (in the heights) provides the needed corresponding term. Possibly, the textual corruption originated because of dogmatic considerations.

13a In order to follow through with this being considered a first-person report, it has been suggested that ויאמר (then he said) should be altered to read וָאֹמַר (and I said); concerning this, see 3a.

13b לאה (Akkadian: *la'û,* "be weak") means "tired, no longer be able to keep at something"; the *hiph'il* correspondingly means "make tired," and yet it can also be used in a declarative sense ("declare one is tired, weak" or "consider one tired" or "weak"). It apparently has to do with a play on the various meanings of the *hiph'il.*

14a On the basis of a large number of MSS, יהוה (Yahweh) is to be read instead of אדני (Lord); see above, textual note 1b, on 6:1.

14b The form-historical parallels mentioned below on p. 307 keep one from interpreting הנה (behold) in the conditional sense, as done by Kaiser and Fohrer (op. cit., 168).

14c העלמה (the young woman) is rendered by Gk as ἡ παρθένος (the maiden, virgin); 'Aquila, Sym, Theod read: η νεανις (young woman, girl, maiden) (Jerome: *adolescentula,* a very young girl; Filastrius Brixiensis: *iuvencula,* a young woman, a maiden); Targ: עולימתא (maiden); Syr *betûltâ* (maiden); Vulg: *virgo* (maiden, virgin).

285

14d Whether the participle is to be translated in a present or a future sense can be determined only on the basis of a full treatment of the entire section. Gk: ἐν γαστρὶ ἕξει (and shall conceive in the womb) (cf. Matt. 1:23); handwritten copies of the Hexaplaric recension: λη(μ)ψεται (conceive) (cf. Luke 1:31); 'Aquila: συλλαμβανει (conceive); Vulg: *concipiet* (conceive, form inwardly).

14e וְקָרָאת (will give him the name) seems to be a second person feminine singular perfect, which is impossible, since the king is being addressed, not the woman. The form should be taken as a third person feminine singular perfect (see Ges-K §74g, Bauer-Leander §54r). Gk reads καλέσεις (you shall call) (see also Matt. 1:21; Luke 1:31), but Gk* reads καλέσει (shall call); GQ and the Lucianic handwritten copies read καλέσετε (you [pl.] shall call); a whole host of other texts read καλέσουσι(ν) (they shall call); Targ: ותקרי (and you shall call); Syr: wᵉnetqᵉrê šᵉmeh (and his name shall be called); Vulg: *vocabitur* (shall be called); Qᵃ renders it as וקרא, which, according to R. Tournay, op. cit., corresponds to the Syr and Vulg and is to be pointed as a *puʿal:* וְקֹרָא (and he will be called), but which can also be read as וְקֹרָא: "and one will call" (see 9:5; H. W. Wolff, op. cit., 9, note o; and G. Rinaldi, *BeO* 10 [1968] 134). Just the multitude of the abberations from the MT makes one suspicious. It happens quite often in the OT that the mother gives the child its name, particularly when she can thank God for his divine intervention; see Gen. 16:11; 29:32—30:24; Judg. 13:24; 1 Sam. 1:20; cf. Matt. 1:21. L. Dequeker (*VT* 12 [1962] 331–335) opts for the pointing וְקָרָאתְ (and you shall call); concerning this, cf. passages like Gen. 17:19: שָׂרָה אִשְׁתְּךָ יֹלֶדֶת לְךָ בֵּן וְקָרָאתָ אֶת־שְׁמוֹ יִצְחָק (Sarah your wife shall bear you a son, and you shall call his name Isaac); in addition, cf. the giving of names in Hosea 1, Luke 1:13, and, above all others, Isa. 8:3, according to which Isaiah, and not his wife, names the child. In addition, this pointing is impossible, since giving the name is part of the sign which is offered to Ahaz (see also Th. Lescow, op. cit., 177, note 20). One should stay with the Masoretic pointing. It is not permissible to agree with H. Donner, op. cit., 9, who slices through the Gordian knot and abruptly arrives at the reading וְקָרָאתִי (and I will name), which would make it apparent to every reader that Immanuel is the son of Isaiah.

14f F. Zimmermann (*JQR* 52 [1962] 157) suggests changing the name so that it reads עַם נוֹאָל, "foolish people," an enticing emendation, but one which does not take 8:10 into account.

15a–a Verse 15 is considered by many to be an addition; see Gottwald, op. cit., 40; C. A. Keller, *Das Wort Oth als "Offenbarungszeichen Gottes"* (1946) 108ff.; G. Fohrer, *ZAW* 68 (1956) 54–56; Stamm, op. cit. (*Immanuel-Weissagung und Eschatologie*) 443, note 18, and the commentaries; on the basis of text-critical evidence, however, there is no reason to object to this verse (see below, p. 288).

15b The exact meaning of חמאה is disputed. There is no doubt that some type of milk product is intended. The translators vacillate between: sweet cream (cream), thick milk (so HAL [= KBL³]), sour milk, and butter. KBL¹ suggests "sweet, fresh, still-soft butter." Dalman also comes to the conclusion (*AuS* VI, 307ff.), primarily on the basis of Prov. 30:33, "that the ancient translators were indeed correct when they translated this as *'butter,'* only that this butter was not to be thought of as completely hardened" (311). He had himself had the experience "that the sheik in Muḥmās, along with thick bread, set out a bowl with honey and liquid cooking butter mixed together, into which the bread was to be dipped."

15c לְדַעְתּוֹ (that he might learn) is translated in Gk as πρὶν ἢ γνῶναι (before knowing), but by Sym as εις το γνωναι (so as to know), by Theod as εν τω γνωναι (in order to know), in Vulg: *ut sciat* (that he might know). Differences in the translations demonstrate uncertainty when trying to understand the passage, but do not presuppose a different original text. ל with the infinitive can indeed have a temporal sense: "at that time, there, when"; cf. the lexica. Without a doubt, the most likely interpretation is to take the infinitive construct in the final sense; on this, see Duncker, op. cit.

17a For יהוה (Yahweh), Gk reads ὁ θεός (God). Qᵃ reads, before יביא (will allow to come), an additional ו (*Waw*), which is to be translated "but" (cf. H. W. Wolff, op. cit., 10, note r). Gk offers the reading ἀλλὰ ἐπάξει (but he will bring upon).

17b–b "And upon the house of your father" is a clumsy phrase since, just previous to this, the discussion had been about the people. H. W. Wolff, op. cit., 10, note s, removes ועל עמך (and upon your people); it is also possible that ועל בית אביך (and upon the house of your father) is not part of the original text either.

17c–c This is generally considered to be an addition, justifiably so, since the words seem clumsy and mention what was supposed to be secret according to the original prediction. However, the gloss ought not be eliminated solely for text-critical reasons.

Form

[7:1–17] There is no general agreement about where the section ends. There can be no doubt that a definite break in thought comes between vv. 9 and 10 and, if the text is not altered, v. 10 leaves one with the impression that it provides a (rather awkward) redactional seam (see above, textual note 10a). Thus Kaiser is of the opinion (similarly, Fohrer and Porúbčan, op. cit.) that vv. 10–17 indeed seem to belong, based on their content, with the verses which precede them, but that the new beginning in v. 10 suggests strongly that the scene which follows should be separated, both in terms of time and locale, from that which precedes it. That makes little sense, since the sign is clearly connected with the message delivered to Ahaz in vv. 4–9: Signs never have meaning in and of themselves, but only as they are connected with a message from Yahweh (see C. A. Keller, op. cit., *Oth,* 144f.). The same discussion has been held concerning the passage in Genesis 15, a discussion based on the passage's form history (concerning the analysis, see Wildberger, op. cit., *ZTK* 65 [1968] 142–147); the debate is over whether vv. 7ff. are to be taken as separate from vv. 1–6 from the outset, which does not work in that passage either, even though v. 7 plainly starts afresh. Isa. 7:9 does not arrive at a satisfactory conclusion for the story: The listener/reader still must find out whether Ahaz allowed himself to be brought to faith or what reaction the prophet had if Ahaz refused. For this reason, the section 1–17 should be considered as a unit in regard to its place and time. Of course, the original text has not come to us without some alterations. As was noted above (see textual note 1a–a), v. 1 comes from 2 Kings 16:5 (the designation of time, אז [then], which begins that sentence and which was originally also part of the original passage in Isaiah, is replaced by more precise dating: ויהי בימי אחז, in the days of Ahaz, etc.). Utilizing this sentence from the book of Kings furnishes some evidence that a real attempt was made to set the prophetic traditions into their proper historical time frame, so that the prophetic books were read along with the corresponding historical books. Here, in a small way, the same thing happened as took place with 2 Kings 18:13, 17—20:19, a much larger passage which was inserted later as an appendix to the book of Isaiah. In addition, not only are v. 4b (see above, textual note 4b–b) and most clearly v. 8b (see above, textual note 8b–b) to be taken as glosses, but most likely v. 15 is also to be handled as a foreign element within the original story. The extraordinary event of giving the name demands that the reason for it follow immediately afterwards (cf. Gen. 16:11 and see below, p. 307), but this is not provided in any way by v. 15; however, with

כי (for) as an introduction, it does follow in v. 16. Another reason which suggests v. 15 be considered a later composition is the fact that both of the infinitives מאוס (to reject) and בחור (to choose), in marked contrast to v. 16, are written in *plene* form. This means that v. 15 ought not be used when attempting to explain what the Immanuel sign meant according to Isaiah's own understanding.

Verse 17 is a problem all by itself. Other attempts to understand this notwithstanding, the most natural explanation is that which sees the verse proclaiming a disaster for Judah, the likes of which had not been experienced since those most unhappy days following Solomon's death, when the unity of Israel was broken. In that case, however, the content seems to be in sharp contrast to the verse immediately preceding, which speaks about the disaster which will come upon Judah's enemies. Some have tried to circumvent this contradiction by removing the conclusion to v. 16: "both the kings who cause you to shudder" (as, recently, also Fohrer), so that v. 16 would then also have to be understood as an announcement of judgment against Judah. On the other hand, some have suggested that the first section of the chapter reaches its conclusion in v. 16, so that v. 17 is to be interpreted as the introduction to vv. 18ff. (e.g., Gray, ad loc.). However, most have generally opted to take v. 17 as an integral part of 7:1/7:10ff. (thus, among other scholars, Graham, op. cit., 205; Wolff; Kaiser; Eichrodt). And yet, the problem is so closely linked to the interpretation of vv. 10ff. that it can be solved only within the context of a detailed exegetical study of the entire passage (see below, pp. 315f.).

After the glosses which have been mentioned are removed, vv. 2–16 remain as clearly part of the original unit. The section contains the report of an unknown person who describes Isaiah's confrontation with King Ahaz at the time when the conflict broke out with the Arameans and Northern Israelites, usually designated the Syro-Ephraimitic War. Therefore, it is the central section of the so-called memorial record of Isaiah, which concerns itself with the activity of the prophet during this very time period (6:1—9:6; see above, p. 252). In the context of this memorial record, this section must have originally been written as a first-person report, not a third-person report. In chap. 6, this was the case and, in 8:1, 3, 11, 16–18, the first person "I" appears once again. It would thus seem most likely that 7:1–16(17) was also constructed as a first-person report (see Duhm, ad loc., and Budde, op. cit. [*Erleben*] 1f.). In order to recover and restore this section, it would take only very minor changes in v. 3; see above, textual note 3a. And yet, it would be most remarkable that, in the transmission of the text, such a mistake as this could have been perpetrated with absolutely no evidence left from the original reading at all. Why would it not have been possible for Isaiah's disciples, if not Isaiah himself, to have preserved such a third-person report within this memorial record?

[7:1–9] After a brief orientation to the situation, in which Isaiah confronted King Ahaz (v. 2), what follows is the prophet's commissioning (v. 3), introduced with the well-known formula ואמרת אליו (and say to him) at the beginning of v. 4, which introduces the actual message from Yahweh. In vv. 7–9, we are apparently presented with a second scene, in which we have the description of the situation, in the form of a causal clause (vv.

5f.), incorporated into the message from Yahweh. Because of this, there is a quite complicated structure in which, in the very middle of the message from Yahweh, viewed in a formal way, a messenger speech is quoted, introduced in fact by the formula כה אמר אדני יהוה (thus says the Lord Yahweh). This caused Saebø to connect the causal clause in vv. 5f. with what precedes, in order to preserve vv. 7–9 as an independent message from Isaiah, even if it does deal with the same situation and has the same basic theme (op. cit., 69). And yet, there are difficulties which result from this interpretation when one attempts to make sense of vv. 7–9; this would seem to suggest that it is better if one abandons any attempt to separate these two parts.

[7:4–9] The message from Yahweh which the prophet is to proclaim to the king is an oracle of salvation. The indicator which provides decisive proof for this conclusion is the admonition "do not fear for yourself" (see J. Begrich, "Das priesterliche Heilsorakel," *ZAW* 52 [1934] 81–92 = *Gesammelte Studien zum Alten Testament,* TBü 21 [1964] 217–231). It is already made clear in v. 4 that particular importance is attached to this challenge, surrounded by three other parallel imperatives, and the reason for alarm is specifically mentioned. But it is impossible that this message from Yahweh comes to an end with this admonition. Within the structure of an oracle of salvation, after the challenge to proceed without any fear, a statement follows, either in a nominal form or in the perfect, e.g., "I am with you" or "I have redeemed you" (see Begrich, op. cit., 82f./219f.). This element is missing here. However, it is included in an indirect way in the name of the child of the עלמה (almah), to be named עמנו אל (Immanuel), and also within v. 9, insofar as the verse alludes to the election of the house of David (see below, p. 290). After the basic promise has been made, formulated as a clause using the imperfect, a specific promise follows, announcing salvation, in this case, the proclamation that the plans of the two enemies of the Davidic house will be foiled. It is part of Isaiah's way of reshaping the form, as it has come to him, that the message from Yahweh does not end at this point but harks back once again to the admonition to go forth without fear.

Oracles of salvation can be delivered in various circumstances, either to individual important personages or to the people as a whole. The present passage from Isaiah has recently been interpreted in light of the so-called war addresses, which belong to the circle of traditions associated with holy war (G. von Rad, *Der Heilige Krieg im Alten Israel* [1951] see pp. 70ff.). Such a speech has been preserved for us in Deut. 20:3f. and appears elsewhere most often in the deuteronomistic writings: Deut. 7:16–20; 9:1–6; 31:3–6, 7f.; however, it is already recognizable in Exodus 14, where it can be reported, following the account about the fulfillment of the oracle, that Israel believed in Yahweh (see 13f. [J], 31). One can compare this with Deut. 1:29–32, where it is observed that Israel did not believe in Yahweh in spite of a favorable oracle. Thus, it seems that one can find an exhortation to believe (האמין) or that belief is expected when oracles of salvation are delivered at the beginning of a war. But to be informed that Isaiah shapes his message in the form of the "war address" to Ahaz does not provide a completely satisfactory explanation: Isaiah is not a charismatic leader, not a spokesman for Yahweh in a holy war, who turns to address the people. His oracle is addressed to the king. It has already been observed many times, and furnished with even more evidence by Würthwein, that vv. 7–9 are to be interpreted on the basis of the traditions about the Davidic covenant (op. cit., 60ff.). תֵאָמֵנוּ (you will not remain) in v. 9b is linked to the promise made to the house of David, already fulfilled to some extent (and certainly reenacted over and over again in the kingship festivals), assuring them that their dynasty would endure: לְפָנַי וְנֶאְמָן בֵּיתְךָ וּמַמְלַכְתְּךָ עַד־עוֹלָם (and your house and your kingdom shall be made sure forever before me) (2 Sam. 7:16; emended text, see BHK; see also Isa. 9:6; Ps. 89:5). But this background is also necessary if one is to understand completely vv. 8a and 9a. These components, from these two verses, force the hearers to draw one further conclusion: "For the head of Judah is Jerusalem, and the head of Jerusalem is the Davidic king," that is, the very king whom Yahweh calls his son (2 Sam. 7:14; Ps. 2:7), whom he has assured of his mercy (Isa. 55:3; Ps. 89:3), and the one to whom he promised his continual faithfulness (אֱמוּנָה) (Ps. 89:2 and passim). If the Davidic King Ahaz earnestly considers this promise of Yahweh, which still applies to his house, then there is no reason why one should fear. It is on this basis that Isa. 7:3–9 is designated an oracle of salvation for a king, one who has been specially chosen by the deity, as great danger of a war threatens.

We have parallels for this type of an oracle in ancient Near Eastern literature. In his inscription, which was found in Afis, Zakir, the king of Hamath, reports, in a striking parallel to that which is reported in Isaiah 7: "Barhadad, . . . king of Aram, united . . . a group of ten kings against me. . . . All these kings laid siege to Hatarikka. . . . But I lifted up my hand to Be'elshamayn, and Be'elshamayn heard me. Be'elshamayn [spoke] to me through seers and through *diviners . . . : 'Do not fear,* for I made you king, and I shall stand by you and deliver you from all *[these kings, who] set up* a siege against you!'" (*KAI* no. 202; quoted from *ANET²* 655). Of course, there is no explicit mention here about belief or trust in so many words. But this is a very common occurrence in similar oracles from Assyria. Thus, e.g., Ishtar of Arbela assures Esarhaddon: "Your gracious leader am I, who unto protracted days, everlasting years have *fixed* your throne under the wide heavens"; and she summons him: "'*Fear not, O king,*' I said to you, 'I have not abandoned you. *I have given you confidence.* . . . In Arbela my mercy is your shield'" (*AOT²* 282; quoted from *ANET³* 450). One notes that here also (as in Isa. 7:9) the discussion centers on the steadfastness of the king's throne. Another indication that this type of oracle had already achieved a fixed form long before the time of Isaiah can be found in a most surprising example, which we have from a letter of the Hittite king Suppiluliumas (ca. 1375–1335) to Niqmadd of Ugarit: "Even if Nuhassa and Mukis are at war with me, even so, Niqmadd, *you are not to fear them [lâ tapalaḫšunu]; have confidence for your own self.* . . . If you pay careful attention, O Niqmadd, to the words of the great king, your lord, . . . you, O king, will see the kindness which the great king, your lord, will give you as a gift. . . . Then you, O Niqmadd, will *have confidence [amāte ša šarri rabî bêlika taqâp]* in the future in the words of the great king, your lord" (J. Nougayrol, *Le Palais Royal d'Ugarit* IV [1956] Text 17: 132, pp. 35–37; concerning this, see *ZAW* 67 [1955] 265).

It is really not all that surprising that Isaiah reminds Ahaz of the covenant with David in his message from Yahweh: He is using the form of an oracle of salvation addressed to kings. We can find a comparable parallel in the OT in a place where one would hardly expect it: in Gen. 15:1ff. (on this, see H. Wildberger, op. cit. [*ZTK*] 65, 142ff.). In v. 1b one finds a clear, though very short, form of such an oracle: "*Fear not,* Abram, I am your shield; your reward shall be very great." O. Kaiser ("Traditionsgeschichtliche Untersuchung von Genesis 15," *ZAW* 70 [1958] 107–126) and H. Cazelles ("Connexions et structure de Gen. XV," *RB* 69 [1962] 321–349) have both demonstrated that the promise ("shield" and "reward" are used in the sense of a soldier's pay, a present made to the victorious commander-in-chief) is to be understood based on its background in the oracle to a king. When faith is mentioned, it is also linked to its usage in this type of oracle.

Therefore, there can be hardly any doubt that Isaiah models his address according to the pattern of the oracle of salvation, delivered to kings at a time when there was a threat of war, and that, already at that time, part of the technical vocabulary in this genre included the theme "faith." It must be asked whether this assessment would also apply to the motif of the "son" who is to be born. In Genesis 15, of course, Abraham does hark back to the promise when he interrogates and receives an answer from God (אשר יצא ממעיך, which shall come forth from you [v. 4]), and it belongs quite generally to the thought world connected with the traditions about kingship (זרע אשר יצא ממעיך, your offspring who shall come forth from your body [2 Sam. 7:12]). It will be necessary to come back to this problem when an attempt is made to answer the question about the identity of Immanuel. It is not surprising that an oracle of salvation would be reinforced by a sign: Gideon demands a sign after he has been assigned the task of delivering Israel (Judg. 6:16; for other examples, see Keller, op. cit. [*Oth*] 23ff.), and even the shepherds in the fields, who were encouraged with the words "be not afraid," were offered a "sign" (Luke 2:12). Just as Gen. 15:7ff. ought not be separated from 15:1–6 (that is to say, the basic Yahwistic material for both parts of the chapter; on this, see Kaiser, Seebass, Snijders), in the same way, the prediction about Immanuel is not to be separated from the message of Yahweh to Ahaz in 7:4–9. Certainly one might object first of all that it should have been mentioned, immediately after v. 9, that Isaiah had carried out the command which was given to him, but that Ahaz responded with skepticism. Budde (op. cit. [*Erleben*] 44f.) explains this gap as a redactional way to shorten the original text. It is more likely that W. Baumgartner has a more correct explanation for the apparent unevenness, treating it simply as the unique way in which the Hebrews told stories ("Ein Kapitel vom hebräischen Erzählungsstil," FS H. Gunkel, FRLANT 36/I [1923] 145–157, see pp. 146–148).

Meter: The attempt by Procksch to read vv. 3–17 metrically is unconvincing. This is a prose account. Even in the oracle, one can be sure that a metrical analysis is possible only at its high points: in v. 7b, one should read לֹא תקוֹם ולֹא תהיֹה, in other words, both times accenting לֹא (not). In vv. 8a and 9a, there are 2 parallel three-stress bicola, forcing one, in one's own mind, to add a third line to it, without which the causal clause could not be understood, namely:

(ו)רֹאשׁ יְהוּדָה יְרוּשָׁלַיִם
(ו)רֹאשׁ יְרוּשָׁלַיִם בֶּן־דָּוִד

(and the head of Judah is Jerusalem, and the head of Jerusalem is the son of David). With the very abrupt, short three-stress bicolon, the message ends with v. 9. The stress on לֹא (not), both times it is used, underscores, as in v. 7b, that the divine decision was absolutely inevitable.

Setting

There can be no doubt that the redactor who placed specific details from 2 Kings 16:5 at the beginning of the oracle to Ahaz correctly dated the confrontation of Isaiah with the king. However, since vv. 2–17 are probably a third-person account, the question still remains about whether the section possibly ought to be viewed as legendary. After de Lagarde (*Semitica* I [1878] 9–13) offered his opinion that this section was not to be trusted to be historically accurate, H. Gressmann (*Der Messias,* FRLANT 43 [1929] 237) declared his opinion that the way Isaiah was reduced here to the status of a wonder-worker would establish the fact that this account was nothing more than a prophetic legend. In spite of this, one need not completely deny its authenticity. Kraeling, op. cit., is even more radical, since he says that the history is of the same type as that found in the stories about Isaiah in chaps. 36–39. Already Budde was correct when he spoke out to refute this: "The Immanuel sign, interpreted as a means to put Isaiah's promise in motion" (thus Kraeling), "should really confront the king with utter clarity, convincing Ahaz that he ought not call upon Assyria for help, but rather, only rely on trusting that Yahweh alone would be present to help bring about a victory in the war against Aram and Ephraim, a glorious triumph for the prophet" (op. cit. [*Das Immanuelzeichen*] 42). It is recognized among scholars that Budde successfully defended the historicity of the account, so evaluated even by those who have felt constrained to restructure the third-person account into a first-person account. On the basis of 8:16ff., it can be presumed that the "memorial record," of which 7:1–16 is a part, was composed not long after the Syro-Ephraimitic War. Therefore, that must also be true for the account about the confrontation with Ahaz.

Commentary

[7:1] On the basis of what we have established to this point, we are in the fortunate position of being able to date a prophetic message very precisely, with great confidence. Verse 1, taken from the second book of Kings, comes from the royal records located in the Jerusalem palace. Of course, that does not include the dating "It happened in the days of Ahaz, the son of Jotham, the son of Uzziah, the king of Judah," which replaced the אז (then), which had been used as a connecting link in 2 Kings 16:5 and which one might presume, possibly without the reference to the father and grandfather of Ahaz, had already been placed at the beginning of the account contained in v. 2ff.

Concerning the names Ahaz, Jotham, and Uzziah, see above, p. 5; concerning Rezin, see above, p. 283. Pekah is the short form of the name פְּקַחְיָה (Pekahiah), "Yahweh opens" (the eyes or ears; cf. Ps. 146:8; Isa. 42:7, 20, and often elsewhere), which was the name of Pekah's predecessor (see also Diringer, op. cit., 167, 203f., 353; the Lachish ostracon 19, line 3; and see Tallqvist, *Akkadische Personennamen,* 180). The first part of his father's name, רְמַלְיָהוּ (Remaliah) (see also 2 Kings 15:15–37; 16:1, 5; Isa. 7:4f., 9; 8:6; cf. also Diringer 179, 217), cannot be explained; see above, textual note 1c, and see Noth, *Personennamen* 257, no. 1261a. Ahaz reigned, according to the chronology from Pavlovský/Vogt, which has been adopted (see above, p. 4), from 734/33–728/27. In 2 Kings 15:37 it is reported that pressure from Rezin of Damascus and Pekah of Israel upon Judah had begun while Jotham was still alive. Since there is no reason to question this short notice, it must be assumed that Ahaz faced the threat of confrontation with his northern neighbors already at the very beginning of his reign.

When compared with Isa. 7:1, 2 Kings 16:5 offers a definite plus: וַיָּצֻרוּ עַל־אָחָז (and they besieged Ahaz) (which should certainly be changed so as to read וַיָּ עָלֶיהָ, and they besieged it). According to this, the siege of Jerusalem, which had been dreaded, had actually come, but had apparently not resulted in quick success and soon had to be discontinued. In the book of Kings we are given the reason for the abandonment of the siege: Ahaz had himself sought aid, from Tiglath-Pileser of Assyria, and this latter ruler had immediately seized Damascus (2 Kings 16:7–9). That must have resulted in the siege being withdrawn from the capital city of Judah. A second difference between the two forms of the text is that the book of Isaiah reads לֹא יָכֹל (and he was not able); that is, in contrast to 2 Kings 16:5, it does not read the verb in the plural. That corresponds to the singular עלה (he went up) / יַעֲלֶה רְצִין (Rezin went up); furthermore, the book of Kings has not yet mentioned any assault upon Israel by Tiglath-Pileser; finally, according to the phrase נָחָה אֲרָם עַל־אֶפְרָיִם (Aram has settled itself down upon Israel) in v. 2, Aram, not Israel, was the driving force behind this most unfortunate action against Jerusalem. Concerning other historical problems, consult the literature at the beginning of this section.

[7:2] At the time when Isaiah confronted the king on Fuller's Field Street, the siege of Jerusalem had not yet taken place. Nothing more was known than that Aram had gained a footing in Ephraim (concerning Ephraim, see above, commentary on 9:8a). The pressure of the moment, at which time the prophet sought to prevent the king from taking action without reflection (cf. the "take care for yourself" in v. 4), would be impossible to understand if the problems of that moment were not viewed within their broad historical context in the world scene: Tiglath-Pileser III was a most dynamic personality who had not long ago ascended the throne of Assyria. As soon as he consolidated all authority under his control, he set out with astounding resoluteness to assemble for himself a world-wide kingdom. He had put down an anti-Assyrian coalition in 743 in North Syria, formed under the leadership of Dardur III from Urartu. Five years later, in 738, he had already succeeded in conquering the group of the states allied with Hamath in Middle Syria, which he immediately incorporated, to a large extent, into the system of Assyrian provinces. Among the rulers who declared their loyalty to him by means of paying tribute, one finds reference to both Rezin of Damascus and Menahem of Israel (Annals, line 150ff.; see *AOT*[2] 346; *ANET*[2] 283). In the years which followed, Tiglath-Pileser was once again occupied in the northern part of his kingdom. But in 734, he set forth on a new campaign in the west, which was primarily directed against Gaza (cf. D. J. Wiseman, "Two Historical Inscriptions from Nimrud," *Iraq* 13 [1951] 21–26, and A. Alt, "Thiglathpilesers III. erster Feldzug nach Palästina," *KlSchr* II, 150–162). Already at that time, the coastal region had been torn away from Israel, to whom it had belonged, and had been incorporated into the Assyrian kingdom as the province *du'ru* (i.e., Dor). In this situation, which was already so threatening for the small states from southern Syria and Palestine, Rezin apparently sought to establish an anti-Assyrian front. Pekah had already—if our explanation of the phrase עַל־אֶפְרָיִם (upon Ephraim) is correct—most likely joined in, more or less under duress rather than willingly. But Ahaz of Jerusalem, apparently having correctly sized up the actual strength of each side, had refused to join. Therefore, at the moment in question, Judah was to be forced to become part of the coalition, being forced by threat of armed attack. The objective was to enter Jerusalem by force, bring about the downfall of Ahaz, and install a certain בן־טבאל (son of Tabeel) in his place (v. 6). טבאל (Tabeel) is an Aramaic name (see above, textual note 6b), and there is no doubt that the one who bore this name was one who would carry out Aramean party policy. That does not mean, however, that he was a man who actually was one of the inner circle of Aramean leaders. It would seem to be almost too shrewd a plan to shove the Davidic dynasty off to the side; that dynasty had been in Jerusalem for a very long time and was deeply rooted there. It is possible that there was some attempt to install a man on the throne who would carry out the Aramean policies but who could lay claim to being a member of the Davidic dynasty. Albright's hypothesis has some advantages, suggesting that בן־טבאל (son of Tabeel) might refer to a son of Uzziah or Jotham, in other words, a prince from the Davidic line, but whose mother had come from Tabeel or Beth-Tabeel (see above, textual note 6b, and E. Vogt, "'Filius Tāb'ēl' [Is 7,6]," *Bib* 37 [1956] 263f.). This supposition cannot be elevated to the status of proof positive, since the reading and interpretation of the Assyrian letter which Albright used have their detractors (see H. Donner, *MIO* 5 [1957] 171; in addition, see Stamm, op. cit. [*Die Immanuel-Weissagung*] 441, note 7).

Based on information concerning the events which were taking place in neighboring Ephraim, a futile sense of dismay had seized Jerusalem, even right within the "house of David." According to 2 Kings 16:2, Ahaz was only twenty years old when he became king. Thus, at the beginning of his reign as king, he was certainly still very dependent upon the advice of the people in the palace, particularly his own relatives; they advised him and/or forced him to carry out their directives. The prophet addresses the house of David also in v. 13, even though he had just previously spoken directly to Ahaz. On the other hand, the suffix in v. 2, on לבבו (his heart) must refer specifically to Ahaz, since one cannot rightly speak about the heart of a house. It is not insignificant, for the understanding of this passage, to keep in mind that in ancient Israel one was always seen as embedded within one's "house," just as, on the other hand, the "house" was always represented at any particular time by its "chief leader." Ahaz is not only a ruler, who stands or falls on the basis of his own achievements and the magnitude of his power, but he is also the representative of the dynasty which bears the marks of its own past and is characterized in the present on the basis of its unique relationship with Yahweh. Therefore, it is already of utmost significance that his heart is "shaking," just because a neighboring petty king is making preparations to go up against his city. One "shakes"/"totters" at other times, for example, when one is drunk (Isa. 29:9; 24:20; Ps. 107:27); blind people totter (Lam. 4:14), but also, as the imagery used by Isaiah so graphically demonstrates: The trees of the forest shake when the wind blows. In a situation like this, an inner composure and an outward steadfastness would correspond to the dignity which befits the Davidic king. But Ahaz does not seem to be able to measure up to such a demeanor.

[7:3] At this time, Isaiah is assigned the task of going up to confront Ahaz. It does not seem to be completely clear to us why the confrontation has to take place specifically at the "far end of the water conduit for the upper pool on Fuller's Field Street." It may be that Isaiah was not sent to the palace so that he would not attract attention or so that those people who were in control at the palace would not immediately be able to contradict his recommendation. One cannot be sure of the exact location of the upper pool. One can conclude from the "go out to" that it refers to a particular location which is outside the city walls. A מסלה is not a country road, but it is a street which is carefully constructed with special materials. In addition to this, this is the only time that we find out the name of a street within or near ancient Jerusalem. It must have been a well-known place. According to 36:2, the junior officers of the Assyrian king took their positions at the very same place when the city was under siege. Since the only access available to an enemy army for entry into Jerusalem is on the northern side, one might suppose that the upper pool ought to be sought there, a solution which has been suggested recently once again (Donner, op. cit. [VTSup 11] 11). But even if the lower pool is located at the southern edge of the city, that does not necessarily mean (contra Donner) that the upper pool must be sought in the northern part. An installation which has been constructed for use by fullers, if the fuller's field is there, can presumably be located only to the south. And yet, each of three comprehensive studies of the topography of the city, J. Simons, *Jerusalem in the Old Testament* (1952), L. H. Vincent, *Jérusalem de l'Ancien Testament* I (1954) II/III (1956), and M. Avi-Yonah, *Sepher Yeruschalayim* (1956), offer differing theories. M. Burrows (op. cit., 227) suggests a location in the lower Kidron Valley. It is only there that one finds as much water as the fullers would need to do to their work. That is also the location of עין רוֹגֵל ('Ain Rogel), the fuller's spring (known today as *bīr 'eijūb*); see G. Dalman, op. cit. (*Jerusalem*) 163ff.; in addition, see *BHH* 826f. The practice of fulling is part of the activity connected with producing textiles. The Arabic *kabasa* means knead, and the Akkadian *kabāsu* means to step on, stamp upon; cf. also the Ugaritic *kbs* (on this, see G. Buccellati, *BeO* 4 [1962] 204, and G. Brunet, op. cit.). Stepping upon, kneading, and beating in the water cleanses the cloth and softens it after it has been woven. To accomplish this, the water is mixed with lye (see Dalman, *AuS* V, 145ff., illus. 33, and *BHH* 2134f.). According to 2 Kings 16:3, Ahaz allowed his son to go through fire. For this reason, Steinmann (op. cit., 83) considers it likely that he and his palace officials had assembled themselves out in Topheth, so that he could offer his eldest son there, to Moloch, in an effort to ward off the danger. On the way back, Isaiah would have been waiting for the king between the Hamra-pool (pool of Siloam) and the Rogel spring, at the point where the Tyropoeon Valley opens up into the Hinnom Valley. But the text in Isaiah 7 does not supply any evidence which would justify combining these events. A presupposition which is much more likely is that the king was on an "inspection tour, intending to check out the fortification installations and provisions for water" (Donner, op. cit., 11), when the prophet met up with him.

The king was not unaccompanied on the Fuller's Field Street, as one can already infer from the address to the house of David in v. 13. Isaiah is also not by himself; at the bidding of God, he also brought along his son Shear-jashub. Because of his name, the presence of this child, who was certainly still a young boy, takes on great significance, which presupposes that this boy was known throughout Jerusalem. No doubt he, like Maher-shalal-hash-baz (see 8:1), was to corroborate the prophetic proclamation of Isaiah (cf. Hos. 1:4–9). Of course, the intended deeper meaning is not quite as clear for us as one might hope. There has already been much discussion even just about the way the name is to be understood grammatically.

Generally, this has been translated: "a remnant returns." But if that were intended, one would expect the reverse word order, יָשׁוּב שְׁאָר. Names which have the imperfect following the noun are rare (see Noth, *Personennamen,* 28). Köhler (*VT* 3 [1953] 84f.) therefore chooses to explain יָשׁוּב as a so-called "bare relative clause" and translates: "the remnant, which returns." But then one would have to go on to say that the son's name is not only intended to alert by means of a message about the return of a remnant or of the remnant, but that the son himself represents that remnant (thus also Gunneweg, op. cit., 27f.). But there are absolutely no parallels in Hebrew for this way of constructing names (in 10:21f. שְׁאָר, remnant, must function as the subject and יָשׁוּב, returned, as the predicate). This surprising word order causes one to be much more occupied with explaining why שְׁאָר (remnant) is accentuated: "a remnant (at least) returns" or in a warning, even threatening way: "(only) a remnant returns" (approximately what is said by S. H. Blank, *HUCA* 27 [1956] 86ff.). Concerning this, the question is posed: Is the name intended as a promise or as an admonition, warning, or threat? Or is the concept of a remnant, to speak of it as H. Gottlieb does (*VT* 17 [1967] 441f.), actually two-sided, i.e., does it contain both an "element of judgment" and an "aspect of salvation" at the very same time? At this point, the other question comes up as well: What does שׁוּב mean in this context? Is it an internal or an external return to Yahweh (the latter is approximately what is maintained by Gunneweg, op. cit.)? Is it return in the sense of a conversion or an inward soul-searching? Or is it return in the secular sense (as, e.g., "returning from a battle"; see Blank, op. cit. [*JBL* 67, 1948] 215, with reference to 1 Kings 22:28 and Jer. 22:10)? Finally, שׁוּב also means to turn oneself away, to the side, so that the translation "a remnant turns itself away" would be theoretically possible. Such names, when further clarification is lacking and without knowing more about the situation out of which they developed, can lead to several different interpretations. Of course, the book of Isaiah offers an interpretation in another passage: 10:20–22 (see the discussion there); that passage has "on that day," which means: in the eschatological time of salvation, "that which remains of Israel will turn back to the Holy One of Israel"; this means that Israel will rely upon the Holy One "in faithfulness (or 'in truthfulness')." But v. 22 adds to this that it is in reality a very small remnant to which such salvation will come. But that section can hardly have come from Isaiah; rather, it is a most interesting interpretation, which cannot help determine the original meaning of שְׁאָר יָשׁוּב. It is even more certain that the passages from 11:11–16 cannot be used when one tries to clarify the essence of Isaiah's message. For this passage, "remnant" is a technical term for the congregation of those who were returning from various lands of the Jewish Diaspora (see above, commentary on 4:3; commentary on 6:13; and below, on 28:5). If these passages cannot be of any help, then it is clear that the concept of the remnant does not have the meaning in Isaiah which is usually attributed to it. And yet, Herrmann (op. cit., 127f.) is correct when he refers to 1:21–26. Using the root יתר (remain), which is connected, based on its meaning, with שׁאר (be left, remain), the prophet does speak of a remnant which still remains, and he does so as well in 1:8; 7:22 (?); and 30:17.

But, according to these passages, it is nothing more than an extremely poor remnant, which has just barely escaped from a catastrophe. Isaiah is aware of the sifting process, and one can certainly speak of the "concept of a remnant," in the sense of a group which still remains, if one does not base that solely upon terms like שאר (remain) and שארית (remnant). An indication that Isaiah had a hope such as this can be seen most clearly within the circle of disciples in Isa. 8:16–18 and among the poor mentioned in 14:32, who seek a place of safety in Zion; see G. von Rad, *OTTheol* II, 165f.

Under these circumstances, we will have to attempt to understand the name on the basis of the situation in 7:2–17 (see below, pp. 313f.), which is a precarious thing to do, since the basic understanding of the prediction about Immanuel is controversial in a way which can hardly be matched by any other section of the OT. In spite of that, the following can be said: The son who is able to accompany his father, indeed on such an important mission, must have been several years old. It is likely that he would have been born around the time that Isaiah was called to be a prophet. This means that the name must correspond to Isaiah's proclamation as it applies to his first period of activity. Whether or not one can confidently take שוב (return) in a religious sense (see 6:10), the name is not as a matter of course to be explained as corroboration for Isaiah's proclamation about salvation, but also not (as Blank interprets it) solely as a prediction of disaster. It warns and admonishes. Isaiah will not deny that salvation is possible. But that salvation is linked to a return to Yahweh. And the fact that only a remnant will find the way back to Yahweh ought not cause anyone to be resigned to being disappointed. Thus, the name is meant to say: Only a remnant will turn back through all of the catastrophes which will press in upon Israel, that is, only a remnant will return to Yahweh in faith. This interpretation explains the uncharacteristic word order (but cf. Gunneweg, op. cit., 29, who plainly speaks of a "prophetic ecclesiola," 31). If שאר ישוב is to be understood in the way suggested here, then it makes good sense to take the lad along to the conversation. His name, though it is far removed from a pure and simple prediction of salvation, theologically corresponds exactly to v. 9b.

[7:4] The preferable way to introduce oracles of salvation is with אל־תירא (do not fear for yourself). This encouragement is accented, and made more explicit, by a whole host of other parallel terms in our passage. The heart of the king ought not "become soft" before these two smoking stubs from burning sticks, naturally referring to the two enemy rulers. The metaphor is an outstanding example of just the right choice of words in Isaiah's use of imagery. In the other two places where the word אוד (burning sticks) is also used in the OT, Amos 4:11 and Zech. 3:2, the word refers to a log which has been pulled out of the fire. That is also what is intended here: The stick of wood is no longer burning; rather, it is only smoking a bit, so that one ought to treat it carefully, but it will not be long before it will go out on its own. The interpretive comment: "before the furious rage of Rezin and Aram and the son of Remaliah" is not really the best—not only because it repeats what the hearer or reader already has observed independently, but also because "furious rage" could indeed be very dangerous, if it were not the furious rage of two petty rulers, essentially powerless, whose own thrones were not resting on solid ground.

Isaiah was correct in his assessment of these two opponents of Ahaz. Israel had been weakened by the first campaign of Tiglath-Pileser into Palestine, and the usurper Pekah, who was not, even then, sitting firmly in the saddle, was himself only half-heartedly participating. But Damascus already had the dangerous Assyrians as neighbors, just across the border. The matter had not really been assessed much differently by the palace in Jerusalem; otherwise, Ahaz would have joined the anti-Assyrian front without giving it another thought.

The admonition אל ירך לבבך (do not let your heart despair) has an exact parallel in the "war oracle" in Deuteronomy 20 (v. 3); cf. also Jer. 51:46 (once again, parallel to ירא, be fearful). השקט, "be still," is not actually found in any other "war addresses," but a synonym, החריש (be still), is used in Exod. 14:14. The first imperative used here, השמר (take care of yourself), which carries particular weight, especially since the admonition not to fear must come at the beginning, does not belong to the special language of the oracle of salvation. But what does it mean in this present context? One hardly ever finds this imperative in the OT without details being included about what one ought to protect oneself from (but see 1 Sam. 19:2). It is often used in deuteronomistic terminology, warning someone to be careful not to forget Yahweh (Deut. 4:9, and passim) but also that one should not forget the events of the salvation history (Deut. 4:15) or the covenant (Deut. 4:23), or something like that. Does Isaiah intend to say that Ahaz should not forget the covenant which Yahweh made with David, including its assurance of a dynasty? One must note that the prophet does not speak about forgetting. Opinions of the exegetes range far and wide: Isaiah attempts to get Ahaz to pull back from war and would thus like to get across to him: Watch out that you do not go forward with military preparations; stay away from your intensive activity, which is essentially motivated by fear and faint-heartedness (C. A. Keller, op. cit. [TZ 11] 82). But this is hardly likely if one considers the basic genre being used here. In an oracle addressed to a king, one would be encouraged to trust in God and would receive a promise of his help. But that does not mean that he ought to "do nothing at all." A. Lods (cf. ZAW 51 [1933] 262) believes that Ahaz had come to see whether the provisions for a water supply were sufficient for Jerusalem during a siege. השמר (take care for yourself) would thus mean something like: Guard yourself and keep from looking around for help from strangers; do not overlook the possibilities for defense which are right within Jerusalem; phrased in religious terms this would mean: Do not overlook the protection which has been offered to Jerusalem by its God. But why does Isaiah not say this more clearly? Apparently, it would be because he deals with circumstances which are clearly conceptualized by everyone present, but about which one was not able to engage in public discussion. As Würthwein (op. cit., 53ff.) has explained most clearly, the intended plan must have been to call for Assyria to give aid against the enemy, which was only to be achieved by a de facto submission to the mighty power which was located on the Tigris. That is, in fact, exactly what happened, as the book of Kings informs us (2 Kings 16:7–9). But at the time when Isaiah encountered the king, that decision had not yet been made. One cannot object to this interpretation of the passage by saying that Isaiah could have known nothing about these "secret" plans. There were other times as well when he was very well informed about specific details concerning events as they developed within the palace (cf. passages like 22:15ff.), and he had a good relationship with important people at the highest levels (see 8:2). Thus, the background for 7:2–9 is that there was a plan to reach an accord with Assyria; if this supposition is not on the mark, "the entire passage remains a sealed book" (Kraeling, op. cit., 280). This means that the alternative: trust in God's protection or in human actions (thus Keller, op. cit. [*TZ* 11] 84f.; von Rad, op. cit. [*Heilige Krieg*] 57f.), is a false dichotomy.

There is a third possibility: human action in a calm setting, in fearlessness and in steadfastness of heart. But one must admit that Isaiah's concern is not with issuing a call for an active military resistance; that much he could leave to the king and his advisers. What was important for him was to restrain Ahaz from the most disastrous course, which would have been an appeal to Tiglath-Pileser for help. No matter how radically different one finds the political messages of the individual prophets, at this point one observes a remarkably unanimous attitude: harsh rejection of any military-political pact with the major powers (for Isaiah, see 18:1ff.; 20:1ff.; 30:1ff.; 31:1ff.). In no way is that simply a political program and it is not based upon "an insurmountable calm and impartiality of judgment when it comes to all earthly affairs" (K. Elliger, "Prophet und Politik," *ZAW* 53 [1935] 12), even though one can certainly laud the prophets, after the fact, about this demeanor; rather, it is based upon their religious premises. One cannot speak in this case about covenant ideology, of course (contra Würthwein, op. cit., 57f.). One way or another, even if it does not come through clearly, there is no doubt that the Zion theology is the basis for Isaiah's admonitions.

Isaiah is much clearer when he shows that he is working within the framework of the election of the king. That is the reason why the "house of David" is addressed (cf. Scullion, op. cit., 289f.). To call upon Tiglath-Pileser for help means that the promises which were given to the Davidic dynasty are to be pushed to the side, as if they are inconsequential. It would finally be a pure and simple rejection of the faithfulness of God, upon which the entire survival of Israel depended. However, also on the political level, submission to Assyria was a most awesome, highly precarious step to take. It would be a betrayal of the neighboring kingdom, with which Judah continued to be related because they shared a common destiny and because they shared faith in Yahweh. It was an action which would give up the defensive wall which was provided by the two states to the north, Ephraim and Aram (cf. 17:3), and which shielded Judah from the powers which were in northern Syria and in the Mesopotamian region. And it was a renunciation of one's own sovereignty, the first step toward the eventual demise of Judah. Every future act of resistance against Assyria and the states which would follow as its successors would no longer be legally a battle for one's own independence, but rather rebellion on the part of a petty state which had freely acknowledged the hegemony of the overlord and had placed itself under his protection (cf. even Ezra 4:15). It had already caused problems when Asa of Jerusalem entered into an agreement with Benhadad of Damascus against Israel, 1 Kings 15:18ff., but at that time Damascus had not been quite so obviously the superior partner. However, Assyria was undeniably the mightier power. Ahaz stood at the moment of decision, the likes of which had hardly ever presented itself in Judah's previous history.

[7:5, 6] It is only when we come to vv. 5f. that we discover the plan of the opponents in the war against Ahaz (on this, see above, pp. 293f.). The conjunction יַעַן כִּי (because) (on this, see above, p. 148) most generally introduces the protasis which provides the reason (see 1 Kings 13:21; 21:29; Isa. 3:16; 8:6f.; used differently in Neh. 11:20), which would speak against the thesis of Saebø (op. cit., 58f.) that the causal clause in vv. 5 and 6 belongs with what precedes. The gloss "Ephraim and the son of Remaliah" puts the Northern Kingdom on the same level with Aram, which does not agree with v. 2. One notices that Pekah is referred to here, as also in v. 4, only by the designation "the son of Remaliah." That is a move which clearly expresses disdain (cf. 1 Sam. 10:11; 20:27, 30; 22:12, but also בֶּן־טָבְאַל, son of Tabeel). Pekah was a usurper; he had in fact been a royal servant before he used force to elevate himself to the throne, but he was not legitimately in line to be king (on this, see A. Alt, "Menschen ohne Namen," *KlSchr* III 198–213). This means that Yahweh, the God of Israel, was not backing him as the one guaranteeing that he would remain on the throne.

[7:7] The actual prediction follows now in v. 7: לֹא תָקוּם וְלֹא תִהְיֶה (it will not happen and will not succeed), namely, the evil which Aram had "planned." The verb יָעַץ (plan) reminds one of the עֵצָה (counsel) of Yahweh, about which Isaiah speaks so pointedly (see above, pp. 202f.). Not the plans of human beings, but rather the plan of Yahweh is the one which actually is carried through to the end. It is exactly as Prov. 19:21 says: רַבּוֹת מַחֲשָׁבוֹת בְּלֶב־אִישׁ וַעֲצַת יהוה הִיא תָקוּם (Many are the plans in the mind of a man, but it is the purpose of Yahweh that will be established); cf. also 21:30; Job 8:15. Thus, it seems that Isaiah has used a formulation commonly found in wisdom (which also has an Egyptian parallel; cf. H. H. Schmid, *Wesen und Geschichte der Weisheit*, BZAW 101 [1966] 147). In a similar context, he makes the same observation in 14:24, using הָיָה (it shall be) next to קוּם (it shall stand) in that passage as well; cf. also 40:8 (דְּבַר־אֱלֹהֵינוּ יָקוּם לְעוֹלָם, the word of our God will stand forever); 46:10 (עֲצָתִי תָקוּם, my counsel shall stand); Jer. 44:28ff.; 51:29. In and of itself, קוּם can have a durative sense ("have ability to go on") or an inchoative sense ("just now come into existence"), but the fact that one finds, parallel to תָקוּם (happen), the verb תִהְיֶה (succeed, be) makes the inchoative meaning the more likely one. Therefore, one cannot separate v. 7 from the preceding causal clause, as Saebø does; as a result, it is to be connected with v. 8 ("It shall not be . . . that Aram's head is Damascus, etc.").

[7:8a, 9a] Based on what has just been said, the clauses in vv. 8a and 9a which are introduced with כִּי (for) are not subject clauses (Saebø, op. cit., 63f.), but are supposed to give the reason why the plan of the enemies will not come to pass: They do not have the legitimacy which God alone grants. That needs no further explanation at all in the case of the usurper Pekah. Apparently Isaiah agrees with Hosea's viewpoint about kingship in the Northern Kingdom: "They made kings, but not through me" (8:4; cf. also 3:4; 5:1; 7:5; 8:10; 10:3, 7). Rezin, serving as a king over a people which does not know Yahweh, is naturally unable to claim that he has been endowed with the full power of Yahweh (even though Yahweh, as the lord of all peoples, could certainly *make* it possible for him to be an instrument to carry out his plans, as Isaiah says about Assyria [10:5]).

To this point, the train of thought comes through clearly. And yet, the main topic of conversation is not just the enemy leaders, but also, and to even a greater extent, their capital cities, Damascus and Samaria. One can come to only one conclusion about what this means: They are also deficient when it comes to divine certification; they do not have the same honor as is accorded the city of God, fittingly bestowed on Jerusalem/Zion. Samaria, the capital of the Northern Kingdom, founded by Omri (1 Kings 16:24), could not even lay claim to being a venerable old city. Ahab had built a Baal temple there (1 Kings 16:32). Isaiah leaves no question, in 28:1–4, about his assessment of that city. His contemporary Hosea did not have any different opinion about the city: "I have spurned your calf, O Samaria. My anger burns against them" (8:5; see also 8:6; 7:1; 10:5, 7). It must acknowledge its sin—that it had obstinately rebelled against its God (Hos. 14:1). And both Amos and Micah agree (Amos 3:9, 12; 4:1; 6:1; Mic. 1:5, 6). As in this passage, Samaria and Damascus are also mentioned together in Isa. 8:4; cf. also 10:9 and 17:13, in which the downfall of each city is proclaimed. Concerning Amos's judgment upon the capital city of the Arameans, see Amos 1:3, 5.

We have already established the fact that the clauses in vv. 8a and 9a call for another clause which would continue the thought. But there is obviously no evidence to suggest a textual gap (see above, on the form of vv. 4–9). Isaiah does not need to put into words what is completely obvious to his hearers. Ever since Ewald, it has been repeatedly suggested that the continuation would have to read: "And the head of Jerusalem is Yahweh." But that is unlikely, based on the clauses which immediately precede. Yahweh is, in fact, the head over Israel too and, in a wider sense, over Aram as well. But in Jerusalem, and *only* in Jerusalem, Yahweh had installed his king (Ps. 2:6); there the throne of the house of David was established (Ps. 122:5). Isaiah was certainly no palace theologian who accepted the tradition about the Davidic covenant without any reflection. That is seen clearly in his actions over against Ahaz, as well as in 11:1, where he speaks about a shoot from the *stump* of Jesse. But the king in Jerusalem is not a ruler just like any other power figure or even like a usurper. He is enveloped by the election of his own God, which cannot be ignored as if it did not exist.

[7:8b] The gloss in v. 8b is most puzzling. Sixty-five years, calculated from the time of the Syro-Ephraimitic War, goes far beyond the time when Israel came to its end. Is this a prediction which was never fulfilled? One could indeed use that very fact as a reason for treating it as genuine; why would an author who inserted a prediction after the fact not have been able to figure this out more exactly! Yet, it seems likely that about sixty-five years after the Syro-Ephraimitic War there were indeed some events which took place to which this prediction makes reference. That brings us to the end of Esarhaddon's era and to the beginning of Ashurbanipal's reign. At that time, in connection with Esarhaddon's war against Baal of Tyre and Tirhakah of Ethiopia, there was a renewed effort to resettle foreign groups of peoples in the area around Samaria (cf. Ezra 4:2), and the same type of activity most likely also took place during Ashurbanipal's reign (= Osnappar, Ezra 4:10), which would have been viewed as a serious blow against the effort to preserve the uniqueness of the indigenous population (see A. Alt, *KlSchr* II, 321, note 4; E. Jenni, *Die politischen Voraussagen der Propheten,* ATANT 29 [1956] 18f.; and W. Rudolph, *HAT* 20 [1949]; see Ezra 4:2).

[7:9b] And now, to the famous clause in v. 9b: אם לא תאמינו כי לא תאמנו (If you do not believe, then you will not remain). Every translation struggles with whether one ought to ignore the wordplay or else give a rendering which sounds rather forced. "Wenn ihr nicht vertraut, so bleibt ihr nicht betreut" (if you do not trust, then you won't be cared for) (M. Buber, *Der Glaube der Propheten* [1950] 196) is not exact. "Wer kein Amen erklärt, der kein Amen erfährt" (whoever doesn't give his amen, that one does not experience any amen) (H. W. Wolff, op. cit. [BibS(N) 35] 23) incorrectly leads one to the conclusion that belief consists in saying one's amen to biblical truths; the same assessment holds true for his paraphrase: "If you do not consider the proclaimed word to be trustworthy, then you have lost your chance for your own individual existence continuing." The closest would be the translation: "If you do not believe, then you will not have any permanency." A more attractive rendering is the traditional: "Glaubt ihr nicht, so bleibt ihr nicht" (if you don't believe, then you won't remain). (After Martin Luther and his associates had weighed a variety of alternatives [see WA DB 2:8; 4:45; 11/1:42], we find in the Deutschen Bibel of 1545: "Gleubt jr nicht, So bleibt jr nicht" [WA DB 11/1:43].)

We have already established that 7:3–9 is an oracle of salvation, in the format commonly used when being delivered to kings. It is very obvious why the continued existence of the dynasty would be mentioned in such a message from God, possibly even making the point that it would last forever. The idea that the dynasty would remain firm as a rock was one of the essential elements in the Jerusalem "kingship ideology," and there are other passages, also in this connection, where the root אמן (support, be firm) appears. One must not make too much of the fact that the *niph'al* is used only here, in the wordplay with the *hiph'il* (Fohrer I², 105, note 48).

In an inscription in the Ninib temple in Babylon, Nabopolassar declares: "Whoever is faithful to Bel, that person's foundation stands firm; whoever is faithful to the son of Bel, that one will become very old" (*ša itti ᶦˡᵘbêli kînu ikunna išdašu ša itti mâr ᶦˡᵘbêli kînu ulabar ana dârâtim*), in which case the Akkadian root *kānu* corresponds, as elsewhere, exactly to the Hebrew אמן (support, be firm) (*VAB* 4 [1912] 68, line 36f.); "life" also belongs to the general vocabulary associated with האמין (believe, trust) (cf. Hab. 2:4 and, on this, see H. Wildberger, op. cit. [ZTK (1968)] 140ff.).

The logical conclusion to the sequence in vv. 8a and 9a would be a message of salvation ending with the following assurance: "But the house of David will continue to remain unshaken," i.e., that it is נֶאֱמָן (established, firm). Instead, in its place, one finds a negative-conditional clause construction in v. 9b. That was once all that was needed for Boehmer (op. cit., 86) to say that the clause is not Isaianic, since a conditional reassurance is really no reassurance at all. According to him, if v. 9b were the actual conclusion to vv. 5–9a, where the call to be unafraid is clearly substantiated, then the effect and power of the encouragement which begins the message in v. 4 would be significantly weakened, if not actually nullified. Boehmer did not gain a following. But he was right in pointing out that there is an excessively sharp break dividing vv. 9a and 9b. Verse 9b, if one seriously examines its relationship with vv. 5–9a, is as shocking as having v. 7 follow 5:1–6 in the song of the vineyard. The style of the oracle of salvation is burst by v. 9. It is this modification itself, which essentially destroys the form of the oracle of salvation, that shows what Isaiah accomplished: For him, the promises to the house of David were not perishable—as, for example, Hosea expected nothing more of the kingdom of Israel—but they are framed within the context of faith. The prophecy of salvation is spoken in a very strict sense, without the validity of God's promises being called into question—and the prophecy of disaster is confined within certain bounds, without invalidating the reasons for its very harsh assessment of those who simply wanted to blindly resurrect the traditions about salvation. Salvation and faith belong together. Luther recognized that very clearly: "Sola ergo fides certificat et habet solidum fundamentum. Frustra autem fit promisso, nisi accedat fides" (Hence faith alone makes certain and has a solid foundation. But the promise becomes useless unless faith is added) (WA 31/2, 58, line 3f., quoted from Kaiser [Engl: *Luther's Works* 16, 82]). In actual fact, an oracle of salvation has become a message of admonition or warning. המאמין לא יחיש (he who believes will not be in haste) in 28:16 is also illustrative of the same type of modification of a traditional promise of salvation; the participle replaces a conditional clause in that passage.

But now, what is the more specific meaning of "believe"? האמין is used in an absolute sense and is definitely supposed to be interpreted according to this usage (on this, see H. Wildberger, op. cit. [VTSup 16] 373ff.). The verb is never used in a construction with the accusative, so that Isaiah simply cannot mean: If you do not believe that what I have just spoken to you is a message from Yahweh, i.e., if you do not take it to be true, then your kingly majesty has come to an end. The verb basically means: be solid, trustworthy, as is clear from its use in nontheological passages (Job 39:24 or 29:24, but also Hab. 1:5; on this, see Wildberger, op. cit. [VTSup 16] 376). In this present passage, it helps explain—certainly in a deeper sense—the reason why אל־תירא ולבבך אל־ירך (do not fear for yourself, and do not let your heart despair) was called for in v. 4. It is not simply by chance that certain vocables are found together, but instead, האמין (believe) is used again and again in connection with these and similar terms (on this, see H. Wildberger, op. cit. [ZTK 65 (1968)] 133f.) and means, in the present and in similar passages: "have confidence, overcome all despondency, show steadfastness." One might wonder why האמין (believe) is not used with ב (in), and it has already been suggested (see above, textual note 9a) that, after תאמינו (believe), the following כי (then) should be changed to בי, "in me" (on this, see also Gen. 15:6 and Isa. 28:16 LXX). But this would only weaken its force: "The construction in the absolute conveys to us . . . the absolute nature of what is intended" (M. Buber, *Zwei Glaubensweisen* [1950] 21). It demonstrates nothing less than a deeply rooted reinterpretation of the faith concept when the Chronicler, who puts the word of Isaiah into the mouth of Jehoshaphat, formulates it as follows: האמינו ביהוה אלהיכם ותאמנו האמינו בנביאיו והצליחו (Believe in the Lord your God, and you will be established; believe his prophets, and you will succeed) (2 Chron. 20:20). In that passage, it can only mean "trust the oracle which Jahaziel the prophet has just finished delivering." What is being called for is faith in the prophetic activity; often enough it has been suggested that this is precisely what Isaiah means: Take the prophetic word seriously!

Certainly the question remains about what would be able to empower and equip Ahaz to believe. On the basis of the context, the only possible answer to this is: the promise made to the house of David which has been brought into the light once again in the message of the prophet, in the threatening situation which showed how real it is. The basic assurance within the promise, and the way it is supposed to take on a specific reality within the "oracle," is not based on the content of the faith but rather on the foundation of the faith.

[7:10–11] Based on an analogy with similar passages, following vv. 4–9 there should be an account of how Ahaz expressed his own thoughts, as did Moses (Exod. 3:11) or Gideon (Judg. 6:15), or even, at the very least, some mention that the inner resistance of the king did not remain hidden from Isaiah. The compact descriptive style of our section presumes that this happened here too, without mentioning it (concerning this, cf. 1 Sam. 10:2ff.). In any case, Isaiah attempts to overcome the reluctance and/or the timidity of the king. For us, a *sign* is only an indication, but for the ancient Israelite understanding, it was the beginning, the down payment, the ἀρραβών (earnest money) for what actually was to begin to take place. It was less frequently provided as a message to counteract the suspicion that something was not going to happen. The prophet goes so far as to give Ahaz the chance to choose whatever type of sign should be given. Whatever might be meant by "deep within the underworld" or "high above in the heights" (see, for example, P. Boccaccio, *Bib* 33 [1952] 177f., who suggests taking this as a way to use two opposites to express every possibility), in any case, it is intended to underscore the generosity of Isaiah/Yahweh. Gideon himself also chose what type of sign he would get, of course without being authorized to do so (Judg. 6:36–40). Admittedly, some are of the opinion that this encouragement to ask for a sign is not historical. In light of the offer which Isaiah is supposed to have made to Hezekiah according to 38:7ff., which is certainly legendary, one could indeed not completely eliminate the possibility that what really happened has been spruced up a bit (see de Lagarde, op. cit., 10, and above, pp. 291f.; in addition, see G. Quell, "Wahre und falsche Propheten," *BFCT* 46/1 [1952] 171, note 2). But we do not have any ways or means to verify the exact words used in the discussion between Isaiah and Ahaz. In and of itself, there is no reason to doubt that a sign was really offered. As the sentence now stands, it seeks to state clearly: It should be a sign which is obviously not caused by some trickery on Isaiah's part. But the conjectures of present-day exegetes, about what it might have actually been, are more problematic. Duhm (ad loc.) suggests: "It might have been, e.g., that the earth would split, as in Num. 26:28ff., or that the sun would become darkened." Wolff thinks it might have been lightning or an earthquake, "just like the two signs given to Gideon in Judges 6, fire from the rock and dew from the heavens" (op. cit. [BibS(N) 35] 29). De Lagarde's observation, that Isaiah must have been either a fanatical dreamer or a trickster for him to have made such an offer, was repudiated by Duhm, who made the observation that all of humanity would have fit into such a category of "fanatical dreamers" until the eighteenth century. But de Lagarde was correct in one sense: The "writing prophets" did not have anything to do with working miracles. That would mean that the sign which Isaiah himself offered was something from within the realm of natural occurrences; about this, there is most general agreement among present-day exegetes in spite of all their differences in the exposition of v. 14: It is not intended to announce the birth of a lad born to a maiden. Isaiah would have expected that Ahaz would have asked for a sign similar to what others had already received.

[7:12] Ahaz is not willing to accept the offer: "I will not make a request and will not test Yahweh." (By translating it in this way, one ought not overlook the fact that the Hebrew שאל does not only mean "request" but also "demand, require.") The two verbs are only formally on the same level. The second is explanatory: "Ask" means here to desire to put God to the test. But that would be presumptuous, and a human being ought not be found guilty of such action over against one's God. God can put a human being to the test, that is very much his right (Gen. 22:1; Exod. 16:4; Deut. 13:14; 33:8; Judg. 2:22; 3:14), and the one innocently accused practically demands of God that he would test him (Ps. 26:2). But that Israel "tests" God now and again is a part of its foolish rebelliousness, which gives evidence that one is turning away from reliance upon God. The accounts which furnish examples of God being "tested" by Israel actually describe cases where Israel demands of God some sort of a miracle, Exod. 17:2; Deut. 6:16; Ps. 78:18. But Israel is specifically commanded: "You shall not put Yahweh your God to the test" (Deut. 6:16; cf. Mark 1:12f., and its parallels). In this way, a very important point is brought out clearly, which distinguishes Israelite faith from that of those who lived nearby (cf. also the way Jesus judges those who seek after miracles and demand signs, Matt. 16:4), for whom giving interpretations of signs played an extremely important role.

With his answer, Ahaz is not only thinking on his feet but, according to the letter of the law, is absolutely correct. There is, to a certain extent, some pride on the part of someone who presumes he is on a level above primitive religiosity. Luther says, about the king's answer: "Impius Ahas simulat sanctimoniam, quod metu Dei nolit postulare signum. Sic hypocritae, ubi non est opus, sunt religiosissimi, rursus ubi debeant esse humiles, sunt superbissimi" (Impious Ahaz simulates a holy attitude which says that he does not wish to request a sign because he fears God. Thus, the hypocrites, when it is not necessary, are most religious; on the other hand, when they ought to be humble, they are most haughty) (WA 25, 116, lines 8–11). Some have said that this interpretation treats the king unfairly. Built within the theologically correct answer of Ahaz, there lurks, without a doubt, a lack of the courage which boldly risks acting on his faith.

[7:13] Isaiah's reaction is just as sharp: "Is it too little for you, to weary human beings, that you also weary my God?" It is not because of a careless style that this invective is addressed once again to the collective group, the Davidic dynasty. Isaiah would have been well aware of the fact that it was not the king alone, or possibly not even the king in the first place, who was responsible for the decisions being made hopefully to cope with the threatening situation. But at the same time, the address "house of David" would once again spotlight it for all of the חֲסָדִים (pious) (cf. Isa. 55:3; Ps. 89:25, 34) who rejoiced in having such a dynasty. According to Mic. 6:2f., הלאה, "make weary," is part of the form of speech used in a רִיב (controversy). "He has made me weary," in the context of an accusation, would mean: I have had enough of him and am not willing to allow myself to be insulted by him any longer; cf. Isa. 1:14: נִלְאֵיתִי נְשֹׂא (I am worn out, having to endure them). Using הלאה, one hears an echo of the idea that the partner's patience has finally worn out. But how is it that Isaiah can accuse the king of having wearied human beings? Some commentators (see Wolff, op. cit. [BibS(N) 35] 30; Kaiser, ad loc.) believe it refers to vacillating while making political decisions, which had worn down the resolve of the inhabitants of Jerusalem, finally being torn apart by this wrenching test of their resolve. We simply know too little about the frame of mind within the palace and in Jerusalem to explain this charge with any degree of confidence. One might also remember that the narratives in the Pentateuch depict some situations in which Moses brings bitter accusations against Israel because it has wearied him with its consistently rebellious nature. Elijah says: "It is enough," and wishes for his death, 1 Kings 19:4. Jeremiah laments that he has become weary and hopes that the furious rage of Yahweh would not be held back any longer, 6:11; cf. 15:6; 20:9. These parallels somewhat substantiate the supposition that, when Isaiah mentions the "human beings," he is primarily thinking of himself.

One notices that he uses the formula "my God." Nowhere else does Isaiah speak of Yahweh as "his God"; when he does it here, the way in which he personally lays claim to Yahweh for himself is intended to show that the connection between Yahweh and the house of David has been broken. One might remember the formulation in 2 Sam. 7:14: "I will be his [the 'descendants of David's'] father, and he shall be my son"; cf. Ps. 2:7. Yahweh is and indeed remains God, whether human beings take any note of him or not. Yet, what is of crucial importance is whether he is "my God." But that "my God" comes only within the boundaries of faith. Here, exactly as in v. 9b, treating the promises of salvation as if they have an objective reality is clearly shown to be nothing more than an illusion.

[7:14] "Thus (לכן) Yahweh himself will give you a sign. . . ." The controversy among exegetes concerning the interpretation of this verse, about which more commentary has been written than any other single verse in the OT, begins with the question about whether the sign Yahweh himself will give is indicative of salvation or disaster. If the confrontation with Ahaz takes place, so to speak, under the sign that "only a remnant will return"; if the existence of the house of David is predicated upon its faith, and if Ahaz goes on to make it clear that he is not ready to venture forth

in faith; if Isaiah has just had to accuse him harshly of not only inappro-
priately testing the patience of human beings but also God; and if the
prophet has at least raised a question, by using אלהי (my God) instead of
אלהיכם (your God), about whether the tie between Yahweh and the
Davidic house had not indeed finally been broken—*then* it seems that
this could only be a sign which proclaims disaster. One ought not lay too
much weight upon the formal argument that לכן (thus), as a rule, and
possibly always, introduces a threat in the genuine passages in the book of
Isaiah (on this, see Stamm, op. cit. [*VT* 4] 31), since one would not expect
anything else in the great majority of messages proclaiming disaster. But,
in fact, no one would arrive at any other conclusion in the present *context*
than that it is a message of judgment. "Only a completely deluded
exegesis would see anything but a threat to Ahaz in the words which
follow" (Procksch, ad loc.; see also Guthe, op. cit.).

When, in spite of this, well-known authorities of the OT continue
to be of the opinion, still today, that the sign which was announced must
predict salvation (see, e.g., Hammershaimb, op. cit.; Lindblom, op. cit.;
Coppens, op. cit. [FS H. Junker]; Scullion, op. cit.; in addition, consult
the summaries of research), that is a result of the extraordinary difficulties which are presented for exegesis in the following verses. It is not
without reason that Buber called Isa. 7:14 the "most controversial passage in the Bible" (*Der Glaube der Propheten* [1950] 201). In actual fact,
the one who reads the announcement which follows in v. 14b is taken
completely by surprise: הנה העלמה הרה וילדת בן וקראת שמו עמנו אל (Behold,
the young woman is pregnant and will bear a son and will give him the
name Immanuel). The phrase has not been composed freely by Isaiah,
but uses a particular form, which Humbert (*AfO* 10 [1935] 77–80) called
the biblical annunciation style (it would be better to call it: "an annunciation oracle").

In Gen. 16:11, the messenger of Yahweh says to Hagar: הנך הרה וילדת בן
וקראת שמו ישמעאל כי־שמע יהוה אל־עניך (Behold, you are with child, and shall bear a
son; you shall call his name Ishmael, because the Lord has given heed to your
affliction). In a similar way, the messenger of Yahweh announces once again to
the wife of Manoah in Judg. 13:3: והרית וילדת בן . . . . (but you shall conceive and
bear a son) and repeats in v. 5: הנה הרה . . . וְיָלַדְתְּ בֵּן (emended from וְיֹלַדְתְּ) (for lo, you
shall conceive and bear a son); he would be the one who would begin to free the
Israelites from the control of the Philistines. Cf. also Luke 1:31. The normal form
of the oracle apparently has four elements: (1) a clause which begins with הנה
(behold), which announces the pregnancy and birth; (2) a clause in the perfect
consecutive which instructs the mother how to name the child; (3) a clause,
introduced by כי (for, because), which gives the reason why this name is to be
given; and (4) special additional elements concerning the importance of the son,
including specifics about an extraordinary deed which will be accomplished to
provide help. The texts from Ras Shamra contain passages which remind one, at
least in some ways, of the annunciation oracle of Isaiah; the most important is
found in the Nikkal text line 7: *hl ǵlmt tld b(n)*, "behold, the young wife bears a
son," which, according to the context, is a reference to the moon goddess Nikkal
(on this, see Hammershaimb, op. cit., 13, and W. Herrmann, "Yariḫ und Nikkal
und der Preis der Kaṭarāt-Göttinnen," BZAW 106 [1968] 7). The similarity in the
wording is indeed remarkable, but there is no reference to giving a name and to its
meaning. One must exercise due caution so as not to try to discover any closer ties
(Stamm, op. cit. [*VT* 4]).

The undeniable connection with the other "annunciation oracles," on the other hand, clarifies certain issues: One cannot translate as follows (as, e.g., Kaiser, ad loc.): "When a young woman, who [already] is pregnant, bears a son, then she will call his name Immanuel." הנה (behold), in such instances, introduces a prediction, but this does not mean that one must presume that Isaiah had a vision (contra Wolff, op. cit. [BibS(N) 35] 38f.). Concerning הנה (behold), see above, commentary on 3:1). For the same reason, it is unlikely that העלמה (the young woman) refers to some unspecified woman, instead of to a particular woman, or should be interpreted in a collective sense (L. Koehler, op. cit., 49; G. Fohrer, op. cit., 54). In addition, the form of the address makes it certain that קראת (she shall call, you shall call) is to be taken as a third person feminine singular. The passages which have been consulted do not offer any help with the question about whether הרה (pregnant) is to be translated as present (see Gen. 16:11) or future (see Judg. 13:3); one suspects that the present sense is more likely. But there are still enough other questions which remain.

First of all: What is the meaning of עלמה (almah)? The translation of the word with παρθένος (virgin), which has caused the passage to be interpreted as the account of the virgin birth, is not impossible from the outset. Procksch (ad loc.) offers his candid opinion: "According to the content, the Gk translation παρθένος and Vulg *virgo* is right on target . . . , whereas 'Aquila, Sym, Theod distort the meaning by using νεᾶνις"; cf. also Schulz, op. cit. In the OT passages which use the term (Gen. 24:43; Exod. 2:8; Ps. 68:26), normally what is meant is an unmarried daughter. In Song of Sol. 1:3; 6:8, the word refers to the beloved. Only in Prov. 30:19 could the term be understood to include the idea that this is a married woman (cf. also עֶלֶם, youth, in 1 Sam. 20:22). In I K 204 and III K II 22, however, the *glmt* is clearly the wife (of the king!) who has just been brought home and, just as with *btlt* (virgin, NK 5; the reading is unfortunately not certain; see Vawter, op. cit., and W. Herrmann, op. cit., 5), the word also can be used in parallel with *att* (wife, I K 201). The messenger of Baal, *gapn waugar,* can also be designated as *bn glmt* (son of a *glmt*) (II AB VII 54, Var. 7). Therefore, the OT in no way supports the idea that עלמה (almah) can mean only the young woman up to the point when she bears her first child.

Even if the עלמה (almah) is actually almost always used to designate the unmarried daughter and, in Ras Shamra, *glmt* can possibly be used in parallel to *btlt,* even so, the main point of the term is not that she is a virgin. The basic meaning of the root is apparently "strong, marriageable, fully developed for sexual activity." Scholarly research has thus, generally speaking, given up on the translation "virgin" (cf. even the way 'Aquila, Sym, Theod translate it with νεᾶνις), because it causes one to be mentally ready for an interpretation which is not forthcoming. One ought to stay with the translation "the young woman."

In addition, there is even more dissension about *who* the עלמה (almah) is, and we will have to limit ourselves to mentioning only very few of the suggested solutions:

1. The traditional interpretation of the church, based upon Matt. 1:23, takes the עלמה/παρθένος to be *Mary* and Immanuel to be *Jesus.* In some quarters, it is still considered correct today, even if there are certain reservations and an awareness that Isaiah would have not been able to anticipate the specific way in which the prediction would be fulfilled; see L. Murillo, *Bib* 5 (1924) 269–280; Brunec, op. cit.; Coppens, op. cit.; Herntrich; Junker, op. cit., 181–196; Vella, op. cit.; Young, op. cit.; Eichrodt, *TheolOT* I (1961) 480f. and *Kommentar* I, 90f. The sign which is given to Ahaz makes sense only if it is visible within a relatively

short period of time. Before Immanuel will be able to distinguish between good and evil, the land of both of his enemies will already have been devastated.

2. *The wife of the prophet,* as suggested already by Rashi, Ibn Ezra, Hugo Grotius. In more recent times, J. J. Stamm has come out clearly in favor of this in his research summaries (see above, literature, summaries of research); see also K. H. Fahlgren, *SEA* 4 (1939) 13–24; Gottwald, op. cit.; Jenni, op. cit. (*RGG*[3]). But this is hardly likely. Should a sign such as this make an impact upon King Ahaz? Since Isaiah's wife gave birth to Maher-shalal-hash-baz during this same time period (8:3f.), there is no possible way that one could speak of the birth of another son to Isaiah. (And yet, Gottwald, op. cit., 437, suggests that the עלמה, almah, is the young bride of Isaiah, who had recently become a widower. On the other hand, Salvoni, op. cit., 30–32, would like to equate the עלמה, almah, with the נביאה, prophetess, in chap. 8 and Immanuel with Maher-shalal-hash-baz. He presumes that Isaiah had also cohabited with the prophetess, in addition to being with his wife, and it was that son who would have received the name Maher-shalal-hash-baz from his father at the same time he was given the prophetic name Immanuel by his mother.) Why would Isaiah not simply mention his wife (אשתי) if that is what he meant? Why would he not plainly say that Immanuel was his own son? Above all, it is impossible that the child's father is the same one serving as a messenger of Yahweh to deliver this "annunciation oracle."

3. Some say: *Some woman who happened to be standing nearby,* to whom the prophet is supposed to have pointed with his finger (therefore, the article is used; something similar has also been suggested by Lescow, op. cit., 178f.). One is to presume that women were present when the prophet was engaging in discussion with the king, in fact pregnant women, which does not really correspond to oriental customs.

4. *The collective interpretation: Every possible wife* who happened to be pregnant (or soon would be). This interpretation is widely held today; see, among others, Duhm; Budde; Koehler, op. cit.; Fohrer, op. cit. [BZAW 99], and his commentary; Kaiser. Kruse, op. cit., seeks to modify this interpretation by suggesting the idea that the עלמה (almah) is the "daughter of Zion." According to form-historical research, this is very questionable, as has been mentioned. It is also not to be assumed that Isaiah wants to say that, in the very near future, *all* the women (or *that* particular woman; Isaiah does place the article before עלמה, almah) in Jerusalem would get pregnant, would have sons, and (because it would be fashionable?) would give their sons the name Immanuel. Above all else: then the הנער (lad) in v. 16 would have to be interpreted in a collective sense, which would certainly have been clarified by the use of a plural of the verb, unless one would not take נער (lad) as a reference to Immanuel but, along with Bird, op. cit., to Isaiah's son Shear-jashub.

5. Some have sought to understand the עלמה (almah) as a mythical being. Gressmann's opinion (*Der Ursprung der israelitisch-jüdischen Eschatologie* [1905] 270ff.) is that this is "the mother of the divine child," a figure who appears in popular eschatology; R. Kittel (*Die hellenistische Mysterienreligion und das Alte Testament,* BWAT 32 [1924]), E. Norden (*Die Geburt des Kindes* [1924]), and A. von Bulmerincq (op. cit., 9ff.) all refer to the myth of the birth of a divine child to the virgin, κόρη. But the material which they use for comparison, from the Hellenistic era, is much too late for consideration as furnishing background data for Isaiah's prediction. Further, the Ugaritic texts, which have more recently been employed to interpret the passage (on this, see Wolff, op. cit. [BibS(N) 35] 35f.), are not clear enough and, above all, are too distant from the thought world of Isaiah to expect that they could cast any real light on clarifying the meaning of Isaiah's passage.

6. Hans Schmidt thinks that this is a woman who has been seen by the prophet within *the context of a vision,* a woman who is to be identified with the

mother of the messiah (ad loc.), and Gressmann (op. cit. *[Messias]* 240) suggests: "Isaiah speaks in such a mysterious way about the young woman who is to bear a child; who it is, he does not say, apparently because he himself did not know." In the same way, Wolff (op. cit. [BibS(N) 35] 39f.) suggests that this is a figure seen by the prophet in his vision, and that commentators ought not pursue the question about her identity. Possibly Isaiah's secret about the identity of the mother and child was even hidden from him as well, but obvious to those who heard him. The king and palace would have certainly recognized when the son of the עלמה (almah) appeared and also the sign which came through his mother and even that he was the one to be called by the name Immanuel. Delling (op. cit.) and Prado (op. cit. *[Forschungsbericht]*) are of a similar opinion. Even if it is most difficult for us to make sense of the mystery of the עלמה (almah), that does not mean that the prediction had to have been just as puzzling to those who listened to Isaiah. But it is not normal for prophetic oracles that they would not have an understandable meaning.

Finally, the suggestion has often been made that it refers to *the wife of the king,* and it is in fact this interpretation which has gained ground in recent times. Thus, Buber is of the opinion (op. cit. *[Glaube der Propheten]* 201): "If Ahaz, when he hears *'the almah'* mentioned, knows who is intended (and only then would it be apparent that the sign was meant especially for him), then this could only be a woman who is close to him, and once again, this could hardly be anyone else except the young queen; one might even correctly suppose that, at that time, she was generally known in palace circles as עלמה, 'the young wife.'" In fact, the Keret-texts cited above from ancient Ugarit would lead one to conclude that the young wife of the ruler in Jerusalem was known as עלמה (almah). Those who hold the viewpoint that this refers to the queen include Bentzen (ad loc.); Hammershaimb (op. cit., 20); Lindblom (op. cit., 19); S. Mowinckel (*He That Cometh* [1956] 110–119); Herrmann (op. cit., 139f.), and Scullion (op. cit., 295, 300). Steinmann (op. cit., 90) claims to know even more: The עלמה (almah) is a princess who had just come into the harem of Ahaz, possibly Abi, the daughter of Zechariah, a friend of the prophet; see 2 Kings 18:2 and Isa. 8:3; thus, this would be Hezekiah's mother. Objections have also been raised against this interpretation. Plainly, one must at least admit that the use of קְרָאת (she will give him the name) cannot be used against this solution. It is certainly not outside the realm of possibility that the *mother* named the child, particularly since the king had many wives, and the form of speech in the annunciation oracle shows that this was an ancient custom, which may well have continued to be popular right within the palace (see above, textual note 14e, and Gen. 4:25; 35:18; Judg. 13:24; 1 Sam. 1:20, and often elsewhere, and also cf. F. Nötscher, *Biblische Altertumskunde* [1940] 71). The objection is raised again and again that the chronology would discount the idea that this refers to Hezekiah. But the chronology for this era is by no means clearly established. If the Syro-Ephraimitic War took place in 734/33 and Hezekiah was five years old when he ascended the throne in 728/27, as the chronology of Pavlovský/Vogt used above (p. 4) maintains, then it is at least not impossible that this might refer to Hezekiah. It must be admitted that uncertainty concerning these dates and our lack of knowledge about the relationships which were common among members of a king's family at that time suggest that exegetes exercise great caution in such matters.

As to the identity of the עלמה (almah), the solution which has been suggested here can be substantiated by means of the son's name, Immanuel.

One must speculate about which associations would have involuntarily sprung into the minds of those who were partners in the discussion with Isaiah, as they heard the name Immanuel. Those who are convinced that the collective interpretation is correct, and are also convinced that the sign could point only to a coming disaster, suggest that the name means "May God be with [by] us," which would mean: "May God protect us in the time of terror." Lescow (op. cit., 179f.) takes it to be a cry of terror: "God stand by us!"; see also R. Eisler, *Iesous Basileus ou Basileusas* II (1930) 651ff. Against this interpretation, one must consider the evidence provided by similar names, such as עמדיה (on a seal, see Diringer, op. cit., 218) and עמניה (Elephantine-Papyrus no. 22, line 105; see A. Cowley, *Aramaic Papyri of the Fifth Century B.C.* [1923] 70), in which "without a doubt, the certain confidence of a pious person is being uttered, who knows that he and his people are under the care of the deity, led by him and protected" (Noth, *Personennamen* 160, also refers to Akkadian names such as *nabu-ittija* [Nabu is with you] and *šamaš-ittija* [Shamash is with you]; cf. also the Egyptian name "Amon is with me"; see Preuss, op. cit., 169, and, in addition, Ιεθεβααλ [Baal is with you] in Tyre, 1 Kings 16:31 LXX, and אתבעל [Baal is with you] in the Ahiram inscription, *KAI* no. 1). We have noticed more than once that names in the book of Isaiah reflect the cultic piety of Jerusalem in that era; see pp. 4f. One must ask whether this does not also apply to Immanuel. Wolff (op. cit. [BibS(N) 35] 42) starts out by referring to Ps. 46:8, 12: "Yahweh of hosts is with us." Therefore, one might consider that the songs of Zion serve as the background for the bestowing of such a name (so Rohland, op. cit., 169ff.; see also E. Jenni, op. cit. [*RGG³*]), which is not to be rejected out of hand, since Isaiah was certainly familiar with this world of thought (see most especially 2:2–4 and 7:8a, 9a, where the idea that the city of God cannot ever be destroyed is an intrinsic element). And yet, Wolff is even more to the point when he connects this with the speech forms used for holy war: Judg. 6:12: "Yahweh is with you!" (cf. 13:16; Josh. 1:9; and above all Deut. 20:4: "Yahweh your God is he that goes with you," עמכם). If one understands 7:4–9 essentially to be a "war address," then one will agree with this interpretation. However, we thought that we were more correct when speaking of an oracle addressed to the king and were of the opinion that, in vv. 8a and 9a, but even more so in v. 9b, one could clearly find a reinterpretation of the Davidic tradition. In addition, it is important that the texts cited by Wolff also use Yahweh's name, just as do both of the similar names to which reference was made: עמדיה and עמניה. But Isaiah says Immanu-*el*, even though, except in 31:3, he otherwise never speaks of El. At this point also, he must have been forced to use certain formulations already in existence. Along with Vischer (op. cit., 22) one must take note of 2 Sam. 23:5: בֵּיתִי עִם־אֵל (my house is with El) (before this, read כִּי־נָכוֹן, for indeed, instead of כִּי־לֹא־בֵן, for surely not). Mowinckel (*Psalmenstudien* II [1921] 306, note 1) had suggested that עמנו אל (Immanuel) was an ancient cultic cry and Vischer makes it even more precise: "a cry or outcry within the liturgy of the royal festival of Zion" (on this, see below, p. 318).

It is stated often enough that God is "with" the Davidic kings in a special way: 2 Sam. 7:9; 1 Kings 1:37; Ps. 89:22, 25. But above all the others, 1 Kings 11:38 is the most important passage to be weighed upon the scales: ". . . I will be with you (עמך), and will build you a sure house

(בַּיִת־נֶאֱמָן!), as I built for David." If the sign in 7:14 is in any way connected with the oracle of salvation in 7:4–9, with its prominent conclusion in v. 9b, then the name עמנו אל (Immanuel) must also be interpreted according to its connection with the Davidic traditions. But if that is the case, it is the unavoidable conclusion that Immanuel is the son of the king, and the עלמה (almah) is the wife or at least one of the wives of Ahaz.

But what is the actual sign? It is not an uncommon pregnancy for the עלמה (almah) and the birth of Immanuel in the sense of a virgin birth. One would also not want to place too much importance upon the fact that Isaiah could not have had any way to know whether the עלמה (almah), even if that supposedly referred to his own wife, would have given birth to a son and not to a daughter. (The name עמדיה mentioned above is, after all, also a woman's name; it could also have been possible that a daughter would be given the name עמנו אל [Immanuel].) Gressmann (op. cit. *[Messias]* 238) is of this opinion: "The only wonder that is possible is the birth of the lad Immanuel, for there is no other wonder contained in the oracle." Köhler, op. cit., 49, affirms, on the other hand: "The sign consists of . . . the giving of the name and in the circumstances which have brought it about." In reality, these two are not alternatives: The sign is made up of the pregnancy and the birth itself, but is given meaning in the intended sense when the name is bestowed. But now, if Immanuel cannot be taken as a "cry of distress," the situation, when viewed in light of the circumstances which will exist when the son is given this name, can signal only a time of joy. That in no way depends solely on our understanding of עמנו אל (Immanuel), but is stated *expressis verbis* in the text: The reason for giving the name is stated in the words of v. 16: "For before the lad understands *how to reject the evil and to choose the good,* the land of both the kings who cause you to shudder will become deserted." Whoever considers the sign, which has been proclaimed, to be singularly a threat of disaster gets into real difficulties in light of this verse. One ought not remove it, for it is indispensable, on the basis of its form as a כי-clause, for explaining the meaning of the name. Thus, many scholars, in order to carry through with their own particular theory, eliminate at least the relative clause at the end: "both the kings who cause you to shudder," so that אדמה (land) can be taken to refer to Judah. This is justified by saying that אדמה ("arable land") is not a political term, in the sense of ארץ (territory) (see Procksch, ad loc.). But it makes very good sense that Isaiah speaks of arable land and not about territory in general in this context.

Therefore, this means: As he comes into the world, just a few months later, the עלמה (almah) names her son Immanuel, since she has reason to declare her thankfulness that it has once again been proved that God is with the house of David. The לא תקום ולא תהיה (it will not happen and will not succeed) from v. 7 would have been fulfilled by then.

Up to this point, the sign deals with salvation, which the house of David is to experience. However, we came to a conclusion above which cannot simply be ignored on the basis of what has been said about the meaning of v. 14, namely that, following the hesitation of the king to show the courage to believe on the basis of a sign which was to be offered—and thus to make the correct political-military decision—the only message which could follow would be one which would threaten Ahaz with judgment. This is the dilemma with which one must struggle in any exposition of the text, even if one sets aside vv. 15 and 17 for the time being.

But beneath this difficult exegetical issue, a hard theological problem with which Isaiah must wrestle in his response to Ahaz can now be stated clearly, on the basis of everything presupposed up to this point. He cannot simply announce the end of the Davidic dynasty, since the promise that God will remain with it continues in force. He has just gotten through saying with great certainty: לא תקום ולא תהיה (it will not happen and will not succeed). Is it possible for him now, because of Ahaz's hesitation, to say that the plan of the enemies of Jerusalem will indeed be carried out? Is it true that God's promise no longer remains in effect, because of Ahaz's refusal? Is the faithfulness of Yahweh shown as illusory just as soon as the man to whom it is promised refuses to listen? Should the result simply be an end to the Davidic house, an end to the city of God, an end for Judah? For Isaiah, that is an incomprehensible thought. But on the other hand: Should refusal of the one who carries the promise make no difference? And ought Isaiah be able to announce salvation for Ahaz after he has come out with "If you do not believe, then you will not remain"? That is apparently not a solution which is available to one who seeks to interpret the Immanuel sign. Therefore, there remains only a third alternative, selected basically by many others already: The sign has an ambivalent character. The objection that one has made virtue out of a necessity simply does not hold up: This two-sided aspect corresponds exactly to the ambivalence within the theological situation. It corresponds exactly to the "two-sidedness" of Isaiah's view about the remnant, mentioned above. But it is not a polarity in which the power going forth from each pole is neutralized by the other side. Basically, the sign conveys salvation, but for Ahaz himself it is a severe threat, a threat which paradoxically is visible in the very proclamation that Yahweh will remain true to his promise. According to our understanding of the עלמה (almah), the sign means that the dynasty of the Davidic kings still has a future. But at the same time, it is made very plan to Ahaz how heavily his doubt weighs him down when considered in light of such faithfulness on the part of God. His actions cannot be without bitter consequences.

The correctness of this interpretation will be borne out by the rest of the material in the seventh and eighth chapters, insofar as they are generally assigned to Isaiah: 8:1–4 speaks unequivocally about the catastrophe which will take place against Damascus and Samaria, which shows that the present wording in 7:16 corresponds exactly to what Isaiah anticipated. On the other hand, 7:18ff. speaks of the trouble which Assyria would bring upon Judah. Hammershaimb, who believes a worse mistake could not be made than to take the Immanuel prediction in a threatening or ironic sense (op. cit., 21), is forced to take 18ff. as a reference to the Northern Kingdom (24). That is no solution, however, since in 8:5ff., with all the clarity that one could ever hope for, there is talk of the onslaught of the Assyrians against Jerusalem. Whoever follows any other line of reasoning is forced to come up with these types of ingenious interpretations. The same is true for Lescow, who considers 7:14 an obvious announcement of disaster. He does not permit himself to go so far as to remove the conclusion of v. 16, but is of the opinion that if such a total catastrophe would come upon the royal kingdom of these two enemies, then Judah could not possibly expect to come out of it unscathed; the verse would indirectly still have to be considered an announcement of disaster. He treats 8:4 the same way. This is how radically one must force alterations to the text if it is not recognized that Isaiah could also speak about deliverance and salvation.

[7:15] Up to this point, v. 15 has been purposely left out of the discussion of this section, since the authenticity of the verse, particularly in recent times, has been denied (see above, textual note 15a–a and the discussion of the form of 7:1–17, and Stamm, op. cit. [*TZ* 16] 443, note 18). Leaving for the time being the difficulties connected with translating לדעתו (learn, know), exegetes have given most of their attention to the way in which the "butter and honey" might provide supporting evidence for each one's own interpretation of the Immanuel prediction, whether for salvation or disaster.

For Gressmann, milk and honey are messianic foods and the main type of sustenance in the end time; he refers to Joel 4:18; Amos 9:13; Deut. 32:13, and a wealth of material from the Greek and non-Greek mythologies as evidence (op. cit. *[Messias]* 156ff.). In Babylon, milk and honey (*dišpu* and *himētu*) were often used in cultic activity (Hammershaimb, op. cit., 21, and see Meissner, *BuA* II, 84; E. Dhorme, *RHR* 107 [1933] 107f.; cf. also Scullion, op. cit., 296). Fat and milk are described as signs of strength and superabundance in a hymn of Lipit-Ishtar from Isin, who is able to say about himself: ". . . the man of the field, who there (i.e., in the land of Sumer) is able to pile high the heaps of grain, the shepherd who increases the fat and milk given in the pen, who permits fish and birds to grow in the swamp, who brings in an overflowing steady stream of water in the aqueducts, who increases the abundant yield in the great mountains, that is me . . ." (A. Falkenstein / W. von Soden, *Sumerische und Akkadische Hymnen und Gebete* [1953] 127). In the Mithra mysteries, the abundance of honey as a food for those who rejoice makes them like the gods (F. Cumont, G. Gehrich, and K. Latte, *Die Mysterien des Mithra* [1923³] 145; cf. also Sib. 3:744ff.; 5:28ff.). Whoever interprets 7:14 in a messianic-eschatological sense does not omit v. 15 as evidence. However, at the same time, there are other voices which suggest that thick milk and honey are not in fact foods of paradise, but the poor daily fare of the nomads who live in the wretched conditions found in the steppe (see Guthe, op. cit.; Fohrer, ad loc.; Stamm, op. cit. *[RTP]* 113f.), and yet honey and butter are currently still considered by the Arabs as favorite types of nourishment (see Driver, *JSS* 13 [1968] 39).

It must be admitted that some of the material cited from the study of other religions, used as evidence to support an eschatological interpretation, comes from quite a distance. Yet, it ought not be overlooked in the exegesis of v. 15 and 7:22 that eating butter and honey is clearly understood as describing abundance in the time of salvation (cf. the striking similarity between 7:21f. and the quotation from the Hymn of Lipit-Ishtar above). Even if one maintains that v. 22 (or at least v. 22a; see Fohrer, ad loc.) is inauthentic, the passage still demonstrates that butter and honey were in no way thought to be sustenance for a time of distress. Therefore, the verse seems to fit in well with our interpretation of the meaning of the Immanuel sign. And yet, it also poses difficulties when one tries to make sense of it. In this context, it is not only unnecessary, it destroys the flow of thought and does not fit the sequence found in an annunciation oracle of this type (see above, p. 307). The sentence provides a reinterpretation of the Immanuel prediction. It wants to make the point that, with Immanuel, a ruler is coming who will be equipped with astonishing powers because, already during his youth, he will have been fed with food which was out of the ordinary (concerning the form and meaning of such expressions in promises about sons, cf. K. Koch, "Die Sohnesverheissung an den ugaritischen Daniel," *ZA* 58 [1967] 211–221). For this reason, the sentence is located at the beginning of the interpretation of the passage along messianic-eschatological lines and is to be considered the work of a redactor.

[7:16] However, in v. 16, there is no doubt that Isaiah himself is speaking. It is hard to determine exactly how long Isaiah thought it would take until the child was far enough along to reject the evil and choose the good. Kaiser (concerning v. 15) suggests: "until their [the children's] personal experiences lead to a freedom of choice which is completely developed, which is approximately the case by the twentieth year of life." It is well known that such is not always the case by the twentieth year! But it would seem that "reject" and "choose" are used here in a very generalized sense and would more likely refer to the time when the child begins to be able to make distinctions in its external world (see P. Humbert, *Études sur le Récit du Paradis et de la Chute dans la Genèse* [1940] 92–97; H. J. Stoebe, "Gut und Böse in der Jahwistischen Quelle des Pentateuch, *ZAW* 65 [1953] 188–204, and Driver, *JSS* 13 [1968] 39, who thinks in terms of three years). One might compare Deut. 1:39 at this point. On the other hand, one really ought not use passages such as Exod. 30:14; Lev. 27:3; Num. 1:3, 32, and Genesis 3 really does not provide any help here (for another view, see S. Stern, who also thinks that the age is twenty years, "The Knowledge of Good and Evil," *VT* 8 [1958] 405–418). Isaiah certainly does not want to mention a very specific point in time. But before it comes to that time, the land of those two kings will have become deserted; cf., concerning this, 6:11: האדמה תשאה שממה (the field remains, yet only as desert) and 6:12: ורבה העזובה בקרב הארץ (and the devastation will be massive in the midst of the land). One should probably presume that this refers to a deportation. In the year 732, Damascus fell and did not rise again. Israel was able to come away from that only lightly scathed but, in any case, a large portion of its territory fell to the Assyrians in 732 and the population was quite decimated (2 Kings 15:29) (cf. the annals of Tiglath-Pileser, lines 227–230, *AOT²* 347 = *ANET²* 283).

[7:17] Verse 17 presents problems which are by no means insignificant, both for interpretation and classification. If the ending, את מלך אשור (the king of Assyria), is taken as a gloss, which is how it is taken by almost all exegetes today, it does not seem impossible that the sentence could be taken as a promise of salvation: Days are coming which are full of salvation in a way which they have not been since the time when the kingdom was still united under David and Solomon. As far as Isaiah is concerned, that epoch is practically the ideal era (see above, commentary on 1:26). Will those days return once again? Hammershaimb (op. cit., 22f.) is convinced this is the case and goes further to suggest that it is not too bold to think that it might be suggesting that the Davidic rule could be reinstated over the Northern Kingdom (cf. also Hattendorf, *ZAW* 48 [1930] 324f., and, above all, Lindblom, op. cit., 26f.). In favor of this interpretation, one can show that v. 17 is not connected to v. 16 by a conjunction so that it certainly would be a strong possibility that v. 17 should be considered a continuation of v. 16 or else a more specific explication of it. But it is highly likely that, if Isaiah actually wanted to say what these commentators read into the verse, he would have said something like this: days, which have not been since David or Solomon, or: as Judah was able to rejoice in earlier times (see 1:26; 8:23). A second comment is even more important: The text says: עָלֶיךָ (upon you [sing.]), and that, in fact, means: over (actually in the sense of against) Ahaz. But if the verse is not intended to say something positive, then, in fact, there are difficulties with the transition from v. 16 to v. 17. The problem is made less serious if one reads (see above, textual note 17a) וַיָּבִא with Q^a instead of simply יָבִא and takes it, with Wolff, as an adversative ו (*Waw*): "But Yahweh . . ." Possibly an adversative particle which was even clearer has been lost (cf. Gk). But it is also possible that the text is intentionally quite radical as it goes from a seemingly favorable picture of the future to the harsh reality of the Assyrian threat. In any case, it does not solve anything either to say that the verse is inauthentic or to take it (as, e.g., the *Zürcher Bibel*) as part of the announcement of disaster which follows in v. 18. It is the necessary conclusion to the oracle, beginning so abruptly so that the hearers would be shocked by its unexpected harshness. The sentence is, therefore, in some ways a parallel to v. 9b in which, after what seemed to be comforting assurances in vv. 8a and 9a, the decisive sentence follows, bringing the previous announcement of salvation into a whole new light.

It is only finally at this point that it is really clear what the Immanuel sign truly means: It does in fact speak about Yahweh's faithfulness to the Davidic house; it clearly underscores the fact that Yahweh's message is still in force, which means that neither of the kings who are going against Jerusalem has any real prospects for his plans being successful. But it also reveals how unbelievable it is that Ahaz refuses such obvious faithfulness on God's part. He refuses in the sense that he does not choose to hold on by faith, refuses also as a politician, since he seeks his refuge among the Assyrians, who will bring nothing but days of terror for him in the future. If "and upon the house of your father" is an addition, then the disaster is directed personally against Ahaz, not the Davidic dynasty as a whole, which, according to the opinion of Isaiah, still had a glorious future. On the contrary, the king will have to bear in mind that the people, as well as himself, will have to suffer the bitter consequences of his unfaith. That the people would have to suffer when the ruler turned away would not have been as problematic for those living in the ancient world, who thought collectively; it does cause much more difficulty for humans today, who seek explanations about how God's justice is fairly applied to each individual.

It is most interesting to note in passing that it must have been a severe trauma for Judah, particularly for the Davidic house, when the kingdom was divided. About two hundred years had already passed since the unity had been destroyed. This terrible crisis had still not been forgotten. The consciousness of belonging together had not disappeared in spite of the political division, and the Davidic house had not as yet given up its claim on an undivided kingdom, as is even seen still one hundred more years later, in the politics of Josiah as the Assyrian power came to an end (see Noth, *The History of Israel,* 274).

It is remarkable that the Northern Kingdom is called "Ephraim" in this very context. This makes it clear that the designation does not refer simply to the rump state which was all that was left of the Northern Kingdom after Assyria split off so much of the territory in 732 (see above, commentary on 9:8a). In this connection, the designation "Ephraim" is particularly appropriate, because the leader who caused the split, Jeroboam, was an Ephraimite from Zeredah and had held the office of being in "charge over all the forced labor of the house of Joseph" (1 Kings 11:26–28).

Purpose and Thrust

The passage before us, 7:1–17, presents a host of almost insurmountable difficulties for exegetical study, but it is also extremely important for understanding both Isaiah's message and the history of faith in Israel in general. The hour when the confrontation takes place with Ahaz, by the conduit of the upper pool, is the birth hour for the biblical concept of faith. The question about the traditio-historical background of the oracle which Isaiah was to deliver to the king has shown that the religious use of האמין (believe) must have already been a fixed element in Israel before the time of Isaiah and that the concept of faith had always been an integral part of the oracle of salvation. But Isaiah's contributions are threefold: First of all, he elevated faith to be the decisive criterion for the behavior of worshipers of Yahweh whenever those persons interact with their God. Faith is the only adequate answer for a human being who treats the relationship with God with utter seriousness. Secondly, there is the fact that Isaiah connected faith and promise together inextricably. Faith is in no way frivolous trust or even something like a euphoric disposition; instead, it is solidly grounded in the history of Yahweh with Israel; in the specific case at hand, faith is grounded in the history of Yahweh's relationship with the Davidic house, as it had been formulated theologically on the basis of the tradition about the election of the dynasty ruling in Jerusalem. But election could not simply be placed into a single historical time period and could not be turned into a mere object; it was part of an actual present reality at that very moment, believed in by the one confronted with the prophetic message (see H. Wildberger, op. cit. [*ZTK* 1968]). And thirdly, one is to pay careful attention to the full extent of the concept which Isaiah has in mind when using האמין (believe). His own unique way of employing the term is already seen by his use of the word as an absolute: The problem is not whether Ahaz "believes in God." Naturally, he is a member of the community which confesses faith in Yahweh; certainly he had encouraged cultic relations with Yahweh at the sanctuary in Jerusalem, not to mention the fact that the existence of Yahweh in itself posed a problem for him. What was demanded of him is quite far removed from a formalized confession of faith in Yahweh. What Isaiah thought of his contemporaries who "draw near [to Yahweh] with their mouth" is explained to us in 29:13f. "Faith" is "holding on in quiet trust," which takes into account the reality of the faithfulness of God, the truth found embedded in the promise of election, which assured those belonging to him that help could be counted on in the harsh times destined to come presently. In the second passage where Isaiah speaks of הַאֲמִין (believe), 28:16, the imagery connected with his description of faith is rounded out in the sense that there he connects faith very closely with justice and righteousness.

Is this memorable moment, when Ahaz and Isaiah confront one another, also the birth hour for the concept of a Messiah? Insofar as one considers the Messiah to be the eschatological bringer of salvation, one must avoid attributing this interpretation to the passage. For Isaiah does not await the birth of the Messiah "at the end of days" but in the very near future. In addition, one must note that the Immanuel sign has an ambivalent meaning and is an announcement of coming disaster for the one to whom it is addressed, Ahaz. On this point, Stamm has pointed to what is most important (op. cit. [*TZ* 16] 450f.). In a messianic prediction, salvation can be announced, or judgment can be mentioned, only *before* the decisive turning point which comes with the birth of Immanuel. It is also not mentioned that Immanuel would "save" Israel (cf. Matt. 1:21). His birth and his name are important insofar as they testify to Yahweh's faithfulness, indeed showing a faithfulness which will expose the fact that there will be no salvation for humans lacking that faith (concerning the ambivalence of the sign, cf. the ambivalent meaning of the Lord's Supper in Paul, 1 Cor. 11:29; see also 2 Cor. 2:15f.).

We do believe, of course, that v. 15 can be recognized as an attempt to understand the passage in an eschatological sense. In that effort, the touchstone of the promise is shifted onto the son himself. In 7:14 the portrayal of the Messiah did not carry with it this deeper eschatological meaning, even if emphasis is placed on the son (on this, see G. von Rad, *OTTheol* II, 173f.). In spite of this, the Immanuel passage, even after one distances oneself from more far-reaching meanings which have been given to this passage during the history of interpretation, still has great importance. The name Immanuel, intended as a sign for Ahaz and Israel, points to circumstances in which one can detect clearly the central message of the OT. And what else did the Messiah demonstrate, in his own way, not only by means of his name but also by means of his deeds for Israel, if it was not עִמָּנוּ אֵל "God is with us"?

Disaster and Salvation
"On That Day"

Literature

W. McKane, "The Interpretation of Isaiah VII 14–25," *VT* 17 (1967) 208–219. In addition, consult the literature cited above, vv. 1ff., insofar as those references deal with the entire chapter.

[**Literature update through 1979**: H. Margulies, "Das Rätsel der Biene im AT," *VT* 24 (1974) 56–76.]

Text

7:18 [It will happen on that day:]
  Yahweh will whistle [for the flies which are at the end of the
    streams[a] of Egypt and] for the bees [which are] in the land of
    Assyria.
  19 They will come and will all settle themselves down
    in ravines in the valleys[a] and clefts of rocks
    and in all the thorn-encircled enclosures[b] [and by all drinking
      places[c]].

  *   *   *   *

  20 [On that day]
  the Lord will shave off with the knife,[a]
    which he hired on the other side of the stream[b]
    [with the king of Assyria],[c]
  the head and the genital hair,[d]
    and he will also take away the beard.

  *   *   *   *

  21 [And on that day it will happen:
  Then one will rear a young cow[a] and two she-goats.[b]
  22 And because of the plenteous milk, which they provide,[a] one will
      be able to eat butter.
  Yes,[a] butter and honey will be able to be eaten, by everyone who
      still remains in the land.]

  *   *   *   *

319

23 [On that day it will happen:
In any region,[a] where
a thousand vine branches are worth a thousand shekels,
it will be full of thistles and thorns,

24 only with bow and arrow will one go about in it,]
[for the whole land will be full of thistles and thorns.]

25 [And upon all the hillsides, which one (now) hoes with a hoe, no
one will go there any more, out of fear,[a] because of the thorns and
thistles. It will be pasture for the steers, a trampling place which
will be trampled down by sheep.]

18a יאר comes from the Egyptian (*jtr[w]*, later *jrw*) and refers to the Nile in 49 of 53
occurrences in the OT. In these cases, the rather frequently used plural is to be
translated as "branches of the Nile" or as a plural of amplification (cf. A.
Schwarzenbach, *Die geographische Terminologie im Hebräischen des Alten Testaments* [1954] 64f.).

19a The meaning of בַּתּוֹת is uncertain; see above, textual note 5:6a–a; according to
the Arabic, בתה ought to mean "cut off." Thus, for בַּתָּה, one would suppose a
meaning something like "sudden fall" (Gk: χώρα, region; Vulg: *vallis*, valley).

19b נעצוץ, "camel thorn," *Alhagi Camelorum* fish, according to *Löw* II, 416f.
Saʿadia suggests this is the thorn of Christ, *Zizyphus spina Christi*.

19c Dalman, *AuS* II, 323, suggests that נהללים also refers to thorny bushes or trees,
more specifically, to the licorice, *Prosopis Stephanica*, a bush which can grow to
be one meter high, which would be a good parallel for the thorn of Christ, which
grows to be as much as five meters high.

20a תער (knife) is masculine, based on its use in Num. 6:5; שכירה, which has been
given an article, must therefore be a substantive. This means that תער השכירה is
either to be taken in the construct, meaning "hired knife," or השכירה is in apposition, which further explains the תער: "knife, namely the hired one." In this case, it
is possible that שכירה should be taken in the very concrete sense of "mercenary
army."

20b The נהר is the Euphrates, and everyone would figure out that the wordplay
was referring to the Assyrians.

20c במלך אשור seems to be an after-thought and is an ancient gloss; see above, את
מלך אשור (the king of Assyria), at the end of v. 17.

20d Literally: "their hair of the feet." This is a euphemism; cf. Exod. 4:25 and see
above, commentary on 6:2).

21a Literally: "a young cow from the herd of cattle."

21b Literally: "two of the small livestock."

22a–a This is missing in the Gk, most likely because the copyist's eyes missed
some words (*aberratio oculi*).

23a מקום does not mean, as it is usually translated in this passage, "piece of land."
It refers to a region which is particularly good for planting a vineyard. Qᵃ reads
כול המקום, meaning "every place," whereas the MT intends to say: "in any suitable
place at all."

25a יראת (out of fear) is an adverbial accusative, which provides the reason; see
BrSynt §100c.

Setting and Form

Budde, op. cit. (*Jesajas Erleben*), 58ff., and Rignell, "Das Immanuelszeichen," *ST* 11 (1957) 116ff. consider the entire chap. 7 to be a single
unit, so that vv. 18ff. simply expand, even more, upon what was treated
in a summary fashion in v. 17. Based on what has been stated already, we
cannot agree with that assessment: Verse 17 is short and harsh, but also a

most impressive statement which brings vv. 1ff. to a close. In fact, the repetition of "it will happen on that day" does suggest that vv. 18ff. *presently* seek to be interpreted in connection with the section which precedes them. In addition, in terms of content, at least vv. 18f. and 20 could be seen as providing further specifics about the disaster announced in v. 17. It is also highly likely that this involves two messages delivered by Isaiah in the context of the same situation as the one presumed as the background for vv. 1–17. But the connection is not original. Every word which expands upon the lightning strike in v. 17 can do no more than dimly try to recreate it.

The unit formed by the various sections in vv. 18–25 is also nothing more than redactional. והיה ביום ההוא (it will happen on that day) in vv. 18, 21, 23, but also ביום ההוא (on that day) in v. 20, are typical redactional formulas, by means of which originally distinct units are linked together and expansions are appended. There is reason for one to note the tedious style in vv. 18ff. That is not simply a subjective opinion, as Rignell suggests (op. cit., 116); therefore, one must address the issue of whether these are not, in actual fact, a collection of various types of additions which have nothing to do with Isaiah at all. And yet, the powerful imagery in vv. 18f. and 20 leads one to conclude that Isaiah himself is speaking. And, since the prophet could see a future framed by heavy storm clouds after he broke off his discussion with Ahaz, the content would not deny that Isaiah could be the source of both statements and that both come from the time of the Syro-Ephraimitic War. But the formulas which have been noted show that a reworking most likely occurred and that, in the course of the redactional assembly of the various units, in some cases coming from a later era, other secondary elements were appended. However, a survey of the opinions of exegetes shows that one cannot achieve absolute certainty when trying to sort out what actually comes from Isaiah himself. The following are to be considered as separate units:

1. [7:18–19]   *The Bees from the Land of Assyria*

Setting

One wonders about Egypt and Assyria being mentioned together (in this sequence!). Indeed, exegetes have found that the flies fit in very well to symbolize Egypt or Ethiopia—though the hieroglyphic sign for Lower Egypt is the wasp—and the mountainous region of Assyria is well-known for its numerous bee colonies; see Budde, op. cit. (*Jesajas Erleben*) 60, and Fohrer, ad loc.; cf. already what Cyril of Alexandria says in the quote below, p. 322. But at the time of the Syro-Ephraimitic War, Egypt posed no threat for Judah. According to Budde and Fohrer, Isaiah does not suggest that both of these peoples will do battle against Judah, but that Palestine will be the scene of battle between the two world powers, which Budde thinks actually took place during Isaiah's time, at the battle of Eltekeh (see the "Taylor-cylinder," line 75ff.; *AOT*² 353 = *ANET*² 287). But the text itself gives no indication that such an interpretation is correct. One might ponder the possibility that details about both, i.e. Egypt *and* Assyria, ought to be simply eliminated altogether. But there is another solution which is no doubt preferable: Originally, mention was made only about Assyria being compared to bees. The bee-keeper is able to "whistle" for the bees, intending to try to attract them to a particular location; no one is able to do that with flies. Bees can adapt to life in ravines within valleys, clefts of rocks, and thorn hedges. Certainly one can encounter them at places where one gets a drink, but it cannot be said that they settle down in such places (ונחו!), which means that this reference is also to be considered a secondary addition, inasmuch as נהללים (here: drinking places) is not thought to be another term for thorny ravines (see above, textual note 19c). "Drinking places" fit very well with the mention of flies. Thus, the original message of Isaiah would have read as follows:

ישרק יהוה לדבורה [אשר] בארץ אשור
ובאו ונחו כלם בנחלי הבתות
ובנקיקי הַסְּלַע[ים] ובכל הנעצוצים

(Yahweh will whistle for the bees [which are] in the land of Assyria and they will come and will all settle themselves down in the ravines in the valley and clefts of rock[s] and in all the thorn-encircled enclosures).

Form

Meter: If אשר (which are) is removed from the first line, and the singular is read in the third line, instead of סלעים (rocks), then this short section can be read as 3 five-stress cola.

The message was expanded at a later time, when the Egyptian threat also became much more acute. There is no reason to suppose that this did not happen until the conflicts between the Seleucids and Ptolemies (thus Kaiser, ad loc.). Assyria and Egypt are also mentioned together elsewhere as the two major powers which threaten Israel and Judah: Hos. 9:3, 6; 11:5; 12:2; Jer. 2:36.

Commentary

Yahweh "whistles" for the bees in the land of Assyria (דבורה, bees, is a collective; thus, the verbs in v. 19 are in the plural). In 5:26 the prophet had already used the imagery of whistling for a people to bring judgment upon Judah, and Assyria was also the subject in that passage.

Cyril of Alexandria (d. 444) remarks about the imagery of the bees in v. 18: "This message is certainly based on a comparison which makes use of the experience of the bee-keeper, who would use the sound of the whistle to drive the bees [concerning μυῖα, bees, see Liddell-Scott, *A Greek-English Lexicon* (1949⁹) s.v.] out of the beehives and out into the open field and then afterwards entices them back again" (see Migne, *Patrologia, Series Graeca* LXX [1864] 209). The belief that one would be able to use noise to induce bees, which were swarming about, to settle down in one place was widely known in ancient times and passed on right up to the present. Bacchus travels through the Rhodope Mountains (in Bulgaria) and those accompanying him are striking metal against metal: "Look at that! Summoned by the ringing sound, an unbelievable swarm comes together, and the bees follow the sound which the metal makes. Liber [= Bacchus] collects them, swarming about aimlessly, and shuts them up in a hollow tree and is rewarded by being able to find honey for himself" (Ovid, *Fasti* III, 741–744; translated by F. Bömer, *P. Ovidius Naso. Die Fasten I* [1957]; see further references from antiquity, idem, vol. II [1958] 195). Concerning older and newer methods which are similar, see M. Sooder, *Bienen und Bienenhaltung in der Schweiz,* Schriften der Schweizerischen Gesellschaft für Volkskunde 34 (1952) 190ff. Swarms of bees and swarms of flies are also used by Homer as images of the way swarms of peoples came to attack: *Iliad* II 86f.: ἐπεσσεύοντο δὲ λαοὶ ἠΰτε ἔθνεα εἶσι μελισσάων ἀδινάων ("meanwhile, the people came crowding on. They were like a great swarm of buzzing bees," W. H. D. Rouse, Homer, *The Iliad* [1962] 24); also II 469f.: ἠΰτε μυιάων ἀδινάων ἔθνεα πολλά . . . ἠλάσκουσιν ("like swarms of quivering flies . . . so many were [the Achaians]," ibid., 31f.). Even today, in the mountainous regions of what was once Assyria, cultivation of bees is a very important line of business. But the residents of Palestine also know bees and their peculiarities very well; Dalman, *AuS* VII, 291ff., illuss. 171f.

Naturally, one must recognize that wild bees are meant in this particular passage. They are fond of settling into the crags of rocks, as is indicated in Deut. 32:13 and Ps. 81:17; cf. also Gen. 43:11; Judg. 14:8f.; 1 Sam. 14:27; Ezek. 27:17 (in addition, cf. the wild honey which John the Baptist ate in the Jordan desert, Matt. 3:4; Mark 1:6). It was natural for the ancient Israelites to compare the Assyrians, warlike and bent on victory, with stinging bees which were difficult to fight off and were certainly dangerous, as is shown in Deut. 1:44 and Ps. 118:12. Apparently, Isaiah made use of a common image for a dangerous enemy as he referred to Assyria.

"On that day it will happen" is not to be taken as a reference to the eschatological day of judgment, but simply intends to point out that it will happen at the same time as the disaster announced in v. 17. Naturally, that does not exclude the possibility that, as the term continued to be used at a later time, it was employed when designating time in the eschatological sense.

The יארי מצרים (streams of Egypt) could refer to the branches of the Nile in the Delta; cf. 19:6. But 7:18 speaks of the "ends" of the branches of the Nile, which means that the author has in mind Upper Egypt or Ethiopia. In that region, at the time of Isaiah, Pi-ankhi was ruler, having established the Ethiopian dynasty, invading the Delta in approximately 726/25 (according to others, not until about 715; see W. F. Albright, *BASOR* 141 [1956] 25). It is possible that this addition comes from this same time period, since Ethiopia had attracted the attention of the leading politicians in Jerusalem; see chaps. 18f. As one can infer from 20:4ff., Isaiah did not expect that the Ethiopians would be able to establish themselves in Palestine.

2. [7:20] *The Razor from Across the Euphrates*

Setting

ביום ההוא (on that day) is also an addition here, but it shows that the verse was not originally connected with vv. 18f. Even if במלך אשור (with the king of Assyria) is a gloss (see above, textual note 20c), this message still should be presumed to have originated at the time of the Syro-Ephraimitic War and to be contemporaneous with vv. 18f.

Form

Meter: a six-stress colon (2 + 2 + 2) and a three-stress bicolon.

Commentary

A knife, תער, can refer to one of the tools used by a writer, Jer. 36:23, and can be used, for example, to shave clean the head of a Nazirite when the time of his oath has come to an end, Num. 6:5. But prisoners of war and slaves were also shaved (illus. of an Egyptian shaving knife: *BHH* 1691). It is not correct to take the shaving of the hair as a description of the devastation and depopulation of Judah, as the "shaving off" of the land (so Delitzsch, ad loc.). That would be possible only if v. 20 was originally a continuation of vv. 18f. The shaving is to be taken literally; it is a way to deeply humiliate someone (see above, commentary on 3:17 and 2 Sam. 10:4f.), particularly since Isaiah also mentions cutting off the genital hair and the beard, both of which are marks of honor for the male ("bald head" is a despicable taunt, 2 Kings 2:23). Even more than a harsh destiny in an external sense, this image of the razor predicts deep disgrace, something which would be extremely humiliating for an Israelite.

The razor "has been hired" from the other side of the river. It is possible that one ought to read, instead of עברי נהר, the more common עבר הנהר, since, with one exception (Zech. 9:10), as far as the Euphrates is concerned, the article is always found on נהר (river). In later times, עבר הנהר describes the region west of the Euphrates: 1 Kings 5:4; Ezra 8:36; Neh. 2:7, 9; 3:7; however, in more ancient texts it refers to the land east of this river: Josh. 24:2f., 14f., and often elsewhere; it all depends on where the speaker is standing; see the article "Transeuphrat" in *BHH* 2021. Isaiah does not yet know of the later usage, which goes back to the Akkadian *ebir nâri* (= the Trans-Euphrates region), which means it is obvious that he uses this to refer to the region of Assyria. שכירה (hired) is connected with the same root as שָׁכִיר, which does not refer only to the "day laborer" but also to the "mercenary soldier," and no matter how the expression תער השכירה (knife which he hired) is to be understood grammatically (on this, see above, textual note 20a), this razor refers to the mighty Assyrian army. But who "has rented" the knife? Some think it means Yahweh and use v. 18 as evidence, where the Assyrians are described as rod and staff of the divine wrath. But if this message is really to be considered in relation to the same situation as 7:1–17, Isaiah would be using this scintillating description also to refer to Ahaz, who had bought Tiglath-Pileser's assistance against both of his neighbors with a substantial "gift" (2 Kings 16:8). In this way, Isaiah exposes the complete irony of seeking help: The "mercenary troops," which Ahaz himself had hired at that time, would bring for him and his land imprisonment and humiliation instead of deliverance. According to 2 Kings 16:7, Ahaz pledged his allegiance with the words: "I am your servant and your son."

3. [7:21–22] *Superabundance*

Setting and Form

The exact interpretation of this passage depends on how one answers the basic question about whether it is an announcement of disaster or salvation. Verse 22a is very clear: Where there is much milk, one cannot speak about disaster. Sometimes, therefore, certain scholars bracket off this half-verse from the rest (see Fohrer, ad loc.) and then interpret at least vv. 21b and 22b as an announcement of judgment. If this is the case, then one would have to explain v. 22b in a way much like what is often done with 7:15, saying that milk/butter and honey are the scanty fare which is all that is left when times are very difficult. We have rejected this interpretation for 7:15. It is also contradicted by the fact that the glossator who would have then added v. 22a would have completely misunderstood the half-verse v. 22b which was already before him. This would mean that, at most, v. 21b would be a message of judgment: The land would be so deeply caught up in the war that a farmer could do no more than raise a cow and two goats. In this case, it would be possible that this half-verse could be from Isaiah, later expanded with glosses in v. 22, but that would mean it would have been given the exact opposite meaning. Instead, it is much more likely that v. 21b already begins the message of salvation: It would be true that a person tied down to the land would be able to call only a very little livestock his own, but the land would be so fruitful and the livestock so excellent that a very few animals would be sufficient for providing a family with milk; indeed, there would be enough milk left over so that one could make butter (concerning the use of the same imagery in the hymn of Lipit-Ishtar of Isin, see above, commentary on 7:15). If this is the case, the same individual who inserted v. 15 would be responsible for inserting vv. 21f. Of course, it is not impossible that 7:22b comes from a still later expander than v. 22a, from someone who was thinking of 7:15 and wanted to refer again to honey as a food of the coming time of salvation.

Commentary

Even if v. 21b is already part of an announcement of salvation, this interpretation still presumes that the land has been devastated. One must, so to speak, start over from the beginning again. The population has been reduced once again to a very minimal level of existence. One cannot really say that they are like "nomads," since a cow does not belong to such a life-style. But it is important to note that the exegetes vacillate, because of vv. 21b and 22b, about whether this intends to speak of salvation or disaster. Even if one takes into account that "milk and honey" are gifts which make the land of Canaan a most desirable place, it is still striking that the expectation is that salvation will take place within such narrow bounds. One could suppose that someone else would have used his palette to paint a picture of joys which are found in paradise. But the hope of salvation in ancient Israel, over and over again, finds satisfaction in the context of an amazingly limited field of vision; one might compare this with 4:5; Amos 9:11ff. Because of this, the hermeneutical question is very difficult to answer—that is, whether such expressions are simply to be taken literally or whether one must try to search out a deeper meaning. If butter and honey will provide the Immanuel child with food, which is to suggest that they will transmit to him powers which are beyond the ordinary, this passage might also have been depicting a type of sustenance which would afford someone wonderful powers. But the text does not give any direct indicators to warrant such an interpretation, and the fantasies of one who reads the Bible can go in whatever direction one desires.

4. [7:23–25] *Thorns and Thistles*

Setting and Form

"These verses are so cumbersome stylistically that they can, in no way, be from Isaiah" (Fohrer, ad loc.; see also Duhm, for a similar view). Of course, one can ask at this point also about whether one of Isaiah's comments has been radically altered by reworking and expansion. It could be that the original wording was something like: יהיה כל־מקום אשר שמה יבוא ובקשת בחצים יהיה ולשית לשמיר כסף באלף גפן אלף שם־יהיה (In any region where a thousand vine branches are worth a thousand shekels, it will be full of thistles and thorns, only with the bow and arrow will one go about in it). But even in this form, it would be difficult to say that this came from Isaiah: It is hard to establish a metrical pattern; the threefold repetition of יהיה (it will be) can hardly be attributed to Isaiah; אשר (which) is a prosaic element; and לשמיר ולשית (thistles and thorns) seems to have been borrowed from 5:6. Therefore, we can thank a redactor for already reshaping words from Isaiah in vv. 23 and 24a. Someone still later added vv. 24b and 25 to that. The expression שמיר ושית (thistles and thorns) had made an impression upon him, but he in turn takes it in reference to the entire land. It would not satisfy him even if only hunters were able to move about among the thicket of the thistles and thorns: Absolutely no one is to be able to go about in the land. Of course, he does say in v. 25b that it will still serve as pasture land, but apparently only because he does not want to go beyond יהיה למרמס (it will be given over to be trampled) in 5:5. One sees again and again how those who expanded the authentic passages from Isaiah, as in this case for the song of the vineyard, used the book as a quarry, from which they mined vocabulary for their own use—not only to show that they had read Isaiah, but also so that they could clothe their ideas with his authority.

Commentary

McKane (op. cit., 216) believes, in opposition to practically all the commentators, that vv. 23f. also ought not be taken as a threat, saying that there is absolutely no lament about Canaan becoming a place for hunting and grazing; rather he believes that these verses express the belief that Canaan was the promised land of the people of God, even without grain, wine, and oil. It seems to him to be too much that an addition (or two of them) follows once again with predictions of disaster, after the prediction of salvation in vv. 21f., which itself does not come from Isaiah. In spite of this, McKane is not correct. It may be that there were certain circles in Judah, also in later times, who held high the nomadic ideal, but even this group would not wish for Canaan to become steppe once again. In fact, the expanders must have consciously set out to use ideas from the song of the vineyard, but were intending now to say the exact opposite. We have to satisfy ourselves with the fact that the expanders and redactors of the book of Isaiah did not worry about making sure that they were maintaining a smooth flow of ideas within the synthesized version of the whole book; each one of them added whatever seemed important to him, in his own situation.

The precise interpretation of the imagery in vv. 23 and 24a encounters certain difficulties. Questions have been correctly raised about the high value of the grape vines: 1000 plants = 1000 shekels. That is an exorbitant price; according to Lev. 5:15, one could buy a ram for two shekels (cf. *BRL* col. 177). There is also no clear indication about why a vineyard with 1000 grape vines is mentioned. In actual fact, there is no intent to speak about the price of the grape vines, as if one would be ready to pay out a very great sum of money for a product of the highest quality. Rather, it is the price of the piece of land which is at issue, upon which one could plant 1000 grape vines. "Still today, one calculates the value of a vineyard in Lebanon and in Syria according to the value of the individual grape vine" (Delitzsch, ad loc.). But even if it is understood in this way, the price is unusually high. To be sure, the Song of Solomon speaks about a vineyard from which Solomon can get a yield worth 1000 shekels (8:11), but that is a royal vineyard which is certainly of sizable proportions. (In addition, it is not certain whether "vineyard" in that passage should be taken in a literal sense or whether it serves only as an image for "young girl" or "harem"; cf. G. Gerleman, BK XVIII, 222.) The author of this section has the following in mind: Even an area where the price of land goes far beyond what is usually paid for it, because it has a particularly attractive location or because the ground is of the highest quality, will be abandoned, to be overrun by thistles and thorns. One will be able to get into such an area only to use bow and arrow. That obviously does not mean that one would seek out every last hiding place of an enemy to hunt him down, but that the vacated land would be given over to whatever grew wild (on this, see 5:5) and thus, that it would be traversed only by hunters (concerning arrows and bows as equipment for the hunt, see Dalman, *AuS* VI, 330ff. and cf. the art. "Jagd," *BHH* 792; concerning שמיר ושית [thorns and thistles], see above, commentary on 5:6).

When someone has already allowed such an expensive vineyard to be overrun with thorny undergrowth, then it is quite clear that "the entire land would be thorns and thistles." But the very fact that v. 24b expresses something which is so obvious shows that the verse is a typical gloss. This same tendency to generalize about what had originally been singled out as a striking example of something unique is also seen in v. 25: It is, blandly put, "all the hillsides" which will no longer be traversed by anyone. This glossator is not even satisfied to allow hunters to be able to patrol in such a region. He raises the threat still another notch: Thorns and thistles have grown so rapidly that absolutely no one is able to get into the undergrowth. In fact, "thorns and thistles" are so abundant in Palestine that it can be very difficult to forge a path through them; see, for example, Budde, op. cit. (*Jesajas Erleben*) 64f. and illuss. 67–74 in Dalman, *AuS* II; no one ought to be blamed for hesitating to travel through such a region. It is obvious that animals do not hesitate to go into such a place to find themselves food. However, the expander is not thinking about wild animals, but rather about cattle which would get into the thicket.

Purpose and Thrust

[7:18–20] One can easily understand why attempts have frequently been made to establish that 7:18–25, one way or another, comes from a single speaker. However, the above analysis has shown that only two of the messages, vv. 18f. and 20, can be shown with some confidence to have come from Isaiah. In addition, one has the impression that these are also nothing more than fragments; in any case, they are only threats of judgment and no reasons for the threats are furnished. Yet, it is not Isaiah's style to announce a threat without mentioning why it is going to come, since he is not a mere predictor but a prophet. Obviously, the redactional bracket ביום ההוא (on that day) connects these words with 7:1–17. And if our conclusions above concerning תער שכירה (the knife which he hired) in v. 20 prove to be correct, then the disgrace which Assyria brings upon Judah is to be seen as the consequence of Ahaz's faithless politics. But it still seems that the redactor who added vv. 18–20 here was interested only in an unadorned announcement of judgment.

[7:21–22] With the announcement of salvation in vv. 21f., the expander is just as clearly interested only in what the future would bring. He intends to speak words of comfort, apparently in light of a virtually total depopulation of the land, which suggests the events of 701, or maybe even more likely, 587: There is a possibility that one can go on living. If one is satisfied enough with things as they are, then one can still rejoice in the fullness of the blessing. But the author never once mentions that it is God who opens that door; he says nothing more than that this hope applies to those who are still left in the land. He does not say that this is the remnant which returns because of the judgment or that those who are still remaining are the remnant which has been cleansed and made holy by God (see 4:3). In addition to this, the "salvation" about which he speaks consists in nothing more than "material" goods and there is nothing which would indicate that this has anything to do with a new relationship with Yahweh. Whoever is still left in Israel will be able to go on living. That seems to be a very meager message. But one can think of situations in which admonitions to believe or to repent are not particularly fitting and where theological reflection is out of place but where the simple declaration that there will be a way which will lead into the future, even after all the destruction, is the message which fits best.

[7:23–25] It is thus all the more disconcerting that the entire section vv. 18–25, which would seem to suggest that it should be understood as a kerygmatic unit, cannot conclude with this decisive glimpse into the future, but reverts once again to a very harsh threat of disaster. That is particularly striking, since it is generally the case that such additions to the original text of the book of Isaiah try to add detail to the picture of the coming time of salvation. But it must be noted that the authors of this final section use the vocabulary from the song of the vineyard, 5:1–7. Indeed, they do not want to try to get rid of the previous message of salvation. But a protest is implicit in these final additions—in fact in the name of their master Isaiah himself: In light of a situation marked by a most radical depopulation, which they faced with all of their people, they believe that there is nothing more important than to recognize that the judgment which Isaiah had proclaimed had actually come, in all of its harshness. It would simply not be appropriate to be already looking for a better future when it was of the utmost importance that they take seriously what was happening in the present. It is most amazing that Israel allowed itself to be so unbelieving when confronting the divine judgment. How could a better future be coming if Israel did not know about the holiness of God? Because of that holiness Israel was responsible to honor God, with greater honor than it should ever give to what could be done by humans.

Isaiah 8:1–4

Speedy Plunder—Swift Pillage

Literature

K. Galling, "Ein Stück judäischen Bodenrechts in Jesaja 8," *ZDPV* 56 (1933) 209–218. L. G. Rignell, "Das Orakel 'Maher-salal Has-bas'. Jesaja 8," *ST* 10 (1957) 40–52. J. Schildenberger, "Durch Nacht zum Licht (Jes 8,1—9,6)," *Sein und Sendung* 30 (1965) 387–401.

Concerning the text: B. Stade, "Zu Jes. 8,1f.," *ZAW* 26 (1906) 135–137. P. Katz, "Notes on the Septuagint. I. Isaiah VIII 1a," *JTS* 47 (1946) 30–31. F. Talmage, "חרט אנוש in Isaiah 8:1," *HTR* 60 (1967) 465–468.

Concerning individual motifs: P. Humbert, "Mahēr Šalāl Ḥāš Baz," *ZAW* 50 (1932) 90–92. S. Morenz, "'Eilebeute'," *TLZ* 74 (1949) 697–699. A. Jirku, "Zu 'Eilebeute' in Jes. 8, 1.3," *TLZ* 75 (1950) 118. E. Vogt, "'Eilig tun' als adverbielles Verb und der Name des Sohnes Isaias' in Is 8,1," *Bib* 48 (1967) 63–69. I. Hylander, "War Jesaja Nabi?" *Le Monde Oriental* 25 (1931) 53–66. C. B. Reynolds, "Isaiah's Wife," *JTS* 36 (1935) 182–185. A. Jepsen, "Die Nebiah in Jes 8:3," *ZAW* 72 (1960) 267–268. H. Donner, *Israel unter den Völkern*, VTSup 11 (1964) see pp. 18–30.

[Literature update through 1979: G. W. Ahlström, "Oral and Written Transmission: Some Considerations," *HTR* 59 (1966) 69–81. M. A. Loisier, "Witness in Israel of the Hebrew Scriptures in the Context of Ancient Near East," diss., Univ. of Notre Dame (1973).]

Text

8:1 Yahweh spoke to me: "Take for yourself a ªlarge tabletª and write upon it with a 'disaster' stylus:[b] For ᶜMaher-Shalal Hash-Bazᶜ
2 (Speedy plunder, Swift pillage). • Then ªI 'selected' for myself reliable witnesses, Uriah, the priest, and Zechariah, the son of
3 Jeberechiah.[b] • Afterwards, I drew near to the prophetess. Then she became pregnant and bore a son. And Yahweh spoke to me:
4 "Give him the name Maher-Shalal Hash-Baz. • For before the lad is able to call out 'father' and 'mother,' someoneª will bring the riches of Damascus and the booty of Samaria to the king of Assyria."

1a–a גליון גדול (large tablet) is translated by Gk as τόμον καινοῦ μεγάλου (a piece of a new, large [papyrus sheet]) (some handwritten copies read τομον καινου χαρτου μεγαλου, a piece of a new large papyrus sheet, or something similar; see Ziegler). 'Aquila: διφθερωμα⟨μεγα⟩(⟨large⟩tanned skin); Sym: τευχος μεγα (large book); Theod: κεφαλιδα μεγαλην (large chapter, head); Targ: לוח רב (large tablet); Syr: *gᵉlājūnā rabbā* (large tablet); Vulg: *librum grandem* (large book). Thus, the versions differ in the way they translate גליון, though they all read גדול (large). Galling (op. cit.) seeks to interpret גליון on the basis of 3:23, the only other passage in the OT where it occurs. Since the word clearly refers to a type of garment in that passage, it would be possible that it should be taken to mean a sheet of papyrus in 8:1, since there is some evidence that papyrus was also used in some cases in the manufacture of clothing (see S. Krauss, *Talmudische Archäologie* I [1910] 141, and Pliny, *Natural History* XIII, 22). Instead of גדול (large), Galling conjectures גורל, lot, used in a context referring to a piece of ground which has come to someone by lot, so that he translates גליון גורל in a very loose sense, as "public property deed" (so also Kaiser). It is possible that καινοῦ (new) in the Gk could have resulted from a misreading of the Greek word κλήρου (lot) (so Katz, op. cit.). Galling, in his interpretation of the passage, understands this as a reference to officially recording the members of the family, by means of which the claims of the individual for land and soil would be legally documented. But the harsh sound of the interpretation forces one to examine this more carefully: In 3:23, גליון should probably be changed to read גלמים (outer garments) (see above, commentary on 3:23), which means that that passage cannot be used to explain גליון (tablet) in 8:1. Moreover, if used for a notice which has the express purpose of preserving the message of Isaiah for future times, a sheet of papyrus would not be particularly suitable. One must be especially cautious when altering גדול (large), which is so universally attested, in order to read גורל (lot). In actual fact, Isaiah wants to use his inscription to attract the attention of the people of Jerusalem, and therefore it would make sense that whatever the גליון is, it would be something which would catch one's eye even from a distance (Driver, *Semitic Writing* [1954²] 80 and 229 thinks that it is a placard). The fact that papyrus would hardly ever be written upon with a stylus (חֶרֶט from חָרַט, dig in) would also discount Galling's interpretation. What seems best is to stay with the traditional translation of גליון as "tablet" (cf. KBL and *HAL;* see also לוּחַ, tablet, in Hab. 2:2). Driver (*JSS* 13 [1968] 40) thinks that it is a wooden board with a layer of wax over it, such as have been found in Nineveh.

1b The exact meaning of חרט אנוש ('disaster' stylus) is also unclear. The literal translation, human stylus, is not very satisfying. It is true that Exod. 32:16 speaks of מכתב אלהים (the writing of God), but there, God himself does the writing, and besides, the reference there is to the divine script, not to a divine stylus (on this, see Stade, op. cit., 135). Thus, some have decided to translate חרט אנוש as "common script," using Deut. 3:11 and 2 Sam. 7:14 to substantiate it; in these passages one finds mention of שבט אנשים/אמת-איש, which supposedly means a "common cubit"/"common rod." But אמת איש refers to a man's cubit and שבט אנשים refers to a human rod in contrast to *divine* judgment. Procksch and others have suggested that this might refer to various styles of writing, in a way which would correspond to the hieratic and demotic scripts in Egypt, and Fohrer even thinks that אנוש refers here to "what one might call an old-fashioned man, who does not know the modern style which trained officials use when writing" (ad loc.). But we have no information at all about various writing styles in ancient Israel, neither in the OT nor from archaeological investigations. However, more than anything else, these interpretations are all problematic since חרט does not mean "script" but "stylus." H. Gressmann (*Der Messias* [1929] 239, note 1), responding to these various solutions, suggested pointing אֱנוֹשׁ (human) to read אָנוּשׁ; on the basis of this emendation, he translated it "with a hard stylus." That fits very well in the context, but אָנוּשׁ does not mean hard, but rather unable to be saved, unsalvageable. Thus, Galling (op. cit.) would rather translate חרט אֱנוֹשׁ with the meaning "indelible script" (similarly, Kaiser). This interpretation also fits very nicely into the context, but this also does not account for the fact that חרט means stylus, not script. Moreover, one cannot find evidence for how the meaning changed from "disaster bound" to "indelible"; this does not seem to be a very likely solution. For the same reason, the suggestion of Talmage is just as doubtful (op. cit.), as he suggests אָנוֹשׁ should be interpreted on the basis of the Akkadian *enēšu* and the Arabic *'anuṭa*, "be weak." Isaiah would have been using a wide, pliable, soft pen, so that he could write clearly enough to make it easy to read. In fact, one may be on the right track when pointing this אָנוֹשׁ, but one must stay with the meaning "disaster bound." A stylus, in and of itself, neither brings joy nor disaster, but when it is used to write down a message which announces disaster, then one might term it a "disaster stylus." That this is the right direction to take can be supported by 1QM 12:3: חיים בחרט למו חרתה שלומכה ברית (the covenant of your peace is written with a stylus of life). If one can speak of a stylus of life, then one can certainly also speak of a stylus of disaster.

1c–c The common translation of מהר שלל חש בז as "rob-soon—hurry-booty" takes both of the verbal elements in the name as imperatives. That is a bit forced in the case of חָשׁ (swift). Jirku (op. cit.) has suggested that מהר should be explained on the basis of the Ugaritic *mhr*, warrior, soldier (on this, see Aistleitner, *Wört* n. 1532, and A. F. Rainey, "The Military Personnel of Ugarit," *JNES* 24 [1965] 17–27, s.v. As a foreign word, it is also found in the Egyptian texts; see A. R. Schulmann, "*Mhr* and *Mškb*, Two Egyptian Military Titles of Semitic Origin," *ÄZ* 93 [1966] 123–132, and A. F. Rainey, *JNES* 26 [1967] 58–60), and he would translate it: "Warriors of booty, hurrying for robbery." That sounds forced and everything speaks in favor of מהר (hurry) and חש (swift), both on the basis of their meaning and because of the grammatical form, being parallel; in addition to this, Isaiah uses מהר (hasten) and חוש (come quickly) together in 5:19. חָשׁ could be taken as a perfect (he was swift), so that מַהֵר (to hurry up, be swift) would be pointed as a perfect also: מִהַר (he hurried up) (thus, H. Torczyner, *MGWJ* 74 [1930] 257). However, it is more likely that these are actually participles. In this case, מהר stands in place of מְמַהֵר, which is certainly possible grammatically (see Ges-K §52s; see also Zeph. 1:14). The short forms of the participles were chosen so that the name would not appear to be too long. Vogt (op. cit.) has pointed out that מהר (hurry) is often used in the sense of an adverb, "quickly, soon, right away" (cf. Joüon, Gr §102e). If that is the case, the main verb which one would expect would follow right after מהר (hurry) could simply be omitted. The participle would only be employed in place of the imperfect due to a desire for brevity, so that מהר שלל (hurry-up-booty) would actually stand for שָׁלָל ⟨יִשָּׂא⟩ יְמַהֵר (he hurries [to seize] booty), which means that the verb נשא (bring, take) in v. 4 would already be anticipated mentally at this point. The double name, which could have some connection with the double enemy, could thus be translated something like: "Very soon, booty, shortly, someone will carry off spoil." This attempt runs into trouble, since one would expect a transitive verb instead of חוש (swift). Thus, one should literally interpret the name to mean something like "Quickly is the booty, hurrying the plundered goods." (This is only a summary of a select number of suggestions, in the interest of brevity.)

2a Instead of וָאָעִידָה (then I selected), Gk reads καὶ μάρτυράς μοι ποίησον (and appoint for me witnesses), Targ וְאַסְהֵיד (and I made witnesses), Syr *washed lî sāhdē* (and I brought for myself witnesses), so that it has often been suggested that the imperative וְהָעִידָה (and appoint witnesses) ought to be read instead of the MT form, supported seemingly by Qᵃ (והעד, and bring witnesses). However, on the basis of analogy with the verbs in v. 3, it still seems preferable to follow the Vulg (*et adhibui*, and I summoned) and to point this וָאָעִידָה (see Stade, op. cit., 136f.).

2b Instead of יברכיהו (Jeberechiah), Gk reads βαραχιου (Berechiah), which would suggest the original was also ברכיהו (Berechiah [Berechyahu]). But the less common form of the name with the imperfect of the verb is to be preferred. The reading in the Gk may be based on ברכיה (Berechiah) in Zech. 1:1 or ברכיהו (Berechyahu) in Zech. 1:7.

4a Concerning the use of the third person singular when speaking of an indefinite subject, "someone," see Joüon, Gr §155e.

Form

Prose is used in 8:1–4. On the basis of its first-person style, it claims to have been written by the prophet himself, which has not been seriously questioned by study of the text.

The short account divides into two parts (1 + 2 and 3 + 4). In the first, the prophet is given a command to write למהר שלל חש בז (for Maher-Shalal Hash-Baz) on a tablet. The second part speaks about the procreation and birth of a son, who is to be given this very same name, מהר שלל חש בז, so that its kerygmatic sense might be given full meaning. Both parts are united, since both mention this name. However, one must wonder whether they belonged together from the very beginning. Would it have been possible for the prophet to have received this command to write an inscription like this upon a tablet with a disaster stylus and to bring in witnesses to observe this action, without knowing the meaning of what he was to write, moreover, without knowing that a son would be born to him who was to bear that name? This difficulty has caused Duhm, Marti, Rignell (op. cit.), et al., and recently Kaiser as well (see each, ad loc.), to treat v. 3 as a pluperfect: "and I had brought myself near to the prophetess," whereas Gray switches the two parts around: vv. 1f. come *after* vv. 3f. But if the pluperfect had actually been intended, then one would expect something like ואנוכי קרבתי (and I had drawn near) (see Procksch, ad loc.; Galling, op. cit., 214, note 1; cf. also S. R. Driver, *A Treatise on the Use of the Tenses in Hebrew* [1892³] §76, and Donner, op. cit., 19ff.); one would have to consider וָאֶקְרַב (afterwards, I drew near) as "narrative." But it hardly makes sense to switch around the two parts. If the son had already been born, or if the birth was at least immanent, then there would have been no need to publish the name by placing it on a large tablet or to bring in witnesses. The most likely interpretation leads instead to the conclusion that writing down the name took place not only before the birth, but also before the conception, in which case it can be presumed that the prophet was commanded to use this particular name right after he had received the command to inscribe the tablet. He himself, no doubt, was well aware of what the name meant (for another view, see Vriezen, VTSup 1 [1953] 209, note 2). The people of Jerusalem were certainly also in a position to know what the name was supposed to signify, being well aware of the position which Isaiah took during the current conflict. The prophet was not to be forced to wait until the name was given to publicize this most shocking sign, since he wanted to summon the people to make a decision *now,* not first after several months had passed. "The tablet, as it were, took the place of the as-yet-unborn son" (Vogt, op. cit.). On the other hand, the birth and giving of the name which had been inscribed on the tablet would give the prophecy even greater authority. Therefore, the section is one unit. The command from God has been separated so that parts of it are in both vv. 1 and 3b, but only because the events are described in the order they actually took place.

Setting

Naming both of the witnesses shows that the message was to be an appeal to those groups which were in political control. Since, as in 7:1ff., Damascus and Samaria are mentioned together and, as in that passage, both of the kingdoms are threatened with downfall, 8:1–4 must also belong to the time of the Syro-Ephraimitic War. Thus, this section also belongs to the "memorial record," which assembles into one place Isaiah's proclamation which was spoken during that era which was so critical for Jerusalem (see above, on the form of 6:1–13). It seems likely that 8:1ff. is to be dated somewhat later than the Immanuel prediction. Since the prophet did not accomplish his purpose during his discussion with the king, he now turns to a wider public. It seems that Ahaz vacillated for a long time, until he finally decided to make the grave decision to become subject to the king of Assyria. The critical situation seems to have lasted longer than most normally think; on this, see Donner, op. cit., 59ff. But in any case, 8:1–4 comes so close to the events of 7:1ff. that the עלמה (almah) of 7:14 cannot possibly be the "prophetess" in 8:3. If the *almah* is to be considered to be Isaiah's own wife, as some suggest, then the נביאה (prophetess) in 8:3 must be another wife of the prophet, and one is then given free rein for fantasizing about Isaiah's family relationships.

Commentary

[8:1] In v. 1, Isaiah uses the formal language used for symbolic actions; see Hos. 1:2: קח לך אשת זנונים (take to yourself a wife of harlotry); Ezek. 4:1: קח לך לבנה (and you, take a brick); Ezek. 4:9: קח לך חטין ושערים (and you, take wheat and barley); Ezek. 5:1: קח לך חרב חדה (and you, take a sharp sword); cf. also 1 Kings 11:31; Jer. 13:4; 25:15; 36:2, 28; 43:9; Zech. 11:15. When comparing the exact wording in the formulation, the passage which is closest to this one in Isaiah is Ezek. 37:16: קח לך עץ אחד וכתב עליו ליהודה (take a stick and write upon it, "For Judah"). Based on these parallels, it is likely that the writing upon the tablet was seen as a symbolic action. But that applies only in a provisional way. One might say that it is a sign which prepares for the actual sign, which was that the son is to be given a special name. In so many words, Isaiah says in 8:18 that his children (their names) are "signs from Yahweh."

Unfortunately, there is no way to determine more exactly what a גליון (here: large tablet) is (see above, textual note 1a–a). We do not know if the tablet was made of wood, leather, or clay. Ezek. 37:16 speaks in a similar situation about עץ (a stick), but Ezekiel does not seem to be referring to a tablet, but rather to a ruler's staff (see Zimmerli, *Ezechiel*, BK XIII, ad loc. [Engl: *Ezekiel 2*, 273]). According to 4:1, Ezekiel had made use of a brick instead and was "to scratch upon it" a city (Hebrew חקק, cut in, inscribe, is a synonym for חרט, from which the חֶרֶט, stylus, in the present passage is derived). Just as little can be said about where one would have placed the tablet so that it would be prominently visible. Since it was to be very large, it was probably to be placed out in the open, where it would be easily seen, possibly at the entrance to the temple. Hab. 2:2 supplies evidence for the custom that the Jerusalem prophets wrote their revelations upon tablets (לֻחוֹת) and, in fact, in a script which would be easy to read (cf. the way גליון, tablet, is referred to in the Targ as לוח, tablet). In Sir. 12:11, we come across the expression מגלי ראי (text emended), "the one who cleans the mirror" (so KBL). According to this, it is possible that the גליון is a tablet which has been "cleaned," that is, polished smooth, so that it would be easier to inscribe something on it.

Just before the inscription "Speedy Plunder—Swift Pillage," a ל has been placed, which one might understand, in analogy with the ל upon seals, to be the ל *possessoris* (of possession), for which ליהודה (for Judah) and ליוסף (for Joseph) can be cited from Ezek. 37:16 as a parallel usage; cf. on this Zimmerli, *Ezechiel,* BK XIII, 909f. (Engl: *Ezekiel 2,* 273f.). It would probably be better to be more prudent, as is Ges-K §119u, and to speak of a *lamed inscriptionis,* meaning "which concerns" or "in reference to," a use which intends to do no more than establish a very loose connection with what follows (concerning the discussion about the meaning of ל on jar handles, see S. Moscati, *L'epigrafia Ebraica Antica* [1951] 85–89).

The name of the son, both in terms of its form and its meaning, is completely different from the normal way in which names were given in ancient Israel. Noth, *Personennamen,* 9, considers מהר שלל חש בז (Maher-Shalal Hash-Baz) as one of the names which are "the result of artistic formulation or what a writer might invent and therefore, such names do not really belong to the actual names which were really in use in Israel." In spite of this, one must ask whether the name is a completely spontaneous construction of Isaiah's. Humbert already (op. cit., 90–92) noted that the expression *ỉs ḥ3k̠* was used in a stereotypical way in the documents and inscriptions of the eighteenth dynasty and Morenz (op. cit.) has very carefully compared Egyptian materials with the names in Isaiah. Grammatically, *ỉs ḥ3k̠* uses two imperatives, which are to be translated something like "hurry, take spoil." But, in actual fact, the combination is treated as a substantive, as, for example, in the sentence: "His majesty brought him (the Nubian rebels) as prisoners of war, all of his people as *ỉs ḥ3k̠*" (= as "speedy plunder"). One cannot refer to this substantive usage in Egypt and simply conclude thereby that Isaiah was using imperatives instead of participles. But it is likely that there is indeed a connection between מהר שלל חש בז (Maher-Shalal Hash-Baz) and *ỉs ḥ3k̠,* since the Egyptian phraseology and/or its translation as a military expression could very well have been a commonly known term in Jerusalem during the time of Isaiah. In any case, the throne names for the Messiah in 9:5 (see H. Wildberger, *TZ* 16, 314–332) show that, at the very least, Isaiah presumably could have known of terminology such as this. Naturally, however, nothing more is explained by this than the striking form which the name took. The message, intended to bring about a response, must be interpreted solely within the context of the historical circumstances and the relationship with the rest of what Isaiah proclaimed.

The doubled form of the name corresponds to the *parallelismus membrorum,* which is common in the Hebrew language. שלל (plunder) and בזז (pillage) are also parallel in Deut. 2:35; 3:7; 20:14; Isa. 10:6; Ezek. 29:19; 38:12f. On the other side, מהר (speedy) and חוש (swift) are also parallel terms. It is very difficult to differentiate the meaning of the two verbs. The certainty of the proclamation is strengthened by the fact that it is doubled, and the fact that the change will take place very soon is accented as well.

[8:2] Isaiah brought along witnesses. The fact that there are two of them corresponds with the Israelite system of justice; see Deut. 17:6; 19:15. The prophet accents the fact that they are נאמנים (reliable); there is no doubt that they would have also been known as trustworthy individuals among the wider public. For this reason, he records their names. There is also a reference to a priest named Uriah in 2 Kings 16:10ff. This is the one who saw to it that an Assyrian altar was constructed in the forecourt of the temple, at the command of Ahaz, serving as the altar upon which the king would make his offering in order to proclaim that he was a vassal. Thus, we do not have any reason to suspect that he was a friend of Isaiah's and like-minded. Rather, he was apparently the chief priest at the Jerusalem sanctuary. When Isaiah set up the tablet someplace in the temple area (on this, see above, commentary on 8:1), then Uriah would certainly have had to give the go-ahead. Since this individual was such a highly placed personage, it is very likely that the other one, Zechariah, the son of Jeberechiah, would have been the father of Ahaz's wife, who was the mother of Hezekiah and whose name was Abi or Abijah; this would mean that this Zechariah was certainly close to the palace and to official politics in Jerusalem; see 2 Kings 18:2 and 2 Chron. 29:1. That they were both ready to do what Isaiah asked, in spite of it all, shows the kind of respect which he commanded in Jerusalem. It is certainly possible that Isaiah himself, from his own background, belonged to the upper echelons of leadership within the capital city (see above, commentary on 7:4). But that he would have been installed into an office to serve as one of the leading court prophets, as Becker (op. cit., 21) suggests, is of course not nearly so likely. Both of the witnesses bear names connected with the name Yahweh. Uriah would mean something like: "Yahweh is light," concerning which one can refer to Isa. 10:17 and Ps. 27:1 (see also Noth, *Personennamen,* 168f.). Zechariah means: "Yahweh has remembered"; cf. passages such as Ps. 74:2, 18; Lam. 3:19; 5:1. As for Jeberechiah, the verbal element is in the imperfect. Such ways of constructing names can certainly be found in more ancient times, but they are much more common just before the exile. It is a name which expresses a wish, meaning: "May Yahweh bless"; see Ps. 67:7f. and Ps. 115:22f. The names fit right in with what was normal in Isaiah's time (see above, commentary on 1:1) and help one to recognize that the leading figures in Jerusalem at that time were obviously moving within the circles of cultic piety which we know from the Psalms.

Why does Isaiah find it necessary to call in witnesses? It is hardly just because they could attest to the fact that Isaiah was the author of the inscription, and it is also not just because they could help explain to the public what the proclamation meant. It is much more likely that it is so that the specific point in time, when it was written down, could be witnessed. Before the son would be born, the situation within the political power structure could have radically altered. But Isaiah wishes to leave absolutely no doubt about what he proclaimed, at a very specific point in time, concerning the fall of Damascus and Samaria, at which time those who were in Jerusalem were still free to make decisions. He is absolutely sure about this matter and takes a chance, really functioning as a "prophet." The cause of his self-confidence, whatever it was, is not spelled out in this present context; he does not seem to feel constrained to give the reasons why he held this vision of the future, but is content simply to state his claim that Yahweh had spoken to him.

When Isaiah summoned the witnesses, he apparently reckoned with the fact that his proclamation, calling for a reorientation of the official political stance in Jerusalem, would not prove successful. Calling upon these two well-known personalities would accomplish the same thing as the preservation of the revelation, the sealing up the instruction with his disciples (v. 16). Even if the prophet met with absolutely no response, it was still important for Jerusalem to know that Yahweh had not allowed his people to be without any clear instruction. And even if Isaiah did not have the power to alter anyone's thinking on the matter, his activity was at least aimed at bringing about the hardening of the people on that day.

[8:3] It is only after he has inscribed the tablet that the prophet draws near to his wife. קרב (draw near) is also used in other cases which describe the act of coming together for sexual activity: Gen. 20:4; Lev. 18:6, 14, 19; 20:16; Deut. 22:14; Ezek. 18:6. When using נביאה (prophetess), Isaiah can only be referring to his wife. But it is most unlikely that he uses that title for her just because she is his wife (contra Duhm, Procksch, et al.). And it is just as unlikely that one can conclude from this title that Isaiah considered himself to be a נביא (prophet). It is possible that Isaiah's wife, as Hulda at the time of Jeremiah (see 2 Kings 22:14), might have held the position of cultic prophetess at the sanctuary in Jerusalem. Since Isaiah placed high value on the temple, in spite of the hesitations which he expressed about the cultic piety, it is certainly not an impossibility.

In Israel, it was not customary for a woman to be referred to on the basis of her husband's title. מלכה (queen) does not furnish evidence to the contrary, since the wife of a king of Judah or Israel is never referred to as a queen in the OT; it is handled differently only when one comes to Song of Sol. 6:8 and the book of Esther, where Vashti and Esther are called queens (passim). It would be still more unlikely that the wife of a prophet would be called a נביאה (prophetess). In addition, Isaiah stays away from using the title נביא (prophet) for himself (see above, commentary on 1:1); he considers himself a seer and not a *nabi*. On the other hand, the OT makes frequent reference to prophetesses: Miriam, Exod. 15:20; Deborah, Judg. 4:4; Hulda, 2 Kings 22:14 = 2 Chron. 34:22; Noadiah, Neh. 6:14. For complete discussion of this matter, see Hylander, op. cit., 53–56; Reynolds, op. cit.; A. H. J. Gunneweg, *Mündliche und schriftliche Tradition der vorexilischen Prophetenbücher*, FRLANT 73 (1959) 102f.; R. Rendtorff, *TDNT* VI 804; Jepsen, op. cit.; concerning Mari, see A. Malamat, VTSup 15 (1965) 220f.

ותהר ותלד (then she became pregnant and bore a son) sounds very much like the Immanuel prediction in 7:14. Also in this case, Isaiah uses the annunciation oracle form (concerning this, see above, commentary on 7:14), which accounts for the fact that he took an oracle which had come to him, concerning the birth of a son, and recast it in narrative prose (concerning this, see Vogt, op. cit., 68). In v. 3bβ, the second half of the oracle, the command to give the name is still reported in the form of direct address. The value placed on the birth of a son and naming the child is treated here, as well as in 7:14ff., as a "sign" which demonstrates the reliability of Isaiah's message.

[8:4] The justification for giving this most shocking name begins with the exact same expression as found in 7:16: כי בטרם ידע הנער (there: for before the lad understands). The reference to time is formulated somewhat differently here: "For before the lad is able to call out 'father' and 'mother' . . ." A child would be able to say "father" and "mother" at an earlier age than, as it is formulated in 7:16, that child would be able to reject the evil and choose the good. But the references are left somewhat vague in both passages, certainly handled this way by Isaiah on purpose. But 8:4 makes it very clear that one cannot interpret 7:16 as referring to a young man who is entering into adulthood.

It is only at this point that one understands exactly what the inscription on the tablet means: The riches of Damascus and the booty of Samaria will be brought into the presence of the king of Assyria. In contrast to 7:17 (את מלך אשור, the king of Assyria) and 8:7aβ, here the specific reference to the expanding world power headquartered on the Tigris would seem to be original. The capital cities of the two kings who were oppressing Judah would fall in a very short period of time. There was no cause for alarm in Jerusalem and the call to Assyria, which had not been thought through very carefully, was completely unnecessary. The חיל (riches) of Damascus, parallel to the שלל (plunder) of Samaria, must refer here to the possessions and riches of the people of Damascus even though, in Neh. 3:34, חיל שמרון (army of Samaria) is used as a designation for the upper echelons of power in Samaria (see KBL). The formulation לפני מלך אשור (to the king of Assyria) helps one to recognize that a triumphal march is meant, at which time the booty of war was carried into the presence of the victor (cf. ANEP illuss. 303f.).

Isaiah's prediction came true. In 732, Tiglath-Pileser III of Assyria conquered Damascus and sounded the death knell for the final time for the kingdom of the Arameans of Damascus, which had played such a leading role in the Syrian region during the previous two centuries. Israel was reduced in size, so that only the mountainous region of Ephraim-Manasseh was left (2 Kings 15:29). Tiglath-Pileser himself describes it: "Israel [lit.: 'Omri-Land' *Bît Ḫumria*] . . . all its inhabitants [and] their possessions I led to Assyria. They overthrew their king Pekah [*Pa-qa-ḫa*] and I placed Hoshea [*A-ú-si-'*] as king over them" (annals fragment, quoted from *ANET³* 284 = TGI [1968²] 58f.; see also *AOT²* 346f. = *ANET³* 283).

Purpose and Thrust

These two symbolic actions, the inscription upon the tablet and the naming of the son, can only be understood and can only make sense in connection with Isaiah's other proclamations at the time of the threat from Aram and Israel. Taken by itself, the prediction of the downfall of Damascus and Samaria sounds surprisingly abrupt and, if one wants to separate it from the rest of what Isaiah had to say about that political and military situation, one could get the impression that Isaiah was only interested in knowing in advance what would happen in the future. The theological position on which he bases what he says is not evident; there is no clear statement about exactly what Isaiah wants to accomplish with these symbolic actions; and there is also nothing mentioned about the *conditio fidei* (condition of one's faith) as in 7:9. But one ought not draw any false conclusions from that. As in other cases, signs are not to be separated from the message they are to convey. A "sign" is a signal light and stubbornly insists on reflection, in the case of the inscription upon the large tablet just as much as when one is called to ponder the meaning of the naked and barefoot prophet (chap. 20). It demands that the wider public enter into conversation with the prophet and, in a way which is different from a message which is spoken quickly and soon forgotten, it pricks like a thorn, long after the initial event is past. From the very beginning, Isaiah would not have deluded himself into thinking that Jerusalem would have altered its basic political stance because of the viewpoint he had shared and, at the very latest, he would have had to have known by the time his son was born that the die had not fallen the way he thought it should have. In spite of that, he still gave his son the name which had been given to him at the first. Even if he had not been able to forestall or rescind the fatal decision to call upon Assyria for help, even then Maher-Shalal Hash-Baz could still accuse the people which had made a decision to go against Yahweh and had not found itself in a position to nor was of a mind to rely on faith. God's people had been correctly instructed, but they had rejected that instruction. The son of Isaiah, with his strange name, would be a witness to that fact as long as he lived.

At first glance, 8:1–4 seems to set forth a prediction of salvation: Isaiah announces the downfall of the enemies who were oppressing Judah. But after what has just been said, this is once again not a situation in which one can impose the schema which hunts for either salvation or disaster. To be confronted so clearly with God's will to save and then still to choose the way of unbelief could only result in a disastrous future, the seeds of which already had been sown. Because of this, we are in the same ambivalent situation as that which characterized the Immanuel prediction, with scholarship having pointed out clearly enough that one simply cannot use alternative categories to show that this predicts either salvation or disaster. Isaiah's offer of salvation was not accepted and he became just what had been said about him in his commissioning, according to 6:10: a preacher who would bring about the hardening of the people.

Isaiah 8:5–8

Shiloah Waters
and Euphrates Flood

Literature

O. Schroeder, "ומשוש eine Glosse zu רצין," *ZAW* 32 (1912) 301–302. K. Fullerton, "The Interpretation of Isaiah 8:5–10," *JBL* 43 (1924) 253–289. K. Budde, "Jes 8:6b," *ZAW* 44 (1926) 65–67. A. M. Honeyman, "Traces of an Early Diakritic Sign in Isaiah 8:6b," *JBL* 63 (1944) 45–50.
[**Literature update through 1979:** H. G. May, "Some Cosmic Connotations of Mayim Rabbîm, 'Many Waters'," *JBL* 74 (1954) 9–29. O. Kaiser, *Die mythische Bedeutung des Meeres in Ägypten, Ugarit und Israel,* BZAW 78 (1959) (passim). J. Bauer, "Altsumerische Beiträge 1–3," *WO* 6 (1970/71) 143–152.]

Text

8:5,6   [And Yahweh went on and spoke further with me:] • Because this people scorns the waters of Shiloah which flow along gently, but 'melt because of the pride' of Rezin[a] and the son of Remaliah,[b]

       7   • therefore,[a] behold, 'Yahweh'[b] will let the great and mighty waters of the Euphrates River rise up [over them][c] [d][, the king of Assyria and all of his glory].[d]
               It rises above all its channels
               and overflows all its banks

       8   and goes upwards over Judah, inundating[a] and overflowing, it reaches[b] even to the neck,
               [But it will happen that his outstretched wings will fill your entire expanse of land, Immanuel.][c]

6a ומשוש את רצין, "and the joy with Rezin" (concerning the vocalization of this name, see above, textual note 7:1b), is syntactically difficult and does not make any sense. It has been suggested that את רצין ובן רמליהו (Rezin and the son of Remaliah) be removed and that מסוס (dissolve, melt) (see 10:18) be read instead of משוש (rejoicing) (Hitzig, Giesebrecht), so that it would be translated something like: "the water which is softly flowing and running off on its own." That is impossible, since the waters of Shiloah are a symbol of Yahweh's protection of

Jerusalem, about which it cannot be said that it "runs off on its own." It is just as impossible that משוש (rejoicing) is a gloss for the supposedly original רצון ("satisfying"), misread as רצין (Rezin), and to be removed (O. Schroeder) or that one should read משה (pull out, specifically out of the water) with Honeyman instead of reading משוש (rejoicing). The emendation of משוש (rejoicing) to read מסוס (dissolving) is probably on the right track, to be pointed מָסוֹס (to melt). For the following את ([the mark of the direct object]), it has been suggested that לפני (because of, before) be read, but it would be closer to the original text to adopt the suggestion that מִשְׂאֵת (because of the pride of) be read (מש being lost by haplography; on this, see Budde, *ZAW* 44, 65–67).

6b Qᵃ reads ואת בן (and the son) instead of ובן (and son), which would make sense right after משׂאת (because of the pride of), which is just before רצין (Rezin), misread as את ([the mark of the direct object]).

7a Gk, Syr, Vulg do not read ו (*Waw*) before לכן (therefore); however, this "*waw* apodosis" is not impossible; see Joüon, Gr §176.

7b Qᵃ seems to have read יהוה (Yahweh) instead of אדני (Lord), but it inserted אדוני (Lord) above the line.

7c עליהם (over them) is an interpretive comment which comes too soon, even if one follows the Gk (ἐφ᾿ ὑμᾶς, upon you) and reads it עליכם (upon you); cf. v. 7b and, on this, see Fullerton, 263f.

7d–d This is an ancient addition which furnishes more concrete details, but it is not to be contested on text-critical grounds.

8a A number of MSS and Syr read ושטף (and inundated), which is essential if one wants to read the perfect. But there is much to be said for reading שטף (to inundate) and עבר (to overflow) as infinitive absolutes (Vulg reads participles: *inundans et transiens,* inundating and crossing over); concerning this, cf. J. Huesman, *Bib* 37 (1956) 287.

8b Gk seem to have had a different text to work with here: καὶ ἀφελεῖ ἀπὸ τῆς Ἰουδαίας ἄνθρωπον ὃς δυνήσεται κεφαλὴν ἆραι ἢ δυνατὸν συντελέσασθαί τι (and he took away from the Judean land a man who will be able to raise a band of men or accomplish some mighty thing), but there is no reason to take that as the preferred reading; in addition, it should not be taken, as does Eichrodt (ad loc.), as an expansion of the MT, to be inserted into the text.

8c In v. 8b, it is strange that Immanuel is directly addressed without any transition. In Syrʰ and the Lucianic handwritten copies of Gk, σου (your) is missing after χώρας (land). That hardly justifies the conclusion that the text originally read only ארץ (land), and thus that the suffix כ (your) should be presumed to have been originally the particle כי (because [God is with you]).

Form

Verse 5 is a redactional link, connecting vv. 6ff. to the section which precedes them. The original message begins in v. 6, introduced with a causal clause. It is constructed just as 29:13f. is, where a clause giving a reason is introduced by יען כי (because) and is followed by a threat beginning with לכן (therefore) (see also 30:12f. and 3:16, where, of course, לכן, therefore, is left out). The causal clause takes the place of the reproach, which so often either precedes or follows a prophetic threat (see above, p. 147, 3:17).

Whether one also considers v. 6b to be an original part of this threat depends on the interpretation and/or reconstruction of the text. On the other hand, v. 7aβ, את מלך אשור ואת כל כבודו (the king of Assyria and all of his glory), though a very accurate interpretation of the imagery of the stream which will bring a flood upon Jerusalem, still must be considered a gloss which disrupts the flow from the metaphor to its explanation, which is found in vv. 7b and 8 (see above, on the form of 7:1–17). Verse 7b seems to fit best right after 7aα.

There is once again much debate about whether one ought to consider v. 8b as part of the original message, which could be possible only if the conclusion of the message is considered a threat. However, that raises significant problems, as will become apparent in the discussion below, so that it is better to treat it as an interpretive comment about the original threat.

K. Fullerton, in a very extensive study of 8:5–10, has made the suggestion that v. 8b should be separated from the preceding message, but then should be connected with vv. 9f. He believes that it is a message of Isaiah, which belongs chronologically to the same time period as 7:4–9. The suffix on אַרְצֶךָ (your land) is to be taken as referring to King Ahaz, who would be addressed here just as in 7:4ff. And yet, the imperatives at the beginning of v. 9 show clearly that a new section begins at that point; there is no doubt that v. 8b should be considered the conclusion for vv. 5–8a.

Meter: Verses 5, 6, and 7aα are prose. However, beginning with v. 7b, the prophet uses the poetic form, as the parallelism in the two halves of the verses clearly shows (three-stress bicola). In v. 8a, the original message comes to a close with 3 two-stress cola (2 + 2 + 2). One can hardly read v. 8b metrically.

Setting

The analysis just presented has shown that the threat was originally in vv. 6, 7aα, 7b, and 8a. No one contests the fact that this comes from Isaiah himself.

The message presumes that the diplomatic decisions made in the palace to deal with the Syro-Ephraimitic War had gone against Isaiah's recommendation. The prophet no longer felt constrained to refer to the imminent destruction of Aram and Damascus and to issue a call for holding on in faith. The dice had been tossed; now the grave consequences of the wrong decision are first sketched out. Therefore, the message must have been spoken some time after that of 8:1–4. It would seem that Tiglath-Pileser had already begun to seize control.

Commentary

[8:6] The meaning of the entire section is made more difficult by the uncertainty concerning the text in v. 6b (see above, textual note 6a). Instead of the construct state מְשׂוֹשׂ, which is syntactically impossible before את ([the mark of the accusative]), if one reads the absolute form מָשׂוֹשׂ, one could, if need be, translate it as follows: "and there is joy with Rezin and the son of Remaliah." But that simply makes no sense in the context: Who in Jerusalem was supposed to rejoice along with Rezin and the son of Remaliah, when everyone was apparently living in utter terror before the two of them? In order to accept that interpretation one would have to presume, already at this point, that הָעָם הַזֶּה (this people) would refer to the population of Samaria or to the entire Northern Kingdom, an interpretation originally suggested by Jerome (Migne, *Patr. Lat.* 24, 119) and adopted once again in recent times (on this, see Fullerton, 256, note

5). But that also must be rejected, if one takes v. 6a into account. The people who reject the softly flowing waters of Shiloah can only be the population in Judah/Jerusalem. According to the textual reconstruction suggested above, v. 6b should be taken as part of the original message, without thereby forcing one to suggest that הזה העם (this people) must be interpreted in a most unexpected way in reference to the North. Isaiah often uses this expression (instead of עַמִּי, my people) to refer to Judah/Jerusalem (cf. above, 6:9) whenever he issues a reprimand. The people, by their own actions, had brought their relationship with Yahweh into question.

The הַשִּׁלֹחַ מֵי (waters of Shiloah) are mentioned only in this passage in the entire OT. Neh. 3:15 mentions the הַשֶּׁלַח לְגַן־הַמֶּלֶךְ בְּרֵכַת, "the Pool of Shelah of the king's garden." שֶׁלַח must mean "water canal"; cf. Akkadian *šalḫu*, "watering pipes" and *šiliḫtu*, "water course"; see also the *pi'el* of שִׁלֵּחַ, used in the sense of "make springs gush forth" in Ps. 104:10 and Ezek. 31:4. But it is certain that this שִׁלֹחַ (Shiloah) does not refer to the so-called Siloam tunnel, which empties into the Pool of Siloam across from the present-day town of Silwan. That was first built under the direction of Hezekiah and one could not say that the water flows only very sluggishly in that! One must rather think in terms of a canal which would bring the waters of the Gihon (called today either *'ēn 'umm ed-daraǧ* or the Spring of Mary) along the eastern slope of the city down toward the south. Two such aqueducts have been found in that area (see Vincent/Steve, 289ff.; Simons, *Jerusalem in the Old Testament* [1952] 175ff., and M. Burrows, "The Conduit of the Upper Pool," *ZAW* 70 [1958] 226). Isaiah would have been thinking of the second of the two, which Schick found in 1886. In some places, it was open to the air; in other places, it was covered over with flat stones. It was about 1.75 meters deep and about 30–50 centimeters wide. Openings on the side toward the valley show that it served as a means of irrigating the Kidron Valley. In the south, it flowed into the *birket el-ḥamra* (see illus. in *BHH* 1796). Weill examined the pitch, which initially amounts to an average drop of only 4–5 meters per thousand meters; only toward the southern end does this increase to an average of 5 meters per hundred meters (see Simons, op. cit., 178). It is easy to understand how Isaiah could speak about the softly flowing waters of Shiloah.

The Gihon, from which the waters of the Shiloah canal flow forth, is the only perennially flowing spring in the area around Jerusalem. The city depends upon it for its existence and it is because of this spring that the city was founded upon the relatively low-lying southeastern hill. There was genuine pride about it in Jerusalem and it was the reason for the comment, in the portrayal of paradise: "a river whose streams make glad the city of God," Ps. 46:5. Isaiah, of course, is not speaking of the Gihon (the name means "bubbler"), but rather of the canal, since it occurred to him that he could speak of the "softly" flowing waters. At this point, one comes to the question about the more exact meaning of the imagery. It must be understood in connection with its opposite, the depiction of the bursting floods of the Euphrates, which would overflow its banks and would even flood the land of Judah. The Targum offers this interpretation in its translation: "As this people has rejected the kingdom of the house of David, which ruled over them gently, like the waters of Shiloah which flowed so gently forth, and found favor in Rezin and the son of Remaliah . . ." This interpretation has gained a following from time to time in the recent past (see Fullerton, 257, note 11); if true, the interpretation would intimate that the Davidic dynasty either was in a considerably weakened position or was so designated because of its peace-loving nature. But this is simply not the case here. If, according to 7:6, the enemies of Ahaz had considered installing Tabeel as king in Jerusalem, it may indeed be true that a small minority in Jerusalem were of the same opinion but, all in all, the large majority of the people had undoubtedly agreed with the political stance of the palace. It was not rejecting the kingdom, but Yahweh. What that means is shown more clearly by Isaiah's use of the verb מאס (scorn). In 5:24, Isaiah mentioned scorning the תורה (torah) of Yahweh of Hosts, in 30:12, the scorning of "this message." According to this, the imagery does not so much speak of "Yahweh as the one who delivers out of all distress" (Kaiser, ad loc.) or the gentle, quiet leading God gives (Fohrer, ad loc.) or something similar, but specifically of the rejection of the message from God, presented by Isaiah as a way to deal with this very situation. However, behind the actual message of the prophet, as is shown in 7:4ff., one finds Israel's traditions about holy war, the invincibility of the city of God, and the election of the Davidic dynasty. To reject the דבר יהוה (word of Yahweh) which was delivered by Isaiah includes saying "No" to all of the elements of faith which are presupposed thereby. One wonders whether Isaiah chose the imagery of the waters of Shiloah because it would cause one to associate the waters with these various traditions. The Gihon had indeed played an important role in the royal rituals; cf. 1 Kings 1:33f. (see M. Noth, *Könige,* BK IX, ad loc.) and possibly also Pss. 65:10; 110:7 (see Kraus, *Psalms 60–150,* ad loc. and *Psalms 1–59,* p. 312). It seems to have been used symbolically for the river of paradise (see Ps. 46:5) and, according to the later expectations concerning salvation, the water from the temple spring was to create conditions like those in paradise throughout the land (Isa. 33:21; Ezek. 47:1–12; Joel 4:18; Zech. 14:8). However, since the discussion is about Shiloah and not the Gihon, it remains unclear whether such associations can be made. It is important to note that לאט means lightly, softly, gently. In contrast to the might of Assyria, which those in Jerusalem thought would provide security, the message of Yahweh is nothing spectacular. It demands that one be resolute, even in situations where humans would be close to despair, and it is "only" a message, to which assent is given by faith alone, believing that it describes what will really come to be. One might think of Elijah at this point, who did not encounter the presence of Yahweh in the storm, not in the earthquake, and not in the flood but in the קול דממה דקה, in the "Stimme verschwebenden Schweigens" (1 Kings 19:12, according to the German rendering of M. Buber/F. Rosenzweig = a voice within a suspense-filled silence).

If the text of v. 6b has been reconstructed correctly, this clause continues the thought from v. 6a still further. Scorning the message from Yahweh corresponds to "melting" before a pompous human being. The *qal* of מסס (melt) is used elsewhere only in 10:18, a passage which unfortunately is also not very clear. On the other hand, the *niph'al* is rather common, also when used metaphorically, in which case the subject is usually לב or לבב (heart); cf. Josh. 2:11; 5:1; 7:5; Isa. 13:7; 19:1; Ezek. 21:12; Nah. 2:11; Ps. 22:15. In all of these passages, it is fear of the might of the enemy which makes the heart "melt." It seems that the metaphor belongs to the material commonly used in connection with holy war. (In Deut. 20:8, one finds the *hiph'il* פ״ המס לבב, lest the heart of his fellows melt as his heart, within the context of a "war address," spoken to the אִישׁ יָרֵא וְרַךְ לֵבָב, man that is fearful and fainthearted.) But the authenticity of 8:6b is not in doubt and the mention of Rezin and the son of Remaliah certainly causes no problems. Budde's emendation which reads מִשְּׂאֵת (because of the pride of) is less certain. But the thought could certainly be attributed to Isaiah: Instead of human beings bowing before God and placing trust in the one "who alone will be exalted" (2:11), they allow themselves to be swayed by human power, even one which comes on the scene in a most arrogant way.

[8:7aα] Isaiah does not mention that Ahaz, because he was afraid of his two neighbors to the north, had turned to Assyria for help. But that is, without a doubt, the specific background to the accusation that he had scorned Yahweh. Judah would have to discover now that whoever trusts in human power brings upon oneself the curse which results in one's own downfall; cf. 20:6; 30:1ff.; 31:1ff. As v. 7aβ points out very clearly, it is this same Assyrian king, into whose arms Ahaz had thrown himself in his despair, who would flood the land of Judah with his mass of troops, which would come like a river overflowing all of its banks. העלה (let rise) is used frequently when one refers to allowing a storm to form, Jer. 10:13 (Q) = 51:16; Ps. 135:7; however, it is also used of troops, Jer. 50:9; 51:27; Ezek. 26:3; 39:2; cf. also 2 Chron. 36:17. Opposite the מי השלח (waters of Shiloah) are the מי הנהר (waters of the river), in which case הנהר (the river), as often in the OT, refers to the Euphrates. Even though Assyria is situated on the Tigris, the Assyrians were pressing in from just across the Euphrates, from the area around Carchemish, on into the region of Syria and Palestine (see 7:20, but also Dan. 10:4).

Water which surges mightily furnishes imagery very similar to a powerful enemy army which presses forward. עצום can mean both "powerful" and "numerous" and is often chosen by someone describing an army, Deut. 4:38; 7:1; 9:1; 11:23; Josh. 23:9; cf. most especially Joel 1:6; 2:2, 5, 11. The word belongs to a stereotypical list of terms selected when depicting an enemy of Israel. The more powerful the enemy, the more impressive the victory of the people and/or the help of its God. Isaiah uses this manner of speaking, but turns it into its opposite: Jerusalem will be handed over, without protection, to this massive army.

[8:7aβ] The gloss in v. 7aβ uses the term כבוד (glory) to describe the unheard-of force of the enemy as it storms forward. The term is very hard to translate in this case, since it refers not only to the splendor of the enemy's external appearance but also to its intense inner power. The Assyrian kings made quite an effort to praise how the splendor (Sumerian: *me-lam;* Akkadian: *melemmu* or *melammu*) of their lord Ashur had overpowered the enemy or even that the "splendor" of their own sovereign authority had destroyed the enemy (see, e.g., *ANET*³ 287a and 287b = *AOT* 352; in addition, see the prayer in *AOT* 251f.). It may be that the glossator had terms such as these at his disposal.

[8:7b] Verse 7b continues the imagery of v. 7aα: The water rises above all of its אֲפִיקִים (channels). The Euphrates can divide itself into several branches and there are canals which branch off from these. However, when the snow melts in the mountainous regions of Armenia, the water overflows all of its banks. It is also not rare for inundations to occur in Palestine (Dalman, *AuS* I/1, illus. 16). In Hebrew, in addition to גדיה (banks), there are other words for "shoreline," such as שָׂפָה (bank) and חוֹף (shore, coast). גדיה is related to the Arabic *ğadda,* "cut off," chosen here because it specifically refers to steep slopes along the riverbank, which normally protect against overflowing.

[8:8a] In fact, the mountainous regions of Judah will be flooded over with this water. The verb חלף (go upwards over) can be used to describe a quick downpour, which comes up very unexpectedly, but also quickly dissipates (see Song of Sol. 2:11). Isaiah also uses שׁטף (inundating), which has a very similar sense, in 28:2, 15, 17, 18; 30:18, where mention is made of Yahweh's intervention by using the imagery of a storm which tears everything up (cf. also עבר, pass through, in 28:18f. and, in addition, see 10:22; 43:2; 66:12). The imagery of the Euphrates, overflowing its banks, apparently without being noticed by Isaiah and those of his listeners who were close to him, shifts over to the portrayal of a most violent downpour. The Assyrian kings were also fond of using the storm to describe their war activities in their inscriptions. For example, Shalmaneser III writes: "descending upon them like Adad when he makes a rainstorm pour down" (*AOT* 341 = *ANET*[3] 277); Nabonidus says about the fall of Nineveh: "The king of Babylon carried out the assignment from Marduk with great power, like a deluge" (*AOT* 362).

"Up to the neck" is how far the water would reach. This image, also used in 30:28, is based on experience. Drought is greatly feared in Palestine; the people suffered time and again from too little water. That the water reaches to the neck is the climax, not the antithesis; this means God would not let his people go completely under, but would already be coming to help them when the danger was at its high point (so J. Meinhold, *Der Heilige Rest: Studien zur israelitischen Religionsgeschichte* I/1 [1903] 114). The passage must not, of course, be interpreted to mean that Judah would completely perish as a result of this flooding, leaving no remnant (see Fohrer, ad loc.); the theme of the section concerns the enormity of the distress to be caused by Assyria, which would bring Judah into very great danger.

[8:8b] If one wishes to consider v. 8b as the original conclusion to vv. 6–8a, then one is forced to take this half-verse as a threat. Thus Eichrodt interprets it: "Just as an eagle descends upon its booty, very powerfully beating its wings, so the masses of the Assyrians which are invading will completely cover 'your land, O Immanuel'." But if one uses this interpretation, one notices the abrupt change of imagery, so that Fohrer, even though he thinks in terms of a dragon which will cover over the entire land, is unable to treat the clause as Isaianic (similarly, Duhm). Such hesitations could be overcome if one would be able to explain that כנפים are the branches of a river which has overflowed its banks (so Delitzsch, ad loc.; see also KBL). But the Hebrew does not have any evidence for such a use. It is just as unlikely that the כנפים are supposed to refer to the "wings" of the Assyrian army. In contrast to the Latin *ala* (wing), כנף (wing) is never so used with a transferred meaning.

There is no doubt that a large bird is being depicted, made clear by the term מֻטָּה, "breadth of the span," that is, the span of the wings. The only question is whether one must take this in a threatening sense. Some have used the negative references in Hos. 8:1 and Ezek. 17:1ff. to support that point of view. However, in contrast to those passages, Isa. 8:8b does not speak about a bird which rushes down upon Judah, but rather about one which extends its wings out over Judah. This passage can thus be explained as similar in usage to Ruth 2:12; Pss. 17:8; 36:8; 57:2; 61:5; 63:8; 91:4 (on this, cf. L. Delekat, *Asylie und Schutzorakel am Zion-heiligtum* [1967] 212–215); Matt. 23:37 = Luke 13:34. The suffix on כנפיו (his wings) must therefore refer to Yahweh. Just like a great bird which extends its pinions over the nest where its young are, in the same way Yahweh protects the land in its entirety (so Marti; Gray, et al.; cf. also the similar imagery in Deut. 32:11).

But if this is the case, then it is impossible that v. 8b belongs to the original text of 8:5ff. Indeed, it is not impossible that this half-verse is a fragment of an authentic message of Isaiah from a completely different context. But it is more likely that it is rather to be considered another one of the many additions which are frequently encountered in the book of Isaiah, additions which alter the interpretation of the prophet's threats. The one who adds this justifies his opinion with a reference to Immanuel. Because of this, we have an ancient attestation to the fact that this personage was perceived to be a guarantor of salvation for Judah (see above, 7:15). But this passage does not have a savior in mind, who comes out of the heavens, but rather looks for a political ruler or spiritual leader of Israel, one who is accorded this title of honor.

Purpose and Thrust

The section vv. 6–8a shows how Isaiah's assessment of the political circumstances was right on the mark, insofar as it anticipated the political and military consequences. Assyria is on the ascent and cannot be stopped. Aram and Israel still furnish a protective wall against the expanding might of that nation headquartered on the Tigris; see 17:3. "Insofar as Judah helps to remove both of the northern neighboring states, it tears down the dam with which it could protect itself from the Assyrian flood" (Fohrer, ad loc.). Isaiah's political suggestions were not unrealistic. However, this section does not scold the people because of a disastrous political stance, but accuses the people of having such a flawed trust in Yahweh. The reason for the wrongheaded politics was the lack of faith. From that flows every type of disaster; indeed, the actions which come when one is afraid because faith is lacking virtually court disaster.

The expander in v. 8b robs the threat of its sharpness. There is no doubt that he did not find himself in the same circumstances as Isaiah. He knew that Judah had been spared in the war during the thirties and that it had survived when Damascus and Samaria were destroyed. And he would certainly have already known that Judah had suffered greatly during the invasion of Sennacherib, but that it had also come out of that catastrophe. In fact, in every case, the waters had reached all the way up to Judah's neck. But this commentator wanted to point out that Yahweh's protection, which was over his people, had manifested itself again and again as a real power. That which was attested in the name Immanuel, "with us is God," had shown itself to be the truth upon which one could build. He would have felt that he had been authorized to add in his corrective, on the basis of the Immanuel prediction, without having been aware of the ambivalent character of that sign. In reality, his way of thinking is not from within the context of the proclamation of Isaiah, but from within the cultic piety of Jerusalem, which Isaiah used only after reflecting about which modifications were needed.

The Plan of the Peoples

Literature

K. Fullerton, "The Interpretation of Isaiah 8:5–10," *JBL* 43 (1924) 253–289. K. Budde, "Zu Jesaja 8, Vers 9 und 10," *JBL* 49 (1930) 423–428. H. Schmidt, "Jesaja 8, 9 und 10," *Stromata, Festgabe des Akademisch-Theologischen Vereins zu Giessen*, G. Bertram, ed. (1930) 3–10. M. Sæbø, "Zur Traditionsgeschichte von Jesaja 8:9–10," *ZAW* 76 (1964) 132–143. H. M. Lutz, *Jahwe, Jerusalem und die Völker*, WMANT 27 (1968) 40–47.

Text

8:9 'Get yourselves close together'ᵃ you peoples—and be terrified,
   listen attentively, all distant points of the earth!
 Gird yourselves—and be terrified,
   gird yourselves and be terrified!
10 Forgeᵃ a plan—it will break in pieces,
   assemble to make an agreement—it will not come to be!
 For with us is God!

9a Gk reads γνῶτε (know) for the disputed word רעו (break), thus reading—as also L—the Hebrew form דְעוּ (know). Some recent commentators have followed this reading: Gray, Buhl, Procksch, Bentzen, Kissane, Kaiser, Fohrer (1st ed.), Driver, *JSS* 13 (1968) 40, et al. But this emendation is not satisfactory. Who is supposed to be recognized? Syp reads ἀκούσατε (hear) (see Ziegler). Indeed, that is a clear parallel to האזינו (give ear) (see Isa. 1:2, 10; 28:23; 32:9), but one would have great difficulty understanding how שמעו (hear) could be misread as רעו (break). Moreover, v. 9aα does not seem to be parallel to v. 9aβ, but to vv. 9ba and 10a. W. Thomas (*JTS* 36 [1935] 410) also alters the text to read רעו, not derived from ידע, "to know," but according to the Arabic *wada'a*, "quiet, be still," and translates: "be ye reduced to submission. . . ." But that does not establish a parallel to התאזרו (gird yourselves) and עצו עצה (forge a plan). The same is true of the Syr: *zû' (zw'w)*, "tremble." Thus, it seems best, at the very least, to stay with the consonantal text of the MT. רעו seems to be an imperative masculine plural from רעע I. Assuming this, it can be translated "rage" (Duhm, Feldmann, et al.) or "treat godlessly" (Rignell, op. cit., Literature, 8:1–4, p. 44), or something similar. But "rage" is a questionable translation and "treat godlessly" once again fails to fit in with the parallel terms. Still others compare it to רעע II (an Aramaic term for the Hebrew רצץ, "shatter"). Sæbø adopts a suggestion, made earlier by Schmidt (7f.), by which he derives רעו from רוע; in spite of the fact that this root does not exist in the *qal*, he translates this "raise the battle cry" (so also Lutz, similarly Fohrer, 2d ed.). This rendering actually fits well with the vocabulary used in this context. More importantly, it corresponds with the readings in 'Aquila, Sym, Theod: συνα-θροίσθητε (assemble); Targ: אתחברו (gather together); and Vulg: *congregamini* (congregate). These versions apparently thought רעו was a form of רעה II. It must remain an open question whether רעו is to be pointed רְעוּ or whether the *hithpa'el* of this root should be read here.

10a עֻצוּ is not based on the normal form, from יעץ (advise), but rather comes from the rarely used alternate form עוץ (counsel, plan) (see Judg. 19:30). There is no need to alter the pointing to read it as if it were the normal form עֻצוּ.

Form

Concerning why this section is not connected with v. 8b, see above, on the form of 8:5–8. There is no question that a new unit begins with v. 11.

In his very extensive treatment of this section, Sæbø has come to the conclusion that Isaiah in 8:9f. "has taken the ancient form of the *'call to battle'*" (on this, see R. Bach, *Die Aufforderungen zur Flucht und zum Kampf im alttestamentlichen Prophetenspruch*, WMANT 9, 1962), "imitating it, applying it to a current political event, and calling it out in disdain and mockery against enemy peoples" (141); on this, cf. Jer. 46:3–6, 9; Joel 4:9ff. According to Kaiser (ad loc.), on the other hand, what is behind this message is the belief that the city of God is invulnerable, as it has been expressed in Psalms 46, 48, 76. In fact, עמנו אל (Immanuel) corresponds quite closely to the refrain in Psalm 46: יהוה צבאות עמנו (Yahweh of Hosts is with us) (vv. 8, 12). For still another view, Bentzen already identified points of contact with Psalm 2 in his commentary (70). Thus, a clear decision about the traditio-historical background of the passage is quite difficult, but is also not necessary. We have noted that in 7:4ff. some terms from the holy war tradition are linked with some from the Zion and kingship traditions. One must remember that the institution of holy war had long since ceased in actual practice; yet, elements from this tradition were apparently incorporated into the Jerusalem cultic traditions.

Meter: V. 9a: a three-stress bicolon; v. 9b: a two-stress bicolon; v. 10abα: a three-stress bicolon; v. 10bβ: a three-stress colon which brings it to a close, carrying greater weight because of its position (cf. Ps. 46:8, 12, where a second phrase follows).

Setting

The question about authenticity has been vigorously debated. Among recent commentators, Hertzberg, Kaiser (1st ed.), Eichrodt, and Lutz consider both of the verses to be from Isaiah and cite Duhm, Procksch, Schmidt (op. cit., 10), Steinmann, Kissane, Lindblom, et al. for support. But there is also an impressive list of those, beginning with Stade (*ZAW* 4 [1884] 260, note 1), who do not think that either verse is from Isaiah: Budde (*Jesajas Erleben* and *JBL*), Gray, Marti, Mowinckel, Fohrer, et al. The question is closely tied in with another: To whom are the verses addressed? The present context would lead one to believe that Assyria is meant, but the plural עמים (peoples) makes that unlikely. More than anything else, if this message does indeed refer to Assyria, it certainly would not fit into Isaiah's proclamation during the time of the Syro-Ephraimitic War. According to the previous message in vv. 5ff., Isaiah had declared that Judah would be severely oppressed by Assyria. There-fore, vv. 9f. have often been explained with reference to Aram and Israel. This is also not an obvious solution. Why would Isaiah not specifically mention these two countries, as he does at other times, but rather speak of "all distant points of the earth"? Fullerton (287) tries to get out of this dilemma by removing the phrase "listen attentively, all distant points of the earth"; Eichrodt (ad loc.) speaks about pressures in general which had come upon Judah (similarly, Rignell, 44); Donner (VTSup 11, 26f., 60) supposes that the anti-Assyrian coalition in the years 734/33 "was far more extensive than the information provided by the Old Testament sources would indicate." Finally, Saebø thinks that form-historical con-siderations indicate the reasons that references in this genre are very general (141). In addition to the questions which are raised by the lack of specific references in 8:9f., which would speak against its authenticity, it would seem that the promise of never-ending salvation in these two verses would indicate that they are not genuine. "Never had he [Isaiah] ever promised the people of Israel Yahweh's protection so uncondition-ally as they faced threats from the whole world" (Budde *[Jesajas Erleben]* 80). But passages such as 8:1–4 show that it is at least possible that Isaiah could promise unconditional protection for Jerusalem. When Fohrer (ad loc.) says that the message is related to the concept of the onslaught of all the peoples, as the final age begins to take shape, he goes beyond what is in the text; there is no reason to explain this message on the basis of the eschatology of the postexilic era. The vocabulary and style are decisive and show that Isaiah is the author.

The vocabulary: חתת (be terrified) is actually one of Isaiah's favorite terms; see 20:5; 31:9; the *niph'al* in 30:31; 31:4 (Job 9:3). מרחק (distant points) is found in 5:26 (emended text); 10:3; 30:27; these are just from passages which are clearly Isaianic. Concerning עצה (plan), see above, commentary on 5:12b and on 5:18f. Concerning the phrase עצו עצה (forge a plan), one might refer to העצה היעוצה (the purpose that is purposed) in 14:26. יעץ (plan) and פרר (break in pieces, annul) are also parallel to one another in 14:27. The phrase לא יקום (it will not come to be) is the opposite of 7:7 and 14:24. Finally, the little phrase כי עמנו אל (for with us is God) is linked to the name of the son of the עלמה (almah) in 7:14; on this, see also Lutz, 44. In addition to the close ties which are seen in the vocabulary, the *style* is also typical: The ironic use of the imperative is exactly parallel to 6:9b. This same style is also used in 29:9a: "Stare at one another—and be in a stupor! Look around you—and be blind!"; cf. also v. 9b.

Therefore, one should stay with the assessment offered by Procksch (ad loc.): While clearly recognizing that there are many ways in which this section does not fit into the framework of the rest of the chapter, he could yet say: "It is Isaianic in every way, so that there can be no question that it might not be genuine."

In light of this, we must still deal with the very difficult problem of how to assign this passage to its correct historical setting. Schmidt thinks it belongs to the time of Sennacherib's march (10). Based on the content, these verses are quite close to 17:12–14 where, except for passages which are not considered authentic, the material belongs to the second period of Isaiah's activity, that is, the years 721–710. Both solutions are possible; neither can be proven to be correct. Possibly Fullerton, 274f.; Lindblom (*Immanuel*) 33; Saebø, 142, et al. are right when they link these verses with 7:4ff. The reason why Isaiah speaks about the peoples here may have its basis in the fact that he is presenting to the people of Jerusalem concepts which had been part of the phraseology of Jerusalem theology for a long time. But if this interpretation is correct, then there is no way vv. 9f. could follow directly after vv. 6–8a chronologically. It is most likely that these two verses come from the beginning of the crisis, even before any decisions had been made in Jerusalem.

Commentary

[8:9f.] It is a well-known motif in the theology of Zion that the peoples gather together to storm the city of God or to bring about the downfall of the king who is ruling there (though the use of the verb רעה II, get close together [or התרעה, be companions; on that, see above, textual note 9a], is, of course, unique. In place of that, Ps. 2:2 uses נוסד, take counsel together [or נועד, assemble by appointment; see BHK], and it is also noteworthy that the emendation התיעץ, conspire against, has been suggested there as a parallel term. Ps. 48:5 also uses נועד, assembled, and, as a parallel, חבר, unite, be joined, has been conjectured, the same verb which the Targ uses in Isa. 8:9 to translate רעו, get close together). The peoples have seen very clearly that storming the city of God is a most difficult undertaking and can only succeed if they unite their forces. For this reason, this is publicized "to all the distant points of the earth"; concerning this motif, cf. 5:26 (emended text); 10:3; 13:5; 46:11; Jer. 4:16; 5:15. One ought to get oneself ready for war; it makes good sense when Schmidt (8) translates התאזרו as "put on the weapons." A passage like Jer. 46:3f. speaks in much more specific terms than does this passage about being armed for the decisive battle. A most important moment for preparation is the war council meeting of the opponents who have banded together (cf. 7:5 and the conjectural reading in Ps. 2:2, mentioned above). As a parallel to עצו עצה (forge a plan), v. 10b reads דברו דבר (assemble to make an agreement). There is a similar expression in Hos. 10:4. There the indefinite term דברים (mere words) is given a more specific focus with שָׁוְא אָלוֹת (empty oaths) and, in addition, דברו דברים (utter mere words) is used parallel to כָּרוֹת בְּרִית (make covenants). For this reason, Saebø translates דברו דברים as "conclude an agreement" (139).

Thus, one can forge plans, in fact, not only for the battle, but even now already for the time after the victory has been achieved, as if this were a foregone conclusion. But that is like making out the bill without the owner being there: The undertaking will run aground, as Isaiah proclaims by effective use of the three imperatives. That the plans of the enemy have been judged to be a failure from the very beginning is similarly pointed out in Pss. 2:3ff.; 46:7, 10, and 48:6ff. as well. The meaning of the verb חתת (be terrified) oscillates between breaking someone physically and breaking someone down mentally; cf. 7:8; 20:5; 30:31; 31:4, 9; 37:27. Verse 10a says that the plan of the enemies will not come to fruition, just as is true in 14:27, since no one can thwart Yahweh's decisions.

The reason why the plans of the peoples will come to naught is plain and simple, for Yahweh is with the people of Jerusalem/Judah: עמנו אל (Immanuel). It was suggested, as was true when 7:14 was discussed above, that the little phrase might have come from the Jerusalem liturgy. If 8:10, as seems likely, precedes 7:2ff., then Isaiah had already called upon his hearers to have faith when he used this little confession, even before his momentous meeting with Ahaz, so that the name Immanuel is simply corroboration for this message.

Purpose and Thrust

This study of the text has shown that these verses are to be understood as related to the Jerusalem salvation traditions. Based on the content, and partially also the vocabulary itself, it is rather close to 7:4ff. There is one important difference, which has caused some commentators to deny that the passage is genuine: The promise is not linked to faith in so many words. But if these verses are really from Isaiah, then they are not to be interpreted as if they provide an all-encompassing truth that the people of God are being offered everlasting protection for absolutely every situation, from all types of hostile threats; instead, the passage must be interpreted according to the specific focus it has, for that particular situation which it addresses. *Now,* Isaiah charges the people, it makes sense that one be very serious about belief in Yahweh's protection; *now* one has to and ought to cling to the עמנו אל (Immanuel). At first, the prophet did not have any reason to speak about what would result if Israel, as the people of God, refused the offer—which is different from the situation in chap. 7, where Ahaz responds with his No, not a completely unexpected response to Isaiah. Thus, 8:9–10 does not really contradict 7:1–17. In a double sense, Maher-Shalal Hash-Baz, the son of Isaiah, was a sign of the promise which Yahweh had offered his people but, when the sign was finally given, it was in response to Israel's refusal to take hold of what this promise declared. In the same way, Immanuel was indeed a sign, intended as a way for Yahweh to strengthen his people in a difficult time by means of prophetic instruction; in actuality, it would serve to remind the people of their refusal to hear and to believe. It is easier for us to see how the Immanuel prediction and its meaning would have been immediately clear to those who had been confronted at the upper pool if we are able to presume, on the basis of 8:9f., that the promise of עמנו אל (Immanuel) had been an important component in the preaching of Isaiah, even apart from the way it is used to name the son of the עלמה (almah).

Yahweh, the True Conspirator

Literature

G. Stählin, *Skandalon*, BFCT II/24 (1930). F. Häussermann, *Wortempfang und Symbol in der alttestamentlichen Prophetie*, BZAW 58 (1932). G. R. Driver, "Two Misunderstood Passages of the Old Testament," *JTS* NS 6 (1955) 82–84. W. I. Wolverton, "Judgment in Advent," *ATR* 37 (1955) 284–291. L. G. Rignell, "Das Orakel 'Maher-salal Has-bas'. Jesaja 8," *ST* 10 (1957) 40–52. N. Lohfink, "Isaias 8,12–14," *BZ* NF 7 (1963) 98–104.

Text

8:11   [For][a] thus said Yahweh to me, as[b] the hand grabbed hold[c]
         'and restrained[d] me from' going in the way of this people:
   12   You are not to identify everything as conspiracy,[a]
         which this people calls conspiracy,
         and in the presence of what drives them to be afraid, you ought
             not be afraid
         and ought not shudder![b]
   13 Yahweh of Hosts,
         he 'is identified as conspirator,'[a]
         he is your fear
         and he is your 'shuddering'![b]
   14 He will become 'conspiracy,'[a]
         will be a stumbling block
         and will be a slipping rock
         for both of the houses of Israel,[b]
         will be a trapping net and will be a throwing stick
         for the inhabitants[c] of Jerusalem.
   15 [a]And many will slip on them,[a]
         fall and break apart,
         will be struck and will be caught.

11a כי (for) is a redactional transitional element.
11b BHK³ reads בחזקה (when grabbing hold) with B; BHS, with L, C, Qᵃ, and many handwritten copies, reads כח' (as [the hand] grabbed hold), which is probably correct; see also the Syr.

11c In this case, חֶזְקַת (grab hold) is a *qal* infinitive; see Bauer-Leander §43g; cf. Dan. 11:2; 2 Chron. 12:1; 26:16.

11d וְיִסְּרֵנִי (and he will instruct me) has to be analyzed as a *qal* imperfect from יסר "instruct." But the imperfect cannot be correct in the context and the *qal* form of the root יסר is rare. Targ reads ואלפני (and he taught me; Vulg: *erudivit me* (he has instructed me), which would suggest reading it as וְיִסְּרֵנִי (he has instructed me). And yet, it has been suggested, since the time of Gesenius (*Kommentar* I 132, note 2), that it be pointed וַיְסִרֵנִי (and he restrained me) (from סור, turn aside; see Sym: και απεστησε με, and he hindered me, and Syr *nasteni,* he turned me aside), which is now supported also by the Qᵃ (ויסירני, and he made me turn aside) and is the preferred reading.

12a If one stays with the reading תקדישו (you shall regard as holy) in the MT in v. 13, then it seems one ought to alter קֶשֶׁר (conspiracy) to read קָדוֹשׁ (sacred), or something similar. But Isaiah is addressing a group of people not considered as part of העם הזה (this people), which means that he is speaking to a group comprised of his trusted associates. Therefore, he would hardly have to say to members of this group that they ought not consider everything holy which the people of Jerusalem consider holy. Instead, it is much more likely that תקדישו (you shall regard as holy) in v. 13 is a corruption of the reading תקשירו (you shall identify as conspiracy); it is indeed possible that it is a conscious alteration, changed by someone who found the statement offensive. The translation of קֶשֶׁר is debated. The basic meaning of the root קשר is "bind together"; Gk translates it in this passage as σκληρόν (hard); for this reason, G. R. Driver, 82f., believes that קשר ought to be translated "knotty affair, difficulty"; Lindblom (see above, literature, 7:1–17), 29f., and Kaiser, ad loc. ("entanglement"), treat it much the same. However, the substantive קשר means "conspiracy" in all the other OT passages where it is used (see Targ: מרוד, rebel). Even Driver is guilty of tending to soften the harsh statement in v. 13 ("he is identified as conspirator").

12b Instead of לא תערצו (you ought not shudder), Targ reads: ועל תוקפיה לא תימרון תקיף (and you shall not call the strong strong); thus, it seems to have read a substantive here (parallel to מורא, fear, in the first half of the line), so that the second colon might have read וְאֶת־מַעַרְצוֹ לֹא תַעֲרִיצוּ, and in the presence of his shuddering, you ought not shudder (see BHS). But it remains a question whether one ought to expect such strict parallelism.

13a Concerning the change in the text to read, instead of תקדישו (him you shall regard as holy), rather תקשירו (you shall identify as conspiracy), see above, textual note 12a. Driver translates: "you will find difficult"; Kaiser: "you shall consider it complicated"; Procksch alters אתו (him) to read אִתּוֹ (with him) (see also BHS) and translates it: "with him you should conspire," in which case he also changes the train of thought, in an unacceptable way.

13b After the substantive מורא (fear), the participle מערץ (shuddering) does not seem to fit very well. Since the *mater lectionis* is missing, it seems that it really ought to be pointed מַעֲרָצְכֶם (your shuddering) (see Duhm, Buhl, 'Aquila: θροησις [terror]; Sym Theod: κραταιωμα [fierce one]; Vulg: *terror vester* [your terror]; cf. Rahlfs-Lütkeman, in *Mitteilungen des Septuagintaunternehmens* I/6 [1915] 301, note 323).

14a מקדש (sanctuary) is not a parallel term to אבן נגף (stumbling block) and צור מכשול (slipping rock) (the translation by Wolverton, 288f., "taboo-place," is a makeshift translation and should not be adopted). Gk translates ἁγίασμα (sanctuary), but it does so in such a way that it makes it the direct opposite of the following parallel terms! In reality, the mistake is to be located in מקדש (sanctuary) itself, which, as תקדישו (him you shall regard as holy) in v. 13, is most likely a dogmatic corrective. Targ reads פורען, "retribution"; Procksch eliminates ולאבן נגף למקדש (for a sanctuary and a stumbling block) altogether; normally the reading מוקש (lure, snare) has been adopted instead of מקדש (sanctuary). Yet, if that is the case, מוקש (throwing stick) in v. 14b is anticipated prematurely. Driver, op. cit., 83, suggests מקשיר or something similar, which he translates as an abstract term ("cause of difficulty"). One might suppose that Driver has correctly sensed what the original text has in mind and yet, based on what has been explained above, מקשר should still be translated "conspiracy" (parallel to מַעֲרָץ, shuddering, in v. 13, to be pointed מקשָּׁר).

14b For לשני בתי ישראל (for both the houses of Israel), the Gk reads ὁ δὲ οἶκος Ιακωβ (the house of Jacob). It is quite astonishing that the MT speaks of *both* of the houses of Israel, especially since this is used parallel to יושב ירושלם (inhabitants of Jerusalem). For this reason, Stade and Marti choose to read לאיש יהודה (to the man of Judah) and Procksch, staying closer to the transmitted text, reads לבית ישראל (to the house of Israel). And yet, corresponding to the situation, the parallelism might be a bit looser here.

14c For the singular יושב (inhabitant), many MSS, and also Gk, L, and Sym, read יושבי (inhabitants of).

15a–a Some (e.g., Duhm, Leslie) suggest eliminating the beginning of v. 15, but כשל (slip) is necessary, since it picks up on מכשול (slipping [rock]) in v. 14.

Form

The message in 8:12–15 is a warning and a threat. In contrast to similar passages, an introduction is included. Because of the substance of this passage, it is possible that the uncommon expressions used to describe Yahweh constraining Isaiah speak about the deeper reality connected with being a prophet; he had been seized by Yahweh.

One notes the wordplay between הקשיר, קשר, and מקשר; ירא and מורא; העריץ and מערץ; מכשול and כשל; מוקש and נוקש; one also notes the alliteration between מורא, מוקש, and נוקש; between מערץ, מקשר, מכשול, and מוקש; and between ונשברו, ונוקשו, ונלכדו, and ונפלו.

Meter: One is able to discuss the meter only if one begins with v. 12b. It is very irregular. Verse 12b: a five-stress colon; v. 13: 2 two-stress bicola; v. 14: 3 two-stress bicola. The closing verse is constructed with 3 two-stress cola.

Setting

Without question, the passage is authentic. It also has as its background the Syro-Ephraimitic War. But here, it is not the general public which is addressed, but rather a circle of trusted friends, who are being encouraged to distance themselves from the widespread cry of panic in Jerusalem. Indeed, in the first place, the message from Yahweh provides instruction for the prophet himself: He should prevent himself from going "the way of this people" (concerning העם הזה, see above, commentary on 8:6). Yahweh himself points out which station the prophet is to take during the time of bewilderment and consternation which follow the news about the events taking place in the north (cf. 7:2).

Commentary

[8:11] In the introduction, Isaiah describes briefly how it happened that he was led to speak the following admonition and threat; Kaiser (ad loc.) actually identifies this as a "prophetic confession." The prophet emphasizes the fact that the message of Yahweh came to him at a time when "the hand" reached out and seized him. He does not mention, as one might expect, the hand of Yahweh and does not say that the seizing caught hold of him. This terse formulation appears to be a code used to describe the basic experience of a prophet who was receiving a message; apparently Isaiah is using a formula which had long since come into general use, serving as a description of the prophetic experience (on this, see W. Zimmerli, BK XIII/1, 47ff. [Engl: *Ezekiel 1,* 117ff.]). In 1 Kings 18:46, the hand of Yahweh coming upon Elijah refers to when he was seized by the Spirit; in Deut. 32:36 and Josh. 8:20 it refers to being completely filled up with an extraordinary power (יד, hand, can also mean "power"). The hand of Yahweh came upon Elisha "as the minstrel played the chords," 2 Kings 3:15, after which he was able to deliver the desired oracle; on this, cf. Ezek. 1:3; 3:22; 33:22. Whereas the formula which is used in these passages is היה יד יהוה על (the hand of Yahweh was upon), in 8:1, Ezekiel says that the hand of Yahweh "fell" upon him. The closest parallel to the way Isaiah formulates this is found in Ezek. 3:14: ויד יהוה עלי חזקה (the hand of Yahweh being strong upon me); see also Jer. 15:17. Because Isaiah limits himself to the bare mention of the "hand" and does not even go so far as to mention that he himself was the object of the seizing, his listeners are brought into the arena of that which is full of mystery, that which takes place which cannot be analyzed rationally; one cannot miss seeing that he is hesitant when it comes to articulating what one basically cannot put into words. But there is no doubt that an ecstatic experience is being described. Elisha needed music in order to induce it and, when this formula is used in Ezek. 3:14, the prophet is carried away by the Spirit. Duhm (ad loc.) thinks that this refers to the prophet being semicataleptic, against which the human spirit would seek to protect itself, bitterly and fiercely, as one would whenever any power sought to inflict harm. Volz (*Der Geist Gottes und die verwandten Erscheinungen* . . . [1910] 70, note 1) favors explaining this as referring to being transported in a trance. And yet, the data for determining exactly what happened are simply too limited (concerning this issue, see F. Häussermann, 22–24). Far more important than the psychological classification, one must arrive at a theological appraisal of what is said: The word presses mightily upon the prophet (cf. Jer. 15:16; 20:7). It does not only determine what he is to say but it also identifies the "path" which he is to follow. There is no doubt that this present passage does not deal with an experience which took place only one time; one must presume that an experience of this type lies behind every message which the prophet spoke in the name of Yahweh.

[8:12–13] Those who are addressed, citizens of Jerusalem, who can be approached with "instruction" from Isaiah, are not to identify everything as קשר (conspiracy) just because the general populace would so label it. As explained already, there is no reason to render this term in any other way than as "conspiracy." קשר describes a political conspiracy which has the goal of overthrowing a ruler, inciting to rebellion, as is seen in Absalom's insurrection against his father in 2 Sam. 15:12, the downfall of Athaliah in 2 Kings 11:14, and the downfall of Hoshea brought about by Assyria in 2 Kings 17:4 (see also Jer. 11:9: insurrection against God; Sir. 11:31: insubordination within one's own family). For an analogous use of the verb, see 1 Kings 15:27; 16:9; 2 Kings 10:9; 15:10, 25, and often elsewhere. It is very rare (cf. Neh. 4:2) that the word is used to describe the menace caused by an external enemy (on this, see Lohfink, op. cit., 100). Therefore, it is highly unlikely, as Rignell (op. cit., 45) suggests about the present passage, that Isaiah's contemporaries were terming the common advance of Aram and Israel against Judah a "conspiracy"; it is much more likely that, within Jerusalem, there were rumors circulating about a plot being hatched against the house of the king and his associates. According to 7:6, the enemies had planned to install the "Tabelite" in Jerusalem as king. In case this actually might have been a member of the Davidic family (as suggested above, commentary on 7:2), even if he had been born of a foreign mother (concerning such an occurrence, cf., e.g., Ashur-uballit's interference in Babylon during the time of Burnaburiash and after his death; see E. Cassin, *Fischer Weltgeschichte* 3 [1966] 25–27), one can certainly presume that, along with the military pressure from the outside, an internal rebellion would have also been planned. Something like this would have relieved the enemies of their concerns about a protracted siege of the very well-protected city of Jerusalem, one with an uncertain outcome. When such an attempted overthrow became known, it must have been quite a shock for both the palace and the people in general. In Isaiah's opinion, it apparently had no prospects for success. But it certainly cannot have been the prophet's intention to dispense a pill which would have a calming effect upon the terrorized inhabitants of Jerusalem. Whoever was concerned for the welfare of the city should be very unsettled—not because a collaborator like the Tabelite had planned an overthrow of the house of the king and had thought of opening the land to the enemy, but rather because *Yahweh himself was the conspirator.* One must let this message stay just like it is, in its terrifying harshness, seeming to border on slandering God himself. קֶשֶׁר (conspire) presumes that one is presently in a relationship where loyalty has been pledged. Jeremiah's laments about how Israel had destroyed its relationship with Yahweh through conspiracy (11:9) are not all that astonishing. However, in this case, Isaiah forces the people to think about whether it is not possible that Yahweh himself would get sick and tired of his people, just as a people might at times get disgusted with its royal house. Would it not be possible that he could finally begin to deal with Israel just as a conspirator would? One must naturally keep in mind that this most disconcerting thought would be set in motion by the very use of this catchword קֶשֶׁר (conspiracy). It is not part of God's nature to be a conspirator against his own people. In the same vein, "stumbling block," "slipping rock," "trapping net," and "throwing stick" are not consistent with Yahweh's essential nature. The theme of this present passage is not found in these terms, but in the sentence: "Yahweh of Hosts, he is your fear, he is your shuddering" (concerning מוֹרָא, fear, see 29:13; concerning יהוה צבאות, Yahweh of Hosts, see above, commentary on 1:8–9 and on 6:3). If Israel runs aground, it will not be because of its external or internal foes, not because of its political situation, but because of its God.

[8:14–15] The threat which follows points this out very forcefully. In actual fact, what is meant has already been announced in 8:7, 8: Assyria will invade Judah. But Isaiah would protest also here that this could not be Israel's מוֹרָא (fear). If these threats are posed, then it is because Yahweh has reason to bring his people to judgment.

The following expressions must be observed to see how they contrast with the cultic theology of Jerusalem (on this, see L. Alonso-Schökel, "Stilistische Analyse bei den Propheten," VTSup 7 [1960] 154–166; see p. 161). This type of theology proclaims: Yahweh's messengers protect the pious, so that their feet do not *strike against a stone* (פֶּן־תִּגֹּף בָּאֶרֶן רַגְלֶךָ, Ps. 91:12); Yahweh is praised as a *rock* (צוּר, 1 Sam. 2:2; Ps. 18:3, 32, 47 = 2 Sam. 22; on this, see H. J. Kraus, BK XV/1, 142 [Engl: *Psalms 1–59,* 259]; in addition, Ps. 19:15 et al.); he is צוּר עֻזִּי (my mighty rock) in Ps. 62:8 or the צוּר יְשׁוּעָתִי (rock of my salvation) in Ps. 89:27 and in similar passages. In other passages, Isaiah himself is able to say that Yahweh is the rock of Israel, 30:29. צוּר (rock) seems, in fact, to have been an epithet of the God of Jerusalem, as one may assume on the basis of names such as פְּדָהצוּר (Pedahzur), אֱלִיצוּר (Elizur), צוּרִיאֵל (Zuriel), and צוּרִישַׁדַּי (Zurishad- dai) (see also the acoristic צוּר, used for the place name בֵּית צוּר, Beth Zur; cf. the Aramaic כֵּיפָא, rock; on this, see Noth, *Personennamen,* 129; ברצר KAI no. 215, line 1, and H. Schmidt, *Der heilige Fels in Jerusalem* [1933] 87ff.). The one who prays to God confesses the belief that the enemy will slip and fall, e.g., Ps. 27:2 (כָּשְׁלוּ וְנָפָלוּ, stumble and fall), and נִשְׁבַּר (be broken) is also used in this sense, e.g., Isa. 28:13; Jer. 48:4, 17, 25; 50:23; 51:8, 30. God can rescue someone from the trapping net which is used by a fowler (מִפַּח יָקוּשׁ, snare of the fowler, in Ps. 91:3; cf. 124:7); on the other hand, one prays that God would be willing to offer protection from the trapping net and the throwing stick of the evildoer, Ps. 141:9; cf. 69:23. In light of this background, Isaiah's threat takes on such a harsh meaning: That which is offered to one who is pious, in time of need, as an assurance, is now torn from that person's hand by Isaiah; that which is the basis for one's confidence has now been turned into its opposite. Such a person's faith is not made more sure, but is disclosed as being illusory. The unsuspecting pilgrim in the temple confronts the jealous God from Sinai!

פַּח (trapping net) and מוֹקֵשׁ (throwing stick) are both pieces of equipment used when hunting birds and also for catching small wild prey. פַּח is translated in the Gk as παγίς, "trap," a meaning which has also found its way into German translations (cf. the Arabic *faḥḥum,* which means "net, trap, snare," and see also Dalman, *AuS* VI 338). Actually, the פַּח is a hinged net. It is made of two frames, each of which has a net stretched over it. It is set up as one would set a book open halfway. When the bird settles on the trigger point, then a simple mechanism is tripped, which causes the two halves to clap together, so that the bird is caught (see *AOB* 182 = *BHH* III 2111 and cf. Ps. 124:7; Prov. 7:23). It is more difficult to establish the exact meaning of מוֹקֵשׁ. The Gk translates it as κοίλασμα, "hollow, pit," which would lead one to think of a snare pit; however, a more precise meaning of the word simply was not available to the translators. Basically, יקשׁ, as the related root נקשׁ, seems to mean "strike down," or something similar (cf. the Aramaic נקשׁ, knock, in Dan. 5:6, and the Syriac *neqaš,* "strike"), so that the מוֹקֵשׁ is really the wood used in a trap or for throwing, in the form of a weapon, something like a boomerang, which seems to have been a common implement used by hunters. (In Syriac, and as a loanword in Arabic, one finds *neqôšâ,* "wood used for striking"; this wood was used to ring bells in eastern places of worship, instead of a gong. Ps. 64:6 would not contradict this meaning, since טמן [contra Driver, *JBL,*

133] does not mean bury, but means hide; see also H. W. Wolff, *Amos,* BK XIV/2, 223f. [Engl: *Joel and Amos,* 185f.] and *BHH* II, 792; *BRL* 288f.) It is true that the participle יוֹקֵשׁ and the substantive יָקוּשׁ seem to have become general terms, used when describing birds being caught; cf. Ps. 124:7, where the "soul" is compared to a bird, able to escape from the פַּח (snare) of the יוקש (fowler). It is possible that מוקש (throwing stick) is also used at times in this general sense. The *niph'al* נוקש has been translated by some as "caught, be entangled"; see KBL and Ges-Buhl. But, in this present passage, that is what the following word נלכד means, linked with פַּח (trapping net), while נוקש (be struck) picks up on the previous word מוקש (throwing stick), and is to be translated "knocked down, having been hit." The meaning of מכשול (slipping rock) and מוקש (throwing stick) merged in the NT word σκάνδαλον. Initially, this Greek vocable meant "the stick in a trap"; then, in a transferred sense, "scandal, irritation"; on this, see G. Stählin, 10ff. and *TDNT* VII, 339f.

In such a shocking way, Yahweh is revealed to "the inhabitants of Jerusalem." And yet, the previous parallel said "both of the houses of Israel." The judgment applies to all of Israel. No one in Jerusalem should think it possible to stand by as merely an observer of the tragedy of the Northern Kingdom and to stay untouched; cf. 8:5ff. The expression "both of the houses of Israel" is found only in this one passage in the entire OT. In this situation, when the clouds of disaster can already be seen as they form over the Northern Kingdom, Isaiah wants to stress the fact that both of these individual countries belong together, like two houses, in which sons of just one father live in close proximity. Isaiah also mentions the house of Judah (in parallel with יושב ירושלם, inhabitant of Jerusalem) in 22:21. But Jeremiah is very fond of this term. He views the interrelatedness of the tribes as the interrelatedness among members of a family. Of course, more frequent reference is made to the בְּנֵי יְהוּדָה (sons of Judah) or the שֵׁבֶט י (tribe of Judah). But this term בית ישראל (house of Israel) is also common (Exod. 40:38; 1 Sam. 7:2; Isa. 46:3, et al.; cf. also *Bît-Humria* in the Assyrian inscriptions; see, e.g., above, commentary on 8:4). One rather common and apparently very old term is בֵּית יוֹסֵף (house of Joseph), Gen. 50:8; Josh. 17:17 (on this, see Alt, *KlSchr* I, 189); 18:5; Judg. 1:22f., 35; 2 Sam. 19:21; 1 Kings 11:28; Amos 5:6; Obad. 18; Zech. 10:6; this is used to demonstrate the closer ties between the tribes of Ephraim and Manasseh. בית (house) seems to be most often chosen for contexts where an effort is made to prevent the break-up of a people who are still united. It is a compromise for Isaiah to refer to the two houses of Israel in this present passage: The reference takes into account the fact that there has been a political division, and yet it underscores the fact that the two houses are interrelated in terms of their responsibility and destiny.

[8:15] Many will slip and fall. One ought not make too much of "many," as if to say that it does not mean "all." As Kaiser (ad loc.) rightly notes, "the Hebrew *rabbîm,* in contrast to its equivalent in German, is not to be interpreted in a partitive sense, but rather in a generalizing way"; one might compare the use of רבים in the Qumran texts to designate the entire membership of the community. On the other hand, the sentence should also not be interpreted as a proclamation of the last judgment which would bring about a complete annihilation of the people. One ought not miss the בם (them) after וכשלו (will slip): Israel will come upon "them," that is, upon the "stumbling block" and on "the slipping rock"; namely, it will fall upon its own God.

Purpose and Thrust

This section allows us to recognize the unprecedented tension within Isaiah's thinking about God. This God, whose faithfulness is certain, whose promises concerning Israel and Judah/Jerusalem cannot be invalidated, is still the only power whom his people must fear with utter seriousness. Either Israel would fear Yahweh and take seriously its knowledge about absolute security being completely hidden within his desire for their salvation—which meant that it was not to bow down before any human powers, was not to permit itself to fear their intrigues—or the people would allow itself to be so impressed by the power which humans were loosing against it that it would make God its enemy, from whom there would be no escaping.

It was made clear above that the section, on a formal level, presents a combination of an admonition and a threat. But what is the overall scope of this section? Apparently it is not just a proclamation that many would slip and fall. In fact, it is the circle of disciples who are addressed, from whom the prophet could expect a favorable hearing. Isaiah confesses that he himself had been hindered, when he had an experience "as the hand grabbed hold," so that he could not "go in the way of this people"; he apparently would like to reach the point where those who were listening to him would also allow themselves to be restrained. They were to turn over that which made them afraid to Yahweh and thus keep themselves from joining in with other voices which were sounding the alarm which went forth throughout the population. The threat of judgment which follows this functions to bring the consequences of a false decision before their eyes. It was a matter of salvation or downfall, life or death.

From a text-critical standpoint, תקדישו (you shall regard as holy) in v. 13 and מקדש (sanctuary) in v. 14 cannot be viewed as original. No matter what the reasons are for the original text having been altered, the introduction of the term *holiness* provides the correct interpretation for the text. Reference has already been made to the dynamic character of the concept of holiness (see above, commentary on 6:3). If one has a real knowledge about the holiness of God, this passage shows how one can see through someone who is gullible enough to trust in cultic piety. But just because Yahweh is the Holy One, one must not shrink back in fear because of what causes "this people here" to be afraid; one is able to preserve one's confidence and have help to hold on in faith in the midst of a world which grasps lamely for anything when crippled by desolation and defeatism.

Paul combined Isa. 8:14 with 28:16 in Rom. 9:32f. As far as he was concerned, Christ was the λίθος προσκόμματος (stone that will make humans stumble) and the τέτρα σκανδάλου (rock that will make them fall) (cf. also 1 Peter 2:8), and for him the actual σκάνδαλον (stumbling block) was the message about the cross (Gal. 5:11). In this sense, he went far afield from the literal sense of the passage in Isaiah—and yet, at the same time, he ingeniously grasped the depth of the paradox which the prophet posed: The σκάνδαλον (stumbling block), upon which humans stumble—or by means of which they find life—is the message which comes from the God who revealed himself to Israel; thereby, the apostle, going beyond the paradox found in the OT, interprets this as follows: The message is from the God who decisively revealed himself on the cross.

Isaiah 8:16–20

The Sealing of the Admonition

Literature

F. M. Avanden Oudenrijn, "L'expression 'fils des prophètes' et ses analogies," *Bib* 6 (1925) 165–171. J. Boehmer, "'Jahwes Lehrlinge' im Buch Jesaja," *ARW* 33 (1936) 171–175. L. Rost, "Gruppenbildungen im Alten Testament," *TLZ* 80 (1955) 1–8. S. Gozzo, "Isaia profeta e i suoi figli 'segni e presagi in Israele'," *Anton* 31 (1956) 215–246; 355–382. L. G. Rignell, "Das Orakel 'Maher-salal Has-bas'. Jesaja 8," *ST* (1957) 40–52. H. L. Ginsberg, "An Unrecognized Allusion to Kings Pekah and Hoshea of Israel," ErIsr 5 (1958) 61*–65*.

Concerning the text: G. R. Driver, "Hebrew Notes on Prophets and Proverbs," *JTS* 41 (1940) 162–175. P. W. Skehan, "Some Textual Problems in Isaia," *CBQ* 22 (1960) 47–55. G. R. Driver, "Isaianic Problems," FS W. Eilers (1967) 43–57.

Concerning אוב: A. van Hoonacker, "Divination by the Ôb amongst the Ancient Hebrews," *ExpTim* 9 (1897/98) 157–160. A. Jirku, *Die Dämonen und ihre Abwehr im Alten Testament* (1912) 5–11. H. Schmidt, "אוב," in FS K. Marti, BZAW 41 (1925) 253–261. I. Trencsényi-Waldapfel, "Die Hexe von Endor und die griechisch-römische Welt," *AcOr* (Budapest) 12 (1961) 201–222. H. Wohlstein, "Zu den israelitischen Vorstellungen von Toten- und Ahnengeistern," *BZ* NF 5 (1961) 30–38. Idem, "Zu einigen altisraelitischen Volksvorstellungen von Toten- und Ahnengeistern in biblischer Überlieferung," *ZRGG* 19 (1967) 348–355. M. Vieyra, "Les noms du 'mundus' en hittite et en assyrien et la pythonisse d'Endor," *RHAs* 19 (1961) 47–55. F. Vattioni, "La necromanzia nell' Antico Testamento," *Aug* 3 (1963) 461–481. H. A. Hoffner, Jr., "Second Millennium Antecedents to the Hebrew 'ÔB," *JBL* 86 (1967) 385–401. F. Schmidtke, "Träume, Orakel und Totengeister als Künder der Zukunft in Israel und Babylonien," *BZ* NF 11 (1967) 240–246.

[**Literature update through 1979:** J. A. Thompson, "A Proposed Translation of Isaiah 8:17," *ExpTim* 83 (1971/72) 376. C. F. Whitley, "The Language and Exegesis of Isaiah 8:16–23," *ZAW* 90 (1978) 28–43.

Concerning אוב: M. Dietrich, O. Loretz, and J. Sanmartin, "Ug. ILIB und hebr. '(W)B 'Totengeist'," *UF* 6 (1974) 450f. G. Schwarz, "'. . . zugunsten der Lebenden an die Toten'?" *ZAW* 86/2 (1974) 218–220. H. P. Müller, "Das Wort von den Totengeistern, Jes 8,19f.," *WO* 8/1 (1975) 65–76.]

Text

8:16 I bind up the admonition,[a] 'affix the seal'[b] of my instruction within
17   my disciples[c] • and shall hope in Yahweh, who hides his face from

363

18 the house of Jacob, and will trust confidently in him. • Behold, I and
my children, whom Yahweh has given to me, are signs and markers for warning in Israel
> from Yahweh of Hosts,
> > who dwells upon Mount Zion.
> > > *　　　*　　　*

19 [And when they speak to you: Consult the spirits of the dead and
the spirits who tell the future, who whisper and mutter; should not
a people consult its ancestral gods, that the living (turn themselves
20 toward) the dead? (So answer): • To the instruction and to the
admonition!ᵃ Indeed, one ought to speakᵇ to the one who (in reality) has no power to conjure awayᶜ (the disaster) in a way consistent with this message.]

16a Ginsberg, op. cit., 62*, on the basis of a reference to the Old Aramaic *'ddw,*
"fortune teller," which is used parallel to חזון (vision) (see *KAI* 202A 12), suggests
reading, instead of תעודה (admonition), rather תְּעֻדָּה (fortune telling), a completely
unnecessary alteration to the text.
16b חֲתוֹם (bind up) seems to be an imperative. If this is the case, it must be dealing
with a message of Yahweh to Isaiah, and the למדי must be Isaiah's "pupils," which
is the approach that Boehmer follows (171f.). 'Aquila, Targ, and Vulg also read
the imperative, but this is impossible in light of the prophet's "I" in v. 17. In
reality, the infinitive absolute חָתוֹם (seal up) should be considered as the original
reading, for which evidence is also furnished by the *mater lectionis.* But then, צוּר
must also be read as an infinitive absolute (certainly not from צרר, bind, but more
likely [contra KBL] from the less common form צוּר, bind).
16c For למדי (my disciples), Gk reads τοῦ μὴ μαθεῖν (= מְלַמֵּד, not to teach); Syr links
the word with what follows; yet, the MT is the preferable reading. There is no
justification for eliminating the word. The alteration suggested by Tur-Sinai
(*ScrHier* 8 [1961] 175) is to read למדיה, which, according to his translation, means
"their cords" (cf. = למדים in the Mishnah); this alteration is also to be rejected.
20a The way one translates תורה (instruction) and תעודה (admonition) here
depends on the answer to the question about the origin of the section. If one
assigns it to the late postexilic age, one might be able to translate the words as,
respectively, "law" and "revelation."
20b It is possible that one should read the singular instead of יאמרו (they speak).
But the plural might also be a way of expressing the indefinite "someone."
20c The common way שחר is translated, as "dawn," somehow does not seem very
convincing. Gk reads δῶρα (bribe), Syr *šuhda* (bribe) (Hebrew שֹׁחַר, present,
bribe). Driver (*JTS,* 162, and FS W. Eilers, 45) refers to the use of the *pi'el* of שחר
(seek diligently [RSV: for which you cannot atone]) in Isa. 47:11 (KBL: "charm")
and also cites the Syriac *šḥr (pa'el),* "control, force," and the Arabic *sḥr* II, which
has the same meaning. Whoever would swear and would consult the dead wishes
to set magical powers in motion. Some details of Driver's interpretation of this
section are suspect, but his reference to Isa. 47:11, similar in content, is helpful;
שחר is therefore to be translated with "charm," "have power to conjure away
[disaster]".

Form

Originally, vv. 19f. were not the continuation of vv. 16–18. The only
question is whether vv. 19f. (or v. 19 all by itself) are a message which was
initially independent and came into existence without any connection to
vv. 16–18 (which, under certain circumstances, could even have come
from Isaiah), or whether both of these units are only supplementary

additions, by a later hand. Apparently, the second option seems more likely: In v. 20, the same terms recur, תורה (instruction) and תעודה (admonition), which are also used in v. 16 but in the reverse order and with a different meaning. Since תעודה is found otherwise only in Ruth 4:7 (manner of attesting), it means that this is not pure chance: A glossator is at work; he has taken both of the terms, but now, because of the new situation which he sees, he has filled them with new meaning.

The previous section began in v. 11 with a testimony which has been termed a "prophetic confession." This formal designation is appropriate also in the case of vv. 16–18 (on this, see Lindblom, op. cit. [Literature for 7:1–17] 46). Just as the "confessions" of Jeremiah betray a familiarity with the songs of lament in the Psalms (see W. Baumgartner, *Die Klagegedichte des Jeremia,* BZAW 32 [1917] chap. 4, and G. von Rad, "Die Konfessionen Jeremias," *EvT* 3 [1936] 265–276 = TBü 48, 224–235), this section from Isaiah is also reminiscent of certain formulas which are expressions of confidence in the Psalms (on this, see below, commentary on 8:17).

Meter: Verses 16–18a are in prose; however, it is certainly an elevated prose, as is shown by the lack of an article on תעודה (admonition) and תורה (instruction). On the other hand, the festive close in v. 18b is a three-stress bicolon. Other autobiographical accounts of the prophets are also cast in prose; cf. 6:1ff.; 8:11; Jer. 11:18ff., et al. No one attempts to discover any metrical structure in the addition in vv. 19f.

Setting

There has never been any question that vv. 16–18 come from Isaiah. The prophet draws a very definite line that marks the end of a very specific period of his activity; in fact, unless we have been completely misled, that line marks the end of the time when he fought the hardest to be heard, during the time of the Syro-Ephraimitic War. That which follows in his "memorial record" does not apply to Judah any longer, but to Israel; see below, on the setting of 8:21–23aα. Isaiah had not gotten his point across with his message; instead, the very opposite happened: As the story about his call already made clear, his activity only brought about further hardening. When he takes another opportunity to speak, then it is to make clear that he will not keep silent because he admits defeat or even because Yahweh had led him in the wrong direction; he knows that his message still has a future. In fact, it seems that Isaiah was not active from 732 until the year Ahaz died (see 14:28–32). Even the addition in 19f., which sounds very much like the passage 47:10b–12 in Deutero-Isaiah, might come from the period of the exile. When ancient, well-established order disintegrates, then the dark side of popular religion rears up into the light, having been shunted off, up until that time, into an unnoticed little corner of life.

Commentary

[8:16] The interpretation of בלמדי (here: within my disciples) is of decisive importance for the understanding of v. 16. Some have suggested that it means: "for preservation with . . ."; Isaiah had written down (or dictated) his words and given the sealed written scroll to his disciples; see Duhm and Mauchline, ad loc.; Schildenberger, 394. If such were the case, we would have some long-sought evidence which would show that the prophets wrote down their own messages. But the text does not mention that his words were written down; nor does it speak of a scroll, nor of anything being delivered to the disciples to be preserved. Besides, would the only task for the disciples be to protect a sealed scroll? There are others who have translated it: "with my disciples," namely, "in their presence, together with them" (Dillmann, Kaiser, ad loc.), or "through my disciples," that is, "with their help" (Hitzig, Ewald, ad loc.). But one cannot be satisfied with these attempts to alter the wording of the text, and it is simply not an acceptable alternative to follow Fohrer's approach, cutting through the Gordian knot by simply eliminating בלמדי. In reality, the tying and sealing up can only be meant in a metaphorical sense (see, e.g., Gray, Feldmann, Herntrich, Hertzberg, Procksch, Leslie). But it is not easy to clarify the exact interpretation of the imagery. Letters and documents were in fact affixed with a seal; see, e.g., Isa. 29:11; 1 Kings 21:8, and, above all, Jer. 32:10–14, 44; one could also place scrolls in pottery jars to preserve them, as the finds at Qumran demonstrate. But would someone have also tied these documents or letters? In any case, we do not find out anything about that in the OT. (Furthermore, it would seem that written scrolls would have first come into use at the time of Jeremiah; see Jer. 36:4ff.; *BHH* III, 1732f.) There are other things in the OT which are tied up, e.g., gold in a purse (2 Kings 5:23; 12:11; cf. also Deut. 14:25 and Ezek. 5:3; on the use of the related word צרר bind, tie up, see Hos. 4:19; 13:12, et al.). The substantive צְרוֹר practically means "purse" (cf. the Arabic *ṣirârun,* "purse for money"). One can also say metaphorically that a purse holds some abstract entity, as in the case of Job, who laments that his transgression was sealed up in a bag (חָתֻם, 14:17), or in Sir. 6:16, which compares a trusted friend with a purse, in which "life" (חַיִּים), that is, salvation and happiness, are concealed. Thus O. Eissfeldt (*Der Beutel der Lebendigen,* BAL 105/6 [1960] 26f.) is right when he suggests that one ought not think of a leather or papyrus scroll being tied up, but rather that a purse is tied up. Just as someone puts something particularly valuable into a tied up or sealed purse for safe-keeping, Isaiah wants to deposit his valuable treasure, his admonition and instruction, within his disciples. In this way, the בלמדי (within my disciples) makes good, clear sense. Cf. the similar concept in 2 Cor. 3:2; Deut. 32:34f.; Ps. 40:9; Prov. 3:3; 6:21; 7:3.

Isaiah describes his message as תְּעוּדָה (admonition) and תּוֹרָה (instruction). See above, on the form of 1:10–17 and the commentary on 2:2b–3, for the use of תּוֹרָה (instruction, torah). תְּעוּדָה (admonition) is found elsewhere in the OT, in addition to v. 20, only in Ruth 4:7, there in the sense of verification, specifically that someone will waive all the rights and responsibilities of being a redeemer. That corresponds to the denominative meaning of the *hiph'il* of עוד: "be a witness" (from עֵד, "witness"); see 8:2. The basic meaning of עוד seems to be "go around, repeat" (Ugaritic *t'dt* means "message"; see Driver, *Canaanite Myths,* 152, note 22), and one could use the *hiph'il* meaning of the verb (i.e., "warn, admonish") for this present passage; cf. Amos 3:13; Jer. 6:10; 11:7; 42:19. As is shown by Pss. 50:7 and 81:9 (see also 1 Sam. 8:9), the verb can be used when one paraphrases to describe the activity of the speaker at the covenant festival, the one who confronts the people with the will of Yahweh. The verb was apparently considered to be apt for describing the entire scope of prophetic responsibilities, and it would not be at all surprising if תעודה (admonition) was in frequent use as a way to depict the prophetic task (on this, see also Driver, FS W. Eilers, 44). This word is very similar in meaning to what was in mind when the prophets referred to תורה (torah), and this is particularly true for Isaiah; cf. also the use of the related term עֵדוּת (decree), e.g., Ps. 81:6. That Isaiah uses precisely these two terms to characterize his message is very helpful for understanding how he viewed himself.

Already in 8:11, one finds out that a group of trusted companions had allied themselves with Isaiah. These associates are called למדים (disciples) here (derived from למד, learn, just as the NT μαθητής, disciple, comes from μανθάνω, learn). The specific usage "associate, disciple" is found elsewhere only in Deutero-Isaiah (50:4 and 54:13), but, in those passages, it does not designate the disciples of a prophet, but rather those of God. The passages show that a למד (disciple) is not so called because his master teaches him, but rather because he has been brought into a fellowship with him; on this, cf. the use of לֻמֵּד (who are accustomed to) in Jer. 13:23.

It is hard to know exactly what can be said in more specific details about such a circle of trusted companions. In 1 Sam. 10:5, 10, a חֶבֶל (band) of prophets is mentioned. But it is very unlikely that one would actually take this to refer to a prophetic school, in the sense of an established institution (on this, see A. Jepsen, *Nabi* [1934] 167 and 194). In 1 Kings 20:35; 2 Kings 2:3, 5, 7, 15; 4:1–38; 5:22; 6:1; 9:1 there is mention of בְּנֵי הַנְּבִיאִים (sons of the prophets) (see also Amos 7:14), which would lead one rather to think of a somewhat looser association. In any case, it is certainly out of the question that Isaiah had an esoteric group of "learned ones" or that he had formed a conventicle of the pious, possibly so that he could introduce them to the technique by which one could receive revelations or so that he could impart to them, much like an Indian guru, basic lessons about God, the soul, and salvation. In a way similar to the other prophets, he stood alone, in an isolated position of importance, but his message was always applicable to matters which were out in the open, directed to the people and the leaders who were responsible for them. Of course, this does not rule out that people gathered around him, from whom he would have received a favorable hearing. If from time to time he addressed them only, that was as a last resort, as the present passage helps us to recognize. One must be very careful when making statements, as Procksch does, "that the prophetic family was at the very same time the core group which would become a core group of God's people" and that, growing "within the shell of 'Ισραὴλ κατὰ σάρκα [Israel according to the flesh], an 'Ισραὴλ τοῦ θεοῦ [Israel of God] empowered by faith" was developing (see also Budde, *Jesajas Erleben* 88, and A. H. J. Gunneweg, *VT* 15 [1965] 31, both of whom suggest that what is described here is the *ecclesiola* which is taking shape within the *ecclesia;* cf. the cautionary and carefully weighed reflections of L. Rost, 4f.). Pulling back into the narrow circle is simply a tactical maneuver, for the purpose of being ready at any time to come out into the open among the people of the entire community.

[8:17] "Sealing up" his message within the disciples means that Isaiah estimates it will be a long time before what he said will take full effect; indeed, he might possibly not even be alive any longer when the message which he proclaimed would come to fruition. But he confesses his confidence, as would someone who prays a psalm of lament: "I will hope in Yahweh"; "I will trust confidently in him." It is particularly clear, with the use of קוה (trust confidently), that this term is rooted in the songs of lament; see Pss. 25:3, 5, 21; 27:14; 69:7–21; 130:5, et al.; cf. also Jer. 14:22. Actually, חכה (wait) is found only in the song of thanksgiving, Ps. 33:20, and in the historical psalm, 106:13, but there is no reason to doubt that it was also used in the expressions of confidence within the songs of lament; cf. Hab. 2:3 and Zeph. 3:8. Both of the verbs bring out the tension implicit in this type of hope; see the Arabic *haka'a,* "punish," and the Hebrew קו, "[outstretched] measuring line." Both terms are very close to what Isaiah means when he uses האמין (believe); cf. H. Wildberger, *ZTK* 65 (1968) 137f., and the terms used in 30:15. This sounds just like the pious person who speaks in the songs of lament, who is filled with tension because Yahweh has hidden his face from him: Pss. 10:11; 13:2; 27:9; 44:25, et al. On the other hand, in a song of thanksgiving one looks back upon the time when Yahweh hid his countenance, Ps. 30:8, or the one who is praying confesses that, in spite of the way it looks, God has not hidden from him, 22:25. But these motifs are used by Isaiah in a new way, as is very characteristic of him: He does not hope, as the pious one who prays, that he himself will physically get "rescued," but he plans to await the fulfillment of the message which has been proclaimed. And he does not say that God has hidden his face *from him* but rather *from the house of Jacob;* on this, cf. C. Westermann, "Das Hoffen im Alten Testament,' *GesSt* TBü 24 (1964) 219–265, esp. 257; concerning the designation house of Jacob, see above, commentary on 2:5.

What does it mean when Yahweh *hides his countenance* from Israel? In any case, it does not mean that Yahweh's rule remains an unfathomable mystery. When God lifts up his countenance upon his people, that means his grace goes forth for them. But when he hides his face, then he gives them over to terror, to being lost (see Pss. 104:29f.; 143:7; Deut. 32:20; Jer. 33:5; Mic. 3:4), which concretely means in many cases that they are given over into the hand of the enemy (e.g., Ezek. 39:23f.). It is possible, since Isaiah speaks of the house of Jacob, that he has in mind the deep encroachment of Tiglath-Pileser into the Northern Kingdom in 732. And yet, he considers both of the individual states to be a single spiritual unity (see above, on 8:14). But if it is true now that Yahweh has withdrawn his saving presence from his people, the prophet will still remain one who has hope and indeed—if this is not paradoxical enough—one who still has hope in this very God who has hidden his countenance from the house of Jacob. It is not misleading to mention, in this connection (see Procksch, ad loc.), Martin Luther's *deus absconditus* (hidden God).

[8:18] In this way, the tying up and sealing of the message practically becomes a symbolic action which intends to make the point that the promise bound up inside still has validity. But since the contents of the message are no longer declared publicly, it is necessary to have signs that will remind people of the message. Isaiah is in the position to point out these signs: himself and all of his "children, whom Yahweh had given him." Some commentators want to take the "children" to mean the disciples, to whom reference had just been made (e.g., Budde, *Jesajas Erleben,* 90; Lindblom, 49f.). That would be possible if Isaiah had referred to them as בנים, sons; however, there is absolutely no evidence that ילדים (children) can have this transferred meaning. Hence the term must refer to the physical children of the prophet (on this, see C. Keller, *Das Wort OTH* [1946] 94f.). If these are to serve as אתות (signs) and מופתים (markers), then it is certainly, in the first place, on the basis of their names. We know two of them: Shear-jashub and Maher-Shalal Hash-Baz (see above, commentary on 7:3; textual note 8:1c–c). The second of these two names very clearly has the characteristics of a promise, but the exegesis in 8:1–4 showed that it had to be used within the context of an accusation against Jerusalem, because Jerusalem had refused to believe. We believe that the sign connected with the first son, Shear-jashub, must be interpreted as a warning (see above, commentary on 7:3). But if it was a warning to avoid the wrong decision *beforehand,* it also could have been an indicator for the house of Jacob, which was under judgment at that time, that there would also be a new future in store. The ambivalence which has been so frequently observed in Isaiah's proclamation is obvious here as well: One can find in the names, which are to serve as signs, an indication that judgment will soon come, but also that salvation can be expected. These are admonitions in any case: Israel's future is to be decided by its relationship with Yahweh.

To what extent is Isaiah himself a sign? Some have also studied the meaning of his name: "Yahweh has bestowed salvation"; see above, commentary on 1:1. But interpreting his name as a sign is questionable; ישעיהו (Isaiah) is not a name which would attract the particular attention of the populace. The prophet is a sign and an admonition by the very fact of his existence. Everyone would be reminded of his message every time he appeared publicly in Jerusalem. But then one must also say more specifically: The children are also signs just because they exist. The reason they serve as signs is pointed out initially when they are given their names. On the other hand, what Isaiah's existence meant had long since been recognized as *coram publico* (public knowledge), because of his public activity.

The relative clause אשר נתן לי (whom [Yahweh] has given to me) is not an insignificant detail when it comes to arriving at this interpretation. Yahweh had given the children to Isaiah, and, therefore, it is natural that they were in service to him. This is not referring to a "miracle," as it is usually translated, unless one would describe it as a miracle that there was a real application of the word of God, clearly seen in the workings of everyday life; on this, see above, pp. 305 and 312. The word מופת (marker, wonder, sign), the etymology of which has not yet been clarified, is used here in Isaiah for the first time (see also 20:3). In seventeen passages out of a total of thirty-six, it is used with אות (sign); this is the case, except for the two passages from Isaiah, only in the speech which is typical of the deuteronomistic writings. Of course, in the postexilic era, מופת is used to describe a miraculous sign; e.g., Joel 3:3; on this, see H. W. Wolff, BK XIV/2, 81 (Engl: *Joel and Amos,* 67f.).

Concerning יהוה צ׳ (Yahweh of Hosts), see above, commentary on 1:8–9 and on 6:3. (צבאות) מעם יהוה (from Yahweh [of Hosts]) is typical of the vocabulary used by Isaiah; see 7:11; 28:29; 29:6; otherwise, it is used only in 1 Kings 12:15. By using השכן בהר ציון (who dwells upon Mount Zion) in apposition in the second colon, there is no doubt that Isaiah is employing a liturgical formula; on this, see above, commentary on 6:1, where reference has already been made to 31:9 as a parallel: יהוה אֲשֶׁר־ אוּר לוֹ בְּצִיּוֹן וְתַנּוּר לוֹ בִּירוּשָׁלָם (Yahweh, whose fire is in Zion, and whose furnace is in Jerusalem).

The notion that Yahweh dwells upon Zion is the result of the transfer of the concept of the mountain of God, now referring to Jerusalem. Zion is "the city of God, the holy habitation of the Most High" (קְדֹשׁ מִשְׁכְּנֵי עֶלְיוֹן), Ps. 46:5; see also 48:2, 4; 76:3; 84:2; 87:1–3. Psalm 74, which laments the destruction of the sanctuary, uses the exact same phraseology as is found in Isaiah: הַר־צִיּוֹן זֶה שָׁכַנְתָּ בּוֹ (Mount Zion, where thou hast dwelt), v. 2; cf. 135:21 (read there בציון, in Zion, instead of מציון, from Zion); concerning the concept in general, see A. Kuschke, *ZAW* 63 (1951) 84–86; G. Fohrer, *TDNT* VII, 307ff.; W. Schmidt, *ZAW* 75 (1963) 91–92. The transfer of the ark to Jerusalem (see Ps. 132:5–13) gave the basic justification, one might say, for the theological claim made concerning the city, and, at the time of the construction of the temple of Solomon, there was a very conscious effort to claim that Jerusalem was the place where Yahweh had his dwelling (cf. 1 Kings 8:12). Except for Isaiah, the concept is seldom mentioned by any of the pre-exilic prophets (but see Amos 1:2). On the other hand, we find it, even though it is in the context of an eschatological reinterpretation, in Ezek. 43:7, 9; cf. also 20:40 (on this, see Zimmerli, BK XIII, 1079f. [Engl: *Ezekiel 2,* 415f.]); in addition, already in an apocalyptic context, it is found in Joel (2:1 and esp. in 4:17, 21; on this, see H. W. Wolff, BK XIV/2, 98f. [Engl: *Joel and Amos,* 81f.]), but it is also to be found in the other exilic and postexilic prophets (Obad. 16f.; Isa. 56:7; 57:13; 65:11, 25; 66:20; Zech. 2:14; 8:3; 9:8). In Deuteronomy, it is found in the more refined formula which states that Yahweh has permitted his name to dwell "there" (12:5, 11; 14:23, et al.), and in the priestly writings, there is an interpretation which follows the lines of Ezekiel: Yahweh certainly dwells in the temple, but that means that he has allowed himself to dwell among his people, Exod. 25:8; 29:45, and often elsewhere.

Since the expression before us was not formulated by Isaiah, one must exercise caution in assessing what it meant for his theology (on this, cf. below, 28:16). But it is also not as if he was categorically rejecting the whole idea. "Yahweh has founded Zion, and in her the afflicted of his people find refuge," 14:32. He can certainly proclaim the harshest judgment against Jerusalem. But he never proclaimed a complete end for the city (on this, see Th. C. Vriezen, "Essentials of the Theology of Isaiah," FS J. Muilenburg [1962] 128–146; see pp. 128–131). Therefore, it is possible that the collection of his messages from the time of the Syro-Ephraimitic War, in spite of the fiasco which he endured from a political point of view, came to its conclusion with the sound of a confession of hope.

[8:19] The expander of the text in vv. 19f. did not interpret v. 16 in the metaphorical sense suggested above, but thought in terms of an actual written תורה (instruction, torah), though he did not use this term to refer to the Pentateuch but to the legacy of the prophetic movement. He had in mind that someone who was barely surviving in the era of disintegration and instability in which he lived would be sustained by holding on to this inheritance. And, in fact, he saw himself at odds with a movement of his day which sought help from the spirits of the dead.

Unfortunately, neither the origin nor the actual meaning of the term אוב is as clear as one would wish. As in 19:3 and 1 Chron. 10:13, this present passage speaks of "inquiring" of the אבות (spirits) (דרש, seek, in Deut. 18:11; and in 1 Chron. 10:13, שאל, inquire), just as one would otherwise speak of inquiring of a deity (see 19:3, parallel to דרש אל הָאֱלִילִים, they will consult the idols). These parallels, the way the term is further clarified by ידענים (spirits who tell the future), and the entire context in which the message is presented in this particular passage leave no doubt that the term refers to the "spirit of one who is dead," as is also the case in other passages (Lev. 19:31; 20:6, 27; 1 Sam. 28:7f.; Isa. 29:4). This way of explaining the meaning causes problems in a host of other passages, because they mention clearing away (הֵסִיר, 1 Sam. 28:3; בִּעֵר, 2 Kings 23:24), exterminating (הִכְרִית, 1 Sam. 28:9), and manufacturing (עָשָׂה, 2 Kings 21:6) the אבות (spirits of the dead). These are all verbs which, above all in the Deuteronomist, can be used in similar contexts to refer to the gods, really to the images of the gods. From this, the conclusion has been drawn that אוב actually refers to a cultic installation, which played a role when one sought to make inquiries of the dead (Jirku, op. cit., 6ff.). Schmidt, op. cit., 259ff., is even more specific, thinking this refers to a whirling piece of wood. Certainly, something like this could be used to drive spirits away, but not conjure up spirits (see K. Budde, *ZAW* 46 [1928] 75f. and *Jesajas Erleben* 92, note 2). Wohlstein, *ZRGG* 19, 348–352, suggests one begin with Job 32:19, where אוב, without question, means "wine bottle." In order to bridge the gap between "wine bottle" and "spirit of the dead," reference has been made to the Syriac *zakkûrâ*, "spirit of the dead," which T. Nöldeke (*ZDMG* 28 [1874] 667, note) derives from the Arabic *zukra*, "small skin bottle." But this explanation of the Syriac *zakkûrâ* is doubtful and, while it is possible that one could arrive at the meaning of "wine bottle" by thinking that someone might try to conjure up a spirit in a drunken ecstatic frenzy, this could hardly be the circumstances in which one would attempt to inquire of the dead. The lexicographers generally identify אוב in the Job passage as אוב I, standing by itself. The attempts of many, in both ancient and modern lexica, to differentiate two different meanings for אוב II are more promising, namely "spirit of the dead" on the one hand and "conjurer/conjuring" on the other (Ges-Buhl, Zorell, Baumgärtel in *TDNT* VI 364f.). But even that does not work for passages such as 2 Kings 21:6: One cannot actually "manufacture" a conjurer and it is not very satisfactory to translate it "stop a conjurer of the dead" *(Zürcher Bibel)* or "order [a spirit of the dead]" (KBL). The conclusion is unavoidable: אוב—just as אשרה (Asherah), which can be used both to identify the cultic pole and also the goddess which is represented by it—is also used on the one hand to describe some implement which could be used when summoning the dead for help and on the other hand could be used to describe the actual spirits of the dead.

Which of these two meanings is more original could possibly be discovered if one were able to clarify the etymology of the term. If one does not try to explain the etymology of אוב I when seeking the source of אוב II, then one can look for help from the Arabic *'âba*, "return again," reminiscent of the French *revenant* (ghost, spook) (see van Hoonacker, op. cit., 157f.; Eichrodt, *TheolOT* II [1967] 212–216; W. F. Albright, *Archaeology and the Religion of Israel* [1968⁵] 148ff.;

Kaiser, ad loc.). On the other hand, C. J. Gadd, *Ideas of Divine Rule in the Ancient East* (1948) 88f., has called attention to the Sumerian *ab, ab-làl,* which in one passage of the Sumerian version of the Gilgamesh Epic (Akkadian Tablet XII, line 79f., see *AOT* 185 = *ANET* 98) means "hole," in the very special sense of the opening in the floor through which the spirit of dead Enkidu climbs up (concerning this phenomenon, see Trencsényi-Waldapfel). M. Vierya sought to provide further evidence by referring to Akkadian and Hittite texts (in the latter, the key word *âpi* indicates that it is a loanword from the Hurrian; see also J. Friedrich, *HdO,* Section I, Vol. II, parts 1 and 2, no. 2 [1969] 23), as well as by reference to the Ugaritic *'eb* (see also C. Rabin, *Or* 32 [1963] 115f., and Hoffner's summary of the argument). Of course, F. Vattioni (477ff.) has presented objections to this argument and has pointed out that there is no passage in the OT which would ever require the meaning "hole" for אוב. And yet, once again, one should compare the context in which אוב is found in Isa. 29:4 and note the way the term, as it is used in 19:3, is translated in the Gk: τοὺς ἐκ τῆς γῆς φωνοῦντας (those calling out from the earth) (cf. comments made already by van Hoonacker, op. cit., 159). In summary, it is not surprising that one would no longer be aware of the original meaning of a loanword, lost when the word was borrowed. In any case, it seems quite likely that Israel adopted the term—and certainly also the rites which went along with it—from its surroundings, and it is therefore easy to understand why there would be such a harsh reaction to making inquiry of the spirits of the dead.

The terms which follow are hardly intended as designations for other categories of spirits; they expand upon what is meant by אבות (spirits of the dead) (which is even more important since a foreign loanword is involved). In eleven of sixteen cases where אבות (spirits of the dead) are discussed, they are mentioned in conjunction with the ידענים. For this parallel term, KBL gives the meaning "fortuneteller." But if the אבות are not those who conjure up the dead, but rather the spirits of the dead, then one would also have to translate ידענים as *spirits* who tell the future (see Ges-Buhl and Zorell). They are called "the ones who know," because they know what is hidden from human beings on earth. Thus, a South-Arabic demon who gives oracles is called *ḥawkim* (from the root *ḥkm;* see M. Höfner, *Wörterbuch der Mythologie,* 1, Part I, 1965, 510). Or possibly one might be reminded of the Arabic genie, about whom it was believed that such a one would be able to help the wise gain wisdom; see A. Schimmel, *RGG³* II, 1299; D. B. Macdonald, *Encyclopédie de l'Islam* II (1965) 560f. And naturally, it is not surprising that Enkidu, the spirit of the dead, is able to inform Gilgamesh how the underworld functions (Tablet XII, line 86f.). As "ones in the know," with powers on a higher level, the ידענים (spirits who tell the future) would be able to disseminate information about the future, but would also be able to instruct someone about the way one could ward off disaster; cf. 1 Sam. 28:15; Isa. 19:3. In Assyria, the interpreters of dreams, inspectors of offerings, and the *eṭemmu* (spirits of the dead) were all consulted about future activities of the god Ashur; see F. Schmidtke, op. cit., 245f. (with additional examples). They chirp or whisper (מצפצפים is onomatopoetic) or they mutter (מהגים; הגה is a term which is used to describe the moaning of a dove, but see also Ps. 1:2 and Josh. 1:8). Gk translates ידענים as ἐγγαστριμύθους (ventriloquist) and the two participles which follow as τοὺς κενολογοῦντας οἳ ἐκ τῆς κοιλίας φωνοῦσιν (those who talk emptily, those who speak from the belly). Secretive muttering describes how one hears an oracle from the spirit of the dead; cf. 29:4 (שחח *niph'al,* "make subdued sounds"). In the pre-Islamic period, it was sometimes described by the use of the word *haǧâ',* and it would seem that this word is the technical term for old Arabic proverbs, *hiǧâ'* (see I. Goldziher, *Abhandlungen zur arabischen Philologie* I [1896] 69 with note 4, and Wohlstein, op. cit., 351f.).

The continuation of this difficult passage in v. 19b seems to reflect the ideas of the opponents of Isaiah: Those opponents seem to suggest that it is only natural that an עם (people) would turn to its ancestors, so why should one not do something which is so normal (cf. 1 Sam. 8:5)? By the very way it is formulated, one notes how difficult it was for Israel to reject the practice of consulting the dead, a common activity throughout their region. עם is not used here to mean "people" in a political-national-istic sense but, as in Jer. 37:12; Ruth 3:11, in the more ancient meaning of "tribal community."

The spirit of the dead is also called אלהים (Elohim) in 1 Sam. 28:13. It would seem that the Akkadian word *ilu* might possibly have this meaning in some personal names (see J. J. Stamm. *Akkadische Namenge-bung* [1939] 283f.; in addition, see *CAD* I/J, 102; in response to this, see W. von Soden, *OLZ* 57 [1962] 485). It is presumed that there must be some point of contact between the two communities if the dead can be consulted on behalf of the living, which means that the translation "ancestral gods" seems justified. The dead are ready to intervene on behalf of, בעד, the living. One might compare, in addition to דרש בעד (inquire for; 2 Kings 22:13; Jer. 21:2), also the expressions התפלל בעד (he will pray for; Gen. 20:7, and often elsewhere); העתיר בעד (make entreaty for; Exod. 8:24); זעק בעד (cry to; 1 Sam. 7:9); בקש בעד (besought [God] for; 2 Sam. 12:16), and similar formulations. Though commonly perceived in this way elsewhere, the spirits of the dead are not to be understood here as threatening powers, but as "protecting gods" who look out for the welfare of others, from whom one can expect solidarity, a relationship which seeks the welfare of the clan.

[8:20] As is generally acknowledged, some parts of the text in v. 20 are somewhat uncertain, and no interpretation can be anything more than an attempt. If one bases the interpretation on the traditional translation of שחר as "dawn," this must be understood as symbolic of hope, support for which one might find in Job 3:9; cf. also Isa. 58:8. If this is the case, one would expect at least some indication that this is what is intended (cf. also Westermann's thoughts, TBü 24, 236, note 9). As has been stated above (see textual note 20c), it is preferable to follow Driver, who refers to Isa. 47:11. In that context, it is announced to Babylon that all of its magical arts (כְּשֶׁף, v. 9) and exorcisms (חֶבֶר, v. 12) and all of its wisdom and knowledge (דַּעַת חָכְמָה, v. 10) have failed. "Evil shall come upon you"—לֹא תֵדְעִי שַׁחְרָהּ, "you know no magic to counteract it," 11aα. In 11aβ, there is a parallel for this: לֹא תוּכְלִי כַּפְּרָהּ, "you will not be able to expiate." According to this, Babylon has wearied itself in vain with its magical arts (v. 15; read there שַׁחֲרָיִךְ, your eager seeking, instead of סֹחֲרָיִךְ your traveling about). Those who are addressed in the text of 8:19f. now find themselves in a similar position: Disaster has broken in upon them. And they take flight, to use practices similar to those employed in Baby-lon; they turn to the אבות (spirits of the dead), to the ידענים (spirits who tell the future). But the author calls them to order: Magical arts cannot cast a spell to ward off their troubles. There is only one who can help, whose path Isaiah had clearly pointed out; it is worth turning back to תורה (instruction) and תעודה (admonition). We would have to know more about this unknown author in order to discover what exact data he had in mind when he used these terms, which he borrowed from Isaiah; see above, commentary on 8:16. The fact that he reverses the order shows that his primary interest is in the תורה (instruction, torah). But we can at least say this much: He demands that the hearers turn back to the transmitted prophetic *message;* cf. Zech. 1:6.

Finally, a question all by itself concerns how כדבר הזה (consistent with this message) is to be understood. Some have translated it as "so," and connected it with תורה (instruction) and תעודה (admonition). But someone who was involved as a successor to the prophetic movement would hardly have thought that anything could be accomplished by simply reciting these two words. If, as pointed out above, vv. 19f. are a conscious addition to vv. 16–18, then this כדבר הזה (consistent with the message) might refer back to that entire section, so that the author would specifically be thinking of Isaiah's confession there, the confession that one could hope in Yahweh who dwells upon Zion.

Purpose and Thrust

There are times when the prophet can speak no more, but must just keep silent. Isaiah is not an official who has to carry out his responsibilities no matter what the circumstances; instead, he is one who has been freely called by God and can afford simply to wait for Yahweh. In fact, he takes into account the possibility that during his own lifetime his message cannot accomplish what was intended. If that were true, then others could possibly keep alive his message, so that his concerns might be heard—when the time was ripe.

This passage does not deal with Isaiah's withdrawal from the public arena of the history of God with Israel. He and his children remain "signs and markers for warning." That which is most necessary has been said; he and those who belong to him will function as a *signum* which cannot help but be noticed, which could result in an obedient response. The names of his children are strange enough so that someone could hardly keep from asking about their meaning when meeting them. Also, whenever the prophet appeared in his home town, it left such an impression that he continued to be a thorn in the side of its residents. There are situations at the far edge of prophetic activity, situations in which the message remains in effect simply by the very fact that the sign is still there (one might compare Hosea's marriage and the names which he gave to his children).

Isaiah wants to wait and hope. For what? The exegetes usually say: for the predicted disaster to finally come (see Fohrer, ad loc.). If Isaiah had proclaimed nothing but disaster during the time of the Syro-Ephraimitic War, then this explanation would be indisputable. Of course, then one would be left with a ludicrous impression of Isaiah: a prophet who delivered his prophecies like one would read minutes of a meeting, who was now hoping for and waiting for Yahweh's actions which would fulfill what was announced, similar to Jonah before the gates of Nineveh. Then it would be difficult to deal with this text as it now stands: Why should Isaiah call upon the God who dwells on Zion? He apparently does it because Yahweh of Hosts is the God of Israel. Even if Yahweh is a stumbling block and a slipping rock for the people who dwell upon Zion and has reason to hide his face from the house of Jacob—still, in spite of all this, the final goal for his journey with Israel is salvation. Some day Isaiah's message would receive a hearing; Israel would once again fear Yahweh; Yahweh would once again allow his countenance to shine upon his people, would smash to bits all the plans of the nations, and the "With-us-is-God" (7:14 and 8:10) would once again become a truth attested publicly by everyone. Therefore, it is not impossible, but rather corresponds to Isaiah's theology, that the prophet brings his activity to a close in the years 734/33 with this daring hope expressed in 9:1ff.; on this, see Lindblom, op. cit. (in Literature for 7:1–17) 49.

The expander who added vv. 19f. updated the message of Isaiah at a time when there was a need to challenge the practice of conjuring up the dead, which his contemporaries had embraced in the hope that this might be the way to ward off disaster in their own time. In an impressive way, he commands those who have been blinded to return to "scripture and tradition." That does not actually contradict what Isaiah says, just as long as one hears, from the tradition, both the promises and demands of the living God. But if the transmitted word is handled as a collection of holy sayings from God, which can give one confidence simply by having them and using them alone, then Isaiah is basically misunderstood. Yahweh is not a God who, like other friendly spirits, simply can be expected to guarantee protection for his people without question, and still less is he a God who allows himself to be manipulated by magical practices. He can wait until Israel has finally understood what it means that he is their Lord. He can hide himself, but in the very fact that he keeps himself hidden, he remains the God of Israel.

Isaiah 8:21–23aα

Oppressive Darkness

Literature

L. G. Rignell, "Das Orakel 'Maher-salal Has-Bas'. Jesaja 8," *ST* 10 (1957) 40–52. H. L. Ginsberg, "An Unrecognized Allusion to Kings Pekah and Hoshea of Israel," ErIsr 5 (1958) 61*–65*. P. W. Skehan, "Some Textual Problems in Isaia," *CBQ* 22 (1960) 47–55. A. Guillaume, "Paronomasia in the Old Testament," *JSS* 9 (1964) 282–290. G. R. Driver, "Isaianic Problems," FS W. Eilers (1967) 43–57.

Text

8:21 . . . .
[a]and he passes through it,[a,b] oppressed and hungry.[c]
And when he hungers, he becomes very angry[d]
and curses his king and his God.
And he turns himself toward what is above
22 and looks to the earth[a]—
but, behold: distress and deep gloom
and oppressive darkness[b]
[c]and no beam of light in depth of night.[c]
* * * *

23 [For there will be no escaping[a] for that one, who is oppressed by him.[b]]

21a–a Nothing is said to identify the subject of עבר (he passes through) and the referent for the suffix on בה (through it). Not only the general understanding of the text, but even the text-critical work is made much more difficult by that fact. Unfortunately, the ancient versions are not at all helpful. One is also conscious of the fact that the text can hardly have come to us intact, so that one ought not make any far-reaching proposals for emendations which have only slight support in the text as it presently stands.
21b It has been suggested that one read, instead of בה (through it), rather בָּאָרֶץ (in the land) (see BHK³ and BHS). But since this is certainly only a fragment, the suffix on בה (through it), referring to something now lost, could have actually referred to ארץ (land) or some similar word, but could hardly have pointed back to תעודה (admonition) (בה: "according to it"), as Rignell, op. cit., 49, suggests.
21c Guillaume, op. cit., 289, suggests that רעב (hungry) is to be understood in light

376

of the Arabic *ra'ib* ("frightened, weak, cowardly"), but Hebrew does not use this word in this way. The fact that Isaiah uses this same root (רעב) twice, in the same breath, is a very effective stylistic technique and is not to be treated as a completely unnecessary repetition (Guillaume).

21d Qᵃ reads יתקצף (he will become angry), replacing the perfect consecutive with the simple imperfect. One can see in the Qumran literature that the perfect consecutive is already dying out (on this, see especially E. Y. Kutscher, *The Language and Linguistic Background of the Isaiah Scroll* [1970]). Guillaume, op. cit., 289, finds fault with this, reading קצב instead, referring to the Arabic *kaṣuba*, and translates it "emaciated," which once again is highly unlikely, since there are no examples of that usage in the Hebrew.

22a Qᵃ הארץ (the land); on this, see Kutscher.

22b KBL suggests reading, instead of מְעוּף (gloom), the form מוּעָף (gloom) (as in v. 23). Since the substantive can be derived from the root עוּף II, "be dark," the construct state מְעוּף (gloom) is certainly possible (even if one would expect to find מְעוֹף instead; see Joüon, Gr §88Le).

22c–c אפלה מנדח might mean "[he is] thrust out into the darkness." Gk reads σκότος ὥστε μὴ βλέπειν = Hebrew מֵרְאוֹת אֲ' (darkness so that one cannot see). Guillaume, op. cit., 289f., also interprets this in light of the Arabic lexicon, making use of *nadaḥa,* "stretch out," taking מנדח as an adverbial accusative and thus rendering אפלה מנדח as "widespread darkness"; see the similar interpretation offered by Driver, op. cit., 46. In this case also, making use of the Arabic seems too risky. In light of the similar vocabulary in Amos 5:20 (note there ואפל ולא־נגה, and gloom with no brightness in it), it may be that מְנֻדָּח, as has often been suggested (see the references in Gray, ad loc.), should be changed to read מִנֹּגַהּ with no beam of light).

23a MT means something like: "For that which is darkened is not dark for the one, the one for whom oppression comes in a moment upon her," which makes no sense at all. The sentence would seem to offer a comment on the phrase מעוף צוקה (oppressive darkness) in v. 22. Some have thought it best to take it as a question, reading הלא (is not) instead of לא (not) (something similar is done by Duhm: "For does not one have a mental derangement, when that one has anxiety?"). Guillaume, op. cit., 290, refers to Vulg (*et non poterit avolare de angustia sua,* and will not be able to hurry away from his distress), which does not derive מוּעָף from עוּף II (be dark) but from עוּף I ("fly") and translates לא מועף, on the basis of the Syriac-Arabic *'awwafa,* "make free, let loose," as "there is no escape"; so also Driver, op. cit., 46, 49. Since עוּף, meaning "to fly," is a much more widely used Hebrew root than עוּף II, "be dark," it would seem that the glossator misunderstood the usage of מוּעָף (gloom) in v. 22. Guillaume's suggestion has the advantage that it does not require one to alter the text at all.

23b מוצק (oppressed) is a *hoph'al* participle from צוק (bring into straits), not a substantive (see KBL).

Form

The fragmentary character of this section is a problem in and of itself. Skehan, op. cit., 48ff., suggests inserting 8:21f. between 14:25a and 25b; the בה (through it) in 8:21 would supposedly make reference to the ארץ (land) in 14:25. In addition, he suggests emending v. 22, on the basis of 5:30b, and reads here: *we'el 'ereṣ yabbît wᵉhinnēh ṣārāh waḥᵃšēkāh wᵉ'ôr ḥāšak bā'ᵃrîpêhā* (and looks to the earth and behold, distress and deep gloom, and light grows dark in its clouds) (50). But such drastic alterations of the transmitted text are much too arbitrary. One must simply live with the fact that the original context, in which this section once belonged, can no longer be identified.

Verse 23aα apparently furnishes another example of the glosses which are so common in the book of Isaiah (so Gray, Duhm, Procksch, Steinmann, Kaiser, Fohrer, et al.). It is typical here, as above in vv. 19f., that a term is utilized from the immediately preceding two-verse section, even if it is in a different form or with a different meaning: מָעוּף/מוּעָף (gloom/escaping) and צוּקָה/מוּצָק (oppressive/oppressed); see above, vv. 19f. For this reason, it is almost universally recognized by scholars that there is a gap between vv. 23aα and β; this means that v. 23aβb does not provide a smooth continuation of v. 23aα. Ginsberg is an exception (see also Kaiser); he reads לוּ (if) for לא (not) (see Qᵃ), לֹה (to him) for לָהּ (to her), and כְּעַתָּה (as now) for כָּעֵת (at the time of), and translates: "For if there were glimmering for him for whom there is straitening," and continues in β: "[only] the former [king] would have brought shame upon the land of the Zebulunite. . . ." But a very cumbersome sentence results from his reconstruction, which makes sense only when the bracketed words are included; without these additional words, it would not make any sense at all; on this, see J. A. Emerton, "Some Linguistic and Historical Problems in Isaiah VIII.23," *JSS* 14 (1969) 151–175, see 161.

Meter: The three-stress colon in v. 21 seems originally to have been the second colon of the fragment; a three-stress bicolon follows (with בה, through it, unaccented), then a two-stress colon, which is expanded by means of another two-stress colon in v. 22a to form a four-stress colon, and there is good parallelism between the 2 two-stress cola. Then, in v. 22b, if one does not consider והנה (but, behold) in establishing the meter, a six-stress colon is used $(2 + 2 + 2)$, providing a very effective conclusion.

One cannot detect it in English, but there are examples of imitative play on words: עבר and ירעב/רעב; alliteration: קלל/התקצף; מעלה/מלכו; צוקה/צרה; מנגה and מעוף; in addition, there is a pair of words which sound very similar: אֲפֵלָה/חֲשֵׁכָה; and finally, the gloomy vowels in מעוף, צוקה, and נגה paint a melancholy scene: The message, metrically constructed in a very artistic way, concludes in a way which is verbose and very macabre sounding.

Setting

Since we are dealing with what is nothing more than a fragment and there is no way to establish an identifiable historical setting, the decision about whether the passage is genuine is also made more difficult (see Marti, Gray, Duhm, Fohrer). On the basis of meter and style, it is typical of Isaiah; the content includes nothing which could not be said by Isaiah and mention of the king in the passage shows that it must come from before the exile. The vocabulary also tilts the scales in favor of Isaiah as the source. It must be admitted that עבר (pass through) (see 8:8; 28:15, 19; 29:5; 31:9); רעב (hunger) (see 9:19; 29:8); קלל (curse) (see 8:23; 30:16); and חשכה and נגה (deep gloom and beam of light) (9:1) do not prove all that much. But the phrase בארץ צרה וצוקה (through a land of trouble and anguish) in 30:6, and particularly צוקה (oppressive) (also with צרה, distress), found elsewhere only in Prov. 1:27, speak very much in favor of judging it authentic. למעלה (what is above) reminds one of the use of that term in 7:11 (on this, see below, commentary on 8:22). Since Isaiah is so fond of using the light/darkness metaphor, it would not surprise us that he would use the *hapax legomenon* מעוף (darkness). Thus, except for the gloss in v. 23aα, there is nothing which would speak against this being considered Isaianic.

The section apparently deals with a group of people who are under severe political pressure, and have problems with hunger as well; most likely they were going through the land in search of sustenance in some place or another. As they were doing this, such an overwhelming anger took hold of them that they began to curse their king and their God. Naturally, one cannot eliminate the possibility that the reference is to a Davidic king in Jerusalem, even though in such a case it would be very difficult to fit this message into the time of Isaiah. It would be much easier if one presumes that this sentence refers to a king in the Northern Kingdom. This could be Hoshea, the final king, who caused the downfall of the Northern Kingdom when he severed his vassalage to Assyria. However, since this passage is part of a collection of the messages of Isaiah from the time of the Syro-Ephraimitic War, it would be more likely that this refers to Pekah, whose misguided political moves brought about the loss of the northern and eastern parts of his land. We discover in the messages of the prophet Hosea just how bitter certain circles of those faithful to Yahweh were when they assessed kingship in the Northern Kingdom, since it seems that Hosea's polemics focused on Pekah; see, above all, 10:3–7; on this, see H. W. Wolff, BK XIV/1, 224 (Engl: *Hosea,* 173), and W. Rudolph, KAT XIII/1, 195. Admittedly, there is no evidence for this thesis, but one must remember that the connecting v. 23aβb speaks about the destiny of the Northern Kingdom, specifically about the section of the Northern Kingdom which had been appropriated by the Assyrian king in 732, and 9:1 refers to "the people who went through darkness," almost certainly the inhabitants of that region who were now in a servant relationship and under severe pressure. It can certainly be admitted that it would make sense for the "memorial record" to conclude with 8:16–18 (on this, see above, on the setting of 8:16–20). But it would not be any less fitting that additions could have been appended to the collection, a collection in which Isaiah spoke of the destiny of the brother kingdom in the north, about which he had said in 7:16 that it would soon be devastated.

Commentary

[8:21] If we have correctly determined the temporal and historical setting for this section, then the subject of the verb in vv. 21f. would be some of the inhabitants of those territories which had come under the political control of Assyria. נקשה (oppressed) reminds one of the formula used for the hand of an enemy resting very heavily (קשה) upon a land (see Judg. 4:24; Isa. 19:4, and cf. 1 Sam. 5:6). One does not need additional proof to show that the "hand" of Assyria was very heavy upon the newly integrated provinces. Of course, it also rested very heavily upon what was left of Israel, now actually a vassal state. But in connection with the catastrophes of war, problems of hunger and epidemics often cause more grief than the actual battles. Amos 8:11f. provides a very telling description of someone wandering aimlessly, while seeking for bread throughout the land (see also Amos 4:8; and in addition, Gen. 12:10; 26:1; 2 Kings 8:1). According to 1 Kings 18:5ff., the king himself went about through the entire land with his "steward" (read נעבר בארץ, let us go through the land, in v. 5, on the basis of Gk) as they searched for water and fodder for the animals. In the same way, there were some who were going throughout the land of Israel to find what was absolutely necessary for survival. One can imagine that this search met with little success. In this situation, from which there seemed to be no escape, the people, who had been beaten down and misled and were suffering the awful consequences of the short-sighted policies of those groups which led Israel, vented their intractable anger by letting go with curses upon the king and were not even hesitant about including God himself in their maledictions. קָצַף does not mean the quick flash of anger which is a response to someone's misconduct, but that deep anger which wells up within a human being who knows that he or she has been cheated and betrayed. It is easy to understand how deeply disappointed the people would have been with the king, after the terrible conclusion to the anti-Assyrian activities. But there were some who thought that Yahweh also had deceived them. That would not have been their view simply because it was generally thought that one had a right to expect his protection; there is no doubt that there were prophets, whom Hosea specifically mentions (see 4:5), who had awakened the hopes which now had proved illusory. False "theology" caused some to strike back at God himself. The facts which contradict such a theology do not often enough lead one to think more deeply about God; rather the human being often lets this false image of God lead to dishonoring God still more. One must naturally also take it into account that the king serves as proxy for God. Basically, things were no different in Israel than in Judah. Therefore, cursing the king was at the same time blasphemy against God. It was a life and death matter when Naboth was accused of having cursed God and the king (1 Kings 21:10, 13, here using the euphemistic term בֵּרֵךְ, bless). The book of the covenant had already stated this clearly: אֱלֹהִים לֹא תְקַלֵּל וְנָשִׂיא בְעַמְּךָ לֹא תָאֹר (you shall not revile God nor curse a ruler of your people), Exod. 22:27; see, in addition, Lev. 24:15; Ps. 10:3; Job 1:5, 11; 2:5, 9; Jer. 10:11; concerning this, see J. Hempel, "Die israelitischen Anschauungen von Segen und Fluch im Lichte altorientalischer Parallelen," *ZDMG* 79 (1925) 20–110; = "Apoxysmata," BZAW 81 (1961) 30–113; see pp. 91ff. = 97ff. If blasphemy is punishable by death, then someone who curses the one who has "earthly" responsibility for this power cannot be treated any less seriously. This is because the king, as the representative of Yahweh, is the one who is responsible for world order, which has to be functioning correctly, since that is the first requirement if a blessed life is to follow. Cf. when Shimei curses David, 2 Sam. 16:5ff., and the sustained impression which this incident left, 2 Sam. 19:22 (מָשִׁיחַ!, messiah!); 1 Kings 2:8. Hempel (op. cit., 98, note 309a) furnishes examples from Israel's surroundings. If there is no reported reaction from the representative of this "order," that only goes to show how completely this system had fallen apart already.

[8:22] One does not only utter curses, but also looks around for help: "He turns himself toward what is above and looks to the earth." In 7:11, Isaiah offered the king a sign "deep within the underworld" or "high above in the heights." Instead of Sheol, here he mentions the earth (but one must also remember that אֶרֶץ can also designate the underworld), whereas in both passages לְמַעְלָה (toward what is above) is used when speaking of the realm above. In this particular passage, one probably ought to take it to mean something like the following: One seeks in the heavens above and on the earth below for some sign of a coming change in fortune. It is possible that this means careful observations which seek omens (flight of birds, movements of or constellations of stars, or something similar; cf. also Ezek. 21:26; on this, see W. Zimmerli, BK XIII, 490 [Engl: *Ezekiel 1, 443f.*]).

However, no trustworthy sign is to be discovered; for there is nothing but oppression and darkness (cf. Is. 5:6). The very mention of צרה (distress) (from צרר, "be tight"; cf. Gk θλῖψις, affliction) calls attention to the confining pressure of the moment. The parallel term צוקה (oppressive) underscores this thought (Gk: ἀπορία στενή, confining difficulty); cf. how the two expressions are used in Prov. 1:27. חשכה (deep gloom) and אפלה (depth of night): These belong to the terminology used to describe the Day of Yahweh (cf. Zeph. 1:15; see the use of צָרָה, distress, and מְצוּקָה, anguish, there as well; see also Joel 2:10; 3:4; 4:15; Isa. 13:10), which Amos had already characterized as darkness, not light (concerning the Day of Yahweh, see above, commentary on 2:12aα). Indeed, the Day of Yahweh is virtually the יום צָרָה, day of distress; cf., in addition to Zeph. 1:15, also Nah. 1:7; Hab. 3:16; Obad. 12, 14; Isa. 33:2; 37:3. In the background of the reference to light/darkness, there is a motif which anticipates that the stars will lose their brightness on the יום יהוה (Day of Yahweh). With a transferred meaning, this idea is found in the threats which accompany the curses in Deut. 28:15f.: "You shall grope at noonday, as the blind grope in darkness," v. 29. Isaiah is not talking about the Day of Yahweh at this point, but he was aware of the mythological concepts connected with it and he uses them here as he paints the picture of the present troubles, for which no comfort could be offered.

[8:23aα] With this, the message ends. Whether it once ended with some words of comfort cannot be determined. As it is at present, it provides the melancholy foil for the prediction of salvation which will follow. However, before that, there is one more gloss, in the first part of v. 23. It reiterates: There is no escape for the one who is oppressed by this darkness. Some have thought it possible that this is from the same hand that wrote the conclusion of chap. 7, which radically cut off every possibility of hope. It is certainly not true that those who added comments in the book of Isaiah were only interested in predictions of salvation. They could also boldly call attention to the disastrous future which lay in store for Israel, with incisive severity.

Purpose and Thrust

Because of the difficulties pointed out above, which make it hard to determine the historical setting, it is also more difficult to arrive at the exact meaning of the text. And yet, the basic message, depicting a situation with no escape, into which human beings allowed themselves to be driven, is not dependent upon such an exact dating. Objectively speaking, the situation was already almost hopeless. But it was essentially hopeless only because humans had reacted to it in a completely false way. They were disappointed; believing that they had been deceived and that they had every right to strike out in a blind rage, they sought "scapegoats"

381

and placed the blame on the king and God. It is typical of the false responses which humans make in such circumstances that people would turn against God instead of revising their own image of God, drawing out the necessary consequences in terms of a new way to relate to him. In reference to the king, this "anger" does not seem to have been misplaced, at least not if Pekah is the king to whom reference is made. Not only Hosea, but Isaiah also had called for a renunciation of this king and others as well. In spite of that, Isaiah saw the desire to affix blame upon the kingship as a sign of complete disorientation. The root problem: Israel's renunciation, which rejected its status as the people of Yahweh, was not to be solved by hurling curses against the king. Those who want to make the "king" alone answerable for this completely mishandled situation reveal that they are fleeing from the responsibility which each individual has to carry, and such funneling of blame is too facile a solution to the problem of who is guilty. As long as the individual does not see that this way of handling the matter is incorrect, all attempts to look around for a glimmer of hope are in vain. In the harshest way possible, Isaiah confronts his listeners: Such a delusion can only result in אֲפֵלָה מְנֻדָּח (no beam of light, in depth of night), in circumstances where things become darker yet, which the prophet can depict only by using the imagery which describes a darkening of the entire cosmos.

According to the present context, this section has been inserted just ahead of the "messianic prediction," which apparently speaks in a completely contradictory way about the shining forth of the light. In this way, the *lux in tenebris lucet* (light which shines in the darkness) is depicted in a well-honed paradox: The light shines into the darkness which seems to be incapable of being illuminated and hope is injected into a situation where there was no longer any cause to hope; salvation comes into view in circumstances which were far beyond the point of rescue. Only the freedom of the mercy of God would be able to resolve this paradox.

Isaiah 8:23aβ—9:6

The Great Light

Literature

W. E. Barnes, "A Study of the First Lesson for Christmas Day," *JTS* 4 (1903) 17–27. R. H. Kennett, "The Prophecy in Isaiah IX 1–7," *JTS* 7 (1906) 321–342. W. Caspari, "Echtheit, Hauptbegriff und Gedankengang der Messianischen Weissagung Jes. 9, 1–6," BFCT 12 (1908) 280–320. F. E. Peiser, "Jesaja Kap. 9," *OLZ* 20 (1917) 129–139. W. E. Erbt, "Zu F. E. Peisers 'Jesaja Kap.9'," *OLZ* 21 (1918) 78–81. H. Schmidt, *Der Mythos vom wiederkehrenden König im Alten Testament,* Schriften der Hessischen Hochschulen, Universität Giessen 1 (1925) 11–13. K. Dietze, "Manasse, eine chronologische Untersuchung zu Jesaja 9:1–6," *Festschrift des Bremer Gymnasiums* (1928) 245–281. H. Gressmann, *Der Messias,* FRLANT 43 (1929). G. von Rad, "Das judäische Königsritual," *TLZ* 72 (1947) 211–216 = *GesSt,* TBü 8, 205–213. S. Mowinckel, "Urmensch und 'Königsideologie'," *ST* 2 (1948) 71–89. M. B. Crook, "A Suggested Occasion for Isaiah 9:2–7 and 11:1–9," *JBL* 68 (1949) 213–224. A. Alt, "Jesaja 8,23—9,6. Befreiungsnacht und Krönungstag," *KlSchr* II, 206–225. H. Ringgren, "König und Messias," *ZAW* 64 (1952) 120–147. M. B. Crook, "Did Amos and Micah Know Isaiah 9:2–7 and 11:1–9?" *JBL* 73 (1954) 144–151. L. G. Rignell, "A Study of Isaiah 9:2–7," *LQ* 7 (1955) 31–35. W. Vischer, "Die Immanuel-Botschaft im Rahmen des königlichen Zionsfestes," *TZ Zürich* 45 (1955). S. Mowinckel, *He That Cometh* (1956) 102–110. H. Ringgren, *The Messiah in the Old Testament* SBT 18 (1956). J. Lindblom, *A Study on the Immanuel Section in Isaiah,* Scripta Minora Regiae Societatis Humaniorum Litterarum Lundensis 4 (1957–1958). L. Alonso-Schökel, "Dos poemas a la paz," *EstBib* 18 (1959) 149–169. J. Coppens, "Le roi idéal d'Is., IX, 5–6 et XI, 1–5, est-il une figure messianique?" Mémorial A. Gelin (1961) 85–108 (literature!). H. J. Kraus, "Jesaja 9, 5–6 (6–7)," *Herr tue meine Lippen auf,* ed. by G. Eichholz, vol. 5 (1961²) 43–53. H. P. Müller, "Uns ist ein Kind geboren . . .," *EvT* 21 (1961) 408–419. W. Zimmerli, "Jes 8,23*—9,6," *Göttinger Predigt-meditationen* 16 (1961/62) 64–69. W. Harrelson, "Nonroyal Motifs in the Royal Eschatology," FS J. Muilenburg (1962) 147–165; see pp. 149–153. H. W. Wolff, *Frieden ohne Ende,* BibS(N) 35 (1965). J. Scharbert, *Heilsmittler im Alten Testament und im Alten Orient* (1964). S. Herrmann, *Die prophetischen Heilserwartungen im Alten Testament,* BWANT 85 (1965) 131–135. J. Schildenberger, "Durch Nacht zum Licht (Jes 8,1—9,6)," *Sein und Sendung* 30 (1965) 387–401. Th. Lescow, "Das Geburtsmotiv in den messianischen Weissagungen bei Jesaja und Micha," *ZAW* 79 (1967) 172–207. J. Becker, *Isaias—der Prophet und sein Buch,* Stuttgarter Bibelstudien 30 (1968) 22–27. J. Scharbert, *Der Messias im Alten Testament und im Judentum: Die religiöse und theologische Bedeutung des Alten Testaments* (1967) 49–78. J. Vollmer, "Zur Sprache von Jesaja 9:1–6,"

ZAW 80 (1968) 343–350. J. Coppens, "Les messianisme royal," *NRT* 90 (1968) 491–496 = "Le messianisme royal," LD 54 (1968) 77–82. W. H. Schmidt, "Die Ohnmacht des Messias," *KD* 15 (1969) 18–34. J. A. Emerton, "Some Linguistic and Historical Problems in Isaiah VIII.23," *JSS* 14 (1969) 151–175 (literature!).

Concerning the text: F. Zorell, "Vaticinium messianicum Isaiae 9,1–6 Hebr. = 9,2–7 Vulg.," *Bib* 2 (1921) 215–218. G. R. Driver, "Isaianic Problems," FS W. Eilers (1967) 46–49.

Concerning individual motifs: C. F. Burney, "The 'Boot' of Isaiah IX 4," *JTS* 11 (1910) 438–443. H. Torczyner, "Ein vierter Sohn des Jesaja," *MGWJ* 74 (1930) 257–259. N. H. Snaith, "The Interpretation of El Gibbor in Isaiah ix. 5," *ExpTim* 52 (1940/41) 36–37. W. H. McClellan, "'El Gibbor'," *CBQ* 6 (1944) 276–288. H. Wildberger, "Die Thronnamen des Messias, Jes. 9,5b," *TZ* 16 (1960) 314–332 (literature!). H. A. Brongers, "Der Eifer des Herrn Zebaoth," *VT* 13 (1963) 269–284. B. Renaud, "Je suis un Dieu jaloux," LD 36 (1963), see pp. 118–126. G. del Olmo Lete, "Los títulos mesianicos de Is. 9,5," *EstBib* 24 (1965) 239–243. G. Fohrer, art., "*υἱός* B," *TDNT* VIII 340–354, esp. 349–352.

Concerning comparative material from religio-historical studies: S. Morenz, "Ägyptische und davidische Königstitulatur," *ÄZ* 49 (1954) 73–74. E. Brunner-Traut, "Die Geburtsgeschichte der Evangelien im Lichte der ägyptologischen Forschungen," *ZRGG* 12 (1960) 97–111, practically identical with idem, "Pharao und Jesus als Söhne Gottes," *Antaios* 2 (1960/61) 266–284. Idem, *Altägyptische Märchen* (1965²), see pp. 76–87. H. Brunner, *Die Geburt des Gottkönigs, ÄA* 10 (1964).

[**Literature update through 1979:** S. Amsler, *David, Roi et Messie*, ChT 49 (1963). A. Soggin, *Das Königtum in Israel: Ursprünge, Spannungen, Entwicklung* (1967). E. Lipiński, "Etudes sur des textes 'messianiques' de l'Ancien Testament," *Sem* 20 (1970) 41–58. J. Mauchline, "Implicit Signs of a Persistent Belief in the Davidic Empire," *VT* 20 (1970) 287–303 (294–299 concerning 8:23). E. Lipiński, "An Israelite King of Hamat?" *VT* 21 (1971) 371–373. H. Graf Reventlow, "A Syncretistic Enthronement-Hymn in Is 9:1–6," *UF* 3 (1971) 321–325. H. Cazelles, "De l'idéologie royale," *JANESCU* 5 (1973) 59–73. R. A. Carlson, "The Anti-Assyrian Character of the Oracle in Is 9:1–6," *VT* 24 (1974) 130–135. J. Coppens, *Le messianisme et sa relève prophétique. Les anticipations vétérotestamentaires. Leur accomplissement dans le Christ*, Bibliotheca Ephemeridum Theol. Lovanensium (1974).

Concerning the text: J. A. Emerton, "Some Linguistic and Historical Problems in Isaiah VIII 23," *JSS* 14 (1969) 151–175.

Concerning individual motifs: M. Treves, "Little Prince Pele-Joez," *VT* 17 (1967) 464–477. W. Zimmerli, "Vier oder Fünf Thronnamen des messianischen Herrschers von Jes 9,5b.6?" *VT* 22 (1972) 249–252. J. G. Heintz, "Le 'feu dévorant' (dans l'AT)," *Le feu dans le Proche-Orient antique* (1973). K. Luke, "The Names in Is 9:5b," *LivWord* (1973) 169–182. Z. Meshel, "Was There a 'Via Maris'? (Is 8:23; Ez 41:12 . . .;)," *IEJ* 23 (1973) 162–166. K. D. Schunk, "Der fünfte Thronname des Messias (Jes IX 5–6)," *VT* 23 (1973) 108–110. G. Scipione, "The Wonderful Counselor, the Other Counselor, and Christian Counseling (Is 9:6)," *WTJ* 36 (1973s) 174–197. D. Grimm, "Die hebräische Wurzel pl' und ihre nominalen Ableitungen im Alten Testament. Eine lexikalische Untersuchung," diss., Halle, typescript (1977).]

Text

8:23aβ, b   As the previous time[a] brought humiliation to the land[b] of Zebulun and the land[b] of Naphtali, so the future one[c] will bring glory for
the way of the sea, the East-Jordan land[d] and the peoples' province.

*   *   *   *

9:1   The people, which went through the darkness,
    sees a great light,
the ones who live in a land of darkness,[a]
    a light shines forth over them.

2 You make much 'of the jubilation,'ᵃ
  the joy is great,
One rejoices before you,
  as one rejoicesᵇ in the harvest,
as one is jubilant
  when the booty is divided.
3 For the yoke, which weighed heavyᵃ upon him,
  'the pulling bar'ᵇ upon his shoulder,
the staff of his taskmaster
  you have smashed as on the day of Midian.ᶜ
4 For every boot, which stomps on in with a roar,ᵃ
  and (every) robe which is rolled aroundᵇ in pools of blood,ᵃ
falls to the firebrand,
  will be consumed by the fire.
5 For "to us a child is born,ᵃ
  a son is given to us,
and the sovereign authorityᵇ came upon his shoulder
  and as his names, 'oneᶜ calls out':
ᵈplanner of wonders,ᵈ
  God's hero,
everlasting father, prince of peace,
6   'greatᵃ in (his) sovereign authority.'
And as for peace
  (there will be) no end
over David's throne
  and over his royal kingdom,
since he fortifies and supports it
  with justice and righteousness
from now on
  even into eternity."
The zeal of Yahweh of Hosts
  will accomplish such a thing.

23a B begins chap. 9 with כעת (as the [previous] time); on this, see below, on form (in what follows, "23aβb" refers to the verse from כעת on). עת (time) is otherwise feminine; possibly there should be changes, to read the feminine ראשונה (previous) and אחרונה (future); cf. Driver, op. cit., 46; Emerton, op. cit., 156ff. In any case, it will not work to follow Budde (*Jesajas Erleben,* 99ff.), who takes הראשון (the first) and האחרון (the latter) as subjects, in which case, according to his view, the "first" would be Tiglath-Pileser and the "latter" would be a future oppressor.

23b Qᵃ reads ארץ (land) instead of ארצה (to the land), which had been suggested as an emendation even before the Qumran writings became known. The alteration is not absolutely necessary. Yet, ארצה (land) is hardly an Aramaic form (so Kaiser); instead, it is an "old, hardened form" of the accusative or else a locative; cf. Ges-K §90f.; L. G. Rignell, *ST* 10 (1956) 51, and Emerton, op. cit., 152f.

23c If Yahweh is to be taken as the subject of הקל (brought humiliation) and הכביד (will bring glory) (or is to be added, as is done by Alt, Kaiser, et al.), then one would have to alter האחרון (the previous) to read בָּאחרון (in the previous [time]). But it simply makes no sense that the word יהוה (Yahweh) could have dropped out of the text, nor that a new unit could begin without any mention of the subject. Certainly, Yahweh is the "theological" subject of the sentence, but it is clear that the name of God is mentioned intentionally only at the very end of the section (9:6).

23d It has been suggested that מֵעבר (from across) be read instead of עבר (East-Jordan, [across the Jordan]), which would make it necessary to insert ועד (and toward) directly before גליל הגוים (the peoples' province, [Galilee of the nations]); see, e.g., Fohrer, ad loc. But the דרך הים (way of the sea) actually goes all the way to the sea, not only as far as the "people's province."

9:1a צלמות (darkness) was understood by the versions to have been a composite word, formed from צל (shadow) and מָוֶת (death): Gk: ἐν χώρᾳ καὶ σκιᾷ θανάτου (in the region and shadow of death); see Matt. 4:16; Luke 1:79; Targ: טולי מותא (shadows of death); Syr: ṭelālê mawtâ (shadows of death); Vulg: umbra mortis (shadow of death). In spite of this unanimous tradition, the word should be interpreted on the basis of a connection with the root צלם, "be dark." Hebrew is not familiar with composite words of this type and, in the other places where the word is found in the OT, the meaning "darkness, gloom" is likely correct; this is also suggested here by the parallelism. The word should be pointed either צֶלְמוּת or (more likely) צַלְמוּת (on this, cf. D. W. Thomas, JSS 7 [1962] 191–200).

2a לא הגוי (the people not) makes no sense. Concerning the attempts to make sense of the MT as it is, see Rignell, LQ 7 (1955) 33 ("Thou hast made the not-a-people great") and H. W. Wolff, op. cit., 53ff. A number of MSS, Q, Targ, Syr read הגוי לו (the people to him), but these variant readings are just as unsatisfactory. In general, it is conjectured that one ought to read הַגִּילָה (the jubilation) (cf. in v. 2b).

2b In the word שמחת (as one rejoices), S. Rin (BZ NF 5 [1961] 255–258) would like to identify an old absolute ending of the plural. But it is not impossible to have the construct state before a prepositional construction; see BrSynt §71d.

3a Concerning סָבְלוֹ (weighed heavy upon him), cf. Ges-K §93q.

3b מַטֶּה, "rod," does not furnish a good parallel for על, "yoke." On the other hand, מוֹטָה (bar of yoke) and על (yoke) can be used interchangeably; cf. Jeremiah 28; in addition, see also Lev. 26:13 and Ezek. 34:27. Therefore, as Studer already has suggested (JPT 7 [1881] 161), מַטֶּה (rod) ought to be altered to read מוֹטָה (pulling bar) (see also Isa. 58:6, 9).

3c Qᵃ reads מדים (Madim); see Μαδιαμ (Madiam) in Gk.

4a The notion that ברעש (with a roar) and בדמים (in pools of blood) are to be eliminated, on the basis of the meter (Procksch), is mistaken. Gk and Targ seem to have read בְּרֶשַׁע, "with evil," which Tur-Sinai ("A Contribution to the Understanding of Isaiah I–XII," ScrHier 8 (1961) 177) considers to be correct, but this distorts the impressive imagery.

4b It is a completely unnecessary "emendation" to alter מגוללה (is rolled around) to read מְגֹאָלָה "soiled" (Zorell, op. cit., 217, and Procksch), in spite of the Syr (mᵉpalpal, wallow [in blood]).

5a Note the alliteration in ילד ילד לנו; concerning the play on words, cf. BrSynt §38c.

5b The hapax legomenon משרה is translated by Gk as "sovereign authority" (ἀρχή); yet, there are difficulties with the derivation of the word if one uses this pointing. Gray (comm.) connects this word with שרר, "rule," and שׂר, "prince" (Akkadian: šarru, king) and has suggested that it be pointed מְשָׂרָה or מִשְׂרָה. Qᵃ reads משורה; therefore, the MT ought to be pointed מְשָׂרָה; concerning this, cf. F. Nötscher, VT 1 (1951) 302, and G. R. Driver, VT 2 (1952) 357.

5c The subject of וַיִּקְרָא (calls out) is not named. Gk (καλεῖται, will be called), Syr ('etqᵉrî, will be called), Vulg (vocabitur, will be called) all took the word as a passive (וַיִּקָּרֵא?). It is possible that Duhm can help at this point (ad loc.), suggesting that one read an ordinary imperfect (וְיִקְרָא), unless one follows Qᵃ, which reads the perfect consecutive; on this, see below, p. 401.

5d–d Gk reads μεγάλης βουλῆς ἄγγελος (messenger of great counsel), a rather free rendering which gives it a different meaning. In what follows, it "translates" ἐγὼ γὰρ ἄξω εἰρήνην ἐπὶ τοὺς ἄρχοντας εἰρήνην καὶ ὑγίειαν αὐτῷ (for I will bring peace upon the rulers, peace and healing to him). 'Aquila, on the other hand, offers the reading θαυμαστος συμβουλος ισχυρος δυνατος πατηρ ετι αρχων ειρηνης (wonderful, counselor, mighty, powerful, father, still a ruler of peace) (similar readings in Sym and Theod; cf. Ziegler). It is worth noting that none of these attempts render אֵל as "God." And yet, Origen (under ·⁕·, other textual evidence is in Ziegler) reads, on the basis of the MT, as an addition to Gk, θαυμαστος συμβουλος θεος ισχυρος (wonderful counselor, powerful God). Targ: מפלי עיטא אלהא גיבירא קיים עלמיא משיחא דשלמא יסגי עלנא ביומוהי, "wonderful counselor, mighty God, who lives for ever, the Messiah, in whose days peace will become great over us." Vulg: *admirabilis, consiliarius, Deus, fortis, pater futuri saeculi, princeps pacis* (admirable, counselor, God, mighty, father of the future age, prince of peace) (Zorell, op. cit., 218, speaks in favor of a corresponding number of six names in the MT, based on metrical considerations). There is no cause for making any changes in the text, but the versions give evidence for the helpless situation in which the people found themselves in ancient times, seeking the meaning of the names "of the Messiah." Concerning the translation which is suggested here, see below, pp. 403ff.

6a למרבה (note the final *Mem* in the middle of the word) presents difficulties. Some MSS, Qᵃ, and Q all read למרבה (for much), but this does not help out much. Gk: μεγάλη ἡ ἀρχὴ αὐτοῦ (his reign is great); Sym: επλησθη η παιδεια αυτου (and his child will be filled). 'Aquila and Targ also read something similar; Vulg: *multiplicatum eius imperium* (his rule—multiplied). On the basis of these versions, some have chosen to eliminate לם as a dittography and then to read what remains as רַבָּה: "great is the sovereign authority" (others read לְמוֹ רַבָּה [for him—greatness] or לוֹ מְרְבָּה [to him—increase]). But Alt, op. cit., 219, recognized that one ought to expect five "throne names," on the basis of the Egyptian pattern, and that a part of a fifth name is in the damaged למרבה. He opts for מַרְבֵּה הַמִּשְׂרָה, "one who increases the kingdom," or, as the translation above would suggest, רַב הַמִּשְׂרָה (great in [his] sovereign authority); on this, see below, p. 405.

Form

The first challenge, very difficult to solve but still very important for the interpretation of this problematic section, is to determine the boundaries. There is no question that a new unit begins with 9:7. However, it is very difficult to determine where the present message of promise begins. Even the versions are not uniform: Gk takes 8:23aβb with 9:1ff. (see also B and Vulg). The solution is made even more difficult by the fact that 8:23aβb brings with it questions about its own text, and its interpretation is not clearly established; yet, one will have to agree that 8:23aβb belongs with 9:1–6.

In recent times, A. Alt has energetically defended this viewpoint. He begins with the poetic form of 9:1–6, where he identifies, along with Duhm (*Jesaja*[2] and [3]), four strophes, each with 10 cola of two stresses each. He claims to have found an additional strophe with the same structure in 8:23aβb:

הֵקַל יהוה		כְּעֵת הָרִאשׁוֹן
וְהַר גִּלְעָד		עֶמֶק הַשָּׁרוֹן
וְאַרְצָה נַפְתָּלִי		אַרְצָה זְבֻלוֹן
דֶּרֶךְ הַיָּם		וְהָאַחֲרוֹן הִכְבִּיד
גְּלִיל הַגּוֹיִם		עֵבֶר הַיַּרְדֵּן

Yahweh brought humiliation	/	As the previous time
and Mount Gilead	/	for the lowland of Sharon
and to the land of Naphtali	/	to the land of Zebulun
to the way of the sea	/ thus, in the future he will bring glory
for Galilee of the nations	/	for "across the Jordan"

He arrives at the suggested expansions based on reflection about the objects of הכביד (will bring glory), which, according to their sense, would have to correspond with designations for particular geographic regions in the first half of the verse.

But this very clever reconstruction is a bit too daring. It must be questioned even because of the presupposition which guides Alt's emendations, that a regular pattern exists within both the strophes and the verses of 9:1–6. It would be better to avoid adopting any textual changes for 8:23aβb—not because the tradition, as it has come to us, is above suspicion, but because none of the suggested emendations is particularly convincing and, in certain cases, arbitrary conjectures are made which prematurely determine the interpretation of 9:1ff. (concerning the various conjectures, see Emerton). As 8:23aβb now stands, one can hardly read it as if it has metrical structure. But that means that, on the basis of meter alone, one cannot show that it is to be taken with 9:1ff. In fact, it is not completely out of the question that an original poetic form of v. 23aβb has been distorted, but it is also possible that the section 9:1–6, which is most poetic, was furnished from the very beginning with a prosaic introduction. But the use of the so-called prophetic perfect in 8:23aβb, as in 9:1ff., and a theme which is common to both, speaks in favor of taking these as connected: Harsh oppression is followed by freedom; having been brought very low in the past, there is new honor in the future. The conclusion, 9:6bβ, seems to clarify further the topic introduced in 8:23aβb, where one misses any mention of Yahweh as subject. Detailed exegesis will have to determine whether the main objection to the unity of this section holds up, namely, that 8:23aβb speaks about the northern province of Israel, whereas the birth of the child who will sit upon the throne of David must speak about what will take place in Jerusalem (see, for example, H. W. Wolff, op. cit., 61).

It is also difficult to clarify the question about the genre of the section. Yet, one can begin with v. 6bβ: קִנְאַת יְהוָה צְבָאוֹת תַּעֲשֶׂה־זֹּאת (the zeal of Yahweh of Hosts will accomplish such a thing). Under no circumstances should this be considered a secondary addition (see, for example, Renaud, op. cit., 121f.). This definitely identifies the section as a promise. One should pay careful attention to the use of a series of perfects (in v. 5aβb, it is admittedly an imperfect consecutive, but see the textual note 5c). And yet, the perfect consecutive in v. 4 (see also the infinitives at the conclusion of v. 6) shows that, to some extent, the events which are described also have a future dimension (see Lindblom, op. cit., 33). The perfects are used because the fulfillment of the promises has already been assured, based on what has already happened, namely, that the child has been born. Exegetes are quick to speak about the hymnic style of this passage. But in an actual hymn, Yahweh is spoken of in the third person, whereas he is addressed in the second person in 9:2. Such perfects are much more fitting in a song of thanks (see Mowinckel, op. cit., 102; Lindblom, op. cit., 34f., and C. Westermann's differentiation between declarative and descriptive praise, *The Praise of God in the Psalms* [1965] 15–35, esp. 19ff.). The relationship between this and a song of thanks is also obvious to anyone who takes note of the individual motifs; see below, commentary on 9:1. To be sure, the second part of this section no longer uses the terminology which links this to the song of thanks. But one would not expect it to be any different, since the reason for the thanks is most extraordinary: the birth of the royal child. The motifs in use here are those of the royal ideology of Jerusalem and/or the ancient Near East. Therefore, this means: The promise in 8:23aβb—9:6 (or, as the case may be, in 9:1–9:6) employs the form of a song of thanks, in which concepts generally found in the traditions of royal ideology have been adopted (cf. the "eschatological song of thanks" in chap. 12 and see Kaiser, op. cit., 99).

Strophes and meter: The division of the poem by Duhm, as it has been summarized above, results in four strophes with the exact same structure, but this requires too many alterations to the text. As is shown by a passage such as the "song of the vineyard," one cannot count on Isaiah to follow either a rigid structure in the strophes or to use a single verse length (concerning meter and style, above all, see L. Alonso-Schökel, op. cit., 151ff.; concerning vv. 5f., see also Renaud, op. cit., 120f.). Of course, one can identify strophes which consist of sense units. The *first* one is in v. 1: 2 three-stress bicola; a *second* in v. 2: 3 three-stress bicola; a *third,* introduced by כִּי (for), in v. 3: a two-stress bicolon and a three-stress bicolon (in which case the stresses are as follows: הִגְגַּשׂ בּוֹ; a *fourth,* introduced by the second כִּי (for), in v. 4: a three-stress bicolon and a two-stress bicolon (כֹל, every, being possibly a secondary insertion); a *fifth* in v. 5: opening with a three-stress bicolon in v. 5a, then a five-stress colon, a two-stress bicolon and (together with the emended beginning of v. 6) a second two-stress bicolon (?); a *sixth,* which should probably be accented as follows:

אֵין־קֵץ	וּלְשָׁלוֹם
וְעַל־מַמְלַכְתּוֹ	עַל־כִּסֵּא דָוִד
בְּמִשְׁפָּט וּבִצְדָקָה	לְהָכִין אֹתָהּ וּלְסַעֲדָהּ
וְעַד עוֹלָם	מֵעַתָּה
תַּעֲשֶׂה־זֹּאת	קִנְאַת יְהֹוָה צְבָאוֹת

As is always the case when dealing with Isaiah, the length of the verse is closely correlated with the content: The 2 three-stress bicola in v. 1 are illustrative of the terrific pressure brought on by the distress, the *o*-sound underscoring the gloomy circumstances. The 3 two-stress bicola in v. 2, with the many *i*-sounds (one should observe the pattern of alteration between *i* and *a* sounds), help to point out the bursts of joy uttered by those who are breathing a sigh of relief after the pressure is gone. In the third strophe, the *o*-sounds remind one once again about the weight of oppression and hardship which had to be endured in order to be made free of the pressure. This is also why there is a return to the three-stress bicolon in the second line in v. 3 and the first line in v. 4. In the first line of v. 5, one notes the many times ל is used, which would, so to speak, make sure that the jubilant shouts are heard. The very short lines which report the throne names allow every single name to have its full impact. The double accent which is given to מֵעַתָּה (from now on) insures an adequate depiction of the hope for a long-lasting peace (see also the upbeat tone of אֵין קֵץ, no end, in v. 6a): The promise is set forth with calm assurance. One would indeed expect the last line, which offers an interpretive comment, to be of a different meter than the two-stress bicola which precede it, and this difference certainly ought not lead one to the conclusion that it is thus not genuine (see Renaud, op. cit., 121ff.).

There are some further unique stylistic elements to be mentioned: In the second line of v. 1, the exact parallelism is interrupted by the anacoluthon which fits perfectly with the light breaking forth. The many vocables used as symbols of foreign domination in v. 3—yoke, pulling bar, staff, that which weighs heavy—all help to describe the ways the people had to suffer ever-increasing indignities. The personification of the soldier's boot in v. 4 characterizes the enemy force as a power which has no mercy, is inhumane, and is not susceptible to any emotions of compassion. The song is thus not only very important because of the nature of its content, but also because it is a pearl of Hebrew poetry.

Setting

The authenticity of the section has also been questioned, just as was the case for 2:2ff.; see, most recently, Vollmer. Since the relationship between 8:23aβb and what follows is not established, at first, 9:1–6 will be studied independently. Among recent scholars, Duhm, Kissane, Steinmann, Lindblom, Eichrodt, Kraus, Müller, Zimmerli, Wolff, Kaiser, Leslie,

Eissfeldt *(Introduction),* Herrmann, von Rad, Schildenberger, Mauchline, Montagnini, Becker, Coppens, et al. consider it to be Isaianic, whereas Marti, Gray, Mowinckel, Fohrer, Lescow, Treves, Vollmer, et al. consider it to have come from another author, generally a later one, and most often date it in the postexilic era.

The reasons for denying the authenticity are manifold and the weight given to various reasons has changed during the history of the study of the text. Marti cites six points which he considers to be sufficient as reasons for his point of view: (1) Isaiah had not set his hope on the house of the king or on a political organization, but rather on a religious fellowship (at which point Marti makes reference to 8:16–18)—completely missing the point about the nature of Isaiah's message, which could have never spoken of faith without a link to some political reality. (2) The "jealousy of Yahweh" was not a motif which gave any comfort to the older prophets, but is a motif which first brings hope for Israel at the time of Ezekiel. But the only way in which one could deny that such a thought would be appropriate for Isaiah would be if he would be characterized as someone who only announced doom. What he proclaims for Assyria in 30:27–33, for example, should certainly be interpreted, based on its subject matter, as the "jealousy" of Yahweh against Israel's enemies; see also Zeph. 1:18 (3:8) and cf. Brongers, op. cit., 279. (3) The entire people, not only a group from within its midst, finds itself in a miserable situation; thus, the message could not possibly be appropriate for the time of Isaiah. But that is a matter of interpretation and must take into account the specific details which one encounters in 9:1. (4) The family of David, at the time when this prediction was made in 9:1ff., did not have any family members reigning any more. But this section does not mention anything about that matter. (5) Neither Jeremiah nor Ezekiel seems to have known anything at all about such a promise. We do not know anything about that, but it is clear that the pre-exilic prophets made no attempts to quote the prophecies of their predecessors. (6) The section is placed at the conclusion of a small collection, which, as the others, seems to demand that one look toward a future time when there would be joy (on this, see G. Fohrer, *Studien zur alttestamentlichen Prophetie,* BZAW 99 [1967] 117ff., esp. 125). But one must be careful how such a schematization is used; even if the section did play a role as these small units were put together, there is still no proof that all of the concluding sections which have a hopeful outlook must be treated as inauthentic.

These reasons, typical of the ones used in the initial phase of literary criticism, simply do not hold up and do not play a very important role any longer. Mowinckel, op. cit., who is not completely ready to deny that Isaiah is the author, sees as the main reason for such denial the fact that the author here, contrary to what is otherwise always true of Isaiah, does not link the promise to any confession and repentance (109f.; similarly Lescow, op. cit., 186f.). One cannot counteract that argument here by citing 2:2ff. and 11:1ff., since those who deny 9:1ff. to Isaiah also deny that the other two sections are authentic. In fact, it is basically correct to say that, for Isaiah, there is no salvation without confession and repentance (Lescow refers to 30:5 as a key verse; see also G. Fohrer, FS W. Eilers [1967] 66f.). The only question is whether he felt it absolutely necessary to speak explicitly about that in every situation and in the presence of every single group of listeners. He certainly does not mention it in passages such as 14:24–27 or 30:27–33, and even in 31:4ff. the main emphasis is placed on the promise; what is more, even in cases where the call to repentance is mentioned, it is still not formulated so as to make it the basic prerequisite for Yahweh coming to help.

If one considers the passage to be inauthentic, then assigning a date poses a most difficult problem. Mowinckel (op. cit., 110) thinks this comes from a group of Isaiah's disciples, so that the message was linked with the Isaianic traditions at a very early stage of development. Lescow suspects that the poem reflects on Sennacherib's pull-out and could very well have come from the circles of the prophets of salvation in Jerusalem. Fohrer and others think that this is a postexilic eschatological prophecy. But none of these situations furnishes a close parallel to Isa. 9:1ff. The ideology of kingship, which has been recorded in vv. 5f., is found else-where primarily in the kingship psalms, which are considered today, in contrast to earlier phases of literary criticism, to have originated at the time when the kings were actually ruling. Isa. 7:1ff. provides sufficient evidence that Isaiah knew about the carefully shaped religious viewpoint concerning kingship which was held by those in the palace in Jerusalem, and had struggled with that interpretation in light of the actual historical circumstances. (This section should not be interpreted on the basis of what it would mean in later eschatology.) The concepts connected with kingship, as they are depicted by the "throne names," would probably not have been quite as real during the time after the exile, so that a later prophet could not have expected his listeners or readers would have understood what he meant as regards these concepts. In fact, the versions show that those who confronted this text in a later time were basically lost when it came to getting at what was originally intended (concerning the messianic ideas in the postexilic era, see Coppens [LD 54] 31ff.).

As far as the vocabulary is concerned, Lescow himself concludes that there is "nothing in terms of the actual speech which can be used to clearly show that Isaiah is not the author." The terminology, as a matter of fact, is exactly what Isaiah uses elsewhere: concerning אור (light) and חשך (darkness), see 5:20; for הרבה הגילה (make much of the jubilation), cf. הרבה תפלה (pray over and over) in 1:15; for הגדיל השמחה (the joy is great), see 28:29; for קציר (harvest), see 17:5; 18:4f.; for שלל (pillage) see 8:1–4; 10:2; for מטה (pulling bar) and שבט (staff), see 10:5, 15; 28:27; 30:31f.; for שבט (staff) being used just by itself, see 14:29; for חתת (smash), see 8:9; 30:31; 31:4; for שרפה (firebrand), see 1:7; for מאכלת אש (consumed by the fire), see 9:18; for ילד (child), see 8:18 (object of נתן, give); for על שכמו (upon his shoulder), cf. 22:22; for קרא שם (call out his name), see 7:14; 8:3; for פלא יועץ (planner of wonders), cf. 28:29; 29:14; for גבור (hero), see 3:2 (cf. 5:22); for אב in the sense of "father of the peoples," see 22:21; for עד with the meaning "eternity," see 30:8; for שר (prince), see 3:3, 4, 14; for כסא (throne), see 6:1; for משפט (justice) and צדקה (righteousness), see 5:7. Even if there are fewer references to contacts with the rest of the tradi-tions of Isaiah in vv. 5f., that is because Isaiah makes use of traditional terms in that section, terms already available to him. In any case, the findings, in terms of vocabulary, are such that, if someone wants to deny that the passage comes from Isaiah, there must be other absolutely con-vincing arguments (for a different view, see Vollmer).

If the passage comes from Isaiah, then the message must fit into a very specific historical constellation—of course during the time of Isaiah. But when one attempts to identify the particular circumstances, then one must remember that the actual historical moment in which many messages of the prophets were spoken either cannot be identified or can be identified only with relative certainty. Statements which sound very vague to us would have doubtlessly been very lucid for the listeners who were very familiar with the way they related to particular events of their own day.

In 8:23aβb it is announced that a major turning point is at hand. The specifics are detailed in 9:1–4: It will take place as a people now sitting in darkness will be freed. This promise breaks down into three parts, 8:23aβb, 9:1–4, and vv. 5f. The message could come to a conclusion with v. 4; one does not really expect it to continue after מַאֲכֹלֶת אֵשׁ (consumed by the fire); cf. a passage like the conclusion of 30:27–33. Because of this, the question is raised about which of these smaller units make the main point. In vv. 1–4, the major turning point to be anticipated will come when Yahweh frees the people. But in vv. 5f., it seems that great salvation comes not because of Yahweh's help, but at the birth of the prince. However, the כִּי (for), at the beginning of vv. 5f., shows that the second part is subordinated to the first. Contrary to what some others have suggested, this כִּי (for) is not of equal importance with the other two uses of the particle, at the beginning of vv. 3 and 4. What is described by vv. 1–4 is not present reality (concerning the perfects, see above, on the form of these verses). But even v. 5a speaks about an event which has already occurred, and both vv. 5 and 6 (up to וְעַד עוֹלָם, even into eternity) apparently mention the reason why the people might be open to this great hope. Of course, it is not the deepest reason—that is the קִנְאָה (zeal) of Yahweh—but it is the reason which one can comprehend intellectually. In other words: The birth of the royal child is—just as the birth of Immanuel in 7:14—the "sign" which is able to help everyone recognize what Yahweh's faithfulness is all about. What is different from 7:14 is that the sign is only expected there, but here it has already become real.

But does the nature of this promise make any sense, based on the text of Isaiah? What is the great turning point which is announced in 8:23aβ—9:4? Most interpreters, even those who deny that this is from Isaiah, lean in the direction of suggesting that Assyria is the enemy whose yoke is to be broken. The Akkadian loanword סְאוֹן (boot) has been frequently cited as an indicator that this is what is meant (on this, see below, commentary on 9:4). In actual fact, it is very likely that Isaiah did not just happen to use an Akkadian word by chance. Another point must also be noted: Isaiah's other depictions of the mighty Assyrian empire (5:26–29; 10:3f.; 10:28–34; 14:24–27; 17:12–14) fit very well with the description of the enemy in this passage; one might also refer to 10:27, where a commentator specifically refers to Assyria by using 9:3.

Who is the one who is addressed in this message? In connection with his interpretation that 8:23aβb refers to the Assyrian annexation of northern and eastern Israel in the year 732, Alt (op. cit., 221f.) suggests that heralds had come into that area from Jerusalem, to announce the imminent deliverance of that region. However, even if one ignores the fact that it would have been highly unlikely for such a message to receive a favorable hearing in that region, which had been occupied by an enemy, it is even less likely that there—at a time when the Northern Kingdom as such had not yet come to its final end—the message about the birth (or, according to Alt: the enthronement) of a new member of the Davidic family would have been seen as providing much comfort. But, above all else, it would seem that there is hardly another option except to take לנו (unto us) in v. 5a as a reference to the inhabitants of Jerusalem/Judah. There have been frequent attempts to connect this message with some particular calamity there. But that causes certain problems: It is true that the cities of the land of Judah came under the foreign domination of the Assyrians when Sennacherib went up against Jerusalem and the heavy hand of Assyria was also upon Jerusalem in the days which followed (see the Taylor-cylinder III 12ff.; *AOT* 353f.; *ANET* 288). But 22:1ff. seems to make it most unlikely that Isaiah would have spoken in such hopeful tones so soon after 701. Because of this, others (see Wolff, op. cit., 62) focus rather on the time between 705–701, as Hezekiah prepared for battle against Assyria. However, that would mean that Isaiah was chiefly to blame for Hezekiah's rebellion against Assyria, which does not seem likely. Thus, one must still side with Alt and conclude that Isaiah announces the deliverance of the subjugated territories in the Northern Kingdom from Tiglath-Pileser. This interpretation seems to make sense by the very fact that 9:1–6 comes at the conclusion of a collection of messages from Isaiah, from the time just before and after 733. Evidence to support this comes from the mention of the day of Midian in v. 3. It would not make any sense for Isaiah, who hails from Jerusalem, to refer to something linked to the Gideon traditions if he was speaking about an event which concerned Judah/Jerusalem. Even if the inhabitants of that region are not directly addressed, the prophet still makes reference to their distress. Because of the sympathy which the people of Jerusalem felt during the present oppression of the Northern Kingdom, the loss of that territory must have caused deep dismay. We can say, then, that 8:23aβ— 9:6 is the message which Isaiah spoke when addressing that situation.

Commentary

[8:23aβb] In addition to the textual difficulties, the understanding of 8:23aβb is made more problematic by uncertainty about the meaning of the two verbs הקל and הכביד, and additionally by the problem of what is meant by their use as perfects. There is no question that הקל can mean "lighten" or "make lighter" (1 Sam. 6:5; Jonah 1:5, and often elsewhere). But it is just as obvious that it also means "treat despicably" (2 Sam. 19:44; Isa. 23:9; Ezek. 22:7). The same is true of הכביד, which means, on the one hand, "make heavy, put on a heavy burden," or "make stubborn," but, on the other hand, at least in Jer. 30:19, means "make important, bring honor." Therefore, these two verbs can certainly be used as parallel expressions. However, the fact that earlier time is contrasted to later time eliminates this possibility (for a different view, see Ginsberg, "An Unrecognized Allusion to Kings Pekah and Hoshea of Israel," ErIsr 5 [1958] 61*–65*; Emerton, op. cit., 156ff.). But how might one understand them as terms which set up a contrast? Is the difficult way things turned out in the past contrasted with the easy time which one will have in the coming time of salvation, or is it just the opposite? The first possibility seems the most likely (see above, commentary on 1:26, concerning the antithesis of earlier/later time). הקל, whenever it is used in the sense of "lighten," uses מִן (from), without exception, whereas, when it means "treat despicably," as in the present passage, it is simply rendered with the accusative (Ezek. 22:7 with בְּ). On the other hand, it can certainly be said that a yoke can be made very "heavy" upon a people (1 Kings 12:10, 14, and often elsewhere; cf. also Hab. 2:6), but it is never said that the people itself or its land will be "made heavy." A study of the linguistic usage of the two verbs shows very clearly that v. 23aβb must be describing the announcement of a sudden change, from disaster to salvation.

There is still the problem with the tense. It would seem that the solution just offered would be at odds with the use of הכביד (here: will bring glory) in the perfect. And yet, this stands exactly parallel to the perfects in 9:1ff., and should be interpreted here in the same way as in those verses (see above, on the form of this passage). It is possible to use the perfect because the birth of the royal child is the event which already sets this radical shift in motion.

Even if Alt's textual reconstruction, outlined above, remains somewhat uncertain, he has still basically pointed to the right way to understand these verses. The "humiliation" of the tribal territories belonging to Zebulun and Naphtali, which Isaiah mentions, refers almost certainly to Tiglath-Pileser's conquest of the Israelite region, as described in 2 Kings 15:29. There, of course, Gilead is also mentioned and nothing in v. 23aβ corresponds with that. Thus, it is possible that the present text we have from Isaiah has come to us in a shortened form, as Alt suggests. But the prophet is also not under any obligation to chart out the exact borders of the territory he has in mind. And yet, v. 23b, which reiterates which territory is to receive honor, does mention three areas and the East-Jordan territory is described as עבר הירדן. E. Forrer (*Die Provinzeinteilung des assyrischen Reiches* [1921] 59ff., 69), on the basis of a very detailed study of the Assyrian annals, found out that, at that time, not only were Galilee and the land east of the Jordan incorporated into the Assyrian empire—a fact which had long been known from 2 Kings 15:29—but the coastal regions of Palestine, insofar as they belonged to Israel, were also incorporated into that empire (concerning this, see also A. Alt, "Das System der assyrischen Provinzen auf dem Boden des Reiches Israel," *KlSchr* II, 188–205). In fact, according to him, one must take into account that three Assyrian provinces were established: *du'ru* (= Dor, today *el burǧ* near *eṭ-ṭanṭūra*), *magidū* (= Megiddo, today *tell el-mutesellim*), and probably *gal'azu* (= Gilead; see 2 Kings 15:29). Apparently, that would correspond to Isaiah's גליל הגוים (peoples' province [Galilee of the nations]) (i.e., *magidū*) and עבר הירדן (East-Jordan land [across the Jordan]) (i.e., *gal'azu*). Then, דרך הים (way of the sea) would refer to the territory of the province *du'ru*. Connections have often been made between the דרך הים (way of the sea) and the *via maris*, that is, with the road, as it was later named, going from Damascus through the East-Jordan land and Galilee (see R. Hartmann, *ZDMG* 64 [1910] 694–702 and *ZDPV* 41 [1918] 53–56). And yet, this designation first came into common use in the late Middle Ages and, if this is the case, it is difficult to figure out what is meant by עבר הירדן (across the Jordan) and גליל הגוים (Galilee of the nations). Procksch (ad loc.) helped his case by positing alterations, reading מֵעֵבֶר and גְלִילָה, and translated: "from the land east of the Jordan for the sea road to the region of the heathen," which sounds very artificial. דֶּרֶךְ הַיָּם must refer to the coastal regions south of the Carmel range, as far as Jaffa, which has been referred to at other times as the plain of Sharon.

הַכְבִּיד (will bring glory) can be explained as a denominative from כָּבוֹד (glory) (cf. the *pi'el* כִּבֵּד, honor, glorify; Akkadian *kubbutu,* "treat with honor"). If one studies the verse in isolation, then one must ask how Isaiah could have risked speaking so soon after 732, in such clear tones, about the hope that the lost territory of Israel would be freed. But if the verse is interpreted in connection with 9:1–6, the answer is clear: The birth of the successor to the throne had given Isaiah increased confidence in the faithfulness of God as it applied to Israel. As 7:17 and other passages indicate, the Northern Kingdom played a significant role upon the horizon of his faith.

[9:1] As has been stated above, the prophet uses the vocabulary found in a song of thanks to set forth his promise in vv. 1f. in greater detail. Naturally, this is the reason it is so difficult for us to determine the exact historical situation. Ps. 107:10 speaks of the יֹשְׁבֵי חֹשֶׁךְ וְצַלְמָוֶת, those who were "prisoners in affliction and in irons," but who are now to praise Yahweh, since he has delivered them from both of these troubles (v. 14); cf. also Pss. 23:4; 91:6; 138:7; Job 29:3. On the basis of passages such as Ps. 107:10, 14 and Job 10:21f., אֶרֶץ צַלְמָוֶת (land of darkness) is another way to refer to Sheol. Whoever has to wander in "darkness" is, for all intents and purposes, already in the realm of the underworld (see J. Herrmann, *OLZ* 19 [1916] 110–113 and Chr. Barth, *Die Errettung vom Tode in den individuellen Klage- und Dankliedern des Alten Testaments* [1947] esp. 80). The OT does not only speak of human beings who are close to death finding themselves already in Sheol, but can say the same thing about those who are harshly oppressed by their enemies (cf., as an example, Ps. 18:18, in connection with vv. 5f.).

Since Isaiah uses motifs from the song of thanks, it would be expected that he would now report that Yahweh had freed his people from the bonds of the underworld; cf. Ps. 107:14. He phrases it differently: "they have seen a great light" and "a light shines forth over them." There is a good reason for that: In actual fact, the deliverance has not yet taken place. And yet, in the middle of all the darkness, the people sees a light; see Pss. 27:1; 36:10; 56:14, and cf. 89:16. "Light" is a symbol for the saving presence of God; for one who has lived in integrity, light shines in the darkness (Ps. 112:4; cf. Job 18:5). There is a place of security upon Zion, since Yahweh has fire (אוּר) there (Isa. 31:9). Or: Yahweh is the light of Israel, which will become a fire, which will burn and consume the enemy (10:17). Therefore, whoever "sees a great light" ought to have confidence, even in the darkness in the realm of the dead, to know that the protecting and saving presence of Yahweh is there and one can thus break out in a song of thanks, even if present distress has not as yet been eliminated. The closest parallel to the way terms are used in 9:1 is found in Ps. 18:28f. (= 2 Sam. 22:28f.): "Thou dost deliver a humble people . . . thou dost light my [the king's!] lamp (תָּאִיר), the lord my God lightens (יַגִּיהַ) my darkness." Since Psalm 18 is a "song of thanks of a king" (on this, see

Kraus, BK, ad loc.), it can be presumed that v. 1 already has the events of vv. 5f. in mind: The great light, which gives one cause to hope for a great deliverance, has really already begun to shine, since a child has been born in the royal palace and now shines forth into the darkness of the current pressure-filled days. At most, however, the listeners would have had only some vague notion that this was meant. (Contra Müller, op. cit., 409, there is no mention of an epiphany in v. 1—it does not speak about the appearance of Yahweh, but rather speaks about Yahweh's saving presence.)

[9:2] As is common in a song of thanks, v. 2 addresses Yahweh directly. This makes it clear that God is the actual subject who will bring about the events which are to take place; rather than addressing Yahweh directly, the rest of the verses, except for v. 6b, describe the specific details about what has happened or is about to happen (concerning the alternation between the second and third person, see Gunkel-Begrich, *Einleitung in die Psalmen* [1933] 47). Joy and jubilation have been made great by Yahweh. Whereas שמחה is a term meaning "joy" in a very general sense— in v. 2b the joy at the time of harvest is mentioned as an example—גיל (jubilation) is much more specific; it, along with its derivatives, is used primarily as a technical term within the language of the cult and refers especially to joy before God (cf. לפניך, before you, in v. 2b or a phrase such as אֶל־אֵל שִׂמְחַת גִּילִי, to God my exceeding joy, in Ps. 43:4). Certainly גיל can also refer to the jubilation which a human being expresses as, for example, when someone has overpowered an opponent (Ps. 13:5). But it is much more frequent that one is jubilant about Yahweh's help (יְשׁוּעָה) (Pss. 9:15; 13:6) or about his grace (חֶסֶד) (31:8). Above all, one should pay particular attention to Ps. 21:2: יְהוָה בְּעָזְּךָ יִשְׂמַח־מֶלֶךְ וּבִישׁוּעָתְךָ מַה־יָּגֶיל מְאֹד (In thy strength, the king rejoices, O Yahweh; and in thy help how greatly he exults!). As in that passage, where the king rejoices and is jubilant because of the victory which Yahweh has granted him, so also in this passage the people at the time of Isaiah rejoice at the birth of a new ruler—because that creates a mood of hope for deliverance from the hardships caused by the oppressor.

The magnitude of the joy is underscored by comparisons with two types of rejoicing: rejoicing at harvest time and rejoicing when spoils are divided. קציר refers to the harvest of cereal grains; cf. the jubilation when one brings in the sheaves, Ps. 126:6; see also Pss. 4:8; 65:14, and Dalman, *AuS* III, 43. Since rejoicing when dividing the spoils is used only for comparative purposes, one ought not conclude that Isaiah is raising hopes for spoils of war (and v. 2b cannot be used to justify translating אבי־ עד in v. 5b with "father of booty"). Concerning the expression חלק שלל (when the booty is divided), see Judg. 5:31; Isa. 53:12; Prov. 16:19; concerning the entire matter, cf. Num. 31:25–47; Deut. 20:14; 1 Sam. 30:2f.; 1 Kings 20:39f.; 2 Chron. 20:25, but also Isa. 8:1, 3, and 10:2, 6. The warrior, if he is not a mercenary, can hope to receive only a portion of the spoils as remuneration for all of his effort and peril. Referring to spoils of war can be used to spurn one on to be brave (2 Kings 3:23). If someone has taken much booty, then that person might put on a banquet feast (1 Sam. 30:16). There is hardly any other joy which compares with dividing up the spoils (Ps. 119:162; Prov. 16:19; on this, see C. F. Burney, *JTS* 11 [1910] 438–443; de Vaux, *Ancient Israel,* 255f., and *BHH* 236).

[9:3–5] That about which one is to rejoice has not as yet been mentioned. The three clauses which begin with כִּי (for) (vv. 3, 4, 5) furnish the details. The first two say: One ought to rejoice, because foreign domination has been thrown off. As was explained above, this deliverance is still to come in a future time. For this reason, the third כִּי-clause is added as well: One ought to rejoice already now, with abandon, since Yahweh has, so to speak, by means of the son from the line of David, provided a guarantee that there will be a future deliverance.

[9:3] In the entire OT, סֹבֶל (which weighed heavy, burden) is used only in the book of Isaiah (10:27; 14:25), in each case with the transferred meaning foreign domination. The related term סֵבֶל (load, burden) refers to forced labor (1 Kings 11:28; Ps. 81:7; see also Neh. 4:11), which is easy to understand, since prisoners of war and forced laborers were, first and foremost, used for hauling heavy burdens. The "yoke" is much more frequently used as a symbol of foreign domination (Isa. 47:6, and often elsewhere) and for servitude in general (e.g., Jer. 30:8; concerning a yoke being broken to demonstrate deliverance, see Jer. 28:2, and often elsewhere; concerning the form and use of the yoke, see G. Schumacher, *ZDPV* 12 [1889] 159–163; Dalman, *AuS* II, 99–105 and illuss. 21ff. and *BHH* 869). נגש (taskmaster) designates the one who prods pack animals (see Job 39:7) or the overseer of the slaves (see Exod. 5:6, 10, 13f.), but it is also a term for the one who wields power (see above, 3:12), and especially for that particular ruler who misuses the power which has been given to him; see Isa. 14:2, 4; Zech. 10:4. Corresponding to this, the שבט does not refer to the shepherd's staff (Ps. 23:4) nor to the teacher's (Prov. 13:24, and often elsewhere) but it is the staff of the ruler (Gen. 49:10; Judg. 5:14; Isa. 14:5; Amos 1:5, 8; that is, it is the scepter; see below, commentary on 10:5 and *BRL* 329ff.; *BHH* 2234 and F. Willesen, *JSS* 3 [1958] 327–335). Unfortunately, these metaphors do not furnish any specific information about the actual type of oppression and, since they can be used in a very general sense, one must be very careful not to press them too far for help with the identification of historical circumstances. Since Yahweh is the subject of החתת (you have smashed), this verse also does not help with specific details about the way the expected deliverance will take place. It is enough that one knows that Yahweh's zeal for Israel has certainly not been paralyzed.

"As on the day of Midian" accents the fact that the deliverance will take place, even if human beings would give it little chance for success. Yahweh acts in wonderful ways (see below, p. 403, פלא יועץ, planner of wonders). Because the reference is so brief, one cannot know if Isaiah knew the traditions about Gideon's battle in the exact form in which they have come down to us in Judg. 7:9ff. There, of course, the victory is described completely as the activity of Yahweh (see 7:22), and there are also other places where Isaiah views Yahweh's help as a sudden and surprising intervention on the part of God, in situations which look hopeless; see 14:25; 17:13; 29:6f.; 30:31f. The motif belongs to the terminology connected with holy war (see G. von Rad, *Der heilige Krieg in Israel* [1951] 9). It may be that the concept of a battle for the well-protected city of God, away from which the enemy is scattered, may play a role as well; cf. breaking the weapons in Pss. 46:10; 76:4, and, on this, see Müller, op. cit., 409ff.

[9:4] The images of the soldier's boot, which tramples around very noisily, and the robe, which is rolled around in blood, are unique and are beautiful examples of the powerfully imaginative expressions to be found in the way Isaiah speaks. But why are the boots and robes of the enemy not simply taken and used by the victors, particularly since mention has just been made of dividing the spoils? According to the regulations connected with holy war, the property of the enemy was under the ban (see Josh. 7:23ff., where a robe is also mentioned, along with other articles), and what is under the ban is to be burned; cf. Josh. 11:6, 9; Hos. 2:20; Ezek. 39:9f.; Ps. 46:10 (on this, see Kraus, BK XV/1, ad loc.).

סאון (boot) is connected with the Akkadian *šēnu* (also *mešēnu*); see also Ahikar 206 and, according to Kraeling, possibly *ArPap* 2:5 (משאן) and possibly also the Ugaritic *s'n;* on this, see J. Friedrich, *Or* 12 (1943) 20. Concerning מאכלת אש (consumed by the fire), see above, commentary on 9:18. The expression fits well with והיה לשרפה (falls to the firebrand). But one ought to note that, according to the royal psalm of thanks, Psalm 18 (v. 9 = 2 Sam. 22:9), which refers to the appearance of Yahweh when he hurries to the aid of the king, a destroying fire will come forth from his mouth (אש־מפיו תאכל). According to the other song of thanks of a king (Psalm 21), fire consumes the enemy when God appears (v. 10: ותאכלם אש . . .). That confirms the fact that vv. 1–4 are connected basically, in traditio-historical terms, with expressions which are common in the song of thanks of a king, even if there are elements of holy war which are inserted as well.

[9:5, 6] This joyful hope is appropriate because of the event of the birth of the royal child. At least, that is the traditional way the section has been understood—and v. 5aα practically forces one to accept this conclusion. However, v. 5aβb seems to have in mind the act of enthronement for a new ruler: The names which are given to the child are just like the "great names" which were given to the Pharaoh in Egypt when he was enthroned (see below). In the same light, the phrase "the sovereign authority came upon his shoulder" (cf. the imperfect consecutive) seems to be out of place in the context of a ceremony celebrating a birth.

These observations caused Alt (op. cit., 217ff.) to interpret v. 5aα ("to us a child is born, a son is given to us") on the basis of Ps. 2:7; thus he believes reference is being made to the action of adoption of the king as the son of God, within the context of the ritual of celebration at the enthronement. This interpretation is misleading, since this is the only explanation which seems to preserve the unity of the entire section so that it fits one specific time period. But this is simply untenable. Certainly, the king can be called the son of Yahweh, but he cannot simply be called a son. He is never called a ילד, "child," or even "child of Yahweh." ילד (child) stands at the beginning and cannot be understood, by forcing the *parallelismus membrorum,* to be vaguely synonymous in meaning to בן (son); on this, see Coppens, *Mémorial A. Gelin,* 99ff. and *Messianisme,* 80;

Kraus, op. cit., 45ff.; and Lescow, op. cit., 183f. Further, 7:14 speaks of the anticipated birth, not about Immanuel being enthroned. It would be difficult to understand the great event in 9:1ff. as the enthronement instead of the birth, providing, as it does, a demonstration of the trustworthiness of the promise to the house of David. Names such as Jonathan ("Yahweh has *given*") have the intention of giving evidence of one's thankfulness on the occasion of the birth of a son and, in 8:18, Isaiah speaks of the children, ילדים, whom the Lord *had given* him. According to Alt's interpretation, Yahweh himself would have to be the speaker in vv. 5f., which would mean that an oracle of God is being quoted. But then, one would not expect לנו (to us) but rather לי (to me), since, unlike 6:8, there is no evidence here that this describes an assembly in the presence of God, which could have justified reading לנו (to us). But even if one ignores לנו (to us), the passives which are used in the expressions make no sense since, according to Alt, it would be saying something such as: "I have installed a son for myself"; see Ps. 2:6. These reflections also call Lescow's argumentation into question, since he cites 1 Kings 13:2 as evidence that this passage does not deal with the birth but with the appearance of a "shoot" from the Davidic family line (op. cit., 184f.).

There is no question that v. 5aα speaks about the birth of a child, through whom the house of David is assured that the line of succession will continue. However, in opposition to the traditional interpretation, this birth is not in the distant future but has possibly already occurred, as the imperfect consecutive וַתְּהִי (came) clearly demonstrates. For human beings under the pressure of hard bondage, it would be small comfort to expect that some time, after decades or centuries, a sudden change would result in life getting better.

Of course, there is no evidence in the OT that the birth of a child in the royal palace was celebrated as a saving event. The basic attitude of the Israelite faith, which by and large kept a somewhat cool distance from the institution of kingship, would also not lead one to presume that the birth of a prince, even if he would be heir to the throne, would have been accorded strong religious value. But no one could doubt that, at the very least, those who belonged to the palace circles would have festively greeted the birth of a princely heir. The royal psalms show that the ancient Near Eastern viewpoint about sacred kingship was not completely unknown. Thus, it might be presumed that it was not only when a king was enthroned (Psalms 2, 110) but also on the occasion of a celebration of the birth of an heir to the throne that elements of kingship ideology, as confessed in the region surrounding Israel, would have also come into play.

Great expectations were attached to the arrival of a king in the ancient Near East, as is illustrated by the prophecy of the priest Nefer-rohu to king Snefru (fourth dynasty; see *AOT* 47f. = *ANET*[3] 445f.). After the depiction of the evil time of lawlessness in the "land of topsy-turvy," it is said: "A king will come, belonging to the South, Ameni, the triumphant, his name. He is the son of a woman of the land of Nubia; he is one born in Upper Egypt. He will take the [White] Crown; he will wear the Red Crown.... Rejoice, ye people of his time! The son of a man will make his name forever and ever.... And justice will come into its place.... Rejoice, he who may behold [this] ..." (cited from *ANET*). This text was composed during the second half of the second millennium, but it is based on earlier copies and, in fact, it does not speak of the birth of a royal child but of that child's appearance in Egypt. The case is different with the "Myth of the Birth of the Pharaoh": At the exact moment of the procreation by the action of the god, the oracle goes out: "It has been spoken by Amon . . . to her [to the king's wife and king's mother] Jahmes: Hatshepsut-Henemet-Amon is the name of this son [sic, even though one would expect 'daughter'; these sentences are very stylized], whom I have placed in [your] body. . . . She will carry out the beneficial actions of this kingdom throughout the whole land. My Ba belongs to her, my [power] belongs to her; my appearance (?) belongs to her. . . . I have united the two lands for her, with all her names upon the throne of Horus the living one. I will attach my protection to her daily, together with the god of each respective day" (H. Brunner, op. cit., 43f.). After the birth, the majestic god comes to see his beloved daughter. He acknowledges that she is his child: "*njnj* [actually: 'welcome'] my daughter from my body, Maat-Ka-Re, my brightly shining likeness, who has gone forth out of me. You are a king, who takes both lands as a possession, upon the throne of Horus, just as does Re. . . . I hereby give you all life, all welfare, all health, as your protection" (ibid., 109f.; see also 121). And in a further scene the god says: "Be welcome before me, be welcome in peace. . . . You are a king, who conquers and who appears eternally upon the throne of Horus the living one. She is kissed, she is hugged, she is taken upon the lap, [for] he has taken a fancy to her above all other things" (ibid., 117f.). With this action, the legitimacy of the heir to the throne is apparently recognized. Once again, in a later scene, which takes place under the sun disk, the child is officially accorded the future honors of a king: "He gives all life, all continuation and all welfare, all health, all largeness of heart upon the throne of Horus, since she leads all the living, since she possesses the crown, . . . since she rules over both of the lands in largeness of heart" (ibid., 149; see also 193. Cf. also E. Brunner-Traut, "Die Segnungen des Gottes Ptah," *ZRGG* 100 and G. Roeder, *Urkunden zur Religion des alten Ägypten* [1923] 158–163).

It goes without saying that there is considerable distance between Isaiah's promise and this highly mythological text. Isaiah says nothing about the procreation of the son by a divine father and 9:5f. is also not a divine oracle, but rather reflects the attitude of the palace as it is openly proclaimed to the public. But it is certainly possible that one should reckon with the possibility that oracles in the royal palace accompanied the birth of a prince, which might not have sounded all that different from the Egyptian traditions. In any case, these Egyptian texts are instructive when one seeks to understand the message of Isaiah. Above all, it is important to see that, as is true for the Egyptian texts, there is mention of according kingly honor already at the time of the birth—without being ignorant of the fact that there would have to be a long wait until that child was enthroned.

Brunner, on the basis of the rather unclear description of the Egyptian events, posits some "act of putting on clothing" under the winged sun disk, which means that "there might be some form of 'investiture'" (150f.). This would explain how Isaiah could say, right after the announcement of the birth of the child: "and the sovereign authority came upon his shoulder." This sentence does not assert something about enthronement but must be interpreted as an act of investiture, by means of which the child is officially elevated to the status of crown prince and is proclaimed the future ruler. There is no doubt that there was a corresponding rite, namely, the bestowal of the ruler's insignia. Duhm and Marti (ad loc.) think that it was a prince's robe, placed around the shoulders of the child.

It is more difficult to understand how Isaiah could mention the throne names, which so clearly belong to the festival of the enthronement in Egypt (see Wildberger, op. cit., 325ff.). The difficulty is exacerbated if one accepts the suggestion (see above, textual note 5c) to read, instead of the imperfect consecutive וַיִּקְרָא (and he called), rather the simple imperfect יִקְרָא (and he will call) or accepts the reading in Qᵃ, וקרא (and he will call). It is quite easy to understand how there could be a shift in pointing, right after the previous וַתְּהִי (came, was). Of course, this conjecture is not beyond doubt; it is also not absolutely necessary for the understanding of the text. Bestowing an important name, which underscores the importance of the child, plays a significant role already at the time of the birth, as the quotations from the "Myth of the Birth of the Pharaoh" demonstrate. Moreover, it is not all that certain whether it was even a practice that throne names were conferred in Jerusalem (cf. Wildberger, op. cit., 319ff.), and, if this practice did occur, magnificent names, such as are used in the present passage in Isaiah, were certainly not generally bestowed upon the king. One must suppose, whether one leaves the imperfect consecutive וַיִּקְרָא (and called out) or not, that Isaiah adapts a practice which was common within the palace but, because of his hope for a new era, takes the essence of the practice and radically reshapes it. If one leaves the text as it is, then this depicts what already took place at the celebration of the birth of the successor to the throne, who was accorded certain titles already at that time, similar to those which were given the Pharaoh in Egypt when he was enthroned.

Therefore, one might venture the following conclusion: 9:5 must be understood as a prophetic imitation of a proclamation from the palace in Jerusalem; this imitation follows the pattern of what took place, soon after the birth of a royal child, on the occasion of his investiture with the honors due to a crown prince. In connection with this, Isaiah used formulations which surpassed what was commonly used in the palace—and which also went beyond what was generally accepted in Israel—but which were at the same level as the concepts about sacral kingship in Egypt, even though we cannot be sure of exactly how he came to know those specific details. In any case, one must remember that Solomon married an Egyptian princess and that Jerusalem was under the overall control of Egypt until it was conquered by David.

For Isaiah the birth of the child and the proclamation that he would be the successor are both a sign and downpayment that Israel could have hope and that foreign domination would not be an unalterable part of its destiny. If succession is ensured, that means the covenant bond between Yahweh and the house of David is still in force. In turn, according to the way the ancients thought, that meant world order was intact and peace could flourish. The kingship is what guarantees this order. Wherever it was able to carry out the specific functions which were assigned to it, then justice, righteousness, and "peace with no end" (v. 6) would some day of necessity be completely realized. Even if that applied in the narrow sense only to the לנו (to us) in the palace, it really applied at the same time to the people as a whole.

The sentence: "And the sovereign authority came upon his shoulder" must be viewed as contrasting to the מוטת שכמו (pulling bar upon his shoulder) in v. 3 (see textual note 3b). What does it mean even now, if peoples rage and nations make plans in vain (Ps. 2:1), as long as the representative of Yahweh carries out his duties in Zion! It has often been noted (see Caspari, op. cit., 290f.; von Rad, *TheolOT* II, 172; and idem, op. cit., 210/213) that the issue is not about the kingly rule but about the משׂרה (sovereign authority) of the one who brings salvation (and thus, it is not about the *king* of peace but about the שׂר שׁלום, prince of peace). That is hardly based on a skepticism which reacted against the kingdom as such, but is the result of how this institution was conceptualized in the ancient Near East. The earthly king is the representative of the heavenly מֶלֶךְ (king), his stand-in on earth (see H. Wildberger, "Das Abbild Gottes," *TZ* 21 [1965] 245–259, 481–501; see 484–488). With respect to the people, he is the מֶלֶךְ (king), but in his relation to God, he is the שׂר (prince), the "representative who rules Yahweh's kingdom." It is completely appropriate that Isaiah, who himself designates Yahweh as the מֶלֶךְ (king) (see above, on 6:5), sees the king in the role of שׂר (prince). Thus, this usage of משׂרה (sovereign authority) and שׂר (prince) is not intended as a deprecation of kingship. That is plain as soon as one sees that v. 6 speaks about the ממלכה (kingdom) of David, without any disclaimers. The ruler in Jerusalem is much more than a king with his own absolute power or one who rules by the will of the people; he carries out God's dominion upon the earth.

Gressmann, *Messias,* 245, already observed that one ought to presume that the practice of giving titles to the Egyptian kings had some impact on giving the names to the royal child in 9:5b. Von Rad (*TLZ* 72 [1947] 215/211f.) thought that it was possible to demonstrate that granting names belonged to the ceremonies connected with the celebration of the enthronement and that, at least in a formal way, Isaiah was dependent upon a tradition which had its roots in Egypt. Finally, Alt, op. cit., 219, pointed out that at least those names which were difficult to understand on the basis of traditions connected with Israel's faith might be rooted in Egypt, and he based that opinion on both the form and the content of the names. In Egypt, bestowing "great" names was a fixed component of the so-called royal protocol (on this, see *RÄRG,* art., "Krönung," and cf. 2 Sam. 7:9 and 1 Kings 1:47). In fact, the full title consisted of five parts. For example, for Harmhab, they were as follows: (1) Mighty Bull, Ready in Plans; (2) Great in Marvels in Karnak; (3) Satisfied with Truth, Creator of the Two Lands; (4) Zeserkheprure (= Beaming Is the Nature of Re), Setepnere (= Chosen by Re); (5) Mernamon (= Loved by Amon), Harmhad (= Horus at the Festival), given life (see Breasted, *ARE* III §29; Wildberger, op. cit., 327). A general survey of all the material shows that practically all of the elements of the throne names have close or distant parallels to the titles bestowed in Egypt and, since none of those names which are placed in this pattern corresponds to any known Hebrew names, there can really be no doubt that the "messianic" names are somehow related to the titles bestowed in Egypt (see also Morenz, op. cit., 74), no matter how difficult it is for us to show the intermediate steps in the process. (For all that, the practice of bestowing such titles was also known in Canaan: *b'l sdk skn bt mlk tġr mlk bny* [Dahood: Legitimate Lord, Governor of the Palace, King of the City, Builder King]; Ugaritic Text 185, lines 4–7; on this, see M. Dahood, *Psalms* I [1966] 11.) In Isaiah's case, whatever would recall the polytheism of Egypt or would not fit in with Israel's faith has been meticulously removed.

Understanding these titles furnishes enough problems, just in terms of the grammar, as has been shown by the uncertainty about how to define the limits of the text and the numerous translation suggestions; on this, see the commentaries of G. del Olmo Lete. Apparently, the names are not all constructed the same way grammatically (that means, they are not all in construct state relationships, as is clear in אֲבִי־עַד, everlasting father, and שַׂר־שָׁלוֹם, prince of peace). The Egyptian names also show a variety in their structure.

The first name is פֶּלֶא יוֹעֵץ (planner of wonders). In order to give it its correct meaning, one must refer to passages such as 28:29 (הִפְלִיא עֵצָה, wonderful in counsel) and 29:14 (see also 25:1: עָשִׂיתָ פֶּלֶא עֵצוֹת, thou hast done wonderful things). Taking these into account shows that פֶּלֶא יוֹעֵץ cannot be divided into two separate titles ("wonder, counselor"), that the name is not to be explained as a noun clause ("the one who gives counsel is a wonder") and is not to be taken to be in the construct state (*"prodigio de consejero,"* a wonder of a counselor; del Olmo Lete, 241; see also Coppens, *Mémorial A. Gelin,* 97, note 34; G. Jeshurun, *JBL* 53 [1934] 384), and shows that יוֹעֵץ cannot be taken in apposition to פֶּלֶא ("a wonder, [namely] one who gives counsel"). פֶּלֶא (wonder) is an accusative object, which is put in the initial position to accentuate it (cf. a phrase such as תְּשֻׁאוֹת מְלֵאָה, full of shoutings, in 22:2). The normal translation of יוֹעֵץ as "one who gives counsel" does not catch the right meaning of the word. The king does not dispense any counsel, but is a ruler, who (as can otherwise be said about Yahweh) plans wonderful, astonishing things (יעץ, counsel, see 28:29) and naturally is also in the position to carry such things out, as noted already by G. Jeshurun. Concerning עֵצָה (counsel), see J. Fichtner (op. cit., Literature, 5:8–24; 10:1–4) 41, the commentary, above, on 5:12b, and Wildberger, "Jesajas Geschichtsverständnis," VTSup 9 (1963) 83–117 (cf. also the titles of Harmhab, to which reference was made, using the names "Ready in Plans" and "Great in Marvels," and see Wildberger, *TZ* 329, note 68). "The messiah had the character, helped by the spirit of counsel, chap. 11:2, to make great decisions, which he would also be able to carry out as אֵל גִּבּוֹר [God's hero]" (Duhm, ad loc.). That the king could be described in just this particular way, as the יוֹעֵץ (planner, counselor), can be proved by Mic. 4:9; cf. also Job 3:14. Normally, of course, God is the only one who makes wonderful plans. Yahweh is the הָאֵל עֹשֵׂה פֶלֶא (the God who workest wonders), Ps. 77:15; see also v. 12; Isa. 29;14; 31:1. When פֶּלֶא (wonders) is used, this is not in the sense of one who does miracles but, on the one hand, it points to the "great deeds" within the history of salvation (Exod. 15:11; Ps. 78:12, and elsewhere) and, on the other hand, it points to rescuing someone out of the type of distress which causes the one who is praying to turn to God in the songs of lament (Pss. 4:4; 17:7; 31:22; cf. 88:11). If the "Messiah" is called the פֶּלֶא יוֹעֵץ (planner of wonders), that means that one can expect him to perform extraordinary deeds within history, similar to God's help as it is given on the "day of Midian" or deliverance from the foreign yoke as proclaimed in vv. 3f.

The second name is אֵל גִּבּוֹר (God's hero). This is also not to be divided into two parts ("God, hero"; thus G. Widengren, *Sakrales Königtum* [1955] 55) and, on the basis of Deut. 10:27; Jer. 32:18, and Neh. 9:32, one also ought not interpret this as a sentence name ("God is a hero") or in a construct-state relationship ("God of a hero" or "hero God"). גִּבּוֹר (hero) is most generally an adjective; see, e.g., אִישׁ גִּבּוֹר (strong man), 1 Sam. 14:52. Del Olmo Lete, op. cit., 240f., suggests interpreting

אל on the basis of the Ugaritic *'ul,* "might," and translates it "strength of a war hero." In spite of the formula יֶשׁ לְאֵל יָד (it is in my power), Gen. 31:29, and often elsewhere, or passages such as Ps. 88:5, it is impossible that the word could mean "strength" in the present combination. אל גבור means nothing less than "mighty God." Of course, in the passages to which reference has been made, Yahweh is called האל הגבור (mighty God); at most, one might ask in connection with Isa. 10:21 whether אל גבור refers to the king and/or the Messiah. But this parallelism corresponds, once again, to the ancient Near Eastern concept of kingship, according to which the king can be depicted by using the same predicates as the divinity whom he represents. Thutmose III can say of himself: "Re himself installed me. . . . I was introduced with all the signs of honor due to a god. . . . His own titles were conferred upon me" (Breasted, *ARE* III §29). The divinity of the king in the ancient Near East is not in any way seen as an encroachment on the majesty of the gods. So that one can avoid a misunderstanding, the Pharaoh in Egypt is often called the "image" of the divinity; cf. Gen. 1:26; 3:5; Ps. 8:6 and, on this, see Wildberger, *TZ* 21 (1965). And it is very obvious that Isaiah has no intention of calling the uniqueness of Yahweh into question, just as a passage such as Ps. 45:7, which practically designates the king as אלהים (divine), would not do this. אל (El) or אלהים (Elohim) can be used in the OT in a rather free way, in the sense of divine beings; see Duhm, ad loc., who refers to Gen. 32:25ff.; 33:10; 2 Sam. 14:17, 20; Zech. 12:8. To designate the "Messiah" as a גבור (hero) is less surprising; see passages such as Pss. 89:20 and 45:4. But in Ps. 24:8, Yahweh is once again called גבור (mighty) and naturally, one can also speak of his גְבוּרָה (might); see, e.g., Isa. 33:13; 63:15; Pss. 54:3; 89:14. The heroic abilities of gods and kings are praised everywhere throughout the ancient Near East; concerning the Mesopotamian region, see, e.g., A. Falkenstein / W. von Soden, *Sumerische und Akkadische Hymnen und Gebete* (1953) 139; for the Egyptian region, see passages such as the beginning of the victory song of MernePtah, *AOT* 21.

אבי־עד can only mean "father of eternity." Without ever being tired of repeating it, the king in the ancient Near East is promised "eternal life." Gressmann, *Messias,* 245, already identified the Egyptian royal titles "prince of eternity" and "lord of unendingness." "As long as the heaven endures, you will endure. . . . Your length of life shall be for all eternity, the length of Re's life as king of both of the lands" (Roeder, op. cit., 72). The courtiers can flatter him by describing his life as continuing ". . . until the ocean (marches) on foot, until the mountains stand up, to go forth and travel by ship . . ." (ibid., 77). But the OT also wishes for the king "eternal life," Ps. 72:5, 17 (see Kraus, BK XV, ad loc.); 2 Sam. 7:16; cf. Pss. 21:5; 132:11–14. Understanding אב (father) is more difficult, chiefly because, when dealing with concepts connected with kingship, God as the father and the king as the son are coordinated terms; see 2 Sam. 7:14. And mention has just been made of the birth of the ילד (child) and בן (son). And yet, the Pharaoh in Egypt is not only called the son but also the "father." Isa. 22:21 shows what sense אב (father) has in the present context: The royal chamberlain plays the role of "father" for the inhabitants of Jerusalem and the house of Judah, which means that he is responsible for making sure that they are protected and that all goes well for them. In connection with Yahweh, the king is indeed the "son" but, in the relationship with the people, he is the "father" in approximately the same way one might speak of "city fathers" in English.

The easiest title to understand is "prince of peace." Alt translates it "welfare official" (op. cit., 219). שלום (peace) should not actually be considered as the opposite of "war." But as is shown by the relationship with vv. 1–4, the basic sense here speaks of peace as freedom from foreign powers who make war; it is guaranteed by a legitimate kingship. A parallel to שר־שלום (prince of peace) is certainly the זֶה שָׁלוֹם in Mic. 5:4 ("lord of peace"?; the text is uncertain), and one is also reminded of the name Absalom. Unfortunately, it is completely uncertain whether "Solomon" was a throne name of David's successor, as Honeyman suggests ("The Evidence for Regnal Names among the Hebrews," *JBL* 67 [1948] 13–25; see 22f.). One need say no more about the king being the one responsible to preserve peace (see Ps. 72:3, 7). But naturally, it is also, and indeed primarily, Yahweh who is the guarantor of peace; cf. the name of the altar in Judg. 6:24, יהוה שלום (Yahweh is peace).

In light of the fact that the royal titles in Egypt have five parts, we assume that there is a fifth name lurking within the apparently damaged beginning of v. 6, which possibly read something like רב המשרה (great in sovereign authority). This emendation is supported by texts written in Egypt. A title of Amenhotep IV reads: "Great in Kingship in [Karnak]" (Breasted, *ARE* II §934; concerning the construction, see also such connected terms as רַב־כֹּחַ, "great in power," Ps. 147:5). Greatness in one's rule is promised to the king again and again in the OT; e.g., Pss. 2:8; 72:7ff.; on this, see Kraus, BK, XV, excursus 1 on Ps. 2:10. Jerusalem is the city of מֶלֶךְ רָב (the great king), Ps. 48:3 (cf. designating the Assyrian king as the *šarru rabû,* great king). Indeed, it may be that Yahweh is meant in Ps. 48:3, not the king; see also Pss. 47:3; 95:3. But if the divinity is the "great king," then it is a natural consequence that his representative on earth is to be praised as "great in his rule" (or, more exactly: "great in his governorship").

What is said about the reign of the future king in v. 6 evolves from the function of the ruler and is based on the throne names: "As for peace, there will be no end over David's throne and over his royal kingdom." Connected with the entire prediction, it would seem that the name "prince of peace" is the most important. Even if, as has just been suggested, שלום (peace) initially refers to freedom from the distress caused by an enemy, the entire expanse and depth of everything which belongs to this must still be taken into account. שלום (peace) provides a foundation for stable order, opening up the possibility for further flourishing developments. Then, the prediction about the child continues: "since he fortifies and supports it with justice and righteousness." The ל before the two infinitives is not final and is also not consecutive, but rather identifies attendant circumstances (see KBL, 465b; Joüon, Gr §124o). It is said of Solomon: He sat himself down upon the throne of his father David, and his kingly rule was greatly strengthened (וַתִּכֹּן מַלְכֻתוֹ מְאֹד, 1 Kings 2:12; see also v. 45. הכין [to fortify it] in the present prediction of Isaiah corresponds essentially to נאמן [be established] in the so-called prediction of Nathan, 2 Sam. 7:16; see above, on the form of 7:4–9 and commentary on 7:9b). But not only the steadfastness and the permanence of rule, but צדקה (righteousness) and משפט (justice) are also part of the foundation, as depicted in the received tradition: Ps. 89:15: צֶדֶק וּמִשְׁפָּט מְכוֹן כִּסְאֶךָ (righteousness and justice are the foundation of thy throne); see also 97:2; Prov. 16:12; 20:18. Of course, the passages in the Psalms speak of the throne of God, but that once again simply points to the statements which describe the correspondence between the divine and human kingdom. H. Brunner, "Gerechtigkeit als Fundament des Thrones," *VT* 8 (1958) 426–428, pointed out that the king's throne in Egyptian depictions rests upon a pedestal which is fashioned in the form of the hieroglyphic sign which is the symbol for *m3'.t,* "righteousness, truth, just divine order." The pedestal is a simplified form of the ancient hill from which the creator god began his work of establishing the type of order which created borders and set limits. *m3'.t* can only be rendered in Hebrew as צדק (righteous) or צדקה (righteousness). If צדקה (righteousness) is the pedestal of the royal throne, that does not only mean that the throne itself will not totter, but that the kingship assures on-going, God-given order in the world, upon which peace, flourishing growth, joy, and blessing all depend (on this, see H. H. Schmid, *Gerechtigkeit als Weltordnung,* BHT 40 [1968] esp. 83–89). However, preceding צדקה (righteousness), משפט (justice) now stands clearly as the most important term. That means that such a basic order becomes visible in the administration of positive aspects of justice, in the sense of a system of justice which allows the insignificant and weak to receive their due as well, in both the political and economic realm (concerning משפט, justice, and צדקה, righteousness, see above, commentary on 5:7b).

It is surprising that, after mention has already been made of the "everlasting father" and the "peace without end," the motif of duration is picked up again, in such rich tones, at the end of the actual prediction: מעתה ועד־עולם (from now on, even into eternity). One must take into account that some of these phrases were used in a very formalized way. All the same, "eternity," in the sense of a strict eschatology, cannot be meant (for another view, Fohrer, *Komm.* 1², 138f., 143; on עולם, eternity, see E. Jenni, "Das Wort Olam," *ZAW* 64 [1952] 197–248, and *ZAW* 65 [1953] 1–34). But it must already be observed that the greatest accent is laid on the sudden change which ushers in the circumstances which are being anticipated.

The concluding sentence, "The zeal of Yahweh of Hosts will accomplish such a thing" holds on to the idea that Yahweh is the provider of the promised salvation, indeed, Yahweh alone. The surprisingly far-reaching expressions about the successor to the throne could arouse the impression that he is the great bringer of salvation. Isaiah protects his message from any such misunderstanding. Since he seems bound to using these exact words, one has an indirect indication that he is not composing vv. 5f., but is adapting long-established traditions. The confidence of faith rests on the solid foundation of God alone or, to be more exact: on Yahweh's קנאה (zeal). The oldest passages which connect the root קנא (be zealous) with Yahweh are Exod. 20:5; 34:14, and Josh. 24:19. Based on these, one presumes that this statement underscores Yahweh's claim to be the only one who has anything to offer when he is compared to all the other gods. But one must note that the קנאה (zeal) of Yahweh does not, as one might suspect on the basis of the frequent translation "jealousy," direct itself against the gods, but rather against unfaithful Israel, which has fallen under their sway. קִנְאָה (zeal) is also not by any means to be taken merely in a negative sense, but can also be used in the *bonam partem* sense, which then means "be zealous," "care deeply for." This is always in the sense of a passionate activity from deep within, which accompanies particular deeds. Where zeal is in action, there is no paralysis, no half-hearted lame effort. The same clause about the קִנְאַת יְהוָה צְבָאוֹת (zeal of Yahweh of Hosts) is also found elsewhere, in Isa. 37:32 (see also 2 Kings 18:31); it seems to be a fixed expression, by means of which the reliability of the prediction is affirmed. "Qin'âh is the totality, the embodiment of all of his [Yahweh's] powers and abilities. . . . A simple *v^eja'aṣ jhwh zô't* would have been enough here. But the more expansive paraphrase has the purpose of laying particular stress on the potency of Yahweh" (Brongers, op. cit., 279). In Isa. 42:13, furthermore, it is Yahweh the גִּבּוֹר (mighty man) whose קִנְאָה ("desire for battle") is mentioned and, in 63:15, Yahweh's קִנְאָה (zeal) is mentioned parallel to his גְּבוּרָה (might). That means that Yahweh's zeal is apparently very much a live topic wherever anyone wants to speak of him as *the* God who hurries to help his people as a hero in battle (see also Isa. 26:11; 59:17; Ezek. 36:5, and elsewhere, and cf. Renaud, op. cit., 126). One can thus practically say: The zeal of Yahweh describes his divine behavior, which he displays as אֵל גִּבּוֹר (hero). Certainly it is not just by chance that קִנְאָה (zeal) is attributed specifically to Yahweh of Hosts (concerning this designation for God, see above, commentary on 1:8–9 and commentary on 6:3).

Purpose and Thrust

This section, 9:1–6, is targeted for a time which addresses a situation full of distress brought on by foreign domination, under which Israel, or at least a portion of it, had to suffer. The message is thus not about an absolute, unalterable, eternal plan of salvation wrought by God. Even if it is incorrect to connect this message with events surrounding the loss of the territory of Israel to the Assyrians, the "darkness" through which the people were traveling would not refer to the human condition in general. Concerning a related issue, this means that the discussion is not about redemption in general, but about an admittedly surprising turn of events within the course of history, an event which could be compared to the "day of Midian" and would call for open celebration.

For this turn of events, the people are purely and simply to thank their God. There is no mention of any active cooperation on the part of the people. The explication of the text showed that a deliverance is being discussed which is analogous to the "salvation" spoken of in Israel's songs of thanks, providing the reason for praising God. But calling to remembrance the way the Midianites were pushed back shows that human activity is not to be completely excluded. There is no more reason to speak about Isaiah calling for quietism here than there was in connection with 7:4ff. But, of course, the confidence can be directed only toward God, and the honor is due exclusively to him.

Concerning other sections in which Isaiah announces deliverance from foreign oppression—30:27–33 comes closest to 9:1–6—what makes this present promise unique is the addition of vv. 5f., where mention is made of the birth of a royal child. According to the evidence which was set forth in the exegetical study, the meaning of this most remarkable addition lies in the fact that it seeks to encourage, so that one trusts the promise just made: By means of the birth of a successor to the throne, Yahweh has once more proclaimed his faithfulness to Israel. The reference to this event serves the same function as the announcement about the Immanuel sign in 7:14. And the message, about which testimony is offered here, is finally the same as there: "With us is God."

Is the child whose birth is announced in 9:5 the son who was promised to the עַלְמָה (almah) in 7:14? Some interpreters suggest as much (see Budde, op. cit., 111; Procksch; Steinmann; Vischer, op. cit., 46; Lindblom, op. cit., 34; H. Ringgren, *The Messiah in the Old Testament* [1956] 30). But in light of the many questions which must remain unanswered, one should proceed at this point only with the greatest caution. However, no matter what, Isaiah is talking about the birth of a crown prince, from the house of David. It has either already taken place or, if ילד (child) and נתן (give) in v. 5a are to be interpreted as prophetic perfects, it will happen in the very near future. That being the case, this section does not speak about a savior at the end of time. In addition, since the help is to be expected from Yahweh alone, it would seem impossible to continue to designate 9:1–6 as a messianic prediction. But one cannot be so quickly done with the issue. In fact, the birth of the royal son is, just as Immanuel in 7:14, to be interpreted as an אות (sign), but not in the same way we understand "sign." It is not only an indictor that Yahweh will act consistently, according to his promises, but is itself already a reality, which can mean nothing less than salvation (on this, see C. Westermann, *Blessing in the Bible and the Life of the Church* [1978] 31f.). Yahweh's zeal for Israel is set in motion. Admittedly, it is not in a chronological but rather in a qualitative sense that the birth of the child is actually an "eschatological" event. It is an assurance that the salvation will really take place.

It is for this reason that Isaiah is able to confer upon the child names which far transcend the historical importance of any of the Davidic kings. One can understand why exegesis has continually suggested that an end-time, mythical figure is envisioned at this point (H. Gressmann, *Messias,* 245; Fohrer, ad loc.), or why the thesis has been brought forth once again that 9:5b deals with names of God himself (Rignell, op. cit., 34), just as, on the other hand, it is easy to understand why some try to remove the mythical import of the names of the child, so that they are left with an innocuous meaning. In reality, the names which have been adapted from the ancient Near Eastern ideology of kingship are used with the intention of testifying to the presence of the transcendent God in the midst of the history of this threatened people of Israel. That which is said about the son of the king in 9:5f. is basically not on a different level than what is said in some of the kingship psalms. When God, according to Psalm 110, says to the Davidic king: "Sit at my right hand," the king in Jerusalem is addressed as the vizier of God. And when Yahweh is able to address the Davidic king as his son (see 2 Sam. 7:14; Ps. 2:7, and elsewhere), then it is not a very big step for him to openly be called a divine being. "Eternity" is also promised for the dominion of the king in other places in the OT, on a seemingly far too grandiose scale. Because of this, it can be assumed that one could have heard predictions from the palace prophets in Jerusalem whenever a successor to the throne was born, probably not sounding all that different from the present words from Isaiah. It would have been unthinkable for Isaiah to make use of the royal ideology from the palace in Jerusalem, an ideology which had unmistakable ties to the concepts of sacral kingship in the ancient Near East, if he had not agreed with the fact that the kingdom of David functioned as a sign and gave expression to Israel's election. Even Ahaz's apparent rejection was incapable of shaking Isaiah's faith. Isaiah does not stand alone in the OT in his assessment that the Davidic kingdom provided the entry point for the divine grace; one might compare Mic. 5:1ff. and Amos 9:11ff. But he is very much at odds with other witnesses to the faith of Israel, above all Hosea. Just as he is able to confer upon Yahweh the title מֶלֶךְ (king) and just as he made use of the ancient Near Eastern motif of a divine mountain in his proclamation, so also, he risks making use of the concept of the kingdom as a "sign" of the saving presence of God among those who belong to him. But Isaiah gave a significant Yahwistic cast to the closing sentence as well, speaking of the zeal of Yahweh as the only real grounds for hope, thus adapting, also there, the mythical traditions about sacral kingship. There is a sharp and clear dividing line which separates these hopes from those regarding what could be expected of the saving actions of the Pharaoh in their broadest sense. The Davidic king is not the bringer of final salvation, but is rather the one who gives the assurance that God has and will still provide salvation. If this is true, one can no longer characterize the throne names as titles which are terms of honor for the king; they are, in harmony with the name Immanuel, actually reinterpreted to become bearers of the message about the great light which will stream forth from God himself, over the people who are in darkness. They praise God, who has raised up this sign (see 11:10) of his faithfulness in the midst of Israel.

We have already mentioned that the widespread term "messianic" is problematic as a designation for this present section. There is no place in the OT which speaks of a מָשִׁיחַ (Messiah) as a savior figure who comes forth out of the transcendent regions and brings world history to an end; see Gressmann, op. cit., 1f. The child, about whose birth Isaiah speaks in this passage, will sit upon the throne of David in Jerusalem. Yet, without a doubt, his birth is a salvation event. The future ahead of him will be more than just a drawn out continuation of the present; it is indeed still history in the normal earthly-human realm, but it is at the same time fulfilled history. What is expected is an on-going condition of salvation (שלום, peace, shalom); cf. the majestic conclusion מעתה ועד עולם (from now on even into eternity). In this connection, the terms messianic and eschatological take on their proper sense.

Was Isaiah's expectation fulfilled? The provinces which Tiglath-Pileser incorporated into his empire were not freed. And whoever the ילד (child) and בן (son) might have been, the hopes which had been brought to life by his birth were only partially fulfilled. But Isaiah's predictions about a ruler from the house of David were not simply put on a shelf after the downfall of the Davidic kingdom, not even when the attempt to restore the Davidic kingdom under the influence of Haggai and Zechariah went for naught. The author of the gospel of Matthew saw the fulfillment of 8:23aβb and 9:1 when Jesus appeared publicly in Galilee (Matt. 4:15f.) without, of course, making use of the overall witness provided by this pericope, and Zechariah's song of praise (Luke 1:79) refers to 9:1, but once again, without giving this passage a specific christological interpretation. On the other hand, Luke 1:32f. alludes to v. 6 and makes the claim that the fulfillment of the prediction of Isaiah took place when the son of Mary was born.

(For 9:7–20, see above, pp. 218–245.)
(For 10:1–4, see above, pp. 213–217.)

Assyria's Arrogance

Literature

K. Fullerton, "The Problem of Isaiah, Chapter 10," *AJSL* 34 (1917/18) 170–84. P. W. Skehan, "A Note on Is 10:11b–12a," *CBQ* 14 (1952) 236. H. Tadmor, "The Campaigns of Sargon II of Assur," *JCS* 12 (1958) 22–40, 77–100. J. Schildenberger, "Das 'Wehe' über den stolzen Weltherrscher Assur," *Sein und Sendung* 30 (1965) 483–489. B. S. Childs, *Isaiah and the Assyrian Crisis*, SBT 2/3 (1967), esp. 39–44. G. Fohrer, "Wandlungen Jesajas," FS W. Eilers (1967) 58–71, here 67–70.

[**Literature update through 1979:** E. Haag, "Prophet und Politik im AT," *TTZ* 80 (1971) 222–246. D. N. Freedman, "The Broken Construct Chain," *Bib* 53 (1972) 534–576. W. Janzen, *Mourning Cry and Woe Oracle*, BZAW 123 (1972), see esp. 54ff., 61f.]

Text

10:5 Woe to Assyria, to my rod of anger,
  [a]in whose hand is my staff of malediction.[a]

6 Against a malicious people I let it loose
  and against the nation, with which I have to[a] be angry, I send for him,
  To despoil[b] the spoil and to plunder the plunderings
  and to trample it down[c] like dung in narrow streets.

7 But *it* does not think of it thus,
  and its inclination does not go that way,
  rather, it has in mind to annihilate and to exterminate peoples—not just an insignificant number.[a]

8 For he says:
  "Is not every one[a] of my princes a king?

9   Is not Calno[a] as Carchemish
  or Hamath as Arpad[b]
    or Samaria as Damascus?"

* * * *

10 [a][As my hand grasped for these idol kingdoms[b]—and their idols are indeed more numerous than those of Jerusalem and Samaria—

11 Can I not, as I dealt with Samaria and its idols, also deal the same way with Jerusalem and its idol images?][a]

411

12 ᵃ[And when the Lord completes his entire work upon Mount Zion
   and in Jerusalem, 'he will'ᵇ bring forth the fruit of the arrogance
   of the Assyrian king and the haughty pride of his eyes,
13 for he says:]ᵃ

         *   *   *   *

    "By the power of my hand I've done it
      and by my wisdom, for I am smart!
    I eliminateᵃ the borders of the peoples,
      and their storehousesᵇ I plunder.ᶜ
    ᵈI knock downᵃ 'into the dust' 'the cities'
      . . . their inhabitants. . . .ᵈ
14 And, just as into a nest, my hand grasped
      for the wealth of the peoples.
    And, as oneᵃ gathers together abandoned eggs,
      I have gathered together the entire earth.
    And there was no one there, who struck with the wings,
      or who opened up the beak and peeped."
15 Shall, therefore, the ax glorify itself over against the one who cuts
      down with it,
    or does the saw magnify itself over against the one who pulls it?
    ᵃ[as if the staff should swingᵇ the one,ᶜ who liftsᵈ 'it'
      or the stick should lift up one who is not wood?ᵉ]ᵃ

5a–a The second line in v. 5 makes no sense (a suggested translation such as that of von Orelli ["he is a staff, since through their mediation comes my ill-will"] ought not be followed). Normally, הוא בידם (it is in their hand) is eliminated and instead of מַטֶּה (staff), the construct form מַטֵּה (staff of) is read. However, if that is done, the second half of the verse is too short. Ginsberg, *JBL* 69 (1950) 54, suggests that the מ in בידם (in their hand) is an enclitic *Mem*, removing the letter and also הוא (it). It would be better to follow Driver, *JTS* 34 (1933) 383, who reads ⟨ו⟩ ומַטֵּא זעמי הוא בידם and translates it: "And the rod of my wrath—it is in their hand." Since, in such genitive relationships, the suffix on the genitive governs the entire thought (so J. Weingreen, "The Construct-Genitive Relation in Hebrew Syntax," *VT* 4 [1954] 50–59), מטה זעמי is to be translated "my staff of malediction" and, correspondingly, שבט אפי as "my rod of anger" (concerning this translation of זעם, malediction, see below, commentary on 10:5).

6a Concerning the construction עם־עברתי (the nation with which I have to be angry), cf. Joüon, Gr §129g.

6b Concerning the form of the infinitive (שְׁלֹל instead of שֹׁל), cf. Joüon, Gr §82k.

6c One should read the *Kethib* לְשִׂימוֹ (to trample it down).

7a Targ translates לא מעט (not just an insignificant number) as לא בחים, "without consideration"; on this, see S. Speier, *TZ* 21 (1965) 312f. and cf. Hab. 1:17b.

8a Concerning יחדו (every one), cf. M. D. Goldman, *AusBR* 1 (1951) 63, who points out that יחד does not only mean "together" but also "alone, separate(ly)."

9a כַּלְנוֹ (Gk: Χαλαννη); in Amos 6:2, it is pointed כַּלְנֵה (Calneh); in cuneiform, it is either *kullani* or *kulnia* (see below, commentary on 10:9); no doubt, the Masoretic pointing is imprecise.

9b Varᴷ\ᵃ and otherwise in the OT, this is pointed אַרְפָּד (Arpad).

10f.a–a Verses 10 and 11 are glosses; see below, on form.

10b It has been suggested that one read האלה (these) instead of האליל (idol), which could be justified if vv. 10f. would be considered Isaianic and would link up directly with what now precedes them. However, it seems that vv. 10f. are an addition, stating that their idolatry caused these cities to fall, which would be most unusual in the middle of the Assyrian's boastful speech. One must stay with האליל (idol).

12f.a–a This verse has also been inserted into the text; see below, on form.

12b The first person in אפקד (I will bring forth) disturbs the train of thought since, in the previous temporal clause, Yahweh is spoken of in the third person. Gk reads ἐπάξει (he will fix, establish); there is little doubt that the MT ought to be changed to read יפקד (he will bring forth), as is done by most commentators.

13a Possibly, instead of ואסיר (I will eliminate), the imperfect consecutive ואסיר (I have eliminated) should be read (see Syr, Targ, Vulg, BHK, and BHS) and then, naturally, also in 13bβ, it should read ואוריד (and I have plundered). This alteration is not absolutely necessary, and it is possible that one might conjecture that, instead of וַתִּמְצָא (my hand grasped) in v. 13, one would read וְתִמְצָא (and my hand will grasp).

13b One should read וַעֲתִידֹתֵיהֶם (their storehouses), along with the Kethib; Qere עַתּוּדֵי, "their rams," in the sense of "their leaders," does not fit very well into the context.

13c Many MSS read שׁוֹסֵיתִי, which is the normal way of writing the verb (*po'el* of שסה, plunder, which corresponds to the Arabic third root form).

13d–d 13bβ is, without a doubt, a very badly damaged text; one suspects we have nothing more than the torso. Gk reads: καὶ σείσω πόλεις κατοικουμένας (and I will shake inhabited cities); Targ: ואחיתית בתקוף ית יתבי כרכין תקיפין ("and I let the inhabitants of fortified cities fall with great force"); Syr: wᵉkabšet mᵉdînātâ dᵉjā-tᵉbān (and I subdued the cities which were inhabited); Vulg: *et detraxi quasi potens in sublimi residentes* (and I have pulled down, as a mighty power on high, inhabitants). According to the Gk and Targ, one would suspect that the text read something like וָאוֹרִיד בֶּעָפָר עָרִים ... יוֹשְׁבֵיהֶם (and I brought down, into the dust, cities . . . their inhabitants) (see Marti); a complete reconstruction of the text is out of the question.

14a The subject of the infinitive in Hebrew is quite often an unnamed "someone"; Joüon, Gr §124s.

15a–a Verse 15b is probably a gloss; see below, on the setting.

15b Concerning the infinitive construction, cf. BrSynt §45.

15c Instead of ואת (and the), on the basis of many MSS and editions, one ought to read את (the).

15d Some MSS, Syr, Vulg read the singular (מְרִימוֹ), which is probably correct; cf. Gk.

15e E. Robertson, *AJSL* 49 (1932/33) 319f., suggests that, instead of the rare לא עץ (not wood), one read instead: לְחֵ(וֹ)ץ, "oppressor." This alteration is not likely since the discussion is apparently about those who use their hands to work with their tools, rather than about political relationships.

Form

There is no doubt that a new section begins with הוי (woe) in v. 5. But there is a difference of opinion about how far it extends; the woe-oracle in v. 5–15 seems to continue naturally with the threat introduced in vv. 16–19 by לכן (for). But these verses are very likely an addition, inserted by another hand; concerning this, see below, on 10:16–19. Someone might object that the woe-oracle about Assyria needs to be followed immediately by a threat of judgment. Such expansions, normally introduced by לכן (for, therefore), are indeed possible (about this see the discussion above, on the form of 5:8–24; 10:1–4), but it is by no means necessary; wherever הוי (woe) is sounded forth, disaster is essentially already being set in motion.

No doubt, vv. 10–12 are an insertion; v. 13 (beginning with בכח, by the power; כי אמר, for he says, at the beginning, is transitional) provides the natural continuation of v. 9. These three verses are prose (in spite of the metrical arrangement found in BHK and BHS). It is most unlikely that Isaiah would have put the words in v. 10 into the mouth of the Assyrian. The phrase מצאה ידי (my hand grasped) has been borrowed by the expander from v. 14.

Though more recent exegetes are rather unified in their opinion about v. 10, many still believe that v. 11 can be considered to be Isaianic (so Marti, Procksch, Hertzberg, Kaiser, Fohrer, Schildenberger, op. cit., 485, and, most recently, also Childs, op. cit., 42f., of course only after he eliminates ולאליליה, and its idols, and ולעצביה, and its idol-images). It is not impossible that the sentence could have come from Isaiah, but it also interrupts the flow of what precedes and follows: The theme of the section is not the threat to Jerusalem but rather the arrogance of Assyria, which has manifested itself against all the peoples and not just specifically against Jerusalem. The verse may be attributed to the same author who wrote v. 10 (so Gray, Duhm, Herntrich, et al.). The fact that the transition from v. 10 to v. 11 is not smooth can be attributed to the ineptitude of the glossator.

On the other hand, v. 12 does not fit together with either v. 10 or v. 11, but it also cannot be considered a continuation of vv. 5-9. It also can hardly have come from Isaiah (see below, commentary on 10:12), which is what one suspects just because of its prosaic form. In any case, it is to be taken by itself and does not belong to the context of the woe-oracle against Assyria.

By their very nature, woe-oracles are very short; one must name the one about whom the woe is uttered, and the one addressed must be characterized briefly, so that the woe seems justified. In this case, the basic form has been expanded. Before the expected description of the downfall of Assyria follows, in vv. 7-9 and 13f., the extent of the task for which Yahweh had selected Assyria is paraphrased in vv. 5f. The characterization of Assyria is handled by the use of imperfect clauses (whereas the normal rule is that the person addressed in the woe is described more specifically by the use of participles in apposition; see 5:8-24; 10:1f.). Then, in vv. 8f and 13f., Isaiah gives the Assyrians, actually, the Assyrian king, the chance to speak for himself—an approach which permits the true nature of his opponent to be unmasked, a tactic the prophet uses again and again; e.g., 3:6; 4:1; 5:19; 22:13; 28:15; see above, commentary on 5:18f. Finally, v. 15 tries to show that the accusation against Assyria makes sense, since it uses a comparison which shows the absurdity of Assyria's conduct.

The poetic power of Isaiah's speech comes out very clearly in this section as well. The prophet is brief and concise as he characterizes the instructions to Assyria by means of the two metaphors "my rod of anger" and "my staff of malediction." He is right on the mark when he uses the imagery of someone gathering eggs to portray this world power's wantonness as it robs and plunders; and he is likewise on the mark when he compares the way Assyria mocked its weak opponents to harming defenseless birds, which cannot even risk making a peep. And, in the place of reflection about the reprehensible nature of the Assyrian pride, he speaks of the ax which praises itself instead of praising the person who wields it when cutting something down.

The meter of the section is very consistent, a rarity, composed almost solely of three-stress bicola. Only v. 6b should be read as a four-stress bicolon or as 2 two-stress bicola. By means of that technique, the first section of the message is clearly demarcated from the following accusation. In the second line of v. 13, עתידתיהם (their storehouses) is to be given two stresses; the third line, which has come down to us in only a fragmentary form, probably was also originally a three-stress bicolon. On the other hand, the last colon in v. 14 is to be read as a seven-stress colon; once again, in the lower portion of this section, this divergence in the length of the verse points out the end of the section. Finally, in v. 15, there are 2 three-stress bicola, but the cola are longer than in the rest of the poem, which means that the progress in thought development is reflected in the external form of the message as well.

Setting

Disregarding vv. 10–12, no one has questioned this as an authentic passage from Isaiah, except for v. 15. Concerning this last verse, Marti thinks that it would fit better with v. 11, Duhm, that it is all a "theological argument." But it is hard to see why v. 15 should be considered "a later judgment about the unreasonableness of Assyrian arrogance" (Marti). The verse fits very well with the theme of Isaiah's woe-oracle, and it is an element of Isaiah's style that he uses proverbial sayings in his proclamation. Nevertheless, v. 25bβ,γ should be treated as a secondary, explanatory gloss to v. 15a, bα. מטה לא־עץ (stick, not wood) sounds rather strange and can hardly be attributed to Isaiah; it is a clumsy attempt to connect v. 15a, bα with v. 5. Above all, the line is not only unnecessary but just about completely obscures the clear imagery which precedes it, which does not need any clarification anyway. Once again, it is certainly Isaiah's style that he could leave his listeners with a simply stated question in 15a, bα; cf., as an example, the way he leaves the reader to his or her own thoughts in 5:29, without any comment.

There is considerable uncertainty about the question of the temporal order of events described in this section. If one considers v. 11 as Isaianic, then one would conclude that it comes from a time when there was a fear that the destiny of Samaria would also overtake Jerusalem. If this is the case, then one would most likely consider it as originating at the time of Sennacherib's invasion into Judah; see Duhm, Marti, Schmidt, Steinmann, Balla, Pfeiffer (*RSO* 32 [1957] 150f.), Fohrer, Eichrodt, Wright, Leslie, Eissfeldt, et al. Since, with the exception of Damascus which had already fallen to the Assyrians in 732, all of the cities in the region of Syria which are mentioned in v. 9 had fallen to Assyria between 722 and 717—that is, during the early period of Sargon—Kaiser, Procksch, Fischer, Ziegler, et al. think it is probably from the years 713–711, when Ashdod started a rebellion against Assyria. However, if, as has been explained above, v. 11 is not Isaianic, then every reason to connect this with Jerusalem is gone. One would expect some specific reference if the message originated during a time when there was an acute threat against the city. But one suspects that Isaiah spoke this particular message at a time when the Assyrians had become the unchallenged overlords of Syria, and it would certainly have been correct to presume that they were making plans to engage in combat with Egypt for control of the entire world. If this be the case, then one would think of the time of Sargon II (722–705), who attributed to himself the victory over Samaria

(*ANET* 284–287 and cf. *AOT* 350–352) and had just recently consolidated his empire by crushing every rebellion in Syria/Palestine. More specific details will be mentioned in the exegesis of the individual verses; see below, commentary on 10:9.

Commentary

[10:5] According to Isaiah, Assyria, which had once again become a world power during the time of Isaiah, had been given the task of bringing the wrath of Yahweh upon Israel (and, one would have to say in this connection: against all peoples). For the prophets, the wrath of Yahweh upon people is a reality, hanging over them like the sword of Damocles; cf. 5:15; 9:11, 16; 10:4; see also 10:25 and 30:27 and, on this, see above, commentary on 9:11b. שֵׁבֶט can refer to the scepter of a ruler, as in Gen. 49:10; Num. 24:17; Judg. 5:14; Isa. 9:3; 11:4; 14:5; Amos 1:5, 8, and often elsewhere. Since Yahweh is "king," his שֵׁבֶט (rod) can certainly function as a symbol of his power as a ruler. Nevertheless, the book of Job also speaks about Yahweh's שֵׁבֶט (rod), 9:34 and 21:9 (cf. also 37:13), but there the background for the imagery about God is in his role as a teacher; cf. Prov. 13:24; 22:15; 23:13f.; 26:3; 29:15; however, in addition to other passages, also 2 Sam. 7:14; 23:21; Isa. 14:29.

Parallel to שֵׁבֶט אַפִּי (rod of my anger), Isaiah also mentions מַטֶּה זַעְמִי (my staff of malediction). These two phrases are not exactly synonymous. מַטֶּה (staff) can also be used when designating the scepter of a ruler, Jer. 48:17; Ezek. 19:11–14; Ps. 110:2, but this can hardly refer to the stick in the hand of the teacher (the word is not found in Proverbs). It apparently refers most specifically to the divining rod, as it is used, among other places, by the magicians in Egypt; Exod. 7:12. But Aaron and Moses also use one; Exod. 4:2–4; 7:9–20; 17:5, and often elsewhere; it can virtually be called the מַטֶּה הָאֱלֹהִים (rod of God) (Exod. 17:9). Thus, one can also speak of מַטֶּה־עֹז (mighty scepter); Jer. 48:17; Ezek. 19:11; Ps. 110:2, the staff which has magical powers within it. As Moses, according to Exod. 17:9, holds the staff of God in his hand and places the onrushing enemy under the ban, in this same way Assyria is given Yahweh's magical rod. This interpretation is supported by the meaning of זַעַם. KBL and HAL offer the translation "malediction," in which case the logical subject is always God, except for Hos. 7:16. Passages such as Isa. 30:27 (Yahweh's lips are full of זַעַם, indignation); Jer. 15:17 (the prophet feels that he has been filled with Yahweh's זַעַם, indignation); and the expression זַעַם לְשׁוֹנָם (insolence of the tongue) in the Hosea passage show that זַעַם, as is commonly done (see Ges-Buhl, Zorell), cannot be translated "anger" or "fury"; one must recognize that this word is making reference to curse-laden maledictions, which are uttered in wrath (cf. Num. 23:7f., where the verb זַעַם, denounce, is parallel to אָרַר, curse, and קָבַב, curse; Prov. 24:24 is similar). If אַף (anger) describes an emotional action, then זַעַם (denounce) is the way it is expressed verbally; it is the word which sets the disaster in motion. However, the concept of the staff of God in human hands, easily seen as having magical connotations in Exod. 17:9, has now become nothing but a simple metaphor, since Assyria's powerful army has actually become the tool being used to carry out God's mission.

[10:6] In v. 6, the commissioning of Assyria is paraphrased by the use of the two verbs שלח (let loose) and צוה (send for) (for these used in parallel, see also Jer. 14:14; 23:32). Yahweh does not have to act directly when carrying out his will. He is surrounded by heavenly powers, whom he can "send"; see Gen. 19:13; Mal. 3:1; Pss. 78:49; 103:20f., and often elsewhere. The natural forces are at his beck and call: fire (Amos 1:4, 7, 10, 12; 2:2, 5) or lightning (Job 36:32, and elsewhere), natural catastrophes, epidemics, wild animals, the sword, or simply the curse. In place of these powers, prophets can also appear (passim). But at a time when mythological thought was on the wane, Yahweh sends an earthly enemy to carry out the full consequences of his judgment; Deut. 28:48; 2 Kings 24:2, just as is the case in the present passage from Isaiah. In the same way, Yahweh can "command" (צוה) his angelic powers, chiefly so that those who belong to him can be protected (Ps. 91:11). It is striking that the OT regularly speaks about "commanding" the נָגִיד (prince) of Israel; 1 Sam. 13:14; 25:30; 2 Sam. 6:21; 1 Kings 1:35; cf. also 2 Sam. 7:11. צוה על עמו ישראל (appoint over his people) must have practically been a fixed formula for commissioning a נגיד (prince) as a tool for the deliverance of the people (on this, compare W. Richter, "Die *nāgīd*-Formel," *BZ* NF 9 [1965] 71–84). It is hardly just by chance that Isaiah used this same terminology when he told how Assyria was ordered to serve as a tool of judgment against Israel. But, instead of עמי (my people), he says עם עברתי (the nation with which I have to be angry) and, parallel to that, גוי חנף (malicious people). חנף was also used by Isaiah in 9:16 (there: godless) to designate the people who had become estranged from God; see above, commentary on 9:16aβ; there, in fact, it is part of his exposition about the wrath of Yahweh. He speaks of Yahweh's עברה (fury) in 9:18. With the exception of these passages in Isaiah, the OT mentions עֶבְרַת יהוה only as part of the formula יום עברת יהוה (day of his fierce anger); Isa. 13:13; Ezek. 7:19; Zeph. 1:18. The wrath which was to be released against Israel's enemies on the Day of Yahweh was now directed against Israel as well, since they had actually become the "people of his fury" (cf. דּוֹר עֶבְרָתוֹ, the generation of his wrath, in Jer. 7:29).

The charge to Assyria was far-reaching according to v. 6b: It was to "despoil spoil" and "plunder plunderings" (concerning שלל, spoil, and בזז, plunder, see above, commentary on 8:1; both of these are also used with an internal object, using nouns of the same root along with the verbs, in Ezek. 38:12), and Israel was to be trampled "like dung in narrow streets." In "the song of the vineyard," Isaiah had threatened Judah/Jerusalem that it would be delivered over to be trampled, מרמס (see also 28:18); in the present passage, Assyria is commissioned to carry out this trampling. The addition, כחמר חוצות (like dung in narrow streets) underscores the fact that Assyria is permitted to go to great lengths to carry out this punishment (cf. the similar expression כַּסוּחָה בְּקֶרֶב חוצות, in the middle of the narrow streets just like dung, in 5:25).

[10:7] One might think that, in light of such terminology, this could refer only to a judgment which would result in absolute destruction, to be inflicted upon all nations. But v. 7 very specifically excludes that as a possible interpretation. Assyria had exceeded the limits which were imposed upon the task it was assigned and had flattered itself by thinking it could use its absolute power to completely destroy (השמיד, annihilate, and הכרית, exterminate) its opponents. As an unrestrained, bloodthirsty brute, it lived life as if it were an unrestrained orgy of destruction, driven to rob and seize, overstepping all bounds of what was right, which might have restrained it from murdering entire peoples. The גוים לא מעט (not just an insignificant number), at the end of v. 7, alludes to the great number of peoples who had fallen victim to Assyria's unbounded desire to conquer land. One can just imagine what feelings would have been aroused in Jerusalem every time the news came that Assyria had taken still more territory. Both of the verbs, חשב (think) and דמה (have an inclination), accent the fact that there is decision and planning (in 14:24, Isaiah uses דמה, have an inclination, purpose, along with יעץ, plan), and לבב (mind, heart) does not mean anything like what one would intend when speaking of "heart" in English; instead, it focuses on the cold calculating עצות (plan) of Assyria, whose own final downfall is announced in 14:24. In fact, there can be no doubt that Assyria followed a definite plan during the time when Isaiah was active, with a carefully laid out policy to conquer land and construct an empire.

What is meant by השמיד (annihilate) is seen most explicitly in the OT as it is used in Deuteronomy (out of sixty-eight occurrences, twenty are found there, another seventeen in the Deuteronomic History; of twenty uses of the *niph'al*, eight are in Deuteronomy and two in the Deuteronomic History); it "designates within the context of the Yahwistic holy war the complete annihilation of the enemy" (H. W. Wolff, BK XIV/2, 204 [Engl: *Joel and Amos,* 168]). A similar distribution is found for הכרית (exterminate): seventy-eight times in the OT, twice in Deuteronomy, eighteen times in the Deuteronomic History (נכרת, be cut off, sixty-seven times in the OT, of those, nine times in the Deuteronomic History). Both of these verbs are used, on the one hand, for describing "exterminating" the peoples of Palestine but, on the other hand, just such an "extermination" is threatened against Israel in case it is unfaithful. Therefore, Isaiah uses the deuteronomic theory of the complete destruction of the peoples just as infrequently as the idea that Yahweh could completely write Israel out of the book of history.

[10:8] The pride of Assyria is illustrated in vv. 8f. and 13f. by quoting the proud thoughts of its king. Such speeches which praise oneself, offered by kings, virtually seem to have achieved a fixed form, which Isaiah employs at this point. One might compare a passage such as Ezek. 27:3: "I am a luxury ship, completely beautiful" (emended text); Ezek. 28:2: "I am a god! I sit in the seat of the gods, in the heart of the seas!"; or Obad. 3: "Who will bring me down to the ground?"; cf. also Isa. 14:13; Jer. 46:8; Ezek. 35:10ff. This praise of oneself seems to shift very quickly to mockery of the gods of the enemy; cf. 1 Kings 20:28; Ezek. 35:13, which also furnishes the pattern which guided the glossator in vv. 10f. On the other hand, one can also speak this way when accusing an enemy of pride because he praises himself (see Jer. 46:8 and cf. 28:2), just as the expander does in so many words in v. 12 (on this, see Childs, op. cit., 88f.).

The Assyrian praises himself: "Is not every one of my princes a king?" Maybe Isaiah knew that in Akkadian, *malku* or *maliku* corresponded to the

Hebrew מֶלֶךְ, which means prince or king of a city, whereas *šarru* corresponded to the Hebrew שַׂר, which designated the king of an entire land. In any case, the Assyrians allowed the conquered little kings in the Syrian region to keep their proud title מֶלֶךְ. Thus, one of the vassals of Tiglath-Pileser, Panammu of Sam'al *(senğirli):* "I ran by the wheel of my lord, the king of Assyria, among mighty kings (מֶלְכִן רברבן), possessors of silver and possessors of gold" (*KAI* no. 216, lines 8ff.). Or Ashurbanipal reports: "During my campaign, twenty-two kings from the seacoast, from the midst of the sea, and from the inland region, servants submissive to me, brought to me their weighty gifts and kissed my feet" (Streck, VAB VII/2 [1916] 9).

In v. 9, Isaiah allows the Assyrian to praise himself for all of his conquests, with Carchemish, Calno, Arpad, Hamath, Damascus, and Samaria being mentioned as examples.

[10:9] The destiny of these cities during the Assyrian period is rather well known to us. Carchemish (Assyrian: *karkamis, gargamiš,* or something similar; presently *ğerāblus*) is on the middle Euphrates, on the present-day border between Syria and Turkey, having been an important center of late Hittite culture; it was vanquished by Sargon in the year 717. It had already been dependent upon Assyria in earlier times, but had secretly established ties with Midas of Phrygia, which Sargon used as the reason for subjugating it and incorporating its territory as a province of his own state (see his annals, *ANET* 285).

Calno, not to be confused with the Calneh which was, according to Gen. 10:10, apparently in the land of Shinar (called כַּלְנֵה, but this supposedly resulted from a textual corruption), but identical with the כַּלְנֵה (Calneh) mentioned in Amos 6:2, cannot be located with certainty; it might be the city in northern Syria which is called in Akkadian either *kullani* or *kulnia* (concerning its location, see K. Elliger, FS Eissfeldt [1947] 97, who seeks its location along the coastal region near Antioch, whereas others, e.g., W. F. Albright, *JNES* 3 [1944] 254f., identify it with Kullanköy, north of Aleppo, while I. J. Gelb, *AJSL* 51 [1934/35] 189–191, thinks he has discovered it 16 km. south of *tell refad*). It had already been conquered by Tiglath-Pileser in 738, but might have been taken once again in 717, when Carchemish fell (see Procksch, ad loc.).

Arpad (Akkadian *arpadda*) was certainly located at what is known today as *tell refad* (also written as *refād, erfād,* or *rif'at*), 30 km. north of Aleppo. Just as Calneh, it had already been conquered by Tiglath-Pileser, actually in the year 740, after a two-year siege, but later it also was drawn into the rebellion led by Hamath in 720; see Sargon's annals, *ANET* 284f.; *AOT* 349f. In the OT in general, as in the present passage, it is always mentioned together with Hamath (2 Kings 18:34 + 19:13 = Isa. 36:19 + 37:13; Jer. 49:23). If this was the most important city on the northern high plain of Syria, then Hamath, presently called *hama,* on the Orontes, was the most important in the mid-Syrian interior region. Its hour came in the year 738. The Assyrians reduced its size at that time so that it was left with little more than its immediate surroundings. In 720, Ia'ubidi of Hamath, in a pact with the other Syrian states, sought to break away from Assyrian control. That attempt failed and Hamath was finally integrated into the Assyrian empire.

Damascus (Akkadian *dimašqu,* or something similar), the capital city of the Aramean state which bordered on the southern edge of the territory of Hamath, had been continually under pressure from Assyria since the time of Shalmaneser III (Battle of Qarqar, 854). In 732, it was conquered by Tiglath-Pileser, who had been asked for help by Ahaz of Judah (see above, commentary on 7:4; cf. *AOT* 346), and from that time on served as the capital city of one of the four provinces which were formed when the Aramean kingdom was divided. Isa. 17:1–3 shows how closely Isaiah had followed the fate of Damascus and how critical he thought the fall of that city was, also for Israel.

419

Finally, Samaria (Akkadian *samerina,* or something similar), the capital city of the Northern Kingdom, fell into the hands of the Assyrians in 722, after a three-year siege. According to 2 Kings 17:6, this took place still during the time of Shalmaneser, whereas Sargon II attributes the conquest to himself in his own annals, adding: "I led away as prisoners [27,290 inhabitants] . . . and [settled] therein people from countries which [I] myself [had con]quered. I placed an officer of mine as governor over them and imposed upon them tribute as [is customary] for Assyrian citizens" (*AOT* 348; *ANET* 284). But it is likely that the city was already conquered during the lifetime of Shalmaneser and that Sargon can claim credit only for establishing order once again (see Tadmor, op. cit., 33–40 and cf. R. Labat, *Fischer Weltgeschichte* 4 [1967] 58).

The list is arranged geographically and depicts the unstoppable advances made by the Assyrians as they headed from north to south, in fact, right up to the northern border of Judah. That it begins with Carchemish—it could have begun with Sam'al, which came under Assyrian control in 738—is probably related to the particularly deep impression which this would have left in Jerusalem, as this well-fortified city fell. Hope that one could erect some bulwark against the Assyrian advance was lost after its downfall. It is very likely that the conquest of these two cities, Calno and Carchemish, in 717 was the specific reason for this message from Isaiah. But then, one must suppose that the other cities are mentioned because of events which took place for them during roughly the same time period, or not too long before it, which would include events connected with the rebellion of Ia'ubidi of Hamath, who had entered into a partnership with Hanno of Gaza, joined also by Arpad, Damascus, and Samaria. (Concerning vv. 10–12, see below, pp. 422–424.)

[10:13] כי אמר (for he says) at the beginning of v. 13 picks up the כי יאמר (for he says) from the beginning of v. 8, after the interruption in vv. 9–12. It is clear that it is secondary, as is seen just by the fact that the tense is different. If we ignore that phrase, then v. 13 furnishes a nice continuation to v. 9. If it had appeared that the king in vv. 8f. was just reporting on the list of cities, none of which was willing to knock heads with him, now he starts to praise himself in plain words: "By the power of my hand I've done it" (cf. Deut. 32:27). Meaning much more than "hand" would in English, יד symbolizes power (see above, commentary on 8:11); in fact, it can be used to mean "strength" (see 2 Sam. 8:3; Isa. 28:2; in 2 Kings 11:7, יד actually refers to a detachment of soldiers).

However, along with physical power, there is the closely allied wisdom. In the ancient Near East, it was generally acknowledged that it was one of the charismatic abilities possessed by a king; see 11:2. Ashurbanipal, for example, praises himself, since Nabu has given him wisdom, just as Ninib [Ninurta] and Nergal had given him bravery and incomparable power; see VAG VII/2 (1916) 255. This wisdom manifests itself in drawing up great plans (see above, v. 7, and cf. a similar portrayal of Tiglath-Pileser III in R. Labat, op. cit., 51–58, and cf. פֶּלֶא יוֹעֵץ, planner of wonders, in 9:5) and gives the king the ability to be prepared to deal with the day to day problems which are part of a great empire; cf. 1 Kings 3:9; Prov. 25:1.

"I eliminate the borders of peoples" would hardly just mean that he conquered territories of other peoples and made them subject to him. Assyria instituted a policy which was extremely threatening to the continued existence of the peoples, taking certain groups from the conquered regions into exile and resettling the land with groups from other parts of the empire as part of an overall political plan to achieve long-term pacification within the newly won regions, as is illustrated by the fate of the Northern Kingdom after the fall of Samaria (2 Kings 17:6, 24). But it also did not avoid the practice of establishing new borders for the conquered groups of peoples, as is exemplified by Sennacherib's description of the siege of Jerusalem: "His towns . . . I took away from his country. . . . Thus I reduced his country" (*AOT* 354; *ANET* 288). However, the "borders" of the peoples had been firmly established by the deity, once and for all time; each people had its own "inherited property" which had been assigned to it by the Most High (Deut. 32:8). The borders of the earth were as firmly established by God as the paths of the stars and the passing of the seasons (Ps. 74:16f.). The borders of a city, established on the basis of the four directions, "exist on the basis of a direct relationship with overall world order; the city is divided into four parts, just as is the world" (G. van der Leeuw, *Phänomenologie der Religion* [1956²] 454). Merely infringing upon the borders of someone's property would put one under a most terrible curse: Deut. 19:14; 27:17; Job 24:2; cf. Prov. 22:28; 23:10 (see the parallels with Amen-em-Opet, *AOT* 40 = *ANET* 422). Thus, Assyria shaped a policy which did not only include the normal policies of conquest, but went further to commit unheard-of deeds of wickedness. The verb שׁסה (plunder) is apparently to be understood in this way as well. It is seemingly a stronger word than שׁלל (spoil) or בזז (take booty). Certainly there would always be plundering, an unavoidable phenomenon which accompanies war and, according to v. 6, Assyria did nothing to stop war booty from being seized. But it can hardly be just by chance that 13bβ uses a different term than 6bα. Seizing gold, silver, weapons, and similar things is not the same thing as plundering the food supplies which have been set aside, without which the population would be left to die of starvation. Deut. 20:19 forbids the destruction of the fruit trees around a city at the time of a siege. But Tiglath-Pileser boasts in a report about his campaign against Damascus: "His gardens, vegetable plants beyond number, I completely destroyed, I did not leave a single [tree]" (*AOT* 346; concerning Shalmaneser, see *AOT* 343). Unfortunately, the text in v. 13b is damaged. Destruction of cities during wartime is certainly not out of the ordinary. But the text seems to be speaking about complete eradication. Once again, Tiglath-Pileser praises himself, at the time of the conquest of the territory belonging to Damascus, saying that he had so completely destroyed 592 cities that they looked like "hillocks after a major flood." Assyria had resorted to practices which were unrestrained, going far beyond what was proper, beyond what could be considered permissible for the victor according to any generally accepted standards.

[10:14] The impudence with which Assyria went about doing what it wanted is illustrated by Isaiah as he uses the imagery of one who gathers eggs, one who plunders the nests of birds. Young shepherd boys may have amused themselves by seeing who could collect the most eggs. Although gathering "abandoned eggs" probably did not cause any problem, Deut. 22:6f. forbids chasing the mother bird away so as to plunder the nest of its eggs or of its young. In just such a thoughtless way, the Assyrians were plundering the cities of their enemies. And their blows stunned so much that no one would have risked striking back with a wing or opening the mouth to let out so much as a peep. Concerning צפצף (peep), see above, commentary on 8:19.

It is possible that the Assyrian kings used this same imagery in their own reports; in any case, we find a similar way of saying the same thing: "Himself [Hezekiah] I [Sennacherib] made prisoner in Jerusalem, his royal residence, like a bird in a cage" (*AOT* 353; *ANET* 288). "I smashed like a flood-storm the country of Hamath in its entire [extent]" (*AOT* 350; *ANET* 284). Or: "I [Sargon] caught, like a fish, the Greeks [Ionians] who live [on islands] amidst the Western Sea" (*AOT* 352; *ANET* 285). "I [Esarhaddon] spread my wings like the [swift-]flying storm[bird] to overwhelm my enemies" (*AOT* 356; *ANET* 289). "They [the enemies of Ashurbanipal] threw down the inescapable net of the great gods, my lords" (VAB VII/2 [1916] 37), and the like. One might compare this with the characterization of the Chaldeans in Habakkuk, esp. 1:8, 14f.; 2:5.

[10:15] Isaiah coaxes his listeners to decide for themselves what judgment would be fitting for the Assyrian hybris which he described. He does this in the most sublime way, in the form of a question, which forces the partners in the discussion to give their own answer to the question; cf. Jer. 2:11, 14; 13:23. It is possible that he quotes from a proverb in v. 15a, bα or makes use of an image which was available to him from "wisdom," used whenever there was a need to show that an action done in arrogance was reprehensible. In any case, and this is important theologically, Isaiah argues by referring to the structure of world order, in which everything has its place, and therefore, its proper function. The tool does not have the right to boast to the one who gave it its proper reason for existing by picking it up in the first place; the same applies to the human being who seeks to rise up in boastful pride against the one who first gave that person's life both form and meaning. Even the king of a world empire is bound to the "order" which he neither established nor can remove at will. He was to remain within the exact boundaries of his *missio*. On the basis of the context in which this message is now found, a considerable dislocation has taken place: World order does not rest within itself. It is established by God, and whoever collides with it must deal with Yahweh, the God of Israel, "who dwells upon Zion."

[10:10f.] In the section which is before us, Isaiah himself does not mention why Yahweh's wrathful judgment was to be carried out against Israel. The expander in vv. 10f. seeks to fill in this gap: It is because of Jerusalem's idolatrous worship. And what foolishness such idol worship was! Indeed, Jerusalem had witnessed the fact that numerous gods of the Syrian states had been unmasked as powerless when confronting the onslaught of the Assyrian might. And it had also seen how Samaria had been brought to shame by its idols. And yet now, it believes that it will be able to stand up to the provocation of this world power on its own, with the help of its idols. The addition seems to attempt—too late though—to explain why Jerusalem, the city of God, in spite of all the promises which had been given to it, had been laid just as low by the enemy as all the other cities: It had trusted, just as the others, in idols. The designation for these idols, אלילים, was taken by the expander from Isaianic traditions; see above, commentary on 2:8. But he is quite at home with the terminology used in the polemic against idols and also mentions פסילים and עצבים. פסילים is connected with the verb פסל, "hew out, hew," while עצבים is from the root עצב, "shape, give form." It would be sheer speculation for one to attempt to elucidate or to investigate the difference in meaning between these two designations so as to explain why it mentions the פסילים (idols) of Samaria but the עצבים (idol images) of Jerusalem. The polemic against the פסילים (idols) is deuteronomic (Judg. 3:19, 26; Deut. 7:5–26; 12:3; see also 2 Kings 17:41 and cf. Jer. 8:19); on the other hand, עצב (idol images) is found primarily in Hosea's polemic (never in Deuteronomy or the Deuteronomist). The inserted material is certainly not typically "deuteronomistic," but it may still come from the time after the fall of Jerusalem (see האלילים, idols, in the Holiness Code: Lev. 19:4; 26:1, and, in Ezekiel, 30:13). The speeches of the Rabshakeh (Isa. 36:14–20 = 2 Kings 18:19–25 and Isa. 37:10–13 = 2 Kings 19:10–13) are examples of the way in which one would generally poke fun at the weakness of the gods of a people which had been laid low; the motif seems to have played a role in political propaganda; cf. 1 Sam. 4:3ff. and, in addition, Eichrodt, *Kommentar* II, 237.

By means of the addition (vv. 10f.), not only is Isaiah's train of thought interrupted, but what he intends to say is twisted around: Whereas Isaiah raises a woe-oracle against Assyria, because it has acted contrary to the task for which it was commissioned, this addition portrays Assyria as the legitimate executor of judgment upon the people of Jerusalem, because they served idols.

[10:12] On the other hand, the glossator to whom we apparently are indebted for v. 12 understood the sense of Isaiah's woe-oracle very clearly. Whereas Isaiah had only indirectly portrayed the hubris of Assyria, by quoting the words of its king, this person speaks of it directly, using Isaiah's phrase גדל לבב (arrogance, big heart) (on this, see 9:8) and תפארת רום (haughty pride) (concerning תפארת, boast, see 20:5; 28:1, 4; concerning רום, pride, see 2:11, 17; concerning רום עינים, haughty eyes, Prov. 21:4). But תפארת (haughty pride) is the term most frequently chosen by those who reworked the book of Isaiah (3:18; 4:2; 13:19; 28:5; in addition, there are passages in Deutero- and Trito-Isaiah). Mentioning the pride of foreign peoples is part of the way one announces disaster for them; see Jer. 48:29f. Wisdom speaks frequently of the "fruit" of one's deeds or one's conduct; see above, commentary on 3:10–11. Besides the expander's familiarity with Isaiah, he is also at home with thought patterns used by prophets of salvation and by wisdom (*Chokma*), for whom the evil consequences of arrogance provide a favorite theme. And yet, for them as well, false actions do not automatically result in disaster; rather, Yahweh is the lord of judgment; *he* punishes Assyria (concerning פקד, afflict, see above, commentary on 10:3a).

Accounts with Assyria will be settled "when Yahweh completes his entire work upon Mount Zion and in Jerusalem." בצע *pi'el,* in the sense of "complete," is also found in Lam. 2:17 and Zech. 4:9. Skehan thinks that v. 12a came into being on the basis of phraseology in v. 11b (both texts mention ירושלים, Jerusalem; עשה [deal with] is referred to again by מעשה [work] and יבצע [complete] is עצביה [idol images] read backwards), which would mean that the author of v. 12a composed this passage on the basis of what he read in v. 11b. That is possible, and would show—as one can presume anyway—that vv. 10f. were already present in the text used by the expander who inserted v. 12, which may explain the way glossators went about their work.

Since בצע (complete) is used in Zech. 4:9 to describe the completion of the temple, it seems likely that one might also presume this present passage refers to completing the work of reconstructing the temple on Mount Zion at the time of Haggai and Zechariah. Thus, it is not about the final completion of Yahweh's plans for Jerusalem, nor simply about the destruction of the heathen encamped in front of the city (Marti, ad loc.), nor about the eschatological time of salvation (Fohrer, ad loc.). Of course, both of the prophets mentioned here were waiting for a decisive change of events in the realms of the foreign peoples at the time the temple was completely rebuilt, and this expectation seems to have precipitated Isa. 10:12 as well. מלך אשור (king of Assyria) would seem to be a code name for the great king of Persia. Thus, v. 12 might well be an attempt to update Isaiah's criticism of the great powers in light of the actual situation during that particular era. It also explains why the glossator would expand on the text just after vv. 10f.: He concurs with the judgment of punishment which had taken place in Jerusalem/Zion but yet, he wants to testify to the fact that the matter did not reach a final conclusion at that point: Building the temple meant that Yahweh once again wished to dwell in the midst of his people and would crush his enemies.

Purpose and Thrust

There is no doubt that 10:5–9, 13–15 is not the first message which Isaiah spoke about Assyria, as can be seen by comparing passages such as 5:26–29; 7:18–21; 8:1–4, 5–8. Isaiah had always looked upon Assyria as Yahweh's tool to carry out his judgment. But now he raises up a woe-oracle against it. Some commentators find that to be a complete break in Isaiah's thought, others say it is completely "impossible" (on this, see K. Fullerton, op. cit., 176), and there are still others who conclude that all the passages in the book of Isaiah which speak of the downfall of Assyria and the salvation of Jerusalem are to be considered to be from someone other than Isaiah (K. Fullerton, "Viewpoints in the Discussion of Isaiah's Hopes for the Future," *JBL* 41 [1922] 1–101, esp. 44ff.). On the other hand, someone like R. Kittel is of the opinion that the present passage is "one of the most original, powerful speeches of Isaiah, being at the same time a first attempt at a philosophy of history, in a grand style, constructed on the basis of the moral order in the world, within the realm of history: World history is world judgment" (*Geschichte des Volkes Israel,* II [1925⁶] 386, note 1; see also G. Fohrer, FS W. Eilers, 67–69). The section is, in actual fact, extremely important for interpreting Isaiah's understanding of history. At the very least, it is a misunderstanding to speak about a change in Isaiah's assessment of Assyria. He never glorified Assyria. He does not need to take anything back from what he said about the Assyrians; instead, he can only continue to corroborate what he had said in his earlier messages about Assyria, namely, that it was a "rod" in the hand of Yahweh. Isaiah never doubted that this world power was under the authority of Yahweh and was thus expected to carry out his will. But this in no way means that Yahweh would simply place his stamp of approval upon whatever Assyria did, and here Isaiah expands on what had been mentioned earlier. Even this world power was not exempted from living within the order which had been established for the whole world and, if it lived at cross purposes with this order, it invited a "curse" upon itself. This section gives evidence for the remarkable thought processes of this prophet. He starts out with purely theological premises (one might even say he begins with a dogmatic preconception): Yahweh, who alone is exalted, is lord of the world and *cannot* allow Assyria's use of power and arrogant manner to go unpunished. It fits completely with this type of order that this is a woe-oracle without any explicit announcement of judgment. Isaiah does not know anything specific about that, how and when Assyria's fall would actually occur; at that time, there were as yet no signals pointing out the weaknesses in the country on the Tigris. But the prophet had not been led in this direction by any empirical observations, on the basis of which one would offer an "update" on the political and military situation. He can only testify: Such arrogance would explode and shatter apart. Woe to the power which so shamefully misuses the commission it received from Yahweh!

Isaiah measures this mighty foreign power with the same measuring rod which he had laid upon Israel/Judah; arrogance must be brought low; it is almost one of his favorite themes (see above, on 2:6ff.; 3:16f., 24; 9:7ff.). But is it appropriate that Assyria be measured by the same norm as Israel, the people of Yahweh? The same problem is posed by the "oracles against the foreign nations" in Amos (Amos 1:3—2:3; on this, see also H. W. Wolff, BK XIV/2, 209f. [Engl: *Joel and Amos,* 172f.]). Already in 2:6ff., Isaiah had spoken about human beings/a man "bowing" and "being brought low." The exegesis has shown that Isaiah was moved at that point to argue on the basis of the thoughts which are found in wisdom. Assyria does not know Yahweh, but it certainly does know a lot about the world order which he established and which he sanctioned. The fact that the ax does not seek to boast against the one who swings it was also known in Sargon's city Dur-Sharruken. Those peoples who do *not* know Yahweh cannot try to offer the excuse that they do not know anything about this order (on this, cf. Rom. 2:1ff.).

If one brackets vv. 10–12 from the discussion of Isaiah's message, it is clear that the prophet did not first begin to raise concerns about Assyria's actions when the Assyrians began to threaten Jerusalem. Both vv. 13 and 14 say very clearly that Assyria's outrageous actions are judged in and of themselves, not just because of its treatment of Israel. Just the opposite: Isaiah establishes the fact that Assyria's mission to carry out God's judgment against Israel had not given it a free hand to mistreat other peoples. Assyria had ridden roughshod over basic rights of those peoples. Injustice remains injustice and murder of peoples is murder of peoples, whether that means Carchemish or Samaria or whomever else had been taken in battle. Jerusalem is not even mentioned. But the fact that Samaria was the last of the cities listed shows that Isaiah was deeply affected by the fate of the Northern Kingdom.

The glossator wants nothing to do with this world-wide review of the fate of the peoples. He is interested only in Jerusalem. This is understandable if, as we believe we have shown, he wrote this after the destruction of Jerusalem by the Babylonians. And it is remarkable that he still maintains that Jerusalem deserved its fate, just as much as all the other groups of peoples. The second glossator draws a conclusion from Isaiah's woe against Assyria, a conclusion which Isaiah had not said in so many words: The judgment against Assyria means there is a prospect for a reprieve for Jerusalem. With this, he helped to determine the shape of the concept to be used in apocalyptic, according to which judgment upon the world power would, in and of itself, be a transitional phase on the way to the final establishment of complete salvation.

The Great Fire of God

Literature

K. Fullerton, "The Problem of Isaiah, Chapter 10," *AJSL* 34 (1917/18) 170–184.
O. Sander, "Leib-Seele-Dualismus im Alten Testament?" *ZAW* 77 (1965) 329–332.
    Concerning the text: E. Robertson, "Some Obscure Passages in Isaiah," *AJSL* 49 (1932/33) 313–324; esp. 320–322. G. Schwarz, "'. . . das Licht Israels'?" *ZAW* 82 (1970) 447–448 (on 10:17a).

Text

10:16 For this reason [the Lord]^a Yahweh of Hosts will allow
    a leanness^b to come upon lush stretches of land,
and in the midst of its splendor there will break out^c
    a conflagration, just like a raging fire.
17 And the light^a of Israel will become fire
    and its holy one will become a flame.
They will ignite and devour its thorn-choked undergrowth^b
    and its thistles^c on one day.
18 ^aAnd the majesty of its forests and orchards
    will be destroyed along with root and branch.^a
    ^b[It will be like when a weak person despairs.]^b
19 And whatever remains of the trees^a of its forest
    will be easy^b to count,
(without effort) a child could make a list^c of them.

16a האדון (the Lord) is missing in some MSS and in Gk and should probably be removed; see Marti and G. R. Driver, *JSS* 13 (1968) 41.
16b משמן (leanness) in the singular is used as an abstract term in Isa. 17:4 ("fatness, stoutness"), but in Ps. 78:31 it is plural משמנים (strongest), used with בְּחוּרִים, "company of youths"; KBL refers to the Arabic *samîm,* "nobleman"; it is possible that the word could mean "important, noteworthy people" in this passage. Then, כבוד (splendor) in v. 16b would have to be understood as an abstract term which is used for a concrete one; cf. Fohrer and see above, commentary on 5:13. And yet, the plural in Gen. 27:28, 39 and in Dan. 11:24 means "fruitful regions." Without a doubt, this interpretation fits the best in the context of Isa. 10:16ff., which speaks about the destruction of part of the landscape (for a different view, G. R.

Driver, op. cit., 41f.). That viewpoint is not contradicted by רָזוֹן, for which the translation "consumption" has been suggested, since the meaning "leanness" can certainly be used when describing a geographical area (cf. the adjective רָזֶה, [poor] land, in Num. 13:20). Therefore, in v. 16b, כָּבוֹד (splendor) speaks of the majesty of the land, just as v. 18 does.

16c Targ reads מִיקַד (burning) instead of יְקֹד (conflagration); it is possible that the word should be pointed יָקַד, as is done in BHK and BHS.

17a Instead of אוֹר יִשׂ׳ (light of Israel), some have suggested reading צוּר יִשׂ׳ (rock of Israel) (see BHK³). In light of 30:29 and 2 Sam. 23:3 (cf. also Deut. 32:4, 15, 18, 31), it would seem that this change should be adopted. Yet, Ps. 27:1 (cf. also 36:10) shows that אוֹר יִשׂ׳ (light of Israel) is not automatically excluded from the ways one could designate God, which also eliminates the need for Schwarz's suggestion that one ought to read אֱלֹהֵי יִשׂ׳ (God of Israel).

17b שִׁית (undergrowth, thorn bushes) is found only in the first part of the book of Isaiah; see above, commentary on 5:6; the form with a suffix is used only here (concerning the pointing שִׁיתוֹ, instead of שֵׁיתוֹ, see Ges-K §93v; the uncommon form שִׁיתוֹ might have been chosen because it sounded similar to שָׁמִיר, thistles).

17c Concerning שָׁמִיר (thistles), see above, commentary on 5:6.

18a–a Gk reads two verbs here: ἀποσβεσθήσεται (will be extinguished) and καταφάγεται (will be devoured). It is possible that, instead of וּכַרְמִלּוֹ (and its orchards), a second verb had been read (something like יִצַּת, kindle, burn), and yet, that remains dubious. The same holds true for the suggestion in BHS that מִנֶּפֶשׁ וְעַד בָּשָׂר (with root and branch) should be removed from the text. One must presume that this was a common way of speaking, similar to "head and tail, branch of the rod and bulrush stem" in 9:13. Instead of יִכְלֶה (will be destroyed), Sym reads ἀναλωθήσεται (be wasted, expended); Vulg: *consumetur* (be consumed); Bruno (263) suggests reading יִכָלֶה, "he goes under" (certainly this should read יִכָּלֶה; see also Kaiser, ad loc.); Driver, op. cit., 42, and BHS suggest reading a *pu'al:* יְכֻלֶּה (be consumed), which yields the same sense. Indeed, one must finally come to the conclusion that there should be a change in the pointing, since, on the basis of the feminine בֹעֲרָה (ignite) in v. 17b, one would have expected a transitive *pi'el* form תְּכַלֶּה (will come to an end).

18b–b The meaning of the verbal root נסס in the *qal*, used only in this present passage, remains uncertain; possibly the text has been damaged. It has been common that some scholars have related נסס to the Syriac *nassîs* or *nᵉsîs*, "sick" (and some, in fact, have compared it with the Greek νόσος, sickness; see T. Nöldeke, *Mandäische Grammatik* [1875] [= 1964] XXX; other views are already found in *ZDMG* 40 [1886] 729, note 2; in addition, Duhm, ad loc.). G. R. Driver (*JTS* 34 [1933] 375 and *JSS* 13 [1968] 42) refers to the Akkadian *nasâsu* I, "to sway to and fro, to tremble," and II, "wave [the hair], flap"; in addition to this, one should compare the *hithpolel* in Ps. 60:6 and Zech. 9:16. This interpretation (see also *AHW* 806a) is preferable to deriving the word from נֵס, "standard" ("as when one who carries a standard despairs"!). Concerning other attempts to emend and interpret the text, see Robertson, op. cit., 320–322.

19a It is not only unnecessary to read, instead of עֵץ (tree), the construct state plural עֲצֵי (trees of) (see BHK), since עֵץ is used frequently in a collective sense and is even used as a collective with the plural of the verb, but it is virtually impossible that עֵצִים means "sticks of wood" or "species of wood."

19b מִסְפָּר does not only mean "number" but also, in a more narrow sense, "a small number"; cf. Deut. 33:6 and phrases such as אַנְשֵׁי מִסְפָּר, "few men," Ezek. 12:16.

19c The Hebrew imperfect can be used to express a condition; see Ges-K §107x.

Form

The section which begins with v. 16 is connected with the preceding section, vv. 5–15, by means of לָכֵן (for this reason) (see above, on the form of 10:5–15). According to the present relationship, which is no doubt only redactional, 10:5–19 forms a unit, to be understood in its entirety as a threat against Assyria. From time to time, some more recent scholars still consider the relationship to be original—Steinmann, for example, who believes that vv. 16–19 speak about Sennacherib's army. According to this opinion, it would fit right into the logic of the oracle that Yahweh would smite the army of the Assyrians with a sickness in order to strike down the pride of its leader (similarly, Mauchline, Montagnini). But 10:5ff. comes to a fitting conclusion in v. 15. Secondary links are common between independent sections, joined by means of לכן (for that reason), which is also the case when a section is provided with an interpretive addition; see, e.g., below, on 10:24; 28:14.

Meter: Verses 16 and 17 are each made up of 2 five-stress cola (v. 16a, without לכן, for this reason, and האדון, the Lord; v. 16b breaks after יקד, break out; כיקד אש, just like a raging fire, is to be counted as one stress). Verse 18a could possibly be read as a three-stress bicolon (v. 18b is a gloss); v. 19 would seem to be a six-stress colon (2 + 2 + 2).

Setting

Verses 16–19 are a threat of judgment. If one does not consider the relationship with 10:5ff. to be original, then there is no announcement of the reason, which is certainly not impossible, though it does not follow the normal pattern. If 10:5–15 is separated from vv. 16–19 there is an equally unsatisfactory result: There is no clear picture about who is to receive this judgment. Already in 1780, J. B. Koppe (in his observations concerning the translation of R. Lowth, *Jesaja,* vol. II, 182ff.; see K. Budde, *ZAW* 41 [1923] 194) expressed the opinion that the section vv. 17–23 "was a completely independent fragment, which did not describe the overthrow of the Assyrians, but the downfall and devastation of the Judean state itself." O. Procksch, in a very similar way, suggests that vv. 16–19 refer to Israel as a whole and dates the message to Isaiah's early period. His view is that the "description of the landscape" portrayed in vv. 16–19 would not fit very well with the description of Assyrian troops on the move and advancing toward Jerusalem, "since one would hardly think that this depicts a moving forest such as the one in Birnam" (Procksch, ad loc.; he already made this point in "Die Geschichtsbetrachtung bei Amos, Hosea und Jesaja," diss., Königsberg [1901] 41, note 3; see also K. Budde, op. cit., and O. Eissfeldt, *The Old Testament. An Introduction* [1965] 307f.). The observation is a pertinent one, but it cannot be used to show that the judgment applies to Israel.

The question about who is addressed is made more complicated by the related question concerning authorship. Procksch is very convinced that Isaiah is the author and it seems that some commentators find it easier to consider Isaiah as the author if the threat is directed against Israel (in which case it would specifically zero in on the Northern Kingdom), rather than if such a radical devastation of its entire land is proclaimed to Assyria. Indeed, one ought not exclude that possible interpretation a priori. Questions about Isaiah's authorship are raised primarily on the basis of style. On the one hand, the individual elements in the images are uneven: In v. 16, Yahweh sends "consumption" through the fields, which are then compared to how they would look after a conflagration. But in v. 17a, Yahweh is not the one who sends the fire; he himself is the fire and flame. According to v. 17b, this fire consumes thorn-choked undergrowth and thistles but, according to vv. 18f., the majesty of the forests and orchards is eradicated. That leads one to the conclusion that a smorgasbord of disparate elements from different sources has been assembled to depict a judgment scene. This impression is strengthened by the observation that terms appear here which are used elsewhere in the book of Isaiah, but are used by and large in a different sense.

Concerning שִׁלַּח (will allow, send) in v. 17, one should compare v. 6. Using רָצוֹן/מִשְׁמָן (lush land/leanness) together is reminiscent of 17:4b (וּמִשְׁמַן בְּשָׂרוֹ יֵרָזֶה), and the fat of his flesh will grow lean; the parallel term כָּבוֹד, splendor, in v. 16b also has a parallel usage in 17:4), but מִשְׁמָן is found here in the plural and has taken on the meaning "lush stretches of land." It is possible to show that מִשְׁמָן (lush, fat) is simply a borrowed term by the fact that it does not fit the way the author visualizes the judgment; he thinks of a powerful conflagration which devastates the entire land and all of its vegetation. In 9:1, Isaiah had spoken about the light which would go forth over the people in darkness; in this case, light is a fire which singes the enemies of Israel. אוֹר יִשְׂרָאֵל (light of Israel), as a designation for God, might be reminiscent of Isa. 31:9, which speaks of Yahweh having a furnace (אוּר) upon Zion. The author of 7:25 already enjoyed using שָׁמִיר (thorns) and שַׁיִת (thistles) in 5:6 (and 9:17); 9:17 is used here, even though it fits very poorly with the parallel term כָּבוֹד (splendor). It is from there that both of the verbs בָּעַר (ignite) and אָכַל (devour) have been taken. On the other hand, בְּיוֹם אֶחָד (on one day) may have been taken from 9:13, a verse which also may have suggested the phrase (root and branch); see above, textual note 18a–a. כַּרְמֶל (orchard) is a favorite term for those who expanded the book of Isaiah (16:10; 29:17; 32:15f., and cf. 37:24). The same holds true for שְׁאָר (whatever remains) (cf. 10:20–22; 11:11, 16; 14:22; 16:14), which may come from 17:3. יַעַר (forest) once again points back to 9:17. The image of the lad who can count all the trees which are left may have been suggested by 11:6 (at least, that is what Marti, Duhm, Kaiser, and Fohrer assume, ad loc.).

To be sure, the connections are uncertain in some of these cases but, in spite of that, after an examination of the vocabulary, there is no doubt the author knew the textual traditions passed on from Isaiah. His use of 9:17f. and 17:3f. is particularly apparent (as also 5:6). Since he does not mention the subject about whom he speaks, he shows that he clearly had 10:5ff. in mind in his expansion, introduced by לָכֵן (for that reason). This means he wants his words to be understood as an explication which further details the preceding threat of judgment against Assyria. Whether he meant the historical Assyria, which came to its end when the Medes and Neo-Babylonians rebelled, remains an open question. It is more likely that Assyria is a code-word for whichever world power was playing a leading role in world history at the time of the author. Actually, commentators generally opt for quite a late date (see, e.g., Fohrer). Duhm, along with others, thinks that it speaks to "the new Assyrians, Syria, the kingdom of the Seleucids, confusing the older, pillaging world power with its heirs in the 2nd century," a confusion which one also encounters in many other places in the OT. Kaiser thinks the author is dealing with concepts characteristic of the apocalyptic writings of scribes, which would mean that the section contains the type of "expectations which are given more definite expression in the apocalypse of Isaiah (24–27) and in the book of Daniel." It is true that one might sense that this is similar to passages such as the apocalypse of Isaiah, but typical apocalyptic themes from the book of Daniel are very different. Thus, it may be that the addition comes from the (late) Persian era.

Commentary

[10:16] שָׁלַח (allow, send) is a technical term used when powers are sent by Yahweh in order to carry out his will (see above, commentary on 10:6). In the present example, רָזוֹן (leanness) is mentioned first, which is to invade all of the fruitful portions of the land. We do not find out how this was actually expected to take place. A piece of very rich land could be worn out because someone foolishly mismanaged it or might be wrecked because a great number of stones and rocks were cast upon it. This is immaterial to the author, who goes on, without any problem, to use the imagery of a raging fire. To be sure, he does say בִּיקֹד אֵשׁ "*like* a raging fire," which could then be interpreted to mean that "raging fire" might depict the רָזוֹן, the destruction of the land. But that would be a very strained comparison and, according to vv. 17f., this interpretation is highly unlikely; בִּיקֹד אֵשׁ (just like a raging fire) is to further strengthen the preceding word, יְקֹד (conflagration). The imagery that the ground is impoverished is too weak for the author, so he replaces it with the harsher image of a fire which sweeps through forest and field, universally feared in the dry areas of the entire Mediterranean region and frequently having spelled disaster for Palestine. מִשְׁמַנָּיו (lush stretches of land) is mentioned again with the use of כְּבוֹדוֹ (its splendor). כָּבוֹד (splendor) is often used to describe the luxuriant growth of trees, pointing to their life and strength (Ezek. 31:18; cf. Isa. 35:2; 60:13). The entire "majesty" of the land—clearly identified in v. 18 by reference to the trees and orchards—falls victim to the fire which Yahweh is kindling (on this, cf. Amos 7:4).

[10:17] Verse 17 takes this even further: Yahweh, "the light of Israel," does not only send a conflagration but he himself becomes fire and flame. The designation "light of Israel" is only found here. But there are similar formulations elsewhere: According to 2:5, the house of Jacob is to wander in the light of Yahweh; in 60:1, Israel calls its God אוֹרִי (my light) (cf. also vv. 19f.); according to Mic. 7:8 and Ps. 27:1, Yahweh is the light of the pious (on this, see above, commentary on 9:1). Yahweh as the light of Israel characterizes the saving protection under which his people are able to live, attested in the theophoric personal names which are constructed with אוּר (light): אוּרִיאֵל (Uriel), אוּרִי (Uri), אוּר (Ur), אוּרִיָּה(וּ) (Uriah); on this, see Noth, *Personennamen,* 168, and S. Aalen, *Die Begriffe "Licht" und "Finsternis" im Alten Testament, im Spätjudentum und im Rabbinismus,* SNVAO 1951/1 (1951) 79ff.; in addition, cf. the lexicon articles by S. Aalen in *TDOT* I 147–167 (see 160f.), and M. Sæbø, *THAT* I, cols. 84–90. But this light which protects Israel can also serve as a fire, as a flame, which singes the land of Israel's enemies. In a way which is different from that in 9:17, where the evil of Israel burns like a fire which consumes thorns and thistles, here Yahweh himself brings on the great divine judgment directly—and, in this case, not against Israel but against its enemy. The concept that Yahweh is a consuming fire undoubtedly has a rich history. This is certainly related to the idea that lightning was described as the fire of Yahweh (Num. 11:1; 1 Kings 18:38; 2 Kings 1:12; Job 1:16). Ezekiel speaks about the "fire of his wrath" (אש עברתו, 21:36; 22:21–31; 38:19), and the priestly writings know that Yahweh's כבוד (glory) upon the mountain looked like a אש אכלת (devouring fire) (Exod. 24:17). But it had already been said in Deut. 4:24; 9:3, and Isa. 33:14 that Yahweh was an אש אכלת (devouring fire) (cf. Heb. 12:29). One suspects, on the basis of 33:14, that this side of Yahweh was symbolized by the "eternal" flame burning upon the altar (cf. the parallel there, "everlasting burnings"). On the other hand, Deut. 9:3 suggests that speaking of Yahweh as an אש אכלת (devouring fire) was originally one element in the general conceptual framework of holy war: As a consuming fire, Yahweh devastated (by means of lightning) the enemies of Israel, since they are also his enemies (cf. Exod. 15:7). It is very interesting how the terms אור (light) and אש (fire) are connected in this passage: The light which streams forth around Yahweh and/or the light which he himself *is* distributes blessings all around and yet, at any time, could become the destroying elemental power, fire, which destroys everything hostile to God. Concerning קדוש ישראל (the Holy One of Israel), cf. above, commentary on 1:4.

[10:18] As mentioned above, the fact that this fire consumes thorns and thistles belongs to the terminology which the expander adopted. That is actually said in v. 18: The majesty of forests and orchards will be destroyed, even to the point of "every root and branch." מנפש ועד בשר (root and branch) must have originally referred to the types of living things which were made of נפש (spirit) and בשר (flesh). But since the expression was used on a higher level of speech, it can also be used here to describe the devastation of the cultivated lands; see Sander, op. cit., 330.

[10:19] Verse 19 once again underscores the severity of the judgment. When there is a forest fire, there may be some isolated trees which stay standing. But they are very few in number; a young child, who has barely learned how to write and count, could easily be far enough along to record their number (in addition, this provides evidence that everyone in ancient Israel had at least some basic idea about how to write; cf. Judg. 8:14).

[10:18b] The gloss in v. 18b goes completely beyond what the imagery intended to convey. Duhm thinks that the proverbial expression מנפש ועד בשר (root and branch, from spirit to flesh) in v. 18a suggested the imagery of being consumed once again, using an "atrocious association of ideas." It may be that the glossator really took רזון (leanness) in v. 16 to mean the type of consumption which could befall a human being and felt justified in making his observation. In any case, one must concede to him that he found it necessary to depict not only the course of events which the catastrophe took but also its shocking effect upon human beings, who could only dissolve (that is what נסס means) into nothingness, completely bewildered by such an event.

Purpose and Thrust

In order to understand this section, one must be reminded of what was said above in the discussion of the "setting." Verses 16–19 seek to reactualize the message of Isaiah concerning the Assyrians, for their own particular situation. Whether, as we have presumed, the suffixes on משמניו (its leanness) and כבודו (its splendor) (v. 16) really refer to the Persians or possibly to another historical power is finally not all that important. It is clear that the author wants to give evidence to his contemporaries which proves that the hubris of human power will finally be broken by Yahweh. Since he does not mention the power to whom he is referring, but chiefly because he uses Isaiah's message of judgment without deeper examination and applies it to his own time, he dehistoricizes Isaiah's message. What the prophet had once said about Assyria or, as the case may be, what he intended to say according to the viewpoint of the expander, still applied in the present and would always apply. Since history always stands under Yahweh's on-going desire for righteousness, the same thing can be repeated time and again, in similar situations: namely, Yahweh's might will remain in force in spite of all opposition. It is important for the author to accent the fact that Yahweh is utterly serious about this.

Isaiah presumes that the judgment will take place in the very near future, within the course of history, but because the peoples themselves are tools which Yahweh uses to carry out his wrath, here the completion of the judgment takes place solely as a matter handled by Yahweh. In this way, historical thought has become remythologized and comes ever closer to an apocalyptic view of history. And yet, the author does not maintain, as apocalyptic does, that the power and glory of ruling the world will be transferred to Israel. But what it would be like when the change in fortune in Israel's history finally arrived was seemingly treated by someone else, who wrote down his ideas in the verses which follow.

Isaiah 10:20–23

The Return of the Remnant

Literature

U. Stegemann, "Der Restgedanke bei Isaias," *BZ* NF 13 (1969) 161–186.

Text

10:20 On that day it will happen: At that time the remnant of Israel and all
of those from the house of Jacob who fled will no longer lean upon
the one who smote them, but will support themselves in truth[a]
upon Yahweh, the Holy One of Israel.

21 A remnant will return, a remnant of Jacob, to the mighty God.

22 For even though your people Israel was as the sand by the sea,
even so it is only a remnant from it[a] which will return.
Extermination is decreed, overflowing with righteousness.

23 Truly, [a]assuredly determined destruction[a] is what [the Lord][b]
brings to completion, Yahweh of Hosts, in the midst of the whole
earth.

20a According to Procksch and Schmidt, באמת (in truth) is to be removed; it is
surprising that it is placed at the end of the sentence and yet, it was probably put
there intentionally, for emphasis. Gk translates this τῇ ἀληθείᾳ (for truth), which
does slightly alter the meaning; see H. Wildberger, art. "אמן," E III/1, *THAT* I, col.
201.

22a בו (from it) is not to be taken with what follows (contra G. R. Driver, *JSS* 13
[1968] 42 and BHS); it has a partitive sense: In Israel's midst, there are only a few
who are able to make a decision to return.

23a–a כלה ונחרצה means, literally: "destruction and closed in" and is to be taken as
a hendiadys.

23b אדני (the Lord) may be a replacement here, as in other cases (3:17f.; 6:8; 7:14;
8:7; 9:7–16), for Yahweh, but then, "Yahweh" stayed here in the text as well. Gk
reads, instead of אדני יהוה צבאות (the Lord, Yahweh of Hosts), only ὁ θεός (God),
which cannot have been the original reading; most of the textual witnesses from
the Hexaplaric recension read κυριος (Lord).

Form

By means of the formula והיה ביום ההוא (on that day it will happen), this

434

section is connected with the preceding one, but that formula still betrays this as an addition. Here one finds added information concerning what is missing when one reads about the announcement of judgment against Assyria: a message about the state of health and/or conduct of Israel. Verses 20–23 presume the existence of vv. 16–19. But it is not likely that the same author has written something once again; if he had wanted to say something about Israel, he would have connected it more closely with his message of judgment against Assyria.

Verse 24 begins anew with the messenger formula, and the theme in vv. 24ff. is so different from vv. 20–23 that one certainly cannot presume any original connection with what follows either.

In addition, there is also nothing which says that vv. 20–23 form a unit. As an example, Procksch concludes that vv. 20f. contain ideas which are like Isaiah's, even though the authenticity of the text is uncertain, whereas vv. 22f., on the other hand, are a later addition. The first part is optimistic; the latter part is pessimistic. One cannot totally reject these observations. Even if one thinks that vv. 20f. might come from Isaiah, one ought not exclude the possibility of a break coming between vv. 21 and 22, which might point to different sources for the two parts. And yet, these verses do hold together on the basis of the common theme of the "remnant of Israel" and can be understood as a reflection upon this concept, the first part centering upon the sincerity of the return and the second part noting that it is frankly only a remnant which can be counted upon to return.

Meter: BHK, at least on the basis of the way it was printed, considered vv. 20–22 to have a metrical form; BHS does not go that far. Certain parts do suggest a metrical speech pattern; this is clear in v. 21 (a six-stress colon: 2 + 2 + 2) or in v. 22b (a four-stress colon); however, in general, an elevated prose style is used.

Setting

In a way which is similar to the preceding section, the question of authenticity must be raised here as well. If one denies it to vv. 16–19, there is still the possibility that one might consider the introductory formula at the beginning of v. 20 as secondary and then presume that a redactor took an authentic message of Isaiah and connected it with the preceding expansion to the text. However, from the context, that is hardly likely. Yet there are other reasons which speak against Isaiah as the author. For one, there is the historical question: If this comes from Isaiah, who might be the מכה (the one who smote), upon whom Israel had leaned? Duhm points out the problem in this way: "Ahaz relied upon Assyria (II Kings 16) but was not attacked; Hezekiah, on the other hand, was attacked, but he did not rely upon Assyria." Hezekiah, of course, did trust in Egypt for help, but then they shamefully left him in the lurch, though Isaiah could hardly have said that Egypt had attacked Judah. Steinmann (ad loc.) tried to date vv. 21f. to the year 739, when Menahem of Israel paid tribute to Tiglath-Pileser of Assyria. That is not very likely, since Israel had not as yet been attacked by Assyria and there was absolutely no reason to speak of a "remnant" of Israel. Finally, Procksch explains: "The מַכֵּהוּ is the Assyrian taskmaster, whose scourge caused Israel to be deeply wounded (9:3), but Ahaz relied on this same master in Judah." However, that explanation distorts the main point being made, that Israel was attacked by precisely that power in which it had placed its trust. One must conclude that this is from an author who is very familiar with the terminology used by Isaiah, but who utilizes it as building blocks for erecting a unique structure to express his own thoughts.

In vv. 20f., שאר ישוב (a remnant will return) is used in the positive sense of something which is promised (even though the continuation in vv. 22f. warns about illusions), whereas the expression has a reproaching and warning character when it is used by Isaiah. קדוש ישראל (Holy One of Israel) also utilizes words from the tradition of Isaiah, but Isaiah uses this as a designation of a name of God which exists independently, never simply as an epithet for Yahweh (in 30:15, קדש ישראל, Holy One of Israel, is not used as an epithet but intensifies the majesty of God's name). In contrast to the way of forming a name which uses a clause, שאר ישוב (a remnant will return), the expressions שאר ישראל (remnant of Israel) and פליטת בית־יעקב (a remnant of Jacob) point out that one actually could refer to a real concept of a remnant at the time the author was writing; "remnant" has become a theological term, which has taken on a meaning all its own by the time of this composition (on this, see U. Stegemann, op. cit., 176ff.). אל גבור (mighty God) certainly has its roots in 9:4, but here, it refers to Yahweh, not the Messiah. "As the sand by the sea" is also used in Hos. 2:1; Gen. 22:17; 32:13; שטף צדקה (overflowing with righteousness) may indeed be reminiscent of 28:15ff.; concerning כלה ונחרצה (assuredly determined destruction), see 28:22.

In this case as well, one cannot be definite about the time when this passage came into existence. Most especially, nothing can be said about the identity of the מכֵּה (the one who smote) in v. 21. As is the case with the preceding passage, if one must assign a date, this message might come from the (late) Persian period.

Commentary

[10:20] והיה ביום ההוא (on that day it will happen) is a "formula which introduces an addition"; cf. 7:18, 20f., 23, and, on this, see above, on the setting and form of 7:18–25. It is not to be interpreted in an eschatological sense; it seeks to do no more than date this message to the same time as the preceding section. As was mentioned above, the author takes pains to clarify the theological point of the "remnant of Israel." The theme had been originally stated in the name of Isaiah's son (7:3). Apparently, in Judah this had finally developed into a hard and fast dogma that there would be a remnant of Israel which would consist of those who had escaped the judgment (cf. 11:11, 16). The remnant of Israel, as it is formulated in v. 20, is פליטת בית־יעקב (those from the house of Jacob who fled) (concerning פליטה, escapee, see above, commentary on 4:2). Whoever is left in Zion is holy, according to 4:3, and all who belong to this remnant believe that they have been marked down on the list of the survivors (cf. 6:13). But the author of vv. 20ff. is not in accord with this "remnant-theology." He learned from Isaiah that there can be no reality of salvation if there is no surrender to Yahweh. Therefore, he expresses his own conviction that the remnant will decide "on that day" to turn toward Yahweh. Instead of "believe," as it is used in 7:9 and 28:16, he speaks about "relying upon" Yahweh, to which he appends באמת (in truth), so that no one wrongly concludes that this can be brought about by a simple confession with one's lips. One can quite properly regard the clause נשען על־יהוה באמת (support themselves in truth upon Yahweh) as a fitting paraphrase of Isaiah's way of describing faith (cf. H. Wildberger, art., "אמן," E III/4–5, *THAT* I, cols. 202–204). But Mic. 3:11 makes it clear that נשען על־יהוה (lean upon Yahweh) could be used in the vocabulary of the cult, as an expression of the type of trust which the prophet treated with skepticism. Thus, one cannot be too surprised that Isaiah uses the vocable only when he speaks about *false* confidence (30:12; 31:1). This present passage puts a stop to the threat that Israel would have the type of confidence which is easily achieved, and which is not very challenging; the passage accomplishes this by framing the matter in a negative way: Israel will *no longer* have confidence in the one who had attacked it. True confidence in Yahweh would be quickly manifested in specific instances when one would say no to, and distance oneself from, certain things. The additional caution provided by באמת (in truth) is even more interesting. One could presume this makes use of Isaiah's term האמין (believe). In any case, it is quite close to אמונה (faith) as it is used in Hab. 2:4. This term means that one allows oneself to hear Yahweh's message and stays far from the "crooked path" (see 30:12) which is so easily followed and is characterized by a piety which seems so correct.

[10:21] In v. 21, turning toward God is described as שוב, "turning around." But v. 21 alters the thoughts of v. 20 in another respect. שאר ישוב does not mean, as is assumed by many scholars (Marti, Gray, Duhm, Bruno, Fohrer, et al.): "*the* remnant turns back," but rather "*a* remnant turns back" (Kissane, Herntrich, Hertzberg, Steinmann, Eichrodt, Schildenberger, Montagnini, et al.). As one can determine on the basis of the way the words are arranged, the accent is on the remnant (see above, commentary on 7:3): This means (only) a remnant, not simply everyone who counts himself or herself to be part of Israel. With this, the shift to vv. 22f. is provided. Concerning אל גבור (mighty God), see above, pp. 403f.. If one would identify this term, as in 9:4, with the messianic king, then one cannot translate שוב as "turn back" but rather must translate it as "turn oneself toward." That is not very likely here. But, in spite of that, hardly another solution remains except to explain "mighty God" as a way to speak further about יהוה קדוש ישראל (Yahweh, the Holy One of Israel) in v. 20.

[10:22f.] After the author very clearly corrected the commonly accepted interpretation about the remnant of Israel, he commences to warn against the illusion that the salvation of Israel, for as much of Israel as still remained, could be taken as a sure thing. Judgment takes its course and has to go the full distance, since it is only in this way that righteousness can become real within history. It is unthinkable that Israel as a whole can be spared this necessary process when "assuredly determined destruction" is going forth through the whole earth. Precisely because one can expect a terrible catastrophe for world powers, Israel should know that there is no longer any validity to the formula: there, among the other peoples, disaster; here, among the people of God, perceiving itself a holy remnant, salvation. In 28:22, כלה ונחרצה (decree of destruction) can refer only to judgment upon Israel (in that passage, על כל־הארץ is to be translated "over the whole land" or should be treated as an addition, coming from 10:23; however, בקרב כל־הארץ in the present passage must mean "in the midst of the whole earth"). The author of 10:23 works within the realm of apocalyptic, which can include an all-inclusive judgment of the entire world. But one cannot characterize him as an apocalyptic thinker, since what he inherited from prophetic thought is still too powerful a force.

Purpose and Thrust

After a threat of disaster in vv. 16–19, one would expect in vv. 20ff., where the scene shifts to Israel, that one would find an unrestricted promise of salvation for the "remnant of Israel." But one must pay very careful attention to the way the concept of the remnant is interpreted here. It amazingly follows the same line of thought as is found in Isaiah and calls into question the self-confidence of the postexilic community, which believed itself to have escaped the judgment of Yahweh which was to go forth over the whole earth. Indeed, the author does stay with the idea that Israel has a unique position, and he also does not deny what his predecessor had proclaimed. But he prevents Israel from feasting on the punishment which comes upon others. Fohrer says of him, "He is no prophet," since his message is constructed by and large out of quotations. But he was certainly already a very observant reader of the prophetic message; and, more than that, he preserved what was inherited from the prophets in a time when there was still a very limited understanding about what really was the main concern of the prophets.

No Fear of Assyria

Literature

L. E. Binns, "Midianite Elements in Hebrew Religion," *JTS* 31 (1930) 337–354.
[**Literature update through 1979:** J. A. Soggin, "Tablîtām in Isaiah 10:25b," *BeO* 13 (1971) 232.]

Text

10:24 Therefore, thus says [the Lord],[a] Yahweh of Hosts: Do not be afraid, O my people, which dwells upon Zion, before Assyria, which strikes you with the staff and swings its rod above you [b]according to the manner of Egypt.[b]

25 For in only a short time, then[a] my[b] fury will have exhausted itself

26 and my wrath [c]will completely be at an end.[c] • And Yahweh of Hosts[a] will swing the whip against them as at an earlier time, when he smote Midian at Raven's Rock [and his staff is [b]over the sea,[b] and he will lift it up according to the manner of Egypt].

27 [And it will happen on that day:
His burden will be withdrawn from upon your shoulder,
and his yoke 'will be torn away'[a] from your neck.]

24a For אדוני יהוה צבאות (the Lord, Yahweh of Hosts), Gk reads κύριος σαβαωθ (Lord of Sebaoth), which means that it did not read אדוני (Adonai); see above, textual note 10:16a.

24b–b Procksch considers בדרך מצרים (according to the manner of Egypt) to be a gloss, since this overloads the meter, and believes it originally was only in v. 26. But one does well not to seek any metrical pattern in these verses.

25a The concept which is central to this section is anticipated and is connected with the main clause by means of a ו (*Waw*); see BrSynt §123f.

25b Instead of זעם (fury), based on the Syr (*rwgzj,* my anger) and the parallel with אפי (my wrath), זעמי (my fury) should be read here.

25c–c על תב יתם causes some problems. One could derive תבלית from בלה, giving it the meaning "end, destruction," in which case, one would translate it something like: "and my wrath (goes forth) for destruction." But that is grammatically questionable, and the resultant meaning directly contradicts כלה זעמי (my fury will have exhausted itself), which precedes it. Some MSS read תכליתם (their coming to a complete end) instead of תבליתם (their destruction), derived from כלה (be finished), but this would not alter the meaning all that much. Luzzato suggested that על תבליתם should be divided differently, reading עַל תֵּבֵל יִתֹּם, with the resulting translation: "and my wrath over the whole earth comes to an end." And yet, according to the context, the subject must be the wrath against Israel. Therefore, we follow the emendation which G. R. Driver sufficiently explained in *JTS* 38 (1937) 39 (see also BHS): וְאַפִּי עַל־תֵּכָל יִתֹּם, "and my wrath shall be utterly completed" (in this case, תכל would be an otherwise unused substantive from כלה, to complete).

26a Instead of יהוה צבאות (Yahweh of Hosts), Gk reads: ὁ θεός (God); the Lucianic recension reads κύριος (Lord). It is possible that צבאות (Hosts, Sebaoth) should be removed.

26b–b It has been suggested that, instead of עַל הַיָּם (over the sea), one should read either עֲלֵיהֶם (upon them) or עָלָיו (upon him) (H. Winckler, *Alttestamentliche Untersuchungen* [1892] 177; cf. Marti and Procksch, ad loc.; BHS). But one ought not be surprised that the sea would be mentioned when reference is made to Egypt.

27a Instead of וְחֻבַּל (after moving the *Athnach*), יֵחָבֵל (will be torn away) should be read, as already recognized by W. R. Smith, *Journal of Philology* 13 (1885) 62f. (Gk reads καταφθαρήσεται, will be utterly spoiled.) The rest of the verse should be considered as part of the next section.

Form

The messenger formula at the beginning of v. 24 shows that a new section begins at this point; once again, לכן (therefore) is used here only as a way to link this section with what precedes (see above, v. 16). The new theme also shows that this is not the natural continuation of vv. 20–23.

Verse 27 begins with the "formula which introduces an addition": והיה ביום ההוא (and it will happen on that day); it is most likely that v. 27a is a secondary addition to vv. 24–26, but the clause undoubtedly was always intended as an expansion of vv. 24–26. As was determined above, v. 27a does not end after צוארך (from your neck), but only after the (emended) יחבל (will be torn away). The remainder of the verse is generally considered to be part of the section which follows. Verse 26b presents particular difficulties, since it uses "whip against Midian" parallel to "staff over the sea." It is most likely that this staff (מטה) refers to the staff of Moses, which he raised at the time of the march through the midst of the sea (Exod. 14:16; 4:2–5; 4:17; 7ff.), with some influence possibly also from Exod. 17:5, 9, where the staff of Moses became the rod of God (מטה אלהים). Concerning מטה (rod), see above, commentary on 10:5. However, one must admit that, if this interpretation of ומטהו (and his staff) is accepted, it would then be the second object of the verb עורר (will swing), a rather awkward construction. Therefore, ומטהו על הים is treated in the above translation as a nominal clause: "and his staff is over the sea." But even this does not help one to understand which sea is meant, over which Yahweh raised his staff "according to the manner of Egypt." Procksch makes it easy for himself by emending the text to read וְנָשָׂא מַטֵּהוּ (and he raises his staff). However, instead of accepting such a tenuous alteration of the text, one would be better off considering v. 26b a gloss; בדרך מצרים (according to the manner of Egypt), at the end of v. 24, also hints that this is what happened. As is easily noted when such observations are added to a text, it has not been very carefully integrated into the context.

Meter: BHK and BHS take this section, as do a predominant number of commentators, as prose, but there are some (Procksch, Fohrer, Kaiser, et al.) who believe that they can detect a metrical structure. If that is possible in vv. 24–26, then one should be able to divide virtually any Hebrew text in order to achieve a metrical structure. On the other hand, after excluding the introduction, v. 27a is a four-stress bicolon.

Setting

Opinions of recent scholars about the authenticity of vv. 24–27a are widely divergent. According to Procksch, this section finally provides the original conclusion to vv. 5–15; this means that we would come only at this point to the answer to the Assyrian question; in vv. 5–15, the prophet himself would simply be offering his own opinion. "There are no grounds for denying the authenticity of the passage. Thought and speech have an Isaianic character, Assyria is specifically mentioned as the opponent (v. 24), the images of stick and staff (v. 5) are utilized once again" (ad loc.). Among those who agree with Procksch, one finds Schmidt, Feldmann, Fischer, Kissane, Hertzberg, Leslie, Montagnini, et al. But Eichhorn had already denied that this passage was Isaianic, and he has a considerable following (Marti, Gray, Duhm, König, Herntrich, Eichrodt, Kaiser, Schildenberger, Becker, Fohrer, et al.). The judgment of Procksch, that the language has an Isaianic character, certainly makes sense; however, as in many similar cases, that means nothing more than that someone conversant with the message of Isaiah, which had been passed down, took up pen and ink. "This oracle of salvation . . . also exudes the spirit of zealous study of the written text" (Kaiser, ad loc.): עמי ישב ציון (my people which dwells on Zion) reminds one of 30:19. Reference was made to the שבט (staff) and מטה (rod) of Assyria in 10:5; cf. also 30:31f. One already finds זעם (fury, malediction) and אף (wrath, anger) used together in 10:5. Concerning הכה (strike), one can refer to מכהו (one who smote) in v. 20. שוט (whip) will have been taken from 28:15, 18 (there, of course, carried out by means of the "flood of water"). Verse 27a is practically a direct quote from 9:3. The author was familiar with the exodus tradition; that also speaks against Isaiah as the source, since he never refers elsewhere to the exodus from Egypt in any of his messages. One must also not overlook the fact that חבל (tear off, destroy) is clearly found only in postexilic writings. Finally, the relative closeness to apocalyptic thought weighs as a final argument against Isaianic authorship; this way of thinking is unmistakable in this section. And yet, once again, the date of composition cannot be determined more precisely. Even though Assyria is mentioned, it is not likely, on the basis of the content, that this section was written during the Assyrian era. Assyria serves once again as a code name for another world power and once again one might presume that this also comes from the later Persian era.

Commentary

[10:24] The promise is introduced by the "messenger formula," presenting this as a direct message from God. That corresponds to the fact that messages of salvation begin with the encouragement no longer to be afraid, אל תירא, as is typical of the priestly oracle of salvation (on this, see above, on the form of 7:4–9, and the oracles of salvation in Deutero-

Isaiah, which begin in the same way, in 40:9; 41:10, 13f.; 43:1, 5, and often elsewhere; see also 35:4). Concerning יהוה צבאות (Yahweh of Hosts), see above, commentary on 1:8–9 and on 6:3. Israel is addressed as the people of Yahweh. The suffix on עמי (my people) provides the reason why the people do not need to be afraid: It remains Yahweh's people, stands under his protection, and can be assured of his help; see the address to the people of God as it is connected with the challenge to be unafraid, in 41:8: "But you, Israel, my servant, Jacob, whom I have chosen, the offspring of Abraham, my friend . . ."; and cf., on the other hand, designating Israel as the הזה העם (this people), used by Isaiah when he declares his opposition to a belief in salvation which makes everything too easy; on this, see above, commentary on 6:9ff.; and cf. the name of Hosea's son לא עמי (Not my people) (1:9, and as it is contrasted to 2:1ff.). The common bond between God and the people is further accented by ישב ציון (which dwells upon Zion), an additional descriptive name for God. First of all, Zion (see above, commentary on 2:2b–3) is the place where Yahweh has his dwelling, to which testimony is given in Solomon's speech at the temple dedication (1 Kings 8:13): "I have built thee . . . a place for thee to dwell in [שבתך, be enthroned] for ever." That is where Yahweh's "tabernacle" is, his "tent" (Ps. 27:5; cf. Amos 1:2); and Isaiah himself says that Yahweh dwells upon Mount Zion (8:18: שכן בהר ציון; on this, see above, commentary on 8:18; the formulation ישב ציון, who dwells in Zion, is also found in reference to Yahweh, e.g., in Ps. 9:12). Where Yahweh is enthroned, there his people can live without fear, under his protection. The one who is faithful to Yahweh can be a guest in his tent (Ps. 15:1), and the title בת ציון (daughter of Zion) is clearly conferred upon Israel in Ps. 9:15, that is, within a psalm which identifies Yahweh as the one who dwells upon Zion; cf. Isa. 1:8; 10:32; 16:1; 37:22; 52:2; 62:11; Lam. 2:1, and often elsewhere. Thus, it is certainly possible to address Israel as inhabitants of Zion (Isa. 12:1; Jer. 51:35). In Isa. 30:19, once again within a section which is post-Isaianic, reference is made to עם בציון ישב בירושלם (people in Zion who dwell at Jerusalem) (instead of ישב, will dwell, it should be emended to read ישב, who dwell), and finally, if one wants to be brief, Israel can be simply called ציון (Zion) (Isa. 49:14; 51:16; Jer. 30:17, and often elsewhere). Isaiah himself, who was not shy about saying that Yahweh dwelled upon Zion, would have hardly spoken about *Israel* dwelling upon Zion, since he would not have wanted to contribute to a false notion that Israel could feel itself secure; therefore, this is a concept typically used in the cultic theology of the postexilic era.

[10:25] The author of this section also sees himself confronted with the harsh reality that Israel, the people of Yahweh, has been delivered over to the world power of his day, which he identifies with the symbolic name "Assyria." He begins with what Isaiah said about the Assyria of his day. But the way he varies what had come down to him is very interesting: He does indeed speak about the staff of Assyria, but does not consider it as a tool for Yahweh, used to carry out a justified, needed judgment against Israel; rather, it is a sign of powerful rule. In fact, in v. 25 mention is made of Yahweh's malediction (זעם) and wrath (אף), borrowed from v. 5 (concerning these terms, see above, commentary on 10:5). But they are used by him as if they are absolute entities, types of potential energy which, once set in motion, keep on going until they have completed their task and only then can they return to a state of rest once again (it is possible, according to this viewpoint, that the use of זעם, fury, without the suffix is indeed correct in v. 25). It fits in very well with this understanding of wrath that the verb כלה is used (cf. also the form תֶּכֶל, the emended reading); it means "come to an end" in the sense of "being consumed" (cf. a passage such as Ps. 71:9: "In old age, the vital power of a human being is exhausted"; see also Ps. 143:7 or the *pi'el* "use up" in Ezek. 6:12, and often elsewhere). Indeed, one must not in any way insinuate that the author of this present passage was of the opinion that Yahweh's wrath was a phenomenon without basis and beyond comprehension. But his interests did not follow the same track as the pre-exilic prophets, who held that Israel's conduct was the reason for this "wrath"; for him, it is simply much more important to announce that Israel could anticipate that the wrath of Yahweh would be coming to a final conclusion. He says it very plainly: עוד מעט מזער, "there still remains just [עוד is actually a substantive and means "duration"] a little bit of something very small." It was already pointed out above that עוד מעט מזער (in only a very short time) has been placed at the very beginning of the clause for a good reason: The parameters for this section are set by an announcement that the near future is the time when one can expect deliverance from the "Assyrian" domination. "Using the general tone of a message of salvation, which will be 'soon,' it shows that all true faith is at the same time an expectation that something is going to happen soon (cf. Rev. 22:20)" (so Kaiser, ad loc.). But so that there is no possible misunderstanding about "expectation in the near future," one should not depict this "soon" as a dogmatically well-defined image about how the events linked with the "last things" will unfold, but the author does risk speaking about specific relationships between powers in his own era (cf. 26:20f.).

[10:26a] At the end of v. 24, "Assyria's" violent actions are characterized as בדרך מצרים (according to the manner of Egypt). In this way (it should be noted that Isaiah would not have been able to characterize those actions in a similar manner), the oppression of Israel by a mighty power of that era is compared with the (completely undeserved and in every way unjustified) oppression of Israel by Egypt. "Assyria" brandishes the rod over Israel, just as Egypt had once done. That is not mentioned so as to accuse "Assyria," but rather, so that the way can be prepared for the assertion that Yahweh's help could not be any further removed, during the present time of trouble, than it had been at that earlier time. The author does not fill in all the details, but compares the anticipated intervention of Yahweh with the strike against Midian. Israel knew how Yahweh had come to the aid of his people time and again, in surprising and overpowering ways, and it was to strengthen itself with such knowledge, to have confidence for the future.

It is remarkable that the author of this section knew of such a minor detail as the story about Raven's Rock. This would have come down to him in the written form of the transmitted text in the book of

Judges (Judg. 7:25). In that particular text, it is not said that Yahweh had raised a scourge against Midian. שׁוֹט is the whip of a tyrant (1 Kings 12:11, 14), one who exercises his rule by force.

[10:26b] Parallel to this whip, reference is made in v. 26b to the "staff over the sea," which Yahweh would raise up "according to the manner of Egypt." It has already been determined that this is a gloss, which fits very poorly in the context: In v. 24, the מַטֶּה is the staff which Assyria raises up according to the manner of Egypt, but here it has to mean the staff of God, though it is certainly most strange that Yahweh would raise a staff in a way similar to how it was done in Egypt; what it means to say is that he will do it again, as he once raised it *against* the Egyptians. This gloss can be explained as an attempt to depict the history of salvation in the past as a model for saving events yet to come. Yahweh will act in the future in a way which corresponds to how he manifested himself in the magnificent history shared with his people in the past, which set the norm for the present.

[10:27a] Verse 26a picked up the theme of 9:3. A still later expander attempted once again to actualize the promise made through Isaiah in a still clearer way. He, just as the author of vv. 24–26a, must have thought that 9:1–6 was a prediction about the downfall of Assyria. But now, even though it was a different entity, "Assyria" continued to raise questions about the power and the trustworthiness of the prophetic promises. For that reason, the author assures the reader that the ancient prediction about deliverance for Israel was finally going to become completely realized.

Even though v. 27a is very closely dependent upon 9:3, the changes are most interesting: Instead of the active verb חָתַת (smash), the passive חָבַּל (be torn away) is used and, in the first half of the verse, the expander uses an intransitive verb (סוּר, be withdrawn); his exclusive interest is about how "now" is the time when the fulfillment of the prophetic prediction will take place; he is enticed solely by the events which will come soon and does not focus on the God who is going to bring them to reality.

Purpose and Thrust

Verses 24–26 are introduced by a messenger formula. That is to be taken seriously, even if the exegesis has clearly shown that the author of this section is also an inferior imitator of a creative thinker; he had very assiduously read the "scriptures." He ventures, in the name of God, to summon his contemporaries "not to fear for yourself" and to proclaim the imminent end of the world power which was only relying on its own might. He apparently sees the justification for his confidence to be two-fold: In the first place, Israel is still the people of God, and thus can count on his saving action. Second, he is certain that Yahweh will act in the present, just as he had acted at the very beginning, in the well-known μεγάλεια (mighty works) of the saving history, at the exodus, when the redemption of Israel was the issue, or at the time of Gideon, when the question concerned whether the people could continue to hold on to the land. Both arguments are rooted in the knowledge of the faithfulness of

Yahweh, which allows one to observe the present, oppressive as it is, in light of the saving history. There is a particular understanding of history behind passages such as these. Certainly, history always presents a new face. But, within history, the basic structures repeat themselves, since the lord of history remains true to himself. Because of this, it is possible to see the future in analogy to the past. Promises are not rendered meaningless if the time period in which they were spoken is now in the past. They are repeatedly reactualized.

The expander in v. 27a underscores that fact. But one must critique this very carefully: He does not shape his remarks based on the faithfulness of God and the saving history which testifies about him, but rather, his viewpoint is sharply focused on the word of God which tells what happened at one particular time and has been recounted since then. The notion that Israel knew of the faithfulness of God, and the saving history which provided evidence for it, only through using the transmitted word is not contradictory, but nevertheless, there is a shift in focus, characteristic of the later era.

Isaiah 10:27b–34

The March against Jerusalem

Literature

K. Fullerton, "The Problem of Isaiah, Chapter 10," *AJSL* 34 (1917/18) 170–184, esp. 173ff. E. Jenni, *Die politischen Voraussagen der Propheten,* ATANT 29 (1956). L. Alonso-Schökel, "Is 10, 28–32: Análisis estilístico," *Bib* 40 (1959) 230–236. H. Donner, *Israel unter den Völkern,* VTSup 11 (1964), here 30–38.

 Concerning the text: E. Robertson, "Some Obscure Passages in Isaiah," *AJSL* 49 (1932/33) 313–324; here 322ff.

 Concerning geography: T. K. Cheyne, "Geographical Gains from Textual Criticism," *Exp* V/10 (1899) 228–232. G. Dalman, "Das Wādi eṣ-ṣwēnīt," *ZDPV* 28 (1905) 161–175. L. Féderlin, "A propos d'Isaïe X, 29–31," *RB* NS 3 (1906) 266–273. G. Dalman, "Palästinische Wege und die Bedrohung Jerusalems nach Jesaja 10," *PJ* 12 (1916) 37–57. W. F. Albright, "The Assyrian March on Jerusalem, Isa. X, 28–32," *AASOR* 4 (1924) 134–140. A. Jirku, "Die Zwölfzahl der Städte in Jes 10, 28–32," *ZAW* 48 (1930) 230. A. Fernández, "El paso difícil del ejército asirio," *EstEcl* 10 (1931) 339–348. H. H. Walker, "Where Were Madmenah and the Gebim?" *JPOS* 13 (1933) 90–93. F. M. Abel, *Géographie de la Palestine,* Vol. I (1933²), vol. II (1938²). A. Fernández, "Migrón," *Miscellanea Biblica BUbach* (1953) 138–142. J. Simons, *The Geographical and Topographical Texts of the Old Testament* (1959), here §1588. H. Donner, "Der Feind aus dem Norden," *ZDPV* 84 (1968) 46–54.

 Concerning individual motifs: G. Vermes, "The Symbolical Interpretation of *Lebanon* in the Targums," *JTS* NS 9 (1958) 1–12.

 [**Literature update through 1979:** D. L. Christensen, "The March of Conquest in Isaiah X 27c–34," *VT* 26 (1976) 385–399.]

Text

10:27b [a]He went[b] up from Samaria,[a]
  28   came to Aiath,
    went through Migron,
     at Michmas[a] he entrusted[b] his baggage.
  29 They crossed through[a] the ravine,[b]
     'Geba[c] will be our[a] quarters for the night!'
    Then Ramah[c] trembled,
     Gibeah of Saul fled.[d]
  30 [a]'Cry shrilly,[a] daughter of Gallim!

Listen attentively, Laishah,
give him an answer, Anathoth!'[b]
31   Madmenah got itself far away,
Gebim's inhabitants brought themselves to safety.[a]
32   Yet today, a position must[a] be taken in Nob,
he swings his hand against the mount[b] of the daughter of Zion,
against the heights of Jerusalem.

33 Behold, [the Lord],[a] Yahweh of Hosts
hews the branches off with the pruning knife.[b]
The towering ones are felled
and the lofty ones are struck down,
34 and the thicket of the forest will be cleared away with iron,
[a]and the Lebanon is overthrown 'with its splendor.'[a]

27a–a MT (literally: "a yoke in light of fat") makes no sense and one cannot be confident about being able to recover the original text. There is no doubt that one ought to read, instead of עֹל (yoke), the verb עָלָה (go up), since it is very unlikely that מִפְּנֵי (from [before]) is to be changed. If that is the case, then שׁמן should be taken to be a place name, but we do not know any place with this name. The closest to what is actually written would be the conjecture יְשִׁימוֹן, "desert," which is also the name for a locale, specifically the *gôr-el-belqâ*, north of the Dead Sea, and also for a particular place in the Negev. The latter location is out of the question, the first is not likely, and we know nothing about any other place with this name to be found anywhere either north or east of Bethel. Many read רִמּוֹן (currently known as *rammûn*) (Marti, Gray, Duhm, *Zürcher Bibel,* Bewer, Simons, Donner [VTSup 11, 30], Montagnini). But one must ask how and why the enemy would have come to an out-of-the-way place like Rimmon. More than for any other reason, רמון (Rimmon) is an unlikely reading if (besides the fact that it is called סֶלַע [ה]רִמּוֹן, the Rock of Rimmon, in Judg. 20:45, 47), as seems most likely, Aiath is to be identified as Ai *(et-tell,* near *dēr dubwān).* It is possible that one should read מִפְּנֵי צָפוֹן (from the direction of the north) or מִצָּפוֹן (from the north) (Simons, et al.), but it is orthographically too far removed from the present text, the same being true in the case of Dalman's suggested reading, which does make good sense: מִפְּנֵי בֵית־אֵל (from before Bethel). Whereas מפני שמאל, "from the north," is a suggestion (Dalman [*PJ* 12] 45) which hardly merits consideration, the proposal first made by von Orelli (1904³) that one read מִפְּנֵי שֹׁמְרוֹן (from before Samaria) seems to catch the correct sense of the text and this has found wide support (Procksch, Kissane, Herntrich, Hertzberg, Bruno, Eichrodt, Kaiser, Leslie, Schildenberger, Fohrer). In any case, the enemy was approaching the capital city of Judah from the north, and its rear base camp must have been at Samaria, even more likely because Shechem had already been leveled before the time in question (see G. E. Wright, *Shechem* [1965] 162ff.).

27b Concerning this translation of the perfect, see below, on form.

28a B reads מכמש (this same variant reading is also in 1 Sam. 13:2, 5, 11, 16). The spelling מכמס (in Ezra 2:27; Neh. 7:31) shows that מכמס is the preferred form, but there is no doubt that the differences in spelling reflect different ways it was pronounced (on this, see Joüon, Gr §5 and Meyer I, 1966³, §8, 14).

28b H. Donner (VTSup 11) takes מכמש (Michmas) with the preceding words ("passed over Migron toward M.") and translates what follows as "musters his weapons of war." And yet, פקד only means "muster" in the *qal;* in the *hiph'il,* on the other hand, it means "entrust, order."

29a Since v. 28 is in the singular, one must ask the question about whether, in v. 29, one ought to read, instead of עברו (they crossed through), rather עבר (he crossed through), along with Qᵃ, Gk, Syr, Vulg, Targ (see G. R. Driver, *JTS* 38 [1937] 39). But then one must conclude that לנו (our, for us) in v. 29aβ should also be altered, possibly emending מלון לנו (our quarters) to read מְלוֹנוֹ (his lodging place) or מָלוֹן לוֹ (a lodging place for him) (perhaps in the form מָלוֹן לָמוֹ). However, such alterations in the text miss the point that this uses a very lively style (it is possible, of course, that עברו should be pointed עָבְרוּ, cross through; see below, commentary on 10:29–31). H. Donner (VTSup 11, 30) translates: "passed through the ravine of Geba, set up a night camp" by reading עבר מעברת גבע מלון לן, but he was obviously guided in this by his presupposition that the poem must have originally been composed of only five-stress cola.

29b מעברה refers to a type of passageway through a valley which is traversed only with extreme difficulty.

29c According to H. Donner, the meter and the geographical line of sight caused these two place names to be switched. But here, as elsewhere, the meter should not be used as a determining factor for such changes, and it makes no sense that the geographical line of sight would have made this change likely, since Ramah is actually closer to Geba.

29d G. R. Driver (*JTS* 38 [1937] 39) explains the meaning of this verb by referring to the Syriac *nās*, "shudder" (cf. the Arabic *nāsa*, "swing to and fro, bob, rock"), coming up with a very close parallel for חרדה (tremble) in the first half of the line. But *parallelismus membrorum* is rather loose in this poem and the meaning "flee" for נוס is so common that Driver's interpretation is not convincing.

30a–a קולך is an "effect-causing object with an instrumental meaning" (BrSynt §93n).

30b עניה ענתות must mean: "poor, miserable is Anathoth." Gk reads ἐπακούσεται (will listen); Syr *wa'enī* (and answer). It may be that עֲנִיהָ (will answer) should be read.

31a In every other case, the *hiph'il* העיז is used in the OT in the transitive: "escape, conceal" (cf. KBL); here it is used elliptically (see BrSynt §127b).

32a Concerning the infinitive with ל to express what one must do, see Joüon, Gr §124l.

32b Qere, Qᵃ, Gk, Syr, Vulg are certainly correct when they read בַּת (daughter). One might ask whether the word ought not just be eliminated; normally, the book of Isaiah refers to it as הר ציון (Mount Zion) (4:5; 8:18; 10:12, and often elsewhere), but one also finds הר בת ציון (Mount of the daughter of Zion) (16:1; cf., for בת ציון daughter of Zion, Jer. 6:2; Mic. 4:8). Once again, the meter should not be the decisive factor.

33a האדון (the Lord) is most likely secondary here, as in some other cases in which it seems quite apparent just by observing the transmitted text.

33b מערצה is a *hapax legomenon* and must mean something like "terror" (see מערץ, shuddering, above, textual note 13b, on 8:11–15). But it is recommended that one follow Duhm and read במעצד, "with the knife (whip, pruning knife)" (or possibly במעצדו, with his knife), parallel to בברזל (with iron) in v. 34.

34a–a The second half of v. 34 presents many difficulties. As it stands, MT should be translated "and Lebanon falls because of a majestic one" (or: "mighty one"), in which case it would remain unclear whether the "majestic one" refers to Yahweh or the Assyrian king. Instead of אדיר (splendor), others read קרדום, "ax" (as a parallel to ברזל, iron) (see BHK); Dalman, *PJ* 12, 57, reads עדיר, "pickax" (which is not found in the OT); Ehrlich reads מַשּׂוֹר, "saw"; Guthe reads כְּשִׁיל, also with the meaning "ax"; Tur-Sinai ("A Contribution to the Understanding of Isaiah I–XII," ScrHier 8 [1961] 186) reads באַרד, "with bronze" (based on the Akkadian *arudû*, "bronze"); this means there has been a widespread search for a parallel word for ברזל (iron) in the first half of the verse (cf. also the conjectured word מעצד, pruning knife, in 33). On the other hand, E. Robertson (*AJSL* 49 [1933] 322ff.) would rather read כרמל (garden land) instead of ברזל (iron) and בְּאֶרְזָיו

(cedars) instead of בַּאְדִּיר (with splendor); he suggests that it could be translated: "And he shall cut down the thickets (of the forest) of Carmel. And Lebanon with its cedars he will fell." But it seems that Gk read a plural for אַדִּיר (splendor) (ὁ δὲ Λίβανος σὺν τοῖς ὑψηλοῖς πεσεῖται, but Lebanon with its majestic ones will fall). אַדִּירִים (majestic ones) (or possibly, instead of that, אַדִּירָיו, its majestic ones) could be a play on words on the cedars of Lebanon (see Zech. 11:2 and Ezek. 17:23). And yet, the suggestion by A. Bruno, to read בְּאֶדְרוֹ (with its splendor) (from אֶדֶר, "splendor"; see Zech. 11:13 and cf. Mic. 2:8), seems most preferable. Actually, the way the cedars of Lebanon are adorned is also important here.

Form

Even if v. 27b cannot be reconstructed with absolute certainty, there is no reason to doubt that this half-verse does not belong with the preceding section. One cannot know for sure whether it served as the original beginning for this poem; when the larger unity, 10:5–34, was assembled redactionally, certainly with the overall purpose of speaking about Assyria, it may be that the original introduction fell by the wayside, possibly having done no more than mention the subject under discussion. There has also been disagreement about how far the original section extends. As already done by J. G. Herder (*Vom Geist der Ebräischen Poesie* II/2, Sämmtl. Werke, ed. B. Suphan, 12 [1880] 289), and suggested once again by Bruno, Kaiser takes vv. 33f. (of course, without v. 33b) as providing a negative backdrop to 11:1–9. However, it has generally been presumed in current research that vv. 33f. are a supplementary addition to vv. 27b–32 (Marti, Gray, Duhm, König, Bewer, Eichrodt, Fohrer, et al.), whereas Donner (VTSup 11, 31) takes at least v. 34 as a later addition. The question is complicated still further by the problem of determining who the author might be. Duhm, for example, also considers vv. 33f. to be supplementary, but still considers vv. 27b–32 to be from someone who came after Isaiah. "The poem is rich in wordplays, but empty in terms of content; its entire approach seems to me to be too frivolous for me to be inclined to attribute it to Isaiah." But this assessment, mainly based on aesthetic considerations, is too arbitrary. It could be that the seemingly "frivolous approach" in the poem was chosen consciously, in contrast to the deadly seriousness of the message, in order to bring about obedience most effectively. But Duhm has observed something correctly in this case: If one denies vv. 33f. to the original author, then one gets into considerable difficulty as one tries to put into words what the section is supposed to mean. Then, one can understand Duhm's assessment that the poem is "empty of content." But that viewpoint would be completely unjustified if vv. 33f. are from Isaiah (see below, on the setting).

When a reader attempts to understand these verses, the following alternatives are posed: Do these verses depict an invasion of an enemy which has already begun to occur or, instead, does this describe a vision of the future? In general, most exegetes are of the opinion that this portrays events which were seen in a vision about what was yet to come. J. Lindblom (*Die Gesichte der Propheten,* StudTheol. [Riga] I [1935] 7–28, here 22ff.) speaks of revelatory fantasies taking shape, cognizant of the fact that the vision originated in the author's own fantasies, even if the author considers it to have come by the inspiration of God. One must leave as undecided the extent to which this view into the future and its explanation are based on a revelatory experience and whether one wishes to describe this poem as something more than an anticipatory look at future events. But recently, H. Donner (VTSup 11) has once again spoken out strongly in favor of the opposite viewpoint. He points to the perfect forms in vv. 27b–29a: The enemy has already come as far as Geba and has set up overnight headquarters there. Now of course there are also perfects in vv. 29b–31. But they do not any longer simply depict the campaign itself; they describe what happened as the astonishing march of the enemy left a deep impression on those localities which are closest to the front, Ramah, Gibeah of Saul, Anathoth, Madmenah, and Gebim, whereas the reaction of the population in Gallim and Laishah is described by using the imperatives "cry shrilly" and "answer." On the contrary, according to Donner, v. 32 exposes the enemy's war strategy, whereas the actual message is recorded in v. 33, introduced by הנה (behold) plus participle and continued by perfect consecutive or imperfect forms. One might say, in opposition to this interpretation, that the perfects are so-called prophetic perfects, but one must be very careful when making an assessment by applying this terminology (see above, on the form of 5:26–30), and switching back and forth in the tenses needs further clarification in any case. Yet, tense is not the only significant factor which would lead one to conclude that this describes actual warfare as it is occurring: The enemy had not used the normal route when marching against Jerusalem (see below, commentary on 10:27b–32), but took a roundabout way, east of the relatively convenient main road which ran between Shechem and Jerusalem. The description is surprisingly precise and detailed, in fact, it is the most exact description of an army's campaign against Jerusalem anywhere in the OT. If it was supposed to be a "vision," the author undoubtedly would have avoided such specific predictions, but would have spoken in very general terms about the advance of the foe "from the north." (One might compare the so-called "war-songs" of Jeremiah, in chaps. 4–6.) Thus, one must basically interpret the section in the same way as was suggested by Donner: We are dealing with the depiction of a surprise attack against Jerusalem, which has already reached the border of the Judean territory and has caused a panic among the communities located along the route leading up to the city. It would seem that the enemy has every intention of storming and taking the city ruled by the Davidic family.

Setting

This brings up the most difficult question about this passage, which certainly does not suffer from a lack of difficulties: At which point within the historical time frame of Isaiah might one discover such a campaign against Jerusalem by such an enemy? We do not have a single indication which would identify the fierce opponent which apparently intended to bring the city into its power by means of a very well-planned sudden attack. H. Donner made a concerted effort to interpret this as a particular phase of the Syro-Ephraimitic War, namely, in the same circumstances as were described in 8:5–8 (VTSup 11, 37). That forces him to conclude that the pride which is to be dealt with, according to v. 33, is the hubris of the two neighbors of Judah to the north, both marching against Jerusalem, Israel and Aram (so also Leslie). But there are serious questions to be raised against this interpretation. The section does not belong to the "memorial record" of the Syro-Ephraimitic War (see above, on the form of 6:1–13). There is no visible evidence that the enemy consists of *two* peoples, bound by an agreement. The redactor who placed this section in this location, after the other passages which refer to Assyria in chap. 10, was certainly of the opinion that the enemy here was also Assyria. In reality, if one presumes that Isaiah is the source of the passage, that is the most likely solution.

However, an Assyrian invasion of Judah is known to have taken place in 701, and it is for this reason that many commentators believe this refers to Sennacherib's offensive against Jerusalem (so Steinmann, Pfeiffer [*RSO* 32 (1957) 150f.], Kaiser, Mauchline, Fohrer, Montagnini). That is impossible as well, since that offensive against Jerusalem did not come from the north, but from the southwest, from the coastal region. Procksch (see also Kissane and Feldmann) thinks it refers to the time when Sargon was at the height of his power. More specifically, this could be about the episode when Ashdod rebelled (which Sargon reported in a number of inscriptions; *ANET* 286f.; *AOT* 350ff.; see Tadmor, "The Campaigns of Sargon II of Assur," *JCS* 12 [1958] 79f.). The books of Kings do not report anything about the position taken by Judah during this rebellion against Assyria in the Palestinian region. However, Sargon writes that Iamani of Ashdod was successful in bringing Judah, Moab, Edom, and the inhabitants of the islands, which had been paying tribute and bringing gifts to Assyria up to that time, into the anti-Assyrian front. It would appear that Isaiah was very much involved in this discussion: According to chap. 20, he attempted, with all the means at his disposal, to put an end to reliance on the Ethiopians, who had promised their help to Ashdod, and one suspects that chap. 18, which reports that the Ethiopian envoys appeared at the palace of Hezekiah, is to be interpreted in light of this same situation. One has no way of knowing what Judah finally decided to do. But, in any case, Sargon had good reason to keep a sharp eye on Judah. This present passage may very likely describe precautionary measures which the Assyrian king took to hold the city of Jerusalem in check, which, along with Ashdod, was in sympathy with and under the diplomatic control of the Ethiopians. He allowed (if our textual reconstruction above is correct) troops to march to the northern border of Judah from their original station in Samaria, which at that time served as the capital city of the Assyrian province of the same name. One might presume that, because of such a move, Judah would have been brought to the point of absolute panic and been greatly afraid of an invasion of the capital city. Of course, it never reached that point; otherwise, no doubt, some news about it would have been preserved for us. The enemy troops stayed in Geba, and Judah stayed neutral in the matter of the rebellion led by Ashdod. The purpose of the lightning-quick invasion had been achieved; Assyria had demonstrated its might. Therefore, Isaiah would have spoken the words of this section at the very time when the enemy troops had just made it through the narrow passage, which was difficult to negotiate, the *wādi eṣ-ṣuwēniṭ*, which was between *muḥmās* and *ǧeba'*. But it must be made clear that no claim is being made that one can be confident of determining an exact historical date with absolute certainty.

And now, to return to the question about the authenticity of vv.

33f. If the interpretation which was outlined above is correct, then the message can be understood only in the sense of a threat of disaster against Jerusalem, which had erred by following such a mistaken political course, being both foolhardy and motivated by unbelief. The last two verses of the chapter speak explicitly about this very issue. Since the enemy would come into direct contact with the circles of leadership, which is what the reference to "the haughty" must mean, one would not expect anything different. Both the idea itself, expressed in the judgment against the hubris, and the way it is formulated (cf. the vocables רום, towering, exalted, שפל גבה, lofty ones are struck down) bear the mark of Isaiah (see, e.g., 2:11). There is no reason to deny the two verses to Isaiah, even though one might concede that v. 34 could be a later addition.

Meter: H. Donner (VTSup 11, 38) presumes that he can read vv. 27b–32 as five-stress cola and v. 33 as 2 three-stress bicola. That is accomplished only by rearranging the text in ways which cannot be justified. Verses 27b and 28aα could indeed be taken as the normal form of a five-stress colon; 28aβb and 29a are five-stress cola in the reverse order (2 + 3); 29b and 30a once again are normal five-stress cola; 30b, 31 is a four-stress colon; 31b, 32a is a six-stress colon; 32b once again is a five-stress colon. Continuing to the end of v. 34, there may be 3 six-stress cola (סבכי ⟨ה⟩⟨יער⟩, thicket of the forest, is possibly to be read with *one* stress). And yet, one might pose the question about whether one ought to seek a metrical structure in this section, particularly since here, as well as elsewhere (see above, textual note 29d), there is no recognizable *parallelismus membrorum*. But, in spite of this, it is a most impressive poem. Every individual colon engages the reader: The short lines paint the picture of the enemy going forward by leaps and bounds; the "reversed five-stress cola," in their own way, underscore the lightning-quick advances and the temporary halts at the nearest place one could set up a base of operations. The "six-stress cola" at the conclusion highlight the transition from portrayal to reflection. Delitzsch (ad loc.) ventured the judgment: "The depiction qualifies, aesthetically speaking, as one of the most magnificent artistic endeavors which has ever been produced in human poetry. . . . Up to v. 32a, the description moves along by describing lightning-quick military actions; then it becomes slow-moving and pulsates with anxiety-filled moments."

The poem makes use of a wide range of stylistic techniques connected with alliteration: cf. הרמה חרדה; בנף ינפף; נדדה מדמנה; לנו מלון; מעברה עברו; עלה על עית; עליו קולך בת גלים; עניהו ענתות. One might also take note of the darker tone of the o-vowel, used at the point when the disaster overtakes Jerusalem (on this, see L. Alonso-Schökel, op. cit., 233); in addition, the names are played around with as one would in a folk-etymology; Micah (1:10–15) furnishes a companion piece. (Duhm attempted to replicate this artistic style: "sie passiren *[sic!]* den Pass, Geba gibt Herberge uns, erregt ist Harama . . . Madmena macht sich davon, antworte ihr, Anathoth!")

Commentary

[10:27b–32] Based on the interpretation outlined above, concerning the march of the enemy against Jerusalem, it is only natural that Samaria is mentioned as the point of origin. Certainly Sargon himself was not leading the troops, but rather some officer, possibly the governor of Samaria who had been put in charge of carrying out this action. As might be expected, the enemy army did not meet any resistance before it found itself in front of the walls of Geba; at the beginning, the army moved through what would have been part of the border region of the Assyrian province Samerina. In Geba itself, the people were apparently so over-whelmed that it could be occupied without any apparent resistance.

Study of the text has dedicated much effort to identification of the place names mentioned in vv. 27ff., without arriving at any satisfactory conclusions (see above, the Literature section; as one of the most recent studies listed there, H. Donner's work [*ZDPV* 84] deserves particularly close attention). The first handicap is that, since reading שמרון (Samaria) in v. 27b is only a conjecture, one cannot be absolutely sure about the point of origin for the expedition. The first place name in v. 28, Aiath, is actually transmitted without any textual problem, but it cannot be located with certainty. At an earlier time (Albright), it had been sought at *ḫirbet ḥayyān* (near *dēr dubwān*). But the American probe at the site confirmed what some had suspected on the basis of a surface examination, that there was no settlement there before the time of the Romans (see *BASOR* 183 [1966] 12–19). One should probably consider עית (Aiath) to be a feminine form, derived from the well-known form עי (Ai), and seek its location at *et-tell* (2 km. southeast of Bethel *[bētīn]* near present-day *dēr dubwān;* Abel, *Géogr.* II, 239f.).

The identification of Migron is still less certain (see also 1 Sam. 14:2). A. Alt once suggested that it was *tell-miryam* (*PJ* 23 [1927] 17ff.). But the ceramic evidence remains uncertain and, in addition to that, the location does not prove to be very satisfactory, since the *tell* is not located along the line from Ai to Michmas. To alter the text on these grounds (so KBL) would be permissible only if the reputed identification would be more certain. Donner suggests, as had G. Dalman before him, that this refers to *tell el-'askar,* 750 m. northeast of *muḥmās.*

It is generally accepted that the just-mentioned place name refers to the location of what was once called Michmas, so that we have finally reached a location which is identified with certainty. It is from this place that the enemy set out to traverse the "passage" through the *wādi eṣ-ṣuwēnīṭ,* called מַעֲבַר מִכְמָשׂ (pass of Michmas) in 1 Sam. 13:23. Geba can also be identified with certainty; the location is presently called *ǧeba'.*

Like Geba, the place names which follow doubtlessly refer to places which are in the Benjaminite territory north of Jerusalem. Ramah can be located with certainty, known today as *er-rām,* 8 km. north of Jerusalem and a bit east of the main highway which goes to the north from Jerusalem; Gibeah of Saul, which was located on what is now known as *tell el-fūl,* is about 5.5 km. north of Jerusalem; the highway from Jerusalem passes by on its western edge (on this, see the excavation reports in *AASOR* 4 [1924] and *BASOR* 52 [1933] 6ff.); and Anathoth is identified with what is presently known as *rās el-ḥarrūbe,* 800 m. south-south-west of the present village of *'anāta,* which is 4.5 km. northeast of Jerusalem but is some distance to the east of the highway. Nob is to be sought, with some degree of certainty, in the area around *rās el-mušārif,* 1.5 km. southeast of *tell el-fūl,* but possibly it was on one of the northernmost knolls of the Mount of Olives, near the location of the Augusta-Victoria Hospital. The rest of the little towns cannot be identified with any degree of certainty (concerning these places, see the map on p. 454).

It would seem most likely that the listing of the place names in vv. 29b–32 indicates the route which the troops planned to take from Geba. According to this, they would have had to march due west, so that they could reach the main highway at Ramah, and would then have marched in a southerly direction along this road, in order to pass through Gibeah of Saul and be in the vicinity of the city of Jerusalem when they arrived at Nob. If this is the case, then Gallim and Laishah would be between Gibeah and Anathoth, while Madmenah and Gebim would have been

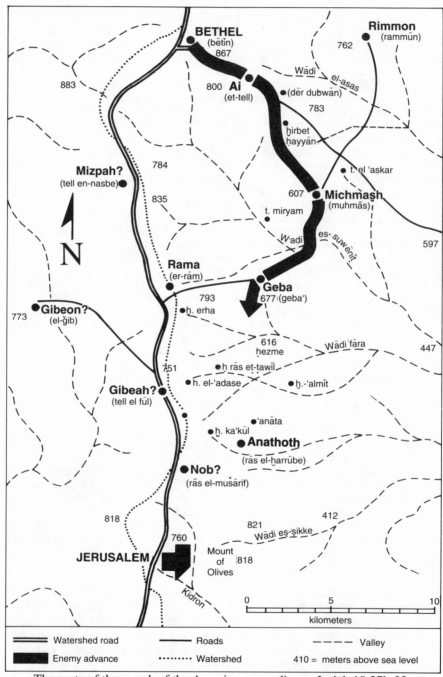

The route of the march of the Assyrians according to Isaiah 10:27b-32.

between Anathoth and Nob. But the out-of-the-way location of Anathoth already goes against this interpretation; even more importantly, it is impossible to align these cities which are mentioned along a line from Geba to Nob. Recognizing these problems, Donner set forth the thesis that the march from Geba to Jerusalem was to proceed along three different routes. Based on this presupposition, taking into account both topographical and archaeological considerations, he concluded that *ḥirbet erḥa* (southeast of *er-rām*), *ḥirbet rās eṭ-ṭawil, ḥirbet el-'adase* (both northeast of *tell el-fūl*), and *ḥirbet ka'kūl* (northwest of *'anāta*) could have been locations for Gallim, Laishah, Madmenah, and Gebim, without trying to be any more exact about identifying the biblical locations with the modern designations for these places. But Donner's thesis—that there were three possible directions in which the march would have gone—is not likely. Isaiah does not want to describe the actual route or the possible routes which could be followed by the advancing army; rather, he simply provides a list of the places where people lived, those who had been thrown into a dreadful panic by an invasion which came to Jerusalem via Geba. Except for the fact that his list proceeds from north to south, one cannot be sure of what principle he followed when listing the cities—if, in fact, he was not simply trying to provide a relatively complete list of all the little towns between Geba and Jerusalem. Since the modern names of the cities do not help in the attempt to more specifically locate Gallim, Laishah, Madmenah, and Gebim, the best one can hope for is that further excavations will clarify the matter. But it may be that these were nothing more than insignificant settlements, the remains of which would hardly be very spectacular.

Even though the identification of the places which were listed must remain to some extent uncertain and to some extent impossible, this still does not alter one's perception that the enemy did not make its advance along the more well-constructed highway, but made its way into Judah through a back entrance. Fohrer thinks that this back road had been chosen so that they could remain under the cover of the mountains for as long as possible. However, from the route which starts at the northern end of the Mount of Olives or from the present-day *rās el-harrūbe,* it is easy to see for quite a distance (on this, see Donner [*ZDPV* 84] 46f.). It is much more likely that one ought to presume that the intention was to find a way around Mizpah (*tell en-naṣbe;* on this, see 1 Kings 15:22 and *BHH,* II, 1228f.), the fortress at Judah's northern border (see Donner [VTSup 11] 36). Of course, according to 1 Kings 15:22, King Asa did not only build Mizpah but also Geba to provide protection on the northern border. But this fortification never seems to have been very important. And yet, one must presume that the very important city of Mizpah played an especially crucial role during unsettled times and the garrison there had important responsibilities. It is possible that the approaching troops were much too weak to be able to force their way through the narrow *wādi ǧilyān* at the eastern edge of the city.

[10:28] In light of the interpretation offered here for this section, it is easy to see why Assyria—taking precautionary measures at a time of political unrest among its vassals in southern Palestine—would have directed its supply camp to go to Michmas. Michmas was a town along the border of the Assyrian province and thus provided a base of operations for invasions into the Judean territory.

[10:29–31] If עָבְרוּ (crossed through) has been transmitted correctly (see above, textual note 29a), then the enemies had already made their way across the *wādi* which separated Michmas from Geba, so that they were now standing on Judean territory—the floor of the valley would have formed the border.

Whether Geba itself had already fallen remains unclear; the prophet allows the enemy to express its intention to set up overnight headquarters at that site. Still less can be said about whether it had gone further into Judah from that place. There is no chance that Jerusalem had been assaulted, but there is no doubt that there was considerable fear in settlements in the territory of Benjamin, certainly very poorly fortified; after the army had circumvented Mizpah, these people were completely at the mercy of the enemy and without any protection. The inhabitants of Gibeah, Madmenah, and Gebim had already fled (on this, see Jer. 4:5ff., 15–18); in the other places, cries of woe filled the air.

[10:32] Before anyone in Jerusalem had recovered from the first shock and before news arrived about the actual strength of the enemy, the people in Jerusalem certainly had to reckon with the likelihood that there would be a surprise attack. But the unsuccessful siege of Jerusalem by Sennacherib shows that Jerusalem was too well fortified to have been conquered without a massive resistance effort. The Assyrians must have been well aware of this. They were happy enough that Judah kept quiet during the time when rebellion had been put down in the land of the Philistines. Ashdod could not actually depend upon any help from Jerusalem, and it also seems that Jerusalem did not come under any particular sanctions after the fall of Ashdod.

[10:33f.] Regardless of whether one takes vv. 33f. as Isaianic or not, it seems that the general inclination has been to assume that these two verses proclaim the failure of this daring and treacherous assault against Jerusalem. If one considers these verses to be a later addition, from another hand, there is hardly another interpretation which would make any sense. The expander would intend to say that the major power from the Tigris region, mentioned already in 10:5–15, was showing its arrogance by moving against Jerusalem and the addition would have been inserted to afford Isaiah the opportunity to announce the downfall of this reckless world power which toyed with whole groups of peoples as one would play with pieces on a chess board. But if one takes these verses to be Isaianic, then one must very carefully weigh the other possibility, namely, that Isaiah enters into judgment of those who were responsible for Judean political decisions. He had done everything possible to keep Hezekiah from relying upon the promises being offered by the Ethiopian envoys and from offering assurances to Ashdod that Judah would help him. It would seem that he had little success with his warnings. It was not his message but rather the vigilance of the Assyrians which prevented Judah from joining in this adventurous rebellion initiated by Ashdod. Therefore, it seems most likely that Isaiah warns the Jerusalem party which was friendly toward Ashdod, being both arrogant and thoughtless, that their efforts would go for naught (one might compare 8:5–8). He uses the imagery employed when one speaks of clearing a thick forest. יַעַר (forest) describes land which has been overgrown with low shrubbery, sometimes very difficult to traverse because the bushes have become so intertwined that they have formed a nearly impenetrable thicket (סְבָךְ, v. 34) (on this, cf. Dalman, *AuS* I, 73ff., esp. 81f., and L. Rost, *PJ* 27 [1931] 111–122, esp. 118f.). But it is possible that some very tall trees could still be seen projecting above this thick, woody ground cover.

Concerning the concept of bringing down the "high," and particularly the terms רוּם (towering) and שָׁפֵל (struck down), one ought to consult what is said in 2:6ff. קוֹמָה (height), יַעַר (forest), and לְבָנוֹן (Lebanon) are also found, together with a derivative of the root רוּם (be exalted), in the taunt song against Assyria, in 37:23f. (cf. also Ezek. 31:3, 10ff., within a taunt song directed against the Pharaoh, and see, in addition, Ezek. 6:3). It is possible that Isaiah uses terminology and imagery which were used in the taunt songs which mocked an arrogant enemy. Lebanon, having vegetation which grew to considerable heights, serves as a common image in the OT for describing height and vital power (Isa. 2:13; Ezek. 31:3). Concerning the types of axes, cf. *BRL,* cols. 62–68.

Purpose and Thrust

No further comments are made concerning the meaning of the imagery about clearing and removing brush from the forest as that might apply to Jerusalem. Quite assuredly, it is *not* said that Jerusalem will be conquered. And yet, it is easy to understand that there must have been fear and trepidation in Jerusalem. Even if the situation did not go to such extremes and never resulted in a massive invasion of the Benjaminite territories, there would have been still been a deafening silence, among those "who had grown very tall" in Jerusalem, when the Assyrians appeared at the border. One can easily surmise that the pressure from the Assyrians would have caused Hezekiah to reorganize his government. At any rate, the influence of the anti-Assyrian group would have become inconsequential at this time and their arrogant activities would have given way to a disconcerting silence. The fact that the king risked listening to their whispered suggestions once again, at a later time, simply shows that human beings are unwilling to learn very much from history and demonstrates how quickly the admonitions of prophets were forgotten.

This present section makes it crystal clear once more that one does not do justice to Isaiah by saying that he is to be treated as if he were a fortuneteller who could announce political and military actions before they occurred. It makes no sense to assess his efforts on the basis of whether the events took place in the exact way he expected and described them. The message of this present passage, and others like it, is the announcement that human arrogance finally shatters. Connected with that, of course, is a conception about political realities which he—along with other prophets—was able to hold to steadfastly, with an amazing certainty: Judah should protect itself from getting mixed up in the affairs of the world powers. The history of the times provided him with plenty of material to justify his theological and political approach: The unexpected and lightning-quick strike of what was just a little Assyrian detachment was enough to destroy the deceptive confidence which was so pleasing to those in Jerusalem, and it revealed the hollow nature of the "arrogant" manner in which the leading circles in Jerusalem conducted themselves. One might compare this with the message spoken by Isaiah in the same situation, in 20:5: "Then they shall be dismayed and confounded because of Ethiopia their hope and Egypt their boast." The alternative to arrogance would have been trust in Yahweh (cf. 7:9 and 31:15). But, in Isaiah's case, it is worth pondering how closely trust in Yahweh—and this is not uniquely true about him among the OT prophets—is linked with a moderate political plan of action, which stays far away from all risky adventures.

Verses 27b–34 bring chapter 10 to a conclusion, being directed against Assyria. The redactor, who placed this section at this point, doubtlessly interpreted vv. 33f., along with the majority of modern interpreters, in reference to the failure of Assyria to take Jerusalem and might have been thinking of Sennacherib's siege of Jerusalem. But the preceding section shows that, by his time, "Assyria" was no longer actually the world empire known to us from the time of Isaiah. Remembering the Assyrian failure at the time of Isaiah would give one courage to rely on the help of Yahweh against whatever world power was in control during one's own lifetime.

Taking this step to reinterpret the message allows one to see how Isaiah was seen as a uniquely important individual, one who certainly did not agree with the presumptuousness of the Assyrians, but was more concerned that Israel, filled with anger because of the outrages being perpetrated by the world power, would not fail to take note of the evil consequences which could result from its own presumptuousness.

Messiah and Kingdom of Peace

Literature

M. B. Crook, "A Suggested Occasion for Isaiah 9:2–7 and 11:1–9," *JBL* 68 (1949) 213–224. Idem, "Did Amos and Micah Know Isaiah 9:2–7 and 11:1–9?" *JBL* 73 (1954) 144–151. L. Alonso-Schökel, "Dos poemas a la paz," *EstBib* 18 (1959) 149–169. S. Herrmann, *Die prophetischen Heilserwartungen im Alten Testament,* BWANT 85 (1965); here, 137ff. J. Schildenberger, "Durch Gericht zum Heil," *Sein und Sendung* 30 (1965) 531–540. J. Becker, *Isaias—der Prophet und sein Buch,* Stuttgarter Bibelstudien 30 (1968), here, 27–30. H. Wildberger, "Jesaja 11, 1–5.9," in *Hören und fragen,* edited by G. Eichholz and A. Falkenroth, vol. 5 (1967) 58–67. M. Rehm, *Der königliche Messias im Licht der Immanuel-Weissagungen des Buches Jesaja,* Eichstätter Studien NF 1, n.d. (1968), here, 185–234. W. H. Schmidt, "Die Ohnmacht des Messias," *KD* 15 (1969) 18–34.

Concerning the text: G. Beer, "Bemerkungen zu Jes. 11, 1–8," *ZAW* 18 (1898) 345–347. G. B. Gray, "The Strophic Division of Isaiah 21:1–10 and 11:1–8," *ZAW* 32 (1912) 190–198.

Concerning messianism: (see also the literature on this theme listed for 7:1–17 and 8:23aβ—9:6). W. Caspari, "Die Anfänge der alttestamentlichen messianischen Weissagung," *NKZ* 31 (1920) 455–481. D. H. Corley, "Messianic Prophecy in First Isaiah," *AJSL* 19 (1922/23) 220–224. H. Schmidt, *Der Mythos vom wiederkehrenden König im Alten Testament,* Schriften der Hessischen Hochschulen, Universität Giessen, 1925/1 (1925). H. Gressmann, *Der Messias,* FRLANT 43 (1929), here, 246–248. W. O. E. Oesterley, "Messianic Prophecy and Extra-Israelite Beliefs," *CQR* 119 (1934/35) 1–11. S. Mowinckel, *He That Cometh* (1956), here, 30ff. F. L. Moriarty, "The Emmanuel Prophecies," *CBQ* 19 (1957) 226–233. W. Koppers, "Prophetismus und Messianismus als völkerkundliches und universalgeschichtliches Problem," *Saeculum* 10 (1959) 38–47. V. Lanternari, *Messianism: Its Origin and Morphology,* History of Religions 2 (1962) 52–72. J. Coppens, *Le Messianisme Royal,* LD 54 (1968), here, 82–85. J. Alonso-Díaz, "Mito o coloración mitológica en la figura del Mesías," *EstBib* 27 (1968) 233–245. J. Coppens, "Les espérances messianiques du Proto-Isaïe et leurs prétendues relectures," *ETL* 44 (1968) 491–497.

Concerning individual motifs: R. Koch, "Der Gottesgeist und der Messias," *Bib* 27 (1946) 241–268. A. García del Moral, "Sentido trinitario de la expresión 'Espíritu de Yavé' de Is. XI,2 en I Pdr. IV,14," *EstBib* 20 (1961) 169–206. G. Ruggieri, *Il figlio di Dio Davidico,* AnGr 166 (1968). S. Plath. *Furcht Gottes,* AzTh II/2 (1963), here, 83f. J. Becker, *Gottesfurcht im Alten Testament,* AnBib 25 (1965), here, 258f. H. R. Balz, "Furcht vor Gott?," *EvT* 29 (1969) 626–

644, here, 629–631. G. Wanke, art. "φοβέω B," *TDNT* IX, 197–205. H. Bruppacher, *Die Beurteilung der Armut im Alten Testament* (1924). H. Birkeland, *ξAnî und ξānāw in den Psalmen*, SNVAO 1932/2 (1933). A. Kuschke, "Arm und reich im Alten Testament mit besonderer Berücksichtigung der nachexilischen Zeit," *ZAW* 57 (1939) 31–57. L. Dürr, *Die Wertung des göttlichen Wortes im Alten Testament und im antiken Orient*, MVAAG 42/1 (1938). F. S. Bodenheimer, *Animal Life in Palestine* (1935). I. Aharoni, "On some Animals Mentioned in the Bible," *Osiris* 5 (1938) 461–478. A. de Guglielmo, "The Fertility of the Land in the Messianic Prophecies," *CBQ* 19 (1957) 306–311. F. S. Bodenheimer, *Animal and Man in Bible Lands* (1960). J. J. Stamm/H. Bietenhard, *Der Weltfriede im Lichte der Bibel* (1959). H. Gross, *Die Idee des ewigen und allgemeinen Weltfriedens im Alten Orient und im Alten Testament*, TTS 7 (1967²). H. H. Schmid. *šalôm. "Frieden" im Alten Orient und im Alten Testament*, SBS 51 (1971) (literature!).

Concerning the interpretation by the Qumran community: R. E. Brown, "The Messianism of Qumran," *CBQ* 19 (1957) 53–82. A. S. van der Woude, *Die messianischen Vorstellungen der Gemeinde von Qumran*, Studia Semitica Neerlandica 3 (1957). J. A. Fitzmyer, "The Aramaic 'Elect of God' Text from Qumran Cave IV," *CBQ* 27 (1965) 348–372.

[Literature update through 1979: B. Celada, "Una profecía altamente espiritual, y una manera general de entender todas las profecías del AT (Is 11,9)," *CB* 24 (1967) 158–162. F. Montagnini, "Le roi-Messie attendu, Is 11,1–10," *Seign* 2/6 (1969) 6–12. F. Lange, "Exegetische Probleme zu Jes 11," *LRb* 23 (1975) 115–127.

Concerning the text: A. García del Moral, "Sobre el significado del verbo nuaḥ en Is 11,2," *MEAH* 10/2 (1961) 33–63. D. N. Freedman, "Is Justice Blind? (Is 11:3f.)," *Bib* 52 (1971) 536. F. Deist, "Jes 11,3a: Eine Glosse?" *ZAW* 85 (1973) 351–355.

Concerning messianism: M. Jenny, "'Es ist ein Ros entsprungen'," *Neue Zürcher Zeitung* 791 (22 December 1968). H.-J. Hermisson, "Zukunftserwartung und Gegenwartskritik in der Verkündigung Jesajas," *EvT* 33 (1973) 54–77, see esp. 58–66. O. Betz, "'Kann denn aus Nazareth etwas Gutes kommen?' (Zur Verwendung von Jesaja Kap. 11 in Johannes Kap. 1)," FS K. Elliger (1973) 9–16.

Concerning individual motifs: R. L. Honeycutt, "The Root Ṣ-D-K in Prophetic Literature,' diss., Edinburgh (1970/71). S. Erlandsson, "Jesaja 11,10–16 och dess historiska bakgrund," *SEÅ* 36 (1971) 24–44. J. Jensen, *The Use of tôrâ by Isaiah*, CBQMS 3 (1973) passim.]

Text

11:1 A shoot will come forth from the stump[a] of Jesse
    and a sprig will 'sprout forth'[b] from his roots.

2 And the Spirit of Yahweh will rest upon him,
    Spirit of wisdom and of insight,
    Spirit of planning and of a hero's power,
    Spirit of knowledge and of fear of Yahweh,

3 [a][and he will have, as his pleasure, the fear of Yahweh.][a]
    [And][b] he does not judge according to appearances[c]
    and does not decide simply on the basis of mere rumor;[d]

4 rather, with righteousness, he helps the lightly esteemed to get
        justice
    and will intervene with equity for 'the poor'[a] in the land
  and he strikes the 'violent ones'[b] with the staff of his mouth
    and kills the malicious one with the breath from his lips.

5 And righteousness[a] is the girdle[b] of his hips
    and faithfulness[a] is the loincloth of his loins.

6 Then the wolf will be a visitor of the lamb
    and the leopard[a] will lie down with the kid.
  Then calf and young lion 'will get fattened'[b] together,
    and a little lad will tend them.

7 Then cow and bear will 'be friends with one another,'[a]
　　and their young will lie down with one another.
　　Then the lion will eat chopped straw like the cow,
8 　　and the suckling will play near the hole of a viper.
　　And toward a young[a] viper
　　a (weaned) child will stretch out its hand.[b]
9 No one shall do anything evil or anything destructive
　　upon my entire holy mountain:
　　For the land will be as full[a] of the knowledge[b] of Yahweh
　　as waters cover[d] the sea.[c]

　　　　　*　　*　　*　　*

10 [And it will happen on that day: Toward the root of Jesse, which
　　stands there like a signal for the nations, the nations will all turn
　　inquisitively, and its resting place shall be glory.]

1a B (see BHK[1,2]) points this גֵּוַ.

1b יפרה, "will be fruitful," is not a close parallel to ויצא (will come forth) in the first half of the verse. The versions (Gk: ἀναβήσεται, will rise up; Targ: יתרבי, will magnify itself; Syr: *nafra',* it budded; Vulg: *ascendet,* will go up) permit one to draw the conclusion that the original reading probably would have been יפרח, "will sprout forth."

3a–a Verse 3a (literally: "and his smell is that of fear of Yahweh") is not satisfactory, even if הֲרִיחַ is translated "have pleasure in," since the repetition of יראת יהוה (fear of Yahweh) interrupts the flow. In addition to this, the second half-line is missing. The versions (Gk: ἐμπλήσει αὐτόν, it will fill him; Targ: ויקרביניה, and he will bring him near; Syr: *wᵉnednaḥ,* "and he gleamed"; Vulg: *et replebit eum,* and it filled him) do not give any real help here either. Emendations such as that suggested by G. Beer (op. cit., 345): והניח בו יראת י' (and the fear of Yahweh will rest upon him) (cf. Ezek. 24:13, MT, and Gk) are not convincing (see also G. R. Driver, *Textus* 1 [1960] 129); there is no doubt that it is actually a dittography from the previous ויראת יהוה (דעת) רוח (Spirit of knowledge and of fear of Yahweh).

3b The ו *(Waw)* before לא (not) is to be removed, as done by a large number of MSS and most of the versions.

3c More literally: "according to that, which his eyes see."

3d More literally: "according to that, which his ears hear."

4a עָנָו, "humble," possibly ought to be changed to read לַעֲנֵי א' (for the humbled of the land) (see Sym: πτωχους, poor; cf. also עֲנֵי עַמִּי, poor of my people, used with דַּלִּים, small one, in 10:2).

4b MT ארץ (earth) disturbs the flow of thought, since the previous verse ends with the same word and רשׁע (malicious one) in the second half of the verse would lead one to expect a different word as a parallel; in addition, it is hard to understand why the Messiah should strike the earth itself, seeing that it is the human beings upon it who have acted wickedly. The almost universally accepted emendation עָרִ(י)ץ, "violent ones," very likely reflects the correct reading.

5a One notes that אמונה (faithfulness) was provided an article; however, one is not used on צדק (righteousness). It should not be added to צדק (righteousness) but rather should be eliminated from אמונה (faithfulness).

5b It seems incorrect that אֵזוֹר (girdle) should be found twice in the same verse. The versions use a variety of words here. G. R. Driver (*JTS* 38 [1937] 39f.) suggests that, for one of the times אֵזוֹר (girdle) is used, אָסוּר (band, bond) should be read instead, which would have the same meaning as the Syriac *'esur,* "band, girdle" (Vulg translates this with *cingulum* and *cinctorium,* with two words for a girdle or sword-belt, which sound about the same but are not quite identical in meaning). This emendation is preferable to what is usually suggested, that one read חֲגֹר (belt, girdle).

6a נָמֵר is not the panther, but rather the leopard, *felis pardus.*

6b It is surprising that v. 6bα has three parts, whereas the other parallel clauses are all composed with two parts each. Gk reads: καὶ μοσχάριον καὶ ταῦρος καὶ λέων ἅμα βοσκηθήσονται (and little calf and bull and lion will be grazed at the same time) (cf. also L) which has caused some exegetes to read יִרְעוּ, "they graze," instead of וּמְרִיא (and fatling). It would be closer to the transmitted Hebrew text to accept the conjecture יִמְרָאוּ, "and they will get fattened." It must be admitted that the verb is not found elsewhere in the OT, but it is found in rabbinic Hebrew and examples have also been found in Ugarit.

7a MT תִּרְעֶינָה (will graze) does not furnish a satisfactory reading; because of the accent, one must take the following word יחדו (with one another) with the second half of the verse; yet, it is absolutely necessary in the first half. With de Lagarde, one really ought to read תִּתְרָעֶינָה: "they will be friends with one another" (*Sem* I [1878] 21); cf. the *hithpa'el* of רעה II in Prov. 22:24: "have friendship with."

8a מְאוּרָה (light-hole) (Qᵃ: מאורות; 1 MS: מאירת, a feminine singular participle in the construct state; see M. Dietrich, *Neue palästinisch punktierte Bibelfragmente* [1968] 52) is translated in the Gk as τρώγλη, "cavern" (L: *cubile,* lair, den; Targ: חור, hole; Syr: *ḥôrâ,* hole; Vulg: *caverna*). Because of that, the conclusion has been drawn that the Hebrew original read מְעָרָה, "cavern," or מְעוֹנָה, "domicile, lair." F. Perles (*JSOR* 9 [1925] 126f.) saw a relationship between מְאוּרָה and the Akkadian *mûru,* "young child" (*AHW* 677), which would make all emendations unnecessary.

8b J. Reider (*VT* 2 [1952] 115) suggests reading, instead of ידו הדה, stretch out his hand, rather יְדַהְדֶּה, based on a connection with the Arabic *dahdah,* "throw stones," or, possibly, "play pebbles." It is true that the perfect form הדה (stretched out) does not fit very well into the context (on this, see below, on form). But it is too risky to presume that this root has the same meaning in Hebrew.

9a Qᵃ reads תמלאה; according to S. Talmon (*Textus* 4 [1964] 117), this is a combination of the third singular perfect and the third singular imperfect, possibly also attested in the reading of the Targ: ארי תתמלי (Behold, you were/will be filled) and the Syr: *deteṭmele'* (who were filled). It is possible that the imperfect ought to be read, but it is more likely that one should leave the MT as it is and translate it in a future perfect sense ("will have become full").

9b דֵּעָה (knowledge) functions grammatically as an infinitive construct and is thus followed by the object in the accusative.

9c Concerning לְ as an accusative particle, cf. Joüon, Gr §125k.

9d Concerning the lack of the article with the participle, cf. Joüon, Gr 138f.

Form

As was mentioned above (see the discussion of the form of 10:27b–34), Herder had already suggested separating 10:33f. from the preceding section, considering it as part of chap. 11. Bruno and Kaiser have agreed with this way of dividing the text. Kissane would like to consider 10:27—11:14 as a unit, but he also moves 10:17–23 and inserts it right after 10:34. Since he wants to presume that Isaianic and post-Isaianic sections are a single unit, one can only conclude that this is a modern attempt to carry out redactional activity. Kaiser justifies his way of dividing this on the basis of relationships in content and because of the same metrical pattern in 10:33a (he removes v. 33b because it has another meter) and 10:34 on the one hand and 11:1, 2, 5 on the other. But it is very questionable whether 10:33a, 34 can actually be read as seven-stress cola (see above, on the meter of 10:27b–34), and, even if this should be the case, it could be purely by chance that one can find seven-stress meter in some of the lines of 11:1f. When one considers the relationship between the content of the two sections, one can certainly recognize that 10:33a, 34 provides a very dismal backdrop for the messianic hopes in 11:1ff. (which might have given the redactor reason to arrange the texts as they are now), but there are no direct connecting links. In actuality, 11:1 presents a theme for which chap. 10 was not prepared: the budding out of a new sprout of David. This theme is still in v. 10. But this verse is an addition, as is disclosed by its introduction, using והיה ביום ההוא (and it will happen on that day). One must consider the possibility that, since vv. 1–16 are introduced by the exact same expression, v. 10 should be considered along with that section (so Kaiser). But v. 10 belongs thematically to vv. 1–9 and apparently intends to expand on the preceding messianic imagery. But it is very clear that there is a different hand at work here, as is shown by the expression שרש ישי (root of Jesse), which imprecisely renders the metaphor in v. 1, and also by its borrowing of the concept of the battle standard from 5:26, but most of all because of the world-wide importance which v. 10 assigns to the Messiah, whereas he is simply a ruler over Israel in the original text (see v. 9). Verse 10 is clearly a later interpretation, written by a different author.

The section begins with the perfect consecutive ויצא (will come forth). Alternating from time to time with the imperfect, this verb form sets the tone for the entire section. Therefore, this very clearly (in this way, it is different from 9:1–6) makes a promise. Naturally, the participle נֹהֵג (leading) in v. 6 does not call this analysis into question, and the same holds true for הדה (stretched out) at the end of v. 8. It is possible that an imperfect form ought to be read in its place (יֶהְדֶּה [?], will stretch out). Concerning the perfect מלאה (has been filled) in v. 9, cf. above, textual note 9a.

What we have here is the prediction about an ideal future ruler, one who is to come from the house of David. Based on content, this comes closest to Mic. 5:1ff. There is no doubt that the prophet makes use of a very well-established genre here as well. The middle section, vv. 3–5, does not speak about the "Messiah" in a way that is any different from how the king is spoken of elsewhere in the OT (see Ps. 72:2, 4, 13). But certainly Psalm 72 and other similar passages are not dependent upon Isaiah (or whoever is actually speaking in this section), but are older, at least according to the history of their transmission. According to Gunkel (*Die Psalmen,* HAT II/12 [1964⁴] 308), this psalm certainly comes from the kingship era; according to Kraus (BK XV/1, 495 [Engl: *Psalms 60–150,* 77]), it is pre-exilic, the same conclusion drawn by Sellin-Fohrer (*Introduction to the Old Testament* [1968] 270). Its "Sitz im Leben" is a Jerusalem kingship festival, possibly at the time of a festival which recurred yearly, though it is more likely that it was used whenever a ruler was enthroned. And yet, one cannot overlook the differences between Isa. 11:1ff. and Psalm 72: There it is a petition on behalf of the present ruler; here it is an oracle about a future ruler. Predictions about a future ruler, whose coming would bring about a time of salvation, were also known among the nations which were Israel's neighbors.

First of all, we refer once again to one of the examples cited above, pp. 399f., from the prophecies of the priest Nefer-rohu (or, the more likely reading, Neferti; see *ANET* 444, note 1). The prophecy deals with the announcement of the appearance of a king who will establish order and justice in the land. He comes from the south, is the son of a Nubian, and is thus a *homo novus,* someone who comes from nowhere. It is possible that Amen-em-het I, the founder of the twelfth dynasty, was greeted by means of this prediction when he was enthroned (so Ranke, *AOT* 47f., note k; however, Snefru, the one who received the oracle, belongs to the fourth dynasty). Predictions of this type were also known in the region of Mesopotamia, even though they were actually often predictions after the fact (but see W. W. Hallo, "Akkadian Apocalypses," *IEJ* 16 [1966] 231–242). That is demonstrated by the collection of prophecies assembled by E. Ebeling, *Keilschrifttexte aus Assur religiösen Inhalts,* H. IX, no. 421 (see also A. K. Grayson, "Akkadian Prophecies," *JCS* 18 [1964] 7–30; *AOT* 283f.; *ANET* 451f., reworked in *ANET* [1969³] 606), where one reads for example: "[A ruler will arise], he [will rule] for eighteen years. The country will live safely, the interior of the country will be happy, the people will [have abun]dance. The gods will make beneficial decisions for the country, favorable winds [will blow]. The date palm and the furrow will bring in good yield. Shakkan [the god of livestock] and Nisaba [the goddess of grain] will [create fullness] in the land. There will be [favorable] rain (!) and high water, the people of the land will observe a festival. That ruler will be killed in an uprising" (*ANET* 606 [slightly altered]). Or, as another example, there is a reference to an oracle meant for the king in a letter to Ashurbanipal: "Ash[ur the king of the go]ds has pronounced the name of the [king] my lord for the kingship over the land of Ashur. In their reliable oracle Shamash and Adad have established for the king my lord, for his kingship over the lands, a happy reign: days of justice, years of equity, heavy rains, waters in full flood, a thriving commerce. The gods are reconciled, divine worship is widespread, the temples are enriched. . . . Old men dance, young men sing, women and maidens are gl[ad (and) ma]ke merry. Wives they take, deck with *ear-[ri]ngs,* beget sons and daughters—the offspring are instructed. Whom his crime had condemned to death, the king my lord has let live; [who] was held prisoner many [ye]ars, is set free; [wh]o were sick many days, have recovered. The hungry have been sated; the lice-infested have been anointed; the naked have been clad in garments" (see *AOT* 328; *ANET*³ 626f.). Reference has frequently been made to the fourth eclogue of Vergil: "Now the last age foretold . . . has come; the great procession of the centuries is born anew. . . . Only do you, chaste Lucina, smile upon the birth of the child; with him the iron generations shall first cease and a race of gold shall arise throughout the world. . . . He—[the child]—shall receive the life of gods, shall see heroes mingled with gods, and himself be seen of them; he shall govern a world to which his father's virtues have brought peace. . . . Of their own accord will the she-goats bring home udders swollen with milk, and herds shall have no fear of mighty lions. Of its own accord your cradle shall pour forth flowers to caress you. The serpent shall perish, and so shall the treacherous poison plant perish; Assyrian spice shall spring up on every soil, . . . the plains will slowly grow golden with tender wheat, the blushing grape will hang from untended brambles, and tough oaks will distil dewy honey" (Moses Hadas and Thomas Suits, eds., *Latin Selections* [1961] 89, 91; the German edition is by H. Schmidt, op. cit., 14f.; critical text and textual edition with commentary can be found, among other places, in H. Holtorf, *P. Vergilius Maro. Die grösseren Gedichte* I [1959] 160ff.; concerning the discussion about how these themes reached Vergil from the Near East, see Gross, op. cit., 53ff. and Díaz, op. cit., 244). For further extra-biblical parallels, see M. Rehm, op. cit., 218–228.

The extensive parallelism of the motifs is unmistakable when these texts are compared. Therefore, there is no reason to doubt that such oracles were to be heard both in the cult and in the palaces of the rulers. And even if what has come down to us is, as a rule, to be judged as predictions after the fact, there were also genuine oracles of this type, which announced a coming one who would rule in righteousness and peace. It is very probable that prophecies of this type were also uttered publicly in Jerusalem. The author of Isa. 11:1–9 made use of one of them, to give shape to his hope for the future, in a way his hearers would easily understand.

Meter: Verses 1 and 2a, bα: 2 seven-stress cola; 2bβ: a six-stress colon; 3b: an eight-stress colon; 4a: a six-stress colon; 4b: an eight-stress colon; 5: an eight-stress colon; 6a: a six-stress colon; 6b: a seven-stress colon; 7a: a six-stress colon; 7b, 8a: a six-stress colon; 8b, 9a: 2 six-stress cola; 9b: a seven-stress colon. Verse 10, up to עַמִּים (nations), is prosaic, then a six-stress colon follows (cf. the somewhat different analysis by L. Alonso-Schökel, op. cit., 152f.). One notices immediately that each verse of the poem is constructed using long lines; it is the intention that this method will accent the importance of what is being predicted. The most important ideas are in the eight-stress cola.

This poem is a pearl of Hebrew poetry. The variety, aptness, and spontaneity of the imagery are astounding: the root out of the stump, the rod of the mouth, the breath from the lips, righteousness as girdle and faithfulness as a loincloth. Above all, one observes that the description of the pastoral scene—that is, the description of the relationship of the animals—is very animated: wolf, panther, young lion, bear, lion, viper, and young viper are juxtaposed with lamb, kid, calf, little lad, cow, cattle, suckling, and child. In this way, every schematization is avoided; every word-pair testifies in its own way that peace has entered upon the scene. One can be sure that these motifs are rooted in a rich and ancient tradition, but the author has successfully created a clear, well-defined image with his own stamp on it. However, one ought not forget that writing fine poetry is not the goal, but that this serves as a way to issue a proclamation. There is no expectation that the listener would just be enthralled by the words and images; rather, it intends to cause people to listen by making use of trusted traditions, set forth in the framework of a message which is being delivered. For the most important part of the message, one might say vv. 3, 4, and 9, the images fade into the background and, without any ornamentation and embellishment, the hearer is told the essentials about what is yet to come. (Concerning the particular stylistic elements, see L. Alonso-Schökel, op. cit.)

Setting

There is considerable disagreement about the question of the authorship of 11:1–9. In that connection, the integrity of vv. 1–9 has also been frequently discussed. The following have come out against Isaiah as the author of the section: Marti, Guthe, Hölscher (*Die Propheten* [1914] 348), Gray, Mowinckel (*Psalmenstudien* II, 308; *He That Cometh* [1956] 17), Budde (*ZAW* 41 [1923] 189), D. H. Corley (op. cit., 224), E. Balla (*Die Botschaft der Propheten* [1958] 475), S. H. Blank (*Prophetic Faith in Isaiah* [1958] 160ff.), Fohrer, et al. But many have also defended the passage as authentic: Duhm, H. Schmidt, König, Gressmann (*Messias* [1929] 247), Procksch, Fischer, Kissane, Hertzberg, Steinmann, H. Ringgren, Eichrodt, Kaiser (vv. 1–8), Mauchline, Leslie, G. von Rad (*OTTheol* II, 169f.), Schildenberger, Montagnini, Coppens (LD 58, 83),

Rehm, op. cit., 192ff. Some are not completely sure or else they attempt to reduce it to an Isaianic core after removing some verses. For example, Eissfeldt concludes, not without considerable reflection, that vv. 1–5 can be attributed to Isaiah, but he wants to separate them from vv. 6–8: In those verses, colors are used which are not otherwise found on Isaiah's palette, but there are some such pictures to be found from a later date which depict a happy final age (*The Old Testament. An Introduction* [1965] 319). Herrmann (op. cit., 131, note 21) and Becker (op. cit., 27f.) have expressed similar viewpoints. As with 2:2–4 and 9:1–6, there is a disagreement here which finally has its roots in differing conceptions about the development of the religious history of Israel and is based on differing understandings of the prophetic movement itself.

That does not prohibit one, also in this instance, from carefully examining the reasons for denying authorship to Isaiah (cf. also Rehm, op. cit., 192f.). Marti (ad loc.) mentions the following points: (1) Isaiah does not look for salvation to come from the monarchy and it seems that in this passage being prepared to serve as the monarch is dependent upon the outpouring of the Spirit. (2) That the Spirit of Yahweh would be bestowed and continue to remain is a sign that this is from a later era. (3) As in 9:1–6, there is no longer a Davidic king ruling (on this, cf. Corley, op. cit., 223). (4) The portrayal of the peace of God, also having an effect upon the natural world, does not fit with the more ancient times. (5) Just as with 9:1–6, there seems to be no time which one can discover which would fit the date when this prediction might possibly have been spoken. Fohrer, one of the newest proponents of the thesis that this is not authentic, adds an additional observation: that the author apparently is at home not only with eschatological theology but also with the teachings of wisdom.

In response, one can say the following: (1) Isaiah is a son of Jerusalem and, even though he had great reservations, as did others, about the monarchy as it actually existed at his own time, he also had great hopes for Davidic rule in the future (on this, see above, on the form of 7:4–9). (2) It is true that one does not find mention of the Spirit of God as an ongoing possession of a human being until the postexilic era (Fohrer refers to the speeches of Elihu in the book of Job). However, there are also outstanding individuals in more ancient times upon whom the Spirit of God came, in fact, upon whom it rested (2 Kings 2:15: נָחָה רוּחַ אֵלִיָּהוּ עַל־אֱלִישָׁע, the Spirit of Elijah rests upon Elisha; in addition, see 1 Sam. 10:6, 10, concerning Saul). In the story about the anointing of David, one reads: "and the Spirit of Yahweh came mightily upon David" (וַתִּצְלַח רוּחַ־יְהוָה אֶל־דָּוִד, 1 Sam. 16:13), in fact, "from that day forward [and after that]." (3). Just as 9:1ff., 11:1ff. does not say that the Davidic kings are no longer in power, but rather that there would be a new descendant who would come forth as ruler, from the ancient family line. (4) The ideal picture of a paradiselike peace of God within nature goes far back in history in the ancient Near East and always came alive once again whenever a new ruler took control. (5) This section, 11:1ff., does not actually provide any indication about the time period of Isaiah's activity to which it ought to be assigned; we must proceed with only some general suppositions (see below, pp. 466f.). But that is not unique (see passages such as 10:27b–34, above). Finally, concerning the objection raised above by Fohrer, one must point out that it has not been clearly determined that the author of this present passage is working with an eschatological theology; in any case, he does not do so in the sense it was used afterwards, by apocalyptic (the difference between this and the later author who wrote v. 10 must also be taken into consideration). It is certainly true that he has firsthand experience with the way of thinking used by wisdom, but that can certainly not be used to weigh against Isaiah being the author, particularly since the kingship ideology betrays wisdom influence in other places as well (cf. passages like 1 Kings 3:4ff. and cf. J. Lindblom, "Wisdom in the Old Testament Prophets," VTSup 3 [1955] 192–204, cf. esp. 198f.; but see also W. Harrelson, "Nonroyal Motifs in the Royal Eschatology," in *Israel's Prophetic Heritage, FS J. Muilenburg* [1962] 147–165, esp. 154f.). On behalf of Isaiah as author, one might begin with the vocabulary. There are very close ties with 9:1–6, but since the authenticity of that section is also a matter of dispute, no comparisons will be made to specific details of that passage. But even if one looks beyond 9:1–6, the use of words is very much what Isaiah would choose: שרש (root) is used by Isaiah in 5:24 and 14:29f. It is typical of Isaiah that he does not only use words derived from חכם (wisdom) and בין (insight), but they are also used together: 3:3; 5:21; 10:13; 29:14; on this, see above, the commentary on 5:21 and on 10:13; in addition, he also uses words derived from forms of גבר (hero) and יעץ (planning) (concerning גבורה, strength, see 28:6; 30:15; concerning עֵצָה, planning, see above, commentary on 5:12b), and, finally, from ידע (knowledge) (see above, commentary on 1:3). דלים (lightly esteemed) and עניים (the poor) are also used together in 10:2 (see also דלים, poor, and אביונים, needy, in 14:30). הכה בשבט (strike with a staff) is also used by Isaiah in 30:31 (cf. שבט מַכֶּךָ, rod which smote you, in 14:29; see also 9:3). For המית (kill), one can compare 14:30; the combination אזור חלציו (loincloth of his loins) is also found in 5:27. אמונה (faithfulness) as the loincloth on the hips of the Messiah corresponds to the encouragement to believe directed toward Ahaz by Isaiah in 7:9; cf. also 28:16 (concerning the vocabulary in vv. 6–9, see below, p. 468).

Thus, the vocabulary in vv. 1–5 points to Isaiah as the author. "The terminology used in these verses . . . embodies the ideal and essentially points to the purpose of Isaiah's message and the way it depicted righteousness" (Herrmann, op. cit., 138, note 44). The theological concepts used here also favor considering Isaiah as the source: Out of the stump, from roots of what has been cut down, a new ruler will come forth. Isaiah recognizes that the way the present Davidic rulers are acting calls into question whether one can count on the ancient traditions of salvation remaining in force. But he will not simply give up on the promise to that dynasty, since the catastrophe which is about to overtake the leadership will open up, at the very same time, the possibility for a new beginning. "The imagery of the rootstock actually appears to employ, much as the idea of refining (1:21–26), a way of thinking which carefully probes into the future, beyond the catastrophe. It is hardly possible to deny that this is Isaiah's way of thinking; he embodied a moderating caution that is one of the marks of great personalities" (ibid., 138).

There is also hardly any justification for separating vv. 6–8 (and thus, naturally, also v. 9). It is certainly correct that Isaiah's "interest [lay] much more in the ethical relationships between human beings than in the relationships among the creatures of the animal world" (Marti). But Isaiah is using a way of thinking which employs traditions which were already available to him. He points out that the central issue for him is what comes through loud and clear in v. 9: No evil will take place upon the entire holy mountain. Certainly there is a break between vv. 5 and 6 as well as between vv. 8 and 9. But v. 9 furnishes the interpretation, which Isaiah himself adds, to the motif about peace among the animals, a concept known by everyone at that time. But this also provides the connecting link for the section vv. 6–8, which at first seems to interrupt and go beyond the boundary of what is discussed in vv. 1–5. If Isaiah obviously makes use of a long-standing description of peace between animal and animal and between animal and human being, then it comes as no surprise when one determines that the vocabulary used here is not typical of Isaiah. In addition, one observes that one could easily expect the terms used here to be employed by any OT writer. Yet, there are still certain noteworthy connections:

Concerning כבש (lamb), see 1:1 and 5:17 (here also גור, be a visitor, sojourn!); concerning רבץ (lie down), 14:30 (in the same line one also finds דלים, poor; see above); concerning כפיר (young lion), 5:29 and 31:4 (here also אריה, lion!). נהג (tend), which is used even less often, is also found in 20:4; concerning שעשע (play), which is also not used very often, see שעשועים (his delight) in 5:7; concerning צפעון (young viper), see the related term צפע (adder) in 14:29; concerning גמל, in the sense of "wean," see 28:9; and, concerning השחיתו (do anything destructive), see 1:4.

However, what is really decisive here is the structure and theme, which are found in such predictions about kings who will bring salvation. They speak, as the examples from the ancient Near East demonstrated above, about a coming ruler as one who will make sure there is righteousness, but also about one who will be a guarantor of freedom; this ruler will not bring freedom just for human beings and for various peoples, but will even effect this in the animal world. The genre itself practically demands that there be a transition from the theme of righteousness to the theme of peace in the transition from v. 5 to v. 6.

If the prediction in 11:1–9 comes from Isaiah, then one must make a very serious effort to identify the time when the prophet might have said this. Since, of course, the passage itself gives no indication, there are some commentators who abandon the effort of trying to determine its date. Duhm made the following decision about 2:2–4; 11:1–8; 32:1–5, and 15–20: "If Isaiah did . . . author these four poems, then this first took place when he was very old, after the storm which came at the time of Sennacherib, not composing for the general public but for his disciples and the believers, not as a prophet who had been sent, but as a prophetic poet; possibly this cycle was his swan song" (written in his comments about 2:2–4). The thought that 11:1ff. might have been, so to speak, a part of his testament, left behind by the aged prophet for a circle of trusted associates after harsh battles and many disappointments were past, is most attractive but cannot be proved. It is easy to see how this message could have been directed toward a small circle of those who thought the same way he did. But that the prophet, so to speak, was also active as a "poet," in addition to his official activities—which would certainly mean that this passage was not intended as a binding message from God—simply makes no sense. Procksch seeks to connect this passage with 9:1ff. and, therefore, also with the Immanuel prediction. There is an obvious connection when one studies the content of these passages. This caused Leslie to presume that both 9:1ff. and 11:1ff. were from the same situation; both sections would have been composed at the time of Hezekiah's enthronement festival. But 9:1ff. does not speak about the crowning of a king but rather about the birth of a crown prince, and 11:1–9 announces the coming of a new ruler, who will come forth from the "rootstock of Jesse," thus, one who might not even have been born yet and, in any case, certainly not one who was ready to assume power. One might presume that 11:1ff. could be assigned to a time slightly before 9:1ff., which would fall into the time when the Immanuel prediction was proclaimed. The promise of a new shoot from the family line of Jesse would then, in its own way, be a response to the faithless actions of Ahaz. It would then make good sense that the prophet would not have been more specific, but would have contented himself with criticizing the royal house by speaking about the stump of Jesse; yet, one must reckon with the fact that he would have also spoken this message in public, possibly even at the time of a royal festival (see Kaiser, ad loc.).

However, maybe there is a still deeper crisis within the Davidic dynasty behind 11:1f., and maybe there is a still deeper and more extensive shock to Isaiah's faith in the Davidic family than Isaiah 7 permits us to recognize. It must have been especially hard for the prophet when he had to live with the fact that Hezekiah did not pay attention when he spoke words of warning at the time Ashdod rebelled against Assyria. In his own way, the king continued the fateful policies of his father, who had turned to Assyria for help, since Hezekiah turned to Egypt/Ethiopia in the same way (on this, see M. Buber, *Der Glaube der Propheten* [1950] 213). It cannot be simply by chance that Isaiah, in defiance of the firmly established ideology of kingship in Jerusalem, does not speak any longer about the house or the kingdom of David (as he had still done in 9:5!) but now speaks of the family line of Jesse. Isaiah's disappointment in Hezekiah must have been even deeper if Isa. 9:1ff. actually does reflect the hopes one had for the crown prince who had been born at the time that was spoken (see above, on the setting of 8:23a—9:6). There is no actual evidence for that, but it would seem possible that 11:1–9 does belong to roughly the same time period as 10:27b–34, so that there is some justification for those commentators who would link 10:27bff. or 33f. with 11:1ff. (on this, see Hertzberg, ad loc.). One is led by 10:27b to suspect that Isaiah had really expected a catastrophe which would destroy Jerusalem. The Davidic family certainly belonged to the "high-minded" and "arrogant," pulled down, according to him, into the depths by the maelstrom of events (v. 33b), no doubt carrying a good share of the blame for the perilous pacts which were made. Isaiah's warning to Ahaz, "If you do not believe, then you will not remain," still hung over the house of David, also after the Syro-Ephraimitic War, even though the rulers in Jerusalem certainly believed that their policies had proved to be correct. In light of this situation, Isaiah had to provide information about whether there was indeed a future for the Davidic family and for Israel as a whole. His answer stated that a new ruler would come forth, in whom the hopes which Israel had for a divinely appointed king would actually come to fruition. But it must be pointed out that the lack of specific details leaves open the possibility that it was at another time of his activity (possibly, as many suppose, after 701) that Isaiah came upon this way of voicing his expectations about what one might hope for concerning the kingship.

Commentary

[11:1] Verse 1a announces the "coming forth" of a new ruler. Because the perfect consecutive is used, the event is clearly set into the context of what was still in the future. For the Immanuel prediction, one must assume that only a very short time period would pass before the son of the עלמה (almah) would be born. In this present passage, the prophet is certainly also not thinking in terms of a far distant future. But one must avoid any attempt to discover the "when"; that is in the hand of God; faith must content itself with knowing that a saving event will still come. Even the verb יצא (will come) is very vague when it comes to identifying the exact time. It can refer to being born (see a passage such as Job 1:21) but also to making an appearance (see Zech. 5:5) and, in Gen. 17:6, יצא מן means "be descended from." The parallel פרח, "sprout" (emended!), says just as little about the manner in which the coming will take place, but does help one to recognize more clearly that there will be an unexpected new beginning. The prediction of Neferti, cited above (pp. 399f.), accents the fact that the ruler who has been announced, who comes from the south, comes from a *new* dynastic house. According to Isaiah, of course, it is not a new dynasty which will provide the king, but he does go back beyond David to relate this ruler to his father, Jesse. Mic. 5:1 speaks in a similar way about the coming (once again, יצא) of a ruler for Israel from Bethlehem and not from Jerusalem.

"He who is to come" is to be called חטר ("rod" (see Prov. 14:3), "sprig, shoot," or, in the next half-verse, נצר, "sprig." The "shoot" does not come forth from a healthy, tall tree and, of course, also not directly from virgin soil, but rather from the גזע, "the tree stump," which means, from the root of Jesse. Concerning this imagery, one might compare Job 14:8: the tree which has been felled can produce once again. "Though its root (שרש) grow old in the earth, and its stump (גזע) die in the ground," it can still bud out with new leaves (פרח) and develop new twigs. That is the wonder to be found in the life force within nature. For Isaiah, it is the way he describes the faithfulness of God, who has חסד (steadfast love) for his עבד (servant) and, thus, for his people. But he does not take the imagery as far as the author of the poetic book of Job: The rootstock of Jesse is not dead. But the very fact that the stump of a tree is able to produce shoots once again testifies to the direct action of Yahweh, which Isaiah terms "wonderful" (28:29; 29:14), without thereby contradicting the general flow of events which take place in nature and history. It is possible that the imagery of a tree is chosen because it is connected with the idea of a tree of life, which served as a symbol for the monarchy (cf. G. Widengren, *The King and the Tree of Life,* UUÅ [1951/4] 50).

One will have to presume that Isaiah had expected the overthrow of the royal family. What would be left would be little more than a stump. Because Isaiah does not, as Neferti, announce that a ruler from an as yet unknown family would come forth, his thinking corresponds to the way one thought about the dynasty in ancient times: One's claim to rule as king had to be legitimized and, for this reason, one needed to demonstrate a relationship to the ancient royal house. Israel's basic rejection of the dynastic principle of succession had led to the change in dynastic leadership that resulted in heavy burdens and unstable circumstances for those seeking just treatment and the resultant disaster convinced Jerusalem/Judah again and again of the basic correctness of its alternate view of the monarchy. One can presume that Isaiah (and his audience) would have had specific expectations connected with the throne of David when he mentioned the sprout from the root of Jesse. But there is no doubt that the issue for Isaiah was deeper than some specific, politically arranged order, more than that he sought to adequately support particular aspirations in that direction. Yahweh's promises to the house of David were valid. Human unfaithfulness had brought their continuing validity into question, but the faithfulness of God remained. Thus, the present formulation gives expression to Isaiah's overall concern that election be understood, clearly demonstrating that the chosenness of the chosen one does not spare that person from fulfilling the demands incumbent upon someone in this office, but, at the same time, that one cannot invalidate the fact that a dynasty is chosen, simply because of the failure of any individual human being.

[11:2] The Spirit of Yahweh rests upon the coming king. It is not a particularly surprising idea that the king will be gifted with the divine Spirit. The king is, by his very nature, a charismatic figure; he has been charged with an extraordinary challenge and must therefore be gifted with extraordinary powers; see 1 Sam. 10:6, 10; 11:6; 16:13, 14; 19:9; 20:23. He is Yahweh's "servant," the official representative authorized to carry out divine rule upon earth. He is the anointed one, and as such Yahweh's Spirit speaks through him (2 Sam. 23:2). Many commentators think that the concepts expressed in 11:2 do not harmonize with the actual concept of kingship in the pre-exilic era, and they base their opinions on the fact that 11:2 says that the Spirit of Yahweh not only comes upon the ruler but *rests* upon him (concerning נוח, rest, in this passage, see A. García del Moral, op. cit., 192f.). Though it might make no sense, one is a king for his entire lifetime; it does not matter whether he takes over the rule in a monarchy which is inherited or else that he is placed on the throne by acclamation after election to the position. This is not contradicted by what we are told about the Spirit of God turning away from Saul (1 Sam. 16:14). That is written from the standpoint of the Davidic dynasty, which disputed the claim of Saul's house that it had the right to rule. And yet, the way Isaiah formulated this comment points out that he is depicting an ideal image of a king. The stability which follows when he is outfitted for his office in this way is also part of this, since only with stability can one expect an undisturbed rule, marked by שלום (peace). According to 1 Sam. 16:13, the Spirit is transmitted through the anointing. However, the anointing produces, one might say, a permanent change in character; cf. 1 Sam. 24:7, 11, et al.

The Spirit of Yahweh gives the king the abilities necessary to carry out the demands of his office. This shows the development in the use of terminology connected with the Spirit. Three pairs of gifts are enumerated, which are bestowed through the Spirit: wisdom and insight, planning and power, knowledge and fear of Yahweh. These are not exclusively, but are primarily, royal *charismata*. Wisdom and insight belong to the aspects of an ideal king (see also G. von Rad, *Wisdom in Israel* [1972] 15f., 21). The "wise woman" from Tekoa boasts about David that he is like an angel of God, being able to distinguish between good and evil (2 Sam. 14:17). A prime example of the same type of discussion is found in 1 Kings 3. Solomon, as a result of his request, is given לֵב חָכָם וְנָבוֹן (a wise and discerning mind) (v. 12); v. 28 establishes the fact that godly wisdom was in him, and 5:9 rounds out the picture: "God gave Solomon wisdom and understanding (תְּבוּנָה) beyond measure, and largeness of mind like the sand on the seashore." One can also recognize from 10:13 just how much the gifts of the Spirit, enumerated in 11:2, belong to the traditional imagery about a king; Isaiah puts into the mouth of the Assyrian the words: "By my wisdom I've done it, for I am smart" (נְבֻוֹן). Prov. 8:15f. praises wisdom: "By me kings reign, and rulers decree what is just; by me princes rule." The king needs wisdom in order to discharge the obligations of his royal rule. Solomon wants wisdom for himself so that he can distinguish between good and evil (1 Kings 3:9) or, as the case may be, to be equipped to rule over his people (which is what שפט means in this passage). However, the observation in 3:28, no doubt from a later time, makes clear, as did the previous description of Solomon's judgment speech, that wisdom was accorded him "to render justice," (לעשות משפט). The same is true in Isa. 11:1ff., in which vv. 3–5 claim that the ruler's wisdom gives special emphasis to the office of king as judge: Above all other tasks, the king carries out divine justice, an emphasis which corresponds exactly to the thought of Isaiah.

On the basis of content, it is obvious that חכמה (wisdom) and בינה (insight) are closely related terms. Nevertheless, one could very well say: חכמה refers much more to the type of wisdom which can handle problems of daily living, whereas בינה refers much more to understanding, identified in intellectual abilities which are necessary for one to see beyond the details of a particular situation, make an appropriate assessment, and come to conclusions about necessary decisions.

The second pair of terms which Isaiah uses to characterize the activity of the Spirit is עצה (planning) and גבורה (hero's power). In a similar way, they appear in Prov. 8:14 as "fruits" of wisdom, those being counsel (עצה) and sound wisdom (תושיה; see also Isa. 28:29), insight (בינה) and strength (גבורה). A parallel to this particular word-pair is found in the two throne names פלא יועץ (planner of wonders) and אל גבור (God's hero) in 9:5; on this, see above, pp. 403ff. It is unlikely here, as in that passage, that one ought to assign the meaning "counsel" to the root יעץ. A king does indeed counsel with his princes and advisers (see 2 Kings 6:8; Isa. 19:11, and elsewhere), but he himself does not give counsel; instead, he makes decisions, he "plans." Normally, according to 2 Kings 18:20 (= Isa. 36:5), רוח עצה speaks of the gift of having the ability to make war plans and to make appropriate decisions about that (cf. Isa. 7:5). Therefore, the connection with גבורה (hero's power) makes good sense (see, once again, 2 Kings 18:20). In connection with this, the king can be called the גביר (hero) (see above, pp. 403f.). It is a stereotype in the books of Kings that the גבורה (might) of a king is mentioned (1 Kings 15:23; 16:5, 27; 22:46, and often elsewhere), which meant that he has proficiency in matters of war. But no matter how clear the OT evidence, Isaiah's references to עצה (planning) and גבורה (hero's power) are simply not about the military prowess of the king. אל גבור (God's hero) in 9:5 is in fact also the שר שלום (prince of peace). Prov. 8:14 shows, as well, that the "civil" application of עצה (planning) and גבורה (hero's power) is certainly possible. Thus, Isaiah makes use of images commonly used when describing the ideology of kingship, but radically reshapes them to convey his expectation about peace.

Without a doubt, the word pair דעת (knowledge) and יראת יהוה (fear of Yahweh) is the decisive terminology for him. That can already be seen in the fact that these do not belong to typical phraseology connected with the ideology of kingship (but see יראת אלהים, fear of God, in 2 Sam. 23:3). Both words are central concepts for describing the Yahweh faith. For Isaiah, above all others, דעת (knowledge) is of the essence; one notes that the term, altered slightly into the form דעה, appears once again in this same section (v. 9) and indeed, at that point, it is not specifically applied only to the king. In 5:13, the substantive דעת (insight, knowledge) is used alone, without being further defined by a genitive form of יהוה (of Yahweh); in 1:3 and 6:9, the verb ידע (has no insight) is used without the accusative of the name of God. Thus, Isaiah has borrowed from the terminology used by wisdom, which deals plainly and simply with knowledge in general (see above, commentary on 1:3 and on 5:13). One suspects that the situation is no different here, that is, יהוה (Yahweh) is only in the genitive relationship with יראת (fear) (on this, see 33:6, where דעת, knowledge, and יראת יהוה, fear of the Lord, are also used together, but are divided by the *Athnach;* for another viewpoint, see Joüon, Gr §129a, 386, note 3). The king simply needs knowledge in general. On the other hand, this knowledge is brought about by the activity of the Spirit of Yahweh, and the parallel term יראת יהוה (fear of Yahweh) shows that this also highlights a relationship with Yahweh. The connection between דעת (knowledge) and יראת יהוה (fear of Yahweh) is very common in wisdom; see Prov. 1:29; 2:5f. But of course, in the very same way, the other gifts of the Spirit are naturally given a new accent by this closing expression יראת יהוה (fear of Yahweh), just as Israelite wisdom as a whole was integrated into the Yahwistic faith because it provided details about יראת יהוה (fear of Yahweh) (see, e.g., Prov. 1:7; 9:10; 15:33). The gloss, the result of dittography in v. 3a, underscores once again the great importance attached to fear of God. יראת יהוה (fear of Yahweh) does not, however, mean fear before God, since it is itself a gift of God; one might say something such as this: It "offers a guarantee that [the Messiah] does not only know the will of God, but respects it as well" (Plath, op. cit., 83f.). And yet, this is also not similar to the English word *awe,* which would be closer to the use of יִרְאֵי יהוה (fear of Yahweh) in the Psalms, which also describes what is meant by the Greek word εὐσέβεια (reverence), being nothing more than a pious attitude about God. Even according to the "last words of David," the מוֹשֵׁל יראת יהוה (one ruling in the fear of God) is מוֹשֵׁל בָּאָדָם צַדִּיק (one who rules justly over men) (2 Sam. 23:3), which means: Whoever rules in the fear of God is a ruler who has concern for righteousness. Certainly this is not all that is meant by fear of God; it refers actually to a basic religious foundational relationship, which becomes visible in the ideal life of one who is wise, in this passage, specifically, the wisdom of a king who is obligated to act wisely; yet, it cannot be separated from the duties of the king as he carries out the obligations of the office of judge in a just way.

The wisdom terms, which Isaiah uses to sketch out what the Messiah will be like, could lead one to conclude that he saw in him the ideal wise person. However, that would intentionally draw the wrong conclusion. The Messiah takes his place as one who is unique, since the gifts of wisdom have been bestowed upon him directly, by the Spirit of

God. He is more than first among equals; he stands in a relationship with the people as God's proxy, has responsibilities connected with an incomparable task, and acts in unquestioned authority. (The concept that every human being will participate in the gift of the Spirit appears at a relatively late time: Ezek. 11:19; 36:26f.; cf. also the theme of the outpouring of the Spirit: Isa. 32:15; 61:1; Joel 3:1ff., and cf. Ps. 51:12; Zech. 12:10; 13:2.)

[11:3–5] The transition from v. 2 to vv. 3–5, that is, from the depiction of the charismatic gifts of the king to those connected with his function as preserver of justice, in no way involves a change of focus, as shown by what has just been said. In addition, the latter function had been expected of a king in Israel for a long time—there was a long tradition that the king was to step forth to bring justice, particularly justice for the lightly esteemed and lowly.

One might indeed wonder about just how responsible the king of Jerusalem actually was in matters of justice and how much influence he could have had in the administration of justice. In Mesopotamia all of the law books of the era were ascribed to a king. To be sure, the kings did not produce them, but they were promulgated under their authority. In Israel, the king did not issue any laws, and when he put a law into effect, as was done by Jehoshaphat, 2 Chron. 19:5ff., or Josiah, 2 Kings 23:1f., it was not his own, but rather Yahweh's or Moses' law. But there can be absolutely no doubt that the king was the highest judicial authority and carried the ultimate responsibility for functions connected with the administration of justice. It is said about David: "So David reigned over all Israel; and David administered justice and equity to all his people" (2 Sam. 8:15; cf., in addition, 2 Sam. 12:1–6; 14:4–11; 15:4; 1 Kings 3:28; 2 Kings 15:5, and elsewhere). Above all, one must take note of Jer. 22:15f.: "Did not he [Josiah] do justice and righteousness? . . . He judged the cause of the poor and needy." In the palace of Solomon, there was a "hall of judgment," in which the king pronounced judgment (1 Kings 7:7). There is no doubt that there was a royal palace in Jerusalem, specifically for judgment, in which all citizens of the state would be able to set forth their cases (on this, see de Vaux, *Ancient Israel. Its Life and Institutions,* 152–157). For this reason, an individual would pray for the king: "Give the king thy justice, O God, and thy righteousness to the royal son! May he judge thy people with righteousness, and thy poor with justice! . . . May he defend the cause (משפט) of the poor of the people, give deliverance to the needy, and crush the oppressor!" (Ps. 72:1f., 4). And, according to Jer. 23:5f., it is expected of the "righteous Branch" (צמח צדיק) that he would act wisely and would establish משפט (justice) and צדקה (righteousness) in the land; see, in addition, 1 Sam. 8:5; 1 Kings 3:6; Jer. 22:3, 13; Isa. 9:6; 32:1; Zech. 9:9; Pss. 45:6–8; 101; Prov. 8:15; 20:8, 28; 25:5.

Israel had the same types of expectations for its king as other peoples in the Near East had for their kings. According to a hymn of Lipit-Ishtar of Isin, the king is the one who ". . . places justice into every mouth, who always makes sure he stands for the one who is righteous, who speaks a just word in matters of justice and decisions. . . . I have established righteousness for Sumer and Akkad, so that all will go well in the land. . . . I, Lipit-Ishtar, have justly led the people" (Falkenstein/von Soden, *Sumerische und Akkadische Hymnen und Gebete* [1953] 129). In the so-called lower entrance inscription of Karatepe, Azitawadda writes: "I destroyed those who were rebellious and rooted out all the evil which was in the land. And I judged the house which I ruled in a friendly way and made goodness the root of my rule" (KAI no. 26, line 8ff.). In Egypt, the Hebrew צדק (righteousness) corresponds roughly to the term *Maat (m ʒ'.t)*: It is a gift from the divinity to the king: "I [Horus] give you *Maat* in your heart, that you may use it." "I [Hathor] give you *Maat,* so that you may live thereby, that you may have a brotherly relationship with it and your heart may rejoice." It is virtually said that the Pharaoh was receiving moral principles "on the basis of his divine nature, very much as one [would receive] a sacrament" (see S. Morenz, *Ägyptische Religion* [1960] 128). Finally, the Persian, Darius, glorifies himself with the words written on the rock-grave *naqš-i-rustām:* "Whatever is just, that I love, injustice, I hate. It gives me no pleasure that the lesser one suffers unjustly because of the greater one, neither does it please me that the greater one suffers unjustly because of the lesser one. What is just, that is pleasing to me. The one who supports cheating is one I hate" (according to E. Herzfeld, *Altpersische Inschriften* [1938] 4ff.). It is said very specifically here that the king knows that he has obligations to protect the cause of justice for the one who is lightly esteemed. But in Ugaritic there are passages which are even closer to the OT. In the Keret legend from Ras Shamra, the king is scolded by his son with the words: "You give in to the most wicked men who have power, . . . you allow your hand to come under the control of injustice, you do not allow the widow to experience righteousness *(tdn dn),* you do not speak justice to the one who suffers in need *(ttpṭ tpṭ),* you do not distance yourself from the one who treads down upon the weak . . ." (the translation is based on Aistleitner II K VI, 43–50; cf. 30b–34). Or one reads: "Danel . . . took his place at the entrance to the gate in the midst of those who were distinguished, who are found at the threshing floor. He decided *(ydn dn)* the cause of the widow and established justice, *(yṭpṭ tpṭ)* for the orphan" (II D, V 4–8; cf. I D, 19–25). In Ugaritic, the word *tpṭ,* which is the equivalent of the Hebrew שפט, also means "judge, help one get justice," as well as meaning to "rule."

[11:3b] The Messiah does not judge on the basis of what his eyes see. That does not only mean that he does not have any regard for a person's importance, that he is completely neutral when judging (see Lev. 19:15; Deut. 1:17; 16:19; James 2:9). If that were the case, then one would have to interpret the second half-verse in such a way that he would also give various parties no hearing. The sense is rather that he does not base his decision upon only the evidence which has been presented publicly, on what he sees and hears; because of the power which comes with his wisdom and insight, he is capable of recognizing what is behind what is seen and heard, what is really real; cf. 1 Sam. 16:7; 1 Cor. 4:3–5; 1 Peter 1:17. "Inspired decisions (קֶסֶם) are on the lips of a king; his mouth does not sin in judgment" (Prov. 16:10); cf. also 25:2f.: ". . . But the glory of kings is to search things out. As the heavens for height, and the earth for depth, so the mind (לֵב, understanding) of kings is unsearchable." Solomon had asked for himself הָבִין לִשְׁמֹעַ מִשְׁפָּט, "understanding, to discern what is right" (1 Kings 3:11), but the knowledge that the Messiah needs to carry out his office is made accessible to him by the Spirit of God. Concerning שפט (judge) and הוכיח (decide), see above, commentary on 2:4a.

[11:4] The overview of the extra-biblical evidence for the king's role as a judge, furnished above, has demonstrated that the messianic ideal, as sketched out by Isaiah, has very deep roots in the ancient Near East (on this, see also E. Hammershaimb, VTSup 7 [1960] 89ff.). But if Isaiah attaches such great importance to establishing justice, for the poor and the lightly esteemed, that is clearly because the entire system of justice had, in plain words, gone to the dogs, as he was forced to lament in some other passages (5:20, 23; 10:2; see also 1:17). But this also corresponds to the OT view of God: Yahweh is a God who time and again functions as the advocate for the lightly esteemed (Pss. 9:10; 68:6; Job 5:15f., and often elsewhere). The king, as עבד יהוה (servant of Yahweh), had to carry out whatever was the will of his divine Lord.

In the passage quoted above from Karatepe, the king praised himself because his reign had fostered friendliness and goodness (נעם). The Hebrew צדק (righteousness) is not, in terms of content, very far removed from that concept (see above, commentary on 1:21). In the present passage, along with צדק (righteousness), one finds the related term מישור (equity). The scepter of the king, according to Ps. 45:7, is a שבט מישור (scepter of equity), and Yahweh himself also judges the peoples with מישור (equity) (Ps. 67:5).

The Akkadian *mi/ēšaru,* or forms which are similar, coincides very closely with the various ways in which the Hebrew צדק (righteousness) is used. One speaks of Shamash as the "king of heaven and earth, lord of justice and of righteousness" *(bēl kitti u mēšari;* A. Schollmeyer, *Sumerisch-babylonische Hymnen und Gebete an Samas* [1912] 107, and often elsewhere). Bel is *šar mēšeri* (righteous ruler) (E. Ebeling, *Literarische Keilschrifttexte aus Assur* [1953] no. 38, line 2). One can speak of "Shamash, the judge *(šapît)* of gods and human beings, acknowledged to be fair" *(ša mēšerum isikšuma, Syria* 32 [1955] 12). Concerning further examples of Akkadian epithets for the king, based on the root *ešēru* (righteous), see M. J. Seux, *Épithètes royales akkadiennes et sumériennes* (1967) 88ff.; concerning the corresponding Sumerian title *sí-só,* see his p. 446.

However, in contrast to צדק (righteousness), the Hebrew word מישור (equity) stresses smoothness, purity (whereas "justice," as it is usually translated here, is more likely what צדק means; cf. the formulation שפט (בְּ)מִישָׁרִים, judge uprightly, in Pss. 58:2; 75:3; 98:9).

The דלים are the socially disadvantaged, people with no influence, to whom no one has to pay any attention. That most of them are also "poor" is practically a given. דל (lightly esteemed) is often chosen to be used parallel to עני (poor, humbled) (Isa. 10:2, and often elsewhere) or with אביון (needy) (e.g., Ps. 82:4). Therefore, it is surely correct that ענוי (humble, the poor) be changed to read עניי (poor, humbled). In fact, in 29:9, ענו (humble) is used with אביון (meek, needy), but that passage should be dated to the postexilic era, at which time ענו, "humble," was used as a designation for the pious (see Bruppacher, op. cit., 67f.), and ought not be changed in that passage. But that means that the corrupted reading, עניי (poor, humbled) becoming instead ענוי (humble), is not just a mistaken reading, but expresses a postexilic piety. (Whoever is convinced that 11:1–9 is postexilic will, as a natural consequence of that position, not change עניי, humble; see Fohrer, ad loc.)

עני (poor, humbled) is, just as דל (lightly esteemed), not (as is the case with רוש, be in want, be poor) primarily an economic term, but is rather a social term (see A. Kuschke, op. cit., 48ff.). The basic meaning of the root ענה is something like "find oneself in circumstances of diminished ability, power, and worth" (so Birkeland, op. cit., 8). That corresponds to the fact that wealth is never treated in the OT as if it opposes God or is objectionable, in and of itself, but only insofar as the power which comes with it leads to unsocial behavior. For this reason, the terms דל (lightly esteemed) and עני (poor, humbled) in v. 4a are juxtaposed with עריץ (violent ones) and רשע (malicious one) in v. 4b (see also ענו, poor, humble, and עריץ, ruthless, in 29:19f.). The עריץ (violent one) has power at his disposal and is so unrestrained that he uses it in unscrupulous ways. One senses that, in conjunction with עריץ (violent ones), not just רשע (malicious one), as in the present passages, is used as a parallel expression (or זר, insolent men; e.g. Ps. 54:5), but also לץ (scoffer) (29:20; and צר, adversary, Job 6:23). When brutality is present, it pairs up with haughtiness, the hubris which brings such disastrous consequences, which Isaiah never grows tired of depicting. But kings have the task of restraining such brutality, as is presumed above by the passage quoted from the Keret legend (see above, commentary on 11:3–5; see also the Darius inscription mentioned there).

The punishment or destruction of those who are brutal and criminal is carried out by the king with the "staff of his mouth," with the "breath from his lips." The way this is formulated betrays an understanding that words are dynamic powers; examples of this are found throughout the ancient world. Prophets "slay by the words of my [Yahweh's] mouth" (Hos. 6:5). The עבד יהוה (servant of Yahweh) in Deutero-Isaiah confesses that Yahweh has made his mouth a sharp sword (49:2). Priest and prophet both have at their disposal a power in the words they use, not known by human beings in general (see how that is still used in this way in Acts 5:1–11). That naturally also applies to the king.

In the OT, similar expressions about the typical king are, of course, very difficult to discover. On the other hand, expressions which correspond to this are frequent in Egypt and Mesopotamia. "Just like the sun god, the king who has the 'Ka' power has all of the special qualities of being filled with divine powers and life powers" (H. Kees, *Ägypten: Kulturgeschichte des Alten Orients* I [1933] 177). On a stele at Kubbân, one reads of Ramses II: "The god of utterance is in your mouth and the one of knowledge is in your heart; the throne of your tongue is a temple of truth, and god sits upon your lips. Your words are fulfilled daily, and your heart's thoughts come to be just like those of Ptah, when he creates artistic productions" (based on Dürr, op. cit., 97). In a letter to Esarhaddon, one reads at the conclusion: "Whatever the king, my lord, has spoken, it is fulfilled just like the word of god" (ibid., 102). And in the words of Ahiqar one is instructed: "Soft is the utterance of a king; (yet) it is sharper and stronger than a [two]-edged knife" (VII, 100; see *AOT* 458; *ANET* 428 and, on this, cf. Jer. 5:14; 20:9; 23:29, as well as Eph. 6:17 and Heb. 4:12).

Even if the OT does not say that the king strikes with his words, it does still say that he has a mighty scepter. According to Ps. 2:9, the king strikes down his enemies with an iron staff (שבט). And, in fact, this emblem of the king's sovereign authority is not only to repulse the enemy from without, but is also to guarantee the rule of justice from within: "Your royal scepter is a scepter of equity (שבט מישור)," (Ps. 45:7). But in this present passage this emblem of the king's power has become the "scepter of his mouth." That is a spiritualization which, in a way similar to the passages quoted above from those who lived around Israel, had possibly also taken on a similar form in Jerusalem's ideology of kingship even before the time of Isaiah. Naturally, royal words are also meant by "the breath from his lips"; see Pss. 33:6; 147:18; Jth. 16:15; 2 Bar. 21:6 (for the ancient Near East, see Dürr, op. cit., 20, 22, 27, and often elsewhere). Along with this, one must take into account the fact that רוח, when connected with the present promise, is to be translated with "breath," though this can also be rendered as "wind," because it deals with an elemental energy. Such a statement is still found about the Messiah in the Psalms of Solomon: "to smash the arrogance of sinners like a potter's jar; to shatter all their substance with an iron rod; to destroy the unlawful nations with the word of his mouth" (17:26f.; [The Old Testament Pseudepigrapha II (1985) 667, 17:24f.]; see also 2 Thess. 2:8; Rev. 19:15). Such statements are rooted in a magical understanding of the word. Therefore one may question how far Isaiah—when he used such formulations—meant them to include the irresistible destroying power of the word. In any case, the Messiah cannot, by his very nature as king, have control over this powerful instrument; instead, it is available only because the Spirit of Yahweh rests upon him, the Spirit of גבורה (hero's power). In this way, the concept of a word which is laden with power has been removed from the world of magic and is now descriptive of fellowship with God. It is possible that for Isaiah the power-laden word of the Messiah is simply his administration of justice, which does not destroy the evildoer directly, but assigns to him, without fail, the punishment which is deserved.

[11:5] Verse 5 underscores what is said in vv. 3 and 4. Righteousness and faithfulness are the girdle and loincloth of the Messiah. The אזור (girdle) (on this, see above, commentary on 5:27) is the "innermost [piece of clothing], the last to be taken off" (KBL). Just as a man binds this article of clothing on himself, and never appears in public without it, this is the way the Messiah is clothed with righteousness and faithfulness.

If צדק (righteousness) was more narrowly defined in v. 4 by מישור (equity), the same is done here by using אמונה (faithfulness). These words are frequently found together in parallel in the OT (Pss. 33:4f.; 36:6f.; 40:11; 88:12f.; 96:13; 98:2f., and often elsewhere; on this, see Wildberger, art., "אמן," THAT I [1971] col. 198). There is no other mention of the earthly king's אמונה (faithfulness) alone or of the צדק (righteousness) and the אמונה (faithfulness) both together anywhere else in the OT; however, an amazing number of such terms refer to Yahweh in Psalm 89, a kingship psalm (vv. 2, 3, 6, 34, 50), and it is noteworthy that the connection between righteousness and faithfulness is also an integral part of the enthronement songs, where Yahweh is celebrated as king or in his role as judge, though that is not a unique function of the king. If now, in the present passage, the same statement is made about the Messiah, that corresponds to what has been observed elsewhere (see above, pp. 403f.) about Isaiah's concept of the office—that is, he applies statements about the divine king, in a transferred sense, to the earthly king. One can ask oneself whether אמונה (here: faithfulness) is supposed to tie in with the demands of faith, to which Isaiah summoned the house of David in 7:9; thus, a question is posed about whether Isaiah wants to say that the faith which he finds so sadly lacking in the family of David might be integral to the very nature of the sprout of Jesse, who is to come in the future. Then one would be justified in translating אמונה as "faith" (on this, see H.

Wildberger, art., "אמן," *THAT* I, col. 198). However, the connection with צדק (righteousness) shows that the Messiah is still being depicted in his function as judge. The אמונה (faithfulness) of the judge is the absolute reliability which a person might count on when in need of help in obtaining justice. Ps. 93:5 says, concerning the decrees of the divine judge, that they are absolutely trustworthy (נֶאֶמְנוּ מְאֹד).

[11:6–8] With the reference to the אמונה (faithfulness) of the Messiah, vv. 1–5 draw to a very acceptable conclusion. With v. 6, a new theme is introduced: the peaceful coexistence of animal with animal and animal with human. There is no more mention of the Messiah after this point. However, the inner connection between these two parts has been pointed out already (above, on the setting). Where a legitimate king is in charge, as the representative of the deity and/or as the guarantor of world order in the righteousness appropriate to his office, the world can recover from its wretchedness; in fact, there can be שלום (peace) throughout the entire cosmos: The lightly esteemed receive their justice; wars come to an end (see 9:6 and the title שַׂר שָׁלוֹם, prince of peace in 9:5); abundant rains will water the meadows (cf. Ps. 72:6); the land will produce its gifts superabundantly (Ps. 72:16; Ezek. 34:26ff.); the herds will be fruitful; on this, see A. de Guglielmo, "The Fertility of the Land in the Messianic Prophecies," *CBQ* 19 (1957) 306–311.

Concerning the ancient Near East, the texts cited above (see the discussion of form) should be consulted. As one example from many, a passage from the song written for Mer-ne-Ptah's enthronement may be added: "O rejoice, you entire land, the beautiful time has come. . . . *Maat* has slain all the lies, the sinners have fallen upon their faces, all of the greedy ones have been repelled. The water stands and does not dry up, and the Nile is carrying along a mighty (flood)" (quoted by Herrmann, op. cit., 346f.). It is not said that the king would take care of everything, but simply that, during the time of his reign, such circumstances would come which would bring blessing. The world order is planned in such a way that salvation is to follow, and salvation would also come wherever it would be respected. What is mentioned in the very short expression in Isa. 32:17 applies: "The work of righteousness will be peace, and the result of righteousness, quietness and trust forever." The only thing which is surprising is that Isaiah would illustrate the coming salvation by using the imagery of peace among the animals. To be sure, the motif itself was not completely unknown in Israel. Hosea speaks about a covenant with the animals of the field, the birds of the heavens, and the reptiles of the earth (2:20; similar to Ezek. 34:25ff.; Isa. 35:9; see also Lev. 26:6 where, in fact, there is a promise that the hazard caused by the wild animals will be solved by their removal, but there will also be a future which is free of danger, one with no threat from beasts of prey [on this, see Gross, op. cit., 83–93]). In the poem *Enmerkar and the Lord of Aratta* (ca. 1700 b.c.e.) one reads: "Once upon a time, there was no snake, there was no scorpion, there was no hyena, there was no lion, there was no wild dog, no wolf, there was no fear, no terror, man had no rival" (text according to S. N. Kramer, *History Begins at Sumer* [1959] 224; see Kramer, *Enmerkar and the Lord of Aratta* [1952] 15, lines 136–140). In the story of Enki and Ninhursag, the paradiselike land of Dilmun is described with the words: "In Dilmun the raven utters no cry, the *ittidu* bird utters not the cry of the *ittidu* bird, the lion kills not, the wolf snatches not the lamb, unknown is the kid-devouring wild dog . . ." (idem [1959] 146f.; also Gross, op. cit., 19). There is a faint echo of the same idea in the Gilgamesh epic: "He eats herbs with the gazelles, with the cow he visits the watering places. With the swarming things in the water his heart is happy" (tablet I, 89–91). Ancient images, about the beginning of time when everything was perfect, are used to portray the messianic peace. What was once a completely perfect real world in the ancient times, when all was intact, would one day come again, when a true protector of the order which God established would take office (concerning similar concepts in Greece, see H. Usener, *Milch und Honig,* Rheinisches Museum f. Phil., NF 57 [1902] 177–195; for Rome, cf. the fourth eclogue of Vergil cited above; see also H. Gross, op. cit., 47–59).

[11:6] The images in vv. 6–8 speak for themselves. The wolf will enjoy it when a delicate lamb provides the type of hospitality and protection which one guarantees a guest (so also 65:25), the very same wolf which is called טֹרֵף טֶרֶף (tearing the prey) in Ezek. 22:27. The leopard which is to lie down with the kid does not have any better reputation, being mentioned together with the wolf in Jer. 5:6 and with the lion and the bear in Hos. 13:7. As late as 1834, a leopard supposedly came into Safad after an earthquake (Bodenheimer, *Animal Life,* 114); leopards could still be observed in Palestine as late as 1911 (*ZDPV* 49 [1926] 251). נהג refers specifically to driving cattle to new, distant grazing pastures; see Gen. 31:18; Exod. 3:1; 1 Sam. 30:20; Ps. 80:2. The lion has become a vegetarian, the young lion (כפיר) roves around in the pasture with the calf, and the old lion eats chopped-up straw like the cow. (In addition, since the כפיר, young lion, is mentioned with the calf, one notes that the word is not used to designate a mature animal; see above, commentary on 5:29.) The bear was also native to Palestine (1 Sam. 17:34; 2 Kings 2:24) and was still encountered in the region around Mt. Hermon as late as the First World War (Bodenheimer, *Animal Life,* 114). The very small child would be defenseless if placed with a wild animal; therefore, in v. 6 mention is made of a "little lad" (one who is old enough to pasture cows; see Gen. 37:2; 1 Sam. 16:11; 17:15), and v. 8 refers to the suckling, יונק, and the weaned, גמול. (The young child was finally weaned when it was about three or four years old; see L. Köhler, *Der hebräische Mensch* [1953] 55.) Suckling and little child are able to enjoy being with what had been, up to that point, most dangerous snakes. Concerning שעשע (play), see above, commentary on 5:7a. Concerning varieties of snakes, the פתן and צפעוני are mentioned. The פתן, according to Aharoni, op. cit., 475, is the cobra *(cobra naja ḥaje).* צפעוני can probably not be identified exactly. H. Guthe, *Palästina* (1927²) 76, mentions, as the most feared, in addition to the cobra, the little horned cerastes and the larger, yellow *daboia xanthina.* According to G. L. Harding, *Auf biblischem Boden* (1961) 18, in Palestine today there are only two poisonous types of snakes, the adder and the horned viper, which are encountered only in the desert.

[11:6–8] The reflections above have demonstrated that the motif of peace among the animals, within a prediction about a future king, is essentially not out of place. But the question must be raised about the significance which this has for the proclamation of Isaiah. Does it deal with a hope which the prophet expects to see actually fulfilled, or are these images simply part of his way of proclaiming a general peace in the salvation-filled future? The problem is similar to the one which was raised in the exposition of 2:2, namely, whether the elevation of Zion over all of the other mountains was meant in a physical or symbolic sense (see above, commentary on 2:2a). If one takes these as literal descriptions, then one must speak of a mythological portrayal of the future (cf. M. Landmann, *Ursprungsbild und Schöpfertat* [1966] 281f., and Díaz, op. cit., 238). Lions do not eat grass and could not be nourished by eating grass; poisonous serpents could not stay alive without using the poison in their fangs to paralyze their victims. If the description is to be understood in a mythological sense, then the author would be—and then this could hardly be Isaiah—in close proximity to the apocalyptic hopes about an entirely new world. M. Buber (*Der Glaube der Propheten* [1950] 215) thinks that "this idyll, where the wild animals are 'guests' of the domesticated ones [could only be] symbolic of peace among peoples, since particular nations were also known by the names of wild animals." Were this the case, then an allegorical interpretation would furnish the key to the text's meaning. It is not very likely that this would be true if it came from Isaiah, and the text itself gives no indication that this is the direction in which it ought to be interpreted; in fact, if the text were meant to be interpreted allegorically, it would be radically different than it is—it would speak *only* of animals and not of the children. Rather than speaking allegorically, Isaiah indicates in v. 9 that he is reinterpreting the ancient mythological imagery.

[11:9] Verse 9 states: "No one shall do anything evil or anything destructive upon my entire holy mountain" (concerning this, see Kissane, ad loc., and M. Rehm, op. cit., 209–218). Some have suggested this verse be separated from the rest (see above, on the setting), just as some have taken verse 9:6 to be an addition to 9:1–5. But in 11:9, Isaiah himself begins to speak and uses his own words to do so. In the future time of salvation, among human beings who are upon Yahweh's holy mountain, there will be *no evil any more* (in Isa. 65:25 as well, this expression is used in connection with peace among the animals). The weak need not fear the powerful any longer, since the powerful are kept within their bounds, and the weak one knows where protection can be found. The harmless one will no longer fall victim to the deceitful, since the deceitful one will no longer have any opportunity to achieve his purpose with tricks and schemes, and the harmless one will have advocates, who will be positioned as a protective rampart because of that person's innocence. Isaiah adds to this: בכל־הר קדשי (upon my entire holy mountain). The first person suffix on קדשי (holy) forces the hearer, who is already rejoicing about the beautiful picture of the future, to be aware that this is not just from a poet, dealing with a completely disconnected vision of the future, but is from a prophet who speaks because of a divine directive. One must assume that the holy mountain of Yahweh refers to Zion/Jerusalem (cf. Pss. 2:6; 3:5; 48:2; 99:9; however, see Jer. 31:23, where the land of Judah is called הַר הַקֹּדֶשׁ, holy hill, and possibly also Ps. 78:54). A prerequisite for this peace, according to v. 9b, is knowledge of Yahweh, which will then fill the entire land. This clause stands in a certain tension with v. 2bβ, according to which the *Messiah* is equipped with the רוח דעת (spirit of knowledge). But it is remarkable that Isaiah averts any eventual misunderstandings in v. 9. The significant factor is knowledge of Yahweh, and knowledge of Yahweh will be available to *everyone*, in fact, "as waters cover the sea." (The clause also is found almost word for word in

Hab. 2:14, but it has probably been inserted there from the Isaiah passage; cf. Sellin, KAT 12 [1929³] and Robinson, HAT 14 [1938], each ad loc.)

[11:10] According to vv. 1–9, the Messiah's importance as a bringer of salvation applies only to Judah/Israel; v. 9, which mentions only the holy mountain of Yahweh, leaves absolutely no doubt about that. However, according to v. 10, the Messiah is there as the banner for the peoples who will draw near to Zion. The fact that he is referred to as the "root of Jesse," not, as in v. 1, as the "shoot out of his stump," shows the careless way this was joined to the rest (cf. also the awkward way the clause is constructed); the expander has no interest in a precise exposition, but rather in an expansion, unless one would go so far as to say a correction, of Isaiah's expectations. The king upon Zion will stand there as a field standard or a signal (concerning נס, signal, see above, commentary on 5:26). It is supposed to show the peoples where they are to gather themselves together (cf. 18:3) and/or where they are to go to direct whatever questions they have. This passage is very definitely intended to be a parallel to 2:2–4—but of course there is the very significant difference that the Messiah does not play any role in 2:2–4. The ancient motif of the peoples paying homage (cf. Pss. 18:44ff.; 72:9ff.; 45:12ff.; on this, see H. Schmidt, "Israel, Zion und die Völker," diss., Zurich [1968] 22–26), according to which they bring their gifts to the ruler in Zion, is now turned around completely: The peoples do not carry their tribute and gifts to Jerusalem, but receive guidance from there. Zion is the center of the world's peoples; there, all the questions which humans have receive their answer, except that here, in contrast to 2:2–4, the answer does not come directly from Yahweh but from the one who has been anointed by him. There is no specific mention about what the peoples have questions about. Is the Messiah a spiritual personage who gives information about questions of law and cult? Hardly. There is no doubt that the Messiah is also thought of in this passage as the one who administers justice and, in fact in this particular case, as the judge who issues decisions concerning particular disagreements among the nations. The peoples come of their own free will; they do not bow down before a power, but before a spiritual authority. The conqueror of the whole world, who shatters "with a rod of iron" (Ps. 2:9; Num. 24:17), does not become a gentle savior, not even actually just a world ruler, but a leader of human beings who rules with full authority.

The section ends with a strange-sounding clause: "and its resting place shall be glory." It makes sense in light of the history of the concept of the מנוחה (resting place). In the first place, the מנוחה is the place of rest for herds. The nomads were very concerned to find such a place; the most desired goal of the wandering people of Israel was that they might come to such a place of rest (1 Kings 8:56; Isa. 32:18; Heb. 4:1ff. and cf. Deut. 12:9; 28:65; Ps. 95:11, and Isa. 28:12). On the other hand, Zion was the "resting place" of the ark (Ps. 132:8, 14; 1 Chron. 28:2). Therefore, it was not that far off the mark to think that Jerusalem would also be the resting place of the king. Whoever comes to the place of rest has reached the goal and can, so to speak, live in the condition of salvation.

It is difficult to determine exactly what the author had in mind by using כבוד (glory). He is certainly not thinking simply of pomp and circumstance, as would be a normal part of life in a royal residence, but might mean that the residence of the king would be the place from which the divine, heavenly glory would break out at the time of salvation. From there, however, it would stream forth across peoples throughout the entire inhabited world.

Purpose and Thrust

In a way which is clearer than even 9:1–6, the motifs of the ideology of kingship in the OT can be found in 11:1–9. But there are particular aspects which must be observed: In the first place, the announcement is about a ruler who comes, not from the house of David, but from the rootstock of Jesse. History will indeed go forward, but not without a sharp break, a time for reaching back to the safe and secure beginnings of kingship in Judah. Besides this, there are characteristic clauses which accent certain things about the king, carefully to be noted. The things about him which make him particularly unique are spiritual gifts from Yahweh—stress is placed upon their permanence and they are components of what is meant by fear of Yahweh. One cannot miss the point that this concentrates energetically on the image of the Messiah as one who provides service, characterized by righteousness. We were compelled to understand vv. 6–8 as a depiction which uses the vocabulary of the paradise myth to announce the radical conquest of evil and injustice. It is just as important that some of the very characteristics one would surely expect in a king are missing. The Messiah is no battlefield hero, and he is also not a world conqueror with a religious bent. עצה (planning) and גבורה (hero's power) have become "civil" virtues. The Messiah is a prince of peace. It is part of Isaiah's "measured reticence," but also his perceptive sensitivity about what could realistically happen, that the Messiah would just rule over the region of Judah/Israel. Most commentators speak of an eschatological expectation. But the problems connected with the term *eschatological* must also be taken into account here: The prophet does indeed speak of a future which will be altered, when compared with the present, but it is still very much a future within this present era (see above, commentary on 2:2a). It is in this framework that one must understand the meaning attached to the term "messianic." The designation "Messiah," which the text itself does not use, can be justifiably used, insofar as this future ruler will bring about a fulfillment of that which Israel's faith had conceived to be the ideal ruler who was to sit upon the royal throne in Jerusalem.

Even though this "image of the Messiah" in Isa. 11:1–9(–10) does not square exactly with general concepts about kingship, and although it is true that in this passage this imagery was subjected to a significant corrective, this is still no indication that this modified messianic expectation has nothing in common with the NT belief in Christ. In the OT itself one finds a substantive parallel to it in Mic. 5:11ff., but beyond this, it is hardly echoed elsewhere. Ezekiel, Haggai, and Zechariah do not make a single reference to Isaiah's viewpoint in their own expectations of a Messiah. But it is obviously utilized in the Qumran literature; cf. particularly 1Q Sb V, 20ff., where mention is made of the call issued to the sovereign of the community, "so that he might establish the royal kingdom of his people even to eterni(ty and judge the needy justly) and legiti(mately) step forward on behalf of (the po)or of the land and each will live before his countenance blamelessly upon all of (one's solid) paths, . . . and he will operate on the basis (of his holy) covena(nt, whenever someone comes who seeks (him). The lord li(ft) you up to the eternal heights and, as a so(lid) tower upon a steep wall, so that (you may strike the nations) by the power of your (mouth), by means of your scepter you will devastate the earth and through the breath of your lips you kill the god(less with the spirit of coun)sel and eternal power, the spirit of knowledge and fear of God. And may righteousness be the girdle (on your hips and trut)h the girdle of your loins . . ." (translation and expansions based on van der Woude, op. cit., 112f.). It is apparent that Isaiah's terminology has been used; however, in his imagery of the king, Isaiah had placed emphasis upon one who establishes righteousness (and, along with that, peace); in the above-cited passage that emphasis is once again abandoned in favor of concepts such as those found in Psalm 2 and other passages. (Concerning the interpretation of Isa. 11:1ff. in the Qumran community, see also 4 Q Mess ar, about which one ought to consult J. A. Fitzmyer.) In the Psalms of Solomon, as the coming of the Messiah is sought, it is said: "Undergird him with the strength to destroy the unrighteous rulers! . . . in wisdom and in righteousness to drive out the sinners from the inheritance; to smash the arrogance of sinners like a potter's jar; to shatter all their substance with an iron rod; to destroy all unlawful nations with the word of his mouth" (17:24, 26f.; see also 29, 36, 39; 18:8f.). It is apparent here as well that the passage is dependent upon Isa. 11:1ff., but in fact the concepts in this passage are more distant from Isaiah's expectations than are those expressed in the Qumran documents.

Without any significant distortions of the text because of the alternate interpretations noted above, Isa. 11:1–10 also contributed to the way the NT described the Messiah; see Rom. 15:12; 2 Thess. 2:8; Rev. 5:5f.; 19:11, 15. But the accord does not apparently go back directly to Isaiah—rather the influence came to the writers of the NT by way of the messianic hopes of Jewish apocalyptic. The seven spirits of the Johannine apocalypse (1:20; 3:1; 4:1; 4:5; 5:6) are not the same as the gifts of the Spirit (it is first in the Gk and Syr, each in its own way, that one arrives at the number seven; on this, see E. Schweizer, "Die sieben Geister der Apokalypse," *Neotestamentica* [1963] 190–202). On the other hand, Isaiah 11 does find an echo in the NT when the gifts of the Spirit, which rest upon the Messiah according to Isaiah, are promised to those who believe in Christ (Eph. 6:14, 17; 1 Peter 4:14).

To show the relevancy of the message of 11:1–9, it can be shown that the Messiah's role was to include progress for the $\beta \alpha \sigma \iota \lambda \epsilon \iota \alpha \ \tau o \hat{v} \ \theta \epsilon o \hat{v}$ (kingdom of God) within historical Israel, which would occur as the divine provision of righteousness became a reality. The gifts of the righteousness of God cannot become a reality unless they are given shape within the socio-economic sphere. The peace which this creates is not the "peace of the soul" for the believer, characteristic of one who survives in the midst of a wicked world, but can be attained only when evil is overpowered, which alone can guarantee that insecurity and fear can be repelled. The anticipated condition of salvation is irrevocably grounded within a knowledge of Yahweh.

Even though, according to the OT, the peoples of the world are clearly on the horizon for the ruler who stands upon Zion (e.g., Ps. 72:8–11, 17), Isaiah's messianic hopes are limited specifically to Israel. However, the meaning of the Messiah for the peoples lies close to the heart of the expander who is at work in v. 10. He does not see the Messiah as a victor and conqueror of peoples, but rather as an adviser and mediator of their disputes. Even the final clause, "its resting place shall be glory," shows this dissonance with Isaiah, whose concern was not about glory but simply about the end of evil among human beings. But it was significant for the expander that stress be placed on the exalted nature of the Messiah—as the representative of Yahweh upon earth, the Messiah would manifest that exalted nature in divine radiance.

Isaiah 11:11–16

Homecoming and Salvation

Literature

See the literature for 11:1–10, insofar as it applies to the entire chapter.

Text

11:11 And it will happen on that day:
'Yahweh'[a] will once again 'raise high'[b] his hand,
to ransom the remnant of his people,
which remained from Assyria [and Egypt]
[and from Pathros and from Cush and from Elam and from Shinar
and from Hamath[c] [d]and from the islands of the sea[d]].
12 And he will set up a standard for the peoples
and will gather together the dispersed[a] of Israel,
and will bring in the scattered ones of Judah
from the four corners of the earth.
13 Then the jealousy of Ephraim will mellow
and the 'enmity'[a] of Judah will be eradicated.
[Ephraim will not be jealous of Judah
and Judah will not afflict Ephraim.]
14 Then they will [a]rush over the 'slope' of the Philistines[a] toward the
sea,
together they will completely plunder the people of the east.
They will stretch out their hands[b] toward Edom and Moab,
and the Ammonites will obey them.
15 And Yahweh 'dries up'[a] the tongue of the sea of Egypt
and brandishes his hand over the Euphrates [b]by means of the
power of his storm[b]
and breaks it up into seven streams,
so that one can cross over it with sandals.
16 Then a road will come into being, for the remnant of his people
who will be left in Assyria,
just like there was one for Israel,
when it came up out of [the land of] Egypt.

11a Instead of אדני (Lord), along with numerous copies, one should read יהוה (Yahweh) here.

11b MT: שֵׁנִית, "for the second time," is superfluous when used with יוֹסִיף (happen once again), and yet, one anticipates that there ought to be a verb before ידו (his hand). Gk reads προσθήσει κύριος τοῦ δεῖξαι τὴν χεῖρα αὐτοῦ (the Lord will stretch forth his hand again). BHS suggests reading שְׂנּוֹת ידו; on the basis of the Arabic *sanija*, "be high," this would mean "lift up the hand." However, there is no evidence for a Hebrew word שׁנה with this meaning. One should also reject the reading יד, which hardly ever means "love," as suggested by A. Fitzgerald, *CBQ* 29 (1967) 369f., who points it יְדוֹ (his love) and, without altering it in any other way, translates it "he will add to his love the second time—he will love (them) all the more the second time." It is possible that one ought to read, instead of שֵׁנִית ידו, rather what is in v. 15: הֵנִיף ידו (brandishes his hand), but it is more likely, based on the actual writing of the individual letters, according to 49:22, and often elsewhere, that this should be emended to read שָׂאֵת ידו (raise high his hand).

11c It is surprising to find Hamath, a city in the middle of Syria, mentioned along with world powers, especially since we know nothing about any Jewish exiles who would have been relocated there. Cheyne, et al., suggest reading אַחמתא; see C. Cornill, *ZAW* 4 (1884) 93; this would mean that one would read Ecbatana here, which would seem more likely in a text which appears to be comparatively young, rather than accepting the conjectured reading מֵחִתִּים, "from the Hittites." However, Hamath is very likely, *pars pro toto,* a way to designate the entire Syrian region and should thus be left as it is.

11d–d מֵאִיֵּי הים, "and from the islands of the sea," is not found in the Gk (though it is added into the Hexaplaric text). This is most likely a later addition, intended to complete the list of lands, since Jews were also dwelling along the coastal regions and on the islands of the eastern Mediterranean.

12a Concerning נִדְחֵי (the dispersed) (without the *Dagesh forte*), see Ges-K §20m.

13a P. Joüon, *Bib* 10 (1929) 195, proposes reading, instead of צֹרְרֵי (enemies of), which does not fit very well with the abstract קנאת (jealousy), rather צְרָרֵי (enmity of) (an abstract plural in the same form as, e.g., מְגוּרים), meaning "enmity," whereas Procksch takes צֹרְרים itself to be an abstract plural (cf. חֲבָלִים, "union," in Zech. 11:7). In any case, one should presume that the original text had a word with the meaning "enmity."

14a–a If כָּתֵף (slope) in the absolute state is correct, then this should be translated: "And the Philistines will flee over a mountain slope toward the sea." But, according to the context, the Ephraimites and Judeans have to be the subject of the clause. F. Wutz, *BZ* 18 (1929) 27f., thinks that, instead of בכתף (over a mountain slope), one ought rather read בְּפֶלֶךְ, alters וְעָפוּ to read וְצָפוּ, and translates it: "They travel on Philistine rafts into the sea" (for צוף, he refers to the Syriac *ṭwp,* "travel by ship"; for פלך, he refers to the Arabic *fulk,* "ship, raft"). Finally, J. Komlosh suggests translating עפו with "they destroy," based on the Aramaic. These suggested emendations are all much too speculative; it is better to stay with the MT. However, since כתף can hardly be in the construct state, it has to be pointed כְּתֵף (cf. Vulg: *in umeros Philisthiim,* into the shoulder of the Philistines).

14b Instead of מִשְׁלוֹחַ, as read in the text of BHS, many copies and editions, as well as BHK³, read מִשְׁלוֹחַ.

15a MT והחרים, meaning "and he will banish," makes absolutely no sense and cannot be left as is, in spite of the suggestion of H. J. Stoebes (*TZ* 18 [1962] 399f.) that one cannot expect the images all to match up exactly in secondary interpretations of the text, such as this. G. R. Driver, *JTS* 32 (1931) 251, refers to an Akkadian root *ḥarāmu,* which supposedly means "to cut off, cut through" (cf. *AHW* 323: *ḥarāmu* II, separate). But it is also not fitting in this case that one postulates a Hebrew word, on the basis of a similar word in another language, even though it is not found in Hebrew, particularly when this suggested meaning does not fit very well in the context. Gk reads ἐρημώσει (will strip bare); Targ: וייביש (and he will make dry); Syr: wᵉnahreb (and he will make desolate); Vulg: *desolabit* (will desolate), which would suggest that the Hebrew was originally והחריב, "and he will allow it to dry out."

15b–b Up until now, no satisfactory solution has been found for explaining בְּעָיָם רוּחוֹ. Gk: πνεύματι βιαίῳ (violent wind); Targ: במימר נביוהי, "through the word of his prophets"; Syr: bᵉ'uḥdānâ dᵉrûheh, "with the power of his wind"; Vulg: *infortitudine spiritus sui* (in the strength of his spirit). Some have related בעים to the Arabic ġāma, "be covered with clouds" and "be plagued with a burning thirst" (substantive ġajm, "cloud, anger, thirst"), and suggest that בעים could be translated as "glowing passion." J. Reider (*HUCA* 24 [1952/53] 87) also favors a connection with this Arabic root, but translates it "with the violence of his wind." Even though this rendering agrees with the Syr and Vulg, this derivation remains highly speculative. The interpretation offered by H. Geers, *AJSL* 34 (1917) 132f., is also questionable: He takes בעים as an adverb from the root בעה (see 30:13; 64:1), meaning "beyond the normal, energetic, strong, powerful." However, if one accepts this interpretation, it causes syntactic problems in the clause; the same is true of the suggestion made by Hummel (*JBL* 76 [1957] 94f.), who takes בעים as an infinitive absolute from בעה (boil up), followed by an enclitic *Mem* (resulting in the attempt to translate it: "boiling of water"). Finally, Tur-Sinai (*ScrHier* 8 [1961] 188) refers to the Akkadian *ûmu* and on that basis presumes there is a Hebrew word עַיִם, meaning "storm." Because of the uncertainty, in fact the virtual impossibility, of such conjectures, one does well to leave the MT as it is. However, on the basis of the versions, it seems that the translation "by means of the power of his storm" is justified.

Form

Whereas the secondary addition, v. 10, continues to speak about the prediction of a sprout coming from the rootstock of Jesse and gives it its own unique interpretation, there seems to be no direct connection at all between vv. 11–16 and vv. 1–9. In addition to this, v. 11 begins with the well-known והיה ביום ההוא (and it will happen on that day) (on this, see above, on the setting and form of 7:18–25 and on the form of 10:20–23): vv. 11–16 are likely from a different hand than v. 10. However, the section presumes that v. 10 is already there, since it takes up the topic of the נס (signal), which points out how the peoples are to come on their way up to Jerusalem (as v. 10 itself had already picked up from 5:26).

On the basis of content, this prediction is divided into four parts: vv. 11f.: the return of the exiles; v. 13: the overcoming of the "jealousy" between Ephraim and Judah; v. 14: the display of the power of the "redeemed" people; vv. 15f.: the roads for the returnees. The fourth part picks up again on the theme of the first, so that the section comes to an appropriate conclusion.

This prediction, which is itself to be dated as late (on this, see below, on the setting), has been expanded still once more. ומאיי הים (and from the islands of the sea) is not found in Gk and thus inserts one final expansion. But the list of the lands, no doubt, is already expanded secondarily after the mention of Pathros (Duhm, Procksch, Condamin, Feldmann, Steinmann, Fohrer, et al.). In vv. 15f., the discussion is just about Mesopotamia and Egypt and, if the entire list of names of the lands had been original, then Elam and Shinar would have been included along with Assyria. But one suspects that even וממצרים (and out of Egypt) did not originally follow מאשור (from Assyria) (see Procksch and Steinmann). It is true that v. 16b does speak of Egypt, but only insofar as the expected return home could be compared to the exodus from Egypt. Because it was mentioned here, ממצרים (from Egypt) was inserted into v. 11, though Egypt is a topic for discussion once again in v. 15aα. The length of the verse itself shows that v. 15 is too full. In v. 16b, ממצרים (from Egypt) ought to be read instead of מארץ מצרים (from the land of Egypt) (see the section on meter). Finally, some also consider v. 14b to be an expansion (Duhm, Cheyne, Fohrer, et al.). If the text of v. 13a has been transmitted correctly, then v. 13b is in fact in tension with it, since, if the enemies of Judah have been "purged" from Ephraim, it is superfluous to say that Ephraim will not be jealous of Judah any longer. But this argument loses its force if one accepts what was said above concerning צררי (enmity of) (see above, textual note 13a). But even so, v. 13b looks like an unnecessary gloss to v. 13a, also demonstrated by the vocabulary which repeats the terms from the previous line.

The section is a promise of salvation for Israel, characteristic of these types of additions to the book of Isaiah (cf. 4:2–6; 6:13; 10:20–23, and 24–27a). The secondary passages in chap. 10 have shown that some felt the need to bring up to date, again and again, Isaiah's predictions about Assyria. But it is really only fitting that the prediction in 11:1–9 (with the parenthetical secondary v. 10 already there) would pose the question about what that meant for the present. L. Alonso-Schökel, "Das poemas a la paz," *EstBib* 18 (1959), 168, has already pointed to the correspondence between the "Spirit of Yahweh" in v. 2 and the "hand of Yahweh" in vv. 11 and 15, the just government of the Messiah in vv. 3–5 and the military successes of Judah against its enemies in v. 14, the peace among the animals in vv. 6f. and the reconciliation of Ephraim and Judah in v. 13. But it is also noteworthy that the interpreter demonstrates no interest in the person of the Messiah.

Meter: The section begins with three-stress bicola: two in v. 11 (taking into account that some parts are considered prosaic additions), two also in v. 12 and one in v. 13a (v. 13b betrays itself as prose by twice using the particle את). Possibly v. 14a is also a three-stress bicolon, since ימה (toward the sea) might be a gloss. However, since v. 14b is a seven-stress colon, this might also apply to v. 14a. Verse 15, after the removal of v. 15aα, has 2 five-stress cola; v. 16 closes with a seven-stress colon and a six-stress colon. (Cf. the analysis of the meter, which differs somewhat, in L. Alonso-Schökel, op. cit., 153.)

Setting

In the modern study of the text, there has been almost universal agreement that vv. 11–16 do not originate with Isaiah (but see Fischer, ad loc., and B. Otzen, *Studien über Deuterosacharja,* Acta Theologica Danica 6 [1964] 44). Israel/Judah is living "scattered about" in the diaspora and is to return from the "four corners of the earth." Isaiah could not have anticipated a return from Assyria (the mention of Judah in v. 12 prevents one from thinking exclusively of the Israelites who had been deported from the Northern Kingdom). The jealousies between Ephraim and Judah are typical of the postexilic era; cf. Neh. 3:33ff.; 6:1ff. Verse 14 could not possibly have come from Isaiah, and the use of the traditions from the exodus in v. 16 would be most surprising, since the prophet himself never mentions the exodus from Egypt. On the other hand, the parallelism of a new exodus with that from Egypt is typical of the ideas found in Deutero-Isaiah. Concerning קנה (ransom) in v. 11, one can compare 43:24; concerning נדחי ישראל (the dispersed of Israel), see Jer. 43:5; see also Mic. 4:6; Zeph. 3:19. It would seem that the author of passages such as 43:1–7; 49:11f. (cf. מסלה, highway); 49:22f. (see נס, signal), and 51:9–11 was intimately acquainted with the motif of the reunification of Ephraim and Judah as it is discussed in Jer. 3:18; Ezek. 34:23; 37:15–28. One might doubt whether the same is true for Zech. 10:3–12, since common motifs do not prove that 11:10–16 is dependent upon Deutero-Zechariah, but can rather be explained on the basis of a common source for the concepts, most likely Deutero-Isaiah (on this, see M. Saebø, *Sacharja 9–14*, WMANT 34 [1969] 221ff.). To be sure, the section is later than Jeremiah, Ezekiel, and Deutero-Isaiah, but is certainly older than Deutero-Zechariah. Verse 13 shows that it must come from a time when tensions between Ephraim/Samaria and Judah had reached an acute level: It does not simply deal with a reunification of the two parts of Israel, as is the case for the passages mentioned from the books of Jeremiah and Ezekiel, but rather with a reconciliation between them. Kaiser (ad loc.) thinks this refers to the Samaritan schism (concerning the way in which this came about, see H. H. Rowley, "Sanballat and the Samaritan Temple," *BJRL* 38 [1955] 166–198, here 187ff., and M. Hengel, *Judaism and Hellenism* I [1974] 90ff.). Yet, that is not the only possibility; rather, the opposite is true: After the schism, there was a mutual distancing from one another, so pronounced that each party laid claim to being the true Israel. It is even more true that the time of the Maccabees, as suggested by Duhm and Marti, does not fit here; at most, the most recent additions might have come from that time. It would seem possible to date this to the time of Haggai and Zechariah, but it is even more likely from the time of Nehemiah and Ezra (see Procksch: fourth, or possibly third, century). At that time, the Persians were ready to grant meaningful concessions to the Jews, so that Palestine could provide them with a strong fortress on the border of Egypt (see K. Galling, *Studien zur Geschichte Israels im persischen Zeitalter* [1964] 156). That might have offered extra encouragement for new contingents of exiles from "Assyria" to return. One could object, concerning this attempt to date the text, that the motif of the return of the "dispersed" had become a solid component of Israel's hope for the future; thus, every attempt to find connections with historical events would be problematic. However, since the original form of the message spoke only about a return from Assyria, which would mean that all the additional names which broadened the scope of the text are secondary additions, the hope for a repatriation had not yet apparently hardened into a fixed, dogmatic form.

Commentary

[11:11] The formula "on that day" is also used here simply to connect it with what precedes, that is, v. 10 or vv. 1–10. The expander wants to say: When the new ruler, whose "resting place" upon Zion will be "glory" (v. 10), carries out the functions of his dominion, much more will happen than just what is promised in vv. 1–9 and 10: Israel as a whole will once again be reestablished in its own land. But it is not the king who will set these events in motion, but rather Yahweh himself. He will continue to raise his hand, which means that he will make sure his power takes effect (for another view, see Fitzgerald, *CBQ* 29 (1967) 369f.). Concerning יד (hand) as "might," see above, commentary on 10:13. (שנית, "for a second time," the result of damage to the text, contrasts the anticipated return with the one which already happened, i.e., at the beginning of the Persian era.) In the OT, נשא יד (raise high the hand), with Yahweh as subject, generally refers to raising the hand to take an oath; here, however, a different meaning can be substantiated by the same usage in 49:22 (see the parallel נס, signal, in that passage also). According to this idiomatic usage, the meaning can hardly be distinguished from נֹפֵף יָד (swing his hand) (see above, 10:32) or הֵנִיף יָד (wave his hand), 2 Kings 5:11; Isa. 11:15; 19:16, and often elsewhere. The purpose of Yahweh's intervention is the redemption of the remnant of his people, in fact, the remnant מאשור (from Assyria), which certainly does not mean: the remnant, which Assyria left, but rather those who still remained in Assyria. יוֹסִיף (once again) helps one to recognize that the return had already begun a long time ago, but now there was anticipation that the return would finally reach a conclusion. As is well known, not all of the Jews alive at the beginning of the Persian era came back to Palestine from Babylonian territories (see Noth, *The History of Israel* [1960] 300, 316; J. Bright, *A History of Israel* [1959] 342ff.; concerning the situation of the Jews in the Persian empire, see Bright, 360f.). But it is completely justified to speak of a "remnant" of the people, not only because some of them had returned, but because many descendants of the exiles had been lost from Israel due to assimilation. It may be that others had fallen victim to various outbreaks of enmity against the Jewish people. We would certainly like to know if the author had actual information about whether any descendants of those once living in the Northern Kingdom might have still been alive in "Assyria"; Jeremiah still had some information about those descendants, and he still had hopes for their deliverance (see Jeremiah 30f.).

The return of the remnant is described by the author as being ransomed by Yahweh. In a similar way, Isa. 43:3 speaks of the כֹּפֶר, "ransom money," which Yahweh would pay for Israel (כֹּפֶר means "ransom money" for someone who is under the sentence of death, Exod. 21:30, and often elsewhere). קנה specifically refers to the ransom of a slave (Neh. 5:8) and is thus a closer parallel term for the more frequently used technical term פדה (ransom). Just as this latter term is used, the former can be used to describe Yahweh's ransoming Israel from its servitude in Egypt, Exod. 15:16; Ps. 74:2 (parallel גאל, redeem). In a way which is different from the way "ransom" is used in English, the Hebrew concept includes an actual taking possession of the people when it tells of Yahweh's action of redemption. Some Jews, who had remained in Babylon, even though they had the opportunity to return, certainly must have justified their actions by presuming they could just as easily serve Yahweh in the foreign land as in the old homeland; see also Jer. 29:5–9. But that is an opinion which was never really acceptable to the authoritative circles of the Yahwistic community: If Israel was really to fulfill its mission and realize the full benefits of its faith, it had to be able to live in the land of the fathers, the promised land, free from foreign domination.

Babylon was actually the center of the Jewish diaspora in the Persian era. The main problem, no doubt, was the return home of the exiles who lived there. As was established above (see the discussion of form), ממצרים (from Egypt) was probably already an expansion. Of course, there were Jewish communities in Upper and Lower Egypt, going back to before the exile (see Bright, op. cit., 326f.). As one learns from the Elephantine papyri, the Jewish military colony at Syene/Aswan was under considerable pressure from the Egyptian population at that time. Thus, it is certainly possible, indeed likely, that some of their members hoped to return to Palestine, because they expected persecutions, and that some actually did return, so that the parallel between Egypt and Assyria had actual basis in fact (cf. סינים, which Q^a reads as: סויניים, Aswan, in Isa. 49:12).

It is quite certain that the following, with its detailed listing of many lands, should be considered a later addition. Pathros, Egyptian *p3-r-r3śj*, "the southland," is a reference to Upper Egypt (see Jer. 44:1, 15; Ezek. 30:14, and cf. Gen. 10:14; 1 Chron. 1:12). In light of the community in Elephantine, which seems to have been very important, the mention of Pathros is justified. Bordering on Upper Egypt, just south of the first cataract of the Nile, one finds Ethiopia, that is, Cush (cf. 43:3; 45:14; Ezek. 30:4, 9, and often elsewhere). Cush was certainly part of the world known to Israel, but we do not know of any diaspora Jews who lived there in ancient times. It is possible that there were small groups of Jews who went there—that is, who went south of Egypt proper—from the time of the first campaign of Cambyses to Nubia (ca. 525) and afterwards. Without any doubt, there were certainly Jews in Elam from ancient times, northeast of the lower course of the Tigris, with its ancient capital city in Susa (cf. Isa. 21:2; 22:6; Jer. 25:24; 49:34–39; Ezek. 32:24; Dan. 8:2). According to Ezra 2:7; 8:7; 10:2, 26; Neh. 7:12; 12:42, there was an Elamite family line in Jerusalem, no doubt so called because that is where its members had once lived (W. Rudolph, HAT 20 [1949] 20). Interest in those who had stayed behind in foreign lands would have been kept alive by those who did return. Shinar (see also Gen. 10:10f.; 11:2f.; Zech. 5:11) is the name for Babylon when it is contrasted with Assyria (concerning the identification of שנער with the Babylonian *šanḫara,* the Assyrian *singara,* and the Egyptian *śngr,* see J. Simons, *The Geographical and Topographical Texts of the Old Testament* [1959] §236). This makes use of an archaizing name, characteristic of the way the expander worked.

Hamath is otherwise, in the OT, always the name for the well-known Middle Syrian city (today known as *ḥama* on the *nahr el 'āṣi,* Orontes). It is not impossible that the text has suffered some damage (on this, see above, textual note 11c), but one suspects that maybe Hamath simply stands for Middle Syria (cf. Zech. 9:2).

Finally, the "islands of the sea" are difficult to identify more exactly. These could be the islands of the eastern Mediterranean, but the reference could also be to the peninsulas and other coastal regions. In Isa. 20:6, יֹשֵׁב הָאִי (inhabitants of the coastland) refers to the Philistines; in 23:2, 6, the יֹשְׁבֵי אִי (inhabitants of the coast) are the Phoenicians. Since this expression is used next to Hamath in the present text, one might presume that this refers to the Phoenician-Syrian coastal region. The territories listed here were all within the borders or under the influence of the Persians; there is nothing which points to the diaspora of the Hellenistic era.

[11:12] It is not easy to find one's way back to the ancient homeland from such a distance. Yahweh helps; he sets up a signal (concerning נס, signal, see above, commentary on 5:26), just as Isaiah had announced in 5:26 that Yahweh would set up such a standard for the Assyrians (see also 11:10). The only thing that is remarkable is that the signal is "for the peoples" and not for Israel itself. This must refer to the peoples through whose land the returnees would march. The way this is formulated is dependent upon 5:26; 11:10; but chiefly upon 49:22, according to which the signal means that the peoples, through whose territory Israel is to pass, are to be ready and willing to help.

נדח (dispersed) is most frequently used to refer to an animal which is a straggler (Deut. 22:1; Ezek. 34:4, 16; Mic. 4:6), which also applies to נפץ (scattered) (1 Kings 22:17; Jer. 10:21; Ezek. 34:6, 12, and elsewhere). But both vocables are also used to designate the Jews of the diaspora. Gk favors using forms of the verb διασπείρειν or the substantive διασπορά in its translation; see Deut. 30:4; Isa. 56:8; Jer. 30:21 (= MT 49:5); Ps. 146:2 (= MT 147:2); 2 Esd. 11:9 (= MT Neh. 1:9), and elsewhere. Concerning נפץ (scattered ones), one should compare Jer. 47:15 (= MT 40:15); Ezek. 11:17. In actual fact, these terms are not as appropriate for describing deportees as they would be for describing those who had fled in fear during wartime or who had emigrated because of economic circumstances (Jer. 40:15; Ezek. 11:17; 20:34, 41; 28:25; 29:13). The problems connected with the diaspora did not have so much to do with being forced to live under foreign rule in a strange land, but rather had more to do with being cut off from fellowship with one's people, which the ancient person, having a very strong desire for security and protection, viewed differently from those who live in modern times. Whoever had been torn away from this relationship would feel cut off from the wellspring of life. One notices in the present text that, right next to the masculine נדחי ישראל (dispersed of Israel), one finds that the feminine נפוצות יהודה (scattered ones of Judah) is used. Duhm, Fohrer, et al. translate this "the scattered Jewish women." Procksch offers the observation that the masculine refers to the tribes and the feminine to the cities. Gray refers to 49:22 and 60:4, where mention is made of the return home of sons and daughters. No doubt, both construct states are connected with both genitives: Israelites *and* Judeans, men *and* women, will be "gathered together." The delineation of the two sexes of the two parts of Israel is simply caused by the *parallelismus membrorum* (cf., for example: "A wise son makes a glad father, but a foolish son is a sorrow to his mother," Prov. 10:1).

The two expressions for scattering correspond precisely to the two verbs for "gathering," אסף and קבץ. אסף is primarily used about bringing in the harvest (Exod. 23:10; Deut. 16:13; Job 39:12), but it can also be used for retrieving an ox which has wandered away (Deut. 22:2) or someone who has fled (Josh. 20:4); whereas קבץ refers quite often to reassembling sheep which have been scattered (13:14; 40:11; Jer. 23:3; 49:5, and often elsewhere), certainly a rather frequent task for shepherds in Palestine; see Dalman, *AuS* VI 259, 262f. and illus. 35, also, cf. Luke 15:4–6; 1 Peter 2:25; in addition, this word is virtually a technical term for gathering the exiles together: Deut. 30:3f.; Isa. 43:5; 54:7; 56:8, and often elsewhere.

The return home takes place as the returnees come from all four corners of the world. This observation may have been the reason so many nations were listed in v. 11. But if "Assyria" actually means Persia, then the term does not need to be expanded in any way; besides, just as other similar expressions, it is supposed to describe the totality of redemptive action and therefore needs no itemizing. It had also been said that Israel had been "scattered to all the winds" (Ezek. 5:12; 17:21; Zech. 2:10); cf. also Isa. 43:6 ("from north and south, from distant places and from the ends of the earth"); 49:12; Jer. 31:8; Amos 9:9.

[11:13] The future salvation does not only deal with gathering those who have been scattered but also with the reconciliation between the two divided "brothers." Isa. 7:17 points out how the disassociation of the northern tribes continued to be an aching wound in Jerusalem. Josiah believed that the time had come for the reestablishment of the Davidic kingdom (see J. Bright, op. cit., 300) and, according to Jer. 30:9 (to be sure, a post-Jeremiah passage, see W. Rudolph, HAT 12 [1968³] ad loc.), one was not only to hope for the return of the exiles but also for reunification with Judah. Passages such as Jer. 3:18; Ezek. 34:23; 37:15–28; Hos. 3:5; and Amos 9:11ff. all show a strong desire for reunification within the Jewish community; see also Isa. 27:6 and Zech. 11:7–16. But the present text does not speak of reunification in and of itself, but of overcoming the jealousy of Ephraim and, if the emendation suggested above is correct, overcoming the enmity of Judah. MT must be interpreted in the sense that a peace would be established between the two groups, since the enemies of Judah (in Ephraim) would be purged very abruptly. Actually, repeated attempts were made to eliminate the problem of disunity by means of force—even until the destruction of the temple on Gerizim by John Hyrcanus (128 B.C.E.). But that cannot be the recipe intended by the author of 11:11ff. (then v. 13b would be a false interpretation or maybe a corrective for v. 13a).

The reason for the tension, on the side of Ephraim, is described as "jealousy," certainly on the mark as a way to characterize the feelings of "Ephraim" toward Judah. The inhabitants of the Northern Kingdom could never get over the fact that David transferred the hegemony of Israel to Judah/Jerusalem, and their successors in the postexilic era did not find it easy to concede, without carrying a grudge, that the prerogative for leadership rested with Judah only because of the temple. Judah's relationship with Ephraim is simply characterized by the author as "enmity." That is remarkable, since 11:11–16 certainly comes from Jerusalem. The policy followed there had been based on a sharp separation from Samaria, already since the days of Haggai (2:10–14), and resulted in an extremely tense relationship at the time of Nehemiah (Neh. 3:3—4:17; 6; cf. also Zech. 11:4–17), so that one might reckon with the fact that Judaism found it necessary to protect itself against the loss of its own identity (cf., for example, J. Bright, op. cit., 413ff.), but this was still a heavy burden for the faith of Israel. According to the present passage, there must have been those in Judah who followed a course which acknowledged that Judah also carried a measure of guilt over against Ephraim in this conflict.

[11:14] The author does not extend such thoughts about reconciliation to the relationship with Judah's neighbors. But he would not have found his point of view to be contradictory: The unification of Judah and Ephraim is *one* phase in the reestablishment of the kingdom of David, another of which is the subjugation of its neighbors. The Ephraimites and Judeans go together to storm the western slope of the hill country in the land of the Philistines. Concerning כתף פלשתים (slope of the Philistines), one can compare כֶּתֶף הַר־יְעָרִים (northern shoulder of Mount Jearim) in Josh. 15:10 and כֶּתֶף עֶקְרוֹן (shoulder of the hill north of Ekron) in Josh. 15:11 (on this, see G. von Rad, *PJ* 29 [1933] 33ff.). Next comes בני קדם (people of the east) (concerning this designation, see Gen. 29:1; Judg. 6:3, 33; 7:12; 8:10; 1 Kings 5:10; Jer. 49:28; Ezek. 25:4, 10; Job 1:3). This does not refer to those mentioned next, the Edomites, Moabites, and Ammonites, since they were not only to be subjugated but rather completely plundered. The "sons of the east" are rather the Aramaic peoples, and later, also the Arabic bedouin tribes, in the outlying regions southeast of Damascus (O. Eissfeldt, *ZDMG* 104 [1954] 97–99 = *KlSchr* III [1966] 297–300, and H. Donner, MIO 5 [1957] 175). Their rebellion, chronicled in Jer. 49:28, caused Nebuchadnezzar to take punitive action (cf. the sixth year of Nebuchadnezzar in the "Wiseman-Chronicle," *ANET*³ [1969] 564). In Ezek. 25:4, 10, the prophet threatens that they will inundate Moab and Ammon from the east. Over and over again, they would force their way into settled land, plunder, and then would themselves be subjected to being plundered by an expedition sent to punish them, but it would simply not be possible to apprehend them.

However, the Edomites and Moabites cannot evade the pursuit, since Israel/Judah is משלוח ידם (stretching out the hand). This expression corresponds to the phrase שלח יד, "stretch out the hand," in fact, so that one can take something and make it one's own (see Gen. 3:22). The parallel expression used to describe the Ammonites, משמעת (subjects), can mean a bodyguard (e.g., 1 Sam. 22:14), but here it is used as an abstract term for a concrete term—"those who are obligated to be obedient," that is, those who are the "vassals" (on this, see the Mesha-inscription: כל דיבן משמעת, "all of Dibon was subjugated," line 28; concerning a noun clause of this type, see BrSynt §14bε). The three groups of peoples in the land east of the Jordan, as the Philistines, had all become subject to David (concerning the Philistines, see 2 Sam. 8:1; the Edomites, 2 Sam. 8:13f.; 1 Kings 11:15–18; the Moabites, 2 Sam. 8:2; the Ammonites, 2 Sam. 10:1–5). Israel's rule over these neighbors did not, of course, last very long: The Philistines (with the exception of Gath) declared themselves free from the Davidic kingdom already during the reign of Solomon (2 Chron. 11:8; see von Rad, *PJ* 29, 40); Moab did the same after the reign of Ahab (see the Mesha-inscription); and Ammon also seems to have once again achieved its independence after the division into the two kingdoms. Edom, which had already become independent again during the time of Solomon, was subjugated once more during the time of Joram (1 Kings 22:48; 2 Kings 8:22ff.; cf. also 2 Kings 14:7), and yet, that did not last. But

Israel had never really ever given up its basic claim to this region. The book of Amos closes with a reference to raising up the booth of David, part of which included taking Edom once again and "all the nations who are called by my name" (9:11f.), which would include also the other neighbors who had once been part of the kingdom of David and thus under the lordship of Yahweh. The long-lasting loss of this region was at least in part a result of the split into two kingdoms. Thus, there was hope that the reconciliation of Ephraim and Judah would also make it possible for the kingdom of David to be reestablished according to its ancient boundaries. That was not just a fanatical dream of those who could not forget the greatness of the past: In the postexilic era, Israel was practically defenseless against pressure from neighboring states. Ezekiel had already proclaimed the judgment of God against them (chap. 25). Reference is also made to Philistia in Zeph. 2:4f. and Jer. 47:4f., to Edom in Obadiah, to Moab in Isa. 15f. (esp. 16:5f.), to Ammon in the book of Nehemiah, where Tobiah is frequently mentioned, the Ammonite "servant" (or "official"; see Rudolph, HAT 20, 109, Neh. 2:10). The vision of the future sketched out in 11:14 does not only express Jewish thoughts about power, but must also be understood on the basis of Israel's need to live by its own ideals within safe borders.

[11:15] Verses 13 and 14 are, so to speak, parenthetical; they once again look at events in Palestine. In v. 15, the scene shifts to the return of those who have been scattered. It is a most difficult undertaking for a group of people to migrate over vast stretches of land; natural barriers are practically insurmountable. But from the time of Deutero-Isaiah on, one aspect of the hope for return was the idea that Yahweh would himself accompany his people and would even forge the path for them. At first, mention is made of the provisions for those who are returning from Egypt: Yahweh will dry up the tongue of the Egyptian sea, v. 15aα. As established above (see the discussion of form), an expander is speaking here. The author builds on Exod. 14:21, according to which, as Moses stretched out his hand, Yahweh completely dried up the sea (וישם את הים לחרבה, made the sea dry land; cf. Josh. 2:10). The motif had already been brought to life again by Deutero-Isaiah, not in the sense of a new exodus from Egypt, but rather as the pattern for Yahweh's help during the return from Babylon (50:2; 51:10; see, in addition, Jer. 51:36; Zech. 10:11). But here, Yahweh's drying out the sea is not just a pattern; it parallels the help which Yahweh provides those returning from Mesopotamia. Just as it is important to Deutero-Isaiah, there is no doubt that this passage also views the redemptive action of God as united with his creative activity, which allows him to drive back the sea when he rebukes it (see also Nah. 1:4 and cf. A. Lauha, *Das Schilfmeermotiv im Alten Testament*, VTSup 9 [1963] 32–46). The power demonstrated in the creation, when Yahweh pushed the sea back, so that it would stay within its bounds, is now going to be used by him in a new way, to free his people. It is surprising that the place they will cross through is called the "tongue of the sea of Egypt." According to Josh. 15:5; 18:19, the northern end of the Salt Sea was called the "tongue of the sea." Based on this, it would seem likely that the Gulf of Suez is meant here; no doubt it was thought to be the place where the crossing would occur.

The original text mentions help only for those who are returning from Assyria. Yahweh brandishes his hand over the Euphrates (concerning הנהר as a way to designate this river, see above, commentary on 7:20). The expression הניף יד (brandish the hand) (Isaiah himself says נפף יד, swing his hand, in 10:32; cf. 10:15) might pick up on the synonymous expression נטה יד (stretch out the hand) from the story of the exodus (Exod. 14:16, 21, 26f.; see also 15:12 and the phrase יד נטויה, his hand is still stretched out; see above, commentary on 9:11b). In any case, when the author uses the expression "by means of the power of his storm," he is thinking of the strong wind from the east which made it possible for the Israelites to cross over through the sea, Exod. 14:21aβ(J). Actually, these two expressions, one referring to the upraised hand and the other to the power of the storm, collide with one another, but they were already combined in the story of the exodus. Therefore, it should not bother us that v. 15b continues by mentioning only the upraised hand: Yahweh smites the Euphrates into seven נחלים, "channels," so that there will be no danger to anyone attempting to cross it. This might be reminiscent of Moses striking the waters (Exod. 17:5), but, at the same time, it is also a reenactment of the battle against chaos, at which time Yahweh split the sea (Isa. 51:10; 63:12f.; Pss. 74:13f.; 78:17; 89:11; 106:9; 136:13f.; Job 26:12; Neh. 9:11). This made it possible for one to cross through the sea on dry ground (Ps. 66:6; cf. Isa. 51:10; Ps. 114:3, 5). The author of the present passage seems to have weighed very carefully in his mind that one cannot simply stop the flow of a river, but one could separate it to form several channels (for which the Euphrates itself could have furnished some visible examples), so that one could cross over just wearing sandals (concerning נעלים, sandals, see above, commentary on 5:27).

[11:16] The remnant which was returning home from Assyria would have a מסלה at their disposal (concerning מסלה, "a highway constructed with rocks which are heaped up," see above, commentary on 7:3). There is no question that the author is thinking here about 40:3; cf. also 19:23; 49:11; 62:10, and 35:8 (here מְסְלוּל, highway). The solid roadway which comes from a distant land belongs to one of the traditional elements used when depicting the return home; it is not simply a דרך (way) or a ארח (path) (on this, see K. Elliger, *Jesaja II,* BK XI, 17f.). The pattern which suggested such roadways to the Israelites was the system established by the Persians, the predecessor of the network of Roman roads which connected the various parts of the empire (on this, see A. T. Olmstead, *History of the Persian Empire* [1948] 299ff.).

The comparison in v. 16b is a most surprising one: "just as there were such for Israel when it came up out of the land of Egypt." We do not find out anything about Israel using such a roadway during the exodus from Egypt. But the parallelism between the second exodus and the first seems to have become so strong that aspects of the new exodus were written back into the account of the older one (concerning the problem of the older and newer exodus, see B. W. Anderson, "Exodus Typology in Second Isaiah," FS J. Muilenburg [1962] 177–195, and W. Zimmerli, "Der 'neue Exodus'," FS W. Vischer [1960] 216–227 = *Gottes Offenbarung,* TBü 19 [1963] 192–204.

Purpose and Thrust

This section provides evidence for the hope that there would be a new Israel, which must have occupied the attention of many different groups of the people after the exile came to an end. The imagery of hope, which Isaiah himself produced in vv. 1–9, to which an expander added v. 10, was not enough to satisfy the author of this section. For him, the Messiah was only a sign of the unfolding time of salvation; Yahweh himself would actually make that salvation a reality, in which case the redeemed people shared responsibility for carrying out the details of all the work needed to solidify this. In contrast to Isaiah, but also to Ezekiel and Deutero-Isaiah, the author thinks in a nonhistorical way. Israel is to return home; we do not find out why this is possible, that is, what political circumstances allow it. There seems to be just as little reflection on the author's part concerning whether he thought Israel was ripe for a return home and whether the return was caused by an inner return, personally, or whether this could be expected in response to Yahweh's turning toward them again. He did not even pose the question about whether all the returnees could actually subsist in the ancient homeland. Whereas Deutero-Isaiah solicits trust and readiness for return, both are simply presumed here. However, the references to the first exodus (and thus, indirectly, to Yahweh's actions as creator) and to the original kingdom of David show, at least implicitly, what gave the author confidence in his promise: the knowledge of Yahweh's power and his unity with Israel. He sees the deliverance as an absolutely pure act of Yahweh's grace, concerning which there was no need for reflection, either about the historical time period or about Israel's status at the time. His conceptualization of Yahweh's activity is once again mythic: God will intervene, and this intervention would be simply wonderful, as had been the case in the magnificent history of salvation in the past, which had long since progressed beyond just using basic mythic concepts. There is no inquiry about Israel's faith and obedience. There is just as little mention of the motif of the establishment of righteousness, which was so central to Isaiah's depiction of the future, except that the righteousness of Yahweh would once again be manifested when the kingdom of David was reinstituted. History would no longer unfold as a "conversation" between God and his people (see H. W. Wolff, "Das Geschichtsverständnis der alttestamentlichen Prophetie," in *GesStud* TBü 22 [1964] 289–307, see 307, and H. Wildberger, *Jesajas Verständnis der Geschichte,* VTSup 9 [1963] 83–117, see p. 108), but rather, it would be a schematized fulfillment of promises which had been given in the past. In all of this, the author is far removed from Isaiah; he is already within striking distance of an apocalyptic understanding of history. It is extremely important in his thought that the reconciliation between Ephraim and Judah be an indispensable presupposition for the coming time of salvation, and thus he does not simply wish to shove to one side the guilt connected with that quarrel. His message, without a doubt, caused the Israel of the diaspora never to give up and the Israel of the homeland never to forget the family members who lived far away.

Isaiah 12:1–6

The Song of Praise
of the Redeemed

Literature

L. Alonso-Schökel, "De duabus methodis pericopam explicandi," *VD* 34 (1956) 154–160. F. Crüsemann, *Studien zur Formgeschichte von Hymnus und Danklied in Israel,* WMANT 32 (1969), esp. 227f.

    Concerning the text: R. M. Spence, "Yah, Yahve," *ExpTim* 11 (1899/1900) 94–95. Seydl, "Zur Strophik von Jesaja 12," *TQ* 82 (1900) 390–395. J. Zolli, "Note esegetiche," *Giornale della Società Asiatica Italiana* NS 3 (1935) 290–292. S. E. Loewenstamm, "'The Lord Is My Strength and My Glory'," *VT* 19 (1969) 464–470.

    Concerning individual motifs: Pressel, art.: "Laubhüttenfest," in *Real-enzyklopädie für protestantische Theologie und Kirche,* vol. 8 (1881²) 479–484. D. Feuchtwang, "Das Wasseropfer und die damit verbundenen Zeremonien," *MGWJ* 54 (1910) 535–552, 713–729, and *MGWJ* 55 (1911) 43–63. E. L. Ehrlich, "Die Kultsymbolik im Alten Testament und im nachbiblischen Judentum," in F. Herrmann, ed., *Symbolik der Religionen,* vol. III (1959), here 54–58.

    [**Literature update through 1979:** H. Gottlieb, "Jesaja kapitel 12" (Danish), *DTT* 37 (1974) 29–33.

    Concerning the text: E. M. Good, "Exodus XV 2," *VT* 20 (1970) 358–359 (includes a discussion of Isa. 12:2). S. B. Parker, "Exodus XV 2 Again," *VT* 21 (1971) 373–379 (includes a discussion of Isa. 12:2).]

Text

12:1 And you shall say on that day:
      I thank you, Yahweh, certainly you have been angry with me,
   [a]so turn away your wrath, so that you comfort me.[a]
  2 Behold,[a] God is my help,
      I have confidence and do not fear for myself.
    For my power and my strength[b] is Yah[Yahweh].[c]
      Yes, he has been salvation for me.
  3 So you will draw water with joy
      out of the wells of salvation.
              *   *   *   *

  4 And you will say on that day:
      Praise Yahweh, call out his name!
    Declare among the peoples his deeds.
      Make it known, that his name is exalted.

5 Sing to Yahweh, for he has done exalted things,
    they are to be made known[a] throughout the whole earth.
6 Rejoice and be glad, you townspeople of Zion,[a]
    for great in your midst is the Holy One of Israel.

1a–a It is surprising to find the jussive יָשֹׁב (so turn away) and the imperfect וּתְנַחֲמֵנִי (so that you comfort me) in a song of thanks which begins with אוֹדְךָ (I thank you). Gk reads διότι ὠργίσθης μοι καὶ ἀνέστρεψας τὸν θυμόν σου καὶ ἠλέησάς με (since you had been angry with me and you have turned back your anger and been merciful to me); Syr: w'hpkt rwgzk wbj'tnj (and you turned your anger and you consoled me); Vulg: conversus est furor tuus, et consolatus es me (your anger has been turned aside and you have comforted me). It seems likely that these versions read וְשָׁב (turned back) or וַיָּשָׁב (turned back) instead of יָשֹׁב (turn back), and וַתְּרַחֲמֵנִי (you have been merciful to me) or even וַתְּנַחֲמֵנִי (you have comforted me) instead of וּתְנַחֲמֵנִי (so that you comfort me), resulting in the reading: "your wrath has turned itself, and you are merciful to me" or "and you comfort me." But one must question whether this approach can be used to rob the MT of its bold way of saying that which does not conform to what is usually said. Targ reads the imperfect: יתוב רוגזך מני ותרחים עלי (may your anger turn from me and be merciful to me). Since songs of thanks can also include requests (see H. Gunkel and J. Begrich, *Einleitung in die Psalmen* [1933] 275), the jussive is certainly not impossible here.

2a It has been suggested that, just before אל (God), on the basis of Syr, one should read על (upon) (Q[a] reads אל אל, to God), so that one could translate this: "behold, in the God of my help I have confidence. . . ." If one leaves MT as it is, 2aβ is a clause by itself. If that is the case, one must question whether, in 2aα אל ישועתי (God of my salvation) should be treated as a construct clause (Procksch: "Look, there is the God of my salvation!"; similarly, Marti). But one suspects that this should still be considered a noun clause.

2b זִמְרָת (strength) is a very unusual form (on this, see Joüon, Gr 89n). But it is also found in Exod. 15:2 and Ps. 118:14; in fact, in both cases, it is followed by יה (Yah). Q[a] reads זמרתי (my strength [my song]), inserting a ה at the beginning of the word, placed slightly higher in the text; on this, see S. Talmon, *VT* 4 (1954) 206f., and *Textus* 1 (1960) 163, note 47; in both of the other passages, there are also certain copies which read זמרתי (my strength [my song]); on this, see G. R. Driver, *JTS* NS 2 (1951) 25. MT can seemingly be explained by the fact that, in liturgical usage, the first-person suffix was slurred when pronounced with the following יה (Yah); see also O. Lehman, *JNES* 26 (1967) 98; however, he wrongly attributes this development to "the actual spoken language" (ibid., 94) (handled slightly differently by Loewenstamm, op. cit., 469).

זמרה does not mean "song," as is the rule elsewhere, but rather "strength" (cf. the Arabic *ḏamara*, "drive on," and *ḏimr[un]*, "strong"; Old South Arabic *ḏmr*, and the Amorite *zmr*, "protect"; see J. Zolli, op. cit., 290–292, and cf. KBL[3] concerning זמר III; in addition, note the personal name בעלזמר, B'lzmr, Diringer, *Le iscrizioni antico-ebraiche palestinesi* [1934] 43, and זמריהו, Zmryhu, ibid., 211, and the biblical name זִמְרִי [Zimri]; cf. Noth, *Personennamen,* 176; for another view, see Loewenstamm, op. cit., 465ff.).

2c יה (Yah) is usually eliminated, although it is also used in the two parallel passages, Exod. 15:2 and Ps. 118:14. It should not be eliminated. Rather, the opposite should be done: יהוה (Yahweh), which follows this, should be eliminated (as a dittography of the following ויהי, he has been; on this, see R. M. Spence, *ExpTim* 11 [1899/1900] 94f.).

5a MT allows for a choice between the Kethib מְיֻדַּעַת (known) and the Qere מוּדַעַת (make known); Gk ἀναγγείλατε (carry tidings) = הוֹדִיעוּ (make known). But the Targ reading is גליא (revealed) and Syr is jdj''hj (known), that is, a participle, as in the MT (Q[a]: מודעות). Since the *pu'al* participle of ידע (know) had taken on the

500

special meaning of "someone who is well-known, one who is trusted," the Qere *hoph'al* form should probably be read.

6a On the feminine as a collective, see Joüon, Gr §134c.

Form

[12:1–3] There is no doubt that 12:1 begins a new unit, shown once again by the connecting formula ביום ההוא (on that day); on this, see the discussion of 11:10 and 11:11. However, in this case it is also joined with ואמרת (you shall say), an introduction to "instructions for a herald" (on this, see Crüsemann, op. cit., 50–55). This genre is occasionally linked with elements from an "imperative hymn" (ibid., 19–82). But the imperative part is not specifically found until vv. 4–6, and there, one discovers that the same introduction is used again, though in the plural. Initially, this formula seems simply to introduce a song of thanks of an individual, in which אודך (I thank you) is characteristic, and that also applies to the remarks, introduced by כי (certainly), which speak of the reason for the thanksgiving. But after this, most surprisingly, the jussives ישׁב (turn away) and ותנחמני (so that you comfort me) follow, at least, this is true unless one alters the pointing or takes away the sharpness of the jussives by translating them with simple imperfect forms (so ibid., 227). These forms would be expected in a lament.

Verse 2 can be interpreted as an element from a song of thanks (see Ps. 118:8f., 14; Exod. 15:2a), but it is just as possible that these lines can be interpreted as expressions of confidence within a song of lament (Gunkel/Begrich, 232ff.). Verse 3, however, is a promise, the type one would expect in answer to a communal lament song. Thus, we have a remarkable mixture of form elements before us in vv. 1–3. Basically, one must treat this as a song of thanks offered by an individual. But the form of this type of song has been radically altered, since it will first be sung "on that day"; for this reason, the author returns again to the present, at which time there was nothing to be thankful about; instead, it was time for seeking help, a time for promises to be made with a view to "that day."

[12:4–6] There is disagreement about whether v. 4 begins a new section (on this, see Seydl, who believes that vv. 1–3 and 4–6 can be treated as parallel to one another). The second use of ביום ההוא (on that day) would speak in favor of this viewpoint, as well as the use of the plural ואמרתם (you will say), in contrast to the singular ואמרת (you shall say) in v. 1. In addition, the style in vv. 4–6 is that of an imperative hymn (on this, see Crüsemann, op. cit., 55f.), whereas, in vv. 1–3, one finds the basic structure of the song of thanks of an individual. And yet, vv. 4–6 are still linked to vv. 1–3, since the "you" (pl.) in אמרתם (you will say) is the same as the "you" (pl.) in ושאבתם (you shall draw water) in v. 3, which is not identical with the you (sing.) in אמרת (you shall say) in v. 1. In addition to this, ואמרת ביום ההוא (and you shall say on that day) in v. 1 is outside the metrical structure, whereas ואמרתם ביום ההוא (and you will say on that day) in v. 4 is integrated within the poem. The variety of sources used for the stylistic elements ought not be too disturbing, since vv. 1–3 also show that the author has brought together material from a variety of sources. Thus, vv. 1–6 are to be taken as a unit. The "you" (sing.) who is addressed in v. 1aα turns in v. 1aβ to Yahweh, recites his own confession in the presence of the community in v. 2, announces a promise to this community in v. 3, and then uses v. 4 to call for all to start singing the (imperative) hymn found in vv. 4b–6.

It has been frequently mentioned that chap. 12 is an eschatological song of thanks. That is a correct assessment if the song is to be sung as soon as the salvation promised in chap. 11—that is, return from exile and reestablishment of the "kingdom"—has become a reality. That means: that will take place in a world which has been really changed but is still part of the present world; there is as yet no mention of a completely new aeon. In terms of content, the psalm promises nothing which could not be said in a song of thanks or hymn which focuses on the present. Yahweh is the mighty helper, in whom one can place one's complete confidence.

Meter: (on this, see Seydl) v. 1aβb: a seven-stress colon; v. 2: 2 six-stress cola (after removing יהוה, Yahweh, and placing a double stress on לִישׁוּעָה, salvation); v. 3: apparently, this is also a six-stress colon (with a double stress on מִמַּעַיְנֵי, out of the wells, and after the article on הישועה, salvation, is removed); v. 4: an eight-stress colon (ואמרתם, and you will say, has two stresses) and a six-stress colon; vv. 5 and 6: each is an eight-stress colon.

Setting

Scholars are almost unanimous in their assessment that chap. 12 does not come from Isaiah (on this, see Kissane). The style is that of Psalm literature; there are some places where one can virtually prove word for word borrowing from the Psalter: v. 2b = Exod. 15:2a; v. 4aβ.γ = Ps. 105:1; v. 4b (partially) = Ps. 148:13. As a reason for denying authorship to Isaiah, one also notes the vague paraphrase which describes the salvation yet to come, which can be very easily distinguished from the concrete expectations in 2:2–4; 9:1–6, and 11:1–9. The fact that this section concludes with קדוש ישראל (Holy One of Israel) does not contradict this argument. This way of describing Yahweh is certainly characteristic of Isaiah, but it was hardly his own unique creation (see above, commentary on 1:4) and is also known through the Psalm literature (see 71:22; 78:41; 89:19). It also appears in the parts of the book of Isaiah which are post-Isaianic and yet, it would have been chosen by the author deliberately, by someone who carefully noted the way Isaiah chose his words. Whether this individual should be identified as the expander who speaks in 11:11–16 cannot be determined; however, chap. 12 presumes that 11:11–16 is already in the text. One supposes that the author should be identified as the final redactor of chaps. 1–11; he purposely wanted to conclude this collection with a reference to praising God in the future time of salvation.

Commentary

[12:1aα] The normal formula והיה ביום ההוא (and it will happen on that day) is altered here to read ואמרת ביום ההוא (and you shall say on that day). The introductory formula, which is followed by an instruction to a herald, recasts the song of thanks and makes it a promise of salvation. The "you" (sing.) who is addressed first, the "I" into whose mouth is placed the words which follow, is the same as an "I" who speaks in the individual song of thanks. However, according to the context into which this liturgical piece is inserted, it must be that people alive at the time of salvation are being addressed. This "I" is to be contrasted with the "you" (pl.) in vv. 3ff. One must conclude from this: the "I" is the inner community, which stands alongside the "you" (pl.), that is, the general population of the people of God: The Israel κατὰ πνεῦμα (of the spirit) addresses the Israel κατὰ σάρκα (of the flesh), in order to draw it to a conscious awareness that God's help is being experienced, to which the community of faith can already attest.

[12:1aβb] For the Hebrew הודה, there is no English equivalent which includes all its shades of meaning. It includes confession, thanksgiving, and praise. Praise is shaped as a confession about having experienced God's help when he turned toward Israel and, in such a confession, there is already cause for thanksgiving. Verse 2 speaks clearly about matters which one would expect to find in a song of thanks. But v. 1aβb is very surprising. If one follows the suggested emendations mentioned above, then one could explain it as follows: You have indeed been filled with wrath toward me, but now you have turned your wrath away, and now I can breathe easier again (concerning נחם, comfort, see above, commentary on 1:24b). Thus, praise is not connected with the anger of God, but is offered because the wrath has come to an end, corresponding to the formula: "How long will you be angry with me?" or to another which says that Yahweh will not "be angry forever" (e.g., Pss. 79:5; 80:5; 85:6; cf. SAHG, 333: "How long will you still be angry with me, my lady, and your countenance be turned away: How long will you yet, my lady, be agitated by anger and will your disposition be furious?"). However, it is precisely this background which makes some sense of the MT. One must interpret it as follows: I thank you, Yahweh, that you have allowed your wrath to be loosed against me, for that gives me the confidence to ask that your wrath might now be turned from me and that I might experience your comfort. In this setting, one must presume that the ancient idea about the wrath of the deity is in the background (see above, commentary on 9:11b). Similar to a cloud which brings disaster, it oppresses the human being, and as long as that is the case, there is no chance to breathe more easily. One actually experiences deliverance when the wrath finally lessens in intensity, since then one can relax somewhat from the built-up tension; see passages such as 2 Sam. 12:20ff. The wrath has an objective reality, hovering over the human being who is affected by it; it must be removed if God is to be able to put his grace into effect again. To show how powerfully this concept is still part of this present passage, the hope is not that Yahweh might bring his wrath to an end, but that the wrath itself might turn away.

נחם, "comfort," is not to be immediately interpreted in a "spiritual" sense. It is not only words which are able to provide comfort, but also "your rod and staff" (Ps. 23:4); that is the way Yahweh's protection actually functions. "Comfort" means "help" (Ps. 86:17), "thou wilt increase my honor" (Ps. 71:21); one can speak of the cup of consolation (Jer. 16:7), which means that "comfort" includes granting gifts which can be held in one's hand (see passages such as 2 Sam. 12:24; Ps. 51:3; Job 42:11). In psalms of this style one cannot remove concrete details about the comfort either anticipated or already received.

[12:2] The "descriptive praise" of God in this psalm is unique because of the use of the perfect אנפת (you have been angry); v. 2 shifts to "declarative praise" (concerning this terminology and the linking of the two stylistic forms, see C. Westermann, *The Praise of God in the Psalms* [1965] 116ff.). The presentation formula (concerning this terminology, see above, commentary on 3:1) הנה (behold) furnishes the introduction in v. 2a. Its meaning is similar to כי in v. 2b ("behold," in the sense of: "it is apparent to everyone, it is plain as day"). If the text has been transmitted correctly, then אל ישועתי (God is my help) is a noun clause (see above, textual note 2a; concerning the inverted order, see KBL 239a).

אל, as a designation for God, is very common in the Psalms, which may provide evidence for the effect which Canaanite literature had on the Psalm literature of Israel (cf. אל עליון, God Most High, as a designation for the god of the city of Jerusalem, Gen. 14:18–22; on this, see also F. Stolz, *Strukturen und Figuren im Kult von Jerusalem,* BZAW 118 [1970], esp. 149–180). Here, however, this designation simply furnishes another divine name for Yahweh (see v. 2b) and, in a later stage of development (Qumran literature), it completely supplanted the latter. Once again, it is a very common confession in the cultic literature that Yahweh is help (and does not just grant help); see Pss. 62:3, 7; 68:20; 118:14, 21; 140:8; he does not just help, but rather, one might say that he is help personified (cf. v. 2b: "Yahweh is my power and my strength"). In a very basic sense, ישועה (salvation) is the OT equivalent of the NT term σωτηρία (salvation) (see Fohrer, *TDNT* VII, 970f.). Yet, one could say something here which is similar to what was mentioned about נחם (comfort) above: it applies both to the internal and external aspect of a human being, has both a material and a spiritual value. Its meaning is very close to שלום (peace) and means salvation in the original sense of the German word *Heil:* a completeness, being intact, integrity, thus, a circumstance in which it is completely possible for a human being to become everything that was intended originally (cf. also ὅλος, complete, with the Latin *salvus,* and the English word "whole" with the German *Heil*). Yahweh is "help" since he creates space for an undisturbed development, in which case a complete unfolding of one's whole settled existence is made possible. Verse 2b points this out in sharp detail: Yahweh is the "power" and the "strength" of the one who is praying. This complete line is found, word for word, in Exod. 15:2 and Ps. 118:14. One cannot know whether this borrowing is literary or not; the exact same "corruption" of the word זמרת (strength) could be the result of a secondary adjustment of texts. In any case, the author of Isaiah 12 draws this from his knowledge of the traditions of Israel and, even though ויהי לי לישועה (he has been salvation for me) seems to be based on personal experience, the reason for his confidence is not any personal experience of God, but rather the testimony of the fathers which is repeated; the author thus bases his confidence in statements of faith which have been handed down. The quote may have been occasioned by the use of the key term ישועה (help) in v. 2a.

The knowledge of Yahweh, which was at the disposal of the Israelite who trusted the traditions of the faith confessed by Israelite people, made it possible for the Israelite to overcome fear (פחד) and, therefore, to be able to hold on to his or her faith (בטח). In contrast to the term האמין (believe), which has a similar meaning, בטח (have confidence) is strongly tied to the language of the Psalms (see H. Wildberger, "'Glauben' im Alten Testament," *ZTK* 65 [1968] 129–159). Isaiah himself shuns the use of the verb (but see בְּמְחָה, trust, in 30:15) or uses it only in a negative sense, about someone whose faith provides no justifiable reason to rejoice (30:12; 31:1; 32:9). Yet, it is noteworthy that בטח (have confidence), just as Isaiah uses האמין (believe), is used here in an absolute sense (cf. Jer. 12:5: "consider oneself to be safe"; Ps. 27:3: "maintain trust, remain confident"; Prov. 28:1: "be undismayed," and often elsewhere). With this usage, בטח (have confidence) is the very opposite of פחד (fear) (just as האמין, believe, in 7:9 is the opposite of ירא, fear, in 7:4; in its negative form, this same word describes the behavior of a believer, 27:1).

[12:3] Whereas the psalm uses very common, traditional terminology in vv. 1 and 2, an image used in v. 3 is unique within the OT: "You will draw water with joy." It is possible that the background for this is an actual rite. Drawing and pouring out water "before Yahweh," according to 1 Sam. 7:6, belongs to the ritual on a day of fasting (cf. also 2 Sam. 23:16). Since Yahweh is called the "fountain of living water" (Jer. 17:13; see also 2:13), this metaphor may have developed because there was a source of water close to the sanctuary in Jerusalem, whose water played a role in the cult, celebrating water as life-giving (cf. Ps. 36:10; also 65:10 and 110:7). According to the topography of Jerusalem, this can only be the Gihon *('en 'umm ed-darağ),* at the foot of the southeastern hill (see above, commentary on 8:6). We learn nothing more specific about it in the OT. On the other hand, the Talmud (Tractate Sukkah 4 and 5) speaks of symbolic drawing of water at the time of the feast of the tabernacles, at which point the present passage from the book of Isaiah was sung (on this, see Pressel, Ehrlich, and Feuchtwang).

Pressel (op. cit., 483) describes it as follows: "Concerning the drink offering, which was presented mornings and evenings, accompanied by burning of incense and sounding of the trumpet, in addition to the wine, one also took some water from the spring of Shiloah: in addition to the nine priests who were functioning here, a tenth was added, in order to draw the water with a golden can, which could hold an amount equivalent to the volume of eighteen egg shells; after he had brought it through the water entrance located on the daylight side of the inner court of the temple, then another priest would take it from him with the words from Isa. 12:3: 'You will draw water from the well of salvation with joy!' and the choir of priests, together with the people, would join in with loud voice to sing these words; the priest immediately took it to the altar, went around it from the left side, poured a portion of it into the wine of the drink offering, then the wine back again into the remaining water, poured this mixture out into a silver can and finally, to the accompaniment of music, poured it into a pipe by the altar, through which it then flowed down into the Kidron." It would seem that this is a custom which goes back to very ancient times; it could have already been an existing practice, in some form, by the time this present psalm was written. The Talmud itself describes the rite as follows: "Why does the Torah say, pour the water out on the festival day? God said: Pour the water out before me on the festival, so that you will be blessed with rainstorms during the year" (Rosh Hashana I, 2).

Without too much difficulty, such rites can take on a new meaning. Drawing water from the well of salvation becomes an image for the reception of saving power itself. Although we would think of this as only a symbolic act, it is more than that: It is actually a sacramental action. The salvation transmitted here is something real; it opens up and guarantees "life" in its fullness and power.

[12:4] Those who receive salvation are to share their experiences with others "on that day," by making sure that the deeds of Yahweh are made known to the peoples. The author expresses this with very common expressions (cf. Pss. 105:1 and 148:13). One is to praise Yahweh, call upon his name. קְרָא בְשֵׁם (actually: address *by* name) is a very ancient expression. One must know the name of a deity if one wants to have contact with the deity. But if one knows his name, then one also has access to him, since the mystery of the deity is included within the knowledge of the name; cf. Exod. 3:13ff.; Judg. 13:17. And yet, in this present passage, the formula is no doubt used much more generically, simply to describe the cultic adoration of God. In the song of lament, it means "call upon the name"; here, in the hymn, it means "call the name out loud" (so H. J. Kraus, BK XV/2, 719f. [Engl: *Psalms 60–150,* 310f.]). In actual fact, that takes place in such a way that the עֲלִילוֹת (deeds) of Yahweh will be known to the peoples. One also comes across this idea elsewhere in the Psalm literature; it is not only upon Zion that one should speak of the deeds of Yahweh, but also among the עַמִּים (peoples); see Ps. 9:12 and cf. Ps. 49:2. One might ask whether עַמִּים (peoples) refers to the non-Israelite foreign peoples in a technical sense (Gk: ἐν τοῖς ἔθνεσιν), rather than referring to them simply as fellow citizens within the boundaries of Palestine. However, in light of בְכָל הָאָרֶץ (throughout the whole earth) in v. 5 (on this, see below), this possibility is excluded. According to Deutero-Isaiah as well, it is not only the "servant of God," but Israel itself which has an obligation toward the peoples (55:5). Israel did not need to leave the borders of Palestine in order to fulfill this. "Peoples," "heathen," lived in the midst of Israel; no territory in the postexilic era was exclusively populated by those who believed in Yahweh. It is true, as well, that Judaism had not yet withdrawn into a ghetto; instead, this verse takes up the challenge of what to do with the peoples, and it answers that challenge by saying that one must proclaim the deeds of Yahweh. Ps. 105, from which the author took the quote, is a historical psalm in which Yahweh's עֲלִילוֹת (deeds) are those from the time of Abraham on. But in the present context of the "eschatological" psalm, much like Deutero-Isaiah, it must refer to taking into account Yahweh's recent deeds, connected with the reestablishment of Israel. However this is treated, it is clear that the author seeks to focus on Yahweh's actions *in history.* Since Yahweh brings such deeds to completion, he is held in high regard, his name is "exalted" (נִשְׂגָּב; on this, see above, commentary on 2:17). The gods of antiquity are most competitive with one another; they can rise, become well-known, and then also lose the sympathy of followers, finally sinking into complete oblivion. Their destiny is tied to whatever one can report about their deeds; those connected with the sanctuary knew that proclaiming was part of their task. Yahweh is also brought into this fray, for the benefit of the peoples; he is mentioned in the confession of praise offered by his congregation. In such a context, one can hardly agree that הַזְכִּיר be translated "call into remembrance" (see KBL³). As a synonym of הוֹדִיעַ, it means to "make known" (see Num. 5:15; 1 Kings 17:18; Ezek.

21:28f.; 29:16); the מַזְכִּיר (recorder) is the one who furnishes the report (see J. Hempel, *TLZ* 82 [1957] col. 818). But the שֵׁם (name) of Yahweh, whose greatness is to be made known, is the "powerful means or . . . the power itself . . . , by means of which Yahweh reaches into the world in revelation and allows his protection, help and strengthening to be experienced" (O. Grether, *Name und Wort Gottes im AT,* BZAW 64 [1934] 51).

[12:5] In reality, Yahweh's name is made known within the cult. That is made clear by the third verb which is used to characterize the praise of Yahweh, זמר (sing). It is typical of, and very clearly linked to, the language of the cult and describes liturgical praise accompanied by music. The topic of the עֲלִילוֹת (deeds) is picked up again with the use of גֵּאוּת (exalted things). In and of itself, that is an abstract term, which can be used to describe the royal sovereignty of Yahweh (see Ps. 93:1 and cf. Isa. 26:10), though here one is to consider the deeds which proclaim Yahweh's sovereignty. Once again, in v. 5b, there is another expression of the desire to "make known": The sovereign deeds of Yahweh are to be made known throughout the whole earth. But that does not mean that some were to be sent as Yahweh missionaries throughout the entire world; rather, this is the same as what the expander had in mind in 11:10, that "the root of Jesse" would show the peoples the path to the sanctuary of Yahweh.

[12:6] In v. 6, the poet turns once again to the cultic community of Yahweh in Jerusalem, the יֹשֶׁבֶת צִיּוֹן (townspeople of Zion), who are to rejoice and be glad (cf. יוֹשֵׁב יְרוּשָׁלַם, inhabitants of Jerusalem, which in 5:3 is an expression for the "community of the citizens"; however, see also יוֹשֵׁב צִיּוֹן, people which dwells on Zion, in 10:24; on this, see above, commentary on 10:24; concerning an expression which means the same thing, בַּת צִיּוֹן, Zion's daughter, see above, commentary on 1:8–9). It can also be said that Yahweh dwells upon Mount Zion (on this, see above, commentary on 8:18). That is no contradiction: Where Yahweh's community is located, he is also there in their midst, and the same fact provides the reason why this community has the advantage, since its members are able to live in the very place where Yahweh has his dwelling place. As certain as it is that the truth of Yahweh is to be proclaimed over the whole earth, it is just that certain that Yahweh is and remains the Holy One of Israel (on this, see above, commentary on 1:4), and it is also just as certain that he shows himself to be גָּדוֹל (great) in the midst of Israel.

Purpose and Thrust

Form-historical analysis and the exegesis of individual verses have shown that chap. 12 has been put together by using elements which were either taken directly from the Psalms or which speak the language of the Psalms. Only the introductory phrase, "and you shall say in that day," is absolutely unique to this psalm. Whereas cultic lyric is specifically focused on whatever is presently on the horizon, here one looks beyond, into the future, when the type of salvation which had already been experienced in the present or anticipated in the future would become a new reality. What was said in the remarks about the "purpose and thrust" of 11:11–16 must be reiterated about the verses before us: No reason is given which explains what will cause salvation "on that day"—it is not enough to simply say that Yahweh had been *angry.* The "citizens who live in Zion" are unquestionably an established group, which neither has to repent nor has to be called to faith, but is simply summoned to praise God. For this reason, this song is also a great distance from the message of Isaiah. In one sense, however, it does have an important point of contact with 11:1-9: Just as the prophet used elements linked to the way kingship ideology anticipated salvation, here as well, details which describe salvation, having been uttered again and again in Israel's worship, are projected into the future time when salvation could be once again anticipated. What was expected in cultic lyric is reshaped to become part of a prophetic promise. The introduction in v. 1aα elevates the psalm to the level of "instruction given to a herald."

As far as the content of this instruction, in spite of almost total reliance on the traditions, the author comes up with two surprising points: First, he accepts unconditionally that the wrath of God is the necessary path through which one must come on the way to salvation. Although we cannot date this instruction with precision, we can say that it was certainly composed in the postexilic era, in a time when there was very little to give the people confidence. In spite of this, the author does not complain; nor does he challenge God by saying that he had been angry long enough. He offers thanks. Because Yahweh had been angry, Israel can recognize that he does not want to break off the relationship he has with them and that he has not renounced his plan to bring about a full salvation. When the human being says yes to the chastening of God, that is the first step forward into the "open space" (ישועה), into true freedom; it is a first step toward release from bondage to a destiny which had been difficult to bear; it is the basis for the turn of events, for Yahweh's "comfort." It belongs to the greatness of Israel that, at the time when it lost its status as an independent nation, when it witnessed the destruction of what seemed to be an essential element in its faith, it did not simply disappear, but instead could acknowledge that its own fate was the necessary, and therefore logical, path on the way to eventual salvation.

And now, to the second point: "Declare among the peoples his deeds." The praise of God is to go forth from Zion into all the world. Certainly this does not mean that the inhabitants of Jerusalem were supposed to look for a way to get all the peoples to repent or that they should all be called to accept the Yahwistic faith. All that is demanded is that witness to Yahweh's גאות (exalted things), the message about his עלילות (deeds), will not be kept from the peoples of the world. The "heathen" should also be included in Israel's great jubilation. There is nothing further about the consequences which that might have, and that was not a particular concern for Israel.

This psalm, Isa. 12:1-6, furnishes a conclusion for the first eleven chapters of the book of Isaiah. The redactor, who is responsible for the final form of this chapter, certainly had in mind that it would conclude with this vision of the future. One minute detail can show how reflectively he went about his task; at the very conclusion, he has placed the name which was so central to Isaiah's understanding of God: "the Holy One of Israel."

Manuscript Sigla

'Aquila	'Aquila
B	Codex Vaticanus
C	Codex prophetarum cairensis
Gk	Greek (Septuagint)
Kethib	Kethib (so written)
L	Codex Leningradensis
MSS	Manuscripts
MT	Masoretic Text
Q^a	Qumran text $4Q^a$ (Isaiah)
Qere	Qere (so read)
Sym	Symmachus
Syp	Syriac Peshitta
Syr	Syriac
Targ	Targum
Theod	Theodotion
Vulg	Vulgate

Hebrew Grammars Cited

Bauer-Leander   H. Bauer and P. Leander, *Historische Grammatik der hebräischen Sprache des Alten Testaments* I, Halle 1922.

BrSynt   C. Brockelmann, *Hebräische Syntax,* Neukirchen 1956.

Ges-K   [F. H. W.] *Gesenius' Hebrew Grammar as edited and enlarged by the late E. Kautszch,* second English edition revised in accordance with the 28th German ed. (1909) by A. E. Cowley, Oxford 1910, reissued 1946.

Joüon, *Gr*   P. Joüon, *Grammaire de l'Hébreu Biblique,* Rome 1947².

Meyer³   G. Beer, *Hebräische Grammatik,* 2nd ed. of R. Meyer I (1952; 1966³), II (1955).

Abbreviations

AASOR	*Annual of the American Schools of Oriental Research*
AcOr	*Acta Orientalia*
ÄA	*Ägyptologische Abhandlungen*
ÄZ	*Zeitschrift für ägyptische Sprache und Altertumskunde*
AfO	*Archiv für Orientforschung*
AHW	W. von Soden, *Akkadisches Handwörterbuch* (1966f.)
AJSL	*American Journal of Semitic Languages and Literature*
AnBib	Analecta Biblica
ANEP	J. Pritchard, ed., *Ancient Near Eastern Pictures Relating to the Old Testament*
ANET	J. Pritchard, ed., *Ancient Near Eastern Texts Relating to the Old Testament* (1955²; 1969³ with supplement)
Ang	*Angelicum* (Rome)
AnGr	Analecta Gregoriana
AnnStEBr	Annales de la société d' émulation de Bruges
AnOr	Analecta Orientalia
Anton	*Antonianum*
ANVAO	Avhandlinger i Norske Videnskaps-Akademi i Oslo
AO	Der alte Orient
AOB	*Altorientalische Bilder zum Alten Testament*
AOT	*Altorientalische Texte zum Alten Testament*
ARE	*Ancient Records of Egypt*, ed. J. H. Breasted
ArOr	Archiv Orientální
ArPap	*Aramaic Papyri of the Fifth Century B. C.*, ed. A. Cowley
ARW	*Archiv für Religionswissenschaft*
ASeign	Assemblées du Seigneur
ASTI	Annual of the Swedish Theological Institute (in Jerusalem)
ATA	Alttestamentliche Abhandlungen
ATANT	Abhandlungen zur Theologie des Alten und Neuen Testaments
ATR	*Anglican Theological Review*
Aug	*Augustinianum*
AuS	G. Dalman, *Arbeit und Sitte in Palästina*, 6 vols. (1928–1942)
AusBR	*Australian Biblical Review*
AUSS	*Andrews University Seminary Studies*
AzT	Arbeiten zur Theologie

Abbreviations

BA	*Biblical Archaeologist*
BAfO	Archiv für Orientforschung Beihefte
BAL	Berichte über die Verhandlungen der Sächsischen Akademie der Wissenschaft zu Leipzig
BASOR	*Bulletin of the American Schools of Oriental Research*
BDB	F. Brown, S. R. Driver, C. A. Briggs, eds., *A Hebrew and English Lexicon of the Old Testament,* 1953
BeiKD	Kerygma und Dogma Beihefte
BeiNTT	Nieuw theologisch tijdschrift. Supplements
BeO	*Bibbia e Oriente*
BETL	Bibliotheca ephemeridum theologicarum lovaniensium
BetM	*Beth Miqra*
BEvT	Beiträge zur evangelischen Theologie
BFCT	Beiträge zur Förderung christlicher Theologie
BFT	Biblical Foundations in Theology
BHH	*Biblisch-Historisches Handwörterbuch*
BHK	R. Kittel, *Biblia hebraica*
BHS	*Biblia hebraica stuttgartensia*
BHT	Beiträge zur historischen Theologie
Bib	*Biblica*
BibLeb	*Bibel und Leben*
BibOr	*Biblica et Orientalia*
BibS(N)	Biblische Studien (Neukirchen)
BiKi	*Bibel und Kirche*
BK	Biblischer Kommentar zum Alten Testament
BN	*Biblische Notizen*
BR	*Biblical Research*
BRL	K. Galling, *Biblisches Reallexikon*, HAT I, 1
BrSynt	C. Brockelmann, *Hebräische Syntax* (1956)
BVSAW.PH.	Berichte über die Verhandlungen der sächsischen Akademie der Wissenschaften zu Leipzig. Philologisch-historische Klasse
BWANT	Beiträge zur Wissenschaft vom Alten und Neuen Testament
BWAT	Beiträge zur Wissenschaft vom Alten Testament
BZ	*Biblische Zeitschrift*
BZAW	Beihefte zur Zeitschrift für die alttestamentliche Wissenschaft
CAD	*The Assyrian Dictionary of the Oriental Institute of the University of Chicago*
CB	*Cultura bíblica*
CBQ	*Catholic Biblical Quarterly*
CBQMS	Catholic Biblical Quarterly Monograph Series
ChT	*Cahiers théologiques*
CollBG	Collationes Brugenses et Gandavense
CQR	*Church Quarterly Review*
Diss. Abs.	Dissertation Abstracts
DTT	*Dansk teologisk tidsskrift*
EHPR	Études d' Histoire et de philosophie religieuses
EJ	*Encyclopaedia Judaica*
EphMar	*Ephemerides Mariologicae*
ErIsr	Eretz Israel
EstBib	*Estudios Bíblicos*
EstEcl	*Estudios eclesiásticos*
ETL	*Ephemerides theologicae lovanienses*
EvT	*Evangelische Theologie*
Exp	*The Expositor* (London)
ExpTim	*Expository Times*

FRLANT	Forschungen zur Religion und Literatur des Alten und Neuen Testaments
GesAuf	Gesammelte Aufsätze (collected essays)
Ges-B	W. Gesenius and F. Buhl, *Hebräisches und aramäisches Hand-wörterbuch zum AT* (1921ff.[17])
GesSt	Gesammelte Studien (collected studies)
GLECS	*Comptes Rendus du Groupe Linguistique d' Études Chamito-sémitiques*
HAL	W. Baumgartner et al., *Hebräisches und aramäisches Lexikon zum Alten Testament*
HAT	Handbuch zum Alten Testament
HdO	*Handbuch der Orientalisk.* Leiden
HTR	*Harvard Theological Review*
HUCA	*Hebrew Union College Annual*
IDB	*The Interpreter's Dictionary of the Bible*
IEJ	*Israel Exploration Journal*
IKZ	*Internationale kirchliche Zeitschrift*
Int	*Interpretation*
IZBG	Internationale Zeitschriftenschau für Bibelwissenschaft und Grenzgebiete
JAC	Jahrbuch für Antike und Christentum
JANESCU	*Journal of the Ancient Near Eastern Society of Columbia University*
JBL	*Journal of Biblical Literature*
JCS	*Journal of Cuneiform Studies*
JETS	*Journal of the Evangelical Theological Society*
JNES	*Journal of Near Eastern Studies*
JPOS	*Journal of Palestine Oriental Society*
JPT	*Jahrbücher für protestantische Theologie*
JQR	*Jewish Quarterly Review*
JSOR	*Journal of the Society of Oriental Research*
JSS	*Journal of Semitic Studies*
JTS	*Journal of Theological Studies*
JTVI	*Journal of Transactions of the Victoria Institute*
Judaica	*Judaica: Beiträge zum Verständnis . . .*
KAI	H. Donner and W. Röllig, *Kanaanäische und aramäische Inschriften*
KAT	Kommentar zum Alten Testament
KBL	L. Koehler and W. Baumgartner, *Lexicon in Veteris Testamenti Libros* (1953; 1967ff.[3])
KD	*Kerygma und Dogma*
KlSchr	Kleine Schriften
LD	Lectio Divina
Leš	*Lešōnēnū*
LWC	Living Word Commentary
LQ	*Lutheran Quarterly*
LRb	Lutherischer Rundblick
LV(B)	*Lumiere et Vie.* Bruges
MEAH	*Miscelánea de estudios árabes y hebraicos*
MGWJ	*Monatsschrift für Geschichte und Wissenschaft des Judentums*
MIO	Mitteilungen des Instituts für Orientforschung
MPT	*Manuels et précis de théologie*
MTZ	*Münchener theologische Zeitschrift*
MUB	Mélanges de (la Faculté Orientale de) l' Université Saint-Joseph (Beyrouth)

Abbreviations

MVAAG	Mitteilungen der vorderasiatisch-ägyptischen Gesellschaft
NF	Neue Folge (new series)
NKZ	*Neue kirchliche Zeitschrift*
NovT	*Novum Testamentum*
NRT	*La nouvelle revue théologique*
NTS	*New Testament Studies*
NTT	*Norsk Teologisk Tidsskrift*
OLZ	*Orientalische Literaturzeitung*
Opusc. Romana	Opuscula Romana
Or	*Orientalia* (Rome)
OrAnt	*Oriens antiquus*
OTTheol	Old Testament Theology
Patr. Lat.	J. Migne, *Patrologia latina*
PJ	*Palästina-Jahrbuch*
RÄRG	*Reallexikon der ägyptischen Religionsgeschichte*, ed. H. Bonnet (1952)
RB	*Revue Biblique*
REB	*Revista eclesiástica brasileira*
REJ	*Revue des études juives*
RGG³	*Religion in Geschichte und Gegenwart*, 3rd edition
RHA	*Revue Hittite et Asianique*
RHPR	*Revue d' histoire et de philosophie religieuses*
RHR	*Revue de l' histoire des religions*
Rm	Rassam cylinder
RSO	*Revista degli studi orientali*
RTP	*Revue de théologie et de philosophie*
SAB	Sitzungsberichte der Deutschen Akademie der Wissenschaften zu Berlin
Salm.	*Salmanticensis.* Salamanca
SANT	Studien zum Alten und Neuen Testament
SBS	Stuttgarter Bibelstudien
SBT	Studies in Biblical Theology
ScrHier	Scripta Hierosolymitana
Scrip	*Scripture*
SEÅ	*Svensk exegetisk Årsbok*
Sem	*Semitica*
SNVAO	Skrifter Utgitt av det Norske Videnskaps-Akademi i Oslo
SOTSMS	Society for Old Testament Study Monograph Series
ST	*Studia theologica*
Str-B	(H. Strack and) P. Billerbeck, *Kommentar zum Neuen Testament*
ST (Riga)	Studia Theologica (Riga)
STU	*Schweizerische Theologische Umschau*
StudGen	Studium Generale
SWJT	*Southwestern Journal of Theology*
Tarb.	*Tarbiz*
TBei	*Theologische Beiträge*
TBü	Theologische Bücherei
TBl	*Theologische Blätter*
TD	*Theology Digest*
TDNT	*Theological Dictionary of the New Testament*, ed. G. Kittel
TDOT	*Theological Dictionary of the Old Testament*, ed. G. Botterweck and H. Ringgren.
TGI	K. Galling, ed., *Textbuch zur Geschichte Israels*
TGl	*Theologie und Glaube*

THAT	E. Jenni, ed., *Theologisches Handwörterbuch zum Alten Testament*
TheolAT	Theologie des Alten Testamens
TheolOT	Theology of the Old Testament
ThEx	Theologische Existenz heute
TLZ	*Theologische Literaturzeitung*
TPQ	*Theologisch-Praktische Quartalschrift*
TQ	*Theologische Quartalschrift*
TS	*Theological Studies*
TS-Z	Theologische Studien (Zürich)
TTS	Trierer Theologische Studien
TTZ	*Trierer Theologische Zeitschrift*
TynBul	*Tyndale Bulletin*
TZ	*Theologische Zeitschrift*
UF	*Ugarit-Forschungen*
UgAbh	Ugaritische Abhandlungen
UUÅ	Uppsala Universitets årsskrift
VAB	Vorderasiatische Bibliothek
VC	Verbum Caro
VD	*Verbum Domini*
VP	Vita e pensiero
VT	*Vetus Testamentum*
VTSup	Vetus Testamentum, Supplements
WMANT	Wissenschaftliche Monographien zum Alten und Neuen Testament
WO	*Die Welt des Orients*
Wört	Wörterbuch
WTJ	*Westminster Theological Journal*
WZ-Halle	*Wissenschaftliche Zeitschrift (Halle)*
ZA	*Zeitschrift für Assyriologie*
ZAW	*Zeitschrift für die alttestamentliche Wissenschaft*
ZDMG	*Zeitschrift der deutschen morgenländischen Gesellschaft*
ZDPV	*Zeitschrift des deutschen Palästina-Vereins*
ZKT	*Zeitschrift für Katholische Theologie*
ZNW	*Zeitschrift für die neutestamentliche Wissenschaft*
ZRGG	*Zeitschrift für Religions- und Geistesgeschichte*
ZS	*Zeitschrift für Semitistik und verwandte Gebiete*
ZST	*Zeitschrift für systematische Theologie*
ZTK	*Zeitschrift für Theologie und Kirche*

Index of Hebrew Words

Index of Biblical and
Related References

Index of Names and Subjects

Index of Names and Subjects

Index of Names and Subjects